MW01010580

# SYNDICATED LENDING:
# *Practice & Documentation*

Seventh Edition

Every owner of a physical copy of this edition of

# SYNDICATED LENDING

can download the eBook for free direct from us at Harriman House, in a format that can be read on any eReader, tablet or smartphone.

Simply head to:

**ebook.harriman-house.com/syndicatedlending**

to get your free eBook now.

# SYNDICATED LENDING: *Practice & Documentation*

Seventh Edition

General Editor and Author

Mark Campbell

Author

Christoph Weaver

Hh

HARRIMAN HOUSE LTD
18 College Street
Petersfield
Hampshire
GU31 4AD
GREAT BRITAIN

Tel: +44 (0)1730 233870
Email: enquiries@harriman-house.com
Website: www.harriman-house.com

Seventh edition published 2019



Hardback ISBN: 978-0-85719-682-8
eBook ISBN: 978-0-85719-683-5

British Library Cataloguing in Publication Data
A CIP catalogue record for this book can be obtained from the British Library.

Founding Editor

**Tony Rhodes**

Foreword
(to the Sixth Edition)

**Andrew Bailey**

## Contributors

| | | |
|---|---|---|
| Cameron Andrews | Mark Betteridge | Nisha Bharadwa |
| Peter Brodehser | Dr Doo Bo Chung | Mark Clark |
| Meredith Coffey | Simon Crown | Clare Dawson |
| Dealogic Loans Department | Michael Dicks | Matthew Dunn |
| David Fewtrell | Finastra – Fusion Loans IQ Team | Yves Gerster |
| Julia House | Alper Kilic | Emilio Lopez Fernandez |
| LPC Team | Chris Porter | Jim Skufca |
| Sean Tai | Christian Ulrich | Alban Vital |
| Tessa Walsh | Michael Ward | |

# CONTENTS

# FOREWORD (TO THE SIXTH EDITION)

It is a great pleasure to be asked to write the foreword to the sixth edition of the Euromoney guide to Syndicated Lending. Nearly thirty years ago, my first job in the Bank of England involved the analysis of syndicated lending in the Euromarkets and the implications of these developments for shaping the original Basel capital agreement as part of work done by the Bank for International Settlements. Around fifteen years ago, I assisted Eddie George to write the foreword to the second edition, and it is very pleasing to see the guide is going strong.

The fact that the guide has reached its sixth edition is a testament to the durability and adaptability of the syndicated loan as an instrument. It is a, possibly the, workhorse instrument of corporate financing. The ebbs and flows of its popularity are to do with the passing attractions of alternatives rather than any fundamental weakness in what is at heart a very simple instrument. Moreover, in banking simplicity is a strong virtue; indeed, it is a great pity that it took a crisis of such severity to provide a reminder of this principle.

There is quite naturally a great deal of focus on structural reform of the banking system. The crisis has sadly delivered strong lessons on both the prudential and conduct of business weaknesses of institutional structures and behaviour which were little questioned in the pre-crisis years. Exuberance resulting from the appearance of good times contributed to a lack of questioning of the soundness of structures and practices. The traditional plain vanilla syndicated loan market went through one of these periods when to many it looked like the outdated model.

Today, we place far more emphasis on ensuring that banks can fulfil their role of providing critical financial services to support economic activity, and do so on a continuous and uninterrupted basis. One of those critical services is financing companies around the world that wish to expand and develop either internally or by acquisition. The future of the banking system depends on being able to meet these basic and reasonable needs of society. The demand for such financing is truly global and requires large scale to support major companies. The syndicated loan is still with us, sitting at the heart of corporate financing. Moreover, as the guide once again explains, by their very nature syndicated loans need to be capable of distribution and selling as a means to achieve sensible risk diversification. Likewise, loans must be capable of sensible restructuring in the event of borrowers experiencing difficulties. The Bank of England has a long history of involvement in this area through the London Approach where it can use its powers of persuasion if those are called for and suitable in the particular context. I was responsible for the London Approach during the most stressful period of the financial crisis, and I learned a great deal from the experienced bankers who handle such restructurings, not least the timeless message that the success of the syndicated loan market depends on the clarity and precision of the terms and documentation of loans. It is right that the guide pays due attention to these important features.

I can highly commend the sixth edition of the guide as an important contribution to maintaining the success of the syndicated loan.

**Andrew Bailey**

Deputy Governor,<br>
Executive Director, Bank of England<br>
Managing Director, Prudential Business Unit,<br>
Financial Services Authority

*February 2013*

# PREFACE

Although the cyclical nature of the syndicated credit market is well known to practitioners, few people in 1992, when the first edition was being written, would have expected that there would be a cyclical requirement for new editions of this book. The frequency turned out to be four years each time coinciding with the Olympic Games, but the excitement of the Olympics being held in London in 2012 resulted in the 6th edition being delayed until the following year and now we seem to have settled on a six year cycle. Each new edition, of which this is no exception, has required significant revision in order to bring it up-to-date. This is surely the best prima facie evidence that the syndicated credit market remains healthy, dynamic and creative.

The book concentrates on the EMEA (Europe, Middle East and Africa) market, many of the participants in which are based in London, but refers, where appropriate, to the US and Asia Pacific markets.

So what is this instrument about which so much can be written? In its simplest form a syndicated loan can be presented schematically as shown in exhibit A.

The relationships shown diagrammatically are just the start of the story and, as all practitioners know, each transaction contains its own unique features usually built around variations on the themes set out in this book.

Over the last 25 years, the syndicated loan market as a whole has transitioned from being regarded as the poor relation of the debt capital markets to being in the forefront of the consciousness of many borrowers, banks and other financial institutions and investors. Indeed, in many cases, having the balance sheet committed to a borrower can be a prerequisite for winning mandates in other fields such as bond issues, corporate advisory work, foreign exchange or payments and cash management.

**Exhibit A: The parties to a syndicated loan**

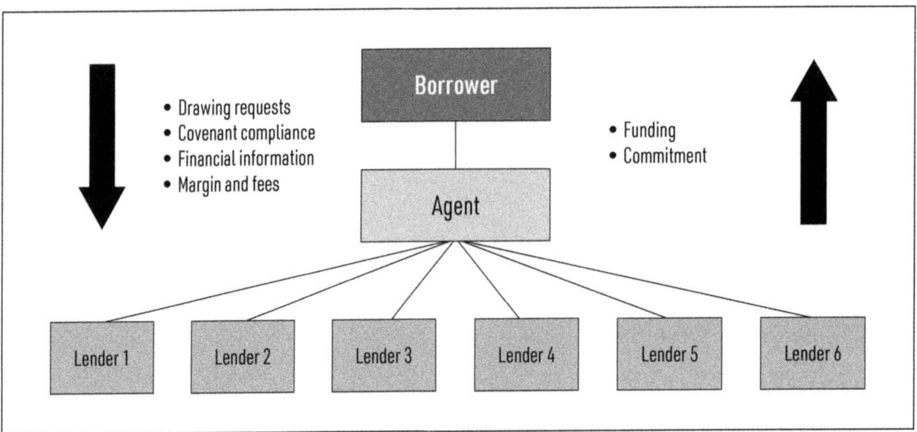


For many years, the largest syndicated loans were arranged in the US domestic market but Europe and now Asia Pacific can also boast some of the largest deals ever arranged, the record being the $75bn deal arranged for AB InBev in 2015.

The technical aspects of syndication and documentation described in this book have been developed, tested and refined in the international marketplace. The widespread adoption of these practices for both primary market and secondary market activity has helped to establish trans-national codes of practice acceptable to and understood by all participants (borrowers, banks and other institutional investors) in the market. The more regulated and traditional domestic markets that, for many years, did not lend themselves to the same degree of innovation and creativity have now followed the precedents set by the international practitioners.

Over the last few years, there has been increasing regulation applied to the loan market and this has had a significant impact on the day-to-day activity for the banks involved in arranging transactions as well as for banks acting as agent throughout the life of the facilities. Just one example is the importance now attached to the various aspects of customer knowledge of all the parties to a transaction both during the primary and secondary market phases.

# ABOUT THIS BOOK

This book starts with an overview of the market from the Loan Market Association (LMA) which has been written by Clare Dawson, Managing Director, LMA.

The reader is then taken through the history and structure of the market before embarking on the various stages of syndicated lending from the opening phase of seeking a mandate and negotiating a term sheet to syndicating, documenting, closing and trading a transaction. As not all transactions terminate in the way originally envisaged, the last chapter summarises the options when restructuring is required.

**Chapter 1** provides a short history of the market commencing with its creation in the 1970s and highlights key changes in the marketplace since then. As this edition is being compiled the market is facing up to what is, perhaps, the most significant single development in that history – the likely transition away from IBOR-based pricing. Since it is currently not clear how the market will handle this (and, indeed, it is not absolutely certain that the transition will take place) the book continues to describe the market as it currently is with pricing in the major currencies being based on IBOR-based benchmarks (plus margin). However, Chapter 1 concludes with a section outlining the importance of IBOR benchmarks to the market; describing the issues with such benchmarks highlighted by the scandals surrounding LIBOR and other benchmarks; dealing with the various regulatory responses to those issues; and, finally, looking at the likely transition away from IBOR benchmarks in favour of interest rate benchmarks tied to so-called risk-free rates (RFRs).

**Chapter 2** provides an overview of the syndicated credit market as it is today. It encompasses statistics on the size of the market, details of where the activity is taking place and in which currencies, and sets out some of the key players based on league table analysis. It comments on the impact of regulations (including the various Basel Accords on capital adequacy) and on the geographic location of the centres of syndication expertise. It concludes with a summary of the way in which banks organise their syndications teams and the technology and information sources they use in order to run this business. This is followed by a number of annexes in which some of the technology providers give their views on how their products can assist market participants. These include brief descriptions of Dealogic Loan Manager and LPC as well as a summary of the Debtdomain platform by Sean Tai of IHS Markit. The Finastra-Fusion Loan IQ team then describe operational best practices in loan servicing systems by reference to Fusion Loan IQ and there is a summary of Bloomberg for Syndicated Loans by Mark Betteridge of Bloomberg. The annexes conclude with a list of relevant information sources.

Chapter 2 also embodies eight supplements written by leading market practitioners covering areas of specific interest as follows:

1. The borrower's perspective by Yves Gerster Global Director for Treasury and Shared Services, Dufry Group.
2. Regional Markets – snapshots of the following regional syndicated loan markets by local experts:
   a. Germany – by Christian Ulrich;
   b. France – by Alban Vital
   c. Southern Europe – by Emilio Lopez Fernandez
   d. Nordic – by Michael Dicks
   e. GCC – by Alper Kilic
   f. Sub-Saharan Africa – by Alper Kilic
3. View of an Institutional Investor by Peter Brodehser, Head of Infrastructure Investments, Ampega Asset Management, GmbH.
4. Loan portfolio management by Dr Doo Bo Chung, formerly Director, Capital and Portfolio Management, Royal Bank of Scotland and Jim Skufca, Managing Director, formerly Head of Strategy and Analytics, Capital and Portfolio Management, Royal Bank of Scotland. This Annex was prepared for the purposes of the Sixth Edition and has been only editorially updated for this edition.
5. A recent history of the European leveraged finance market by Tessa Walsh, Global Loan Editor, LPC.
6. US institutional loan performance: Birth, Growth, Crisis, Recovery and Records by Meredith Coffey, Executive Vice President for Research and Regulation for the Loan Syndications and Trading Association.
7. Explaining loan and recovery ratings by Cameron Andrews, Director, Standard and Poor's Product Management EMEA and Chris Porter, Head of Loan Recovery and CCO Business Development Standard and Poors, EMEA.
8. Financial Regulation and the syndicated loan market by Simon Crown, Partner, Clifford Chance LLP. This also looks briefly at some of the possible effects of Brexit on the loan markets.

The Dealogic league tables and other charts used in Chapter 2 and Supplement 2 were kindly provided by Nisha Bharadwa of Dealogic.

**Chapter 3** introduces two case studies by examining the issues involved in preparing term sheets for two hypothetical borrowers, the first to provide liquidity facilities as a commercial paper ('CP') back-up line, the second for an acquisition financing facility. The transactions envisaged are two of the common types found in the syndicated credit market, the first being a revolving credit facility, the second being a multi-tranche multi-currency facility incorporating term and revolving facilities. These term sheets have been designed to explore, in a practical way, many features which are likely to be encountered in these types of transactions, whilst at the same time keeping them as realistic as possible. The term sheets themselves have been annotated to emphasise and highlight the key commercial points being made in each paragraph. The chapter ends with an explanation of the relevant all-in cost calculations for both transactions from a borrower's perspective.

**Chapter 4** covers the syndication process and all the steps involved. It starts with an assessment of the factors to be considered when deciding to bid alone or in a group. It covers alternative syndication strategies and discusses the activities involved in executing each step in the syndication process. The chapter closes with a worked example of a syndication strategy for each of the transactions featuring in Chapter 3.

**Chapter 5** is based on the offer to arrange the hypothetical commercial paper back-up line for DutchCo described in Chapter 3 and provides a draft facility agreement based on the sample term sheet. The agreement has been constructed in a conventional way and takes the reader through the document by providing pertinent commentary. The agreement, a US dollar denominated standby revolving credit and swingline facility agreement is annotated on a clause-by-clause basis. It uses the standard form developed under the auspices of the LMA.

**Chapter 6** gives the reader a concise explanation of the alternative methods for the effective transfer of assets from one institution to another. This has particular relevance in today's environment as banks increasingly look to the secondary market as a means to manage their portfolios. The Annex, originally prepared by David Fewtrell, Director and Portfolio Manager/Trader, Investcorp Credit Management EU and revised by Michael Ward, Manager at HSBC, provides a worked example of a secondary market trade using LMA endorsed standard confirmations and pricing methodology.

**Chapter 7** is a summary of the steps to be taken when restructuring transactions involving syndicates, draws attention to some of the frequently found pitfalls and offers ideas as to how to avoid them.

A Glossary of Terms is to be found at the end of this book where technical terms and market jargon are explained.

It is assumed that the reader is familiar with the concept of discounted cash flow. The calculations in the worked examples have, when necessary, been made using Excel spreadsheets and, therefore, minor differences in the results might be found if other calculators are used.

Various levels of pricing and interest rates have been used for the examples in this edition but the authors are not suggesting that these rates are the appropriate ones for any particular transaction either at the time this edition is published or at any other time and the absolute levels of pricing and interest rates chosen are not in themselves important. It is essential for a practitioner to use the prevailing rates when working in any real life situation. The methodology does not change, merely the answers.

Square brackets [ ] are used throughout this book to indicate that an insertion is required depending on the circumstances. It is hoped that the type of insertion required in each case is clear from the context and that the reader will realise that, once the insertion has been made, the square brackets drop away.

**Mark Campbell**

General Editor

*March 2019*

# LIST OF ABBREVIATIONS

ACT: Association of Corporate Treasurers

AfDB: African Development Bank

AIIB: Asian Infrastructure Investment Bank

APLMA: Asia Pacific Loan Market Association

ADB: Asian Development Bank

BBA: British Bankers' Association

BIS: Bank for International Settlements

CDB: Caribbean Development Bank

CEDB: Council of Europe Development Bank

EBRD: European Bank for Reconstruction and Development

ECB: European Central Bank

EIB: European Investment Bank

EIF: European Investment Fund

EMEA: Europe, Middle East and Africa

FCA: Financial Conduct Authority

IADB: Inter-American Development Bank

IAIC: Inter-American Investment Corporation

IACPM: International Association of Credit Portfolio Managers

IBRD: International Bank for Reconstruction and Development

IDB: Islamic Development Bank

IFC: International Finance Corporation

ISDA: International Swaps and Derivatives Association, Inc

LIBOR: London Interbank Offered Rate

LMA: Loan Market Association

LSTA: Loan Syndications and Trading Association, Inc

NIB: Nordic Investment Bank

OECD: Organisation for Economic Co-operation and Development

PRA: Prudential Regulation Authority

# ABOUT THE EDITORS

**Mark Campbell** is Special Counsel at international law firm Clifford Chance. He joined Clifford Chance in 1982 and has specialised in international and domestic banking and financial work. He has acted for a wide variety of arrangers of syndicated financing transactions of all types and has advised the Loan Market Association on its standard documentation since its inception. In recent years much of his work has centred around the acquisition finance, leveraged buy-out and restructuring markets. He has contributed to periodicals on financial law and is a regular speaker at conferences on syndicated lending and secondary market issues. Mark took his Law degree at Oriel College, Oxford and is the Chair of Governors for Shapla School, Tower Hamlets and Chair of Trustees at Tower Hamlets Education Business Partnership.

**Christoph Weaver** is General Manager of BayernLB, London Branch. Previously, he was Deputy Head of Loan Capital Markets and Head of Transaction Management at Royal Bank of Scotland. During his time at RBS, Christoph had geographic responsibilities for Germany, Austria & Switzerland, Nordics, France and Southern Europe. He joined RBS in 2004, before which he worked for HVB (now Unicredit) to establish and spear-head their Corporate Syndications Team with additional responsibilities for the financial institutions team and a major focus on European Borrowers. In 1997, Christoph moved to the Debt finance Division of Bankgesellschaft Berlin where he became Head of Syndications, leading a cross border team with a particular focus on borrowers in Eastern Europe, the Nordics and the Near Middle East. Christoph started his career at WestLB in credit before moving on to Syndications where he focused largely on UK corporates and FI's. He was latterly the Course Director of the Euromoney "Syndicated Loans for Practitioners" training seminar. Christoph was born in Germany, grew up in Scotland and was educated in both Germany and the UK where he received a Dipl. Betriebswirt (FH) and a BA European Business Administration.

**Tony Rhodes** is now retired from the finance industry. His last full-time employment (1998–2004) was at HSBC where he was European Head of Debt Capital Markets and Global Head of Loan Syndication. Before this, Tony worked at Credit Suisse (CSFB) for nearly three years where he was responsible for primary and secondary loan syndication in Europe, Middle East and Africa, having previously spent 15 years in a variety of positions in debt capital markets at Bank of America International Limited (BAIL).

Tony started his career in the project finance unit of Shell International Petroleum Company, being based first in London, then in Paris. This was followed by a Paris-based consultancy position after which he moved to Liverpool, England, to join the Treasury Department at Ocean Transport & Trading Limited. His final position prior to joining BAIL was in the project finance unit at Lloyds Bank International Limited.

Tony read Natural Sciences and Business Management Studies at Corpus Christi College, Cambridge, and holds a Master of Arts degree. He was a regular speaker at seminars and workshops on syndicated lending and was the course director and lecturer on the Euromoney training seminar entitled Syndicated Loans for Practitioners for 20 years from its inception in 1990. In addition to being the general editor and author of the first five editions of this book, he was general editor of the book entitled *Encyclopedia of Debt Instruments*, first published by Euromoney Books in 2006, then revised and published as a second edition in 2012.

Tony was a founding director of the Loan Market Association.

# ABOUT THE CONTRIBUTORS

**Cameron Andrews** is a Director responsible for Standard & Poor's Product Management Group in EMEA. Having held a number of positions at S&P, across the Product Management, Media and Marketing functions, Cameron's current role is to maintain and develop S&P's product offerings in Europe, with particular focus on S&P's Rating Evaluation Service, Private Ratings, Loan and Recovery Ratings, Credit Assessments, Private Credit Analysis, Credit Estimates and Mappings. Cameron joined Standard & Poor's in October 2000 as a media manager in the Insurance Ratings Group and prior to joining was a journalist in the financial trade press.

**Mark Betteridge** is the Global Head of Fixed Income and Currency Analytics at Bloomberg. He is responsible for Bloomberg's core debt, treasury, bond, syndicated loan and currency analytics, as well as credit analytics and league table products across the Bloomberg Professional service. Prior to his current role, Mr. Betteridge was responsible for the business development, design, build and rollout of Bloomberg's league tables and syndicated loan products globally. Before joining Bloomberg in October 2009, Mr. Betteridge spent eight years with Fortis – most recently as Director of Secondary Loans – where he managed the team responsible for all secondary loan activity and investor relationships in Europe, Middle East and Asia. Prior to that, Mr Betteridge held a variety of positions at NatWest, within the firm's Structured Finance division. Mr Betteridge holds a Bachelor's degree in Business Economics from Cardiff University.

**Nisha Bharadwa** commenced her fifteen year career at Dealogic in London, working closely with the Heads of Fixed Income and subsequently Equity Capital Markets, Mergers & Acquisitions and Investment Banking Strategy, globally. In 2012, she relocated to Hong Kong and worked across the Asia Pacific region in Hong Kong, China, South East Asia and Australia. Returning to London in 2015, her focus shifted to the growing

European Leveraged Finance Market and developing Dealogic's unique Leveraged Finance platform. Since 2018, she has managed Dealogic's Media presence in EMEA. Nisha studied Economics at the University of Manchester.

**Peter Brodehser** joined the Infrastructure Investments team at Ampega Asset Management GmbH (Germany) in September 2014, tasked with building its debt and equity investment portfolio. Peter is an infrastructure and investment specialist with over 20 years of banking and investment experience, having previously held positions at HSH Nordbank, Helaba and PwC gaining experience in project and acquisition finance, corporate finance and M&A. He has closed various transactions in the transport and energy sector across Europe, Asia and the United States. He holds a BBA degree from University of Applied Sciences Cologne, an MBA from FOM Business School and a PhD from University of Potsdam.

**Dr. Doo Bo Chung** was, at the time of publication of the 6th Edition of this book, a Director in the Capital and Portfolio Management Group (CPM) at the Royal Bank of Scotland's International Banking (IB) division. Doo Bo contributed to the implementation of an Active Credit Portfolio Management capability for the wholesale banking business and led the development of the IB division's integrated capital allocation framework. Doo Bo has a background in academia and risk management having previously worked in ABN AMRO's Quantitative Risk Analytics team. Doo Bo has an MSc graduating cum laude and a PhD degree in Aerospace Engineering both from the Delft University of Technology. Doo Bo was also the National Physics Olympiade champion in Suriname (South America), representing Suriname in the International Physics Olympiade held in Oslo, Norway (1996).

**Mark Clark** is head of the Corporate Loans Agency business at NatWest. He leads a team of industry specialist relationship managers within the NatWest Syndicated Loans Agency market-leading provider of independent, professional agency bank services.

**Meredith Coffey** is Executive Vice President, running the Research and Analysis efforts at the Loan Syndications and Trading Association (LSTA). Ms. Coffey co-heads the LSTA's regulatory and CLO efforts, which help facilitate continued availability of credit and the efficiency of the loan market. In addition, Ms. Coffey heads up a team of analysts that are responsible for analysing current and anticipated market developments, helping the LSTA build strategy and improve market efficiency, and providing commentary through weekly newsletters, periodic conferences and webcasts. Ms. Coffey and the analyst team also engage market participants, press and regulators on issues and developments in the global loan market. By presenting broad and unbiased analysis, the LSTA's research team is a non-partisan voice representing all loan market participants.

Prior to joining the LSTA, Ms. Coffey was Senior Vice President and Director of Analysis focusing on the loan and adjacent markets for Thomson Reuters LPC. Additionally, Ms. Coffey is a frequent speaker at industry events and has authored chapters in several books about the syndicated loan market. She has a B.A. and a graduate degree in economics from Swarthmore College and New York University, respectively.

**Simon Crown** is a partner in the regulatory practice at Clifford Chance, which he joined in 1998. He advises a broad range of financial institutions on regulatory issues, including regulatory capital, market abuse, payment services, mergers and acquisitions and conduct of business rules. Simon is a leading adviser on Brexit. Simon is a member of the City of London Law Society's regulatory committee. Simon has a law degree from the University of Oxford and a post-graduate law degree from University College London.

**Clare Dawson** joined the Loan Market Association in 1999 after spending two years in the syndications department at Sumitomo Bank, working on loans in Europe, the Middle East and Africa. Prior to Sumitomo she spent two years at the British Museum Development Trust raising funds for the Museum's Great Court project. Before joining the British Museum, Clare had spent some eight years at Sumitomo in the international department, including two years at the bank's head office in Tokyo, where she helped establish a syndications desk. In London she worked mainly on origination in various western European and Nordic countries. Clare has an honours degree in Modern and Mediaeval Languages from the University of Cambridge.

Clare is a member of the Sterling Risk Free Rates Working Group and chairs the Sterling RFR loans sub-group. She is also a member of a number of other currency working groups looking at potential replacements for LIBOR.

**Michael Dicks** has been involved in the syndicated loan market since 1982, firstly as part of the team at Midland Bank International syndicating financing for Airbus and other aircraft deliveries, then at Citibank Investment Bank syndicating structured trade finance obligations, before moving to the SEB Group in 1989 when on SEB acquiring full control of Scandinavian Bank in 1990 he was part of the team founding SEB's syndicated Loan practice. He has over the last 30 years been at the forefront of Nordic Corporate syndicated lending fuelling debt funded acquisition sprees and restructurings through the various economic cycles of this period. Michael retired from a 43 year career in Banking at the end of October 2018. Enjoying shooting hunting and fishing he now spends his time between Exmoor and London and enjoys finally being able to spend more time with his two daughters and three Labradors.

**Matt Dunn** is a partner in the finance group of the Irish law firm Arthur Cox in Dublin, where he works closely with the firm's Infrastructure, Construction & Utilities Group on loan and bond financings in the energy and infrastructure sectors, including PFI and PPP financings. Prior to Arthur Cox, he worked as an associate (2007-15) and then partner (2015-18) at Clifford Chance LLP in London, where he advised borrowers and lenders on cross-border acquisition financings, infrastructure and project financings, margin loans and restructuring work. Matt has a BA in Modern History from the University of Oxford and an MSc in Economics from the University of London.

**David Fewtrell** is a Director and Portfolio Manager for Investcorp Credit Management EU having originally joined 3i Debt Management, the predecessor to ICM EU in July 2012. Prior to that he was a Managing Director at HSBC where he headed the bank's institutional loan sales business in Europe. David set up and ran HSBC's secondary loan trading business having started his career at NatWest undertaking a variety of loan trading, credit and corporate banking roles in NatWest Markets and NatWest International. David has over 17 years sales and trading experience in the international syndicated loan and leverage finance market and is one of the pioneers of the modern secondary loan market in Europe. He sat on the board of Directors of the Loan Market Association for over 10 years and was Vice-Chairman between 2006 and 2009. David holds a Banking Diploma from the Institute of Financial Services and is approved to perform the FSA controlled function 30.

**Yves Gerster** is Global Director for Treasury and Shared Services at Dufry, the leading travel retailer which is quoted on the stock exchange in Switzerland. His function, among other tasks, is responsible for group financing which includes syndicated bank debt as well as senior bonds issued in Europe and the USA. He also serves on the council of trustees of Dufry's Swiss pension fund trust and as chairman of Dufry's cyber risk committee. He has 19 years of experience in finance in various industries. He graduated with a degree in economics at the University of Basel.

**Julia House** is a senior associate in the general banking practice of Clifford Chance in London. Julia joined Clifford Chance in 2010 and has worked in the firm's London and Madrid offices as well as spending eight months on secondment to Barclays Bank PLC. Julia specialises in corporate lending and infrastructure finance and has a B.A. in Jurisprudence from Jesus College, University of Oxford.

**Alper Kilic** is the Head of Standard Chartered's Corporate Finance Europe, Loan Syndications Africa & Leveraged and Structured Solutions businesses. He has over 22 years of experience in finance and banking covering USA, Europe, Middle East and Africa. He is also a Board Member for Standard Chartered Yatirim Bankasi Turk A.Ş. He joined SC in 2008 to focus on Structured Trade Finance and Financing Solutions in Sub-Saharan Africa. His deal experience includes structured loans, loans syndications, securitizations and Islamic Finance. He has covered clients across oil & gas, infrastructure, telecoms and FI sectors in different geographies. Alper also has extensive expertise in working with a wide range of Export Credit Agencies, Multilateral Agencies and Development Finance Institutions. Prior to Standard Chartered, Alper worked at Citibank in Istanbul and London for 11 years. He has an MBA from the University of Dallas and a BSc in Metallurgical Engineering and Material Science from the Middle East Technical University in Turkey.

**Emilio López Fernández** has been Head of Corporate Loans for Iberian corporates at BBVA since February 2016. He joined BBVA in 2010 and has been focused on origination and execution of corporate loans for IG and non-IG borrowers in Europe, on both bank and institutional deals. Prior to joining BBVA, Emilio spent 5 years in London at RBS in Leveraged Finance and Corporate Lending. Emilio has both Spanish and French citizenships and holds a Master´s degree in Finance at Sciences Po Paris. He is a Corporate Finance Professor at Universidad de Navarra (Madrid Campus), Master of Banking and Financial Regulation.

**Chris Porter** is Head of Loan, Recovery and CLO Business Development for EMEA at S&P Global Ratings, looking after ratings throughout the region, for corporate and leverage loans plus CLOs. He is also responsible for the coverage of Private Equity houses. Prior to S&P Global Ratings he spend over 20 years in the syndicated loan market, working across many of its different asset classes. His career started in NatWest on the project group that subsequently transformed into Europe's first dedicated secondary loan sales team. His next role was on the primary sales desk, distributing corporate, structured and financial institution loans to European investors. After primary sales, Chris was posted to Hong Kong, where he was responsible for the pricing, structuring and origination of syndicated debt in South and South East Asia. The main focus of this role was to bring debut issuers from Thailand and India to the international loan market. On his return to Europe he became the Head of European Loan Trading for NatWest, taking the team through the integration with The Royal Bank of Scotland, transforming the desk from a back-to-back operation into a full trading book, working mainly in the leverage and corporate markets. At the same time he joined the Board of the LMA, a post he was to hold for ten years. During his time on the Board he co-chaired the Valuation & Trading Practices Committee and chaired a number of working parties, as well as writing the first set of Transferability Guidelines for the LMA. He also held the post of Vice-Chairman of the LMA for two years. After RBS, Chris moved to Bank of Scotland, where he created and headed the Loan Sales and Trading Team.

**Jim Skufca** was, at the date of publication of the Sixth Edition of this book, a Managing Director in the Capital and Portfolio Management Group (CPM) of Royal Bank of Scotland's International Banking Division. Jim has over twenty five years of experience as a credit portfolio manager, trader and research analyst for major financial institutions including Wachovia Securities, Deutsche Bank Securities, Citigroup Securities and Aegon. While at Wachovia, Jim was instrumental in creating and leading the Corporate and Investment Bank's active credit portfolio management effort.

**Sean Tai** originally founded Debtdomain in 2000 and led the company until its acquisition by Ipreo in 2013. Sean's experience in banking led him to develop a product to simplify loan syndication and trading. The first syndicated loan was launched on Debtdomain in 2002 and since then Sean has been instrumental in driving the growth of the company into agency, secondary trading and compliance products. Based in London, Sean has a broad role focussed on developing the Debtdomain business globally. He continues to work directly with many clients globally and hosting industry conferences. Prior to setting up Debtdomain, Sean worked at Macquarie Bank, Standard Chartered and National Australia Bank. Sean has a Bachelor of Economics from the University of Sydney as well as Professional Certification from the Institute of Chartered Accountants of Australia and the Securities Institute of Australia.

**Christian Ulrich** joined Bayerische Landesbank in 1999 and has worked within the Corporate Finance division, in particular syndicated loans, since 2004. From 2011 onwards Christian headed the corporate advisory unit and since 2017 he has served as Head of Corporate Structured Finance with a focus on origination and execution of syndicated loans and corporate acquisition financings for corporate clients. He graduated from University of Gießen, earned a degree in Business Administration and has supplemented his education with an executive course in Management at INSEAD. Christian is married with two children.

**Alban Vital** is Head of Western Europe Origination in the Loan Capital Markets team of SMBC. Based in London, the team is responsible for managing the underwriting, structuring, pricing and syndication strategy of loans for Corporate clients and financial institutions in the region. Alban has over 15 years of experience in the loan market, he has extensive deal experience in M&A financing, corporate leverage, infrastructure and structured finance across various sectors and countries. Before joining SMBC, Alban was part of the Global Loans team of Barclays Capital mostly focusing on corporate leverage syndication. Prior to joining Barclays in 2006, Alban started his career at GE Capital as part of their Financial Management Program and then Capital Markets team. Alban holds an MBA from INSEAD (France), a Master in Management from the CEMS and an Engineering degree with distinction from Université Catholique de Louvain (Belgium).

**Tessa Walsh** is LPC's London-based global loan editor. Tessa has been covering the syndicated loan market in Europe, the Middle East and Africa for more than 20 years and is responsible for editorial coverage for LPC, Refinitiv and Thomson Reuters. Tessa has been published in Reuters, the New York Times and International Herald Tribune and other publications and chairs LPC's European Roundtable, an annual forum that allows loan syndicate heads and leading institutional investors to discuss market developments. Tessa has an M.A. in Philosophy from St Andrews University and a post-graduate diploma in Newspaper Journalism from London's City University.

**Michael Ward**, CFA is a Manager in the European Middle-Market Leverage Finance team at HSBC Bank plc. Before joining HSBC, he was a Vice President at RBS where he oversaw the bank's £4bn global asset deleveraging of its unprofitable loan portfolios across Europe, the Middle East and Africa. Michael has also worked within the bank's Debt Capital Markets division focusing on syndicated loans. Michael holds an MSc in Finance from Warwick Business School, along with a First-Class BSc in Financial Maths & Economics from National University of Ireland, Galway. He is also a CFA charterholder.

# ACKNOWLEDGEMENTS

This is the second edition of this book not to benefit from the direct contribution of Tony Rhodes who edited each of the first five editions, but who has now left the work of updating to others. Nonetheless, Tony's influence on the structure, content and style of the book remains immense and I would like to thank him for his continued advice and support (as well as for his friendship over almost the entirety of my career in the loan market).

As a mere lawyer I could not have hoped to carry on Tony's good work without the support of banking professionals and, in preparing this edition, I have been very fortunate to be able to work with Christoph Weaver of Bayern LB who, together with Richard Bradbury and his colleagues at NatWest and Chris Linnane of Bayern LB have been able to apply their enormous expertise and experience to the task of re-working and replacing large parts of the text to take account of the many changes in the market which have occurred since the previous edition appeared in 2013. I am particularly grateful to Sean Malone at NatWest for enabling members of his team to work on this project.

I would also like to thank my colleagues, Julia House, whose help on both this edition (particularly with the sample term sheets and facility agreement) has been invaluable, Matthew Dunn and Sandra Pask, without whom I would certainly not have been able to cope with the mammoth task of dealing with the manuscript.

The Loan Market Association (LMA) is indisputably the leading trade association for the syndicated loan market in Europe, Middle East and Africa. This book benefits in part from the work undertaken by the LMA and embodies a number of the standard forms that have been developed. The LMA authorised the selective use of this work for which I am deeply indebted as I am to Clare Dawson for writing the introductory review from the LMA.

This market has countless facets and the supplements to Chapter 2 are written in order to offer the reader a broader perspective on the market than would be the case by just concentrating on its technical aspects. My thanks go to Cameron Andrews, Peter Brodehser, Meredith Coffey, Simon Crown, Michael Dicks, Yves Gerster, Emilio Lopez Fernandez, Alper Kilic, Chris Porter, Stephanie Queniat, Christian Ulrich, Alban Vital and Tessa Walsh for their informative, incisive and useful contributions. Dr Doo Bo Chung and Jim Skufca prepared the supplement on portfolio management for the Sixth Edition of this book and, although they were unable to work on this edition, I thank them for their contribution.

I wish to acknowledge the contributions made by Mark Clark of NatWest towards the revision of the section on the agency function in Chapter 4 and by David Fewtrell and Michael Ward in developing a worked example of a secondary trade in the Annex to Chapter 6 as well as by Mark Betteridge of Bloomberg, the Dealogic loans team, the Finastra-Fusion Loans IQ team, the LPC team and Sean Tai of IHS Markit for the Annexes to Chapter 2.

This Seventh Edition benefits from the contributions and comments made in previous editions by individuals who were active players at the time and I wish to record my thanks to them for their professional support; they are listed here alphabetically according to the edition in which they first appeared. Obviously some people, who have had lengthy careers in the syndicated loan market, span more than one edition.

First Edition: Frank Canosa, Alby Cator, David Chandler, Isabel Clapman, Keith Clark, Mike Constant, the late Gerald Doherty, Jim Fuschetti, the late Norbert Hagedorn, Richard Halcrow, Robert Halcrow, Linda Hanson, Morven Hay, Simon Hood, Jiri Huebner, Bernard Hunt, Stan Hurn, Walid Kaba, Len Lizmore, David Lord (late), Hilary McCann, David Morley, Bill Morrow, Spyros Papanicolaou, the late Hugh Paton, David Rimmer, Bill Robinson, Sol Saad, Fabian Samengo-Turner, Zoë Shaw, Duncan Straughen, Eileen Ward, Howard Watson and Jörg Wulfken.

Second Edition: Charles Bennett, Christopher Beresford, Paul Brooker, Noreen Doyle, Chris Elliott, Tim Elliott, Simon Jackson, Bahman Jahanshahi, Grant Johnson, Sidney Kurth, Michael Leemputte, Bruce Ling, Maria Roca, James Saft, Dietmar Stuhrmann, Cathy Weir and Stephen Williamson.

Third Edition: Valerie Amato, Tony Assender, Richard Cartledge, Meredith Coffey, Michael Day, Stephen Fitzmaurice, Ed Flanders, Julian van Kan, Mark Nickell, Andy Smith, John Starling, Paul Tay, Julian Taylor, Ellie Souza and Jo Whelan.

Fourth Edition: Samir Assaf, Alan Christenfeld, Noreen Doyle, Fergus Elder, Elizabeth Gray, William Fish, Ian Fisher, Isabel Fleming, Robert Gray, Philippe Henry, Helen Ibbotson, Jonathan MacDonald, Gráinne Molloy, Gerald Montagu, Ruth Ramsey, Tim

Reid, Geoff Rimington, Tim Ritchie, Scott Talmadge, Tanya Trainer, Rachel Watson, Zvi Wolgemuth and Andrew Yianni.

Fifth Edition: Don Carden, Dan Cohen, Matthew Dunn, Ephraim Ehrhardt, Edwin van Eijbergen, Toby Fildes, Jennifer DeMarco, Felix Geiringer, Darrenth Hawken, Keith Ho, Anna Jakimova, Jasmina Jakimova, Caroline Kennedy, Zey Nasser, Dan Neidle, Sandra Pask, Mark Pesso, Abhishek Pundhir, Jonathan Ready, Michelle Roles, Wendy Rosenthal, Hardeep Sandhu, Steve Schoenhaus, Roger Taylor, Dermot Turing, Paul Watters, Sandy Wax, Christoph Weaver and William Wild.

Sixth Edition: Josie Ainley, Edward Ainsworth, Philip Angeloff, Rick Antonoff, Mark Arbeid, Leah Edelboim, David Felsenthal, Allegra Benitah, Avrohom Gelber, Kevin LeGallo, Nathan Holland, Per Lindberg, Carolina Lopez Perez, Tom Pax, Alexander Riddick and Antonio Stockino.

Seventh Edition: Jeff Berman, Jules Brizi, Simon Crown, Laura Douglas, Asta Evans, Dolly Haastrup-Quornooh, Rui Huo, Robert Johnson, Pierre-Benoit Pabot du Châtelard, Katelijne Ribbink, Titus de Vries, Deborah Zandstra.

Finally, I would like to thank Chris Cudmore and the team at Harriman House, for their support, encouragement and effort in making this Seventh Edition happen.

**Mark Campbell**

*April 2019*

# *Introduction*

# THE LOAN MARKET ASSOCIATION CONTINUES TO EXTEND ITS INFLUENCE

**Clare Dawson**

*Chief Executive,*
*Loan Market Association*

Since the publication of the sixth edition of this book in 2013, the Loan Market Association (LMA) has continued to play an increasingly significant role in the syndicated loan market in the Europe, Middle East and Africa (EMEA) region, and has also extended its documentation and training into a wider range of sectors, geographies and syndicated loan products. Moreover, in the last six years, the loan market itself has continued to face challenges on a number of fronts. It therefore seems appropriate to give once more a brief description of the history and achievements of the LMA, and to offer a view of the changes and trends in the loan market that are influencing the Association's work.

## THE ORIGINS AND DEVELOPMENT OF THE LMA

The LMA was established in December 1996 on the initiative of a number of leading London-based market practitioners, who had come to the view that the syndicated loan market in Europe would benefit from the existence of a trade association that could develop collective solutions to issues which individual market participants would not be able to deal with as efficiently on their own. From the initial membership of seven founding institutions, numbers have grown steadily, and the number of members now stands at over 700, consisting of banks, other financial institutions, law firms and service providers from more than 60 jurisdictions. Members come from across the EMEA region and beyond, emphasising how much the LMA's reputation and influence has grown since its early days, particularly in some of the newer, developing markets.

The initial focus of the LMA was on the newly developing secondary loan market, which, while suffering from inefficiencies and lack of standard market practice, was becoming more important to major banks, as they began to look at ways to improve returns on capital through more active balance-sheet management. It soon became clear that the core goal of the Association was to optimise liquidity, and this continues to shape the thinking of those responsible for taking the LMA forward, whether in the context of the secondary market, or in relation to the LMA's work in the primary market.

As the market has evolved, and the challenges facing it have changed, the LMA's priorities have also adapted to meet the needs of its members. In the current market the main focus of the LMA falls on four areas:

- working to maintain the ongoing attractiveness of the syndicated loan product to an increasing universe of borrowers and lenders
- engaging in constructive dialogue with regulators to ensure that regulation does not have unintended consequences for, or excessively inhibit liquidity in, the syndicated loan market
- bringing the benefits of standardisation and widely accepted market practice across the broad range of syndicated loan products and markets
- working with market practitioners to increase operational efficiency in the syndicated loan market

# DOCUMENTATION

In its early years, the LMA focused mainly on projects relating to the secondary market, developing documentation for trading both par and distressed loans, and standard settlement parameters, as well as launching the secondary loan Valuation Survey. However, as the LMA expanded its remit to cover all aspects of both the primary and secondary loan markets, producing documentation for the primary market became an increasingly important aspect of the Association's work. Initially, a set of Recommended Forms of Primary Document for the investment grade market was produced, covering both single and multi-currency deals and revolving and term loan facilities. Subsequently, additional documents, including options for letter of credit and swingline facilities, as well as term sheets, confidentiality agreements and mandate letters, were added to the set of primary documents.

An important development, which was prompted by the primary documentation project, was the dialogue established with The Association of Corporate Treasurers and the British Bankers' Association. The involvement of the former in the production of the Recommended Forms of Primary Document was undoubtedly an important factor in establishing the documents' credibility with the corporate sector. While the documents are, of course, only the basis of negotiations between borrowers and lenders, the goal was to standardise the boilerplate areas of the documents so that these negotiations can focus on the commercial aspects of individual transactions.

While the vast majority of LMA documentation is governed by English law, which is a widely accepted market standard, the LMA has produced French and German law versions of the investment grade primary document, launched in 2002 and 2007 respectively, with a Spanish law version published most recently, in 2013. It was felt that adapting the LMA documents for these jurisdictions, while maintaining the overall style and content of the English law form, would broaden acceptance of LMA standard documentation in three major markets where many borrowers had traditionally pressed for shorter, less comprehensive loan documentation.

Around three years after the launch of the English law investment grade primary documents, and after wide consultation among market participants, the LMA began to draft a document for the leveraged loan market. A working party of representatives from banks and law firms was formed, and the newly formed Institutional Investor Committee was also invited to review the document. Once again the aim was to produce a template form that would be negotiated to suit each individual transaction – the more complex nature of leveraged loans meaning that the document left considerably more areas blank for negotiation than the investment grade version. After a number of drafts had been reviewed, a finalised document was launched in January 2004.

Following the start of the financial crisis in 2007, after some discussion the decision was made to create an LMA Intercreditor Agreement. Clearly this was an ambitious project: intercreditor agreements are highly tailored to the complexities of each transaction. Nonetheless, our members felt there was a clear benefit to the market from the LMA producing a recommended form that had been thoroughly reviewed for complex issues such as multi-party hedging. After the financial crisis had begun to raise difficult issues between borrowers and lenders, it became clear that the LMA leveraged facility agreement was a robust starting point for lenders to negotiate with borrowers. The intention was that the Intercreditor Agreement should provide a similarly strong framework for negotiation, and when the document was launched in February 2009 it was widely welcomed as a document that had benefitted from detailed discussion of the complicated issues involved by leading practitioners and lawyers. Subsequently, work was undertaken to produce documentation for other structures seen in the leveraged market, including an intercreditor agreement and super senior secured revolving credit facility agreement for use together with a high yield bond.

All LMA documentation is subject to continuous review, to take account of changes to legislation and regulation, judgements in relevant litigation and developments in market practice, as well as simply to incorporate improvements that market participants have identified in the course of using the documents for live deals. Where possible, the boilerplate areas of the different sets of primary documents are kept the same, although differences in the perception of risk, or operational complexity, for example, may result in the parties requiring different positions to be taken in different markets. On the secondary side, the most significant changes were as a result of the decision, taken in 2009, to combine the distressed and par trading debt documents into one combined set, which was launched in February 2010. This included the consolidation of representations and warranties from the previously published par terms and conditions and distressed terms and conditions, as well as a single uniform trade confirmation for par and distressed trades.

After years of focusing purely on documentation for the corporate markets – whether investment grade or leveraged – in 2010 the decision was made to broaden the scope of LMA documentation to include other, specific sectors of the syndicated loan market. As a result, a particularly busy 18 months resulted in the production, during the course of 2012, of a multi-property investment facility agreement for commercial real estate finance, a term loan agreement for use in developing markets, and a pre-export finance facility agreement. Subsequently, the suite of Real Estate Finance documents has been considerably expanded, and a German law Real Estate Finance document has been produced, in both German and English language versions. An extensive set of documents for use in developing markets, under English law, has been published, and since the merger of the African LMA (ALMA) into the LMA in 2014, we have updated and expanded their set of South African law documents, and produced a facility agreement for use under the local laws of a number of other African jurisdictions. With increasing focus from both regulators and investors in developing a European private placement market, we produced an agreement adapted for this market in 2015, in both the loan and bond formats which are used by participants in this market. Finally, most recently, in April 2018 we published a buyer credit facility agreement for use on Export Credit Agency (ECA) backed transactions. This project benefitted from the involvement of most of the major European ECAs, and was an excellent example of cooperation between the public and private sectors on a pan-European basis.

# REGULATION

Ever since the financial crisis of 2008/9, a growing area of activity for the LMA has been communicating with governments and regulators about issues that the Association feels could affect liquidity in the syndicated loan markets. Whilst initially, post crisis, the focus of the regulators was on measures aimed at strengthening the financial system and making similar crises less likely in future, over recent years the range of regulatory proposals has broadened enormously in scope. Much of the regulation proposed is aimed at activities other than lending, but nevertheless has the potential for adversely affecting the ability of both banks and institutional investors to continue to fuel economic growth by lending. FATCA, CLO risk retention rules, sanctions, Article 55 of the BRRD, leveraged loan guidelines and anti-money laundering rules have all had a significant impact on the loan market. The effects of Brexit on the loan market are still unclear, and after the speech by Andrew Bailey, Chief Executive of the FCA, in July 2017, in which he signalled the FCA's unwillingness to support the production of LIBOR beyond the end of 2021, the market, and the LMA, has been devoting huge amounts of time and resource to the question of finding alternative benchmarks. The LMA has been in continual dialogue with regulators, market participants and other trade bodies to ensure that any solutions work for the loan market as well as other products such as derivatives, and to stress the importance of the syndicated loan market as a core provider of funding for corporate activity.

## EDUCATION

Another area in which the LMA has a particularly important role to play is in the field of education, whether it be in terms of training in the use of the LMA documents, or informing the market of the issues and trends of which market participants need to be aware. As the legal and regulatory framework in which loan market practitioners work continues to change, this is an area in which trade associations such as the LMA can add value for the market as a whole, as well as for individual institutions, by ensuring that participants are fully informed of the issues they need to address when transacting deals. The LMA's education and training programme has continued to expand since the last edition of this book. In addition to the members' Documentation Training Days, which have been increased to cover any new documents, the LMA Certificate Course, a one-week introduction to the syndicated loan market, has continued to be extremely successful, and gives those new to the market a thorough insight into the product and market practice. More recently we have developed a three day REF Certificate Course and a Loan Documentation Certificate Course, the latter held both in London and Johannesburg, The overseas seminar and conference programme has also been expanded, and now covers the Nordic region, Central and Eastern Europe, Russia, major African centres and New York, as well as the major Western European financial centres. In all, over 33,000 delegates have attended LMA events since the last edition of this book appeared in 2013, and the annual conference, first held in London in October 2008, is now the largest loans event in EMEA, attracting over 900 delegates from across the region, with, for the first time in 2017, over 300 people watching the live streaming of the conference.

As well as holding this wide range of events, the LMA also produces a number of publications for its members. Close to 10,000 copies of 'The Loan Book', a study of the syndicated loan market through the financial crisis of 2007 to 2009 and the key issues likely to affect it thereafter, have been distributed since its publication in September 2011. Further books, covering developing markets, real estate finance, and a look back at 20 years in the syndicated loan markets, published to coincide with the LMA's twentieth anniversary in 2016, have all proved extremely popular with members. In autumn 2012 'Regulation and the Loan Market', the first of a series of LMA Guides was published, and is now one of over a dozen guides on a wide variety of topics, covering legal, commercial and operational issues. Adding to the relatively small body of published work about the syndicated loan market is another way in which the LMA can promote the advantages of the syndicated loan product, as well as educate market participants about issues they need to be aware of in an increasingly complex environment.

A key development over the last few years has been our increasing use of electronic means of delivering training and knowledge. We have an active webinar programme, with over 30 webinars available covering various LMA documents, legal and regulatory issues and other market developments across a wide range of jurisdictions, with a new webinar being added to our website almost every month. In addition, we have produced a series of short videos featuring interviews with market practitioners about a specific topic. A particularly popular development has been our e-learning course, a web-based course which provides an introduction to the syndicated loan product in the form of 10 modules, each concluding with a multiple-choice test. So far almost 5,500 people have registered and started the course, and over 1,500 have completed all 10 modules. Additional modules covering specific topics will be added over time.

## EXTENDING INTO NEW MARKETS

In 2014, the decision was taken by the Boards of the LMA and the ALMA to merge the two organisations. The ALMA was a small organisation based in Johannesburg, and did not have the resources to cover the African markets much beyond South Africa, and the LMA, which had already run a few events in South Africa, was keen to start covering the continent much more comprehensively. Since then the LMA has updated and significantly added to the ALMA's suite of South African law documents, has produced a facility agreement which can be used under the local law of a number of other African jurisdictions, and has established a programme of training events and conferences in Southern, East and West Africa. Appetite for the LMA's services across Africa is considerable, and the number of members across the continent has increased substantially since the merger.

Another new area for the LMA is Green Lending. In March 2018, together with the Asia Pacific Loan Market Association (APLMA) in Hong Kong, we published the Green Loan Principles (GLP). These were based on the Green Bond Principles previously published by ICMA, but were adapted to reflect the private and relationship-driven nature of the loan market. The GLP create a high-level framework for green lending, and the LMA will continue to work to adapt the principles to accommodate as many different types of loan product as possible, such as general corporate purposes facilities, to open up the market to a wide range of borrowers.

## ON-GOING ISSUES

For both the primary and secondary markets, operational issues continue to pose considerable challenges. As the size of syndicates has grown – in some cases to several hundred lenders of record – agents have sometimes struggled to cope with processing amendments and waivers and executing transfers. In the secondary market, whilst average settlement times have been reducing over the last two years, in part driven by some of the initiatives the LMA has undertaken though its various operations committees, significant delays still occur on many trades. Collation and publication of secondary settlement statistics by the LMA has certainly given more clarity to progress on this front, and provided individual institutions with a benchmark against which to measure their own performance. Creation of an escalation matrix for operations contacts has also been helpful for closers seeking to expedite settlement of a particular trade, or resolve a problem. Commercial service providers have also been developing new products for both the primary and secondary markets, and the LMA has created a Fintech sub-committee to connect members with technology providers.

## LOOKING TO THE FUTURE

Notwithstanding current difficult market conditions, it is possible to identify underlying trends in the market that will continue to affect the work the LMA undertakes. Many of these will be ongoing, such as the increasing globalisation of the market, and the EU's growing importance in shaping the regulatory environment for banks active in Europe. Brexit could, however, over time change the way in which UK and EU regulators approach financial regulation, which may necessitate a two streamed response by the LMA. The LMA maintains an ongoing dialogue with its sister organisations in the United States and Asia, the LSTA and the APLMA, and has co-operated with them on a number of projects in the interests of making it easier to transact cross-border business. With regard to systems solutions to the challenges set by loan settlement/operations, the LMA will continue to work with institutions and vendors in what should be recognised as a medium to long term project.

As the global economy changes, and developing markets become increasingly important both as markets and providers of investment, the syndicated loan market will also see new opportunities open up and flows of capital change. The LMA is already working to promote the acceptance of regional standards in some of the newer markets such as in

Africa and CIS countries, as well as to broaden the membership to include some of the financial institutions in these countries which are starting to look outside their immediate home markets.

Looking forward, provided that the LMA continues to achieve the goals it sets itself, and to add value for its growing membership, there is no reason why the Association should not continue to act as a constructive and influential agent of change in the loan markets across the EMEA, and to feature prominently in future editions of this valuable publication.

# *Chapter 1*

# THE CREATION AND HISTORY OF AN INNOVATIVE MARKET

# THE CREATION OF THE MARKET

In looking at the origins of the international syndicated loans market, the creation of the Eurodollar, the currency used in the embryonic phase of that market, deserves a brief mention.

Dollars have been used by banks based in London and in various other centres to finance international trade for many decades. The dollars used for these purposes were held in US bank accounts, but, as they had non-US ownership (at first, principally European), they became known as Eurodollars.

The offshore dollar market developed and grew in the late 1950s, particularly as a means of financing foreign trade. This market was given tremendous impetus as the risks incurred by certain sovereign borrowers, of holding dollars in the US, became apparent. A dramatic example occurred during the Suez Crisis of 1956, when the US Treasury invoked the Neutrality Act and froze the deposits of the participants in the conflict. Although this was lifted within a few weeks, it had a lasting effect, particularly on the depositors in the Middle East who became converts to the external dollar market. The need for a sophisticated offshore market received another boost when the Soviet Union and others of the Eastern bloc countries recognised the risks associated with the holding of their dollar balances in New York during periods of international tension.

Some would argue that 1958 was the founding year for the Eurodollar as it was during that year that non-convertibility, the last remaining impediment to the growth of the Eurodollar market, was removed. Thereafter it became possible for non-US residents to hold dollar balances, and the major European currencies became freely convertible into dollars. This, 14 years after the event, was the final major provision of the Bretton Woods Agreement to be implemented.[1]

1 The 1944 Bretton Woods Agreement set out to establish a post-war international monetary system of convertible currencies, fixed exchange rates and free trade. To help achieve this, the agreement created two international institutions: the International Monetary Fund (IMF) and the International Bank for Reconstruction and Development (the World Bank) in order to provide economic aid for the reconstruction of post-war Europe.

# DEVELOPMENT OF THE MARKET

Eurodollar availability represented only one-half of a market. Suitable uses for the offshore currency were needed as well. For the market to develop to a significant size, both borrowers and lenders of the newly available Eurodollar deposits had to squeeze into the existing rate structure for dollar denominated deposits and loans available in the well-established US money and capital markets. Soliciting, and then lending Eurodollar deposits, on the basis of an agreed margin over deposit rates provided the basis for the development of a profitable deposit and loan business, which had, at the same time, to be at a competitive all-in cost for borrowers when compared with alternative sources of finance.

Further momentum for the development of the Eurodollar market as the foremost source of international finance came from other directions. In 1964 the Interest Equalisation Tax Act was enacted; it sought to discourage foreign borrowers from tapping the US capital markets, principally in order to assist the US balance of payments but also to encourage Europeans to establish indigenous and reliable sources of long-term finance. The US also introduced the Voluntary Restraint Programme of 1965 and the Foreign Direct Investment Act of 1968, both of which were designed to make a favourable impact on the US Balance of Payments. Opinion is divided as to their effectiveness for this purpose, but without doubt they served to provide an added incentive for the development of a permanent market for offshore dollars free from control of the regulatory authorities.

International banking, particularly the syndicated loan market as we now know it, therefore had its origins in the 1960s. The birth of the Eurodollar and the development of the cross border interbank market gave rise to an opportunity to bring together lenders from different geographical origins into syndicates to participate in loans with a common funding basis and on common terms and conditions. As Paul Einzig explained:

> *'the critical feature in the evolution of the market was the development of a system of raising medium-term credits with adjustable interest periods. Instead of fixing the interest rate for the entire period of a credit, it is adjusted from time to time, on the basis of pre-agreed intervals, to reflect the ever-changing market rates on interbank deposits'.*[2]

This highlighted one of the most imaginative and important mechanisms of the new market. The most common funding basis known as LIBOR (London Inter Bank Offered Rate), was the rate at which time deposits were offered by banks to other prime institutions in the financial marketplace. The popular name for such credits, whether granted by single banks or syndicates, was 'roll-over loans' because, even though they might be

---

2 Einzig, Paul, Roll-Over Credits: the System of Adaptable Interest Rates (London, Macmillan, 1973).

granted for a period of years, they were automatically renewed on modified terms every six months (or other agreed period) when the underlying interest rate (LIBOR) was re-set. The loan, which was thereby rolled over from one interest period to the next until it matured, achieved a flexibility and appeal hitherto unavailable to borrowers.

With LIBOR accepted as the basis rate off which loans could be priced, various borrowers and banks worked together to establish appropriate market practices for arranging medium-term loans for borrowers of differing credit standing. The method adopted was to arrange the rollover loans with their floating (variable) rate of interest and to add to this a margin which would reflect the credit risk of the borrower. By this means, all banks, able to fund themselves in the marketplace at LIBOR (or less), could participate in a loan which used this rate as the basis rate.

LIBOR was subsequently used not just as a basis for interest rates on loans, but also as a key part of the mechanism for huge volumes of derivatives contracts and the subsequent history of the LIBOR rate is dealt with later.

The early loans were nearly all denominated in US dollars which was by far the best developed Eurocurrency. However, as confidence grew, other currencies became available and the market started to permit borrowers to change the currency of outstandings periodically during the life of the loan, thereby creating the multi-currency loan.

Early documentation for syndicated loans was, by modern standards, concise in the extreme: the $1bn syndicated loan arranged by S.G. Warburg for Ente Nazionale per L'Energia Elettrica (ENEL) in 1973 was documented on a mere eight pages. The market has become more sophisticated since that time, so much so that, reflecting the better appreciation of the risks involved in Eurocurrency lending, it is now most unlikely that a full loan agreement can be covered in less than 75 pages using normal fonts. This documentation will also cover the increasingly varied options that are included in syndicated loans, which currently are required to accommodate multi-tranche, multi-currency, multi-purpose, multi-option and multi-borrower situations.

## THE PETRO-DOLLAR

Given that borrowers and banks were working on the development of both the market operation and the documentation of syndicated loans, it was with enthusiasm that the banks took on the job of recycling the proceeds of the oil price rise in 1973. The price of oil quadrupled over a short period of time, but some of the oil-producing countries did not have the capacity to deploy the revenues immediately in their domestic markets. International banks therefore became the recipients of massive dollar deposits (petro-dollars) from these countries and in turn were forced rapidly to look for suitable lending opportunities. Not surprisingly, the oil-importing countries were faced with huge deficits on the oil account due to the large increase in price; as a result, these sovereign states became the borrowers that the banks were so actively seeking. A cycle therefore developed with the oil-producing countries generating unprecedented surpluses on the oil account and depositing a substantial proportion of their revenues with the international banks who then lent the money to the oil-importing countries to pay their bills to the oil producers. This simplified picture of the recycling process illustrates vividly the intermediary role which the international banks so successfully played in circumstances which they had not encountered before.

The seeds of a lending disaster, however, might have been detected in the borrowing activity of the oil-producing countries with large populations and other natural resources. Using oil reserves to support their credit-worthiness, these countries borrowed heavily to finance their infrastructure and natural resource projects.

Countries which were particularly active in this respect included Venezuela, Mexico, and Nigeria but, by the mid-1980s, after a collapse in the oil price, they were all in the process of restructuring their foreign debt.

# THE SOVEREIGN DEBT CRISIS

## Problems in eastern Europe

The borrowing activity of sovereign borrowers in the syndicated loan market was at its peak during the late 1970s and early 1980s. The common view of international bankers was that sovereign borrowers could not fail, and this view was expressed publicly by the senior executives of some of the major lending banks. The 1980s were to tell another story altogether. First there was the crisis in eastern Europe which arose when banks and other institutions became nervous of further lending to the Soviet bloc and its satellites because of the sheer size of their international debt, a problem brought into vivid focus in late 1979 with the Soviet Union's invasion in 1979 of Afghanistan and, less than 12 months later, the start of fundamental political change in Poland which gave rise to the creation of the union Solidarity. Early in 1981 the unthinkable happened: Poland sought to defer payments due under the direct and syndicated loans amounting to some $8bn in total, which had been contracted with western banks. This became the forerunner of the major sovereign rescheduling programmes of the 1980s.

### Latin American countries reschedule their debts

Worse was to come. In 1982 Mexico suspended payments on its $90bn of foreign debt. Mexico's example was followed in short order by many other countries (Brazil, Argentina, Chile, Venezuela, Yugoslavia and Nigeria to name but a few of the more significant cases) seeking to reschedule their debts with western banks. The period of apparently unlimited opportunity for banks to make loans to sovereign borrowers came to an abrupt halt.

The meetings, discussions and negotiations required to secure a rescheduling of debts were immensely protracted and required dedication from bankers, borrowers and lawyers alike. A first principle was that all banks had to be treated equally, which meant that in some cases a participant with a negligible amount of the total debt would hold an effective veto. Due to the time consumed in dealing with literally hundreds of lenders in some reschedulings, the principle of equal treatment in more recent restructuring negotiations has been replaced with the principle of equal opportunity.

## SOVEREIGN BORROWERS TAP THE CAPITAL MARKETS

By the mid-1980s the sovereign borrower had almost disappeared from the marketplace not only because of the difficulties encountered by some countries in their attempts to reschedule debt, but also because alternative markets for credit-worthy sovereign borrowers had developed to the point which made them more cost-effective for core borrowings. Whereas in 1980 the Kingdom of Belgium had been one of the most active borrowers in the syndicated loan market, by 1985 it was tapping the fixed and floating rate bond markets almost exclusively. Borrowers such as the Kingdom of Spain, the Kingdom of Denmark, the Kingdom of Sweden, the Republic of France and other sovereign borrowers, usually acting directly, or through state-guaranteed public sector entities, were all very active users of the syndicated loan market in the early 1980s. By 1985 they were all using sources of finance such as the money markets – through note issuance programmes and the fixed and floating rate Eurobond market.

During the 1980s, new developments started to take place in the financial markets which would have a significant impact on the syndicated loan market. Borrowers found that the short-term money markets were able to offer floating rate funds at a lower cost than loans from banks. One of the first major issuers of paper, the Kingdom of Sweden, managed to establish funding levels substantially below LIBOR through its early tender panel bidding programme. Treasurers, however, had to be able to assure their boards of directors that medium-term liquidity could be guaranteed, despite the disintermediation of banks as the principal source of funding, and so, in parallel, banks started to offer back-stop or standby facilities. Their purpose was to provide alternative liquidity to issuers of short-term paper, a process directly comparable to the practice which had long been established in the US domestic commercial paper market.

The standby facility was used as liquidity insurance extensively during the mid and late 1980s by borrowers who could issue short-term instruments at advantageous spreads, often substantially below the contractual margin for advances under the standby facility. These standby facilities, when combined with the issuance of short term paper, were known under various acronyms such as RUF (Revolving Underwriting Facilities), MOF (Multi-Option Facilities), NIF (Note Issuance Facilities) and BONUS (Borrower's Option for Notes and Underwritten Standby). They were all designed to permit the borrower to obtain funding from sources which were cheaper than bank advances while recognising that banks were the ultimate source of liquidity.

## CAPITAL ADEQUACY CONCERNS

There was a further driving force working to promote the use of the capital markets for funding and to change the role of banks from providers of funds to providers of liquidity insurance. It emanated from the particular treatment by regulators and accountants of undrawn commitments as 'off-balance sheet' items. In the mid-1980s banks providing these standby facilities were not generally required to provide capital to support their commitments, which meant that for many banks the earnings of such facilities were treated as fee income.

The rate of growth of the standby facility started to cause concern among the regulators and this became one of the points of focus for the committee established in Basel, under the aegis of the BIS (Bank for International Settlements) to review and recommend appropriate levels of capital which banks should maintain to support their commitment overhang and lending activity. In December 1987, the committee published its proposals on capital adequacy for banks and established guidelines which were endorsed unanimously by the regulators of the G10 member countries and Luxembourg. The adoption of these recommendations (the Basel Accord), which were to be implemented in accordance with an agreed timetable, meant that the regulators had created a 'level playing field' for major international banks. This common approach fundamentally reshaped the market and changed the banking habits of nearly two decades of bilateral and syndicated lending.

## LEVERAGED DEALS GROW IN POPULARITY

In the late 1980s the US domestic syndication market exploded as a direct result of activity generated by the financing of leveraged buy-outs (LBOs), management buy-outs (MBOs) and leveraged recapitalisations. The process had started quietly in the early 1980s but accelerated at breakneck speed to its climax, culminating in 1989 with the consummation of the $25bn RJR Nabisco buy-out transaction arranged by the specialist house Kohlberg Kravis Roberts & Co. (KKR). This transaction included a $14bn syndicated loan requiring banks to commit of up to $500m each, which at the time was quite exceptional. This level of activity became vulnerable to the potential refusal of banks to accept stretched credit structures. Indeed, it came to an abrupt halt in late 1989, when a proposed management buy-out transaction for United Airlines failed because potential lenders, previously so amenable, finally rejected the aggressive structure proposed by the sponsors. Outside the US this type of lending activity was much more muted until the late 1990s; indeed, until that time, only the UK developed into a remotely significant market for these transactions, and it was never large by US standards.

## THE EARLY 1990S

At the turn of the decade, therefore, a very different banking environment had already started to emerge. The highly profitable (at least in terms of fees) LBO/MBO activity had started its decline. Some major banks in the US were suffering losses – particularly arising from excessive real estate lending extended during previous, buoyant years. The world economy had started slipping into recession, resulting in the requirement to make provisions on a scale not experienced by banks since the height of the sovereign debt crisis. At the same time, some borrowers were becoming disillusioned by the difficulties of dealing with syndicates in times of crisis and were seeking to re-establish old fashioned relationships with a core group of banks. The deadline for banks to comply with the capital adequacy rules, imposed under the terms of the Basel Accord, was also fast approaching.

As a result of all this an increased emphasis was placed by banks involved at all levels in the market on the credit quality of the borrower and the credit structure of each transaction moving away from the *name lending* which was commonplace in the 1980s. The majority of banks, particularly the US banks, recognised the need to obtain higher returns commensurate with the underlying credit and market risks being taken. Asset growth was no longer a sufficient measure for success and indeed many banks had their lending limits cut as head offices worried about meeting the capital adequacy regulations. Outside of the banking world, the first Gulf war occurred and in this downbeat environment volumes of transactions dropped dramatically.

The contraction of appetite combined with asset constraints imposed at head office led to a shift in pricing to higher levels than had been prevalent in the late 1980s.

# THE MID-1990S

The requirement for banks to meet the capital adequacy guidelines by 1 January 1993 was very much the focus until a certain comfort level set in by mid-1993 as most major banks found that they had achieved and even exceeded the minimum levels stipulated. Furthermore, the losses that had been so debilitating in the early 1990s started to decline and the capital positions of many banks improved dramatically. Inevitably, the banks began looking for new lending opportunities and the relatively attractive levels of pricing (for banks) prevalent over the previous two to three years started to crumble.

In many cases borrowers who raised finance in 1994 were able to refinance the same transaction in 1995 at half the price and with the same banks a phenomenon to be experienced again many years later.

During the mid-1990s, the US market started to experience rapid growth particularly in the field of leveraged finance. US banks and foreign branches in the US were now hungry for well-priced assets and the feelgood factors of a growing economy in a low interest rate environment provided the confidence that the proposed business plans were sustainable and deliverable. This encouraged leading banks to take very large underwriting positions which were by and large sold down effectively. This period was also characterised by the growth of non-bank investors who treated leveraged loans as just another asset class, were insistent that loan ratings be provided and looked for relative value against alternative instruments. The funding capacity of these investors enabled the arrangers to offer innovative and aggressive capital structures using *alphabet* tranches, each one embodying characteristics targeted at a specific investor base. This approach was refined during the remainder of the decade and migrated to the European theatre.

# THE LATE 1990S

Acquisition finance was the most important part of the market in the late 1990s. One look at the volume statistics and it is evident that some phenomenal activity took place. It was driven in 1995–7 by the acquisition activity in the US, in particular the revival of the highly leveraged transaction supported by the reopening of the high yield bond markets. Then the UK market started to blossom with the start of a series of jumbo transactions which, whilst not matching the volumes in the US, nonetheless pushed out the limits of experience of European practitioners. Volumes of activity in the UK were undoubtedly helped by the take-over code that obliges a bidder to have committed finance when a bid is launched for a public company. This requires a bank or a small group of banks to sign a loan agreement committing a substantial amount without, in the interests of confidentiality, the possibility of sounding the market or indulging in any pre-placement.

If, in 1997, anyone thought that sovereign debt crises were relegated to the history books, the devaluation of the Thai baht showed that they were out of touch with reality. This devaluation triggered the *Asian crisis* which encompassed South Korea, Malaysia, Thailand, Indonesia and to a lesser extent the other Asian countries. In 1998 the Asian crisis spread to Russia – linked directly to the short-term funding lines made available to many Russian banks from Korean banks that were pulled at maturity. The resulting default and problems in the banking sector created a general loss of confidence in emerging market credits and Latin America was the next to suffer a liquidity crisis. Fortunately, the experiences of the previous sovereign crises meant that the IMF and commercial banks were able to react swiftly to avoid systemic risk. By 2000, the economies of the Asian countries were again starting to grow strongly, while Russia also announced a restructuring deal with the London Club of commercial lenders.

On the corporate front, the market-defining transaction in the field of hostile acquisitions was the financing of Olivetti's bid for Telecom Italia. Olivetti, acting through Tecnost Spa raised €22.5bn for its bid. This was the first major hostile bid in Italy and the size of the transaction exceeded anything previously seen in the European theatre. The arrangers were Chase Manhattan (now JP Morgan), DLJ (merged with Credit Suisse), Lehman Brothers (no longer a separate entity after its insolvency and the sale of its main businesses to Barclays and Nomura) and Mediobanca. The syndication was a success driven by the short maturity profile and the remuneration which surpassed the usual expectations of the European marketplace. The message for borrowers was clear: capacity from the bank market is available, but at a price. This may not be as aggressive as it sounds. Olivetti's plan, evidenced in the maturity profile, was to refinance the loan as soon as possible in the capital markets. Once the Olivetti bid had succeeded, Tecnost tapped the capital markets successfully, thereby reducing its borrowing costs substantially. Thus, although the borrower had to pay up initially for bank balance sheet capacity, the above average returns for the loan participants were short lived. Nevertheless, for some banks the income on this one transaction equalled the annual target income for their syndications teams.

Deals like this were generally well received because borrowers were prepared to pay a pricing premium for the funding capacity and the free call option offered by the banks. This meant that even if the price looked high *out of the box,* the borrowers could hope to refinance in other capital markets before the bank funding had been outstanding for too long and without a pre-payment penalty.

One of the major changes in the bank market in the late 1990s was a growing desire of banks to manage their loan portfolios more actively. This increased requirement for liquidity resulted in the rapid development of a secondary market in loan trading starting as usual in the US and migrating to Europe some two years later. At the outset, the market was chaotic with little or no standardisation of closing procedures or documentation. By the end of the decade, the US, Europe and Asia had each established a formal body to recommend operational procedures and standard form documentation through the LSTA, the LMA and the APLMA respectively. These were enshrined in the transferability clauses of loan agreements in an attempt to obtain more flexibility from borrowers to allow transfers to take place.

Technology also played a role in the development of the syndicated loan market in the late 1990s. The use of internet based systems to launch transactions into the market became increasingly commonplace and the ability to send documentation electronically and receive comments back the same way increased productivity significantly. Initial worries about security were largely overcome.

## THE EARLY NOUGHTIES

The year 2000 was the year that the European theatre finally took centre stage for acquisition financing in the syndicated lending market. It was a year of business opportunity for both borrowers and lenders with jumbo telecom mergers and acquisitions and their related financings providing the foundation for the overall transaction volume. However, in parallel, new global regulations were introduced, notably in the areas of customer knowledge (Know Your Customer or KYC), and banks started to prepare for the introduction of a new Basel Capital Accord (known colloquially as Basel II) to replace the existing 1988 Basel Capital Accord (Basel I).

Record-size deals in 2000 for borrowers in the telecom sector were the €13bn acquisition facility for KPN of the Netherlands which was more than twice oversubscribed, France Télécom which raised in excess of €70bn of commitments for its €30bn facility to back the purchase of Orange from Vodafone, and Deutsche Telekom which raised €12bn and £3.5bn in its dual facility shared between itself and One-2-One. Emphasis for the most part was placed on keeping the average life as short as possible on these transactions by incorporating 364-day tranches and relying on bond or equity markets for the takeout. The Deutsche Telekom transaction did however test the market at the time by including a seven-year tranche which proved difficult to syndicate.

This level of activity proved to be unsustainable. The overhang of telecom exposure at the start of 2001 was a cause of considerable concern to bankers although with the benefit of hindsight this generally proved to be unfounded and the 364-day tranches put in place in 2000 were refinanced successfully. However, with the bursting of the dot.com bubble in March 2001, the subsequent decline in equity values worldwide, the uncertainties created in the wake of the events of 9/11 and the weakness of many of the world's leading economies, merger and acquisition (M&A) activity over the period 2001–03 was more muted such that the investment grade syndication market was forced to focus once more on core financings and refinancings rather than on *event driven* transactions.

After a period of relative calm in the late 1990s, the leveraged loan market made significant progress in terms of size, structure and complexity. During the period 2000–03, there was a steady increase in the use of mezzanine funds for the provision of intermediate capital. As the high yield market regained its poise, the competition between the mezzanine providers and the high yield investors provided borrowers and deal arrangers with real alternatives for structuring new transactions. Two ground-breaking transactions, arranged in 2000, which played a key role for these developments were the leveraged buy-out of United Biscuits (at £1.4bn, a record at the time for a public to private leveraged buy-out in Europe) and the leveraged recapitalisation of Elis (multi-tranche €1bn and $130m which attracted many non-traditional lenders including collateralised debt obligations and insurance companies), the diversified service group, itself previously subject to a leveraged buy-out in 1997.

For banks, the increasing pressure to improve profitability from their wholesale banking business continued to push them more and more towards multi-product relationship banking. The exact definition varies from bank to bank and extends across a mix of banking products from corporate advice through to cash management. The result has been a shift in negotiating style with borrowers (almost) expecting potential arrangers to try to secure other mandates, such as bond takeout mandates, when pitching for financing mandates. Borrowers have been complaisant in this approach in order to secure balance sheet availability at the cheapest price. And with corporate bond markets in receptive mood for most of this period, these arrangers demonstrated their capacity to deliver on these bond market mandates by placing the paper widely and successfully. This forced a competitive response from the traditional M&A houses (mainly US investment banks) which became more or less obliged to commit their balance sheets to underwrite transactions in order to maintain their privileged relationships with their clients. An example of this early in 2004 was the €12bn acquisition financing arranged by BNP and Merrill Lynch (now Bank of America Merrill Lynch) to support Sanofi Synthélabo's hostile bid for Aventis in which the initial underwriting for the full amount was shared in the ratio 2:1 between the two mandated banks. (This financing was later increased to €16bn when the takeover bid became friendly.) The benign credit environment prevailing at that time meant that the sell down risk for such positioning was not unacceptably high.

# THE MID-NOUGHTIES

The period from 2004 to mid-2007 was characterised by a generally benign global economic environment: interest rates were generally quite low, businesses were generally doing well, stock markets had recovered their poise from the downturn in 2001–03 and banks appeared to be generally well capitalised allowing them to go for significant asset growth. This period also saw the expansion of the non-bank financial investor, often referred to generically as 'institutional funds'. As is often the case, these institutional funds had been active for a number of years in the US leveraged loan market before they saw further growth opportunities outside of the US market.

Thus the appetite of investors for new assets appeared during the mid-noughties to be virtually unlimited. Arrangers adopted the business model *originate and distribute* across the widest spectrum of transaction types. Transaction size no longer seemed to be an obstacle and records for deal size were established and broken in rapid succession.

In the investment grade sector, liquidity in the banking market permitted borrowers to refinance deals, signed only a year or two previously, at a reduced cost, with fewer financial covenants (if any) and frequently with longer tenors. For example, in 2004, hypermarket chain Carrefour paid just 17bp over Euribor for its €1.5bn five-year revolver, which was 8bp less than it paid for the €1.5bn five-year tranche of its €2.5bn revolver signed in 2003, and the deal was twice oversubscribed. The deal also featured the 5+1+1 structure whereby the borrower had two one-year extension options available at the end of the first and second years respectively that potentially provides the borrower with a seven-year deal.

But it was in the leveraged sector that the most significant changes took place. Liquidity was no longer just the banking sector plus a few funds active in mezzanine financing but a whole raft of institutional funds actively seeking loans as an asset class. The sheer volume of funds interested in this sector intensified competition to the point where arrangers accepted higher leverage, weaker covenants, the so-called covenant-lite documentation, and in many instances lower pricing (under a reverse-flex clause) due to substantial oversubscription in syndication. The structure of the transactions became more complex as tranches were designed to meet the specific objectives of different investor classes: the so-called 'institutional tranches' with second lien and PIK tranches in many of the larger deals. Notwithstanding the weakening of lenders' positions, the deals were frequently oversubscribed. A detailed description of the leveraged market over this period can be found in supplement 5, and an analysis of US institutional loan and high yield bond performance in supplement 6, both featuring at the end of chapter 2.

A new record was set in the US market in 2006 with the jumbo financing supporting the LBO of HCA Inc for a consideration of approximately $33bn by a private equity consortium of Bain Capital, KKR and Merrill Lynch Global Private Equity. The multi-tranche financing facilities amounted to $16.8bn, the largest ever leveraged loan at the time. This deal was particularly notable for highlighting the depth of the institutional market in the US and the performance of the transaction post-syndication created confidence that these investors would remain active in the sector.

A side benefit of the increased involvement of institutional funds in the loan market was the rapid growth of a secondary market in the leveraged loan sector. Some funds, unable to obtain access to the primary syndication, desperately sought assets for their portfolios from this source and many banks developed a secondary desk specialising in this class of asset.

## WHEN THE MUSIC STOPS...

In July 2007, Charles (Chuck) Prince, then CEO of Citigroup was quoted as saying: 'when the music stops, in terms of liquidity, things will be complicated. But as long as the music is playing, you've got to get up and dance. We're still dancing.' The music was still playing but fading fast. In July 2007, the sub-prime crisis was the trigger for a major worldwide reassessment of credit risk which then developed into a worldwide credit crunch. The sub-prime crisis started earlier in 2007 as a domestic issue in the US as some sub-prime borrowers started to default on their housing loans. Banks, often using third party originators, had been making loans to sub-prime borrowers and had found that, due to the high liquidity of the markets, there was a ready securitisation market for these loans if they were repackaged by splitting them into tranches carrying different ratings. These securitised issues were distributed widely and globally.

But, as more and more defaults on these mortgages occurred and the risk of default on the securitised issues themselves became a realistic possibility, it became clear that there was no precise method for determining which institutions had bought these securitised assets and were holding them in portfolio. As a result, banks became very wary of advancing funds to any institutions that they felt might be overly exposed.

The uncertainty about which institutions were exposed to the sub-prime market translated into a liquidity crisis relatively quickly as banks started to reduce and cancel money market lines to other banks and institutional funds. The interbank market, on which syndicated lending has been based from its inception, almost ceased to function with reports from many banks and financial institutions that LIBOR no longer reflected their funding cost and allegations that some of the banks which formed part of the panel of banks contributing to the calculation of the LIBOR rate were not inputting rates which reflected their own cost of borrowing. As a consequence the Federal Reserve, the European Central Bank and the Bank of England, to differing degrees, opened up funding windows for institutions facing a liquidity shortfall. During this period, a number of suggestions for an alternative to LIBOR that might be more representative of the actual cost of funding were tabled. Regulatory and criminal investigations into the setting of LIBOR (and some other benchmark rates) during this, and other, periods were made public in 2012. These have resulted in some of the institutions which contributed rates as part of the determination of LIBOR being fined significant sums, in the resignation of senior executives from those institutions and in increased scrutiny from regulators and legislators of benchmark interest rates (one of the results of which is the report of Wheatley Review into LIBOR published in September 2012 and which recommended the regulation and reform of the LIBOR setting process). The ramifications of these events for the LIBOR rate continue at the time of writing and are further discussed later in this chapter 2.

It since became clear that the prudence shown in relation to interbank lending was justifiable as some of the most well-known names as well as some of the less well-known names reported very substantial losses from their activity in the sub-prime sector. Indeed, the global distribution of securitised issues was so effective that there were few financial institutions or investors that did not suffer some losses from the sub-prime crisis. Some of the institutions that reported the largest losses had to resort to raising new equity to support their capital base (and capital ratios) and achieved this in a number of ways, for example, via placement of shares with sovereign wealth funds (for example UBS, Barclays, Citigroup) or via the raising of new equity by way of rights issues (for example RBS). In the latter part of 2008, after the demise of Lehman Brothers, many banks were forced to accept government funding in various guises to meet their capital needs (for example RBS, Citigroup, Commerzbank) and others merged abruptly under the duress of the financial crisis (for example Bank of America and Merrill Lynch, Lloyds TSB and HBOS).

The result was quite dramatic. With a weakened capital base and an inability to be certain of funding at LIBOR, many banks, and other institutions, were reluctant to take on new assets, certainly not on the terms and conditions prevailing in mid-2007. Caught on the cusp of the changing market environment were many transactions that had been underwritten in the preceding weeks or months. With investor appetite falling or evaporating completely, arrangers were left with substantial long positions resulting in an overhang of non-placed underwritten deals that lasted well into 2008 when banks started to sell these positions at deep discounts. One of the high profile transactions caught in this maelstrom was the £9bn loan backing the buy-out of the UK pharmaceuticals retailer, Alliance Boots.

Although the momentum from transactions from the first half of 2007 enabled 2007 to record the highest ever volumes of syndicated lending, the fall in transaction volumes and number of deals in the first half of 2008 was quite unprecedented. Notwithstanding the credit crunch, the latter part of 2007 and early 2008 saw some record-breaking transactions. Indeed, in the second half of 2007, ENEL raised €35bn as its part of a joint tender offer with Acciona for all of the share capital of Endesa, a Spanish utility, although this amount was subsequently reduced to €23bn for general syndication. Rio Tinto raised a multi-tranche facility of $40bn for its acquisition of Alcan Inc. which was consummated in November 2007. Late 2007 also saw the largest ever syndicated loan to that date of $55bn for the Australian mining company BHP Billiton to finance its bid to acquire Rio Tinto. It was successfully underwritten, although it was cancelled late in 2008 when the bid failed.

## THE LATE NOUGHTIES

Historically the loan market had always been fairly resilient to systemic 'market shocks'. This time following the collapse of Lehman Brothers in September 2008 and the downfall of major financial institutions (notably Fannie Mae, Freddie Mac, AIG, HBOS, RBS, etc), it was unable to escape the crisis unscathed.

By December 2008 and despite extensive central bank intervention, bank liquidity almost dried up and funding became extremely challenging. Banks, which had been over-reliant on inter-bank markets for liquidity, were facing a dramatic increase in their funding costs because of a loss of confidence in the inter-bank markets and a significantly higher cost of raising money in the capital markets. Market liquidity was further impacted by large withdrawals by investors from US money-market funds.

Pre-credit crunch when bank CDS levels (a benchmark for funding costs) were very low, banks were able to fund themselves at or even below LIBOR. Post credit crunch however, average CDS levels reached c.200bps while 3-month LIBOR stayed close to 100bps. This decoupling from LIBOR meant that banks were lending at a rate below their own funding costs.

In this difficult climate, characterised by rising levels of asset write offs, lenders focused on managing down their balance sheets and lowering their risk exposure. Many banks decided to scrutinise critically their relationships and refocus their activities to support core clients and exit those with insufficient returns from their capital commitment. A number of lenders also retrenched to their domestic markets and exited non-core countries and non-core lending activities. Last but not least the number of market participants dropped markedly during the crisis as lenders merged or were sold off.

The very rapid withdrawal of bank liquidity – as many counterparties (banks, funds, CDOs or SIVs) struggled to or could no longer participate in loans – led to a massive, swift and historic rise in pricing in recognition of the banks' increased funding costs, which were not reflected in the official LIBOR levels. For illustration, average pricing for investment grade borrowers rocketed to a peak of 240bps towards the end of 2008 and even strong investment grade borrowers could not obtain money for longer than three years... Long gone were the days of seven-year tenors and low double-digit margins!

As a result, borrowers shied away from refinancing cheap existing facilities. The syndicated loan market was almost muted and comprised mostly of:

(i) 'club' transactions between the traditional local market lenders,

(ii) amendments, waivers and restructurings to support troubled companies and

(iii) 'forced' refinancings as existing deals reached maturity and bridge facilities could not be refinanced according to the original plans.

Syndication strategies also dramatically changed during the crisis and new approaches were developed to maximise available liquidity.

Due to a more cautious approach from banks characterised by a reluctance to take overly structured or risky exposures, the market witnessed a shift from a classic 'pyramid' syndicate structure with a limited number of Bookrunners at the 'top' and a longer list of Mandated Lead Arrangers and Participants at the 'bottom' of the pyramid to an 'inverted pyramid structure' with a long list of Bookrunners at the 'top' and a more limited number of participants at the bottom of the pyramid.

In a market where club style and best efforts transactions dominated, it became important for borrowers to secure as much liquidity as possible upfront from key lenders ahead of launching any general syndication phase targeting other lenders.

Because of this and due to an inherent uncertainty about banks' ability to deliver, borrowers from time to time had to deal with a larger number of arranging banks. With lenders wanting to differentiate themselves, this resulted in an intense competition for coordination roles with co-ordinators playing the role Bookrunners used to play pre-crisis, although without the much cherished enhanced league table recognition, which remains relevant only for MLAs and Bookrunners.

The crisis also saw the introduction of a number of documentation changes following lessons learned from the failure of Lehman; most notably the protection of both borrowers and bank groups in the event of a defaulting lender and/or an impaired agent. Approved lender language also became more prevalent in documentation, but interestingly banks did not use this opportunity to dramatically improve their documentary protections vis-à-vis the borrowers by way of tighter covenants or additional restrictions as this was predominantly a crisis of the financial sector and banks rather than of the corporate borrowers. The post-Lehman months were also characterised by lenders structuring and providing a number of innovative financing solutions to enable borrowers to mitigate their refinancing risk.

Forward Start Facilities (FSF), which were introduced in late 2008, became widely accepted as an established form of financing for companies faced with challenging liquidity pressures. They allowed borrowers to extend maturity, lock in existing bank liquidity by avoiding early exit by non-core banks, and re-price investors' commitments via the use of a top up margin and a loyalty fee inserted within the FSF documentation.

In January 2009, UK brewer Marston signed the first forward start facility and secured a £295m 3-year extension to its £400m facility due in August 2010. At the time, 3-year money was the maximum lenders were prepared to fund and securing a longer tenor was a significant event. With improving liquidity, however, the use of the FSF tool started to decline progressively as a mainstream tool.

Lenders also started to structure and provide multi-product (loans, bonds, USPP, equity) integrated financing solutions allowing borrowers to tap multiple pockets of liquidity efficiently and diversify away from bank debt.

Debt diversification became a major theme in the post-GFC years. Pre-GFC, European borrowers were over-reliant on bank lending as their main source of capital as evidenced by banks accounting for 70% of corporate risk, with the other 30% sitting with capital markets. The shift to a more bond based model, similar to the position witnessed in the United States, changed the shape of the European loan market. This resulted in a situation where strong corporate credits covered most of their funding needs in the capital markets, leaving the banks only with responsibility for their undrawn backup line requirements.

As a result, bond issuance volumes surged to new record levels in 2009. According to Dealogic, the European corporate bond market experienced record volumes and exceeded the corporate loan market for the first time in 2009 (€557.2bn vs €338.4bn). In contrast, syndicated loan volume in EMEA fell by c. 40% compared to 2008.

Market sentiment steadily improved as the year 2009 progressed. Liquidity recovered sharply and spreads in the loan market tightened. Average tenors in the second half of 2009 increased, with 5-year deals successfully syndicated for strong rated names, although it was not until Philips came to the market in March 2010 with a new 5-year transaction that this tenor returned as a benchmark maturity for good investment grade names. After risk aversion during the first part of the year, the loan market became more open to risk and more transactions for lower rated/unrated borrowers were seen.

# THE 'TWENTY-TENS': THE REVIVAL OF THE LOAN MARKET AND THE RETURN OF BENIGN MARKET CONDITIONS

By 2010, the market was characterised by a dearth of M&A activity, abundance of liquidity (largely due to borrowers refinancing through cash or in other markets and most markedly the various quantitative easing initiatives from the respective central banks in effect pumping liquidity back into the market), an advantageous shift for borrowers in the supply and demand for loans and a need by banks to generate income from fees.

With many banks recapitalised and balance sheets having significantly contracted, the loan market was showing signs of resurgence and lenders started to move out of crisis mode.

This revival was characterised by:

### A steady downward pressure on margins and improved terms for borrowers

As underlent banks competed for business and remained keen to maintain credit support to underpin client relationships, pricing started to fall consistently from the highs reached during the crisis in late 2009. Pricing was driven down by benchmark deals for highly rated companies with margins eventually falling slightly below 30 basis points for multi-year facilities.

Nevertheless pricing still remained significantly above pre-GFC levels. The average margin for investment grade borrowers from 2000-07 was just under 60bps compared to c.100bps in 2010-11.

### A return of longer tenors across the credit spectrum

The five-year tenor became the norm again even for lower rated investment grade names. In November 2010 in France, EDF's RCF refinancing re-opened the market for 5+1+1 year maturities closely followed by Germany's RWE, showing that this development was not restricted to France. While this was initially limited to single A rated names, it eventually extended down the credit curve and entered the BBB rated space.

### A renewed appetite for underwriting

Post Lehman, underwritings disappeared for more than 12 months, until March 2010, when a €4.2bn transaction for Merck KGaA, in support of the acquisition of Millipore, was underwritten by three banks and launched into the market. This was illustrated further by the $45bn jumbo acquisition financing fully underwritten by six banks and supporting BHP Billiton's failed attempt to acquire Potash in September 2010.

### A comeback of borrower friendly structures

While there was a flight to quality during the crisis, looser structures with an absence of financial covenants made a dramatic return post-crisis. The recovery in the non-investment grade loan market also continued with significantly higher volumes.

### A recovery in volumes although funding costs continued to be at historically high levels

Volumes recovered as evidenced by global syndicated loan volumes in 2010 rising by 57% compared to 2009, with $2.92trn worth of loans issuance for the year. It is however worth noting that the vast majority of the business was composed of refinancing of existing facilities and with only limited amounts of 'event driven'/'new money' deals, which were very slow to come back to the market and frequently financed on a 'club' and therefore relationship, basis rather than an underwritten basis.

This trend continued in 2011 when robust loan market conditions prevailed despite volatility in other markets, and broader economic and geopolitical issues, such as the eurozone crisis.

Nevertheless, bank funding costs remained at elevated levels (several times higher than they were pre-GFC). Combined with falling margins as described above, this caused lending to return to uneconomic levels for banks and led banks to target their resources at core clients who were able to offer strong ancillary business. As a result, a divided market emerged whereby two borrowers of the same rating and sector could have different pricing depending on their size and operation and the strength of their relationship bank group.

To address key areas of market stress, lenders developed a number of structural solutions to aid syndication and safeguard liquidity.

- First draw fees and higher utilisation fees (classically between 15bps and 50bps depending on the level of utilisation) were introduced for revolving credit facilities in order to ensure that lenders received an extra margin in the event the facilities were drawn. This was also triggered by certain borrowers drawing undrawn facilities by less than 1/3 and thus avoiding the payment of utilisation fees. This structure has the benefit for borrowers that it does not have an impact on the commitment fee, which is ordinarily calculated as a percentage of the margin.
- From the summer of 2011, US money market funds began to restrict lines of credit to European banks due to concerns over their sovereign exposure. Banks without access to dollar deposits, particularly French and German banks, were significantly affected. To preserve bank liquidity, transactions were structured to address this concern including solutions such as dollar currency premiums, redenomination of dollar tranches into alternative currencies and restrictions on the ability to draw dollars in multicurrency facilities or optionality to participate in non-dollar tranches within a transaction.

- Pre-GFC, acquisition financings were structured with one, three and five-year term bank facilities syndicated in the banking market. Major event driven financings undertaken post-crisis were often structured as bridges to capital markets take-outs and executed with new pricing mechanisms in the form of duration fees, step-up pricing, etc. incentivising borrowers to refinance quickly in the capital markets but without going as far as the classic bridges, which even have 'go to market' clauses to force borrowers to refinance in the debt capital markets.
- There was also evidence of a reluctance to accommodate some specific features in syndicated facilities. Particularly lenders pushed back at participating in swingline loans, due to the significant additional increased cost to the banks for holding these under Basel III, and demonstrated a significant reduction in appetite for fronting bank roles.

In 2012, relatively low deal volumes and the effects of the long term refinancing operation (LTRO) masked the reality and led to a continuation of excess demand over supply in the loan market and generally kept pricing down.

The LTRO is a European Central Bank program providing eurozone banks with a cheap source of financing backed by acceptable collateral such as eurozone sovereign debt. With more than 800 bidders participating in the auction in 2012 (with banks from so-called 'peripheral' eurozone states being the main subscribers), the LTRO provided much needed liquidity (c. €1trn) for the financial system and arguably avoided a second credit crunch.

Low 2012 volumes could be attributable to a combination of (i) very high volumes in 2011 meaning that many borrowers had already refinanced, (ii) a very receptive bond market and (iii) a relative lack of M&A and other event driven activity, which has become a recurring theme; driven by a lack of borrower appetite rather than a refusal by the loan market to support acquisitions.

The EMEA loan market also became increasingly inconsistent in 2012, as witnessed by the massive pricing difference between equivalently rated borrowers in different jurisdictions and very apparent regional variations in the market.

On the one hand, a lack of deal flow and a willingness to support strong relationships was keeping pricing low for some names, while on the other hand peripheral names, which were relying on domestic banks, had to pay a premium to reflect domestic banks' elevated funding costs. A striking example of this was the difference in pricing and terms seen between deals for Henkel (signed in March 2012) and Enel (signed in February 2012). Despite their similar ratings (one notch difference during syndication), the two borrowers priced on dramatically different terms.

## TWENTY-THIRTEEN ONWARDS (2013-18)

The period has been marked by the dominance of US Banks in larger European event driven scenarios with French banks arguably the most active European players in the EMEA market. However, the different markets defined by both regional and borrower categorisation, show many other strong and consistent players in the Bookrunner and MLA roles over the period. Additionally, following the retrenchment of many mid- or smaller sized European banks post GFC a number have now emerged as strong regional players.

## REGULATORY CHANGES LEADING TO INCREASED COSTS

Regulatory changes, notably the introduction of Basel III recommendations (which encompass the increased capital ratios implemented from 2013-18 and the Liquidity Coverage Ratio introduced in stages from 2015), made in an effort to reduce systemic risk and prevent the collapse of another major financial institution such as Lehman Brothers, have translated into increased pressure on bank capital and more onerous liquidity requirements. This has affected lenders and their ability and willingness to lend and has led to increased pressure on pricing of commercial paper backup and general corporate purpose revolving credit facilities. Swinglines which have historically been viewed as a 'free option' for borrowers are now treated as liquidity facilities with banks required to maintain liquid assets representing a percentage of the value of any commitment under such facilities which could be drawn within any 30-day period.

Costs of lending have notably increased. This trend has not however been generally reflected in the pricing of transactions resulting in lenders and relationships being further squeezed. With a continued abundance of willing lenders, borrowers are reacting by continuing to review the size and ability of their banks to meet their requirements and informally allocating ancillary business among those banks.

There is a growing acknowledgement that the relationship model which has developed over the past 20 years or so is under pressure from all sides due to a limited and diminishing wallet available to compensate lenders for the loss leading nature of much of the relationship lending from a significant number of borrowers. This is exacerbated by competition from new entrants to the market bringing digital solutions to products and processes and is likely to lead to necessary adaptations in the future as transactions are refinanced. Changes will, however, occur over a period of time and be specific to each borrower, their wallet, relationships and strategy.

# GROWTH OF THE SCHULDSCHEIN MARKET

The Schuldschein is a private placement loan vehicle in the form of a loan which originated in Germany. They were originally used to lend to high quality (largely public sector) borrowers with minimal documentation (governed by German law). Over recent years this market has not only taken off as an alternative to the public bond market but has also in part replaced the syndicated term loan market for corporates (see also supplement 2.1 to chapter 2). Schuldscheine were traditionally sold to smaller German banks (especially Sparkassen and Cooperative banks) but now represent a form of investment for most banks and many institutions lending to corporates across Europe. In contrast to the syndicated loan, Schuldscheine are not ordinarily linked to relationships and therefore ancillary business. Depending on the investor base, tranches are tailored for either bank or institutional appetite.

# GREEN LOANS

This period has also seen the development of the green loan market, which aims to facilitate and support environmentally sustainable economic activity.

In 2018 the LMA, LSTA and APLMA published a set of 'Green Loan Principles' developed by a working party with a view to promoting the development and integrity of the green loan product.

The Principles create a high-level (voluntary) framework of market standards and guidelines which focus on:

- the use of proceeds for Green Projects;
- the process for evaluation and selection of projects;
- the management of proceeds; and
- reporting practices

This market is still developing, but is another example of the innovation and flexibility which is the hallmark of the syndicated loan market.

# DIGITISATION AND RELATIONSHIP BANKING

The digitisation revolution is also impacting the loan market with new innovations being developed (for instance to identify investor appetite and distribute transactions). The revolution is also affecting the loan market indirectly as other banking products which have traditionally been viewed as part of the parcel of ancillary income are either being provided over digital platforms (thus reducing the potential for income) or are even being provided more competitively by new market entrants. Both scenarios lead to a reduction in the capacity for banks to earn fees and therefore be compensated for the loss leading lending provided on relationship transactions. As this trend develops, the loan market will again find itself needing to adapt to a new environment. History has shown us how this has been achieved over the past 40+ years and the nature of the loan market is that it will again change to meet the requirements of both borrowers and lenders and continue to provide a stable funding platform going forward.

# CODA – IBOR-BASED LENDING COMES TO AN END?

## A MARKET BASED ON IBOR

As will be clear from the description of the creation of the syndicated loan market earlier in this chapter, from the outset the market worked on the principle that pricing would be based on the interest rate at which interbank deposits were offered by banks to other prime banks (IBOR). In most cases this IBOR was set in the London market (LIBOR) although over time IBOR rates have been set in other markets (e.g., Euribor has become the key benchmark rate for euro-denominated loans and domestic IBORs are commonly used for some currencies – such as the Stockholm Inter Bank Offered Rate (Stibor) for Swedish Kröne denominated loans).

This use of IBOR rates as benchmarks for interest rates arose, of course, because in the early days of the syndicated loan market banks actually funded their participations in the loans via the taking of deposits in the interbank deposit market for the relevant currency of the loan. Thus, the IBOR rate represented the cost to the lenders of funding their lending activity and the margin represented their profit. The documentation for transactions reflected this with certain provisions being aimed at protecting that margin over the IBOR (for example, tax gross up clauses – *see Clause 17 of the Dutchco sample agreement in chapter 5*) and others being intended to give protection to lenders if for some reason the IBOR does not represent their funding costs (*see Clause 15.3 of the Dutchco sample agreement in chapter 5*).

Furthermore, many of the mechanical aspects of syndicated loan documentation (timings of notices; day count conventions; definitions of 'Business Day' and 'Month' etc.) are based on practices in the interbank deposit markets and, naturally, the IT systems which have been developed for the market reflect this.

## IBOR DEVELOPMENTS

Of course, although the syndicated loan market began by using IBOR-based rates because banks were funding themselves in the interbank deposit market, there was no requirement that lenders should do so. Indeed, the fact that syndicated loans in, for example, dollars were being priced at an interest rate of US Dollar LIBOR plus a margin meant that there was an incentive to lenders to fund their dollar lending activities at a lower cost than US Dollar LIBOR – and thus increase the profitability of those activities. Over the years banks funded their activities in increasingly diverse and complex ways so that the idea that loans were being funded in the interbank deposit market became something of a fiction. However, it was a useful fiction as LIBOR (and other IBOR rates) were easily ascertainable and understandable rates which (at least until the GFC) were not questioned either by lenders or borrowers. There was a general acceptance that IBORs were at least a good proxy for the funding costs of lenders even if they did not represent their actual funding costs.

In 1986, the British Bankers Association (BBA) took on responsibility for administering LIBOR (collecting the submissions of panels of banks for each LIBOR currency in relation to the rate at which the panel members thought 'interbank term deposits will be offered by one prime bank to another prime bank for a reasonable market size today at 11am'). In 1998 the BBA changed the question asked of the panel banks so that it related to the rate at which they could borrow funds were they to do so by asking for and then accepting interbank offers.

However, the biggest development in relation to LIBOR during the period prior to the GFC was that it was used as the basis for huge numbers (and volumes) of derivative contracts so that the aggregate value of LIBOR related derivatives dwarfed the aggregate value of LIBOR related loan transactions. Federal Reserve estimates as of the end of 2016 indicated that the total gross exposure of contracts referencing US Dollar LIBOR was $199trn of which $190trn consisted of various types of derivatives, and $1.5trn was syndicated loans (with the remainder being a mixture of other business and consumer loans, bonds and securitisations).

LIBOR was also used in a wide variety of other financial instruments so that it was an integral part of the global financial markets.

# IBORS AND THE GFC

The central role played by IBORs (and particularly LIBOR rates) in the financial markets had evolved quietly and almost without being questioned. However, the GFC of 2007 and 2008 revealed a number of flaws in the IBOR benchmarks which had been largely ignored until that point.

In particular:

- IBORs were based on submissions by panel banks made in response to questions about their borrowing costs in the interbank market. In times of financial stress, such as the GFC, liquidity in the interbank market may well (and, in fact, did) dry up so that there may be insufficient actual interbank transactions on which to base a submission and yet panel banks were still expected to make submissions based on their judgement;
- The administration, and submissions in respect, of IBORs were not regulated in any way and yet the huge significance of IBOR rates for the markets meant that there were very real conflicts of interest for organisations and individuals tasked with contributing to the setting of the rates; and
- There were no credible alternatives to IBOR rates.

During the GFC there was a huge focus on IBOR rates as the drying up of liquidity was seen as a sign that banks did not have confidence in the creditworthiness of other banks and that this might lead to a meltdown in global markets.

Following the crisis investigations by regulatory authorities around the world uncovered many examples of attempted manipulation of IBOR rates either to suit the financial interests of individuals or organisations or, in some cases, because submitting banks were nervous about submitting their actual interbank borrowing costs (high at that time because of the GFC) because to do so might be seen as evidence of their uncreditworthiness.

The full facts of the so-called LIBOR scandals are beyond the scope of this book, but the overall effect of the focus placed on LIBOR and other IBORs by the GFC was to cause regulators around the world to consider ways in which they could be reformed or, indeed, whether their place in the financial markets could be taken by more robust benchmarks.

The scandals also caused those financial institutions which had been involved in submitting rates as part of the LIBOR panels to realise that this activity was not risk free. A number of them were fined heavily for their involvement in the scandals and they became reluctant to make submissions.

# IBOR REFORM – 2012-2017

Following the GFC and the scandals relating to IBORs which emerged from it, international regulators started to look more closely at all the benchmarks which underpin the financial markets. In July 2013, the International Organisation of Securities Commissions produced a set of principles for financial benchmarks which have been the basis for reform and regulation of IBORs and other financial benchmarks ever since.

In September 2012 the initial report of the UK regulators, the Wheatley Review of LIBOR, was published. This concluded that LIBOR should be retained as a benchmark rate, but that it should be comprehensively reformed. The BBA was to be replaced as administrator by a new independent entity and the administration of LIBOR and the submitting of rates for its determination were to be regulated. The review identified the lack of sufficient trade data to corroborate submissions by panel banks as a significant weakness and recommended that the publication of LIBOR for certain currencies and tenors where the volumes of trades were particularly low should be discontinued.

The Review also proposed that in the long term alternative benchmark rates should be considered.

The Review led to the discontinuation of LIBOR quotations in Australian Dollars, Canadian Dollars, New Zealand Dollars, Danish Krone and Swedish Krone and the end of quotations for two weeks and four, five, seven, eight, nine, ten and eleven month maturities. As a result, LIBOR would only be available for overnight, one week and one, two, three, six and 12 month maturities in US Dollars, Euros, Swiss Francs, Sterling and Japanese Yen.

This change put focus on the fallback arrangements in loan documentation because these said that where LIBOR for a particular currency or maturity was not available on screen it should be calculated by means of quotations from Reference Banks. It emerged that institutions were unwilling to act as Reference Banks because of concerns about liabilities they may incur. In circumstances where it was not possible to obtain Reference Bank quotations the documentation indicated that rates should be set by reference to the cost of funds of each individual lender. While this might be a suitable fallback in an emergency or on a one-off basis, it would be very unwieldy and virtually unworkable if applied to a large number of contracts on a regular basis. Fortunately, the number of contracts using the discontinued currencies and maturities on a regular basis was not large and it was possible for the problems caused to be fixed. However, it was clear that if the LIBOR for a more commonly used currency, such as US Dollars, were to cease to be published then there would be very significant practical issues for the market.

In 2014, ICE Benchmark Administration (IBA) took over administration of LIBOR (which was often referred to thereafter as ICE LIBOR) from the BBA. In the period from 2012-2017, regulators around the world encouraged the continued reform of IBOR based benchmark rates with the aim of ensuring that they were determined using actual transactional data rather then the judgement of the submitting banks. IBA has, for example, implemented a number of changes to the determination of LIBOR and similar changes have been implemented and/or considered for other IBOR related benchmarks (including Euribor which is the principal benchmark used for Euro interest rates).

## REGULATION

The administration of, and submissions to, LIBOR became regulated under the UK Financial Services and Markets Act following the Wheatley Report and the European Benchmarks Regulation brings activity related to a wide variety of benchmarks under regulation on a Europe-wide basis.

## LIBOR – THE BEGINNING OF THE END

Reform of LIBOR and other IBORs was aimed at strengthening the robustness of those benchmarks and, in particular, at making sure that they were based on actual transactional data. However, the regulators were concerned that it may not be possible for benchmarks based on interbank funding activity to be sufficiently grounded in actual transactional data because the interbank markets continued to be somewhat illiquid. The regulators, therefore, encouraged market participants to consider whether alternative benchmarks might be used.

In July 2017, the Chief Executive of the FCA, Andrew Bailey, made a speech ('The Future of LIBOR') which most commentators believe signalled the beginning of the end for LIBOR as an interest rate benchmark. In that speech he said that, in spite of the various reforms which had been made to ICE LIBOR by IBA, 'the underlying market that LIBOR seeks to measure – the market for unsecured wholesale term lending to banks – is no long sufficiently active … LIBOR is sustained by the use of 'expert judgement' by the panel banks to form many of their submissions'. The continued lack of real transactional data to support the calculation of LIBOR meant that the FCA concluded that it was 'potentially unsustainable, [and] also undesirable, for market participants to rely indefinitely on reference rates that do not have actual underlying markets to support them'.

Regulators had already been encouraging market participants to consider alternative 'risk free' benchmarks and Mr Bailey's speech heralded a period of transition away from

LIBOR and towards benchmarks based on these 'risk free rates' (RFRs) by stating that there would be a voluntary continuation of panel submissions to sustain LIBOR until the end of 2021, but after that time it was no longer intended that the FCA would use its powers to compel banks to submit to LIBOR. Given that it is widely believed that many panel banks currently only submit to LIBOR because they are effectively compelled to do so by regulators, it is generally believed that this means that LIBOR will cease to be published by the end of 2021 at the latest (possibly earlier if suitable RFR alternatives are in place). Mr Bailey left open the theoretical possibility that LIBOR might continue to be published, but the direction of travel was clear.

Although participants in the derivatives market had been planning for the introduction of RFR benchmarks for some time, Mr Bailey's speech came as a surprise to the loan markets and other 'cash' markets. Indeed, the fact that such alternatives had been largely sponsored by the derivatives markets meant that their suitability for the loan market was questioned by many market participants.

## CONSULTATION AND TRANSITION

At the time of writing the loan markets are in a period of consultation as to how loans can transition from being based on LIBOR, Euribor and other IBOR type benchmarks to being based on the RFR benchmarks being established as alternatives. Although, in theory, there is nothing to prevent LIBOR and other IBOR type benchmarks from continuing post-2021 (and, indeed, IBA have indicated that they intend to continue publishing LIBOR) most market practitioners assume either that LIBOR will cease to be published or that, even if it continues, the market will move to using RFR based rates.

As at the time of writing the position with regard to the alternative RFR based rates for each of the five LIBOR currencies is:

| | |
|---|---|
| Sterling | A Working Group on Sterling RFR has recommended that a reformed version of the Sterling Overnight Index Average (SONIA) should be the alternative benchmark for Sterling LIBOR. This rate is based on unsecured overnight transactions. |
| US Dollars | The Federal Reserve's Alternative Reference Rates Committee (ARRC) has selected the Secured Overnight Financing Rate (SOFR – a broad treasury repo financing rate) as the alternative rate for Dollar LIBOR. |
| Swiss Franc | The Swiss National Working Group on RFRs has identified SARON, a secured overnight repo rate, as the Swiss Franc alternative. |
| Japanese Yen | The Japanese Study Group on RFRs has selected TONA (an unsecured overnight rate) as the Japanese Yen alternative. |
| Euro | The Working Group on Euro Risk-Free Rates has announced its recommendation of €STR (an unsecured overnight bank borrowing rate) as the risk-free rate for the Euro area. |

Therefore, RFR alternatives have already been identified and the derivatives markets appear to be well prepared for the transition from LIBOR/Euribor to these rates. However, the RFRs identified so far are not necessarily all suitable to use in the loans market and there will need to be considerable work done before the loan markets are ready to transition away from LIBOR and other IBORs. Indeed, it could be said that such is the dependence of the loan market on LIBOR/Euribor that the transition away from those benchmarks may be the most significant change to the syndicated loan market since its inception as outlined earlier in this chapter.

## ALIGNING RFRS WITH THE LOAN MARKET

There are a number of significant differences between the RFRs which have been selected as alternatives to LIBOR rates and LIBOR. In order to provide for an orderly transition to the use of interest rates based on those RFRs in the loan markets there will need to be work done either to align the RFR rates with practices in the loan markets or to change loan market practices to bring them into line with the methodology being used for the RFRs.

The regulators have recognised this and are consulting with loan market participants and trade associations like the LMA and the LSTA as to how the transition away from LIBOR can best be managed in the loan market. For example, in the Sterling market the RFR Working Group charged with promoting the transition to SONIA has established a sub-group to consider benchmark transition issues in the syndicated loan markets.

At the time of writing the work on transitioning away from LIBOR in the loan markets still has a long way to go, but there are clearly some key issues which need to be dealt with as follows:

Term rates – LIBOR is a forward-looking term rate (in other words a rate fixed for its period to maturity) quoted across a range of maturities from overnight to 12 months whereas the RFRs are all backward-looking overnight rates. From a borrower's perspective one advantageous feature of LIBOR is that the borrower can 'lock in' the interest rate for the term of the interest period it selects so that it can be certain as to the cash outflow required when interest comes due to be paid at the end of the interest period. If RFRs were simply imported unchanged into loan transactions, then this feature would not be available. Either the borrower would have to pay interest on a daily basis or the interest payment could be made on a regular (say monthly, quarterly or six monthly) basis, but without any certainty as to the amounts to be paid because that would depend on the daily fluctuation of the overnight rate. A number of possible ways of dealing with this discrepancy have been considered including:

- calculating a 'term' RFR by averaging the overnight rates over the interest period (but this would still not provide the certainty of a forward-looking rate);
- fixing the borrower's interest cost for an interest period by way of a basis swap (but this involves added complication and cost for borrowers); and
- establishing a variant of the RFR which replicates the forward-looking term nature of LIBOR (but this may not have a sufficient basis in real transactional data to distinguish it from LIBOR).

At the time of writing the jury is out on what solution the market will select although there appears to be a clear demand from loan market participants for the forward-looking term rate option. The same issues apply to all of the RFRs being introduced as alternatives to LIBOR in other currencies.

**Risk Premium** – LIBOR is intended to measure the funding costs of banks and, therefore, includes an element to compensate for the credit risk of lending to a bank on a term basis. However, the RFRs are not intended to include any element of compensation for credit risk. As a result, an RFR should typically be a lower rate than the equivalent LIBOR rate. This means that in the transition from LIBOR based rates to RFR based rates in existing financial contracts it is not possible simply to substitute the relevant RFR for LIBOR because this will almost undoubtedly favour one of the parties to the contact. The various working groups looking at transition are considering how best to bridge the gap which this causes – probably by the determination of a 'risk premium' element intended to equate to the discrepancy in rates at the time of transition.

**Consistency** – One of the attractive features of LIBOR based lending is that a multicurrency facility including all the LIBOR currencies does not have to have a multiplicity of special features relating to drawings in each currency because they are, to a large extent, determined on the same basis (although the day count basis and timetable for Sterling differs from those for other currencies). However, it is likely that many of the features of any RFR based rate will be currency specific. For example, the RFRs are either secured or unsecured depending on currency. This could even result in there being differing margins depending on currency. The working groups on transition will have to look at whether a level of consistency can be achieved across currencies.

**Technology** – The technology platforms for syndicated loans are based on the mechanics of LIBOR and thus, the discrepancies noted above mean that significant changes will be needed to those platforms in order to accommodate the transition to RFR based rates (unless the discrepancies can be eliminated).

## THE FUTURE – THE END OF THE END?

It is likely that by (or perhaps before) the end of 2021 LIBOR, and (perhaps) Euribor, will either cease to be published or will cease to be the preferred rate for use in syndicated loan transactions. At the time of writing the expectation is that the IBOR for each currency will be replaced by rates related to the alternative RFR rates for these currencies identified above.

It may be that the replacement rates will be modified versions of the overnight RFR rates which have been adjusted to include some of the characteristics of LIBOR identified above as being advantageous. During the transition period it is expected that loan documentation will be adjusted in order to be flexible enough to accommodate these new rates. The market will also have to find some way to enable 'legacy' transactions (ones which do not contain mechanisms expressly allowing for the transition to the new rates) to be amended to allow for a move from LIBOR based rates to RFR based rates.

At the time of writing it is probably too early to say what solutions will be found to these issues. However, it is safe to conclude that absorbing these changes requires a huge and concerted effort by market participants.

# *Chapter 2*

# STRUCTURAL ANALYSIS AND RECENT DEVELOPMENTS IN THE SYNDICATED CREDIT MARKETS

The syndicated credit market is one of the largest and most flexible sources of capital in the international financial marketplace. Its responsiveness, capacity, and diversity of participants mean that it is a natural market to which any borrower with significant requirements for capital will turn.

This chapter provides a framework for the study of the syndicated credit market. It reviews the types of instrument found in the market and analyses the principal players – borrowers, arrangers, facility agents and lenders. It also incorporates eight supplements, each written by specialists in their field. The purpose of these supplements is to provide the reader with in-depth commentary on topical or more detailed issues from experienced practitioners in the market.

## DEFINITION

A syndicated credit (this term, rather than 'loan', is used because the syndicated banking market offers products other than loans) is one in which two or more institutions (banks or other non-bank investors, collectively the syndicate of lenders) contract with a borrower to provide (usually medium-term) credit on common terms and conditions governed by a common document (or set of documents). Interest on syndicated loans usually accrues at a variable rate (rather than a fixed rate, which is more usually found in the debt capital markets). This variable, or floating, rate of interest is reset (refixed) periodically; the periods most frequently used are one, three and six months, and are usually selected by the borrower. The borrower usually mandates one or more banks to act as arranger(s) and one member of the lender group is normally appointed by the borrower to act as the facility agent for the syndicate, although the facility agency role can also be provided on a third-party basis (by an entity which does not form part of the lender group). It is the role of the facility agent to coordinate all negotiations, payments and administration between the parties once the contract has been executed and to distribute all financial and compliance information to the lenders.

The aforementioned common terms and conditions apply to all features of the transaction with one exception: the front-end fees. The apportionment of these fees between the arrangers and lenders is the subject of analysis in chapter 4; reflecting the differing role/risk of certain lenders. The lenders that benefit from this disproportionate allocation of fees are those that take increased risk in the transaction, such as those that, for example, take market risk by underwriting transactions.

This broad definition of a syndicated credit embodies the principal features of the product. It is a multi-lender transaction with each lender acting on a *several* basis – each lender acts as underwriter and/or lender, on its own without responsibility for the other lenders in the syndicate. If a lender fails to honour its obligations as a member of a syndicate, the other syndicate members have no legal duty to satisfy these obligations on that lender's behalf. (The facility agent will usually consult with the borrower in such circumstances and endeavour to find a willing replacement lender or lenders – although it is not obliged to do so.)

A syndicated credit is usually of medium-term maturity, that is, between three and ten years, although transactions can be arranged having a maturity as short as six months or as long as 25 years. These are typically driven by sector/sector dynamics, for example, infrastructure/project finance may have a longer tenor in comparison to a typical corporate borrower where currently a maximum five-year tenor is typical.

Lenders in a syndicated transaction agree to participate in the credit facility on common terms and conditions but not necessarily in equal amounts. Indeed, it is quite usual to create different commitment levels and titles (the tickets or brackets) that will co-exist in a syndicate.

The syndicate members agree to common documentation to which the borrower and all lenders are party, knowing that it will govern the contractual relationships throughout the life of the facility. However, because of the *several* nature of the lenders' commitments, a lender accepting this common documentation is not deprived of its ultimate individual right to sue a borrower if a breach of the credit agreement occurs. It is usual, however, to act first through the facility agent and only take individual action when all other courses of collective action are found to be ineffective in securing a remedy.

The facility agent's role is to act as the agent for the lenders (not the borrower) and its duties under the finance documents are typically solely mechanical and administrative in nature. The facility agent's duties are also to coordinate and administer all aspects of the credit facility once relevant documentation has been executed. This will include the disbursement of moneys from the syndicate to the borrower after satisfaction of relevant conditions precedent, and will also cover collection of moneys (essentially commitment fees, front-end fees, interest and repayments of principal) from the borrower on behalf of the lenders. The facility agent will also be responsible for ensuring satisfaction of any conditions precedent and any conditions subsequent (if applicable) and transmitting any post-closing waivers or amendments requested by the borrower and negotiating them with the syndicate members. The responsibilities and role of the facility agent in cases where an event of default has occurred are outlined in chapter 7.

The credit process when evaluating a participation in a syndicated credit is substantially the same as the one a lender would use if it was providing the same loan on a bilateral basis. However, the credit parameters and structural features of a syndicated transaction may be more comprehensive than those for a bilateral facility as they must satisfy the minimum criteria of a diverse group of lenders in the market in order to be successful. One of the advantages that lenders enjoy when they join a syndicated transaction is that they automatically benefit from a common position with their fellow syndicate members. They are, therefore, not vulnerable to a divide and conquer approach that can prevail when a borrower arranges a series of bilateral lines without, for instance, uniform credit covenants. An additional credit aspect for lenders to consider when evaluating a participation in another lender's deal is the quality and market reputation of the arranger. If it is one of the market leaders, it is reasonable for a participant to assume that the transaction will have passed the internal quality checks of that institution and that adequate resources have been applied to the due diligence process. If the arranger has little or no experience of handling syndicated transactions more care may be necessary. In either case, it is *never* appropriate to rely on the name of the arranger to justify a participation in a syndicated transaction and each and every opportunity needs to be evaluated in its own right by participating lenders.

Significant changes in lender behaviour are often first detected in the syndicated markets; these may manifest themselves by the refusal of a lender or group of lenders to participate in certain types of deals. It is only through the syndication market that the nature and depth of changes in strategy, internal policy or pricing requirements can be fully appreciated. The decision by a lender not to renew a bilateral line as a result of such internal policy changes will tend not to be immediately noticed in the market, as it will not normally be made public. Detecting changes in lender behaviour is a vital part of a syndicator's job, and to be successful, a practitioner must create and maintain his or her own network of contacts in order to keep abreast of changes in general market sentiment (although it is important to ensure that such attention to market changes does not cross any boundaries of acceptable behaviour by breaching applicable anti-trust/competition law).

Lenders have many motives for using the syndicated credit market. It may simply be to share a credit risk, the amount of which is considered too large for one lender to book. It may be that a lender is looking to enhance the return on its asset by arranging the deal and taking a disproportionate amount of the fees from the transaction. It may be that a lender is using leadership in the syndicated credit marketplace to leverage the development of other business, or it may be that a lender willing to be a participant finds the market acts as a very efficient source of assets that would otherwise be unobtainable.

The syndication market can be segmented in a number of ways: one way is to distinguish between the primary and the secondary market. The primary market generally comprises the syndication activity prior to the signing, although, in the case of acquisition finance, the financing documents may be signed by one or more underwriters with primary syndication only taking place upon the successful consummation of the bid. Lenders joining a transaction at the primary stage will be original parties to the documentation and will benefit from any publicity associated with the transaction. The secondary market refers to the distribution or selling of a transaction once the primary market is closed. Front running, that is selling the deal in the secondary market before the primary market has closed, falls foul of current market standards and the LMA has issued guidelines on recommended behaviour with many transactions explicitly prohibiting such activity – further discussed in chapter 4. Whilst the syndicated credit market is private, information regarding deals in the primary market is likely to receive more publicity, with the bookrunner(s) providing a coordinated approach to potential lenders on behalf of all the arranger(s) and underwriter(s). This is quite different to the generally uncoordinated approach in the secondary market where individual lenders deal with their proprietary investor bases on terms that may differ from those on offer in the primary market. Chapter 4 describes primary market methodology in detail and chapter 6 describes the principal aspects of secondary market sales and transfer of assets.

The syndicated market can also be segmented into international or domestic transactions. An international transaction for a borrower can be defined as one which is not denominated in the borrower's domestic currency, for example a US dollar loan for an Italian borrower, with the syndicate comprising lenders from several countries, usually including lenders from the borrower's country of origin. Another example would be a transaction involving a borrower in one country enjoying a guarantee from its parent in a different country. (The DutchCo case study explored in chapters 3, 4 and 5 provides an example of this.) A domestic transaction can be defined as one which is denominated in the borrower's domestic currency; an example would be a pounds sterling transaction for a British borrower, but with the syndicate comprising lenders of various nationalities participating through their London offices.

There is a strong positive correlation between the nationality of a corporate borrower and the nationality of mandated lenders (although in multi-lender arranger groups, borrowers often seek geographic diversity). For instance, US banks arrange more transactions for US borrowers than banks of any other nationality. UK banks arrange more transactions for UK borrowers than banks of any other nationality. This fact needs to be taken into account when studying the performance of lenders in league tables. It then becomes obvious why the US banks dominate arranger league tables when the criterion used to measure activity is the value (amount) of deals completed.

One of the strengths of the syndicated credit market is its immense flexibility, not only in the different types of instrument available, but also in:

- the tenor of transactions which, as previously stated, can vary from six months to 25 years;
- the size of an individual deal, which can vary from $20m to $75bn or more;
- the drawdown schedule which can be tailored to meet almost any requirements;
- the currency of outstandings, which can vary from time to time in multi-currency transactions;
- the repayment schedule which can incorporate regular repayments reducing the loan to zero at final maturity, regular repayments but with a balloon repayment at final maturity, a bullet repayment or can be based on an annuity profile;
- the variety of acceptable uses for the proceeds which can range from working capital to project financing, from asset-based loans to commercial paper standby facilities, from acquisition finance to short-term bridge financings.

This flexibility is one of the reasons why the syndicated credit market has remained a dominant provider of capital to the many and varied borrowers that tap it.

# INSTRUMENTS

The syndicated credit market uses many instruments and has developed a stream of new products to meet borrower needs and take advantage of innovation in the markets. Of the instruments described below, the term loan and the revolving credit facility are the foundation of the market and are, without doubt, the most frequently used instruments.

## Term loan

A term loan is for a specific amount of money which is to be repaid in full by an agreed date. The borrower usually has the right to drawdown funds in a single amount or in tranches during the availability period. Repayment of the loan may follow an agreed repayment schedule (amortising term loan) or be in a single amount at the final maturity of the loan (bullet loan). Amounts that are repaid, or pre-paid, that is, repaid earlier than required under the terms of the loan agreement, may not be redrawn. (It is this restriction on a borrower that is the principal distinction between the term loan and the revolving credit.) A term loan may include a multi-currency option to permit the borrower to switch currencies periodically.

## Revolving credit facility

A revolving credit facility is also available for a specific amount of money for an agreed period of time, but, unlike the term loan, it offers the borrower the right (but not the obligation) to drawdown, repay and redraw all or part of the loan at its discretion. When drawing under the facility a borrower must satisfy certain conditions precedent, which are repeated for each subsequent drawing. This occurs because each drawing is technically repaid at the end of an interest period even though it may be redrawn (rolled over) for another interest period if required by the borrower. The revolving feature is usually available throughout the life of the facility. Final repayment of outstandings will be made at the latest on the final maturity date of the facility although, in some transactions, reductions in the amount of the commitments and outstandings under the facility may occur at regular intervals.

## Standby facility

An instrument commonly used by the syndicated credit market is the standby facility, a variety of revolving credit facility. (See DutchCo case study – chapters 3, 4 and 5.) It differs in that, from the outset, it is expected that the borrower will not use the facility for funding, but will keep it undrawn in reserve, as a standby. The borrower usually makes alternative arrangements to secure funding by issuing other instruments to investors such as commercial paper, medium-term notes or bid advances. However, if any of the markets for these instruments collapses or ceases to exist, the standby facility can be drawn down. It is worth noting that this type of standby facility does not enhance the creditworthiness of the borrower in relation to investors holding any outstanding instrument. The ability of a borrower to use the standby facility for funding is governed by the terms of the related documentation. This will usually embody certain events of default which, if they occur, permit lenders, *inter alia,* to decline to advance any further funds. Should an event of default be declared when other funding instruments are outstanding, investors cannot rely on a drawdown under the standby facility as the means of repayment. This feature of standby facilities is of particular importance to the rating agencies when evaluating the strength of the liquidity support provided by banking syndicates to issuers of commercial paper.

## Standby letter of credit

The standby letter of credit can be distinguished from the standby facility in that lenders *enhance* the credit risk of the borrower in relation to a third party. This instrument has been used to support private placements, commercial paper programmes, leveraged leases, export credit-related financings and other structured deals. The purpose of these facilities is to enhance the credit of a borrower thereby allowing access to sources of funds not normally available. The credit enhancement is required because those sources of funds are not prepared, or are unable for legal reasons, to accept the borrower's credit risk alone, but are prepared and/or allowed to take the credit risk of the lenders providing the credit enhancement.

Examples of the use of this instrument can be found in the financing of some projects. Certain sources of funding, such as the European Investment Bank (EIB), can provide funds during the pre-completion phase of a project, usually meaning the construction or installation phase only, if the completion risk is underwritten by a syndicate of acceptable banks. Since such sources of funds are usually very attractive to the project sponsors, it is usually worthwhile to form a syndicate of banks to issue a standby letter of credit in favour of such a lender, which is then prepared to advance the funds.

## Hybrid transactions

As previously stated, the funding from a syndicated loan is structured so that interest accrues at a variable or floating rate, for example LIBOR, which is reset periodically in accordance with the terms of the credit agreement. The funding obtained under such a facility can be combined with interest rate or basis swaps, currency swaps, caps, options and other derivatives to alter its nature to suit a borrower's needs. In some cases, there are reasons, such as complying with regulatory requirements or in the case of leveraged acquisitions and project financings, implementing a contractual hedging strategy, for combining such derivative instruments with the underlying funding at the outset. This permits the borrower to lock in the desired currency and/or interest rate mix at a known cost or subsidy for the life of the facility. The simultaneous combination of funding and derivatives is not, however, obligatory; liability managers can, at any time, enter into, or reverse, their positions to take advantage of market conditions provided that such activity does not breach any covenants embodied in the facility documentation.

The most common types of hybrid transactions are loans combined with interest rate swaps and other derivative products.

## Loans combined with interest rate swaps, caps, floors and collars

Some syndicated transactions, particularly in the fields of project and acquisition finance, rely heavily on the achievement of forecast cash flows to service the debt and assumptions will have been made about the absolute levels of interest rates. The borrower and/or the arranger may take the view that it is imprudent to keep the whole transaction on a floating rate basis. The borrower may be concerned that rising interest rates could jeopardise its ability to service the debt from the cash flows. The arranger may have the same concern and also be concerned that the deal will not sell in the market unless this risk is demonstrably hedged. The prudent course of action may be to convert all or part of the financing on to a fixed rate basis by means of an interest rate swap. This type of swap is illustrated in exhibit 2.1. By entering into the swap, the borrower pays to the swap counterparty a fixed rate of interest over the three-year contract of Rx per cent semi-annually where Rx is the fixed rate of interest. In return, the borrower receives a payment equal to LIBOR from the swap counterparty that, after adding the margin, is used to service the loan.

Some borrowers use other derivative instruments to hedge their interest rate risk. For instance a borrower may buy a cap for the life of the loan that effectively sets an upper limit (or cap) on the level of interest that the borrower must pay in return for payment of an up-front premium. An alternative might be a collar which combines the purchase of a cap with a sale by the borrower of a floor. This would reduce the up-front premium to the borrower and provide the benefit of market rates but also afford protection in a rising interest rate scenario above a contracted level. However, it would also mean that a borrower would not fully benefit from a fall in interest rates below the floor level. As option products, generally involving an up-front premium, these derivatives are only suitable for shorter term loan tenors, such as those associated with acquisition finance rather than long term project financing.

### Exhibit 2.1: US dollar interest rate swap

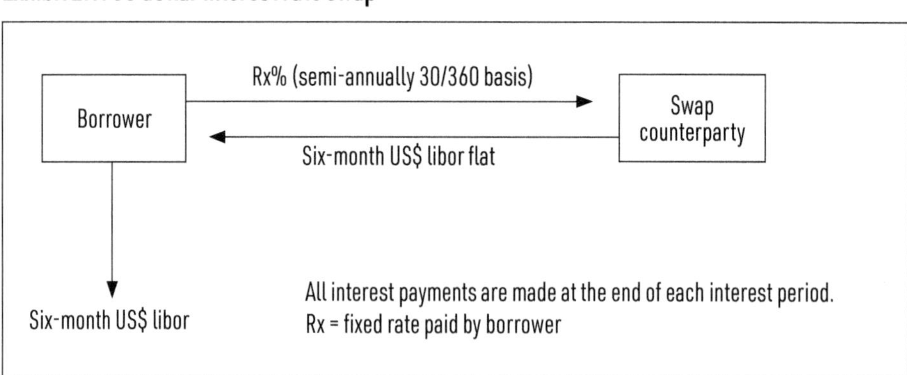

## Other instruments

Other banking instruments which have been syndicated include performance bonds, advance payment guarantees and retention money bonds, all commonly required by project sponsors when awarding large contracts. The market for these instruments peaked during the period of infrastructural development in the Middle East. They are still used for very large contracts. Commercial letters of credit are also syndicated when, for instance, country limits are extremely tight or because certain nationalities of lenders are precluded from such transactions by law or regulation.

# THE SYNDICATED CREDIT MARKET

In the statistical analysis which follows, certain totals may not agree exactly due to the lack of official data and the necessity to use a variety of sources of information. Nevertheless, the trends identified and conclusions drawn are not materially affected by such discrepancies. All amounts are given in US dollar equivalent except where explicitly stated otherwise.

## Size of the market

Over the last 38 years the market for syndicated credits has grown substantially in size as shown in exhibit 2.2.

**Exhibit 2.2: Global syndicated lending (1980 - 1H 2018)**

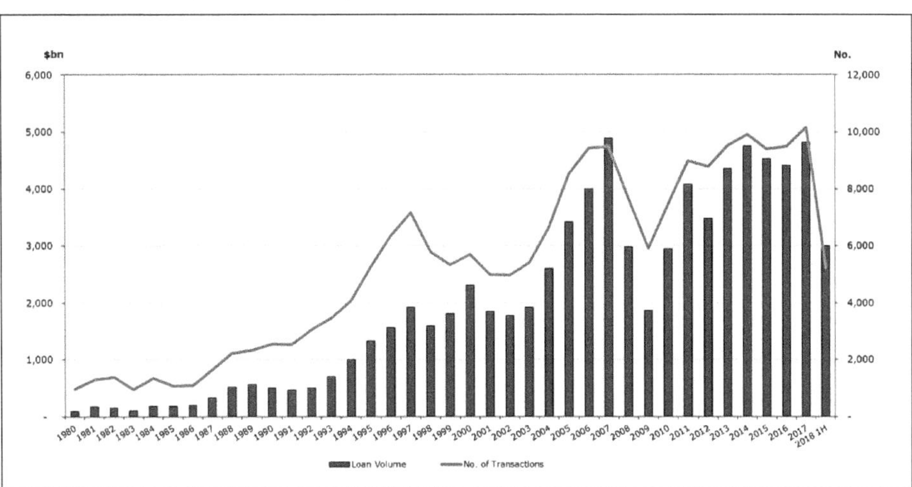


**Source: Loan Analytics, Dealogic**

The total volume (amount) raised in 1980 was a mere $90bn mainly in the sovereign and financial institutions sectors but the market grew rapidly in the 1980s so that by 1989, when a temporary peak occurred, the size of the market was $566bn, predominantly in the corporate sector. New peaks occurred in 1997, just prior to the Asian (Thai baht driven) crisis, at $1,924bn and in 2000, at the height of the telecom and dot.com boom, at $2,314bn. Volumes fell immediately after that, as a consequence of the bursting of the dot.com bubble and the loss of confidence after 9/11, which meant that the market achieved a new high only in 2004 when volumes amounted to $2,610bn. For the next few years new record highs were posted: in 2005 with $3,426bn; in 2006 with $3,999bn; in 2007 with $4,891bn until volumes dropped by almost 39% the following year, amidst the beginning of the GFC which saw the collapse of Lehman Brothers, equity indices plummet and drying up of liquidity in the credit markets. M&A activity started to decline and this coincided with significantly declining volumes in the syndicated loan market, as banks looked to reduce their balance sheets in light of significantly higher funding costs. 2009 to 2011 (from $1,853bn to $4,065bn) saw a recovery in global markets, although sovereign and economic concerns remained. Data from 2012 clearly shows a decline in volume of around 17%, to just under $3,100bn, which coincided with the ongoing Eurozone crisis, debate over the US fiscal cliff and uncertainty over economic growth in Asia. Many borrowers had accelerated refinancings in 2011 fearing a rise in loan pricing which created a deal hole in early 2012 and determined the outcome of the year. However, 2013 was a landmark year. With a strong US performance despite the US government shutdown, the Greek bail-out concluded and central bank liquidity supporting asset values, the global syndicated loan market reached $4,200bn – the best year since the pre-crash boom year of 2007. This was followed up by an even stronger volume of $4,700bn in 2014. A relatively muted 2015 on the back of the collapse in energy prices and further Eurozone concerns saw volume fall slightly, followed up by a further fall to approximately $4,000bn volume in 2016 – a year of both elections in the US and a referendum in the UK, results of both generally surprising the financial markets. 2017 was a benign year with strong global growth, few market suprises and syndicated loan volume returning to growth mode at just over $4,600bn. After a strong 1H 2018, global loan volumes will likely reach their highest ever level in 2018 despite the effects of rising US interest rates, the unwinding of quantitative easing measures in the US and Europe and increasing geopolitical risk.

Although a more comprehensive history of the market is provided in chapter 1, a few of the salient events in the development of the market are recorded here. After the peak of 1989, volumes declined to $494bn in 1990 and to $466bn in 1991. This decline in volume was caused by a number of factors the most important of which were the absolute reduction in the number of corporate and acquisition finance transactions, the impact of the first Gulf war on markets generally, the high loan losses experienced by banks during that period and the concern by banks over the need to meet the capital ratios required for 1 January 1993 under Basel I regulations. Once banks became confident that they were adequately capitalised, fierce competition broke out which translated into increasing volumes of activity in 1993, 1994 and 1995. These were years when many borrowers took advantage of the high liquidity in the bank market and refinanced deals, that had been put in place during the early 1990s, at lower margins and with longer tenors.

In 1995, the market took a new and very promising direction, providing the means by which borrowers in the corporate sector could take advantage of the liquidity in the banking sector to finance their acquisition deals. Instead of being exceptional, the multi-billion dollar/euro/sterling deal became commonplace. One of the first of these jumbos to hit the European market was the $8.5bn deal in 1997 for ICI and indeed this deal was voted deal of the decade in *Euroweek*'s poll published in January 2000. It had all the hallmarks of a market defining transaction because of its size, the secrecy during its conception and in the flexibility of its transferability provisions: it was the first deal to be actively traded in the secondary market in London.

The steady rise in volumes from 1995 to 1997 reflected this new paradigm that the syndicated credit market could finance just about any acquisition envisaged and the mood was positive on both the investment grade and leveraged front as shown by the peak in volumes achieved in 1997. The Asian crisis of 1998 dented confidence around the globe and this pushed volumes lower in the investment grade sector and reduced activity in the leveraged market as well. It was only in 1999 and the record year 2000 that recovery was really seen and this was essentially driven by a frenzy of activity in the telecom sector. (A number of the notable deals have been recorded in chapter 1.)

The events of 2001, the bursting of the dot.com bubble, the collapse more generally in equity values worldwide and the psychological impact of 9/11 meant that confidence was again dented and indeed many commentators predicted recession on a global scale. Low interest rates and buoyant consumer demand in the US market kept the global economy from collapsing but volumes in the syndicated loan market again fell in 2001 and 2002. The pick-up in volumes seen in 2003 was due principally to the refinancing of acquisition-related debt from earlier years and locking in term facilities at a low point in the pricing cycle.

The period 2004 to mid-2007 proved to be another period of rapid and sustained expansion of the market driven mostly by the arrangement of acquisition finance in both the investment grade and leveraged sectors. The growth of private equity funds available for leveraged deals meant that once again, as in the late 1990s, virtually no potential target was out of range and it was the appetite of financial sponsors which was a key driver as shown clearly in exhibit 2.3.

Deals became increasingly leveraged as debt proved to be readily available to support often ambitious acquisitions and they were, for the most part, successfully syndicated with the increasing support of non-bank financial institutions. In addition, the benign economic environment prevailing at the time enabled new and developing economies to benefit from the largesse offered by investors so that growth in regional markets such as the Middle East, central and eastern Europe (but principally Russia), India and Australia saw transactions that dwarfed previous experience. In Europe, there was a change in the mix of countries accessing the market with one of the most significant growth areas being transactions for borrowers in Germany. This was prompted by changing circumstances (regulatory change regarding the state-owned banks), weakness of many German banks over recent years and the decision by German borrowers to be less dependent on bi-lateral lines from their domestic banks and more open to the opportunity of building relationships with international banks.

During the GFC and the collapse of Lehman Brothers bank liquidity was scarce (despite massive interventions by central banks) and funding became extremely challenging. Banks were facing a dramatic increase in their funding costs because of a loss of confidence in the inter-bank markets and a significantly higher cost for raising money in the capital markets. Market liquidity was further impacted by massive withdrawals by investors from US money-market funds. The years 2009–11 saw a recovery in the syndicated loan market with volumes increasing and pricing falling. Large scale acquisition financing became available to corporates once again, displayed by several underwritten deals in 2010, such as BHP Billiton's $45bn facilities to finance a proposed takeover of Potash Corp. The sudden decline in activity in 2012 was caused by many factors e.g., (i) very high volumes in 2011 meaning that many corporates had already refinanced, (ii) a resurgence of the bond markets and (iii) the eurozone crisis. By 2014, global M & A financing of approximately $750bn featured prominently in a post-GFC record annual volume of US$4,700bn made up of deals such as the $36.4bn Actavis/Allergen Inc. transaction, the largest deal of 2014, itself outshone in 2015 by the record $75bn club facility put in place by AB InBev to support the acquisition of SAB Miller. Central bank easing since the GFC supported asset prices during this period with strong liquidity in the loan market providing financing at an increasingly competitive cost and all areas of the US, EMEA and APAC saw significant M & A deal flow in the period 2014–2016. Bayer's $56.9bn funding package to support the acquisition of Monsanto (which was finally completed in 2018) was the biggest deal of 2016 Size, in terms of M & A, does matter and the syndicated loan market's ability and appetite to support the biggest transactions was demonstrated by the $100bn financing commitments agreed by 12 lenders for the aborted Broadcom takeover of Qualcomm in Q1 2018.

**Exhibit 2.3: Global Sponsor backed Acquisition related loan borrowing (2000 - 1H 2018)**

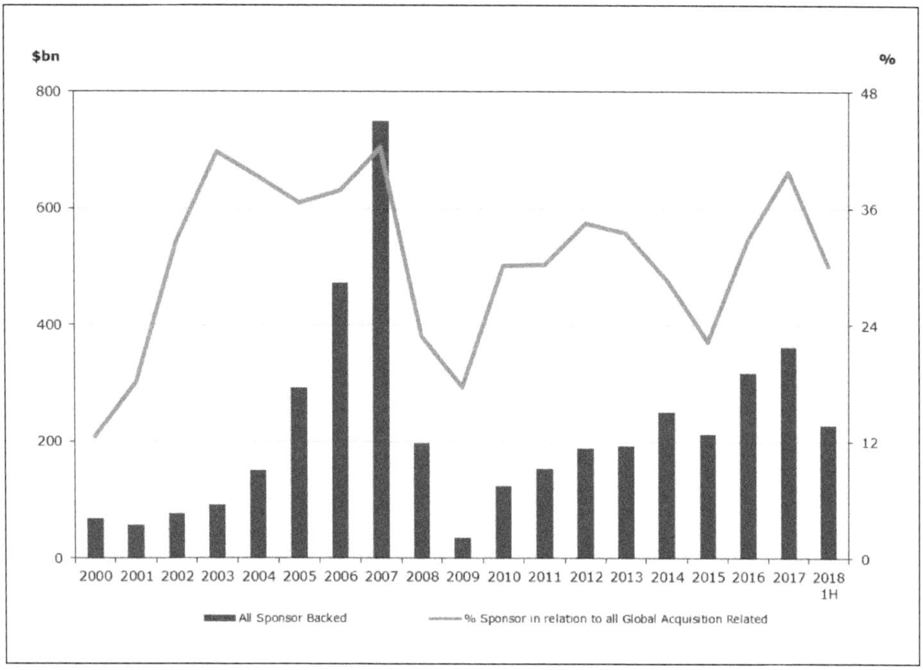

$bn

%

All Sponsor Backed

% Sponsor in relation to all Global Acquisition Related

**Source: Loan Analytics, Dealogic**

## Comparison with the bond markets

There has been significant convergence between the loan and bond markets in recent years as the investor base and the 'book-building' approach to syndication coincided. The bond markets have traditionally provided medium-term and long-term (typically five to 30 years depending on the currency) fixed and floating rate debt to high quality borrowers, typically rated 'AA' or better. Many of these borrowers have also been users of the syndicated credit market in the past. More recently, the debt capital market has expanded to cater for the needs of corporates across the entire credit spectrum including the high yield area where bonds can be issued for borrowers in the single B category. Bonds for this category of issuer have been developing more slowly in the European markets than in the US market although both have had their peaks and troughs over the last few years. Exhibit 2.4 shows the volume of corporate issuers in loan and bond markets for the period 2000 to 1H 2018.

The corporate bond market has been used in recent years for the refinancing of very large short-dated tranches in corporate acquisition transactions arranged in the syndicated loan market. The intention at the outset would be that the bond transactions proceed as soon as practicable post closing of the acquisition and usually within one year (364 days) otherwise the borrower would be required to extend the short-dated tranche by exercising a term-out option, normally an expensive option. As an example, the Project Tennis case study used in chapters 3 and 4 is structured with a bond take-out in mind.

**Exhibit 2.4: Global corporate syndicated loan and bond borrowing (2000 – 1H 2018)**

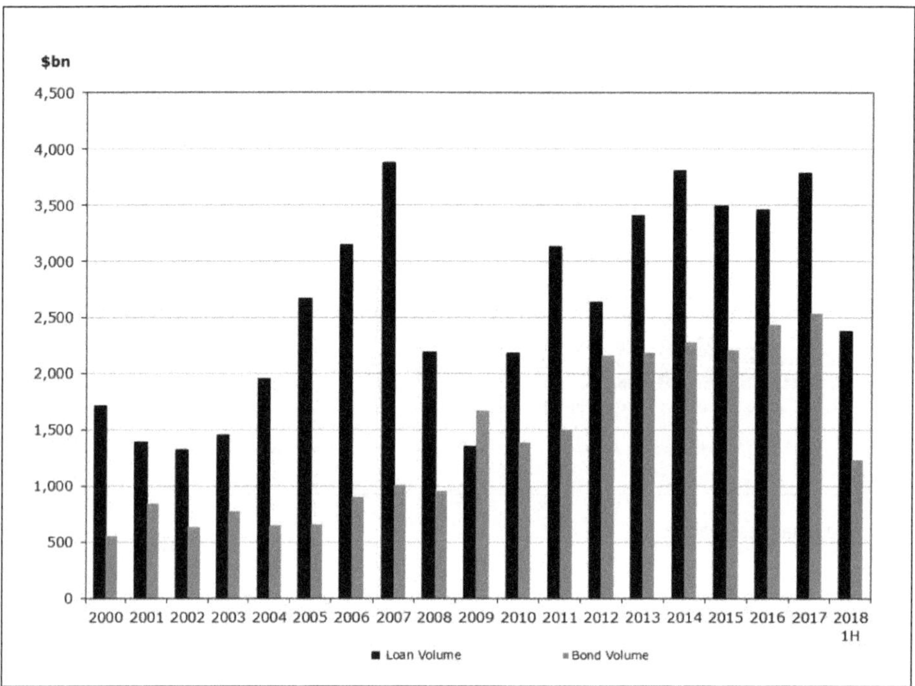


**Source: Loan Analytics, Dealogic**

Over the last few years, the market for high yield bonds has grown steadily, predominantly in the US with issuance of $158bn in 2007 of which just some €25bn was issued in Europe. Until 2009, the high yield bond market in Europe was relatively small and illiquid. As such, it was not considered to be a source of acquisition finance debt where speed and certainty of execution, along with the ability to deliver liquidity in size, are key. However, since 2009, the high yield market has shown rapid growth in both attracting new investors and in providing liquidity to the debt markets. With the capital costs to banks of lending on the rise, investors finding a renewed appetite for yield and significant capital build-up in funds, the high yield bond market is thriving.

The majority of the recent high yield bond surge in Europe has been focused on refinancing but, with the pick-up in new event-driven deals, bridges to high yield bonds are becoming a more popular option (as in the US) to finance new acquisitions by private equity firms and strategic buyers alike. Increasingly in 2010, high yield bonds became an important part of capital structures alongside or, in lieu of, bank lending facilities, in part driven by continuing strong demand by high yield investors for assets, as well as growing interest by issuers in the flexibility afforded by high yield bonds.

The bond markets have also grown in importance in the field of project finance, providing a refinancing alternative when transactions have been rated and this is expected to continue for project deals where the cash flows are both highly predictable and reliable once the construction phase is completed.

Another area of growth has been in the field of securitisations. Many banks have used this market to issue securities repackaging loan assets via conventional structures, for example residential mortgage-backed securities (RMBS), or via highly complex structures such as collateralised loan or debt obligations (CLOs and CDOs). These structured transactions accommodated investment grade and non-investment grade loans as well as highly structured leveraged loans. The growth and use of these structures by many banks and other institutions was one of the key drivers enabling growth of liquidity in the period 2004–07 and their subsequent demise is one of the factors which caused the subsequent shortage of liquidity. The *originate and distribute* business model used by deal arrangers, particularly in the leveraged loan market, during 2004–07 effectively ceased to function during the 2008–11 period around the GFC as seen in transaction volumes demonstrated in exhibit 2.3. The resilience and subsequent growth of the CLO market has been the backbone of the leveraged finance market despite the introduction in 2016 of the Dodd-Frank Act which required a CLO manager to retain a minimum financial interest in a transaction ('skin-in-the-game'). The liquidity provided by these private funding vehicles has supported the growth in leveraged loan volumes since 2011 albeit their liquidity has probably stimulated the growth of 'cov-lite' transactions which have now become the market norm in the US and EMEA regions, in spite of the increasing discomfort of financial regulators.

With the introduction of the market flex clause, there has been convergence of the syndication process in the loan and bond markets. It is too strong to say that the loan market has been giving 'price guidance' to borrowers when launching deals in the market but the use of market flex for upward adjustment of pricing and reverse flex for downward adjustment compare well with the 'book building' techniques used in the bond markets.

# Borrower analysis

## Borrower type

For the purpose of this analysis, three categories of borrower have been identified and used. They are:

- the sovereign sector, which includes sovereign borrowers, quasi-sovereign and supra-national borrowers ('sovereigns');
- financial institutions ('FIs');
- corporate borrowers ('corporates') which also includes private equity borrowers and the vehicles (for example, special purpose companies) used for acquisitions.

Exhibit 2.5 shows a sectoral analysis of the period 2000 to 1H 2018 as well as the proportion of the market taken by corporates and FIs.

**Exhibit 2.5: Global syndicated loan borrowing by borrower type (2000-1H 2018)**

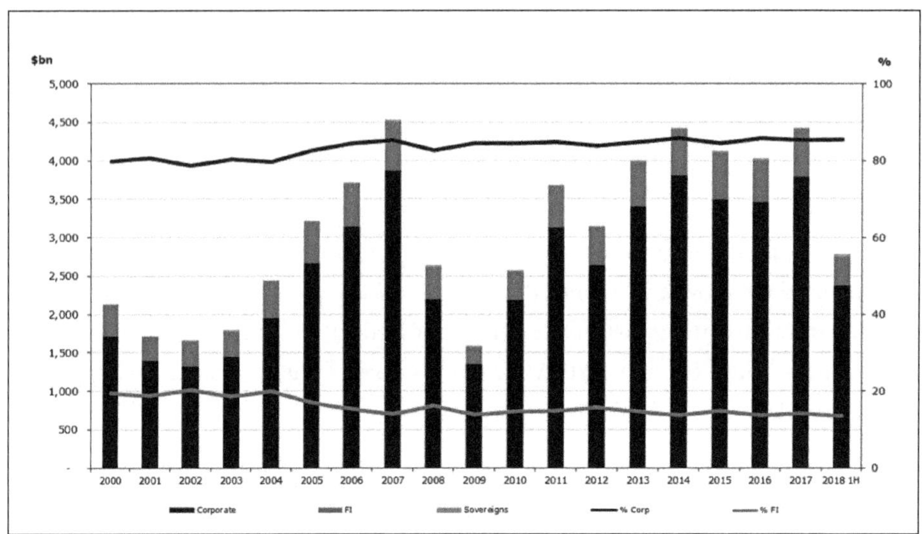


**Source: Loan Analytics, Dealogic**

It shows that corporates were the most active sector of the total market. Indeed, in each of these years the corporate sector accounted for around 80% of the market with core funding and acquisition finance being the most significant uses as shown in exhibit 2.6. Of the remaining two categories, financial institutions have been more active in the syndicated loan market than sovereigns which have largely turned to the debt capital markets for their regular funding needs. FI activity is particularly buoyant in emerging and developing markets such as the Middle East, central and eastern Europe and in the Asian markets.

Exhibit 2.6 also highlights the growth of refinancing activity in the periods 2003-05 and increasingly from 2011 to date. High levels of market liquidity, a hugely competitive global banking market and limited new money demand pressured market pricing over this period, so stimulating refinancing activity. General corporate refinancing, post-GFC, has demonstrated an alternative to the more traditional practice of appointing bookrunners/ arrangers to manage a formal syndication process. Instead, corporate borrowers have largely self-arranged the process (potentially using independent advisers to provide negotiation support). This has been largely due to the growing liquidity in the syndicated credit market post-GFC which diminished the benefit of appointing a bookrunner with strong distribution capabilities. This process also highlighted that in a competitive pricing context, the need for lenders to receive ancillary business opportunities to subsidise a credit price was only ever within the gift of the borrower. Exhibit 2.7 shows the dramatic growth of acquisition financing by region over the period 2000 to 1H 2018.

#### Exhibit 2.6: Global syndicated loan borrowing by use of proceeds (2000-1H 2018)

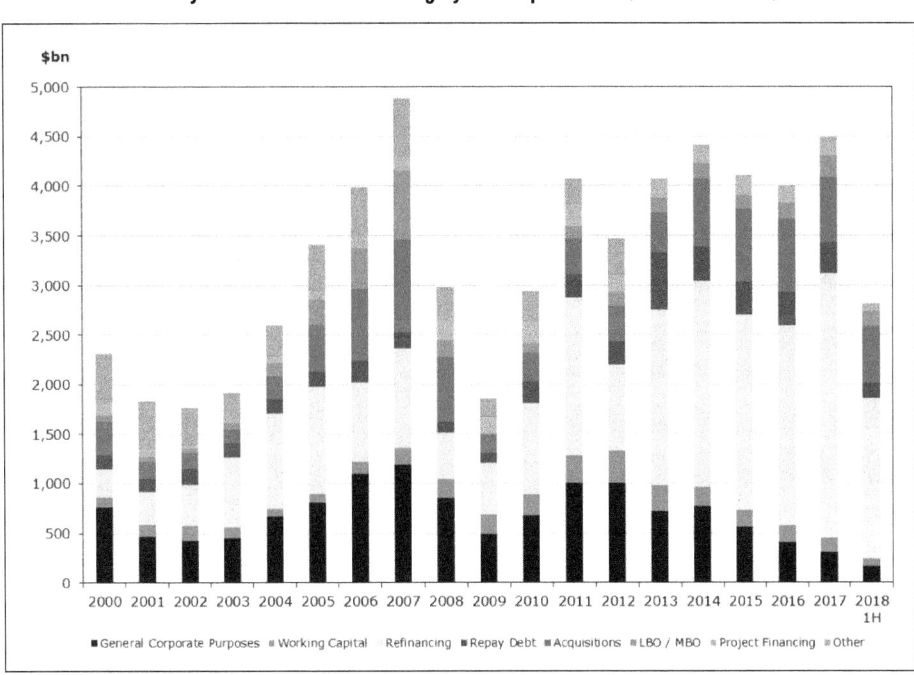


Source: Loan Analytics, Dealogic

**Exhibit 2.7: Global acquisition-related loan borrowing by world region (2000–1H 2018)**

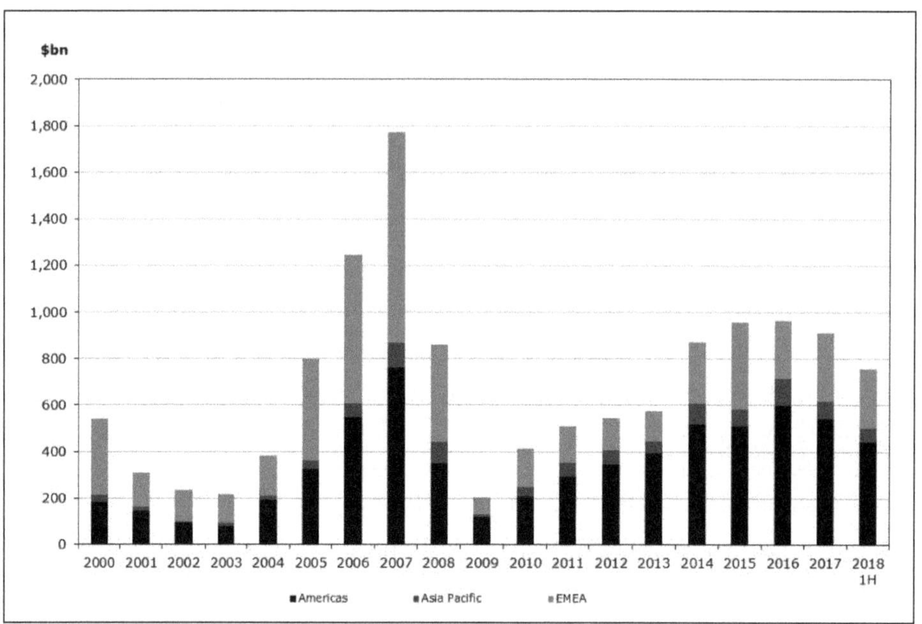


**Source: Loan Analytics, Dealogic**

## Borrower origin

An analysis of syndicated activity by geographic origin of the borrower for the period 2000 to 1H 2018 is illustrated in exhibit 2.8.

**Exhibit 2.8: Global syndicated loan borrowing by region (2000–1H 2018)**

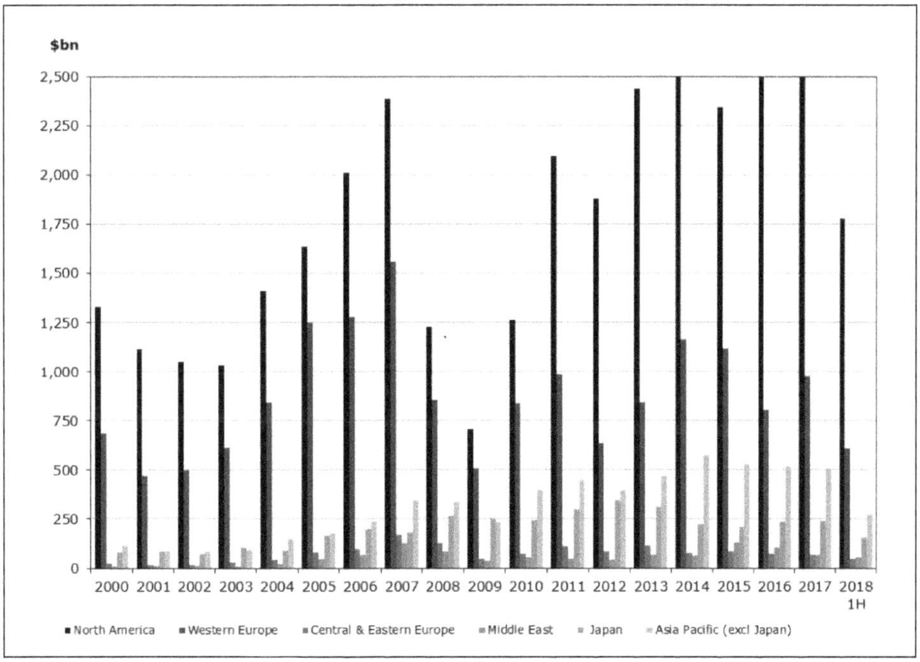

**Source: Loan Analytics, Dealogic**

During this period, borrowers from North America, Western Europe and the Asia Pacific region have accounted for 90% or more of the market, but borrowers from North America dominate the volume statistics. In fact, North American borrowers alone accounted for approximately 50% or more of all syndicated credit activity of which on average 95% is for US names. This explains to a large extent the dominance of the corporate sector as a borrower category (and the dominance of US banks in the league tables, since they are more frequently mandated for these deals than any other nationality of bank). Although the US market has historically been closer to 70% of the global market, its percentage fell to 48% in 2005 as the European market expanded on the back of European corporate activity. Nonetheless, the size of the US market has given market and financial muscle to the leading US banks with the result that innovation and syndication techniques from the US market, particularly in structuring tranches of leveraged transactions that will appeal to institutional funds, have infiltrated other markets. In the past, it has often been the case that such innovations from the US market have first hit Europe and then Asia but in the period 2003–07, with the expansion and global reach of US private equity sponsors, innovations in structures were being disseminated simultaneously across the globe.

The US market can be divided into two main market segments: the leveraged (non-investment grade) and the investment grade segments. It is the leveraged segment that has attracted most interest from non-bank financial institutions and loan funds as they see opportunities to purchase assets in this asset class that are not available elsewhere. An analysis of the performance of US loans (institutional tranches) and high yield bonds is provided in supplement 6 at the end of this chapter.

In Western Europe, the UK used to be by far the most active single source of new business as shown in exhibit 2.9. Over the last eighteen years the importance of the UK has markedly reduced, demonstrating the increasingly international nature of syndicated lending within Europe and the development of important local markets for the product from both a borrower and lender perspective. There has been significant growth in the continental European market for syndicated loans and the market share of European business arranged by UK borrowers has fallen from its peak of 41.6% in 2000 to around 22% currently. Borrowers in France and Germany capture second and third place over the period with the proportion of the market taken up by German borrowers showing the highest (albeit irregular) growth.

### Exhibit 2.9: European loan borrowing by nationality (2000 -1H 2018)

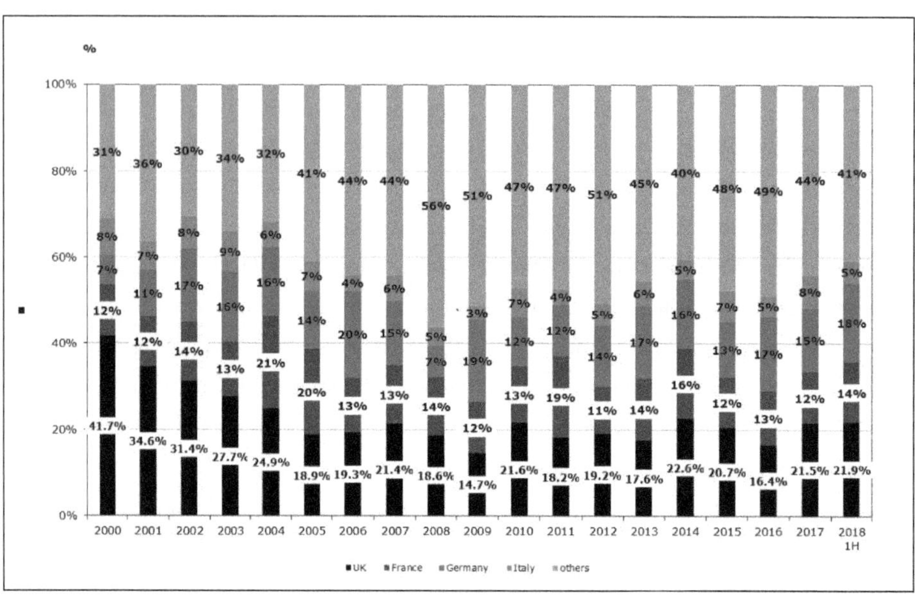


Source: Loan Analytics, Dealogic

In the regional market of Asia Pacific, steady growth was seen until the onset of the Asian crisis which started in 1997. The result was to reduce new deal flow to a trickle in 1997–98 but as exhibit 2.10 shows, after an initial setback at the start of the millennium, there was steady growth in activity over the period 2002–14 (with a slight dip in 2009) since when volumes have been steady. One of the principal drivers has been the opening and growth of the Japanese domestic syndication market for jumbo-sized deals and the use of the international syndication market by Japanese corporates. Another interesting development has been the growth of jumbo acquisition deals in both Australia and India. Whilst Japan's influence on the absolute numbers has stayed relatively consistent since the GFC, most notable is the increasing importance of Chinese borrowers accessing the syndicated credit markets since 2012, having been particularly active in cross-border M & A over the period, e.g., ChemChina's European acquisitions of Pirelli (2015) and Syngenta (2017).

**Exhibit 2.10: Asia Pacific loan borrowing by nationality (2000–1H 2018)**

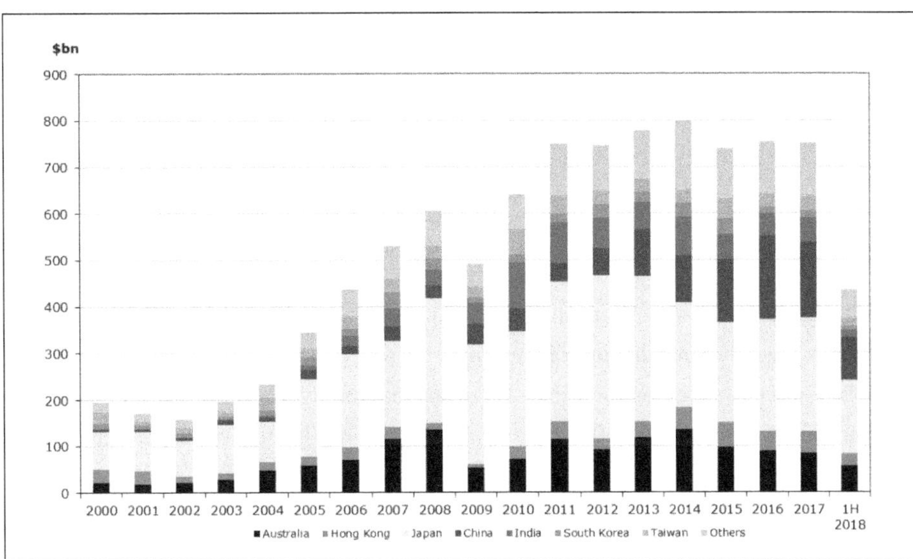


**Source: Loan Analytics, Dealogic**

## Analysis by currency

The US dollar is the currency that has dominated the syndication market since its inception, although its dominance has declined in recent years. In 1980, transactions denominated in US dollars accounted for nearly 90% of all transactions whereas in 1990, the proportion had fallen to approximately 66%. This was reversed in the mid to late 1990s with the US dollar proportion again reaching close to 80% but with the growth of euro-denominated transactions since 1999, the US dollar proportion again fell to close to 60% in 2007 and subsequently below 50% as the effects of the GFC were seen. Levels have since returned to closer to 70%. The breakdown of the market between currencies is illustrated in exhibit 2.11.

**Exhibit 2.11: Global syndicated loan borrowing by currency (2000 - 1H 2018)**

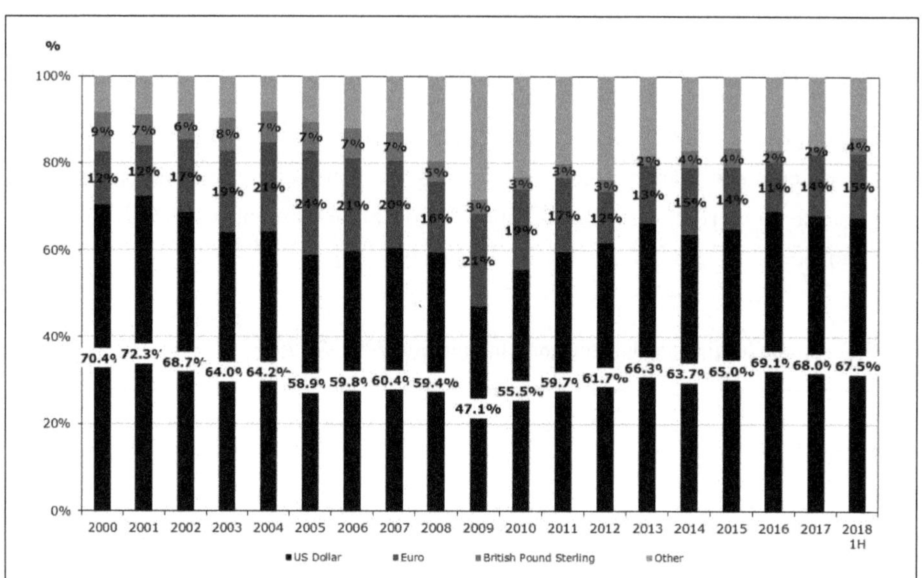


**Source: Loan Analytics, Dealogic**

Historically, the most important alternative currency to the US dollar was the pound sterling but since the introduction of the single currency (euro) in Europe it has fallen to third place and now represents less than 5% of the market. By contrast, euro-denominated loans account for some 15% of the market and there has been a rise in the growth of other currencies (Australian, Hong Kong and Canadian dollars; Japanese yen; Chinese renminbi) as more and more domestic currency transactions have been executed.

The importance of these currencies in international transactions varies considerably. Most transactions denominated in euro and sterling are arranged for borrowers in the Eurozone and UK respectively and are therefore, by definition, domestic transactions. In contrast, the US dollar is used for domestic as well as international transactions and is really the only currency used extensively by borrowers domiciled outside of the US, as an alternative to their domestic currency. It should be noted that many transactions have multi-currency options and therefore the currency of advances outstanding under the facility may well be different from the currency of denomination.

## Analysis of lenders active in the market

There are three principal groups of lenders active in the syndicated loan market. First, there is a relatively small number of banks capable of originating, structuring, pricing and arranging a syndicated transaction. Most of them are prepared to underwrite a transaction and take the corresponding market risk. There is a larger number of major banks and some other financial institutions which are prepared to underwrite transactions but which do not have the desire or the capacity to originate them. Finally, the majority of banks and institutional funds only participate in deals at a level which suits their portfolio, without taking market risk.

League tables, which rank lenders according to certain criteria, are the most commonly used method for estimating market share. They are compiled in a number of different ways by various organisations, none of which are official. Because the data on which they are based only include the publicised deals, the league tables do not provide a totally accurate picture. Nevertheless, when taken over a number of years from a source which has used a consistent methodology, the league tables do enable the most active lenders to be identified. This is the approach adopted for the league tables which follow. The reader can therefore identify the lenders that have shaped the market since the last edition of this book was published in 2013.

The methodology used for establishing these frequently used league tables, the Dealogic league tables, is described in annex 2.1.

**Exhibit 2.12: Top 10 global bookrunners of syndicated loans (2013 -1H 2018)**

| Pos. | Bookrunner | Deal Value ($) (m) | No. | % share |
|---|---|---|---|---|
| 1 | JPMorgan | 2,409,896.28 | 7213 | 11.12 |
| 2 | Bank of America Merrill Lynch | 2,199,277.32 | 7446 | 10.14 |
| 3 | Citi | 1,356,881.41 | 3850 | 6.26 |
| 4 | Wells Fargo Securities | 1,200,502.88 | 5313 | 5.54 |
| 5 | Mizuho | 878,013.72 | 3997 | 4.05 |
| 6 | MUFG | 855,309.36 | 5491 | 3.95 |
| 7 | Barclays | 845,713.82 | 2830 | 3.9 |
| 8 | Deutsche Bank | 761,866.92 | 2734 | 3.51 |
| 9 | RBC Capital Markets | 600,251.03 | 2359 | 2.77 |
| 10 | BNP Paribas | 597,695.04 | 2424 | 2.76 |

**Note: Bookrunner market share is a proportion of bookrunner-led loan volume only*

**Source: Loan Analytics, Dealogic**

Exhibit 2.12 shows the top 10 global bookrunners (now the preferred term for original mandated banks) measured by volume cumulatively for the period 2013 to 1H 2018.

**Exhibit 2.13: Top 10 EMEA bookrunners of syndicated loans (2013-1H 2018)**

| Pos. | Bookrunner | Deal Value ($) (m) | No. | % share |
|---|---|---|---|---|
| 1 | BNP Paribas | 284,750.59 | 1303 | 6.72 |
| 2 | HSBC | 235,444.98 | 1018 | 5.56 |
| 3 | Deutsche Bank | 225,391.29 | 803 | 5.32 |
| 4 | JPMorgan | 206,909.62 | 541 | 4.88 |
| 5 | UniCredit | 201,582.54 | 1043 | 4.76 |
| 6 | SG Corporate & Investment Banking | 193,045.19 | 873 | 4.56 |
| 7 | Credit Agricole CIB | 185,766.50 | 925 | 4.39 |
| 8 | Citi | 185,501.31 | 589 | 4.38 |
| 9 | ING | 174,800.40 | 916 | 4.13 |
| 10 | Barclays | 169,149.98 | 586 | 3.99 |

**Note: Bookrunner market share is a proportion of bookrunner-led loan volume only*

**Source: Loan Analytics, Dealogic**

**Exhibit 2.14: Top 10 Asia Pacific bookrunners of syndicated loans (2013-1H 2018)**

| Pos. | Bookrunner | Deal Value ($) (m) | No. | % share |
|---|---|---|---|---|
| 1 | Mizuho | 600,469.92 | 3016 | 19.93 |
| 2 | MUFG | 373,215.75 | 3808 | 12.39 |
| 3 | Sumitomo Mitsui Financial Group | 368,357.32 | 3438 | 12.23 |
| 4 | Bank of China | 183,225.74 | 782 | 6.08 |
| 5 | State Bank of India | 97,861.44 | 266 | 3.25 |
| 6 | ANZ | 96,397.18 | 493 | 3.2 |
| 7 | Standard Chartered Bank | 69,468.66 | 514 | 2.31 |
| 8 | HSBC | 63,999.36 | 403 | 2.12 |
| 9 | Taiwan Financial Holding Co Ltd | 47,077.98 | 332 | 1.56 |
| 10 | National Australia Bank | 46,541.26 | 205 | 1.54 |

**Note: Bookrunner market share is a proportion of bookrunner-led loan volume only*

**Source: Loan Analytics, Dealogic**

**Exhibit 2.15: Top 10 Asia Pacific (Excl Japan) bookrunners of syndicated loans (2013-1H 2018)**

| Pos. | Bookrunner | Deal Value ($) (m) | No. | % share |
|---|---|---|---|---|
| 1 | Bank of China | 183,225.74 | 782 | 10.75 |
| 2 | State Bank of India | 97,861.44 | 266 | 5.74 |
| 3 | ANZ | 96,258.18 | 492 | 5.65 |
| 4 | Standard Chartered Bank | 69,329.66 | 513 | 4.07 |
| 5 | HSBC | 63,743.65 | 402 | 3.74 |
| 6 | Taiwan Financial Holding Co Ltd | 47,077.98 | 332 | 2.76 |
| 7 | National Australia Bank | 46,541.26 | 205 | 2.73 |
| 8 | Westpac | 46,380.94 | 230 | 2.72 |
| 9 | MUFG | 45,974.92 | 275 | 2.7 |
| 10 | DBS | 45,863.08 | 339 | 2.69 |

**Note: Bookrunner market share is a proportion of bookrunner-led loan volume only.*

**Source: Loan Analytics, Dealogic**

Exhibits 2.13, 2.14 and 2.15 show the same for Europe Middle East and Africa (EMEA) deals, for all Asia-Pacific transactions and for Asia-Pacific (excluding Japan).

It can be seen that the US banks occupy the dominant position in the global league tables, which, as suggested earlier, is a direct result of the size of the US market and the dominance thereof by US banks. It is also testament to the speed of recovery of the US financial sector post-GFC compared, say, to European banks, that the top European bookrunner (Barclays) only took 7th place. Japanese banks came through the financial crisis relatively unscathed (MUFG also taking a substantial shareholding in Morgan Stanley at the time) and it is evidence of their financial strength and maintained global aspirations that Mizuho and MUFG are fifth and sixth respectively. The number of transactions that each bank has arranged and an estimate of market share are also shown.

League tables can be used by banks to promote their capabilities in each of these categories to suit their purpose. Banks use the league tables that illustrate their track record most effectively. For an arranger, it may be important to be in the top five when bidding for a mandate, although rarely will league table standing be more than just one of the criteria used by a borrower when mandating a bank. Some banks will choose to present the league table which measures market share in terms of volume, whereas others may be more favourably positioned when market share is measured by number of mandates. Both statistics are valid: volume of deals arranged can, however, favour a bank which arranges a small number of very large transactions, when set against the record of a bank that has a wide spread of clients but for whom each transaction is relatively small. These alternative analyses enable a bank to make a different case to its clients: the first, that it is highly confident about its capacity to arrange a transaction given its track record in arranging large or jumbo deals, the second that it is demonstrably capable of arranging a syndicated transaction given the number of mandates it has received. A bank that is an active participant can also use league tables to demonstrate its track record as a provider. This can be used to its advantage in order to secure the attention of the principal arrangers when soliciting invitations into transactions.

League tables need to be treated with care. A single, large, transaction early in the year can result in a high ranking position in the volume league tables for the mandated bank(s) although it (they) may not necessarily be regular arranger(s) of syndicated transactions. The implied market leadership can therefore be misleading, even though it is an accurate record of volume year to date. Any borrower using the league tables as a guide to the level of expertise available from a bank seeking a mandate for a syndicated transaction should examine the league tables over a period of at least two to three years to ensure that short-term distortions have been eliminated.

The syndicated credit market can be segmented by category of transaction such as acquisition finance deals, leveraged finance deals, energy deals, airline and aerospace deals, project finance deals and so on. League tables can be created for each of these specific segments which enables banks to identify themselves as a leading 'acquisition or leveraged finance' bank, an 'energy bank', 'airline and aerospace bank' or 'project finance bank', as the case may be. As the reader will realise, league tables must be treated with caution until the underlying methodology in capturing transactions in each category is fully understood.

Not surprisingly, there is a high correlation between the banks that hold senior positions in the arranger league tables and those holding senior positions in league tables of providers that list the banks and institutions most active in committing their balance sheet to transactions, at least in the primary market. Again, care must be taken in the interpretation of these league tables since they do not record subsequent sales of assets in the secondary market once primary syndication has closed.

In the past, there were some notable providers, such as Japanese banks and regional German banks, whose ability to commit to transactions did not, in general, match an ability to secure a corresponding level of arranger mandates. However, many of these banks have now recruited syndication specialists to redress this anomaly and borrowers have been mandating them in this role.

# PRICING

Exhibit 2.16 summarises schematically the credit/pricing cycle of the loan market.

This representation of the market highlights the cyclical nature of the loan pricing cycle an example of which can be seen by examining the market in the period from 2004–2012. During the period 2004 to mid-2007, investment grade borrowers were able to tap the market aggressively, securing lower costs, lower fees and weaker (indeed, in some cases, no) covenants for their facilities as per boxes three, four and five. Because liquidity was available and plentiful during this period, lenders were driven by hunger for higher yielding assets to expand their risk/reward tolerance and the leveraged acquisition market was not slow to exploit this opportunity.

Absolute pricing levels were negotiated to lower levels (either in the bidding process or as a result of applying reverse flex) than had been available historically, where a fairly rigid set of pricing levels had been established for different tranches in leveraged transactions, and weaker covenant structures were negotiated given the intense competition for mandates. Furthermore, leverage ratios increased as banks competing for mandates assumed that investors' appetite would provide the takeout. Until mid-2007, this was largely the case.

The credit crisis of 2007-09 led to a steep rise in pricing due to the rapid withdrawal of bank liquidity and high funding costs (and the market was most closely represented by boxes seven, eight, nine and ten). Pricing hit its peak at the end of 2009 and then came down, particularly for high rated companies. Since this point in the cycle, pricing generally (and certainly in the investment grade segment) has fallen consistently, reflecting continued central bank liquidity supporting asset prices, a global economy recovering from the financial crisis, a low borrower default rate and limited 'new money' credit demand. In 2018, rising US interest rates, the demise of quantitative easing and unwinding of central bank bond portfolios, new fair value accounting rules (IFRS9) and increasing geopolitical risk may be factors in slowing, or reversing, this trend.

**Exhibit 2.16: Loan pricing cycle**

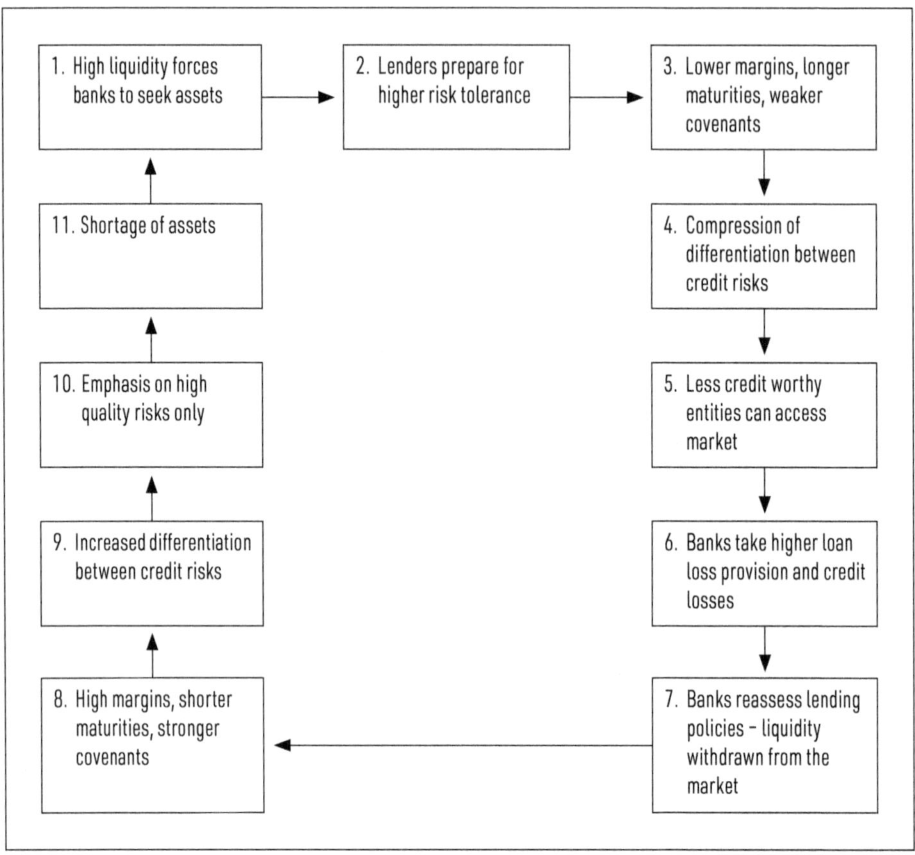


To examine these changes in terms of the cycle, the compression of the differentiation between credit risks (box 4) means that less credit-worthy borrowers are able to access the market but this, after a period of time, can be expected to lead to higher provisioning and indeed some credit losses (box 6), the situation developing in 2007–08. Banks, and more generally lenders (box 7) will then reassess their lending policies (as happened in 2007–08) which is usually translated into more restrictive lending policies with a corresponding withdrawal of liquidity from the market (as happened in 2008). Borrowers then find that lenders require higher margins and fees (box 8), will insist on tougher credit covenants and will reject transactions that do not meet the newly established criteria (hence the upsurge in pricing and rejection of deals that did not take account of changed market conditions which happened in 2008/09).

As credit differentiation increases (box 9) with a greater emphasis on high quality credits, banks start to find that the size of their loan portfolios is diminishing. An apparent shortage of assets emerges (box 11) and with the liquidity in the banking system unsatisfied, banks start to look for new opportunities to lend (box 1). And so the cycle recommences. Although the pricing cycle has been seen to operate in this way, its period is not constant and there is no obvious way to predict the movement between the different phases. As a result, there may be long periods before a move to the next phase is clearly apparent.

If we assume that the correct price (meaning in this context the terms and conditions set out in the term sheet including specifically margin, fees and covenants) of a transaction is the price that the transaction clears the market, that is attracts a syndicate of lenders that matches the expectations of the borrower and the mandated banks, then that price is a function of the demand and supply of those types of assets at the time the transaction is being arranged. At a transaction, or micro level, specific factors based on the type of transaction, the sector, the specific credit features of the deal and the opportunity for lenders to build or extend their relationship will all be factors that are critical in finding that market clearing price.

At the macro level, the price will be set taking into account the overall demand and supply components which are shown in exhibit 2.17.

#### Exhibit 2.17: Factors affecting pricing in the syndicated credit market

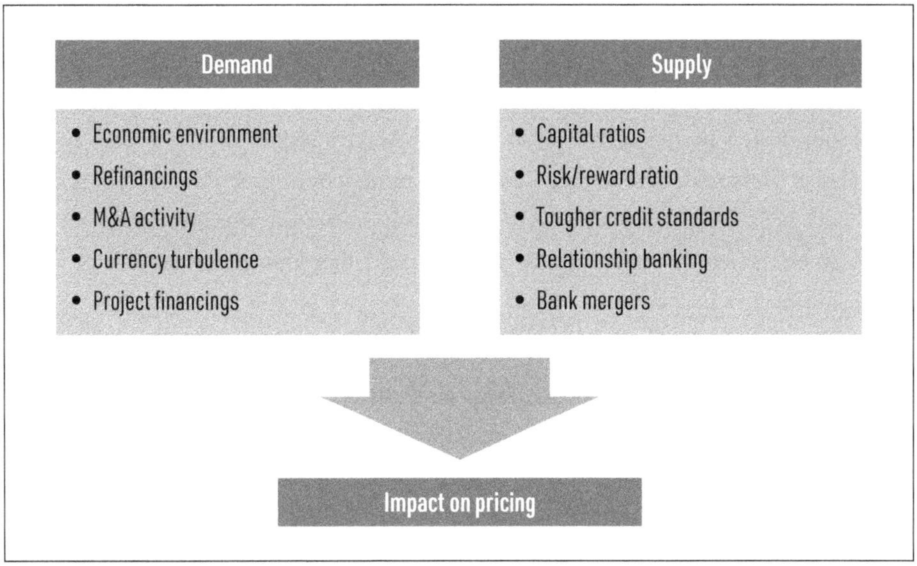

| Demand | Supply |
|---|---|
| • Economic environment<br>• Refinancings<br>• M&A activity<br>• Currency turbulence<br>• Project financings | • Capital ratios<br>• Risk/reward ratio<br>• Tougher credit standards<br>• Relationship banking<br>• Bank mergers |

Impact on pricing

On the demand side, the state of the global, regional and local economy has a direct bearing on the level of syndicated lending activity although efforts to find direct correlation have not so far been entirely conclusive despite the various studies that have been conducted in this field. One of the numerous research attempts culminated with the publication of BIS Working Paper 132. It set out to find significant levels of correlation between developing country economic structure and the pricing of syndicated credits and was published in July 2003. It contained an analysis of the determinants of pricing of 5,000-plus syndicated credits granted to developing country borrowers between 1993 and 2001 and was conducted under the aegis of the BIS by Yener Altunba and Blaise Gadanecz. They found that syndicated loans with riskier characteristics, or granted to riskier borrowers, were more expensive than others, although the effect of purely microeconomic (transaction) price determinants was in several instances weaker when macroeconomic conditions in the borrowers' country were also taken into account. In other words, strong borrowers in weaker countries paid a premium over their peer group in stronger countries. In addition to individual loan or borrower considerations, they found that lenders seemed to emphasise macroeconomic factors to determine the pricing of their loans, such as the level of exports relative to debt service in the developing countries where the borrowers are located. For borrowers in some developing countries, this means restricted access to external financing. They also found that (pricing) discounts are granted on developing country loans provided by small groups or clubs of relationship banks rather than on facilities with the participation of a large number of institutions.

However, experience has shown that during periods of economic growth, investments in new capacity and projects and in the related resources are all drivers of demand for new financing facilities. Refinancings have been mentioned as one of the sources of new business but as the term implies, it is not an increase in overall demand rather a replacement of maturing facilities. The most significant driver of marginal demand is the level of *event driven* activity mainly linked to mergers and acquisitions. The rapid growth of syndicated loan volumes between 2004 and 2007 was directly linked to this type of activity. Finally, although not a main driver of demand, the impact of currency turbulence can lead to emergency loan requirements offering banks the opportunity to provide their services to clients in the sovereign sector.

On the supply side, factors affecting banks' willingness to lend will include capital ratios (the Japanese banks virtually withdrew from the market when they risked breaching the international limits set by Basel I), the prevailing position on the credit/pricing cycle described above, in particular the risk-reward relationship and the appetite for varying levels of credit quality. In recent years, the notion of the relationship has become critical for most major banks with few prepared to lend on a transaction basis. In fact, as banks seek better returns from their lending business it has become commonplace for them to offer a variety of fee-based services to secure complementary revenue streams to supplement loan margins and fees thereby enhancing the return from the relationship for the use of the balance sheet. The form this additional business takes varies substantially depending on the range of services a bank can provide and may include seeking mandates for bond issues, providing corporate finance advice or executing foreign exchange and derivatives trades. The consequence of this approach is that banks may decline to participate in transactions if they believe the overall return from the relationship is insufficient. As reported in the Asian Wall Street Journal in September 2003, Mr Erhard Wehlen, the then treasurer of German engineering group Linde, was quoted as saying:

> *'There are some banks now who are willing to say no…Banks are only giving credit where there is a broader business relationship.'*

The continuous merger of banking institutions is also an important factor on the supply side. Following a number of high-profile mergers there are now fewer banks participating actively in the international syndicated credit markets than was the case in 2000. However, new investors emerged to support the market, notably institutional investors and funds such as collateralised debt obligations (CDOs) and collateralised loan obligations (CLOs). It remains clear however, that these non-bank financial institutions are focused on the higher margin deals (most frequently the higher yielding tranches of leveraged transactions) rather than the low-margin relationship-driven investment grade corporate deals. The collapse of their collective appetite in late 2007/early 2008 brought the market for new leveraged acquisitions to a virtual standstill.

Notwithstanding the above, there is another factor to be taken into account when considering the pricing of an event driven deal which is too large for the usual core banks to provide. This is shown schematically in exhibit 2.18.

**Exhibit 2.18: Factors affecting the pricing of a syndicated loan**

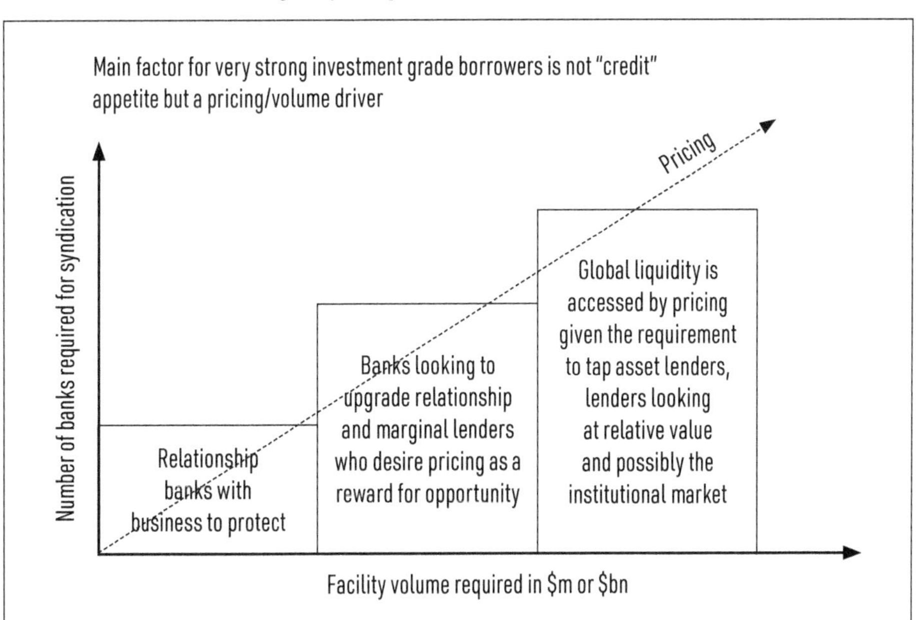

As the size of a transaction increases, the number of lenders required in the syndicate increases accordingly. The lenders/banks can be broken down into three groups: (i) the relationship banks that will participate at almost any price to protect their business with the borrower, (ii) the banks that have serious ambitions to build their business with the borrower and will participate provided the transaction is reasonably priced and structured, and (iii) the banks and other institutions classified as *relative value investors* that will compare the terms and conditions on offer with alternative markets such as the secondary loan market, the secondary bond market, the asset swap market and the credit default swap market. This last group of investors will participate provided that the terms and conditions on offer equal or exceed the alternatives. The market clearing price for a deal in these circumstances is the price that attracts the marginal lender(s), in turn depending on the transaction size and the need to capture banks and institutions from the different groupings. Thus a highly rated borrower may be faced with pricing which is well above its usual pricing if justified by the size of the transaction, and this has been seen on many occasions when pricing jumbo acquisition facilities. The commercial consequence is for multi-tranche structures to be employed with the intention to refinance one or more of these tranches rapidly (typically within one year or sooner) through an asset disposal programme or by tapping the capital markets. It is fair to say that many of the jumbo deals arranged in recent years would have struggled without a 1-year tranche, and most have been satisfactorily refinanced.

## PRUDENTIAL REGULATION OF BANK LENDERS

The syndicated credit market is subject to a wide range of different regulatory requirements. One of the most significant areas of regulation for European lenders which are authorised as banks is capital adequacy. Many of the other areas of regulation are covered in supplement 8 to chapter 2.

The Basel Capital Accord on capital adequacy and prudential regulation of banks, 'Basel I', was published in 1988 and implemented by 1993. Following extensive consultation from 1999 between regulators, practitioners and other interested parties about the introduction of a revised approach, the Basel Committee on Banking Supervision (the 'Committee'), hosted by the Bank for International Settlements (BIS), published a new capital adequacy framework known as the New Basel Capital Accord, 'Basel II', in June 2004. Following the financial crisis, further modifications were put in effect, with the 'Basel III' accord being finalised at international level in 2011. The Basel III modifications were themselves modified (or, in the language favoured by BIS, "finalised") in December 2017 by a package of changes informally known as 'Basel IV' (although BIS treats them as part of the Basel III process).

This section briefly outlines the Basel I approach and describes the key changes implemented, or to be implemented, by Basel II and Basel III (including the 'Basel IV' changes) which affect the syndicated lending market directly. It should be noted that Basel III modifies Basel II but does not replace it so that Basel II remains relevant. It should also be noted that Basel II has not been fully implemented globally so that in some places Basel I may still be relevant.

### Basel I

In 1987, the Committee published proposals for international convergence of capital measurement and capital standards for internationally active banks, which formed the basis of Basel I. The Committee had been established as a result of the growth of such banks' assets and off-balance sheet exposure in a variety of situations which the regulators believed were not adequately supported by the capital of the banks involved.

The objectives of the Committee were to establish a new framework which would serve to strengthen the soundness and stability of the international banking system. The new framework sought to be both fair and to offer a high degree of consistency in its application to banks in different countries – the aim being to diminish an existing source of competitive inequality between international banks.

In developing the Basel I framework, the Committee established credit or counterparty risk weightings, based on the relative risks associated with commitments or off-balance sheet exposures to each type of counterparty, which would have a direct relationship with the level of capital needed to support the risk concerned.

Basel I also set out minimum levels of capital to be held by banks in support of the credit risk inherent in their balance sheets. Eligible capital was split into two categories: tier one (or core) capital, which, broadly, included equity and disclosed reserves but excluded goodwill, and tier two (or supplementary) capital, which, broadly, included hidden reserves, subordinated term debt, asset revaluation reserves, general provisions/general loan loss reserves and hybrid (debt/equity) capital instruments. Basel I stipulated that the minimum standard capital position for banks must be 8% of risk-weighted assets, at least 50% of which must be made up of core (tier one) capital. Supplementary (tier two) capital must amount to no more than core (tier one) capital, and term subordinated debt included in supplementary (tier two) capital must amount to no more than 50% of core (tier one) capital.

The reason why the various iterations of the Basel Accords are examined in a book on syndicated lending is that the arrangers and originators of transactions are required to devise structures that are capital efficient in order to keep pricing at levels which are the most cost effective for borrowers. For instance, while Basel I was in force, commercial paper back-up lines were frequently structured as 364-day transactions rather than the evergreen structures that were formerly used. This was to take advantage of the fact that an undrawn commitment under such a structure benefitted from a 0% credit conversion factor (meaning it would not attract any regulatory capital charge). Pricing reflected this structure and was demonstrably lower than it would be for tenors in excess of one year. This 0% credit conversion factor is no longer available under Basel II or Basel III and therefore the regulatory capital driver for such structures is no longer present (see below for more detail).

## Basel II

During 1999, the Committee issued proposals for the reform of Basel I. The international banking regulatory body proposed to build on the broad success of Basel I, recognising that a more sophisticated approach was required to address both financial innovation and the increasingly complex risks faced by internationally active banks. These proposals formed the basis of Basel II. The UK and the other European Union member states completed the implementation of the Basel II requirements in January 2008. Final rules for implementation of Basel II in the US were announced in June 2012 although implementation has not necessarily produced a level playing field on both sides of the Atlantic.

The Basel II framework was based on three pillars: (1) minimum capital requirements, (2) the supervisory review of capital adequacy, and (3) market discipline, which are discussed in more detail below. The Basel II framework retained the general requirement (set out in Basel I) for banks to hold total capital equal to at least 8% of their risk-weighted assets. As is the case under Basel I, tier two capital must not exceed 100% of tier one capital.

### Summary of the key aspects of Basel II affecting the syndicated lending market

- Introduction of three distinct options for the calculation of credit risk, being the so-called standardised approach, together with two internal ratings-based (IRB) approaches;
- introduction of a 20% weighting for exposures to highly rated corporates and a 150% weighting for exposures to weaker credits under the UK's implementation of the standardised approach;
- introduction of special treatment for securitisation by requiring banks to look at the economic substance of a securitisation transaction when determining the appropriate capital requirement under both the standardised and IRB approaches;
- 0% credit conversion factor (CCF) for undrawn 364-day commitments only if they are unconditionally cancellable without notice, otherwise CCF of 20% applies under the standardised approach and between 0% to 75% for the IRB approaches;

- new specific capital charge for operational risk with three options for calculating the exposure;
- increased scope for recognising guarantees (for example, the provision of a parent guarantee by corporate rated A or higher in respect of a loan from a bank to a lower rated subsidiary may allow a capital benefit under the standardised approach);
- expanded recognition of credit derivatives, guarantees, collateral and on-balance sheet netting as credit risk mitigation tools (however, Basel II requires that security arrangements must be shown by banks to be legally effective in order to benefit from the desired regulatory capital treatment);
- regulators to have powers to impose super-equivalent minimum capital ratios where appropriate; and
- banks using the IRB approaches must use such approaches for actual credit decision-making (and not just for regulatory capital purposes).

## The first pillar – minimum capital requirements

This is the main element of the Basel II framework and is the one that is most relevant to this book. This pillar attempts to differentiate more effectively between levels of credit risk and to give greater recognition to risk management techniques than Basel I.

In considering a comparison of Basel I and Basel II, it is important to note that the concept of a capital ratio where the numerator represents the amount of capital a bank has available and the denominator is a measure of the risks faced by the bank (risk-weighted assets) remained in place. Under Basel II, the regulations that define the numerator of the capital ratio (that is, the definition of regulatory capital) remained unchanged. However, Basel III has redefined this (see below). The proposed modifications occurred in the risk weighting to be applied for particular counterparties and the changes were designed to make the resulting capital ratios more meaningful.

## Rating assessments for credit risk

The Basel I approach to calculating capital for banking book credit risks applied the same risk weightings to all counterparties of the same type. For example, all exposures to OECD banks were risk weighted 20% while all exposures to corporates were risk weighted 100%. This approach was increasingly seen as overly simplistic. Basel II used alternative approaches: a new standardised approach which placed greater reliance on approved internal or external credit assessments (for example, Standard & Poor's and Moody's ratings) to differentiate credit categories, and the IRB approaches (foundation and advanced) which relied on banks' own internally-generated data. Supplement 7 to this chapter explains the methodology used by Standard & Poor's for its loan and recovery ratings.

The latter IRB approaches allowed banks that qualify (i.e., have obtained regulatory approval to adopt an IRB approach) to rely on their own internal estimates of risk components in determining the capital requirement for a given exposure. The estimates of risk adjustment for which this calculation provides were designed to be much more flexible and tailored to the individual circumstances of the bank whose capital requirements are being calculated. It is often the case that a bank moving from a standardised approach to an IRB approach in respect of a set of assets will have a significantly reduced capital requirement.

The differences between the foundation and advanced IRB approaches related to the extent to which a bank is permitted to provide its own estimates of the factors necessary for the IRB calculation. Under the IRB requirements, banks must also categorise their exposures into broad asset classes including: central governments and central banks; financial institutions; corporates; retail; and/or securitisation exposures.

An extract of the risk weightings for different categories of credit quality under the standardised approach are shown in exhibit 2.19.

Under the standardised approach, there are two options for claims on banks: under the first option, all banks incorporated in a country will be assigned a risk weight which is one category less favourable than that assigned to claims on the sovereign of that country except that for claims on banks in countries with sovereigns rated BB+ to B- and on banks in unrated countries, the risk weight is capped at 100%. The risk weight for banks in countries with sovereigns rated below B- is 150%. The second option bases the risk weighting on the external credit assessment of the bank itself. Exhibit 2.19 summarises the weightings for the two options.

Basel II does not, under the standardised approach, take into account the maturity of claims on banks in calculating capital requirements, except for a limited adjustment for short-term claims on banks (which is shown in exhibit 2.19).

It should be noted that the risk weightings under the standardised approach are subject to variation as a result of differing national implementation. The implementation of the Basel II rules in the EU was carried out pursuant to the so-called Capital Requirements Directive.

**Exhibit 2.19: Basel II – Standardised approach – Risk weights**

| Counterparty | | AAA to AA- | A+ to A- | BBB+ to BBB- | BB+ to B- | Below B- | Unrated |
|---|---|---|---|---|---|---|---|
| Sovereigns and central banks | | 0% | 20% | 50% | 100% | 150% | 100% |
| Other banks | Option 1[1] | 20% | 50% | 100% | 100% | 150% | 100%[3] |
| | Option 2[1] | 20% | 50% | 50% | 100% | 150% | 50%[3] |
| | | 20%[2] | 20%[2] | 20%[2] | 50%[2] | 150%[2] | 20%[2,3] |
| **Counterparty** | | **AAA to AA-** | **A+ to A-** | **BBB+ to BB-** | | **Below BB-** | **Unrated** |
| Corporates | | 20% | 50% | 100% | | 150% | 100%[3] |
| Securities firms | | Claims on securities firms to be treated as claims on banks provided they are subject to "comparable" capital requirements to those applied to banks under Basel II. Otherwise, claims on securities firms to be treated as claims on corporates. | | | | | |

1. For exposures to other banks, national supervisors have a choice of two options. The risk weightings for option one are based on the credit rating of the country of incorporation of the relevant counterparty. The risk weightings for option two are based on the credit rating of the relevant counterparty itself.
2. Short-term claims with an original maturity of three months or less.
3. Risk weightings for claims on unrated banks and corporates cannot be lower than risk weightings for claims on sovereign of incorporation.

## Lending secured by property

Lending secured by mortgages on residential property would, under the standardised approach, receive a 35% risk weighting. However, in 2004 the Committee noted that commercial property lending had been a recurring source of problem assets. Therefore 'in principle' a 100% risk weight was normally required for commercial property mortgage loans although there is limited scope for a preferential risk weighting in certain circumstances in some well-developed and long-established markets.

A bank applying an IRB approach under Article 153 of the CRR would be subject to the 'slotting' rules applicable to 'specialised lending', where the lender is unable to estimate the probability of default or its estimates do not meet CRR requirements. The CRR contains a set of risk weights to be assigned to five categories, depending on the underlying credit (e.g., 'strong' and 'weak') and remaining maturity (two categories: less than 2.5 years and 2.5 years and longer).

## Off-balance sheet items

Basel II provided that off-balance sheet items will be converted into credit exposure equivalents through the use of credit conversion factors. Commitments with an original maturity of up to one year and commitments with an original maturity of over one year generally received a credit conversion factor of 20% and 50% respectively under the standardised approach (although certain 'high risk' items may receive a credit conversion factor of 100%). However, any commitments that were unconditionally cancellable at any time by the bank without prior notice, or that effectively provide for automatic cancellation due to deterioration in a borrower's creditworthiness, qualify for a 0% credit conversion factor.

## Short-term committed facilities

As mentioned above, under the Basel I framework, a committed credit line with a 364-day time limit would have been awarded a zero weighting. Following the implementation of Basel II, only commitments which are unconditionally cancellable at any time would attract a zero weighting. In other cases, the weighting would be 20% (or 50% if the original maturity of the commitment exceeded one year) under the standardised approach. Under the IRB approach the weighting would be 75%. These charges reduce the attractiveness of such commitments to banks, given the regulatory capital requirements.

## Operational risk

Basel II introduced a new requirement for banks to hold capital covering operational risk, which is defined as the risk of loss resulting from inadequate or failed internal processes, people and systems or from external events, including legal risk but excluding strategic and reputational risk. Reaching an agreed definition of operational risk, as well as a mechanism for quantifying it and calculating capital requirements for it, proved to be significant challenges in the process of finalising Basel II.

## The second pillar – supervisory review process

The second pillar of Basel II, which contains what is referred to as the supervisory review process, was designed to ensure that capital requirements are appreciated in the context of a broader risk management framework. The supervisory review process centres upon the need not only to ensure that banks comply with their various obligations under the first pillar, but also that they do not rely on capital as the only option when addressing risks covered by the first pillar. The second pillar is also concerned with ensuring that banks address other risks which are not covered, or which are only partially covered, by the first pillar, such as interest rate risk, business risk and strategic risk.

The second pillar contains a number of principles focusing on the need not only for banks to have rigorous internal risk monitoring, assessment and management procedures (including effective board and senior management oversight), but also for effective supervision by regulators who set capital requirements in excess of the minimum standards, assess a bank's level of compliance and take effective supervisory action where necessary.

## The third pillar – market discipline

The third pillar of Basel II aims to encourage banks to monitor and control risk effectively, by obliging them to make a series of disclosures about their risk profiles and regulatory capital procedures which are available to market participants. The ability of market participants to use the information contained in these disclosures to make their own assessment of a particular bank is intended to provide a strong incentive for the bank concerned to be as diligent as possible in complying with the Basel II requirements. The disclosure requirements in Basel II are designed to strike a balance between the need for meaningful disclosure which achieves this end and the protection of confidential and proprietary information.

## Basel III

Basel III was the response of the Committee to the GFC with an aim to amplify existing Basel II requirements and introduce new ones. Basel III is intended to promote a more resilient banking sector, improve its ability to absorb shocks and eliminate systemic risk from the banking sector. Basel III is subject to a multi-year roll-out. The newer prudential metrics, in particular relating to liquidity, will not be fully in force until 2019, with some obligations only taking effect by 1 January 2022. Basel III sets out to achieve its goals by strengthening the global capital and liquidity requirements of banks. As will be discussed below, qualifying capital, risk-weighted assets and the required ratio between the two are all changing: qualifying capital is becoming less flexible and risk weightings are going up. Basel III is not, however, primarily about capital requirements, as the sections on leverage and liquidity ratios below will suggest.

Basel III has been implemented in the European Union by Directive 2013/36/EU (commonly referred to as 'CRD IV'), requiring to be implemented by member states by 31 December 2013, and Regulation (EU) No. 575/2013 (commonly referred to as the 'CRR' or 'Capital Requirements Regulation'), which took effect on 1 January 2014. By contrast to the implementation of Basel II, which gave significant flexibility to member states on implementing various aspects of its requirements, much of the implementation of Basel III is effected via the CRR, an EU regulation which has direct effect and does not require member state implementation in order to be legally effective.

## Capital ratios

Basel III aims to strengthen the regulatory capital framework by raising both the quality and quantity of the regulatory capital base. While the Basel III framework retains the general capital requirement (set out in Basel I and echoed in Basel II) for banks to hold total capital equal to at least 8% of their risk-weighted assets (RWAs), Basel III imposes amendments with regards to its composition. From 1 January 2015, the minimum 'common equity' component was increased from 2% to 4.5% of RWAs and the 'Tier 1' element of the total capital, which includes common equity, was increased from 4% to 6% of RWAs.

The Basel III framework also introduces two additional capital 'buffers' above the minimum capital requirement of 8% of the banks' RWAs. The first buffer is the 'capital conservation buffer' which will comprise of common equity amounting to 2.5% of the banks' RWAs. While, in theory, a bank may allow its equity to dip below the capital conservation requirement, if it does so it will be subject to restrictions on paying dividends and bonuses which will continue for as long as its total equity remains below that level. The second buffer, the 'countercyclical capital buffer', would only be imposed at times of excessive credit growth and at the discretion of national authorities. This buffer comprises of an additional common equity of up to 2.5% of the banks' RWAs. As with the capital conservation buffer, the countercyclical capital buffer became fully effective on 1 January 2019.

EU member states also have the power under CRD IV to apply a systemic risk buffer of 1% to 3% for all exposures and up to 5% for domestic and third party exposures (and even higher if the Commission agrees).

It should also be noted that while the above-mentioned capital ratios are imposed on all banks, certain large banks, known as 'Systemically Important Financial Institutions' or 'SIFI', are subject to further capital charges over and above the Basel minima in an effort to ensure the stability of these institutions.

Article 153(2) of the CRR increases risk weightings in respect of a bank's exposure to another financial institution. This has increased the regulatory capital costs of interbank lending. In addition, Article 153 applies to a broad range of bank counterparties, including 'large financial sector entities' and 'unregulated financial entities'. This means that bank lenders which are subject to Article 153 need to focus on whether the borrower falls within these categories.

## Definition of Capital

Basel III seeks to improve the quality of the banks' capital base by reconsidering what amounts to capital. Basel III reiterates the importance of banks having their risk exposures backed by a high-quality capital base. The GFC showed not only that banks held insufficient levels of high-quality capital, but also exposed inconsistencies across jurisdictions as to what amounted to capital. The topic of defining capital is very complex and only a summary has been included below.

The Basel Committee took another look at the definition of capital and concluded that total regulatory capital will consist of the sum of Tier 1 Capital (going concern capital encompassing Common Equity Tier 1 and Additional Tier 1) and Tier 2 Capital (gone-concern capital). In short, Tier 3 was abolished and greater focus placed on the common equity component of Tier 1 which comprises of, amongst other:

- Common shares issued by the bank that meet the criteria for classification as common shares for regulatory purposes (or the equivalent for non-joint stock companies);
- Certain Stock surplus (share premium) resulting from the issue of instruments included in specific Common Equity Tier 1 criteria;
- Retained earnings;
- Accumulated other comprehensive income and other disclosed reserves;
- Common shares issued by consolidated subsidiaries of the bank and held by third parties (i.e., minority interests) that meet the criteria for inclusion in Common Equity Tier 1 capital;
- Regulatory adjustments applied in the calculation of Common Equity Tier.

Additional Tier 1 consists of the following:

- Instruments issued by the bank that meet the criteria for inclusion in Additional Tier 1 capital (and are not included in Common Equity Tier 1);
- Stock surplus (share premium) resulting from the issue of instruments included in specific Additional Tier 1 capital criteria;
- Instruments issued by consolidated subsidiaries of the bank and held by third parties that meet the criteria for inclusion in Additional Tier 1 capital and are not included in Common Equity Tier 1;
- Regulatory adjustments applied in the calculation of Additional Tier 1 Capital.

Tier 2 capital is no longer divided into lower Tier 2 and upper Tier 2, but comprises of a single set of Tier 2 capital. Tier 2 capital includes:

- Instruments issued by the bank that meet the criteria for inclusion in Tier 2 capital (and are not included in Tier 1 capital);
- Stock surplus (share premium) resulting from the issue of instruments included in specific Tier 2 capital criteria;
- Instruments issued by consolidated subsidiaries of the bank and held by third parties that meet the criteria for inclusion in specific Tier 2 capital criteria and are not included in Tier 1 capital;
- Certain loan loss provisions;
- Regulatory adjustments applied in the calculation of Tier 2 Capital.

## Leverage Ratio

In order to limit the amount of lending done by banks and curb the level of risk in the financial sector, the Basel III framework supplemented risk asset ratios by introducing the concept of a leverage ratio (fully effective from January 2018). The rationale behind the leverage ratio is to restrict the absolute level of indebtedness which a bank may take on. Where a bank takes on matched assets and liabilities, it may well incur little or no risk, but the argument behind the leverage ratio is that sheer size is in itself a risk, and that banks should not be permitted to grow the absolute size of their balance sheet above a certain multiple of their capital no matter how well-hedged they may be. The leverage limit under Basel III is 3% – that is, the bank's gross borrowings should not be more than 33 times the bank's Tier 1 capital. One of the features of implementation in the EU (Part Seven of the CRR) is a prohibition on collateral being used to reduce the exposure value of assets, and a prohibition on loans being netted with deposits.

The US Federal Reserve's implementation of the Basel III leverage ratio with respect to the largest banking organisations provides that a US bank holding company that meets G-SIB (Global Systemically Important Banks) criteria must maintain a supplementary leverage ratio of 5% or else face limitations on its ability to make distributions and discretionary bonus payments. Each insured deposit-taking subsidiary of a G-SIB bank holding company must maintain a supplementary leverage ratio of 6% in order to be considered well-capitalised under the US 'prompt corrective action' framework.

## Liquidity

The Basel III amendments to the Basel II framework introduced two new prudential requirements into the structure of bank supervision. These are the liquidity coverage ratio (LCR) and the net stable funding requirement (NSFR).

### Liquidity Coverage Ratio

The liquidity coverage ratio is a development of a rule to which most banks were already subject. The essence of this rule is that a bank is required to maintain a pool of highly liquid assets which is sufficient to meet the forecast net cash outflows over a 30-day period based on certain regulated assumptions. Among the assumptions are that a bank will be subject to a downgrading by three notches and experience a 30%, 40% or 100% (depending on the type of borrower) drawing of all the liquidity lines which it has granted, unable to raise finance from secured funding on non-government securities and unable to issue commercial paper or access the short-term money market.

Under the previous rules, the level of assets banks held to fund normal outflows was assessed on a behavioural basis by the bank itself. Under the LCR, however, the regulator imposes on the bank assumptions about how fast cash will flow out, and the bank must construct its asset pool accordingly. The LCR ascribes weightings to certain kinds of asset and liability to determine what will lead to an outflow of cash. Having ascertained that amount of outflow, the bank must ensure that it sets aside sufficient liquid assets meeting various narrowly-defined quality criteria to cover the predicted net outflow. Under the LCR requirement, the three main categories of liabilities that will trigger the need to hold liquid assets are undrawn commitments, funding provided to a bank for which the bank has provided security over certain of its assets, and deposits, liabilities and obligations of banks under unsecured funding.

The LCR asset pool must be a real asset pool, in that it must be a segregated and identifiable pool of assets, controlled by the group treasurer as part of the bank's liquidity management activity and completely unencumbered. This means that at least some of the high-quality liquid assets held by the bank will be ineligible for inclusion in the LCR ratio. The overall result for many banks is to increase the proportion of their total balance sheets which is required to be held in the form of highly liquid assets. Since highly liquid assets are invariably low-yielding assets, this imposes a cost on the relevant bank.

The LCR is being introduced in stages. The detailed requirements in the EU are set out in Commission Delegated Regulation 2015/61, which contains the rules governing which assets will qualify as high-quality liquid assets, and how cash outflows and inflows should be calculated. For example, committed liquidity facilities to clients that are not financial customers will be subject to a drawdown rate of 30%.

The LCR has a significant impact on bank lenders in respect of committed undrawn facilities, as these will have to be backed with liquid assets. The LCR also creates disincentives to a bank providing a liquidity facility to another financial institution. In addition, loans are not eligible for inclusion within the liquid asset pool, which may make them less attractive to banks than corporate bonds, which can be eligible.

### Net Stable Funding Ratio

The second liquidity standard is the net stable funding ratio. The NSFR is an innovation in that it seeks to control the extent to which banks rely on short term (sub-one year) funding as a proportion of their overall funding. In effect, it requires a bank to fund the illiquid portion of its asset book with funding of more than one-year residual maturity. The thinking behind 'stable funding' is that some bases on which banks fund their credit activities are less likely to be withdrawn in moments of stress than others. For example, retail deposits are relatively stable, compared with commercial deposits and funding derived from the issue of short-term debt instruments such as commercial paper. Banks will need to demonstrate that long-term assets are funded through relatively stable liabilities.

As with the LCR, the key to understanding the effect of this rule is to consider its assessment of what constitutes 'stable' funding and what constitute 'illiquid' assets (on which see the Committee's October 2014 NSFR paper BCBS295). 'Available stable funding' is calculated by taking various categories of liabilities and multiplying by a particular percentage, depending on the value of that type of liability as a source of stable funding:

- 100% of regulatory capital and liabilities with maturity of one year or more
- 95% of stable (i.e., deposit guaranteed) retail deposits
- 90% of less stable retail/SME deposits
- 50% of corporate wholesale deposits
- 0% of financial institution funding

The working assumption is that over a 12-month period the net outflow will be 5% of retail deposits, 50% of corporate deposits and so on. Thus, the effect of the rule is to put pressure on a bank to fund illiquid exposures with either capital, long-term debt or non-financial sector deposits. The basic requirement is that a bank's 'available stable funding' must exceed its 'required amount of stable funding'.

Stable funding is required to finance those assets which are regarded as not being capable of being liquidated within 12 months without significant expense. This at first sight seems a fairly strange concept, since almost any financial asset is capable of being realised within that period. However, the NSFR bestows the calculus of illiquidity as, for instance:

- 0% of cash and claims on central banks with maturities of less than six months
- 5% of the value of government securities with a maturity of more than one year
- 15% of AA- or more corporate and covered bonds with a maturity of more than one year

- 50% of liquid equities, bonds of between A+ and BBB- and loans to corporates with a residual maturity of less than 1 year
- 65% of high-quality mortgages
- 85% of retail loans with a residual maturity of less than one year
- 100% of everything else, such as assets that are encumbered for a year or more

These percentages are intended to be estimates of the amount of a particular asset that could not be monetised within a 12-month period. The 'everything else' category includes all non-financial assets.

The Committee's 'final standard' on NSFR was published in October 2014, with an expectation of implementation as a minimum standard by 1 January 2018. The EU will implement the NSFR as a binding measure through its reform of the CRR, in a package commonly known as 'CRR 2'. In any event, Article 413 of CRR contains a general requirement that banks ensure that long term obligations are adequately met with a diversity of stable funding instruments under both normal and stressed conditions.

## Large Exposure Rules

Another prudential regulatory regime worth noting is the rules on large exposures. The large exposure rules applicable to EU banks are found in Part Four of the CRR. The large exposure rules aim to limit banks' credit risk, i.e., the maximum loss that a bank may incur, associated with exposure to a single counterparty or set of connected counterparties (counterparties within the same group). Put differently, the large exposure rules flag large exposures and encourage risk diversification. A counterparty is any party to which the bank assumes a credit risk – the most obvious example being a borrower. Under the large exposure rules, exposures to connected counterparties are pooled together and calculated as a single exposure.

According to the large exposure rules, banks must monitor and control their 'large exposures'. A large exposure is defined as the total exposure of a bank to a counterparty or connected counterparties which in aggregate equals or is more than 10 % of the bank's capital base (being the total of its Tier 1 and Tier 2 capital, less deductions). Unless the exposure is exempt, a bank is not allowed to hold a total exposure to any counterparty or connected counterparties that exceeds 25% of its capital base. What is more, all large exposures taken together must not exceed 800% of a bank's capital base.

# LOCATION OF THE MARKETPLACES

There are three principal centres of syndicated credit activity. These are London, New York and Hong Kong. However, there are many other centres where transactions are syndicated either because of the currency of the instrument or more usually because of the location of the borrower. For instance, a US borrower located in California, whose main business is in that state and whose market is principally in the western part of the US, will probably use the regional marketplace based in Los Angeles. An Australian borrower may choose to use the Australian dollar market centred in Sydney. The Japanese market is centred in Tokyo. Other important regional centres include Singapore, Frankfurt, Paris and Toronto. Dubai, and to a lesser extent Riyadh, have become established as regional syndication centres for borrowers located in the Middle East and Gulf region. A detailed analysis of each such regional centre is beyond the scope of this book, but supplement 2 to this chapter contains summaries of the local markets in a number of EMEA regions.

It can be misleading however to place too much emphasis on the geographical location of the syndication centre. In most major international banks, the ultimate decision on whether or not to participate in a transaction is independent of the office to which the invitation is sent. For instance, an invitation, emanating from the London syndications unit of a US bank for a US domiciled transaction, sent to the London syndications unit of a British bank, will normally be passed to their New York office for review and credit approval. The office may need to return the transaction to London for sanction if the size of the commitment being sought is outside the limits held in New York. It is difficult to be certain in which 'market' such a transaction is being syndicated and from the bookrunner's point of view, probably unimportant once the relevant individual contacts have been established with each potential participant bank.

Two quantitative criteria merit discussion as proxies for deciding which is the most active syndication centre. The first is simply the number of banks with offices located in the centre. The second is to estimate the total volume of transactions arranged in that location. Neither of these is entirely satisfactory. The physical presence of a bank in a location is often not a good indicator of its willingness to participate in syndicated credits. For instance, some non-UK banks retain branches in London principally for treasury management purposes with little or no desire to take assets from the syndicated credit market.

The second criterion, that of the total volume arranged in a location, is also unsatisfactory. A single syndicated transaction may be arranged in a number of different countries and an arbitrary allocation of such a transaction to any one location would lead to distortions. The difficulty is illustrated in the example of a US corporation, which is prepared to guarantee its French subsidiary in raising €500m and awards the mandate to a Swiss bank.

The mandated bank syndicates the deal from New York and London (in order to deal with the US and European aspects of the credit) and ultimately signs the deal in Zurich. Because of the nature of the deal, the agent for the loan will be located in Paris. This can be said to be a truly international deal without a single dominant location.

Probably the best indicator of activity is the physical presence of a large number of market practitioners with the appropriate professional infrastructure. A change in the location of such individuals could mean either that the market was decentralising or moving to another centre or both. Indeed, since the late 1990s, there was an ever increasing concentration of syndication teams in London as several major US and continental European banks chose this city to house their specialist teams. This trend is likely to be reversed following the UK's decision to exit the EU, but the extent of the reversal is not yet known.

# TEAM STRUCTURES

## Introduction

The ability of banks to provide a high quality and cost-effective service to corporate borrowers seeking to arrange syndicated loan transactions and to do so as profitably as the market pricing will permit depends on them having experienced and well-organised teams of people with access to the latest technology. In this section the types of team structures commonly employed by leading banks in the market are considered. The types of activities to be undertaken can be summarised as follows:

## Origination (including execution):

- Structuring transactions
- Pitching to clients
- Negotiating documentation
- Product specialisation and expertise
- Preparing information packages for upcoming live deals

## Syndicate:

- Opining on pricing and structuring
- Managing underwriting exposure
- Assessing underwriting capabilities

- Syndication strategy for transactions
- Co-ordinating deal launches and syndication

## Sales:

- Sales to banks and securing commitments
- Maintaining relationships with banks/investors
- Collecting market intelligence
- Input on bank lists
- Answering investor questions
- Secondary loan sales* and sourcing

* May be performed by a separate public loan sales team in some banks.

There are several different team structures covering origination, syndicate and sales, which can involve various combinations, as shown by the team structure examples below.

## Team Structure Examples

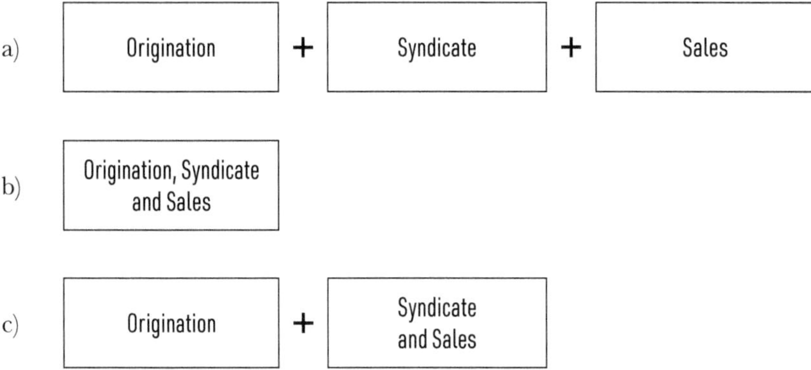


Some banks may keep each area in three separate teams as shown in (a), or may have origination, syndicate and sales responsibilities in one overall team (b). Most banks tend to combine syndicate and sales, and then have a separate origination team (as shown in (c)), whilst maintaining a close working relationship and communication line between the teams.

The team structure combination which banks implement depends heavily on the strategy in the syndicated loan market of the bank and its level of activity in the market. Market volume and trends also have a significant impact on how syndicated loan teams are structured, and will influence structure changes over time. Regulators are also keen to ensure that a syndicate desk is able to maintain an objective view on underwriting risks, particularly in relation to leveraged transactions, which may influence team structure.

## Explanation of Various Team Structures

Keeping all three areas in separate teams (a) can be advantageous for banks that are very active in the loan market, bookrunning numerous transactions when volumes are high. This structure keeps each team focused on its respective roles, and develops specialist expertise in each area. For instance, if a bank has many underwritten deals in the market, the syndicate team can focus on pricing, managing the total underwriting book and providing views on liquidity. The largest and most active banks tend to have this structure. Given a totally different cast of characters, from investors, borrowers and sponsors, distribution mechanism and market dynamics, in many instances leveraged syndicated transactions are managed by their own separate teams – generally structured similarly – but working separately from general syndication specialists. However, outside of leveraged syndicated finance, banks are inclined to move away from this type of structure when volumes drop and the number of underwritten deals falls considerably (a development which was seen in the aftermath of the GFC).

Instead of having the three teams separate, banks with lower levels of activity in the loan market may opt to keep origination, syndicate and sales as one single team. This is particularly common for banks that are not highly active in the market, or which specialise in more limited sectors in the loan market, and therefore do not need significant resources to be able to bookrun many deals. Their loans teams are smaller and more cost-effective, although they may require expansion in the future if the bank decides to become more active in the loan market.

Most active banks in the market choose to have an origination team and a combined syndicate and sales/distribution team. This allows originators to focus on customers, pitching, structuring and documentation of live deals, and the syndicate/sales team to concentrate on pricing, execution and investor coverage. This structure enables those with pricing responsibilities (i.e., syndicate and sales) to be in close contact with bank investors, which should ensure the accurate pricing of transactions. In the current market, there has been substantial growth in alternative distribution channels or transaction/portfolio risk mitigation techniques (e.g., PRI or credit insurance) which may also be managed via the Syndicate or Sales/Distribution activity.

## Team Structures in the Future

Current volumes are expected to remain relatively stable in the coming years, so it is anticipated that the most active arranging banks in the market will continue to follow team structures (a) or (c) whilst less active banks opt for one single combined team (b).

It is to be expected that the syndicated lending market will remain highly competitive over the medium to long term, with banks vying for loan mandates as they seek to use the product to generate cross-sell ancillary opportunities from clients. To this end, efficient and cost-effective team structures will be essential for the active banks in the market. Within this dynamic, technology will continue to play an ever-increasingly important role in order for banks to gain a competitive edge over rivals and reduce costs.

# TECHNOLOGY

The loan market has not historically been naturally an electronic one. Unlike the worlds of bonds and equities, with their relatively straightforward products and large numbers of investors, syndicated loans depend on fewer participants, and on the strength of relationships. It is a personal market, in which individuals still know each other and deals have typically been distributed in telephone conversations or in e-mails, rather than with a couple of mouse-clicks. While a bond syndication may last just a matter of hours, loans are usually less hurried and syndications still last days or weeks. The impact of technology on syndicated lending has therefore been different from that on other asset classes, and the focus is still on the technology aiding communication between people, rather than communication between machines.

It is helpful to look at technology's role in the loan market's recent history. In the first instance, technology helped to improve transmission and reduce the burden of documentation, from borrower documents to confidentiality undertakings ('confis'), to facility agreements, all of which were previously sent around on paper and couriered between institutions.

The ability to improve efficiency by sending information over the cables in syndicated lending first came about with the telex and fax machines. These did not eliminate the paper – in some ways they produced more through duplication, as originals were usually required, but they did speed things up, allowing confi wording negotiations, acceptances and commitment letters to be sent almost instantly.

From the mid-1980s, technology also enabled access to the latest market information from providers such as the Loan Pricing Corporation (now part of Refinitiv) and Capital Data (now Dealogic), which has contributed to analysis used for pitching and investor targeting.

At the start of the 1990s, Computasoft (now Dealogic) launched the first version of LoanRunner, a system which ran on DOS and provided contact management, syndication tracking and joint bookrunning capabilities. Less than five years later, PCs were becoming more advanced, the world wide web was spreading beyond the scientific and academic communities, and LoanRunner was updated to run on Microsoft Windows. Syndications were now being launched and managed on computer systems.

It was adopted widely in Europe, although it did not have the same stronghold in the Americas and, in the late 1990s, Customised Database Systems (CDS) (now Fidelity National Information Services, known as FIS), released a product called SyndTrak, which not only filled the need in the Americas, but eventually replaced much of the LoanRunner footprint in Europe, offering a more up-to-date equivalent.

Around the same time, IntraLinks built IntraLoan, and Computasoft released LoanLink, both of which provided online document distribution systems with linkages to fax and e-mail and marketed themselves on the basis of process improvement and a reduction of courier costs. Arranging banks and investors were already used to documentation being transmitted electronically, so adoption of these systems, particularly IntraLinks, seemed a natural progression. Another company, Debtdomain, also evolved, providing a combination of bookrunning and document distribution capabilities.

A few banks developed their own equivalent loan syndication systems in-house, but Dresdner Kleinwort (now absorbed into Commerzbank) tried to act as a technology provider by offering the use of its system, eLoancoordinator, to other banks. Uptake was not high, partly due to the heavy Dresdner branding of the system.

An emerging market for syndicated loans was now beginning to take shape, and some of the growth was being facilitated by Debtdomain's loan trading platform which, because of the company's Singapore base, was readily accepted by the Asian market. This platform provided an openly accessible list of investors and helped to catalyse activity in this new market, with adoption of Debtdomain becoming almost universal on the emerging markets desks of banks in Europe. The company has since developed its agency and primary syndication solutions and grown beyond the emerging markets.

Although banks were already used to the idea of entrusting private documents to a technology supplier's environment, when using IntraLinks and similar systems, allowing them outside the banks' own infrastructure, Debtdomain pushed the model further, hosting a central system for bookrunning, so banks were now allowing pre- and post-commitment distribution details, including investor call notes, to be held by the technology service provider on one big system also containing other banks' data, but carefully secured to maintain full confidentiality. This model also kept subscriber costs down, as there was only one set of infrastructure to be maintained, and it was not long before Debtdomain was gaining a strong foothold in the corporate syndicated loan market.

It is hard to overlook the role of technology in the operational administration of loans, particularly with ACBS (now a division of FIS) and Loan IQ (originally developed by Deutsche Bank subsidiary IQ Financial, but now owned by Finastra). Both have replaced internally-built systems and delivered significant productivity gains, centralisation and consistency of lending records, reporting capabilities, automation of workflow and the ability to reconcile to a single top-level view.

Agency has another set of needs, addressed to varying degrees by Debtdomain, IntraLinks, Loan IQ and SyndTrak 4, which offer elements of agency-specific functionality, including periodic alerts, enhanced documentation management and systemised amendment voting.

Faster, electronic settlement has seen advances in recent years, with DTCC and Markit collaborating (Markit acquired ClearPar from FIS, and Storm Loan Marketplace) and Trade Settlement, Inc. (TSI) marketing its own offerings.

End-to-end integration of systems, from origination or primary distribution through to closing, maintenance and agency, and with linkages to secondary trading, have long been discussed, but the appetite to spend money implementing what would normally be complex integration tasks, given each banks' pre-existing loans infrastructure, is weak.

Until recently, the technology landscape has remained loans-centric, with most of the application providers being focused significantly more on lending than on any other asset classes and no moves to provide full DCM solutions, integrating bonds and loans for example, despite that being the current structure of some banks' distribution teams. Ipreo, which leads the market in bond syndication solutions, acquired Debtdomain, in February 2013, to capitalise on synergies between syndication processes and provide a single resource for cross-asset sales teams. Ipreo was then acquired by IHS Markit in May 2018 to create a single provider of critical information, analytics and solutions to capital markets participants globally.

Shifts in consumer technologies, with high mobile device usage and adoption of distributed 'cloud' storage concepts now the norm, could influence the design and evolution of the next generation of front-office syndication tools, but neither of these are without control and compliance challenges, and the pace of change within the banking environment is likely to lag behind similar changes in industries with lighter regulation.

Perhaps the future will bring more advanced analytics to support pitching and deal modelling, or increased focus on the economics of syndication, looking more at returns on scarce capital. It would make sense for banks to pursue further efficiencies and connectivity throughout a loan's lifecycle, seeking to integrate loan systems together, and with internal systems for client relationship management (CRM), risk management, accounting, etc., particularly as deal volumes rise again, to minimise the need to vary headcount, and to maximise the value of information held.

Undoubtedly technological developments such as blockchain, artificial intelligence and the increasing sophistication of Optical Character Recognition (OCR) will, in time, become part and parcel of the syndicated credit market These developments can be used to aid the identification of investors for primary distribution, process and review of loan documentation and combine with internal administration systems, so accelerating the primary syndication process, driving faster settlement of secondary trades and easing the credit administration burden.

However, in view of the personal nature of the market, technology is more likely to combine with, rather than replace, such benefits as personal contacts and communication, market positioning or transaction sourcing which a well-connected syndicator can provide, particularly in a dynamic and uncertain market.

In the annexes to this chapter, you will find articles by some of the technology providers mentioned above, giving their views of how their solutions fit market requirements and the future direction of the market.

## SOURCES OF INFORMATION

When pricing a new transaction, one of the first steps is to seek information on comparable deals. However, the syndicated credit market is generally private and pricing and other information may not necessarily be in the public domain. The syndicated credit market has become increasingly sensitive to the disclosure of private (e.g., pricing) information among practitioners following interest (and in certain instances, action) from regulators over the flow or use of private information, or other information exchange between practitioners, particularly where it may have disadvantaged a borrower.

Published reports on current market levels of pricing and structure provide a useful guide during negotiations for a mandate and can sometimes work to the benefit of both borrowers and lenders. However, this source of market intelligence, which can be found on screens or in the specialised magazines, must be treated with caution because banks and borrowers are under no obligation to disclose the details of the transactions on which they are working. Publication of a deal story can be the result of investigative journalism, without the corroboration of any of the interested parties, and may not be accurate or complete.

Historical information on the market is maintained by a small number of commercial sources. One of the most widely used and accurate sources is the one provided by Dealogic. Their Loan Analytics database is updated regularly and it allows subscribers to obtain information on individual deals as well as to analyse past activity according to a wide variety of user-selected criteria. A description of this system is given in annex 2.1.

A selection of the principal sources of information on the syndicated credit market are set out in annex 2.6.

# ANNEX 2.1: HISTORY AND METHODOLOGY OF DEALOGIC LOAN MANAGER

**Dealogic Loans Department**

Loan Manager, a component of the Dealogic platform, provides industry leading coverage of all global leveraged and investment grade syndicated lending, allowing for detailed analysis of the syndicated loans market. The product was originally launched in 1987 under the name Loanware with the help of a number of leading loan market participants and some 30 years later covers more than 200,000 deals and has over 2,000 users.

Like its subscribers, Loan Manager has moved fast to keep up with the latest technological developments and advances in the loans market. While doing so it has adhered to the principles on which it was launched; namely to provide the most accurate and up-to-date information available on all global syndicated loans.

Dedicated teams of researchers are based in the world's main financial centres and are constantly in contact with deal participants. Researchers will track thousands of news sources in over 30 languages on a daily basis to ensure the best possible coverage of international and domestic activity with information updated in real time. Emphasis is put on primary sources and reconciliation with market participants to ensure accuracy of information.

Loan Manager includes a profile of every loan which includes detailed information such as the borrower's business and nationality, the loan type, currency, amount, margin and fee information, syndicate details and key dates. Other information such as borrower ratings and leverage ratios are included where appropriate and available. In total, each loan contains up to 180 fully searchable fields allowing for very specific subsets of information to be retrieved and reported upon.

Intuitive software provides the product with great flexibility. Users can easily filter on numerous variables to quickly identify deals with specific characteristics, analyse comparable transactions, analyse deal pricing and market trends, keep track of market events and rank market participants such as bookrunners and mandated lead arrangers for marketing purposes and competitor analysis.

Loan Manager official league tables are published regularly in leading financial publications such as *Global Capital*, the *Wall Street Journal* and *The Financial Times*. Rankings are produced using market led criteria which is reviewed annually through forums with key loan market participants.

It is thanks to the help and support of banks active in the global loans market that Loan Manager remains an essential analytical product for loan origination and syndicate teams throughout the world.

# ANNEX 2.2: HISTORY AND EVOLUTION OF LOAN PRICING CORPORATION (LPC)

**LPC team**

LPC is the premier global provider of news, data and analysis for the syndicated loan and CLO markets. The brand is known and respected in the global financial markets for the breadth and depth of its loan coverage, with an unmatched 35 years of history, offices in all major financial centres and strong market expertise.

LPC provides state-of-the-art information products and services for syndicators and market professionals. The company was founded as Loan Pricing Corporation in 1985 with a grant from the Rockefeller Foundation to bring transparency to the global syndicated loan market, and was also the first information provider to launch real-time coverage of the EMEA loan market in the late 90s.

Integrated first into Reuters Group, and later into Thomson Corporation, LPC is now part of Refinitiv, following Blackstone's acquisition of a 55% stake in Thomson Reuters' Financial & Risk division in October 2018. Global coverage is supported by LPC's offices in New York, London, Hong Kong, Sydney and Tokyo

The information that LPC supplies is used every day by banks, asset managers, law firms, regulators, companies and other market participants to inform and drive their loan and CLO syndication, trading, market monitoring and research, compliance and portfolio management activities.

LPC offers news, data and analysis covering every region, country and market sector globally. Products and services include print publications and online news, analysis, valuation services and interactive databases.

These include the real time web-based services LoanConnector and Secondary Market Intelligence (SMi) which give access to global real-time news coverage, the DealScan database of terms and conditions on more than 250,000 loans, comprehensive secondary market prices for traded loans, analysis and commentary and market statistics including league tables, comparable pricing and covenants.

Print products include Goldsheets in the US and Basis Point in Asia, which provide news and data on the loan and CLO markets, as well as numerous newsletters and briefings which cover the middle market, leveraged and investment grade markets in depth.

LPC Collateral, a tool to monitor and evaluate CLO holdings, provides up to date, detailed and standardized data on underlying collateral, including accurate and comprehensive asset prices, for more than one thousand CLOs. Trade History and Loan Holdings gives access to more than one hundred thousand loan trade prices and the list of current holders of outstanding loans.

LPC's products provide up to 100 news stories a day globally and access to 100,000 archived stories since 1995 as well as daily pricing on more than 5,000 tranches from the secondary market to 8,500+ subscribers globally. It is part of the IFR Group, which also includes Project Finance International.

# ANNEX 2.3: DEBTDOMAIN[3]

**Sean Tai**

*IHS Markit*

Although Debtdomain is a global platform, it is best known for its role in the EMEA syndicated loan market, both for historical reasons, and its current prominent position in that market. This Annex traces the growth and development of Debtdomain, as it added features and functions in lockstep with the needs of the EMEA syndicated loan market.

## Beginnings

Debtdomain was introduced to the EMEA syndicated loan market as a primary syndication platform in 2003 after starting in Asia-Pacific in 2002.

Prior to the development of collaborative bookrunning technology, many arranging banks in EMEA used an internal, installed (non-web based) application for bookrunning their deals, if indeed they used any system at all – many used spreadsheets. However, these internal bookrunning tools did not support the highly collaborative method of arranging deals that had developed in EMEA, in which several banks work closely together during the distribution phase of the deal, sharing the feedback they receive from the market. This lack of support for collaboration created significant additional work for bookrunners, as they tried to coordinate their efforts during a deal. Moreover, internal bookrunning tools did not communicate or integrate with the document sharing systems that prevailed at that time, with the result that arrangers had to set up and manage each deal via two systems.

Debtdomain's key innovations were therefore:

1. enabling real-time collaboration in bookbuilding among multiple loan arrangers via a hosted, web-based system;
2. combining that feature with secure document distribution (or in today's terminology, a 'virtual data room' (VDR)).

3 Debtdomain is a web-based platform that is widely used by participants in the global syndicated loan market to securely and efficiently collaborate on deals. Since its inception in 2001, the platform has been used by more than 500,000 individuals representing thousands of firms – including loan arrangers, agents, secondary traders, investors, borrowers, lawyers and others – to collaborate on more than 35,000 primary, secondary, agency and other deals.

Being able to instantly pull up a deal status report for complex deals with multiple bookrunners saved junior staff the daily hassle of maintaining and consolidating a 'night sheet'. In addition, borrowers liked the ability to see how their deals were progressing in real time, without having to wait for the bookrunners to compile their separate results into a single syndication status report. This support for real-time joint bookrunning gave EMEA bookrunners, for the first time, a tool that worked the way they did.

Having a single system for both bookrunning and document distribution also offered some important advantages. For one thing, it enabled the distribution team to set up the deal just once – and then to monitor investors' dataroom activity level from within the bookrunning system. It was easy to see when investors had signed the online confidentiality agreement, and then how active they were in the dataroom. Additionally, when an investor was marked as 'declined' in the bookrunning application, the contacts belonging to that investor were automatically removed from the document site.

Importantly, the Debtdomain platform was hosted and accessible over the Internet via a standard web browser. In other words, arrangers did not have to supply costly servers, update software or engage in-house support staff in order to deploy it.

## Evolution into the market standard

The loan market can be slow to adapt to change, and it can take years for new processes to become established. Early adoption of Debtdomain technology for syndication was focused on FI deals for developing market borrowers. These FI deals were mostly arranged out of Frankfurt, Munich and Vienna, and developing-market teams in London. The technology proved particularly valuable for these deals, as they had many joint bookrunners and hundreds of investors.

Over time, the Debtdomain platform was adopted by more arrangers in a wider range of deals and markets. The Financial Crisis focused banks' attention on efficiencies and cost reduction, ironically providing a significant boost to adoption over that period. When the market began to rebound in 2010, the use of Debtdomain technology increased sharply. The 'network effect' meant that joint arrangers were exposed to the system during deals, with other leads who had already started using Debtdomain as their core syndication platform. As a result, by 2012, over 90% of EMEA deals that were launched on a platform were being syndicated on Debtdomain.

Over the years, the use of Debtdomain for sending deal invitations and online confidentiality agreements and signing no-reliance letters, and self-declarations of public/private status went from being fairly novel in 2005, to standard market practice. Moreover, the convenience of having all parties on the platform began to outweigh the arrangers' initial concerns about sharing investor lists and storing contact data 'outside the firewall'.

Deal volumes since 2012 have been fairly flat yet there has been a continued increase in the number of deals launched on Debtdomain. This reflects an increase in the proportion of deals for which a platform is used. Before 2017, around half of all deals were managed via email and spreadsheets, without any online bookrunning or dataroom platform. However, by 2019 the platform utilisation rate in EMEA was approaching 70%, driven by arrangers' desire to both improve productivity and meet internal and regulatory requirements for information security. It is policy in many banks not to email documents to investors without encryption. Running deals by email or spreadsheet is no longer acceptable for many arranger banks. Also, a syndication site is now very much expected by many investors, borrowers and joint arrangers, even for smaller deals.

Use of Debtdomain has also expanded across the EMEA region. More than 10% of EMEA primary deals syndicated via the platform are now for African borrowers, and usage of Debtdomain by GCC based arrangers has also increased significantly.

Use of Debtdomain has also expanded to adjacent capital markets, with over 90% of all German law Schuldschein deals syndicated on Debtdomain.

## The Debtdomain loan investor and contact directory

In order to support real-time joint bookrunning, Debtdomain has also incorporated a shared directory of market participants. After all, for joint bookrunners to set up and run a deal, they need to be able to select from an agreed-upon list of potential arrangers, investors and contacts. The Debtdomain database of market participants grew organically, with arrangers and agents adding new users to the platform in order to run deals. The Debtdomain team enriches the list by 'curating' it to remove duplicate institutions and contacts, as well as maintain fund/fund manager relationships and other data relating to investors.

The Debtdomain contact database has effectively become the centralised directory for the EMEA and global loan market. Today, this database comprises around 500,000 individual contacts at more than 20,000 institutions. The market activity of a larger number of active arrangers and investors enables these contacts to be cleansed regularly for data accuracy and completeness. Most syndication desks globally now use Debtdomain as their main 'address book'.

## Beyond primary syndication

When primary syndication volumes crashed after the market disruption in 2008, the Debtdomain team refocused development and marketing efforts on other functions and phases of the deal that offered the possibility for more stable revenues. In 2009, Debtdomain introduced features related to loan investor CRM, deal pipeline and management reporting, secondary trading and portfolio sales and public/private compliance reporting.

However, the most significant new product area for Debtdomain was (and is) administrative agency services. In fact, Debtdomain revenues from agency are about equal to primary syndication. More than 180 agents globally use Debtdomain, with tools that go well beyond document distribution to lenders – Debtdomain Agency includes a financial monitoring calendar and tickler system, amendment voting and data cleansing tools.

As Debtdomain has extended its reach into the back office, a growing desire for straight-through processing (STP) has emerged. For example, a common request is to connect Debtdomain agency sites to a client's loan administration system, in order to automate deal site access due to changes in lender lists resulting from secondary trades, as well as to populate lender holdings for amendment voting.

Other integration projects that have been completed for clients include:

- feeding documents from Debtdomain to a bank's internal document repository;
- synchronising client human resource records with contacts in Debtdomain to ensure leavers are removed in a timely way;
- connecting Debtdomain's 'Deal Pipeline' system with a bank's internal multi-asset pipeline system.

A new product added in 2014 was datarooms for usage outside syndicated lending. This is a rapidly growing area of business where banks and corporates use Debtdomain for secure document distribution for any purpose.

## Acquisition by IHS Markit

Through the acquisition of Ipreo in August 2018, Debtdomain became part of IHS Markit's Loan Platforms business. This franchise includes ClearPar, Loan Reconciliation, Notice Manager, Loan Reference Data, WSO Agency, and WSO Services. Debtdomain is highly complementary with these platforms, sharing many of the same clients across loans agency, syndication and trading.

Looking to the future, IHS Markit's vision for Debtdomain includes:

1. building an integrated Amendment voting solution leveraging data and workflow tools from other products within the Loan Platforms suite;
2. reducing double-entry by sending primary allocations directly from Debtdomain to ClearPar and then receiving sub-allocations back in order to update Debtdomain Agency sites;
3. integrating Debtdomain into the unified Loan Platforms portal.

The widespread adoption of Debtdomain technology is believed to have had a positive impact on both the development of the market, in terms of improvement in both efficiency and liquidity – core goals shared with the LMA.

# ANNEX 2.4: OPERATIONAL BEST PRACTICES IN SYNDICATED LENDING

## SIX THINGS LENDERS SHOULD LOOK FOR WHEN UPGRADING THEIR LOAN SERVICING SYSTEM

**Finastra – Fusion Loan IQ Team**

In the decade since the global financial crisis, lenders have faced compressed deal margins, prompting a refocus towards boosting profitability through portfolio optimisation. Some are achieving this by reducing risk-weighted assets, some by shifting towards an originate-to-distribute model or by finding ways to increase fee-based income.

At the same time, lenders are placing greater importance on creating and preserving strong customer relationships. Not only in hope of capitalising on new business opportunities, but also because borrowers expect the same level of personalised and convenient services offered by leading consumer technology brands.

But can you achieve portfolio optimisation and improved customer service if your business is built on an immature operating model with manual processes? Probably not.

### Inside an immature operating environment

When administrative agents managing a portfolio of syndicated deals of limited complexity insist on administering them using a 'system' of exhaustive procedural manuals and insecure, disconnected spreadsheets, they expose the borrowers, counterparties, and themselves to operational and reputational risk. While such solutions are generally capable of the basic financial calculations, the risk stems from the reliance on the end user applying the correct rules, performing activities at the appropriate time, and complying with business process and policy.

Immature operational environments do not appreciate the systematic enforcement of fundamental controls such as 'four-eyes' or the division of authority, let alone the more advanced controls needed to manage a complex, time-sensitive business such as sophisticated user-rights and approval models and the automated movement of cash. Paper and spreadsheet-based controls are often introduced to compensate for this lack of systematic control, causing inefficiency, audit issues, and often, further compound operational risk.

Perhaps most daunting of all is the challenge of achieving the required data segregation and security while simultaneously providing a global view of a customer or portfolio to those who need it. These risks drastically limit with whom these agents can do business, the value they can add for their customers, and, consequently, the income the business can generate.

As immature operational environments illustrate, it is not powerful financial calculation, but rather the definition and enforcement of business process – and ideally, best practices – which is the primary value added by a software package which is fit for purpose.

However, if best practices are rigid in nature and universally adopted across the industry, how can an institution hope to develop competitive advantages to differentiate itself from its competition? If the institution cannot create innovative product offerings and business process, does it not risk commoditisation?

## Characteristics of a best-in-class loan servicing solution

When a bank is considering replacing or consolidating their loan servicing system(s), there are several key features and capabilities they should look for.

1. Advanced front-to-back-office capabilities

Following approval and deal signing, the platform should seamlessly transfer responsibility for the regular maintenance of the deal and collateral package to the appropriate back and middle office teams. This ensures the credit is immediately available for trading, reporting and risk management, and eliminates the operational risk associated with the re-keying of data.

As the deal is maintained, the system should provide the front-office with the data needed to manage the customer relationship, and to perform continuous due diligence, monitor covenants, conduct periodic reviews and sanction renewals. Ongoing deal maintenance includes interest and fee accrual and application, invoice generation, management of cash flows and notices between borrowers and lenders, as well as the production of sub-ledger accounting.

Critically, a strong loan servicing solution can effortlessly calculate all participant shares and the principal, interest and fees due to each participant, as well as funding due upon borrower notice of intent to drawdown.

2. Best-in-class loan servicing workflows

Best-in-class servicing workflows leverage the details of the credit agreement, the collateral package, and information provided by the bank's customer information file system to drive data entry validations (including data which is entered into the system via APIs), user workflows and SLAs.

The system should have configurability such that for a specific circumstance, the user can choose to ignore a restriction, in which case the policy violation will be logged, and notifications sent to a pre-defined distribution group. Alternatively, such a violation may simply be defined as requiring an additional level of approval, depending on a variety of configurable conditions (such as the user's outbound cash-flow limits, the status of the loan or customer, and so on).

3. A modern technology stack

To reduce maintenance costs and human capital challenges, a bank's syndicated loan servicing solution should be built on a modern technology stack. Loan servicing solutions built on older technology using arcane programming languages are more expensive, in part due to the cost to recruit and retain the necessary developers to maintain the system. When the necessary talent is recruited, they are often not easily leveraged across a bank's technology team. Also, the underlying technology needs to align with your bank's existing architectural standards.

4. Rich trading functionality

Banks should have a single, real-time view of all back-office transactions that affect a trader's portfolio during the entire loan lifecycle. Multi-currency and multi-branch capabilities can provide users with an up-to-date picture of company-wide performance while industry-standard workflows enable lenders to streamline commercial or bilateral loan booking and processing activities.

5. Strong accounting and audit controls

Accounting functionality should combine online accounting with real-time debits and credits. Configurable parameters can often include multi-branch, multi-business line, and general ledger/subledger with configurable account mapping. Users should have the ability to manage lender shares and portfolio positions across multiple entities, reducing the need for double entry and reconciliation, while providing an extensive audit trail.

6. Advanced collateral management capabilities

Finally, the loan servicing solution should have collateral management capabilities that allow users to efficiently create and manage an increased volume of financial and non-financial assets associated with collateralised loans, such as commercial real estate. Users should be able to capture, maintain, and report on a rich detail of collateral across the portfolio, including asset registration, unit details, rent rolls, and invoices.

## About Fusion loan IQ

As the syndicated loan servicing platform for 18 of the world's top 25 agent banks by loan volume in 2018, Fusion Loan IQ has become the industry standard solution.

# ANNEX 2.5: BLOOMBERG FOR SYNDICATED LOANS

Over the last seven years, Bloomberg's investment in its syndicated loan news, data, pricing and analytics has created a highly valued product whose greatest strength is its integration into a cross asset-class platform with a unique breadth of functionality. Bloomberg's syndicated loan products are widely used across origination, syndication, sales & trading, and by portfolio managers and analysts.

## News

Bloomberg's experienced journalists cover the syndicated loan markets in Europe, Asia and the Americas, with teams focused on leveraged finance as well investment grade loans and Schuldschein. News coverage can be tracked directly on the Bloomberg Terminal or via pop-up or email alerts.

## Data

Bloomberg's global syndicated loans database consists of more than 54,000 active loan tranches (and approximately 160,000 replaced or retired loans), covering nearly 40,000 unique borrowers across more than 200 countries and 100 different currencies.

The loans data team maintains relationships with over 1,100 unique banking entities globally for the procurement of information. On average, Bloomberg adds more than 300 loans per week, or more than 3,800 loans per quarter.

Deal data includes relevant dates and amounts, loan type and purposes, lender lists, primary pricing including grids and fees, amendments, ratings and much more — Bloomberg captures up to 350 unique data points, more than anyone else. All this information is validated with either the arrangers or the borrower and is subject to more than 1,000 logic checks, to guarantee its quality and integrity. No third-party data is ever used to populate the database.

Bloomberg's identifiers (Financial Instrument Global Identifier) cover all global asset classes including Syndicated Loans. They are free to use, free to issue and free to redistribute.

## Secondary market pricing and yield analysis

Bloomberg's message functionality allows investors to capture and compare loan pricing they receive from dealers, as well as to track quotes in real-time on a portfolio basis.

The evaluated pricing methodology (BVAL) provides pricing on over 9,000 syndicated loans globally. BVAL's relies first on market quotes from a variety of sources. In the absence of recent market quotes, BVAL implements relative value comparison of similar loans in the same industry.

Bloomberg calculates loan yield or credit spreads to different potential repayment dates, allowing users to customise the attributes of the loan and create amortisation and margin schedules.

## Integration into the Bloomberg Terminal and Enterprise products

Bloomberg's syndicated loan data is seamlessly integrated into the sophisticated functionality offered by the Bloomberg Terminal, allowing users to:

- Analyse the debt maturity profile and capital structure of borrowers.
- Track credit ratings, bond pricing, CDS spreads, and fundamental data.
- Search the syndicated loan and corporate bond database for comparables, historical issuance trends and aggregated maturity profiles.
- Monitor the loan and bond new issue pipeline and recently priced deals.
- Assess trends in market share with 66 official syndicated loan league tables and the ability to create and save custom tables.
- Send and receive trade confirmations.
- Follow secondary loan markets alongside global equity, FX, fixed income and commodities.
- Book loans into our order management systems and portfolio analytics.
- Download data simply and dynamically to Excel or into in-house databases using Enterprise Data feeds.
- Meet KYC & onboarding requirements faster while staying on top of regulatory changes with our Entity Exchange & Entity Intelligence.

# ANNEX 2.6: SELECTED SOURCES OF INFORMATION ON THE SYNDICATED LOAN MARKET

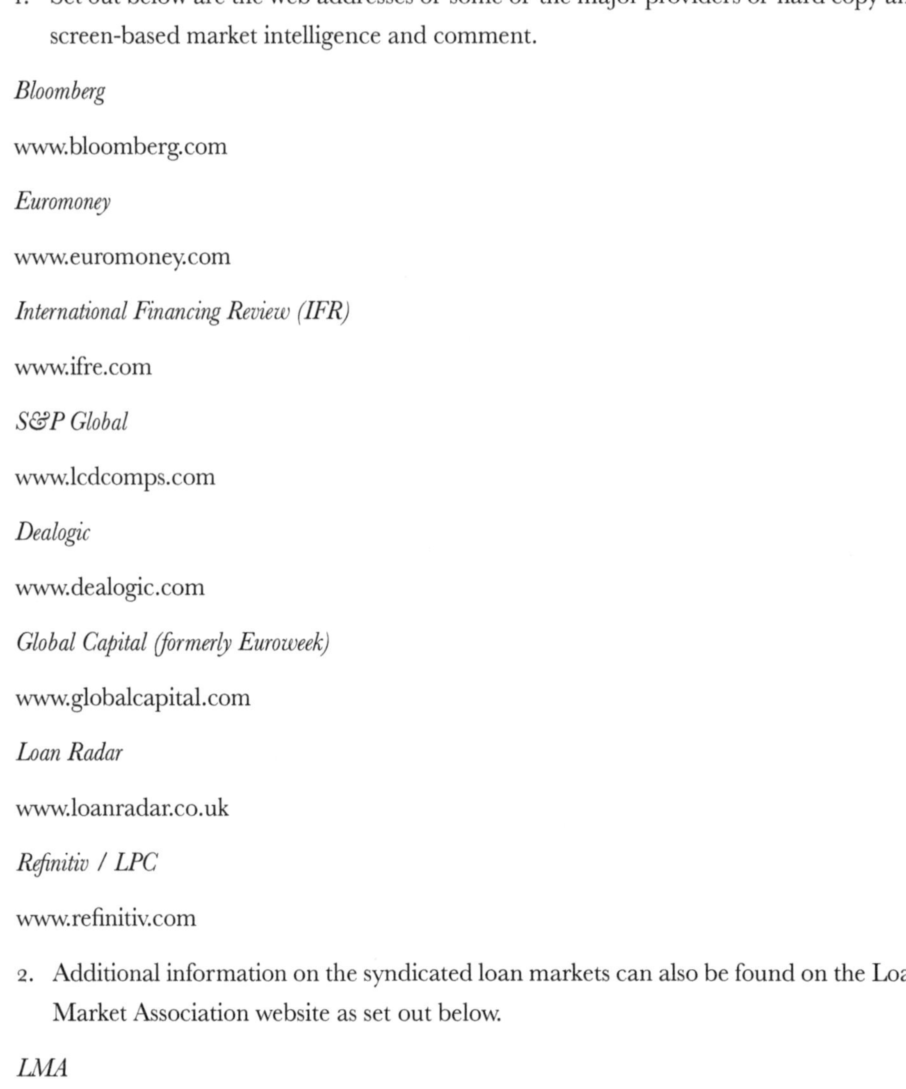

1. Set out below are the web addresses of some of the major providers of hard copy and screen-based market intelligence and comment.

*Bloomberg*

www.bloomberg.com

*Euromoney*

www.euromoney.com

*International Financing Review (IFR)*

www.ifre.com

*S&P Global*

www.lcdcomps.com

*Dealogic*

www.dealogic.com

*Global Capital (formerly Euroweek)*

www.globalcapital.com

*Loan Radar*

www.loanradar.co.uk

*Refinitiv / LPC*

www.refinitiv.com

2. Additional information on the syndicated loan markets can also be found on the Loan Market Association website as set out below.

*LMA*

www.lma.eu.com

# SUPPLEMENT 1: THE BORROWER'S POSITION

**Yves Gerster**

*Global Director for Treasury and Shared Services, Dufry Group*

## BACKGROUND TO DUFRY

Dufry is a hugely successful global retailer and one where you find yourself in one of their retail stores without even trying, at least in airports. When it comes to navigating change Dufry has grown to become the undisputed global leader in travel retail as it is 3 times bigger than the next biggest competitor, operating around 2,200 stores with a turnover of CHF8.4bn and EBITDA of over CHF1bn in 2017. With a diversified global footprint and a presence in 65 countries Dufry has over 20% share of airport retail which is the first thing that springs to mind when thinking of duty free, but Dufry also has a presence on cruise lines, mainly in the Caribbean, at railway stations and downtown such as casinos and leisure resorts.

Dufry has a very strong presence in North and South America. For those frequently travelling to the US, Hudson, their convenience store concept will be familiar. In Europe, large operations exist at London Heathrow, in Spain and Switzerland to name just a few. In Greece, Dufry is the sole duty free operator with shops in Athens and on all touristic relevant islands.

Dufry operates different retail concepts, the most familiar is the general duty free shop with the less obvious being the brand boutique where the whole shop is designed and branded with the corporate identity of one single brand or alternatively a specialised/ theme store which offers products from a variety of different brands belonging to one specific product category.

## HISTORICAL GROWTH STRATEGY

Dufry follows a dedicated growth strategy. Since 2003, Dufry has multiplied its global market share from 3 % to over 20 % through a combination of organic growth and acquisitions. The consistent execution of Dufry's strategy and its focus on profitability has delivered an impressive 20 % average annual turnover growth over the last ten years, along with improving EBITDA margin. In fact, the turnover multiplied 12 times whereas the EBITDA is 20 times 2003 levels.

Just as in the past, Dufry continues to focus on the strategy of profitable growth through further acquisitions and organic growth. In relation to organic growth, travel retail is a fast moving and growing industry driven by a resilient growth in the number of passengers. Annually, according to Airports Council International World (ACI) global passenger numbers are expected to grow by at least 5 % and industry specialists expect the trend to continue.

The industry still has consolidation opportunities with current potential targets operating on more limited regional footprints as compared to the transformational acquisitions of the recent past. Geographically, the key growth region is expected to be Asia and potentially some bolt-on acquisitions with high synergy potential in existing markets.

For all projects, be it organic or acquisitions, Dufry applies a disciplined financial approach. They carefully analyse every project with detailed projections and taking into account the potential worst case scenario.

Further to the steady increase in passenger numbers over time and the financial discipline, Dufry minimises business risk through a highly variable cost structure.

The asset light character of the Dufry business and the variable cost structure helps them to limit the impact of downturns and leads to a strong and stable cash flow generation and a quick deleveraging over time.

Dufry has consistently been a cross-over credit (leverage normally 2x-3x), debt financing the majority of acquisitions (short-term increased leverage to c. 4x), with some equity finance. The company has reasonably high, but manageable, leverage relying on strong cash flow to deleverage. Dufry has resisted higher leverage levels that some acquisitive companies have achieved making them relatively stable and resilient to unpredictable conditions.

# FINANCING REQUIREMENTS

Clearly a strategy such as Dufry has had over many years needs to be financed. This has resulted in 11 major debt transactions completed in the past 12 years (six syndicated loans, four bonds and one equity), although to follow the clear strategy, depending upon the size of the acquisition, Dufry has historically included some element of equity component in the funding mix.

### Exhibit 2.20: Selected Dufry transactions 2006-2018

| 2006 | 2008 | 2011 | 2012 | 2013 | 2014 | 2015 | 2017 | 2018 |
|---|---|---|---|---|---|---|---|---|
| CHF800m | USD1.2bn | USD1.0bn | CHF650m | EUR335m | EUR500m | USD4.4bn | USD4bn | |
| Brasif | Hudson Group | Acquisition South America | Refinancing | Acquisition Greece | Acquisition Greece | The Nuance Group | World Dufry Free Group | Refinancing |

### Exhibit 2.21: Key Dufry financings

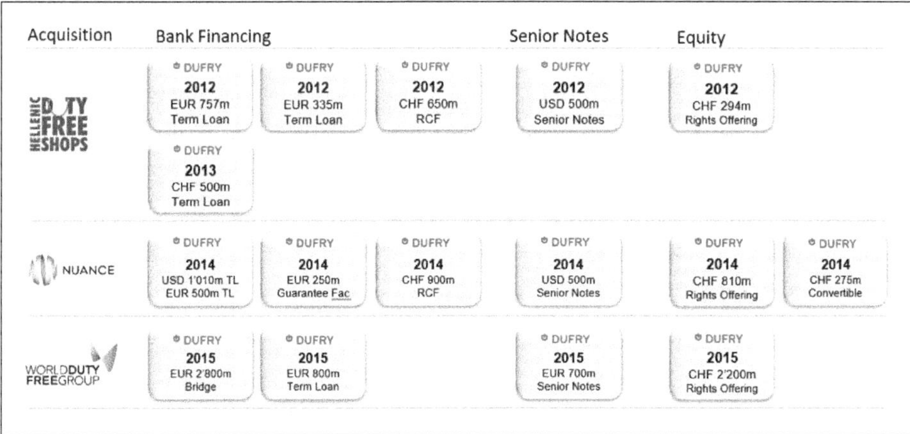


As at the date of this book Dufry has EUR3.3bn in syndicated facilities and EUR1.2bn across two bonds. It has been rated since 2012 and current ratings are S&P BB, Moody's Ba2.

The financings have taken the form of acquisition facilities, full refinancings, debt and equity bridges in addition to the successful use of strategic amendment in the bank financings. With a syndicate of around 30 banks this requires a great deal of management and has been successfully executed at Dufry.

Dufry's business is cash generative and does not require external financing to operate it, but growth through acquisitions needs to be debt funded which means to a large extent, relying on bank debt. In 2012, bonds were added to the funding mix to have a more diversified product portfolio, achieve a more balanced maturity profile and mitigate the refinancing risk. Looking at the different financing elements used for the last three transactions, there has always been an element of bank debt, (at times supported by a bridge) a bond and some equity.

The success of the financings was due to many elements, but in particular to the fact that:

1. a highly disciplined financial approach was adopted;
2. a fair and transparent interaction with all stakeholders was aimed for;
3. promises were kept.

## RELATIONSHIP BANKING

Relationship banking is based on a mutual understanding between the parties and trust about their respective interests with an open dialogue as far as this is possible. Dufry has lived and breathed this relationship banking model consistently for more than ten years, across its transactions. The long standing relationships and a stable banking group have provided additional support. Dufry currently has around 30 banks participating across its syndicated facilities at different exposure levels. Banks at the highest exposure level include Dufry's core banks, there is an additional group of relationship banks with a medium exposure and a third group of new or local commercial banks, some of them pure asset takers, with limited appetite for and access to side business.

In the end, as a borrower, Dufry expects its relationship banks to be transparent and realistic about what they can offer and then be able to deliver when called upon to do so. Dufry understands this is easy for a borrower to expect and the reality can be far more complex.

The biggest advantage for Dufry of this relationship approach is the flexibility available. Due to the personal relationship to individuals at the respective banks, it is possible to act far more quickly. Dufry has arranged for financings, bridges and amendments, all within very short periods of time and without the requirements for heavy documentation or inflexible bureaucracy yet still adhering to the necessary strict regulatory framework. In the case of the World Duty Free acquisition, Dufry informed a small group of core banks about the project on a Saturday and had the firm commitment for the bridge by the following Monday night. The banks committed to participate with around EUR 1bn exposure each without knowing the final structure and terms and conditions of the financing arrangements. This can only be achieved with a relationship banking model and where there is a trustful relationship and a proven track record.

Another example which shows how this relationship works well was the acquisition in Greece in 2012 and 2013, which not only provides a good insight into the Dufry approach, but is also a good example of managing opportunities in uncertain and unpredictable times. In a first step, Dufry bought 51% of the shares financed with debt on group level and refinanced the target's existing debt with a local syndicated facility with Greek banks. The whole structure was ring-fenced and non-recourse against the rest of the Dufry Group. At the same time, Dufry refinanced the group level debt, was rated by the rating agencies and subsequently issued its first bond. To execute such a transaction in a market at a time where foreign companies were tending to pull out of Greece rather than investing in it required a very strong relationship with banks. One year later, as the business had proven to be resilient against the Greek crisis, Dufry bought the remaining shares with cash and shares, replacing the local financing with an inter-company loan.

Relationship banks have regularly supported Dufry through underwriting specific financings. In the past, most of the Dufry financing initiatives were done in relation to an acquisition. It was therefore crucial to have a committed financing in place to de-risk the transaction and also to provide the seller with sufficient comfort that Dufry could fulfil its obligations agreed in the Sale and Purchase Agreement. Dufry has typically addressed this through an underwritten bridge facility or straight with an underwritten bank financing arrangement. When it comes to a new transaction, Dufry has to weigh the costs of the underwriting against the execution risk the company is willing to take should there be no underwriting.

Last year, for the first time, Dufry approached its banks with a non-underwritten transaction for three reasons:

1. No external time pressure as the refinancing was not done in relation to an acquisition.
2. Plenty of liquidity was available in the market and the perception was that there should not be a problem to get the transaction executed smoothly.
3. The close and open relationship with the bank group helped Dufry to make the transaction a success.

At that time, the situation was very different and an opportunity existed to refinance existing transactions, given the borrower friendly capital markets which Dufry saw as an ideal moment to review the debt financing positions with the key aim being to improve commercial terms and move closer towards an investment grade style loan documentation.

In cases where Dufry did go for an underwriting, the sequence was always the same: The transaction was underwritten with around three to four of its core banks followed by a general syndication. Dufry has also seen some two step syndication processes in the past. Typically, the appetite of the banks is pre-sounded before the syndication which allows Dufry to anticipate the market appetite. As a consequence, Dufry can typically work without a market flex. If possible, Dufry has also tried to keep existing facilities in place by amending them to reflect the new scenario.

Although the relationship banking model is highly appreciated, it will be a challenging one going forward. Financing is getting cheaper and thus less profitable for the banks. On the other hand, the ancillary wallet has been shrinking recently with this trend expected to continue. As an example: financial market products are traded in a very competitive environment over online platforms and other non-bank players are entering the market for some products which originally where covered by banks. Additionally, new technology allows the replacement of certain products originally offered by banks.

In Dufry's specific case, this is seen, for example, in credit card acquiring or bank guarantees where insurance companies are playing an increasingly important role. Another important element is technology which replaces services originally offered by banks. An in-house bank for example is reducing the number of bank accounts drastically. There, the banks are not only losing the fees for the accounts and the transfers but are also missing the regular interaction with the corporate which tended to lead to additional business.

Basically, the relationship banking model has a lot of advantages but it is actually the environment which is potentially putting more pressure on the approach going forward unless something changes materially e.g., that the lending product becomes profitable again for banks which would ultimately reduce the pressure on the need for ancillary business to make up the shortfall, which will shrink over time.

## MANAGING BIG BANK GROUPS

Dufry has a large number of lenders, currently 30, and interacts with 150 banks in total through its global businesses. The reason for the relatively large group of 150 banks is the business model. Being a retailer, Dufry needs to work with local retail banks to collect the cash physically from the shops. On that side, it will be difficult to optimise the group and concentrate the operational cash management on just a few banks.

On the lending side, it is difficult to say what the right size would be. On the one hand, the more banks a corporate has, the less it depends on a single name. There is always the risk that somebody drops out in a refinancing. Also, the negotiation power is slightly in the corporate's favour if it has a relatively large group.

On the other hand, to manage a large group is very workload intense. And it will become more challenging going forward. As mentioned before, the ancillary wallet is expected to shrink drastically over the next years.

During the last years, the interest of the banks in participating in Dufry's financing arrangements has increased materially. Dufry never had problems to find new banks but had to work on it. In the last couple of years, this has changed and the interest of new banks to participate in the lending has increased materially. This may have various reasons:

- There is simply too much liquidity in the market and banks looking for some yield have migrated to the sub-investment grade area.
- Also, due to the Dufry growth and track record, they became more visible.
- In the last financing, Dufry had to reject a quite large number of banks which wanted to become part of the lending group.

Probably, most important for Dufry is the ideal mix of banks which cover all the requirements: a small number of best in class investment banks, right mix of geographical footprint i.e., some American, some European and some Asian banks to offer traditional commercial banking. Ideally, there are also banks who are specialised niche players in some products, but unfortunately, there are only few such banks. Banks tend to offer all products and try to pitch for all their products in all markets. Dufry often finds itself in meetings where banks are pitching for totally unrealistic scenarios. In that respect, Dufry has been in communication with banks about some form of rule of conduct, or rules of engagement, which should manage the expectations on both sides.

# DOCUMENTATION AND INCREASED REGULATION

To ensure to comply with the targeted amortisation of debt, Dufry also matches the currencies used on the debt side with the corresponding share of the free cash flow per currency. Although Dufry operates in 65 countries, it is actually purchasing and selling predominantly in USD, EUR and Sterling.

In respect to currencies, Dufry has adapted the documentation in a way to be protected against short term fluctuation of the currencies – EBITDA is typically calculated at the P&L rates (average) and the net debt at the balance sheet rate (single day). To eliminate that particular challenge, Dufry has agreed with the banks to calculate both figures at the balance sheet rate.

A particular situation where this has helped Dufry was in 2016, where after the Brexit referendum sterling lost around 20% value.

Know your customer (KYC) requirements are becoming increasingly onerous. The problems are not the requirements itself but the missing automation or digitalisation, the missing standardisation and the paper based processes. Dufry believes that technology, and especially blockchain, can play a key role to overcome those challenges. Today, Dufry still needs physically to provide passport copies to the lawyers, get them notarised and send them via courier to the respective banks. Dufry is not only doing that once, but delivering the same documents to different banks or stakeholders. In some cases, Dufry is even obliged to deliver the same document to different departments in the same institution! As mentioned before, Dufry works with 150 banks in more than 60 countries. Unfortunately, the requirements vary from country to country, sometimes from institution to institution.

The technology ought to be available, the challenge would be to agree on an international standard and to implement it.

# BANK VERSUS BOND

On balance, evidence suggests a large number of sub-investment grade European corporates still prefer more discrete prepayable bank financings (with maintenance covenants as a trade-off) compared to less onerous incurrence based testing with bonds, with public ratings, and often security, required by non bank investors.

Dufry, as a user of both markets can compare directly and recognises that the mix can work well with both having their advantages and disadvantages. The reason to add bonds to the Dufry funding mix was never a question of not having sufficient access to liquidity, but was always a de-risking strategy in the sense that there was the recognition that relying too heavily on one single source of debt funding was unhealthy. Bonds allow for longer maturities resulting in a more balanced debt maturity profile. Another advantage of mixing bank debt and bonds is to achieve a balanced fixed and floating interest rate mix without the requirement to hedge the interest exposure via derivatives. Also, the incurrence based covenant approach in the bond market provides the borrower with additional flexibility for acquisitions.

This, however comes at the cost of being less flexible when it comes to early repayments. Another disadvantage of the bond is the requirement of external rating and the implications this has on the bank internal rating. The agencies rate Dufry sub-investment grade whereas Dufry has typically been rated investment grade by the banks' internal rating. The external rating puts some pressure on the internal rating.

Another aspect is the documentation. The LMA standard is significantly less complex than the bond documentation.

For Dufry, it is important to have access to both products and this is not expected to change – at least not as long as Dufry has a sizeable debt position.

# SUPPLEMENT 2: REGIONAL MARKETS

## SUPPLEMENT 2.1: REGIONAL MARKETS: GERMAN MARKET

**Christian Ulrich**

*Head of Corporate Structured Finance, Bayern LB*

European corporate financing is widely viewed as being dominated by banks. Traditionally, Germany is characterised by a bank-based financing system where, with a few exceptions, (bilateral) loans have consistently been the most important financing instrument.

In the wake of the global financial crisis, research shows that a shift has taken place in the financing behaviour of corporate borrowers in the eurozone with some country-specific deviations.

1. Corporations raise less funds externally and rely to a greater extent on internally generated funds from their own activities
2. A shift more towards equity than borrowed funds in respect of external funding
3. Bank loans become less important as a financing instrument than other debt-like instruments e.g., debt securities or debt provided by non-banks.

These developments might have been a reaction to experiences of borrowers during and after the financial crisis and seem to be a consequence of temporary financial constraints and restrictive lending practices experienced in the past as well as a preparation for even tighter bank regulation.

So the question is, did these developments effect syndicated lending in Germany and, if so, how?

Within the last two decades the German loan market has developed into one of Europe's largest syndicated loan markets (see exhibit 2.22) with borrowers raising large loans at highly competitive rates. Of course, there have already been mid cap companies borrowing money in the syndicated loan market but the majority of German borrowers were large listed companies or large family-owned companies with international activities. However, in recent years syndicated lending activity has attracted even small and medium-sized companies. Improving market conditions in a highly competitive banking market with domestic and foreign banks providing financial assistance across various products, generating ample liquidity for local companies, was probably a necessary condition. The openness of borrowers of the German Mittelstand to adapt their financing behaviour and their readiness to tap also the syndicated loan market has been a notable change. Actual data and transaction analysis show that even double digit million deals are no longer the sole territory of domestic banks but also foreign banks arrange or participate in them, leading to fierce competition in lending activities. The required funds for the transactions are being provided not only by domestic banks but also by foreign banks who are contributing, large scale, obviously executing their business strategies by targeting small and mid-cap companies in the German Mittelstand. Segmenting transaction volumes reveals that loans with a transaction size of €100m or less have become a significant segment in the syndicated loan market in recent years. Today one can experience that even smaller companies with revenues starting in low double-digit millions use syndicated loans as a main financial source.

**Exhibit 2.22: Germany Syndicated Loan volume 2000 to 1H 2018**

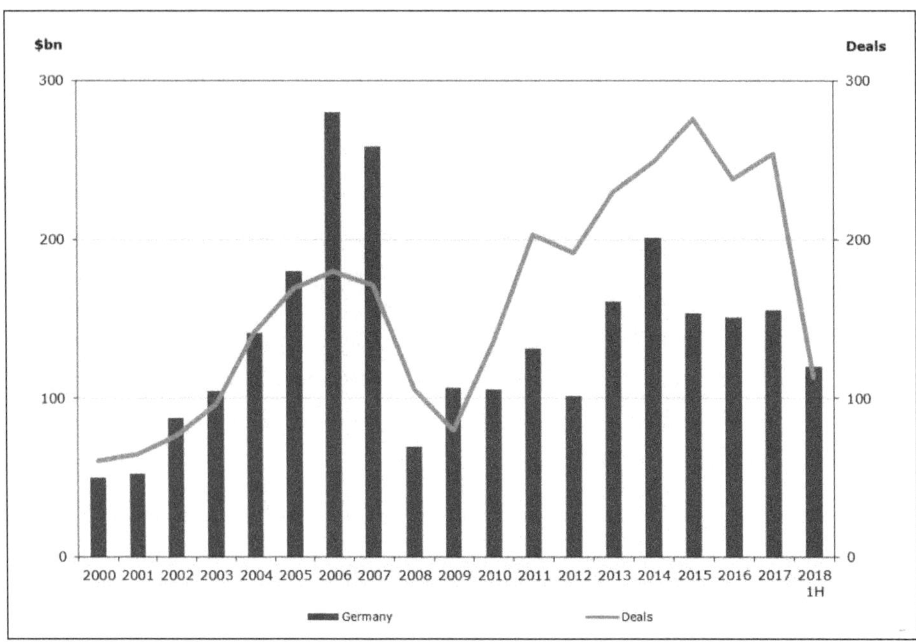


**Source: Dealogic**

Another interesting development in corporate financing has been the occurrence of alternative sources of debt financings. One financing instrument which has hit the market and significantly increased its market share in Germany is the *Schuldscheindarlehen* (SSD). Due to market uncertainties resulting from the impact of the European sovereign debt crisis, public debt markets were shut down for certain periods of time and German borrowers / issuers switched to this financing instrument. It is widely seen and recognised as a supplement to (syndicated) loans and public debt securities and not as a substitute. Additionally, the instrument has been increasingly accepted both by borrowers/issuers due to its comparative pricing advantages to public debt and by investors by gaining access to issuers mostly active in public debt markets. In its initial phase the instrument was used as a primary source for refinancing existing debt. In the meantime, it is used even as a take out instrument for bridge loans in acquisition financing. An increasing number of companies have been using SSD as an instrument in their corporate financing toolbox to address their financing needs. Over the last years, corporates from the rest of Europe and beyond have also started to issue SSD in the market.

Both observations have had an impact on how corporate financing in Germany is looking today. The openness of borrowers of different sizes fuels market transformation, but also offers opportunities for syndicated loans and SSD as well. Compared to other countries in the euro zone it might not be breathtaking, but for the traditional German 'house bank' principle, it marks a major game changer.

# SUPPLEMENT 2.2: REGIONAL MARKETS: FRENCH MARKET

**Alban Vital**

*Head of Western European Origination, Loan Capital Markets, SMBC*

## Evolution of the French market

The French loan market has always been characterised by the weight of its local banks in the economy of the country; four French banks rank in the top ten European banks in terms of their size of the balance sheet.[4] In the first half of 2018, (i) France represents the third country in terms of syndicated loans volume in EMEA (22% of EMEA volumes), after the UK and Germany, and (ii) the top fifteen French transactions accounted for 67% of the total IG syndicated loan volume in France (USD47.7bn out of USD70.4bn). All major international banks are active in France.

Over the last five years, fierce competition between banks and abundant liquidity have led French corporates to refinance their existing debt early and push for better terms and conditions: tighter pricing, looser documentation, removal of financial covenants for IG large corporates and longer maturities –5+1+1–year tenor being the norm for Revolving Credit Facilities (extension options could be used at the end of the first anniversary and/or the second anniversary of the loan).

The market remains dominated by the volume of bank debt vs disintermediated types of financing. Loans still represent c. 60% of corporates' financing means (vs 30% in the USA, for instance). Over the last years though, thanks to the low interest rate environment and the ECB asset purchase programme, this imbalance has been directed towards an increase in the volume of bond issuances in particular for large corporates (see exhibit 2.24). Except for acquisition financing, whereby bridge loan facilities are often used for a short-term period before being refinanced on the debt/equity capital markets, large corporates tend to only have backstop facilities such as revolving credit facilities, and issue bonds to refinance their existing debt.

4 Source: Fédération Bancaire Française, March 2018

## Exhibit 2.23: France Syndicated Loan volume 2000 to 1H 2018

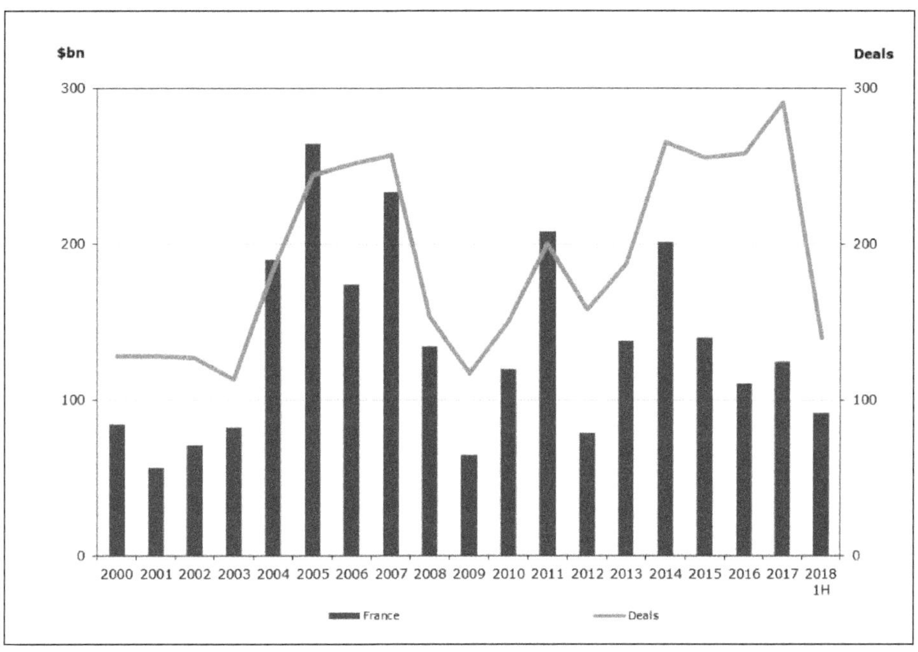


Source: Dealogic

## Exhibit 2.24: NFC debt in France (annual growth rates, as %)

Source: Banque de France, 2018 Markets and Risk Outlook

On the back of a favorable environment, alternative ways of financing have emerged over the last couple of years. *Schuldschein* loans (coming from Germany) and ESG-linked/green loans have been used by corporates to diversify their sources of funding – refinancing of existing debt or acquisition financing for instance (2016 SEB acquisition of the German company, WMF mostly refinanced via *schuldschein* loans and more recently Faurecia acquisition of the Japanese company, Clarion refinanced with a *schuldschein* loan). French banks have followed the trend arranging more and more *schuldschein* and ESG-linked/green loans. The amounts raised on the private placement markets have continued to grow but remain at low development stages compared to the traditional loan/debt capital markets. The development of these new markets has allowed (i) banks to diversify their ancillary business and (ii) corporates to have access to better terms and conditions and longer maturities while enhancing their reputation at the same time.

Since January 2018 for instance, four major French corporates have issued green & sustainable loans for a total amount of EUR3.45bn with pricing being tied to the company's performance on environmental, social and governance metrics (ESG KPIs). These metrics can be measured against an independently management sustainability index. In addition, French corporates have started to implement these ESG KPIs directly in their back-up revolving credit facilities, used for general corporate purposes.

## SMEs - Leveraged market

On the other hand, the SMEs are still relying a lot on banks to cover their funding needs. This is particularly true for LBOs. In 2016–17, France was number one in terms of volume issued (20% and 18% of market share respectively), followed by the UK and Germany.[5]

The lack of transactions and competitive terms and conditions in the investment-grade space has recently led more and more international banks which were previously focusing on large corporates, to participate in the syndicate of mid-cap French corporates. Growth in the leveraged loan market, together with the deterioration of protection through covenant-lite documentation, illustrate this intensified increase in risk taken by investors. Since 2012, spreads have decreased by c. 30% as demonstrated by exhibit 2.25 below.

5 Source: S&P Global, Eur LBO 2Q 2018

**Exhibit 2.25: Weighted average new-issue spreads – France**

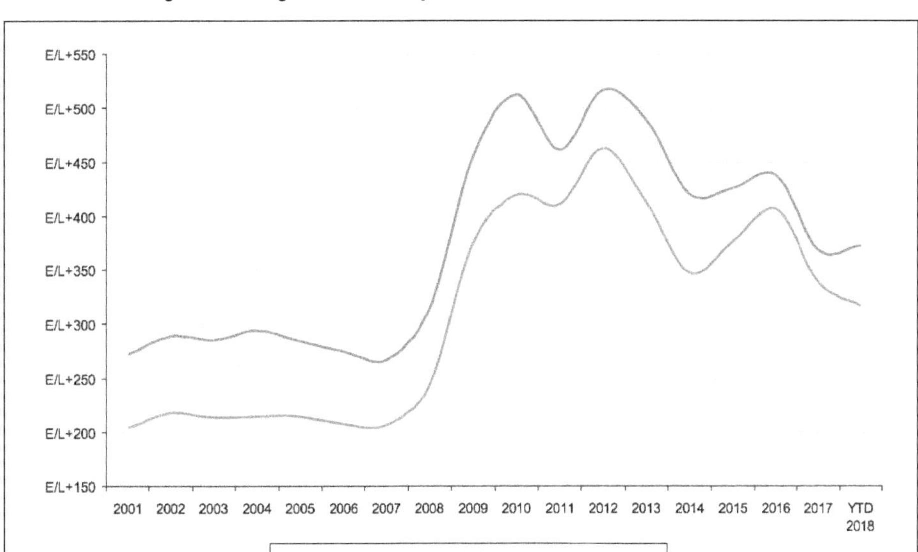


**Source: S&P Global, Eur Senior 2Q 2018**

The French syndicated loan market is evolving with international banks expanding their client base, while alternative ways of financing are becoming more prominent, allowing corporates to be less reliant on banks, diversify their sources of funding and achieve lower spreads.

# SUPPLEMENT 2.3: REGIONAL MARKETS: SOUTHERN EUROPEAN REGION

**Emilio Lopez Fernandez**

*Head of Corporate Loans – Spain and Portugal, BBVA*

The syndicated loan market in Southern Europe has been driven by the strong liquidity available and fierce competition among banks in the last few years, particularly in Spain and Italy.

The 'new money' element has been significantly more relevant after some years with low incidence. The refinancing focus moved from highly rated corporates to cross-over and mid-market companies. Additionally, M&A activity in Spain and Italy had an uptrend during 2017 and the first half of 2018 given the economic recovery and attractive valuations in certain sectors. Acquisition-related activity accounted for nearly 20% share of total volume compared to less than 10% in 2016 and previous years.

However, issuance in both Spain and Italy is still far from the levels reached in other geographies, such as the UK or Germany, where a number of jumbo cross-border transactions were successfully subscribed (BAT, Reckitt, Bayer). Indeed, the only landmark jumbo acquisition in Southern Europe financed in the syndicated loan market in recent years took place in 2018 in favour of ACS (via its subsidiary Hochtief) and Atlantia, for the takeover of the infrastructure conglomerate Abertis for a EUR18.2bn loan consideration.

Sustainable lending should be an area of growth, especially in Spain, where a number of key borrowers have successfully closed innovative deals, in particular Iberdrola, REE and Mapfre. Hera and Generali have also recently opened the way in Italy with ESG (Environmental, Social and Governance) linked facilities.

Although certain similarities exist between both markets, it is important to highlight the respective specificities, especially regarding the banking competitive landscape.

## Exhibit 2.26: Spain Syndicated Loan volume 2000 to 1H 2018

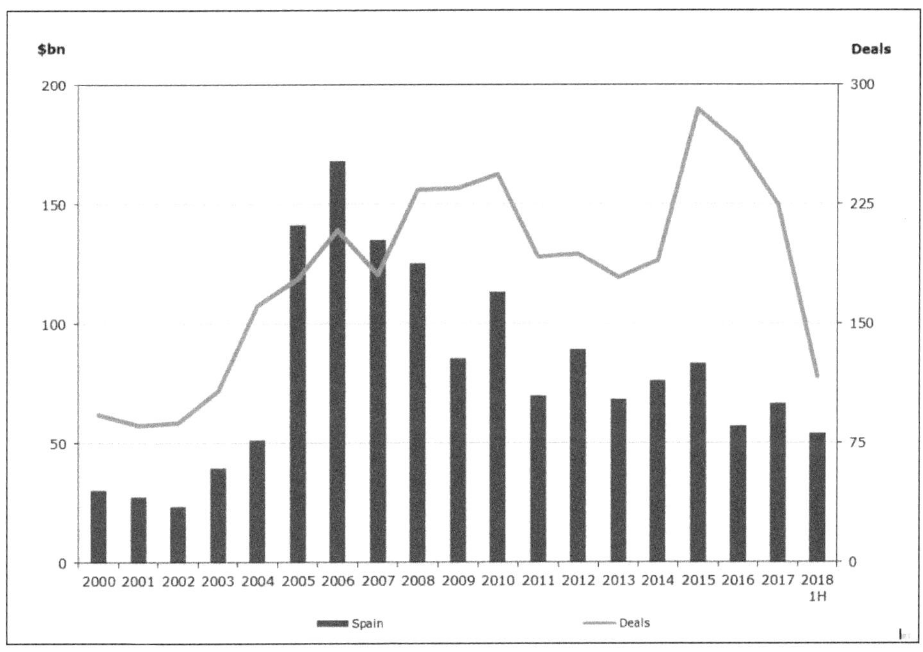


Source: Dealogic

## Exhibit 2.27: Italy Syndicated Loan volume 2000 to 1H 2018

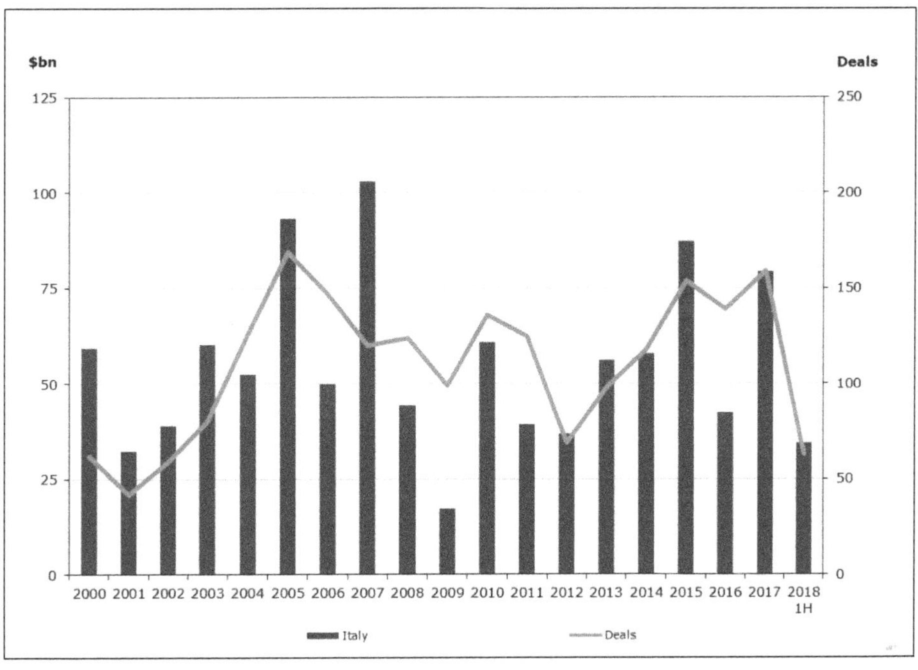


Source: Dealogic

## Investment grade

Pricing-wise, levels reflect ancillary business and not credit on a standalone basis. Peripherals premium was removed for internationally diversified borrowers.

In terms of volume, we have seen some reduction in investment-grade refinancing as borrowers have previously taken advantage of low pricing levels and there is minimal potential pricing improvement after strong downwards pressure since 2013.

In relation to recent market trends, borrowers tend to foster smaller bank groups with a more selective approach focused on lenders' capabilities. However, a number of exceptions remain (Iberdrola in Spain and Enel in Italy). In terms of format, 'amend and extend', instead of straight refinancings have been successful with a push for looser documentation. For instance, some borrowers were able to remove the Euribor floor from their documentation despite current negative rates, even for drawn facilities.

Club deals are also common these days, in particular in Italy, where some international banks are able to participate at similar takes as domestic banks.

In the Real Estate area, it is worth mentioning the rise of *Socimis* deals in Spain. These *Socimis* (e.g., Colonial, Testa, Hispania) are listed trusts generally with an investment-grade rating, which have tapped the loan market to accompany their capital markets strategy.

Most banks are underlent in the investment-grade space, and well-capitalised compared to 2008, though more focused around ancillary business given restrictive profitability requirements.

## Non-investment grade

In the non-investment grade area, we shall distinguish between bank deals, including low-leveraged mid-market, and leveraged lending transactions, both sponsored and non-sponsored, which may require the tapping of the institutional market.

In recent years, the primary issuance market was dominated by the imbalance between the investors' demand and borrowers' supply, which imposed downward pressure on margins, falling to historical levels. These low levels, together with a favourable technical environment (low level of default, minimum volatility, high liquidity) favoured opportunistic transactions. Let us bear in mind that in Southern Europe, the deleveraging of non-investment grade corporates has been very significant post-crisis.

Transactions have seen their structure being loosened with higher covenant headrooms, longer tenors (e.g., six-year amortising facilities are now market standard and even seven year is achievable for BB-implied borrowers), higher balloons (over 30%) and average lives (reaching up to five years). Additionally, strong bank liquidity means that underwriting activity is restricted to sponsor-driven deals and competitive M&A processes.

On the institutional lending side, the market closed 2017 with record volume and issuances, primarily driven by M&A. There was also a significant shift towards increasingly looser structures and downward pricing. For example, average new issue yields for BB range transactions in Spain fell from 301 in Q1 2017 to 279 in Q4 2017. This decrease in yields has affected pricing on Senior CLO tranches, with managers repricing at record low coupons.

The private equity funds have been particularly active, surpassing even pre-crisis levels. 2017 was the year in which the Term Loans B market in Southern Europe was consolidated. In addition to the reduction in cost, the 'cov-lite' format has been generalised, that is, without maintenance covenants.

## Spanish bank competitive landscape

Since the bailout of certain Spanish savings banks in May 2012 (including Bankia, the country's largest mortgage lender, among others) the Spanish banking system has been dramatically transformed via consolidation. From over 50 institutions, there are currently less than a dozen banks which are active in the syndicated loan market.

Santander and BBVA remain the two most active bookrunners and benefit from the widest geographical footprint and product range. For example, in the institutional market, outside international banks, BBVA and Santander are the Spanish bookrunning houses of reference. In relation to sustainable lending, BBVA is the indisputed leading bank and one of the most active worldwide.

Caixabank has filled the gap by being very active in certain segments (real estate, project finance) and regions (Catalonia, Valencia) and due to the significant increase in terms of balance sheet capacity following the integration of several local savings banks. Sabadell and Bankia are also active players especially in the mid-market whilst they have increased their presence with top borrowers (Iberdrola, Telefónica). The rest of the players tend to play passive roles with limited arrangement capabilities.

## Italian bank competitive landscape

In Italy, whilst the process of consolidation of banks has been less significant than in Spain, the syndicated loan market is now dominated by four main players, Unicredit, Intesa-SanPaolo, Mediobanca and BNP-Paribas through BNL. Underwriting activity and bookrunning statistics in all segments have been led by these institutions.

However, the concentration of a number of regional players and the acquisition of others by international banks, such as Cariparma by Crédit Agricole, have converted Italy into one of the most competitive markets in Europe, especially in the mid-market.

International investment banks tend to struggle to access the market other than top borrowers such as Enel and Telecom Italia, partly due to the relatively lower penetration of institutional transactions for leveraged deals.

Further consolidation may be expected of domestic banks in the next few years.

# SUPPLEMENT 2.4: REGIONAL MARKETS: NORDIC REGION

**Michael Dicks**

To understand the importance of the Nordic market (Sweden/Finland/Norway/Denmark/Iceland) in the development of syndicated lending, in the broader context of the European market, one needs to reflect on history and the first period of modern economic growth that Sweden led during the mid to late 1800's.

Sweden developed rapidly in the late 19th century as the demand growth for raw materials (iron ore/wood products etc) morphed into a demand for sophisticated machinery and equipment. External funding had already been used by both the government and private enterprises to develop railways to the mines and forests in the North, and power development via use of Hydroelectricity. The first syndicated bond transactions organised by French/German and British bankers supported this capital import and important infrastructural development. Sweden has the oldest Central Bank, having been established in 1668. In 1866, the Swedish Stock Exchange was established and, in 1897, the Central Bank became the sole issuer of bank notes and the de facto lender of last resort, commercial banks expanded as did the credit capacity to fund industrial development.

Sweden's industrial growth driven by inventors and engineers led to the foundation of companies such as AGA, ASEA, Ericsson, Alfa Laval and SKF amongst others. Swedish banks founded in the mid 1850's played an important part in arranging the inward flow of capital to fund these export orientated industries. Add to this the post WW1 expansion as Sweden had remained neutral, followed by what has been coined the Golden Age of Growth (1950–75). There followed the crisis years of the 80's (in industry) but an explosive growth in real estate investment funded in the late 80's by the first modern day syndicated facilities provided by both local and international banks. This was the same time that the UK market's development of MOF's, NIF's and RUF's accelerated the use of syndicated facilities from the early days of the Euro dollar loan market founded arguably in c. 1973 with SG Warburgs USD1bn facility for ENEL (see chapter 1).

In the late 1980's in Europe, only the UK and Sweden were using the benefits of syndicated credit facilities. The rest of Europe was largely funded by bilateral bank facilities, and local bond or private placement markets with the concept of international bond issuance for industrial financing slowly developing.

The Nordic markets entered the 90's in crisis. In 1990–91 there was a flurry of early syndicated RCF's issued to fund international expansion via acquisitions (Stora/SCA buying in Germany/Switzerland with USD billion-dollar RCF's and large bank syndicates)

However the Real Estate bubble burst in Sweden in 1991/92; the ERM was attacked; Soros staked sterling taking on the BoE; inflation and volatile interest and currency rates created havoc. This was a period of crashes, restructurings but yet rapid growth on the other side of this intense period through mergers and acquisitions. The Nordic phoenix rose from the burning fires and in the following 10 years became second only to the UK in the use of syndicated facilities to fund international expansion. Germany, France and other European countries such as Spain, Italy were until the mid-90's still primarily funded in the bilateral bank and local bond/private placement markets.

The Nordic syndicated markets led the way during the 90's and up to the 2008 global financial crisis in both aggressive pricing (and annual re-pricing!), documentation structure (namely lack of financial covenants) and stretched tenors (standard seven year bullets for most investment grade credits and even an eight year tenor for MoDo at one point). There were 'blips' along the way, notably the Russian/Mexican/Thai financial crisis in 1997, the LTCM crisis in 1998 and the 2000 Telecom/Dotcom crisis (leading to the Ericsson/ABB restructurings in 2002 and more). In general, the Nordic syndicated loan market per se was the leading market in terms of price and aggressive documentation competition, and given the large number of export orientated companies in mainly Sweden and Finland and the expansion of the oil and gas sector in Norway both local and international banks were very focused on client and business development in the Nordic area. Equally for many years during this period the combined Nordic market annual volume statistics were second only to that of the UK (investment grade corporate lending).

**Exhibit 2.28: Nordic Syndicated Loan volume 2000 to 1H 2018**

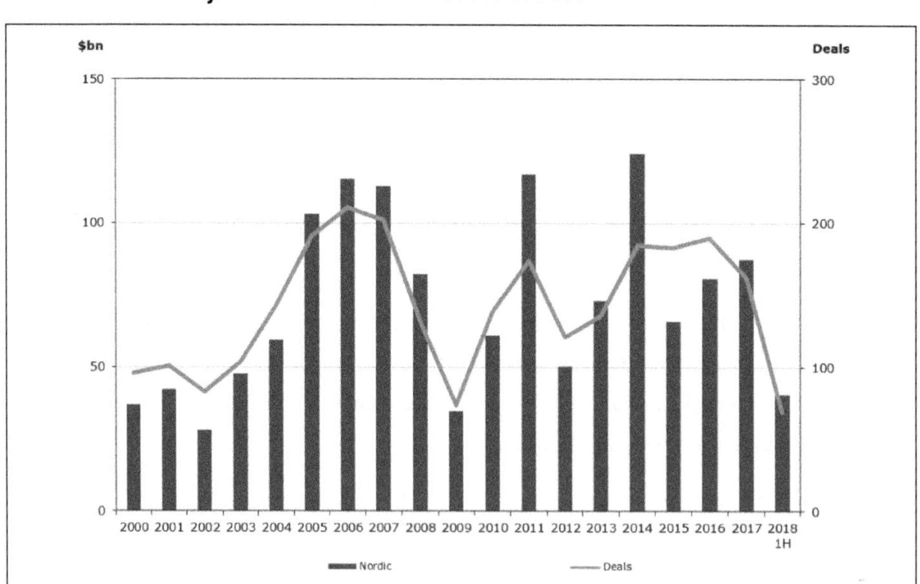


Source: Dealogic

For many Nordic companies during the period from 1994 to date, the problem has been to manage the expectations of their bankers and share the ancillary wallet to compensate for the true cost of relationship lending – low returns on capital. Despite the introduction of the BIS Capital Adequacy regimes and their increasing complexity banks continued to invest in unprofitable Nordic lending relationships, hoping for lucrative international ancillary business. Many remained unrewarded for a very long time. In other European and the UK markets during this time corporate clients had typically been less open to wide bank syndicates, not so the Nordic's where in the mid 90's syndicates of 30 or so local and international banks were not uncommon. Today it can be argued that there is a much more homogenous approach to syndicated standby facilities across the European markets, with corporate treasurers looking to manage, and in some cases tier, their relationship banks into meaningful, mutually beneficial cooperation. Further, the syndicated loan market both before and after the financial crisis in 2008 has proved to continue to be the market that remains open all hours despite market crisis, as the imbalances of market capacity and investor appetite in bond and private placement markets globally come and go (though the 'risk off' scenario has been mainly absent since early 2010 – except for the China currency crisis in 2015–16).

Whilst the above reflects on the trend in non-Private Equity syndicated financing, it is also a fair reflection of the Nordic markets to say that local and international PE houses have benefited from aggressive local practices in the Nordic market, and the local LBO market has grown in tandem with the wider European and global markets where the USA led the way in the 1980's. The first Nordic PE funds were set up in the early 90's and have benefited from close co-operation from their local Nordic bankers initially with a preference for 'closed' club funding solutions. As the PE market has continued to grow in the Nordic's and Nordic PE houses expanded globally, they have equally benefited from the full array of capital market solutions available from the international and Nordic banking community, but are still arguably the most fêted and to a degree 'spoilt for choice' community in Europe.

The Nordic corporate, industrial and PE community was often in the past referred to as a niche market. The definition of a niche is 'a product, service, or interest that appeals to a small, specialised section of the community'. The Nordic borrower/issuer base has always commanded worldwide attention from financiers ever since the first syndicated funding supporting the development of infrastructure in the first and second industrial revolutions in Sweden (1850–90 and 1890–1950). This happily continues today and has been a relatively consistent theme since Swedish Industry discovered the benefits of syndicated lending to fuel global expansion in the early 1990's and the other Nordic countries followed on. Long may this situation continue benefiting Nordic industrial expansion and providing the main Nordic banks with a place in the international financing arena.

# SUPPLEMENT 2.5: REGIONAL MARKETS: GCC REGION

**Alper Kilic**

*Regional Head of Loan Syndications – Africa, Standard Chartered Bank*

The syndicated loan market in the Gulf Cooperation Council (GCC) (GCC Loan Market) consists of the six Middle Eastern countries: Bahrain, Kuwait, Oman, Qatar, Saudi Arabia and United Arab Emirates (UAE). Given the critical role of the hydrocarbon sector within the GCC, oil price volatility has been an important factor in the growth of the GCC Loan Market. As demonstrated in exhibit 2.29, during the 1990's loan volumes were subdued, as was the price of oil. However, as oil prices increased during the early 2000's so did the GCC Loan Market up until the crash of the financial crisis in 2008. Interestingly, the drop in oil prices since 2014 has had the opposite effect on the GCC Loan Market, as GCC sovereigns have tapped the loan market for the first time, thus supporting growth in loan volumes.

#### Exhibit 2.29: GCC Syndicated Loan Issuance 1995 to 1H 2018

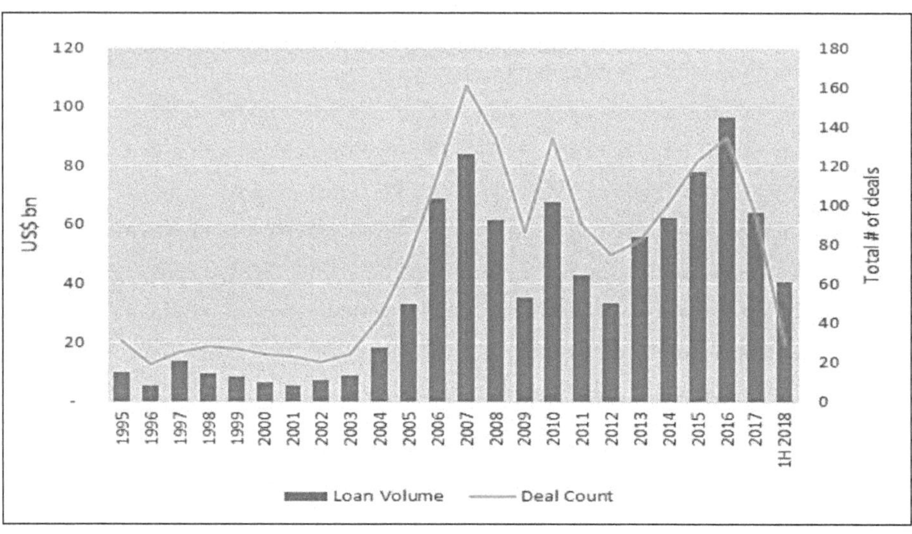


**Source: Dealogic**

Within the GCC, loan volumes have been dominated by sovereign/government related entities (GRE's) and project finance borrowers. Outside this group of borrowers there is only a small group of investment grade corporate borrowers who have tapped the syndicated loan market in meaningful size. This is one of the characteristics of the GCC Loan Market. It is a shallow loan market with loan volumes dominated by a small borrowing base. It should be highlighted that the UAE and Saudi Arabia have historically been number one or number two countries for loan volumes and both are the largest economies in the GCC.

Since the hydrocarbon sector has been the driver for economic growth and the primary source of sovereign revenues within the GCC, it is not surprising that the oil & gas sector has been a significant contributor to loan volumes in the region. Outside the oil & gas industry, key industries that have contributed to loan volumes are telecommunications, transportation, utilities, chemicals and finance (financial institutions and non-bank financial institutions) coincidently all these sectors typically have strong sovereign/GRE connections. Please refer to exhibit 2.30.

**Exhibit 2.30: GCC Syndicated Loan Issuance by Sector 2005 to 1H 2018**

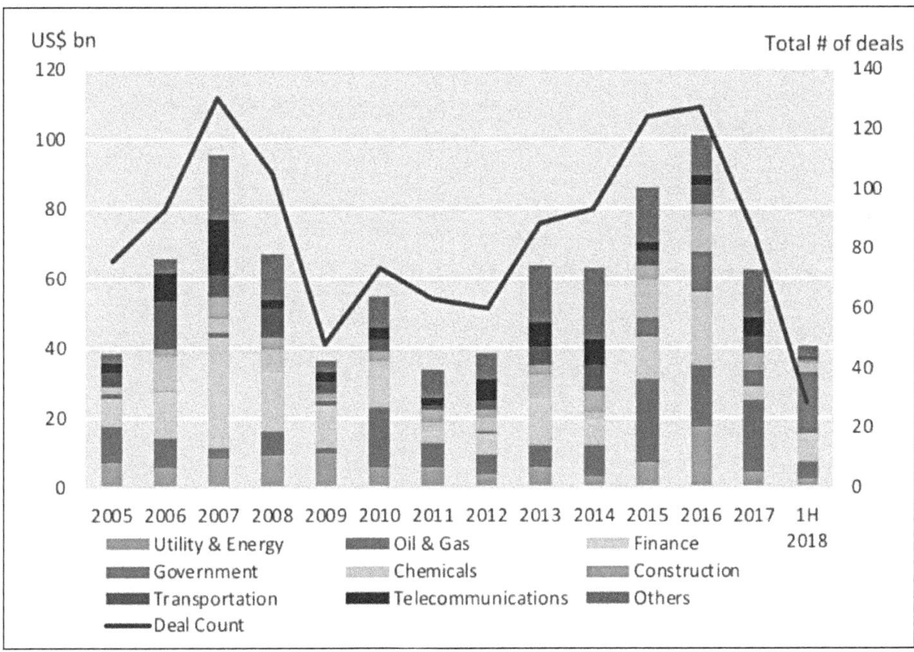


**Source: Dealogic**

The GCC Loan Market is largely dominated by USD denominated transactions, the only exception being Saudi Arabia, since local currency loan issuances have a strong representation. This can be attributed to the financial strength and capacity of the local Saudi Arabian banks versus the international and regional banks in their home market.

International banks have typically been supporters of sovereign/GRE/project finance loan issuance in the GCC, and only a very small group of them have been active further down the credit spectrum. In contrast GCC banks have typically been key liquidity providers outside this borrowing base and down the credit spectrum.

The low oil price environment (Q4 2014 onwards) has asked oil exporting GCC sovereigns to re-evaluate the status of their economies (which as mentioned earlier are hydrocarbon sector centric) and in some cases, push for more economic diversification/alternative financing options and to reconsider the private/public balance in infrastructure financing. All these potential changes will likely have a noticeable impact in the GCC Syndicated Loan Market in the coming years.

# SUPPLEMENT 2.6: REGIONAL MARKETS: SUB-SAHARAN AFRICA REGION

**Alper Kilic**

*Regional Head of Loan Syndications – Africa, Standard Chartered Bank*

The syndicated loan market in Sub-Saharan Africa (SSA) (the 'SSA Loan Market') covers 48 countries split across four regions: East Africa, West Africa, Central Africa and Southern Africa. The SSA Loan Market has grown exponentially since 2005 (see figure 1). While there was a slight downturn in 2008 following the global financial crisis, the market continued to benefit from international investors who looked to the continent in search of higher-yield and high-growth assets. Post-2014 volumes (particularly in West Africa and oil and gas transactions in general) have been negatively impacted by the downturn in commodity prices (see exhibit 2.31). Despite this, loan volumes remained above pre-2008 levels due to the diversity of the SSA loans market. South Africa and Nigeria have traditionally dominated the syndicated loans market in terms of deal volumes. However, both countries have recently been impacted by a combination of volatile commodity prices and in the case of South Africa low growth and political uncertainty. East Africa, largely driven by activity in Kenya, has emerged as a key market for diversification and has benefited from the liquidity shifting away from West Africa.

### Exhibit 2.31: SSA Syndicated Loan Issuance 2005 to 1H 20181

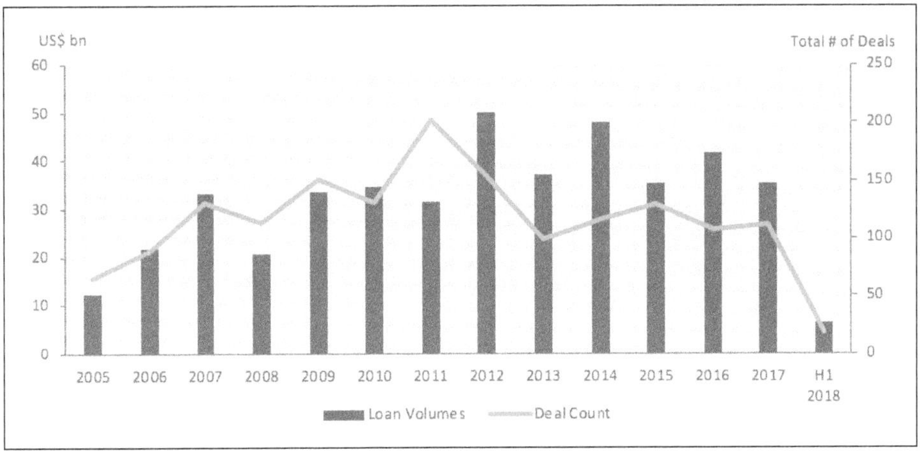

Source: Dealogic

With the exception of South Africa where we see a number of repeat issuers across both corporates and financial institutions, the SSA Loan Market has relatively few entrenched borrowers. The SSA Loan Market (excluding South Africa) is therefore characterised by a diverse mix of more developed markets/issuers and a number of distinct developing markets and smaller players across the region. This diversity can make it difficult for international investors to access the broader market given individual market nuances. As such we see strong international demand for borrowers with multi-jurisdictional presence including the regional African multilaterals like African Export Import Bank, Eastern and Southern Trade and Development Bank (TDB) and Africa Finance Corporation. In terms of transaction value of issuances this has been historically dominated by a small number of borrowers, who have built up their profile with international investors to enable them to raise large amounts on a recurring basis. Most notably in the non-financial institution space, Sonangol having raised more than USD34.4bn in over 37 transactions and Ghana Cocoa Board, raising over USD22.3bn in 30 transactions since 1995. Sonangol is one of the most recognised names in the African oil and gas space. Ghana Cocoa Board has continued to set the market in the agri-business sector with its annual syndicated loan raising upwards of USD1.0bn per year since 2007. The South African banks and regional DFIs contribute to a steady flow of transactions in SSA every year with syndicated loans that attract a large number of investors due to their robust credit quality and the strong relationship banking groups these borrowers have maintained.

From an industry perspective (see exhibit 2.32) we see variation year-on-year highlighting the cyclical nature of the market. The oil and gas sector continues to account for a significant portion of volumes, at an average of 23.1% of total loans volumes from 2005 to 1H 2018. However, increasing infrastructure spending by governments and consistent borrowing by the financial institution sector has contributed to increasing loan volumes even as the oil and gas sector contribution remained fairly stable. In years when oil and gas loan volumes were particularly subdued (for example, 2007 and 2016) we saw an increase in transactions in other sectors as investors looked for diversification in sectors with strong reputable borrowers and attractive yields.

**Exhibit 2.32: SSA Syndicated Loan Issuance by Industry 2005 to 1H 20181**

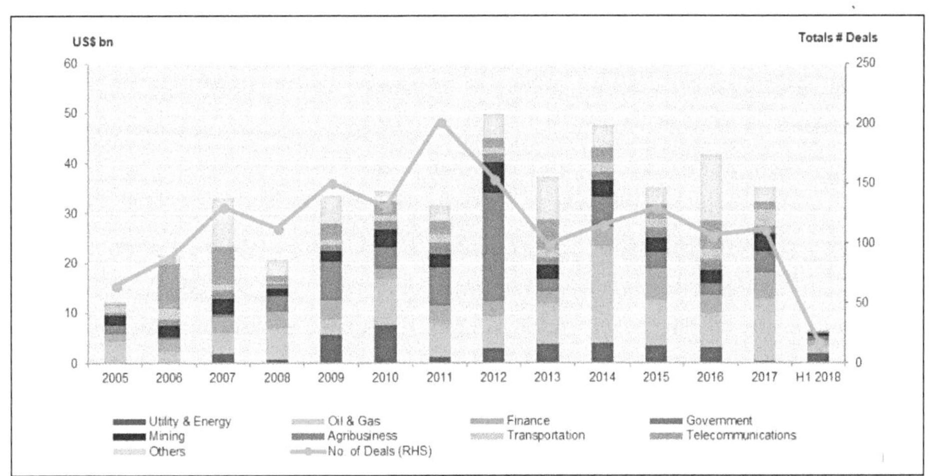


**Source: Dealogic**

# Currency

The US Dollar remains the primary transaction currency in the SSA Loan Market. The West African francophone market sees a number of euro denominated transactions predominantly involving the French banks. Multilaterals and multi-national corporates in the region have also been incorporating euro tranches in their syndicated lending facilities to fund growth in markets like francophone Africa which have euro requirements – one such borrower is African Export Import Bank (Afrexim). In 2017, Afrexim raised €499.5m as part of a USD1.16bn equivalent syndicated loan transaction. There has been an increase in local currency syndicated loan financings in the region. However, local currency lending as a whole remains largely driven by local banks providing bilateral facilities. In terms of local currency syndications the South African Rand market is well developed. However, outside of South Africa there have been limited local currency transactions coming to market. We are however seeing an increasing trend for local currency transactions in the region to help mitigate foreign exchange risk associated with a general depreciation of African currencies against the US Dollar (in 2016 MTN Group raised XOF140bn in Cote d'Ivoire via a local currency syndication and in 2016 Kenya Power and Lighting Company raised KES15.18bn via a local currency tranche under a broader syndication).

## Investors

Investor appetite is relatively diverse (see exhibit 2.33), but has historically been driven by European bank investors, accounting for 41% of loan volumes in 2017. In general South African corporates, banks and regional multilateral financial institutions benefit from the broadest pool of investor support with US, Japanese and European banks providing these investors with competitive funding. As an example, Standard Bank has widened its investor base for its syndicated facility up to 43 lenders as of its USD1.0bn 2017 syndication. This was Standard Bank's 37th syndicated loan transaction since 1995 and during this period its lender base has steadily increased. Sovereign issuers are also able to attract relatively broad investor bases. Liquidity for smaller single country corporates/financial institutions (outside of South Africa) is highly dependent on region, issuer and structure with a more limited pool of investors.

The South African banks have been increasing their share of the SSA Loan Market facilitated through regional partnerships with local banks and strong in-country presence. There is also an increasing trend for arrangers to target specific investor groups (Asia, Middle East) to try and expand the borrower's lender base and attract specific pools of liquidity (see exhibit 2.34). Development Financial Institutions and Export Credit Agencies are also emerging as key partners in the region helping to support the continent's sizable infrastructure investment requirements. Their involvement typically also helps borrowers maximise tenor and lower borrowing costs. These credit enhanced structures also provide investors with significant comfort in alleviating some of the underlying country/counterparty risk in these transactions.

### Exhibit 2.33: SSA Syndicated Loan Lender Nationality 2016 vs 2017

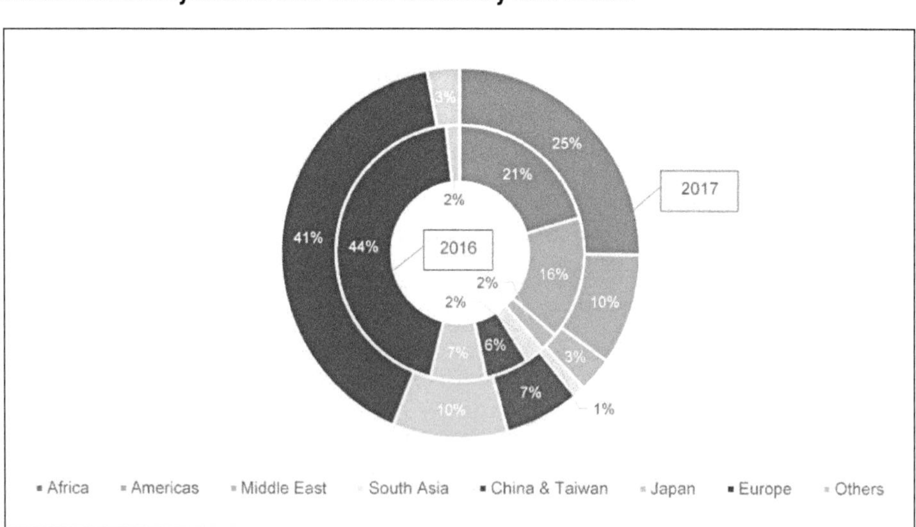


Source: Dealogic

# SUPPLEMENT 3: VIEW OF AN INSTITUTIONAL INVESTOR

**Peter Brodehser**

*Head of Infrastructure Investments, Ampega Asset Management GmbH (formerly Talanx Asset Management GmbH)*

## WHAT AN INSTITUTIONAL INVESTOR IS LOOKING FOR?

The first thing to notice while assessing institutional investors: there is not the institutional investor as such. All institutional investors have in common is that they are organisations that pool large sums of money and are looking to invest them into liquid and illiquid assets. However, their appetite in terms of tenor, risk, minimum yield requirements, currencies etc., is quite different. It is, for example, a myth that all institutional investors are looking for long tenors. It is rather true that especially the life insurance companies are keen for long tenors while, for example, reinsurance companies are in favour of shorter tenors. The trigger for one or the other is on the right-hand side of their balance sheets.

### Tenor

Life insurance companies collect funds from their customers with a weighted average life of about 10–15 years. Furthermore the inflows and outflows of cash are very predictable. Hence long term investments – such as infrastructure investments – are a perfect match for them. Exactly the opposite occurs when reinsurance companies are involved. Their business model requires having huge amounts of liquidity being available in case of an insured event occurring. Hence, they can't afford to allocate a significant part of their portfolio to long term (illiquid) investments. Consequently they are looking for short term liquid assets – ideally listed bonds/stocks.

Industrial insurance companies are somewhere in between. They are not going for 30 years infrastructure PPP transactions, as a life insurance company would do, but their appetite in terms of tenor is definitely longer than a couple of years, normally in the area of 5–10 years.

## Currencies

The same logic applies while looking at other investment criteria such as currencies. European life insurance companies and pension funds will have a strong preference for Euro or Sterling transactions – depending on their liabilities on the right-hand side of the balance sheet. Reinsurance companies and industrial insurance companies additionally have a significant appetite for US-Dollar investments – based on the fact that their insurance business is to a certain level and degree invoiced in US-Dollar. Hence, the trigger is also the currency structure of the liabilities on the right side of the balance sheet.

## Repayment profile

Apart from the view from an asset liability stand point it is important to consider what institutional investors can handle process-wise. It is often said "institutional investors have a preference for bullet repayments". From a commercial stand point, that is not necessarily true. An amortising tranche with a weighted average life of ten years is from a commercial perspective and asset liability standpoint the same as a bullet repayment after ten years. However, the electronic data processing (EDP) systems of an institutional investor are set up to handle and process bullet repayments and, as such, it is easier for them to book it. Consequently, institutional investors do indeed have a preference for bullet repayments, but nearly all institutional investors are in the meantime able to handle and willing to accept amortising structures. That is especially true for infrastructure and real estate transactions. It is just a little more cumbersome for them to book it in their systems.

## Minimum yield requirements

Most institutional investors don't have minimum yield requirements as such but, without a doubt, they require a return to cover their liabilities. For many life insurance companies the return rate to be achieved in total for the liabilities on the right hand side of the balance sheet is at least 2-3%. That percentage can be gained by investing in a broad variety of investments and tenors. Currently, a lot of fixed income instruments struggle to generate a return on or above that target yield, but alternative asset classes such as e.g., infrastructure; real estate and private equity can compensate for these numbers.

In summary, the investment criteria of European-based institutional investors are based on the respective liability structure and the booking systems and lead to the following:

**Exhibit 2.34**

| European Institutional Investors | | Investment Criteria |
|---|---|---|
| 1.) | Life insurance companies and pension funds | Long tenor (10-15 years weighted average life)<br>EUR or GBP (depending on the countries they are active in)<br>Low risk |
| 2.) | Industrial insurance companies | Medium tenor (5-10 years weighted average life)<br>EUR, GBP and USD<br>Medium risk |
| 3.) | Reinsurance companies | Short to medium tenor (<7 years weighted average life)<br>USD, EUR and GBP<br>Medium to higher risk |

# ANY SPECIFIC REQUIREMENTS OF INSTITUTIONAL INVESTORS?

While comparing the view on transactions of institutional investors to banks in respect of loans, one can say that the requirements are very similar. This is because most of the bigger institutions have hired bankers 'to run the show'. As such, the view they will take on structures, security packages, covenants etc., is almost the same as for banks. There are only two aspects which most of the institutional investors will take a different view on:

## Make Whole/Spens Clause

Most of the institutional investors will require a Make Whole Clause, also known as Spens Clause. A Spens Clause guarantees a prepayment penalty in case of an early refinancing to be paid to the investor. The background is twofold: first, institutional investors want to make sure that the main intention of their investment in loans, i.e., to achieve a better match of assets and liabilities, is met. If a transaction could be refinanced shortly after financial close it would jeopardise their investment approach. Hence, a Spens Clause ensures to a certain level and degree that the tenor transformation is reduced as far as possible. Second, a Spens Clause is just another word for the swap breakage costs in the banking world. Consequently institutional investors don't want to accept a structure which is less beneficial for the investors than banks would approve. For technical reasons, almost all of the transactions with a Spens Clause are fixed rate loans. While in theory, it is also possible to agree a Spens Clause for floating rate loans, it is far more difficult to agree a mechanism of calculating it.

Although institutional investors will require a Spens Clause for most of their transactions they have shown a lot of flexibility in negotiating a reasonable package on a deal specific basis and are also willing to consider borrower's needs.

## Transferability

The Transferability Clause stipulates in the loan documentation the conditions for debt providers to sell the loan investment to another investor. Due to regulatory requirements, Solvency I regulated institutional investors can't accept the LMA loan standard with regard to the Transferability Clause if they book a transaction directly on their own balance sheet. The LMA standard says with regard to transferability: "a transfer … is subject to borrower's consent not to be unreasonably withheld or delayed". The critical issue is the borrower's consent. Regulators require institutional investors to be in the position to sell a part of the coverage assets as a whole in case needed without third party consent. The regulator wouldn't accept a third party/borrower's consent – even if it cannot be unreasonably withheld or delayed. That is the reason why the loan documentation is adjusted with regard to that specific clause to the extent Solvency I regulated entities are involved. That requirement doesn't apply in the same manner for Solvency II regulated entities or when the investments are booked via a fund, but exceptions to the rule need to be discussed and addressed on a deal-specific basis.

# LIQUID VS ILLIQUID ASSETS

The most common investment type for institutional investors is liquid assets, i.e., listed bonds and stocks. Due to risk restrictions bonds are considerably overrepresented in their portfolios. Institutional investors have been active in investing in liquid assets for decades. A major part of their portfolio consists of government bonds. The risk assessment for this paper, due to the availability of an external rating, is comparatively easy. Furthermore these assets could be sold within minutes in case of need. As such, it is the perfect instrument for an institutional investor.

But it is fair to say that within the current low interest rate environment it becomes more and more difficult to gain sufficient return to cover the liabilities. The quota of stocks which could potentially cover the liabilities return-wise is restricted, due to risk appetite considerations. government/corporate bonds are either not in the position to cover the liabilities or the rating of these bonds is too low to allocate a significant part of the asset under management to these instruments. Again, a better match of assets and liabilities can be achieved by investing in illiquid asset classes. Consequently, institutional investors have increased their investments in loans in alternative asset classes such as infrastructure, real estate and private equity significantly in the last years.

While investing in alternative asset classes' loans (or, in other words, illiquid instruments), institutional investors try to gain a yield pick-up in comparison to the classic investment targets. However, the yield pick-up is not necessarily based on a higher implied risk. Actually, just the opposite tends to be the case, given the high recovery rates especially for infrastructure investments. The yield pick-up is rather due to illiquidity, duration and complexity. Private placement transactions in the infrastructure, real estate or private equity area are not as liquid as a listed bond but in return the investor is able to gain an illiquidity premium. For example, a debt instrument will provide a yield pick-up due to illiquidity of at least 50–80 basis points in comparison to a liquid instrument with the same risk/rating and a corresponding tenor. In addition, these transactions are complex by nature, but with a qualified team on board, investors are easily able to handle that level of complexity – as banks have already been doing for decades. Furthermore, institutional investors are able to find longer tenors in the alternative investments space, hence they can generate an additional duration premium which is especially attractive to life insurance companies and pension funds. They will be able to generate a duration premium and achieve in one go a better match of the assets and liabilities.

Exhibit 2.35 shows the levers institutional investors can apply while investing in alternative asset classes to generate a yield pick-up:

## Exhibit 2.35: Levers to generate a yield pick-up for alternative asset classes

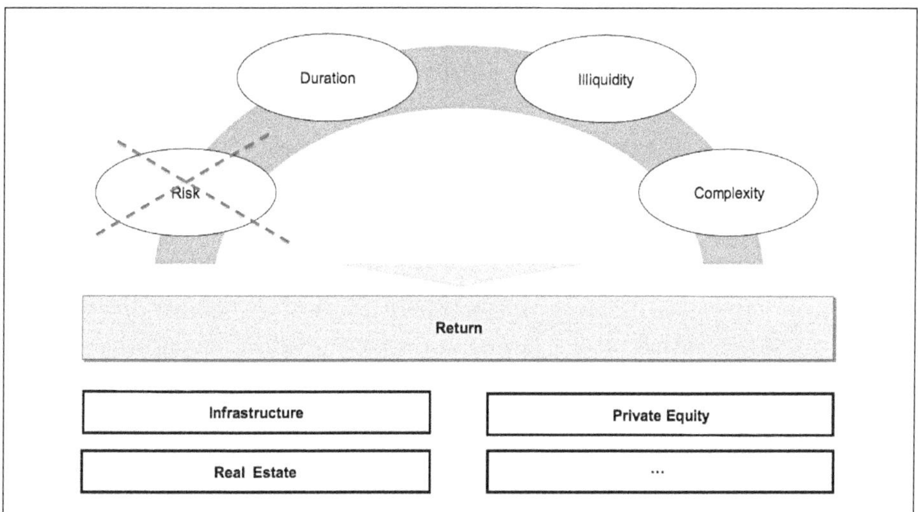

Investing in loans instead of bonds (or the other way round) is always a mixed blessing. Loans provide the following benefits:

- Offer the option to play an active role in the structuring phase and give the investor the opportunity to tailor the investments to its needs;
- Direct access to the senior management of the borrower or the sponsor to build a relationship;
- High recovery rates;
- Enhanced information rights.

Nevertheless, loans come along with the following negative points:

- Relatively low liquidity in comparison to bonds;
- Loans often come with optionalities for the borrower; it is more difficult to reflect these options in the booking systems of an institutional investor.

A couple of years ago bonds were considered as a fixed rate solution while loans were always floating. That is not the case anymore. Most of the loans institutional investors are involved in do have a fixed rate coupon. In long term transactions, they are sometimes combined with (floating) bank tranches. Bank tranches will often provide the short-term financings while institutional investors cover the long tenor tranches.

## WHAT ARE THE DRIVERS OF INSTITUTIONAL LIQUIDITY?

There are predominantly two drivers for institutional investors to join the loan market – especially the loan market for alternative investments: (i) to provide for a better match of assets and liabilities in terms of tenor and (ii) to generate a yield pick-up in comparison to the public bond market. The intention to match assets and liabilities is the main driver for institutional investors to invest in long term loans. As the tenor of the liabilities remains very stable over the period, the liquidity of institutional investors in the market is not really volatile. But it is also true that the low interest rate environment has accelerated investments of institutional investors in loans. In particular, loans in the area of alternative asset classes will help the institutional investors to provide for sufficient return to cover the liabilities.

Movements of volumes should be viewed over a longer period of time. In the 'old days', i.e., before the financial crisis 2007–08, long term lending was predominantly performed by banks. They had the appetite for long tenors and the knowledge to accompany complex transactions. Institutional investors had an appetite for long tenors but were knowledge –

and resource – wise not in an ideal position to invest in such assets. Their home turf was the classic fixed income business, i.e., listed bonds. During and after the financial crisis 2007–08 we could see banks reducing or exiting long term lending. As a consequence, there was a liquidity gap. Complex transactions with a long tenor could not be financed easily. Even the actions of development banks were not in a position to close the gap. Now, as we have already seen for a couple of years, banks and institutional investors are returning to long term lending, but one needs to notice that the long-term lending activities of banks are somewhat cautious (inter alia due to Basel III) while the investment activities of institutional investors are still growing.

**Exhibit 2.36**

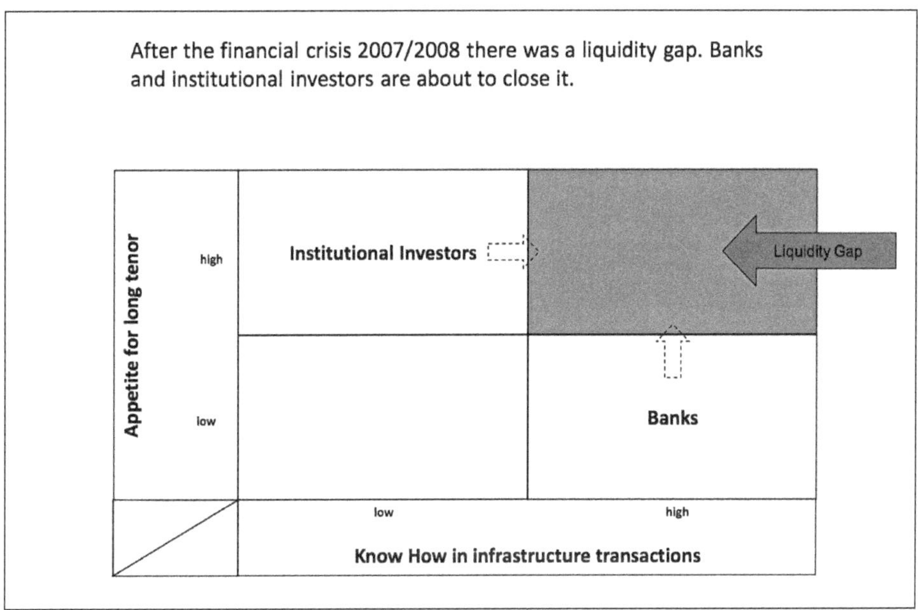


# APPROVAL PROCESSES

The approval process differs significantly from investor to investor. It is also not only a function of investor vs investor, the approval process also varies from product to product. Most liquid asset classes are considered easy to analyse and straight forward. Consequently, the approval process can be done at short notice and in most of the cases without the involvement of senior management. With almost all institutional investors, investment and portfolio managers work within a well-defined framework and approval matrix on a day-to-day basis. Hence, the investment decision can be done at working level within a couple of days. It is however fair to say that this process in the case of most institutional investors, will only be applicable for externally rated and listed bonds/ stocks. Only a small number of institutions, predominantly the smaller and medium sized organisations, also follow that approach for their alternative asset classes. They simply don't have the staffing and the resources available to implement an additional process for alternative assets, a comparably small part of their portfolio. Larger organisations normally do have a modified process for alternative asset classes in place. That process takes into consideration that the complexity of transactions in the alternative investment space is greater. The process foresees that each individual transaction is presented to an investment committee. Some institutions have – just as with banks – a separate credit department providing a second opinion as an integral part of the approval process for each transaction.

The due diligence process which is performed within the frame of the approval process doesn't differ too much from a bank. If the institutional investors take an active role in the structuring process they would like to have direct access to all the relevant project or company documents. On top of that they will appoint external advisors for support in areas such as legal, technical, market, environmental, regulatory etc.

Where institutional investors don't have an active role in the structuring process they will receive an information memorandum to get the due diligence process started. Such a memorandum covers the main aspects of the financing and will provide a preliminary risk assessment. In addition, external advisors will also be involved to support the institutional investor. The approval process in terms of timing will be quite similar to banks.

It is worth mentioning that the insurance companies' asset managers can bring in their own risk analysis experts from the insurance business. That helps a lot in particular while assessing complex infrastructure investments transactions.

# CONCLUSION

There is not the institutional investor as such. The appetite of institutional investors in terms of tenor, risk, currencies etc. is quite divergent. The basis for their individual needs is the structure of the liabilities on the right hand side of the balance sheet. European life insurance companies and pension funds are looking for low risk, EUR/GBP transactions and long tenors. On the contrary, reinsurance companies are focused on EUR/GBP and USD transactions with a significantly shorter tenor.

The requirements of institutional investors with regard to the structure of a transaction don't differ from the view of a bank active in the same sector. The same is applicable for the approval process as most institutional investors hired bankers 'to run the show'.

There are just two points to be considered in terms of structure when bringing institutional investors in: institutional investors will require a prepayment penalty in case of an early refinancing (Spens Clause) to ensure a good match of their assets and liabilities in terms of tenor. The amount to be paid under a Spens Clause corresponds with the swap breakage costs of banks for floating rate loans. Furthermore, the transferability clause, i.e., the conditions for debt providers to sell the loan investment to another investor, needs to be checked from a regulatory stand point on a deal specific basis.

Loans – especially loans in alternative assets classes – provide a perfect match of assets and liabilities in terms of tenor. This is the main reason why the amounts allocated to loans will continue to grow in the years to come.

# SUPPLEMENT 4: LOAN PORTFOLIO MANAGEMENT

**Dr. Doo Bo Chung**

*Director, Formerly Capital and Portfolio Management, Royal Bank of Scotland*

**Jim Skufca**

*Managing Director, Formerly Head of Strategy and Analytics, Capital and Portfolio Management, Royal Bank of Scotland*

NB: This supplement was prepared by its authors for the purpose of the sixth edition of this book and has not been subsequently updated. Except for minor editorial changes it is presented as per the sixth edition.

## INTRODUCTION

This supplement will provide a high-level background on portfolio management, the main techniques and models, and how effective management of the loan portfolio can contribute to overall success of a financial institution.

## THE LOAN PORTFOLIO MANAGEMENT RATIONALE

The provision of a loan requires an institution to allocate balance sheet resources in terms of funding and capital to underwrite the unexpected losses in the portfolio. Loan portfolio management in this context refers to the act of directing these scarce balance sheet resources to optimise shareholder returns within the institution's risk tolerance.

As with many investment management processes, the underlying principle is captured in the age-old adage of avoiding having all of one's eggs in one basket. This underlying principle was formalised by Markowitz in his work on the Modern Portfolio Theory for which he received the Nobel Prize in Economic Sciences in 1990. In short Markowitz showed that while the total returns of a portfolio of assets are the weighted average of asset returns, the risk as measured by the volatility of returns (or standard deviation) is less than the weighted average of the underlying asset volatilities unless assets are perfectly correlated. As the value of individual assets is unlikely to move perfectly in sync, having a large diverse population of assets will decrease risks for a given level of return.

Banks tend to build profitable relationships and develop franchises that naturally tend to focus and concentrate the bank's loan portfolio in a specific sector or geography. Building and maintaining an origination function tends to be relatively expensive with many costs fixed in the near term; expanding it across sector and geography involves countless additional costs such as maintaining banking licences across multiple jurisdictions and attracting talented origination staff to maintain relationships. The high operating leverage creates an incentive for the institution to create additional balance sheet capacity to drive origination. An effective loan portfolio management process can both reduce a portfolio's concentration through proactive risk management and increase origination efficiency by churning the portfolio and reducing its overall cost of capital.

The basic premise of portfolio management is that it requires less capital to operate a well-diversified loan portfolio as opposed to a highly concentrated one. This can be best illustrated through a simple example. Capital is a required buffer against unexpected losses up to the risk tolerance of the institution. Beyond this risk tolerance it is considered uneconomical to hold capital. For this example, assume the institution's risk appetite can be articulated as having no more than a 0.02% probability of default in any given year (roughly equivalent to an AA rating). Now consider a €1bn loan portfolio consisting of 50 assets each with a notional amount of €20m, Probability of Default (PD) of 1%, and Loss Given Default (LGD) of 50%. Assume defaults in the portfolio for this example are not correlated (correlation in effect reduces the number of independent assets). The probability of x defaults or less occurring in this portfolio (Pr(X≤x)) can be written as a binomial distribution.

$$\Pr(X \leq x) = \sum_{i=0}^{x} \binom{n}{i} pd^{i} (1 - pd)^{n-i}$$

Where $n$ is the number of assets in the portfolio, and $pd$ the probability of default. The below table shows the probability of more than $x$ defaults or more occurring (1-Pr(X≤x)).

| Nr of Defaults | Pr |
|---|---|
| 0 | 39.499% |
| 1 | 8.944% |
| 2 | 1.382% |
| 3 | 0.160% |
| 4 | 0.015% |
| 5 | 0.001% |

The institution in this example needs to ensure it has sufficient capital to withstand any event that has a likelihood of occurrence of more than 0.02% to comply with its risk tolerance objective. With 50 assets in the portfolio the likelihood of at least one default occurring is relatively high, even when the individual asset's PD is relatively low at 1%. In this example, the likelihood of one or more defaults occurring in any given year is 8.9%. It is only after four or more defaults that the likelihood of this event occurring becomes less than the risk tolerance level of 0.02%. So, for the institution to meet its risk tolerance objective it will need to budget for four losses less the expected loss which should be considered a cost of running the business. The expected loss in this example is EL = €1bn x 1% x LGD = €5m. The loss equivalent to four assets defaulting is 4 x €20m x LGD = €40m. The capital the institution needs to hold is thus €40m – €5m = €35m.

Now, all things equal, assume the €1bn portfolio now consists of 100 assets of €10m notional each. The probability of *x* defaults or more occurring is given in the table below.

| Nr of Defaults | Pr |
|---:|---:|
| 0 | 63.397% |
| 1 | 26.424% |
| 2 | 7.937% |
| 3 | 1.837% |
| 4 | 0.343% |
| 5 | 0.053% |
| 6 | 0.007% |

With more assets in a portfolio the likelihood of a default occurring in the portfolio increases. However the loss incurred with each default is also much smaller if we assume the portfolio size remains the same. The institution will now need to hold capital sufficient to withstand six defaults occurring in one year. The expected loss remains €5m. The loss equivalent to six defaults however is now 6 x €10m x LGD = €30m. The capital the institution needs to hold is reduced to €30m – €5m = €25m. This simple example demonstrates the benefit of having a more diversified portfolio.

# KEY COMPONENTS OF LOAN PORTFOLIO MANAGEMENT

The aim of loan portfolio management is to construct a collection of loans that minimises concentrations and correlations while maximising returns. Implementation of loan portfolio management across different institutions varies widely. However, there are generally three interrelated activities that are considered part of a loan portfolio management process:

1. Measuring and monitoring against the risk tolerance.
2. Facilitating the onboarding of assets.
3. Managing and distributing excess risk concentrations.

# MEASURING AND MONITORING RISK

Measuring the risk of the portfolio is a crucial first step in loan portfolio management. Developments in loan portfolio analytics have provided loan portfolio managers with increasingly sophisticated tools to identify and measure risk concentrations. Portfolio risk models generally consist of four basic ingredients: Probability of Default (PD), Loss Given Default (LGD), Exposure At Default (EAD) and a correlation model. As modelling approaches have a large influence over portfolio management actions it is appropriate to provide a brief overview of the main modelling approaches.

## Regulatory Capital

There has been an increased focus on the minimum capital level required to support the loan portfolio following the global financial crisis. The following sections provide a brief overview of the regulatory framework and capital models (and further detail is provided in chapter 2 of this book).

The regulatory framework is internationally coordinated by the Basel Committee. The mutually agreed supervisory frameworks from this committee are generally referred to as Basel Accords. There have been three Basel Accords to date. Basel I in 1988 was the first step in aligning measurement of capital across different countries. The accords set minimum capital requirements and introduced risk weightings to measure riskiness of different asset classes (Riskiness of different assets is measured in terms of Risk Weighted Assets (RWA)).

Basel II developed the concept of risk weightings further with better risk sensitivity for weighting riskiness of assets. It also introduced standards for measuring operational and market risk. In terms of credit risk Basel II set out two broad approaches namely the standardised and the internal ratings based approach.

## The standardised approach

In the standardised approach, risk weighting for different asset types are based on their external credit rating.

| Rating | AAA to AA- | A+ to A- | BBB+ to BBB- | BB+ to BB- | BB- to B- | Below B- | unrated |
|---|---|---|---|---|---|---|---|
| Sovereigns | 0% | 20% | 50% | 100% | 100% | 150% | 100% |
| Banks/Securities Companies | 20% | 50% | 100% | 100% | 100% | 150% | 100% |
| Corporates | 20% | 50% | 100% | 100% | 150% | 150% | 100% |

The standardised approach contains only one of the four basic ingredients of the modern portfolio risk model as the credit rating is a proxy for probability of default.

## Internal ratings based approach

The internal ratings based approach allows risk weightings to be more sensitive to riskiness of assets. The internal ratings based approach contains three of the four main ingredients namely the PD, EAD and LGD. Correlation is, in effect, assumed to be fixed. There are two main approaches: a Foundation approach and an Advanced approach. In the Foundation approach the PD is based on internal ratings while the regulators prescribe the LGD and EAD. In the Advanced approach PD, EAD and LGD are all based on internal models. The risk weighting in both IRB approaches are calculated using formulas known as the supervisory formula.

In general, the risk weighting using the supervisory formula leads to lower risk weighing for investment grade names compared to the standardised approach. For speculative credit grades the supervisory formula leads to higher RWAs as risk weightings continue to increase above 150% for the worst credit grades.

### Basel III

The Basel III accord is the latest evolution of the supervisory framework developed by the Basel Committee, which attempts to address the various shortcomings of the existing financial regulations as observed during the GFC. The latest framework keeps the supervisory formulas intact. However, a host of new regulations on capital and liquidity management relevant to the loan portfolio are introduced to ensure that the financial system is more resilient in the future.

New regulations on capital will increase the amount of core capital institutions will need to hold for each unit of RWA. Restrictions on the use of short-term wholesale funding and the requirement to manage liquidity is already increasing funding costs across the industry. While the final result of the new regulations is not yet clear, both increases in funding costs and increased capital requirements are already having a direct impact on managing the loan portfolio's profitability.

### Economic capital

The regulatory capital models contain only three of the four key ingredients of a modern portfolio risk model and various economic capital models have been developed to capture the effect of correlation and concentrations to complement the existing regulatory models. Initially economic capital models were mostly proprietary models developed in house. However, there are now a number of vendors providing a range of solutions either off the shelf or through bespoke development. A popular model class is the Merton model and its variations named after the Nobel Prize winner, Robert Merton. The Merton model builds on earlier work done on the Black Scholes Merton option pricing model and provides a mathematical framework to introduce correlation of asset prices into measuring a portfolio's risk concentrations. Advanced economic capital models can provide portfolio managers with near real-time information on portfolio concentrations and assess each individual asset's contribution to the overall riskiness of the portfolio. This ability to identify risk concentrations is a crucial capability to effectively manage the portfolio's overall riskiness and profitability.

## THE ONBOARDING PROCESS

In the short-term financial institutions' costs are mostly fixed and, given this operational leverage, there is a natural tendency to focus on generating revenues to meet fixed operating costs. On the other hand, the cost of a portfolio's risk concentrations is not immediately apparent and may remain dormant for many years. Warren Buffet is quoted as saying "After all, you only find out who is swimming naked when the tide goes out."

In good times it is difficult to determine whether excessive risks have been taken to meet the near term revenue targets. The onboarding process needs to balance these competing forces as getting this balance wrong could either paralyse the origination process or lead to concentrations that are costly to mitigate. In this section we provide a brief overview of the onboarding process as it relates to loan portfolio management.

The stated long-term Return On Equity (ROE) target for many financial institutions following the GFC is between 10 to 15%. The below example illustrates the difficulty of meeting the ROE target in a competitive loan market. Consider the fact that a €100m five year corporate term loan with a PD of 0.4% and a LGD of 40%, which is equivalent to a typical BBB-rated asset, will require an institution that provides the loan to allocate €80m RWAs using the supervisory formula. Assuming a 10% capital ratio the institution needs to hold €8m of equity capital for the loan. If the loan prices at 100bps net interest margin (i.e., net of funding costs which could be substantial for five year funding given regulatory requirements for liquidity) the gross ROE available from the asset is 12.5% which is insufficient to meet the institution's targets as it will still need to account for operating costs and taxes (the gross ROE reduces to the low single digit percentages once costs and taxes are accounted as most cost-to-income ratios are above 50%). To meet its return targets the institution will need to build a relationship on the back of the balance sheet commitment and cross sell profitable fee business by applying its intellectual capital.

The loan portfolio management process starts with client selection and onboarding. The degree to which the loan portfolio can be shaped decreases substantially once an institution invests in coverage bankers and building relationships with its chosen client base. Its chosen client base will determine the assets it will consider onboarding and set the loan portfolio's main risk profile in terms of sector, geography and credit quality. As such, analysis of the loan portfolio's risk concentrations and diversification needs should inform the client selection and coverage strategy. Once the client base is selected, the asset onboarding stage provides a final opportunity to validate the business case based on real time portfolio risk analysis.

In most institutions the asset onboarding is overseen through a dedicated capital allocation committee or is considered part of a risk underwriting committee's mandate. A number of institutions manage the origination process separately from the loan portfolio management process by applying a transfer pricing mechanism for the cost of managing risk concentrations in the loan portfolio. The fair transfer price, however, is difficult to determine in practice given that a large section of a typical corporate loan portfolio is potentially illiquid. Also great care needs to be taken in identifying risk concentrations using modern portfolio tools such as an economic capital model as these will invariably contain a vast number of simplifying assumptions based on historic observations on asset value correlations and volatility.

Loan portfolio management business models are continuing to evolve and new innovative structures will emerge to balance the needs of portfolio diversification and near term revenue objectives.

## MANAGING EXCESS RISK CONCENTRATIONS

Loan portfolio managers need to constantly monitor the portfolio's risk concentrations. Even with a perfectly balanced onboarding process there will be situations where mitigation and/or diversification action needs to be taken to rebalance the loan portfolio and a sophisticated risk transfer market is a crucial pre-requisite for the development of loan portfolio management as a separate discipline from pure credit risk management. In the past two decades the risk transfer market, and in particular its synthetic variety, has grown exponentially. While the global financial crisis laid bare the risks involved, the credit risk transfer market is likely to remain an integral part of the financial markets. The next sections will provide a high-level overview of the main risk transfer instruments and techniques used by loan portfolio managers to reduce excess risk concentrations and to diversify the loan portfolio.

Credit risk transfer instruments can be categorised as either single name or portfolio oriented with a further distinction possible between cash or synthetic instruments. The two main single name instruments are:

1. Secondary loan sales: A secondary market for loans, while in existence for centuries, started to grow in the late 1970s. Before the 1970s transferring a loan required either the creation of a contingent liability or the legal transfer of the debtor-creditor relationship. Both approaches were considered cumbersome and loans were deemed non-tradeable assets to be held on the balance sheet until maturity.

   The liquidity in the secondary loan market started to improve dramatically with transfer friendly clauses becoming a common feature in loan documentation. From the early 1980s the market volumes grew exponentially and until the development of a synthetic market in the 1990s, secondary loan sales represented the only viable alternative to manage the loan portfolio post-origination. As secondary loan sale transactions are conducted in cash form, a key benefit is that both funding and credit risks are transferred through the sale, which could be a crucial consideration when funding costs form a major constituent of warehousing assets on the balance sheet.

While loan sales remain an important portfolio management tool there are various limitations on the tool's effectiveness. Liquidity for syndicated transactions tends to peak right after successful primary syndications and tails off as relationship banks are topped up on appetite. Beyond the primary market, liquidity is selectively available for specific credits from asset takers (strongly dependent on sector, geography and funding requirements). As asset takers generally require a market clearing yield regardless of the underlying assets' inherent yield, it could be extremely costly to mitigate an unfunded revolver through secondary loan sales where the asset when unfunded, yields a modest commitment fee only. In addition the need to disclose sales to the borrower means there could be negative relationship implications, limiting its use as a portfolio management tool to specific instances.

2. Single name Credit Default Swaps (CDS): a single name credit default swap is a bilateral agreement between two counterparties in which one party (the writer) offers the other party (the buyer) protection against default loss by a third party (the reference name) for a specified period of time in return for premium payments (spreads).

   To illustrate – assume a loan portfolio manager is concerned about credit concentration in Example Co and wishes to reduce this exposure by €100m. The loan portfolio manager enters into a five year CDS contract with Bank X and agrees to pay 150bps per annum quarterly in arrears for the default protection. If Example Co does not default the loan portfolio manager pays €375,000 at the end of each quarter until maturity of the CDS contract. In the event of default the loan portfolio manager will need to pay the premium up to the time of default as this is paid in arrears and receive a payout from the contract. If the contract specifies physical settlement the portfolio manager will have the right to sell a loan or bond to Bank X worth €100m face value for €100m cash. In case of cash settlement an independent agent will poll dealers to determine the mid-market value of the cheapest to deliver security under the contract and the cash payout will be the difference between the face value and this mid-market price. For instance if this mid-market price is determined to be 35 cents to the euro the pay out in this case would be €65m.

   CDS contracts were introduced in the 1990s and gave portfolio managers a powerful tool to diversify the portfolio without impacting the client relationship as contracts remain bilateral and do not have to be disclosed to the client. The CDS market saw tremendous growth through the early 2000s with improvements in liquidity in terms of names quoted and tenor available.

   Although liquidity has continued to improve through the last decade, the number of names actively quoted in the CDS market is still limited to roughly 10% of a typical large corporate loan portfolio with a limited liquidity available for a further 15% leaving limited options on roughly 75% of the portfolio.

Portfolio orientated products allow loan portfolio managers to efficiently mitigate a large number of assets through a single trade. While there are many variations in portfolio oriented products, the discussion here is limited to index trades and securitisation as these are two widely employed portfolio products:

1. Index trades: Index trades allow a loan portfolio manager to diversify or manage a loan portfolio's concentrations in terms of a specific geography, sector or credit quality by taking positions in a CDS index rather than individual names. In general, it is less effective for managing individual single name risks in a portfolio as assets contained in the portfolio are unlikely to exactly match the index. CDS indices were developed in the mid-1990s and typically consist of between seven to 125 individual names depending on geography or sector, which are refreshed every six months. In general, quotes are available for one through five year, seven year and ten year tenors, with five and ten years considered the most liquid. The two most widely quoted indices are iTraxx Europe which contains Europe's 125 most actively traded CDS names and the CDX.NA which contains 125 North American investment grade names. Similar to the CDS market it is, at the time of writing, a predominantly over-the-counter market.

   A loan portfolio manager concerned about the portfolio's concentration in for instance the Telecom Media and Technology (TMT) sector could buy protection through a CDS index with TMT names as underliers. Assume a five year TMT CDS index consisting of 20 names is quoted at 150bps per annum. If the portfolio manager buys €40m of protection this would be the equivalent of buying €2m notional CDS protection on all 20 names included in the index. In this example the loan portfolio manager would pay €600,000 per annum in premium for the protection on the 20 names.

   In the event of a credit event on one of the names the contract will pay out on the defaulted name similarly to the single name CDS contract either through physical or cash settlement, while the premium required will now be reduced to 19 x €2m x 150bps = €570,000 per annum (i.e., 150bps on the remaining 19 names times the notional amount).

   Transacting through a CDS index could be much more effective than executing transactions on a large number of individual names to manage a portfolio's concentration. Executing a large number of trades becomes cumbersome to administer and liquidity is considered to be generally better in CDS indices rather than on individual names.

2. Securitisation: Securitisations can be either structured as cash or synthetic transactions and allow loan portfolio managers to pool and package individual loans together to be distributed as tranches of risks with different credit qualities. In the traditional cash securitisation market the asset is sold to a bankruptcy remote special purpose vehicle (SPV) and the categorisation into varying degrees of subordination allows tranches of different risk characteristics to be created. Although traditional cash securitisation remains an important tool for the loan portfolio manager to distribute an otherwise illiquid asset, it suffers from similar shortcomings to those of secondary sales. The borrower in many cases will need to be notified and documentation issues could prevent assets from being transferred into an SPV.

   In the synthetic structure the assets are referenced through documentation rather than true sale to an SPV and can thus be passed without notifying the borrower. Securitisation can be an extremely effective tool for loan portfolio managers to obtain capital relief, to transfer risk and to create additional capacity to be deployed through origination. The following example demonstrates the underlying principle. A loan portfolio manager wishes to reduce the capital the institution needs to hold on a €1bn portfolio with an average probability of default of 5% per annum (roughly equivalent to a B rating) and a loss given default estimated to be 60% on average. Based on these inputs the risk weighted assets (RWA) using the supervisory formula is €1.76bn (i.e., risk weight 176%). Assuming an equity capital ratio of 10%, the institution will need to hold €176m in equity capital for the portfolio.

   If the portfolio is securitised a subordinated tranche of roughly €200m will result in the remaining tranches to be considered AAA rated, reducing the risk weight on these tranches to a 7% floor. The exact thickness of the subordinated tranche will be dependent on the rating agency securitisation model. However, assuming the issuing institution's models are generally in line with the rating agency's model a subordinated tranche that covers the institution's own calculated equity should result in a very strong rating of the remaining tranches.

   In this example, assuming the entire €200m subordinated tranche is sold off to investors, the RWAs will reduce to €800m x 7% = €56m and the equity capital using the 10% capital ratio to €5.6m releasing €170.4m in capital. The economics of the securitisation is a function of pricing of the underlying assets and where investor appetite can be found for the subordinated tranche. To illustrate this through an example – assume the underlying assets are yielding 260bps per annum net of expected loss and investor appetite for the subordinated tranche can be found for a 12.5% yield. The income generated on the portfolio in this example is 260bps x €1bn = €26m and the yield demanded by the investors is equivalent to 12.5% x €200m = €25m. Passing on the yield required by the investor the portfolio manager in this example is left with €1m of revenues for €5.6m of remaining equity capital (17.8% return on capital excluding cost of funding or taxes). As demonstrated by the above example securitisation could be an extremely attractive tool to release capital on otherwise illiquid assets.

New regulations such as the Volcker rule which prohibits banks from taking proprietary positions are likely to have a significant impact on the risk transfer market. There is increased pressure to move more of the financial derivative markets onto exchanges instead of the current OTC format. The combined impact of the new regulations and capital requirements will lead to reduction in liquidity for certain financial instruments in the near term as it becomes less profitable to make a market in these instruments. As liquidity in certain instruments decreases there is likely to be demand for more securitisations to release much needed capital back into the business.

While it is difficult to predict the longer term impact of the new regulations on the risk transfer market, what is clear so far is that the risk transfer market will continue to influence the development of loan portfolio management and vice versa.

# CONCLUSIONS

The financial industry is undergoing a period of profound change as loan institutions adjust to the new regulatory framework across the globe. Tighter regulations on capital and liquidity are already driving up the cost of providing loans across the entire industry. At the time of writing the full effects of the various regulatory changes are still to be felt with many rules yet to be implemented, but some consequences for loan portfolio management are starting to emerge.

There has been an increased focus on managing a loan portfolio's cost of capital as both funding costs and amount of core capital required are expected to increase over time. Loan portfolios are slowly being positioned away from unprofitable products such as long term financing or the provision of back up liquidity in favour of shorter term trade and working capital financing.

While the focus on the cost of capital has temporarily shifted loan portfolio managers' attention to regulatory capital, economic capital models remain a crucial tool for portfolio managers to identify risk concentrations in the portfolio. Advances in real time risk assessments based on market based signals are providing managers with increasingly powerful tools to risk manage the loan portfolio and assess the risk adjusted returns on individual assets.

As traditional lending institutions are priced out of performing the credit disintermediation function for certain products, loan portfolio management teams are seeking ways to leverage the existing origination platforms to originate assets to distribute to third party investors. Given this context securitisation is likely to be an important feature in loan portfolio management as scarce balance sheet capacity needs to be released to be redeployed through origination. For non-traditional loan investors with low costs of funds and long investment horizons, floating rate assets with a positive risk adjusted spread could represent a compelling investment alternative. There should be an alignment of long term incentives between investors and originating institutions as securitisation becomes an integral part of the loan management process, diminishing the risk of previous excesses.

Loan portfolio management is an evolving field with new innovative business models likely to emerge, providing better alignment of incentives to manage the scarce balance sheet resources and the need to generate revenues. Continuing advances in risk models and the risk transfer market could allow better identification of risk concentrations and better tools to mitigate these once identified. The ability to identify and quantify the cost of risk concentrations should enable institutions more effectively to direct origination resources towards long term profitable client relationships.

# SUPPLEMENT 5: A RECENT HISTORY OF THE EUROPEAN LEVERAGED FINANCE MARKET

**Tessa Walsh, Global Loan Editor**

*LPC (Loan Pricing Corporation)*

## INTRODUCTION

The story of Europe's leveraged loan market divides neatly into the periods before and after the global financial crisis. It highlights many of the themes that defined and reshaped the financial system in the following decade and invites inevitable comparisons.

The market built to a crescendo before the collapse of Lehman Brothers in September 2008 nearly brought the global banking sector down, and its slow recovery and its transformation into a sophisticated institutional market have underpinned Europe's growth.

Leveraged loans play a key economic role by helping to create new companies and reshape existing ones by providing financing to riskier, more indebted companies, including buyouts by private equity firms.

Like the high-yield bond market, the leveraged loan market specialises in lower-rated sub investment grade or 'junk' companies, which are particularly sensitive to the macroeconomic climate and external shocks.

The asset class was at the centre of the global financial crisis, and even held partly responsible for it, due to the exposure of commercial banks, which had provided huge, highly leveraged multi-billion euro loans to back massive private equity buyouts.

European leveraged loans were overshadowed by the ensuing sovereign debt crisis for the next five years and had to seek help from the high yield bond market to tackle a multi-billion dollar refinancing wall as countries' credit ratings tumbled, borrowing costs soared and the euro and future of the eurozone came under pressure.

Regulation swept in as central banks pumped trillions of dollars of cash into their economies and lending stalled as banks introduced tough new capital controls. Tougher regulatory scrutiny encouraged banks to remove riskier term debt from their balance sheets to protect depositors, and higher capital costs under Basel III also reduced their appetite to lend.

This set the scene for the market's next phase of development and the shadow banking sector stepped forward to fill the gap, driving a massive influx of cash as investors targeted higher yielding senior loans due to a lack of alternatives as quantitative easing programmes supported risk assets.

The institutionalisation of Europe's leveraged loan market moved the Continent towards a diversified US-style investor buyside, and demand for loans only increased further as investors rushed to buy floating rate loans to hedge against rising interest rates.

Traditional loan buyers including Collateralised Loan Obligation (CLO) funds developed into larger and more diversified credit managers as cash started to flow into Separately Managed Accounts (SMAs) from pension funds and insurance companies, and global relative value funds positioned themselves to exploit any arbitrage between markets and debt instruments.

Alternative pools of capital also sprang up to challenge the status quo, which allowed the direct lending and private debt markets to become established and thrive, as European middle market companies turned to specialist lenders for capital – at a price.

Institutional investors are more sensitive to market conditions, which drives dynamic pricing that offers higher returns for increased risk. The diversification of the investor base created true pricing elasticity – the ability to find a clearing price for debt – and changed banks' strategy to an 'originate to distribute' model from a 'buy and hold' model.

Consistent availability through volatile market conditions with price flex also allowed Europe's leveraged loan market to compete with the high-yield bond market, particularly after the advent of 'covenant lite' loans in 2014, which offer fewer investor protections.

The developments of the last 20 years have created a more robust, resilient and flexible loan market which is a valuable tool for Europe's economy, and the ability to offer similar products to the larger US market has given European companies a wider range of funding options in their own currencies.

## TODAY'S MARKET

Europe's leveraged loan market is far more complex and diverse than its early days with many more players. Volume more than trebled to $207bn in 2018 after a decade of recovery from a post crisis trough of $67bn in 2009, due to a surge in liquidity and interest in the private market.

The three main themes of the last decade – institutionalisation, price elasticity and the creation of alternative capital pools – have seen the market transition into a real asset class with capital markets style execution – a far cry from its origins as a bank market with fixed pricing.

Europe has continued to move into line with the far larger US market, which saw volume of $1.24trn in 2018. This transition has led to huge changes in how deals are structured and sold, as banks continue to grapple with regulatory and capital issues, as well as changes to how investors manage and raise money.

The main theme of the last decade has been the enormous amount of money targeted at European leveraged loans as central banks' stimulus pushed capital into credit and risk assets, including private equity and private debt markets, as the proliferation and diversification of the investor base created excess liquidity amid limited dealflow.

Private equity firms have also been the beneficiaries of the huge influx of cash, which has helped them raise increasingly massive multi-billion dollar funds in the last five years. The amount of private capital 'dry powder' doubled to $2.10trn at the end of June 2018, according to Preqin.

Most of that money – 58% or $1.2trn globally – was targeted at private equity firms, which raised $426bn of funds globally as of December 2018, $90bn of which was targeted at Europe, according to Preqin. The largest fund raised was $18.5bn for Carlyle Partners VII fund and the ten largest funds raised totalled $125bn.

New money has also been flowing into Europe's leveraged loan market through SMAs for pension funds, insurance companies and sovereign wealth funds. One Canadian pension fund alone had $60bn to put to work in the credit markets in 2018 for example.

SMA volume figures are not available, but participants estimate that it is rivalling or exceeding a record $27bn of CLO funds raised in Europe in 2018. SMAs currently provide roughly 40-45% of institutional liquidity, CLO funds 30-40% (down from 70-80% pre-crisis) and banks provide the remainder, according to market participants.

The development of alternative pools of capital has also funnelled money into leveraged loans, with an estimated $900bn of private capital available globally in 2018, according to Preqin as the shadow banking sector replaced smaller scale bank lending.

The sheer weight of capital flowing into all areas of Europe's leveraged loan market, has boosted capacity and driven the evolution of the market, creating bigger deals with higher leverage that reflect higher valuations in frothy public markets.

The European market has adapted and is now capable of financing massive jumbo deals for single B rated companies of up to €10bn, backed by single private equity firms, and their successful placement has boosted confidence in the European market's capacity and reduced its reliance on the US.

# EARLY DAYS (1997-2004)

European companies were underleveraged compared with US firms in the early 1990s and European banks and investors enthusiastically embraced the concept of leverage – providing high levels of debt to riskier non-investment grade companies, in return for yields of 150bp or more.

An early but flamboyant false start amid late 1980s excesses was followed by a dormant period in the recession of the early 1990s. By 1997 the European leveraged market had been active on a modest scale for a couple of years, but at $14bn, was a fraction of the larger US market at $194bn.

The leveraged market quickly became the most exciting and dynamic area of lending in the long bull run from 1997, driven by huge growth in the private equity sector, and increased more than 20 times from $14bn in 1997 to a record $359bn in 2007 that has never been matched.

Europe was the place to be as companies spun off non-core units and private equity firms created new European leveraged buy-outs (LBOs). Demand for leveraged loans grew exponentially after the advent of Europe's single currency in 1999, which laid the foundations of an institutional market.

Europe's patchwork of domestic markets and legal jurisdictions initially relied on bank and mezzanine investors, who made binary lending decisions after exhaustive credit analysis, but a new breed of yield-hungry institutional fund investors was springing up to buy loans as Europe started its journey to a more flexible US-style market.

Pricing increased and settled on typical LBO structures. Amortising term loan A (TLA) tranches were priced at 225bp, bullet term loan B (TLB) tranches at 275bp, and bullet term loan C (TLC) tranches were priced at 325bp, with maturities of six, seven and eight years.

This winning formula was remarkably to remain unchanged for another seven years, and deals were differentiated by leverage. Amortising A tranches were sold to banks and B and C tranches to investors and deals were fully covenanted.

Collateralised debt obligation (CDO) funds first arrived in Europe from the US in 1999. The funds put loans and high-yield bonds into special purpose vehicles that were then securitised, sliced into debt with a range of credit ratings and sold to investors.

Leveraged loans had been marketed as a low volatility, low correlation instrument, but were now connected to the wider capital markets via structured finance vehicles and a more mobile investor base that looked at loans in a relative value context across asset classes.

US funds started to invest in European assets and €416.5m of European CDOs were created according to Fitch, although a couple of European funds, such as Prudential M&G, were already participating directly via investment portfolios.

Europe's first institutional fund investors spent around €2bn on high-yielding cable and telecom assets in 2000 which collapsed in value later in the year in a major setback. However early 2001 produced Europe's first jumbo LBO – a €1.56bn deal backing the buyout of German industrial gases business Messer Griesheim, which attracted European funds' first significant contribution of €250m.

Although the market produced eight deals over $1bn in 2001, the shock of September 11, 2001's terrorist attacks on New York stalled the market. Volume recovered to close the year 38% higher at $83.5bn as US volume slumped amid the bankruptcy of energy trader Enron.

Activity increased in 2002 after a subdued start as private equity firms sold businesses to each other, often replacing one loan with another in secondary or tertiary buyouts, in a trend that dominated the next five years.

Recapitalisations also gained popularity as sponsors used cheap debt to remove their equity investments and releverage businesses with more debt, and a jumbo €2.22bn LBO for French plug and switch manufacturer Legrand was one of the first deals to be placed entirely with European funds.

The looming second Gulf War frustrated the first institutional investors' attempts to raise more money, but the leveraged market grew another 38% to $123.5bn in 2003 as the institutional market regained the ground that it had lost in 2002.

# RAGING BULL (2004-07)

The raging bull market in European leveraged loans started seriously in 2004 as a shortage of paper and richer European returns started to move the transatlantic markets closer together.

The debt management arms of US private equity firms, US credit managers and credit funds set up shop in London's Mayfair district to snap up well priced and structured European loans, and Europe's non-bank investor base had doubled to around 60 by the end of the year.

The volume of paper placed with funds quadrupled to $29bn by the end of the year and the hunt for paper pushed secondary trading to €38bn, according to the LMA, as loan bids climbed over par on the break for the first time.

CLO funds became the main line of business for more established European fund managers such as Duke Street, ING Capital, Harbourmaster, Alcentra, Prudential M&G and AXA and banks also started to develop and spin off their own CLOs.

Hedge funds and credit funds arrived later in 2004 after securing financing from banks through CLO warehouses and subsequently Total Return Swap (TRS) programmes, using leverage of three to five times to boost returns.

This financing was central to the explosive growth in loans that followed. Buyers were able to maximise returns on a stable asset class in a benign economic environment with low default rates that had yet to see any margin erosion, unlike the US market.

This created seemingly bottomless liquidity as new funds piled into the market in breakneck buyside growth. Private equity firms took advantage of the cheap debt and arranging banks were able to count on the market buying what it was given.

European LBO structures started to change to cater to funds. More debt was pushed into longer-dated TLB and TLC tranches, which were mostly allocated to fund investors in institutional carveouts. Arranging banks boosted their returns by stopping paying front-end fees to funds in February, and reverse price flex arrived in June as margins started to come under pressure.

New higher-yielding layers of subordinated or junior debt were squeezed into LBO structures to maximise debt. Second lien or first loss tranches which pay higher margins to compensate for a second claim over assets in event of a bankruptcy appeared for the first time from the US, along with Payment-In-Kind (PIK) loans and more sophisticated debt tranching.

By mid-2004, leverage multiples were heading towards 1998's previous high and covenant packages were loosening. The market saw its first reverse price flex in June and record secondary prices of 102 in October, as demand stayed strong.

Arrangers tailored deal structures towards funds with reverse flex on senior and junior debt and started to reserve more than 50% of deals for funds with bigger TLB/TLC carveouts. Liquid funds were contributing nearly a third of market liquidity by the end of the year, after providing 20-25% for several years.

Europe continued its transformation towards a more flexible credit-driven asset class in 2005 as deal sizes increased. Leveraged volume hit just under $200bn, as private equity borrowing more than doubled to $143bn, and CLO issuance doubled to €10bn.

Structures stretched by adding more junior debt as deal sizes increased. Repayments were pushed out towards maturity and debt was moved up and down capital structures according to demand.

Primary supply failed to meet the growing demand, however, and the secondary market became a new leveraged distribution powerhouse as investors competed for paper and trading hit €61bn, according to the LMA.

Leverage ratios increased too and covenant packages were squeezed as second lien volume increased fivefold to $6.4bn while mezzanine volume climbed to a record $11.6bn.

Larger TLB/TLC allocations were reserved for nimble funds to speed up turnover and profit for arranging banks, while smaller TLAs and revolving credits were kept for credit-conscious bank investors.

The market cooled in May 2005 when US auto makers General Motors and Ford Motor were downgraded to junk in the US and volatility rose as hedge funds sold high-yield bonds to cover redemptions as Europe saw its first secondary market selloff.

The first of several jumbo loans – €7.55bn of senior and second lien facilities totalling backing Egyptian entrepreneur Naguib Sawiris' bid for Italian mobile telecom company, Wind – had to pay fees to funds and boost second lien pricing to sell the senior debt.

A wave of new issues hit the market in July but reverse flex and high secondary breaks continued as big funds demanded larger allocations for multiplying CLOs, and hedge funds were increasingly active buyers.

A new and more aggressive phase of margin erosion started as 25% of all LBOs were flexed in 2005 with flexed tranches totalled $12.7bn. Private equity firms were asking for more leverage to fund higher purchase prices as deals were snapped up by funds.

Eight funds committed €100m each to a €3.8bn financing for packaging firm Smurfit Kappa, which were the largest fund commitments seen at the time and the year closed with huge new jumbo loans. A €7.22bn acquisition for UK chemicals business Ineos and an €8.6bn take private financing for Danish telecom TDC were held over for the new year.

Any questions about market capacity were quickly dispelled by phenomenal demand in early 2006 as leveraged loans grew another 27% to just under $253bn, with $198bn of sponsor lending, as funds competed for paper in a buyside feeding frenzy.

Attention turned to deal structures as pricing fell. TLAs started to shrink in early 2006 and were replaced by US-style TLB structures, and sponsors also stripped out second lien tranches by year end to reduce funding costs.

Syndication of the Ineos and TDC LBOs coincided with the opening of a huge amount of CLO warehouse capacity. Ineos gathered a mighty syndicate of 51 banks and 150 institutions, some of which had committed through several funds, giving 473 accounts.

TDC, the second-biggest buyout globally since KKR's infamous acquisition of RJR Nabisco in 1989, raised total commitments of €15bn, €3.5bn of which was pledged to its €2.8bn institutional tranches alone, prompting the largest flex of 37.5bp.

Opportunistic private equity firms piled on more debt and leverage and tighter pricing and reverse price flex became normal as the market moved closer to demand-driven pricing. A third of deals were reverse flexed in 2006 and average pricing dropped to 200bp on TLAs and revolvers and a blended rate of 250bp on the TLB/TLC, but demand and secondary prices remained high.

As pricing tumbled, private equity firms introduced amendments and waivers to allow a raft of aggressive bull market features including dividend payments, acquisition add-ons and second-lien taps to boost M&A activity.

Private equity firms teamed up to bid in consortia to bid for larger companies. Around half or $100bn of the $200bn of private equity borrowing was placed with funds, showing an 80% increase on 2005 and secondary trading doubled to €93bn, according to the LMA.

The secondary market was a one-way bet due to captive appetite from CLO warehouses as issuance trebled to €29.5bn, according to Fitch. This kept prices on the most actively traded loans at 101-102 and allowed banks and traders to rely on continual demand.

The strategy was to be as long as possible as secondary prices climbed. Banks made fees from arranging CLO warehouses, and banks with first loss provisions also made money as the loans traded up. The largest managers were running up to ten CLOs and funds were buying more than 50% of deals by the end of the year with carveouts of up to 70%.

To create more longer-dated TLB/TLC paper for funds, bank TLAs were reduced and amortising A loans were removed. This meant that European companies could refinance long before covenants were tested and repayments were due and did not need to generate enough cash to repay debt.

If senior debt was hot, junior debt was hotter. Second lien loans doubled to $13bn and mezzanine climbed 61% to $19bn with a record €1bn mezzanine tranche on Dutch cable company Casema's LBO, as junior debt pricing fell, covenants loosened and buyers started to protest about stretched terms and squeezed margins.

The market's traditional barriers were crumbling but unified protest was unlikely with up to 250 active funds. Banks, however, started to step back from high leverage at the end of the year and some forward-thinking investors started to position for a downturn.

# FINANCIAL CRISIS (2007-09)

2007 began well but Europe's senior syndicators were privately worried that the market was out of control. Junior debt had pushed total debt and leverage ratios to record highs and pricing was still falling. Bankers were concerned that they were taking too much risk for too little return and companies with aggressive business plans would run into difficulties.

Returns and sponsor equity contributions were low, leverage was at record highs and covenants had eroded. Toppy structural features appeared including equity cures, toggles – the ability to turn off interest payments – on second lien and Payment In Kind (PIK) loans, mulligans, which allowed one-off defaults, and ultimately covenant-lite loans.

The introduction of covenant-lite loans in the first half of 2007 marked the peak of the market and leveraged volume rose to a record $359bn in 2007, before the American sub-prime mortgage market wreaked havoc on European leveraged loans.

Early 2007 had a frantic pace that was unhealthy in hindsight. Volume was 105% higher than 2006 after a strong first half, but halved to $115bn in the second half, as sub-prime volatility hit the formerly rock-solid asset class. Liquidity ebbed as funds stopped buying and the market effectively closed.

Volume passed 2006's full-year total in the middle of the year which saw the record buyout of UK pharmaceutical retailer Alliance Boots backed by £9.05bn of senior debt – which came to be known as the deal that broke the market.

Lending to private equity firms shot up to $288bn or 80% of the market, which has never been matched, as sponsors sold businesses to each other, often refinancing the debt within months to cut pricing and loosen terms.

TDC's aggressive repricing in May took pro-rata pricing to 175bp with a blended TLB/TLC rate of 200bp and fund carveouts of 80% to 90% were seen on the deal for German forklift manufacturer Kion.

Low pricing put pressure on the entire CLO model, despite funds' protests and subordinated PIK loans replaced mezzanine debt as sponsors opted for cheaper non-cash pay debt and riskier deal structures. A record €157bn of loans were traded according to the LMA, which has never been rivalled.

Covenant-lite loans were introduced from the US at the end of the first quarter featuring only bond-style incurrence tests and were grudgingly accepted (after first appearing on the VNU World Directories recapitalisation) on deals including the huge Alliance Boots LBO.

Leverage peaked at 6.04 times total debt-to-EBITDA and 4.88 times senior debt-to-EBITDA in mid-June, but directories businesses and strong industrial companies were levered at ten times or more and sponsor equity hit a low of around 16% of deal structures.

Highly leveraged deals with weak structures — particularly covenant-lite loans – failed to sell in June, including deals for Spanish retailer Cortefiel and German cable company ProsiebenSat.1, and fell below par in secondary, in the first sign of trouble.

The peak of the market was over by late June as the US subprime crisis highlighted the risk in the multi-billion euro pipeline of large aggressively priced and structured buyout loans. Hedge funds shorted leveraged loans for the first time and prices tumbled.

An ultra-aggressive covenant-lite loan for Dutch retailer Maxeda DIY was pulled after adding a covenant and a discount to 99.75 failed to generate interest and syndicators wondered whether the massive £9.05bn Alliance Boots LBO was simply too big for the market.

Falling secondary prices virtually closed the market for the first time in ten years. Hedge funds were forced to sell loans to meet margin calls as Europe's new capital markets connectivity worked against it for the first time.

A market repricing left €75–80bn of aggressively underwritten legacy loans trapped in the pipeline and arranging banks with long positions as sub-prime contagion scythed through structured products and liquidity disappeared.

The abrupt closure of the CLO and CDO markets highlighted Europe's reliance on the CLO pipeline. Europe's buyside had grown to around 250 institutional investors, consisting of roughly 60% CLOs and 40% proprietary trading desks and hedge funds.

CLO investors had invested in structured vehicles that suffered sub-prime losses and demand for CLO securities collapsed, including leveraged loan CLOs. Banks alarmed about their mounting loan exposure pulled warehousing lines for new CLOs and closed TRS lines for hedge fund buyers.

The secondary loan market was overwhelmed by selling as average bids fell from 100.7 to 95.7 – a previously unimaginable drop that was caused by the unwinding and liquidation of CLO and CDO warehouses, which was the biggest single surprise of the crash.

Low secondary prices shut the primary market between July and October and syndication of Alliance Boots' £5.05bn of senior debt was put on hold as secondary desks closed in early September after taking huge hits.

Small Original Issue Discounts (OIDs) appeared in Europe for the first time as banks offered fees to funds in a bid to sell the €75–80bn legacy pipeline, which proved unsuccessful as few investors had the money or nerve to buy cheap loans after heavy mark to market losses.

US banks marked down trapped pipeline deals more aggressively in October but many European banks chose to hold the pipeline deals on balance sheet hoping for recovery, instead of taking mark to market losses. Some deals were restructured to include 'toxic' junior debt that was held by arranging banks to reduce leverage.

Secondary prices fell to 96 as the scale of financial write-downs linked to the sub-prime crisis emerged. Investors demanded deeper discounts and some of the pipeline looked unsellable, even at discounts of up to 97.

Europe's top 40 leveraged loans closed the year at 95.5 as confidence ebbed. By the end of the year, European banks had only sold 5% of the pipeline, while more than 50% of the US pipeline had been sold.

If the second half of 2007 was bad, things were about to get substantially worse. Early 2008 started well, as new players tried to profit from lead arrangers' legacy overhang problems and underwrite punchy new deals.

But 2008 will be remembered for only one thing – the collapse of Lehman Brothers in September – which caused the biggest financial crisis since the Great Depression of the 1930s, and continues to influence the European leveraged loan market a decade later.

Mistrust spread through the financial system. Banks had to be bailed out by national governments, global stock markets fell and economic activity sank, which caused a global recession from 2008–12 and pushed Europe into a sovereign debt crisis.

Lehman's failure caused a meltdown in Europe's leveraged markets as banks and investors scrambled to assess exposure and counterparty risk. Liquidity froze and secondary prices plummeted, inflicting deeper mark-to-market losses on investors and new lending stopped.

Secondary prices fell 2,200 bps in the fourth quarter alone amid forced selling, mostly in a bloody October, when prices fell 1,700 bps from 81.84 to 64.78, although much of the damage had already been done.

Europe's first major outflow of capital started when secondary prices breached 90 in January as hedge funds' TRS programmes started to unwind after leverage evaporated. Prices fell again in mid-February to 85.02, triggering forced selling into a weak market as banks dumped CLO warehouses, bringing losses of 10% from the beginning of 2008.

Banks had provided leverage on leverage through CLOs and TRS programmes and even the best loans traded down most heavily as forced sellers dumped their most liquid names. The primary market reverted to an all-bank investor base as institutional investors fled and lending to private equity firms stopped.

Deal launches were delayed in March as JP Morgan bought US investment bank Bear Sterns with a $29bn loan from the Federal Reserve. Underwriting banks realised that the market was unlikely to improve and started to discount the €75-80bn backlog of unsold leveraged loans more aggressively.

Around £4bn of Alliance Boots' record £9bn buyout loan was sold in mid-May at 90 to 91 and another £650m sale followed in June at 92. Citigroup and Deutsche Bank sold loan portfolios to private equity firms with financing, and private equity firms also controversially bought back their own debt.

The primary market could not compete with so many underwriters selling at deep discounts. Although sales as low as 75% of face value were painful, they turned out to be good trades, as over levered deals were restructured with bigger losses in the ensuing economic downturn.

Leveraged volume of $53.45bn in the first half of 2008 was 78% lower than a year earlier and private equity lending of $39bn was 81% lower as sponsors found it nearly impossible to borrow and secondary prices fell again in July to 87.5.

Attention turned to the slowing economy and governments stepped in to support banks in the run up to Lehman's collapse, which was followed by forced mergers between financial institutions and bankers moved into damage limitation mode in a frightening period.

Weekly shocks rocked the markets as banks were re-equitised and renationalised. Banks stopped underwriting and focussed on survival as they struggled to close positions as chaos in the financial sector quickly moved into the real economy.

The Continent started to slide into a double dip recession, dishing out a dose of painful amendments and waivers and the prospect of credit losses amid poor fourth quarter trading numbers. European leveraged loans seemed to be on the edge of a precipice moving into 2009, as low secondary prices implied recovery value and suggested that all leveraged companies were going to default.

Europe's leveraged loan market was one of the biggest casualties of the credit crunch in 2009 due to banks' exposure. A massive technical sell off dragged secondary prices to record lows and closed the primary market for most of the year while central bank liquidity helped prices to rally.

Leveraged loans dropped 43% to a record low of $67bn in 2009, with only $18.5bn of sponsor borrowing and the CLO machine ground to a halt as issuance stopped.

Secondary prices hit record lows of 59.51 in January 2009 and averaged 65 in the first quarter. The market was viewed as oversold and a schizophrenic rally followed which defined the year in the credit markets.

Secondary loan prices were nearly 30% higher by the end of the year as the illiquid European secondary market was as overwhelmed by bargain-hunting buyers on the way up as it had been by sellers on the way down.

The first European restructurings appeared in the first half of 2009 amid an economic downturn, which carried on into 2010 and sponsors battled to keep control of portfolio companies instead of doing new deals.

A dysfunctional loan market was a massive problem for a refinancing wall of up to $470bn of maturing buyout loans that had to be refinanced by 2016, according to KPMG, which forced many issuers into the high-yield bond market for punitively expensive best efforts deals.

Europe's leveraged loan market reinvented itself as a corporate refinancing market for stressed companies. Stronger companies started to issue high-yield bonds, as one of the biggest credit trends of the post-Lehman period started.

Weaker 'zombie' companies were forced to 'amend and extend' (A&E) loans in the second half of 2009, which became known as 'amend and pretend' as bankers hoped that company performance would improve.

The move to high-yield bonds was reinforced by regulation as capital rules made it increasingly expensive for banks to hold riskier term debt, which encouraged banks to adopt a distribution model, rather than lending directly.

The first restructurings including French auto supplier, Autodistribution, were tough debt-for-equity swaps with rock-bottom recovery rates that wiped out junior lenders and also hit senior debt as credit downgrades and rising defaults also started to hurt CLO funds.

Equity prices bottomed in March 2009 and secondary loan prices were 19% higher at the end of the first half, ending a brief window of opportunity from November 2008-February 2009 to invest in high-quality European loans at rock-bottom prices.

Investors took a harder line with sponsors over equity contributions as default rates climbed and took control of companies. Late 2009 saw a wave of amendments and extensions as government stimulus programmes pumped cash into economies and improving company performance slowed restructurings.

Secondary prices rose to 87.4 but the new issue market remained closed. Most European buyouts lined up for some form of covenant restructuring as liquidity improved, which made good fees and allowed banks to avoid further write-downs and losses.

The first senior secured bonds were seen for Virgin Media and Smurfit Kappa in October and November, which was a key theme of 2010. Senior secured bonds had been seen in Europe before but not pari passu or alongside senior loans in a US-style development.

# SOVEREIGN DEBT CRISIS (2010-14)

2010 was a better year despite Europe's escalating sovereign debt crisis. Volume increased for the first time since 2007, but progress was sporadic as looming sovereign bailouts for Greece and Ireland periodically stalled recovery amid fears of a double dip recession.

The high yield bond market kept the leveraged loan market running as it continued to refinance existing loans and the influx of repayments helped to push secondary loan prices closer to par.

Leveraged loan volume climbed a solid 27% from a nine-year low to $94bn – slightly higher than 2002 levels – in a year characterised by refinancing, large corporate M&A loans and a smattering of new buyouts in the second half.

Large leveraged corporate M&A deals started to be sold on both sides of the Atlantic midyear as the transatlantic cross-sell started and bankers played the euro and dollar loan and bond markets off against each other for best price and execution.

New buyouts started to appeared in late 2010 backed by smaller, low levered loans with large equity cheques, which looked attractive in a low interest rate environment with few alternatives and also provided a hedge against inflation.

Two big bouts of volatility around Greece's deteriorating finances in February and May and Ireland's bailout in December ensured that conservative new buyout loans offered higher pricing, but liquidity was still a concern.

No new European CLOs had been issued since Lehman Brothers' collapse in late 2008, but a handful of successful deals including a £510m financing backing KKR's purchase of British retailer Pets at Home showed huge demand.

Hungry investors turned to the US for new deals, which helped to transform the European leveraged loan market from an illiquid clubby bank market to a more fluent, liquid institutional market with a range of US features, including US-style LIBOR floors, ratings and wide distribution to a sophisticated buy side.

A five-point fall in secondary prices in May closed the high-yield bond market as eurozone volatility peaked but a more stable second half saw large leveraged corporate acquisition loans placed with the help of the larger and more liquid US market.

Europe's first crop of new buyouts in September saw strong fund demand and were placed with successively tightening OIDs and the first European LIBOR floors – a US feature which guarantees returns to investors – gave high yields of more than 8%.

Incentives were gradually reduced as demand improved and Europe saw its first secondary breaks over par since Lehman during the fourth quarter. Volatility around Ireland's bailout pushed secondary loan and bond prices lower in early December and banks were reluctant to underwrite bridge loans.

The secondary market recovered to close 2010 higher at 93 and cash from repayments meant that 40% of European CLOs were back in compliance by late 2010, highlighting the resilience of CLO structures.

Europe's intensifying sovereign debt crisis and banks' rising funding costs took centre stage in 2011. Leveraged lending was 46% higher than 2010 and climbed back over $100bn to $140bn, but activity slumped in a volatile and eventful second half after Greece received a €120bn bailout and the European Central Bank started to buy Spain and Italy's bonds.

Investors were flush with cash from high yield bond repayments in a bullish first half. Banks syndicated new deals with higher leverage and lower pricing. Deals were flexed down for the first time since 2007, some of 2009 and 2010's more expensive loans were repriced.

Private equity borrowing more than doubled to $89bn from $43bn, but as Greece hovered on the brink of a default over the summer and contagion spread to Italy and Spain, investors withdrew and the high yield bond market ground to a halt.

The unpredictability of the volatile high yield bond market put more emphasis on amending and extending existing loans, as the refinancing wall moved closer and $33.4bn of leveraged loans were extended in 2011.

Secondary loan prices slumped to 89.6 in the third quarter and arranging banks were caught long for the second time in four years with nearly €10bn of unsold leveraged loans and bridge loans to high bonds in September.

Several deals, including the seven times leveraged buyout of Swedish alarms maker Securitas Direct, had to be restructured with Original Issue Discounts (OIDs) of 98 or adding second lien loans. The €10bn overhang still failed to sell and banks had to take painful losses to sell as yields soared above 10%. Arrangers had $6.4bn of loans left to sell as the year closed, and underwriting ground to a halt.

A second banking crisis started in late 2011 as banks' massive exposure to sovereign bond holdings of indebted peripheral countries was revealed. US money market funds were reluctant to lend to European banks, which raised the cost of dollar funding.

The European Central Bank started a huge infusion of credit into the European banking system under its Long Term Refinancing Operations (LTRO) in December 2011 which helped to stabilise the banking system and extended into 2012.

With so many problems in Europe's banking sector, the hunt for replacement capital took on new urgency as the refinancing cliff moved closer with $41bn of leveraged loans maturing in 2013 and $91.6bn in 2014. CLO consolidation started, as established managers targeted critical mass and a more diversified range of funds instead of just CLO funds.

Potential new European investors including pension funds and insurance companies had been educated about the merits of the asset class since 2008 as a possible alternative for bank capital, but continued to sit on the sidelines.

Mid-market institutional money started to appear from funds like Bluebay, KKR, TPG and Highbridge Capital and more established providers of senior and hybrid debt like Ares Capital and Haymarket Financial also exploited the gap left by banks scaling back as the direct lending market started.

The eurozone crisis continued to curb demand for new loans in 2012 amid an uncertain macroeconomic outlook and volatile markets, as the peak of the refinancing wall drew nearer with $124.6bn of loans maturing in 2015.

Europe's low growth prospects due to the recession and eurozone crisis curbed M&A activity, which helped the market to focus on chipping away at the refinancing wall in an orderly way with the help of the high yield bond market.

European leveraged volume lurched lower again with a 22% drop to $117.4bn as volume returned to 2008 levels amid some frightening moments on the euro. Activity resumed in the fourth quarter as sentiment grew more positive again, after a lull of more than a year since the second half of 2011, and new buyouts reappeared.

Larger European companies were able to get a better price by raising loans in the larger US leveraged loan market, which was less affected by eurozone issues. A hot US market bred confidence in transatlantic distribution and set a more positive tone for the start of 2013, along with a good pipeline of deals.

Some European companies were tapping the US market to price in dollars under New York law to access the covenant-lite market, and several European investors were already buying dollar paper under New York law as supply in Europe remained thin.

Competing against dominant high-yield bonds was a major challenge for the loan market and the rise of bonds and relative value investors increased loans' correlation with the capital markets and boosted volatility.

The rise of global funds also exacerbated this trend. The ability to tap Europe and the US and raise funds including loans, bonds, senior secured bonds and loans allowed relative value investors to take advantage of value without committing capital regionally or being locked in.

With the CLO market still closed, work was continuing on a wide range of alternatives, including low or unlevered funds, listed loan funds, managed accounts and hedge funds.

Pension fund and insurance money finally started to materialise slowly after several years of intensive education about the asset class, but investors were wary due to a lack of clarity about how they would be treated under the EU's Solvency II insurance regulation.

Despite being dismissed initially, direct lending continued to grow and gain ground as specialist funds worked with banks to fill a gap in small scale, higher yielding, credit intensive middle market deals as banks pulled back from lending to small and medium-sized enterprises.

The bruises of the financial and eurozone crises were still on show in early 2013 and some companies were still struggling, but the European leveraged loan market started to rebound and the CLO market reopened.

New CLO funds were printed for the first time since 2008 and 20 CLOs were raised totalling €7.3bn as the market's traditional and biggest buyer base resumed business and activity in high-yield issuance doubled to $121.5bn as the refinancing wall peaked.

European leveraged loan volume hit a six-year high of $191.5bn, showing a 74% increase on 2012, as sponsor volume hit $122bn. This was mostly due to heavy refinancing volume of $127.85bn as pricing started to fall amid more positive conditions, a trend that was to dominate the next five years.

Banks were still facing capital issues with Basel II and were reluctant to lend in the leveraged space and liquidity was still constrained, allowing direct lenders to grow and accelerate, particularly smaller midcap specialists in lending to small and medium-sized companies.

The main event of the year came when US regulators updated US Leveraged Lending Guidelines (LLG) in March in a watershed moment for the transatlantic markets, which brought new levels of scrutiny and changed bank's credit processes, monitoring and reporting globally.

The guidelines were introduced by the Office of the Comptroller of the Currency, Federal Reserve and the Federal Deposit Insurance Corporation to curb systemic risk in the banking sector by reducing banks' ability to underwrite risky loans that they might not be able to sell.

The rules, which imposed a six times leverage limit and also stated that credits also had to be able to repay all senior debt, or half total debt within five to seven years from free cash flow, had an immediate impact on US structures and suddenly put a cap on the market.

Although the impact was initially greatest for US banks, US regulators extended the guidance to non US banks doing business in the US, and US banks also applied the rules globally, which caught the eye of European regulators.

Europe's exposure to covenant lite lending increased with more cross-border deals and euro carveouts of large dollar transactions were seen while European companies continued to use 'covenant loose' structures with limited covenants.

Although 2013 had still been a difficult year, with worries about Italy and contagion issues as Greece went through one of the final legs of its bail out, which caused a couple of violent blips in the market as more aggressive structures were rejected, the year closed with the most positive outlook since 2007 as the eurozone held together and worked through the problems facing the peripheral countries.

## SECOND BULL RUN (2014-18)

The return of M&A in 2014 marked the start of a second bull run in the European leveraged loan market characterised by borrower-friendly terms as interest rates stayed lower for longer and central bank purchases continued to create a positive backdrop for credit and risk assets.

Volume climbed 9.3% to $201bn and more than half of that total – $124bn – was refinancing and repricing, which cemented the downward trajectory for pricing as technical demand overwhelmed deal supply amid a surfeit of buyers, including CLO funds, as volume doubled to $14.3bn.

Europe's first pure covenant-lite loan, an €818m loan backing the buyout of French veterinary pharmaceutical firm, Ceva Sante Animale, was completed in March. The deal was the first euro-denominated loan to be raised for a European company as investors accepted structures with fewer safeguards.

By the end of the year, 15% of loans were cov-lite. Covenant lite loans, which have bond-style incurrence covenants only, helped the loan market to compete with high-yield bonds, which had held the upper hand since the crisis, as bond issuance peaked at $147bn, along with the return of second lien loans in the middle of the year.

Private equity firms prefer the flexibility of loans, which lack the prepayment penalties that bonds carry and second lien loans also help them to write smaller equity cheques thanks to higher debt and leverage.

A downturn in crude oil prices started in the middle of the year amid surging output from OPEC, Russia and US shale producers, which rattled the market before gathering pace at the end of the year.

The market was shaken in September, when Credit Suisse received a warning from the Federal Reserve in the US highlighting problems with the bank's adherence to the US leveraged lending guidelines in a 'Matters Requiring Immediate Attention' letter.

This showed that the regulators were determined to enforce the guidance more strictly and that banks that failed to do so would face penalties, which could include fines or being closed down and banks immediately fell into line.

Stricter application of the rules allowed non-bank lenders, or 'shadow banks' including Jefferies, Nomura and KKR to underwrite more highly leveraged loans and take market share as regulated banks were forced to pass on riskier deals.

Direct lenders made further gains as demand for the product remained strong despite banks' renewed appetite to lend, as new and existing players, such as Alcentra, ICG and KKR raised unlevered funds that targeted returns in the low to mid-teens.

The unitranche product, which combines senior and mezzanine loans, and is best suited to small and medium sized companies grew in popularity, and deal sizes stretched to €250m as alternative lenders' financial firepower continued to build.

The slide in oil prices accelerated at the end of the year after a Saudi-led OPEC decision to keep production high to defend global market share rather than cut output to support prices and volatility rose.

Falling oil prices were supplemented in early 2015 by a dramatic tumble in China's stock market and plummeting oil and commodity prices, but this volatility failed to derail the European leveraged loans market, which continued apace with a third year of gains since 2012.

Volume rose another 15% to $216bn as leveraged M&A of $83.4bn hit its highest point since 2008 after a pickup in the fourth quarter. Worries over the Chinese economy delayed some loans until midyear and a backlog of loans was launched in July, several of which were delayed or flexed in the second half of the year.

EMEA lending plummeted in the third quarter as transatlantic secondary prices fell amid the ensuing volatility and investors refused to buy primary deals that would quickly trade lower. Choppy markets in the US forced banks to pull a $5.6bn buyout of software firm Veritas in November, which threatened to impact the European market towards year-end.

Banks on Veritas lost around $100m each as the US market was caught with long positions, and banks lost a combined $1bn on fees and markdowns, which took until the end of the year to resolve.

In December, the US Federal Reserve started to raise interest US rates for the first time since June 2006, which further increased the appeal of floating rate loans as a hedge against further rate rises on both sides of the Atlantic and exacerbated the supply-demand imbalance.

The ongoing woes of the energy sector depressed the transatlantic markets in the first half of 2016, although Europe's leveraged loan market fared better than the US, as fewer energy companies had issued leveraged loans.

Political headlines grabbed the limelight in a turbulent year, with the shock result of Britain's vote to leave the EU in June, and the election of President Donald Trump in November, however despite these headwinds, disruption proved to be short term and the market quickly recovered.

European leveraged lending fell 33% to $183bn in 2016 compared to a year earlier and volume hit its lowest point since 2012 as acquisitions slowed and opportunistic repricings and recapitalisations took over.

The first half of 2016 saw volume of $79.8bn as pricing widened on uncertainty, but volume rose to $102.9bn in the second half. Deal structures came under pressure as covenant lite loans rose to 41% of the market.

Sponsors pushed more aggressive terms, including the ability to add extra debt or pay dividends, as leverage levels crept higher, catching the eye of the European Central Bank, which had started to look at loans in May 2015.

Meanwhile developments were flying thick and fast as Europe's fund market continued to grow strongly. CLO issuance had been steadily rising and hit $17bn, but CLOs were outgunned as the flow of SMA money accelerated into credit managers' accounts from pension funds, insurance companies and sovereign wealth funds.

Direct lenders started to challenge banks for deals, with the ability to make large contributions and take down large chunks of pre-placed second lien loans, which were designed to compete with high yield bonds and better suited to smaller deals.

In retrospect, late 2017 was the top of the market and European leveraged lending soared 73% to hit a ten-year post crisis peak of $256bn as a repricing frenzy got underway and $161bn of loans were repriced, but demand continued to far outweigh supply.

Cash flooded in as US rates rose three times during the year, further boosting the appeal of floating rate loans. The first half of 2017 saw volume of $142bn as borrowers took advantage of deep liquidity to reprice and refinance existing facilities on a more attractive basis.

Sponsor borrowing hit a post-crisis high of $157bn in a record year for private equity fundraising as the industry raised $453bn from investors globally, bringing the amount of 'dry powder' available to more than $1trn.

The European Central Bank published its guidance on leveraged transactions in May in a bid to take the heat out of the market, and it was implemented in November, ironically just as the US market started to ease its rules.

The guidance noted that the low interest rate environment and search for yield had warranted specific monitoring of leveraged finance exposure after a strong recovery as fierce competition and borrower-friendly structures had led to leniency in credit policies.

While banks were obliged to follow the reporting requirements, the ECB rules appeared to have little effect, and banks paid more attention to their national regulators, such as the PRA in the UK, which were pushing for US-style guidance.

By mid-2017, the market was becoming more aggressive despite continued uncertainty about low commodity prices, European elections and continuing uncertainty around Brexit, Donald Trump and North Korea. Covenant lite lending rose to 76% of the market.

Leverage levels were rising and it was not unusual to see first lien deals with total debt of 7x with increasingly aggressive loan documents as the combination of growth of financing teams at private equity firms and US law firms seeking to gain market share pushed boundaries.

The increased complexity of loan documentation spawned a new industry of covenant research firms, such as Covenant Review and Debt Explained, to analyse documents and help investors to push back against some of the more egregious terms on offer.

Second half volume was lower at $114bn, as sponsors and investors focused on new money transactions and a pickup in event-driven financings, particularly in take-private deals in the second half of 2017, as banks turned more aggressive deals down and were replaced by SMA money.

Large public to private buyouts included a €2.95bn-equivalent financing backing the $5.3bn take-private of payments firm Nets, a $2.6bn cross-border loan backing the buyout of UK-based payment processing company Paysafe and a €1.4bn loan and £266m loan for German generic drugmaker Stada part-financing its €5.2bn buyout.

The market moved into higher gear in 2018 as deal sizes and leverage levels continued to climb, although overall volume was 49% lower at $206bn as volatility rose amid concerns that an economic downturn was approaching.

Banks started to underwrite more highly leveraged buyouts again with leverage of up to 7.75x as it became clear that regulators would not punish lenders and jumbo buyouts reappeared in 'the year of the carveout'.

Companies sold huge units to private equity firms, taking deal sizes ever higher and redefining capacity in Europe's leveraged loan market, which presented syndication challenges as volatility increased in the course of the year.

Investors rebelled over aggressive terms and conditions after a surge in supply in the second quarter, which produced an unusually rapid pricing correction and the transatlantic loan markets also took fright in December amid concerns about a US-China trade war and as the US slowed interest rate rises.

The year started strongly with a huge €5.5bn leveraged financing backing US private equity firm KKR's €6.83bn acquisition of Unilever's margarine and spreads business which sold well, but traded lower in the secondary market. The deal was the biggest new money institutional money capital raise at the time and one of the biggest deals for a European single B rated issuer since 2007.

That record was quickly eclipsed by two huge buyouts. A $13.5bn loan and bond financing for Refinitiv, formerly Thomson Reuters' F&R division was announced in January, which was the biggest buyout since the financial crisis, and a similar $7.6bn financing backing Akzo Nobel's spinoff of its chemicals business followed in March.

Syndication of both deals hung over the market for months, as arranging banks waited for a window of opportunity to launch the massive transactions. Market conditions grew more challenging as a rise in supply in the early summer gave investors a chance to push back against some of the market's more aggressive developments.

Law firms had been haggling to get the best terms for sponsors and documents became a battle ground as investors drew the line over aggressive features that included giving private equity firms more flexibility to make add-on acquisitions, limiting debt repayments from excess cashflow and avoiding using sale proceeds to repay debt or reinvest.

This produced a particularly rapid pricing correction in a more interconnected market of around 100bp within weeks as many investors, including CLOs, were unable to buy paper at 300bp. The speed of the snapback, which matched the high-yield bond market, was attributed to the proliferation and diversification of investors, including more relative value players.

Banks had problems trying to sell inventory over the summer that were exacerbated by higher leverage and weaker terms and private equity firms had to make concessions on documentation, pricing and discounts to get deals over the line and help arranging banks to find often painful clearing prices.

In a key test of liquidity and market sentiment, the jumbo loans for Refinitiv and Akzo were launched after the summer break in September and both deals sold well. Technical factors, primarily huge demand and a small pipeline of deals, overwhelmed concerns over credit, aggressive documentation and worries about an economic downturn at the end of an unusually long economic cycle.

The jumbo loans set pricing at 350-450bp, but the pipeline remained thin. Volatility struck again in December, when slowing interest rate rises encouraged investors to look at better relative value elsewhere and US retail loan funds saw a record monthly outflow of more than $10bn.

European secondary prices lost 233bp from 99.74 at the beginning of November until the end of the year, when prices closed at 97.41, but the impact on the market was limited by a thin pipeline after the syndication of the two jumbo loans.

Lines in the institutional market were blurring as CLO managers added direct lending funds to their multiasset funds and larger middle market lenders such as GSO and Ares were able to make commitments of up to €500m on deals and challenge banks for business as dealflow remained scarce.

In September, the LLG was relaxed when US government agencies said that it was guidance and not a rule, which encouraged banks to arrange more highly leveraged deals, which started to attract a chorus of complaints and criticism as a potential threat.

Regulators and central bankers including the Federal Reserve Chair Jerome Powell, his predecessor Janet Yellen and Bank of England Governor Mark Carney warned of the perils of excess corporate debt in leveraged loans and the potential negative economic impact, while some even compared the asset class to the sub prime market which caused the financial crisis.

## LOOKING FORWARD

The European leveraged loan market not only survived its first crisis, it has thrived and is now a fully functioning asset class. Although central banks' stimulus has extended the credit cycle, a more diverse buyside means that the market is less likely to close in the next downturn.

The amount of institutional money has never been higher in Europe's leveraged loan market. Changes to the investor base in the last decade mean that the market will weather the next crisis better and continue to offer companies more borrowing options.

In perhaps one of the biggest changes since the financial crisis, the middle market landscape has changed from a bank market and handful of funds due to the proliferation of new mid-market lenders and products including unitranche loans and preplaced second lien which have been developed to cater to this demand.

The market has been on a strong upwards trajectory since 2014, with the exception of a couple of blips in late 2015 and 2018 and is better able to price risk, with price elasticity creating a range from 275-650bp depending on the counterparty and quality of the credit.

This bull run since the development of covenant lite in 2014 is the strongest seen since the peak of the market before the financial crisis and invites inevitable comparisons between then and now.

Lower interest rates have reduced the interest burden on companies, but are allowing private equity firms to put more leverage and debt on companies which is producing bigger deals and supporting higher valuations driven by frothy public markets. Despite regulatory attempts to curb it, leverage is at or near historic highs.

Higher multiples and leverage continue to fuel fears that private equity firms could make strategic mistakes or overpay for assets. It also means that sponsors are taking more risk, which could reduce returns on the next generation of mega funds as the next downturn draws closer.

The rise of covenant lite loans has helped the loan market to compete with the high-yield bond market as the two markets have converged, but lenders still have concerns as loan documents are far more aggressive than 2007, which is expected to lead to lower recovery rates in the next downturn as lenders will not be able to take pre-emptive action.

Aggressive terms, such as adjusted EBITDA also create additional 'hidden leverage', which makes it difficult for companies to perform to plan as the original adjustments were too extreme, which could further reduce recovery rates.

Covenant lite loans are also giving private equity firms more control and if companies encounter problems, sponsors will be able to restructure businesses or hand the keys over when there is no value left. Investors are particularly concerned about the extension of covenant lite loans to middle market companies.

The European leveraged loan market is behaving more like a capital market with increased volatility as the growth of specialised financing teams at private equity firms makes sophisticated sponsors more powerful, and a more diverse buyside de-emphasises relationship lending.

The relationship between private equity firms and their lenders is growing more combative and arm's length as a result, as both sides push to see what they can get away with – either more aggressive terms for the private equity firms, or investors pushing back against an underpriced deal.

Europe's leveraged finance market has transformed but it has not yet seen a full credit cycle and the task ahead is to help issuers navigate difficult market conditions and get through the next downturn. Much, however, depends upon the shape of the next downturn.

Manageable default rates and robust CLO structures helped the market through the shock and liquidity freeze of the financial crisis, but more experienced market participants are warning that the next downturn could be more prolonged and persistently low default rates will not be a good indicator.

With few protections, lenders will be able to take little action on covenant lite loans, and the risk of 'zombie' companies is growing. Investors are basing lending decisions on perfect models and projections which means that even a modest downside could put leverage in the 8-9x range, which could be at or through value for lenders.

While a lengthy slide could be manageable, a short and nasty downturn could see highly leveraged deals struggle to refinance, which could lead to another raft of amend and extend deals similar to 2008 again.

The main danger, however, is rising interest rates, which make companies' debt burden less sustainable, particularly if company earnings are also declining, along with higher LIBOR rates which further boost borrowing costs. The jury is out on the availability of covenant lite in tougher market conditions and maintenance covenants could be introduced in some deals.

There is still room for Europe's economy to rely less on banks and more on institutional investors. The European leveraged loan market is still less standardised than the US, although a bigger buyside is creating a more efficient and process-driven market with ratings and pricing grids, as it continues to import the best and worst of the US model.

The drive towards bigger, more complex deals is set to continue as European companies take advantage of enormous interest in the credit market and the huge amount of money that is being committed to an asset class that, for all its ups and downs, is still viewed as very attractive.

Although deal structures are weaker, the quality of assets is better than ten years ago, and demand remains strong for well priced and structured floating rate leveraged loan assets in a low interest rate environment that offers few high-yielding investment alternatives.

More investors are now willing to offer capital to the asset class to develop a strategy and build diversified portfolios that reflect the economy and the ability to put leveraged loans in competition with other non investment-grade asset classes is positive for global managers.

# SUPPLEMENT 6: US INSTITUTIONAL LOAN PERFORMANCE: BIRTH, GROWTH, CRISIS, RECOVERY AND RECORDS

**Meredith Coffey**

*Executive Vice President for Research & Regulation, Loan Syndications and Trading Association*

Today, in 2019, the US institutional loan asset class is over 20 years old. During the past two decades, the market has grown, crashed, faced an existential crisis, recovered and flourished. The story begins in the mid-1990s, when the institutional loan market emerged as a small and idiosyncratic asset class, marked by low volumes, modest trading and little standardization. From 2000-2007, the institutional loan asset class grew rapidly, thanks to its stellar historical risk-adjusted performance, which married moderate returns to very low volatility. Then, in 2008, the loan market – indeed all markets – crashed. But for loans, which had billed themselves as a low-volatility, high Sharpe ratio alternative, the crash was nearly an existential crisis. Nonetheless, the market enjoyed a period of recovery in the ensuing years as investors took comfort in loan and CLO performance during and after the GFC. Ultimately, at the time of writing, the institutional loan market has grown to record levels, nearly doubling its pre-GFC size. But the question going forward is whether the characteristics that made loans so attractive – their low volatility and modest loss experience – will prevail through the next cycle.

## THE PRE-GFC LOAN MARKET: THE SALAD DAYS

In the years leading up to the GFC, US institutional term loans – those non-investment grade term loans structured to be sold to non-bank lenders like mutual funds, collateralized loan obligations (CLOs), insurance companies and hedge funds – enjoyed an enviable performance run.

First, the stability of these loans was remarkable. Being senior, secured, floating rate and generally callable at or around par, their secondary prices seldom fluctuated dramatically. In downturns, their senior and secured nature generally led to high recoveries if a company defaulted. In turn, loan prices seldom dropped as far as high yield bond prices. Conversely, because they were callable near par, their prices seldom climbed much above 100 cents on the dollar. And because they were floating rate, their prices didn't vary dramatically as interest rates moved. All told – and as exhibit 2.37 illustrates – prior to the GFC, this led to very stable prices in the secondary market, particularly relative to their high yield bond cousins.

**Exhibit 2.37: US Loan and HY Bond Index Returns, 1997-2017**

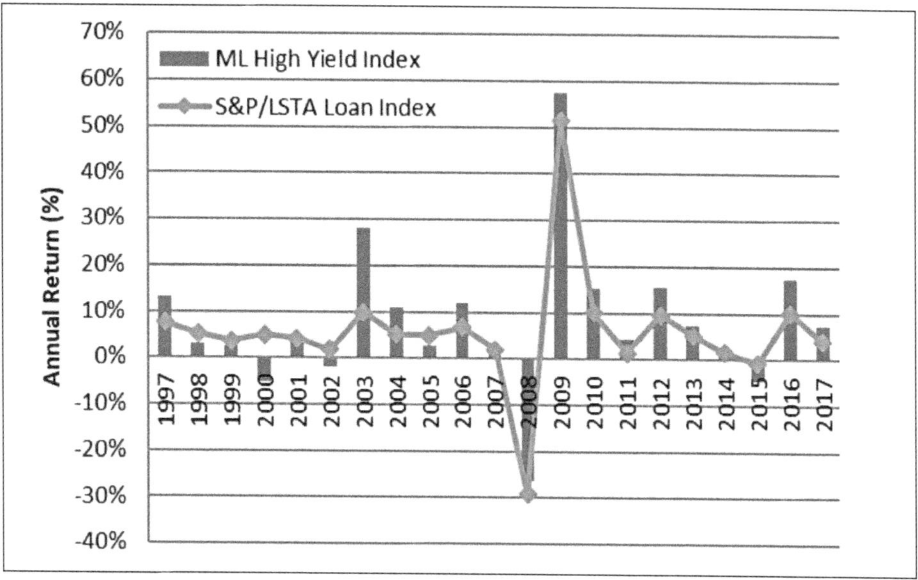


Source: S&P/Capital IQ/LCD, Merrill Lynch

While their price volatility was modest, loans offered respectable returns. Certainly those returns could fluctuate as LIBOR (and LIBOR margins) moved. However, as LIBOR spreads tended to climb when LIBOR fell, these trends often offset each other. Thus, as exhibit 2.37 demonstrates, loans offered more stable returns than high yield bonds; indeed in the decade from 1997 to 2007, loans did not have a single negative year. In contrast, high yield bond returns – though often higher – were much more variable.

**Exhibit 2.38: US Institutional Lending Volumes, 1997-2017**

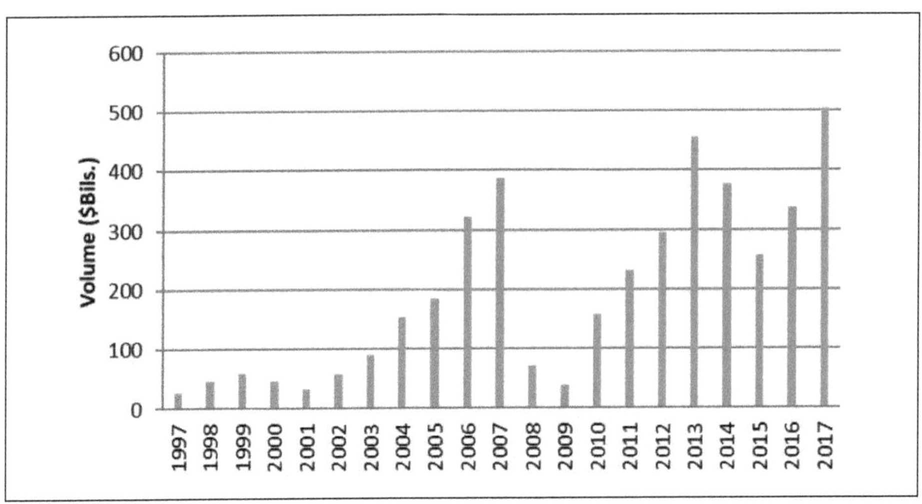


**Source: S&P/LCD**

Thanks to these solid yet stable returns, investors – primarily in the form of loan mutual funds and CLO investors – flocked to the institutional loan asset class, permitting it to grow rapidly. As exhibit 2.38 indicates, new issue institutional lending increased from less than $50bn per year in the late 1990s to more than $350bn in 2007. Thanks to more loans being structured for institutional investors, the overall size of the institutional loan market, as measured by outstandings in the S&P/LSTA Leveraged Loan Index, increased from less than $100bn in the early 2000s to nearly $600bn at its pre-Crisis peak (exhibit 2.39).

**Exhibit 2.39: S&P LSTA Leveraged Loan Index Size**

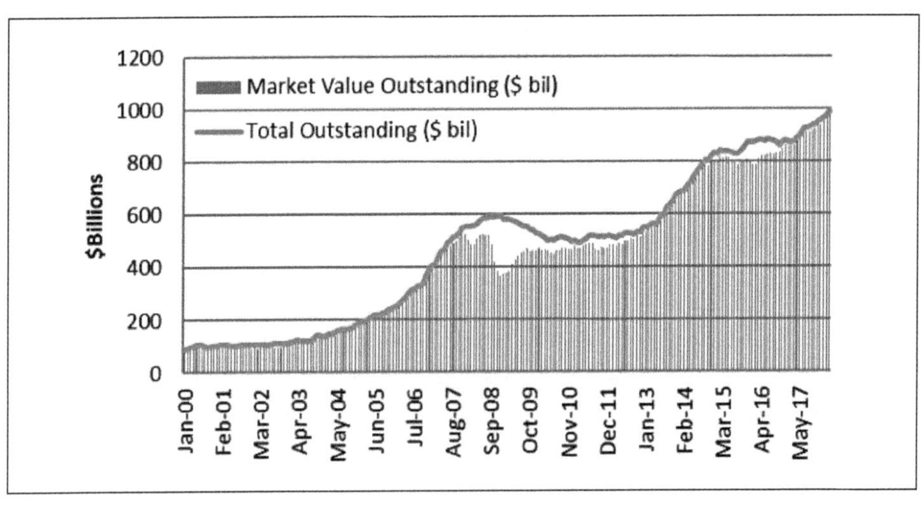


**Source: S&P/LSTA Leveraged Loan Index**

But unfortunately the loan market was swept up in the mania leading up to the GFC, with volumes climbing higher and spreads trending lower. When the music stopped, as Charles Prince famously said, suddenly, abruptly, loans stopped behaving like loans and started behaving like bonds.

# IN A FINANCIAL CRISIS, ALL CORRELATIONS GO TO ONE

The GFC appeared to turn the argument for 'moderate-return/low volatility' loans on its ear – at least initially. As the credit markets began to soften in 2007 and then crumble in early 2008, instead of simply edging down from par, US institutional loan prices slid almost in tandem with high yield bonds – an unprecedented event (see exhibit 2.40). In turn, investors began to question the historical investment thesis of loans. These loans certainly did not appear to be low correlation, low volatility assets.

**Exhibit 2.40: Loan and HY Bond Secondary Market Prices 2005-2017**

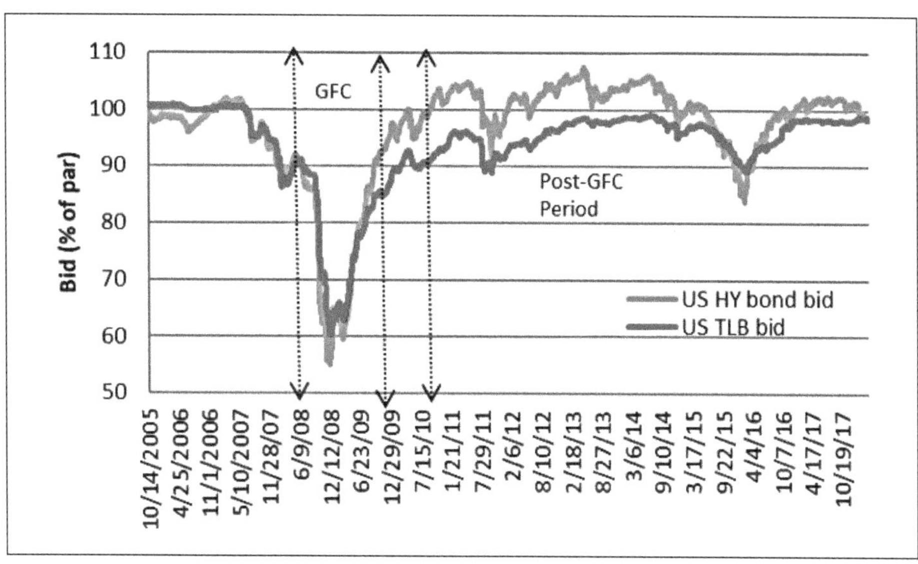


**Source: Thomson Reuters LPC, S&P/LSTA Leveraged Loan Index, BAML HY Bond Index**

There were two factors driving this sharp drop. First, there was the fact that banks were long and wrong, having underwritten – but not yet sold – billions of dollars of loans in the peak period leading up to the GFC. Second, loans were – at least partially – victims of their own historical success. Because institutional loans had exhibited such low price volatility historically, managers were comfortable applying leverage to (or borrowing money to invest in) loans. While this played out just fine for long-term, non-mark-to-market financing (like CLOs), it became problematic for the mark-to-market variety of leverage. In mark-to-market leverage, a manager could borrow money to invest in loans, but would have to provide additional margin if the value of the portfolio dropped too far. This had never been a problem before – loan prices had never dropped en masse before – but all loan prices began to decline in 2008. As loan prices dropped, margin calls were triggered. As margin calls were triggered, this forced managers to sell loans. As they sold loans, prices dropped further, triggering a new round of margin calls. A price spiral ensued, continuing until December 2008, when nearly all of the mark-to-market leverage was wrung out of the system. The average secondary loan price at that point was around 60. This was well below the loan market's previous low (about 88) and not far from HY bonds' bottom (55).

To be fair, this was a short-lived – albeit very severe – dislocation in almost every market. It was, after all, the GFC, the worst crisis since the Great Depression. After the leverage was wrung from the system – and the Central Banks pumped liquidity into the system – prices on both high yield bonds and leveraged loans rebounded rapidly (as exhibit 2.40 further illustrates).

But the statistical damage had been done. Not only was loans' record of only positive returns shattered, but with a *negative* 29% return, loans underperformed high yield bonds in 2008 (exhibit 2.37).

But while such levels of price volatility were new for loans, the fundamental nature of loans hadn't changed. Certainly, at more than 10%, the post-GFC default rate was higher than market participants expected (exhibit 2.41). However, recovery given default was true to historical form, averaging around 80 cents on the dollar. Investors took comfort from this experience, and the loan market began to recover again.

**Exhibit 2.41: US Institutional Loan Default Rates**

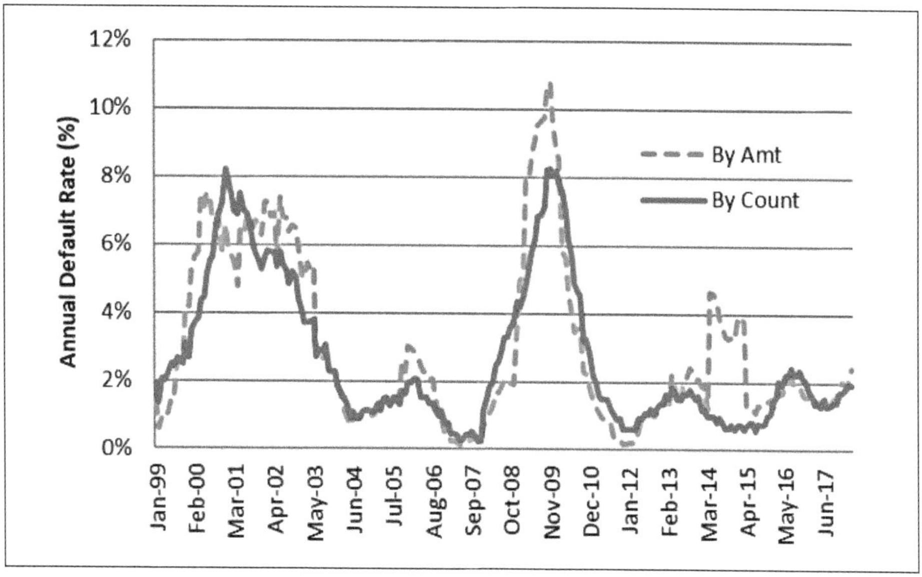

**Source: S&P/LCD**

# THE RECOVERING LOAN MARKET

After the loan market recovered in 2009 from its worst dislocation ever, market participants wondered whether investors would return to the loan market or whether the market would be destined to shrivel into insignificance. The answers, happily, appear to be 'yes' and 'no', respectively. To be fair, the new issue loan market did go on a two year hiatus. After seeing nearly $400bn in 2007, institutional lending fell below $100bn in 2008 and 2009 (exhibit 2.38). Likewise, the S&P/LSTA Leveraged Loan Index – having grown from $250bn to $600bn in just three years – shrank significantly. As exhibit 2.39 demonstrated, the face value of index outstandings dropped from nearly $600 bn at the end of 2008 to $500bn in 2010. But even as the face value of the index declined, its market value climbed from below $400bn in late 2008 to nearly $500bn by early 2011.

Moreover, after that two year hiatus, the institutional loan market began to grow again – with a vengeance. By 2013, institutional lending and the size of the Index had recovered to pre-GFC levels. And that was just the beginning.

Despite the volatility of the GFC period, investors that stayed the course enjoyed very solid performance and very modest actual losses. In addition, Central Banks around the world were cutting interest rates to de minimus levels and priming the pump through quantitative easing. Investors, flush with cash, looked for somewhere to put it to work. Many of them landed in the US institutional loan market.

**Exhibit 2.42: Cumulative CLO issuance, mutual fund flows (Jan-2011 to Dec-2017)**

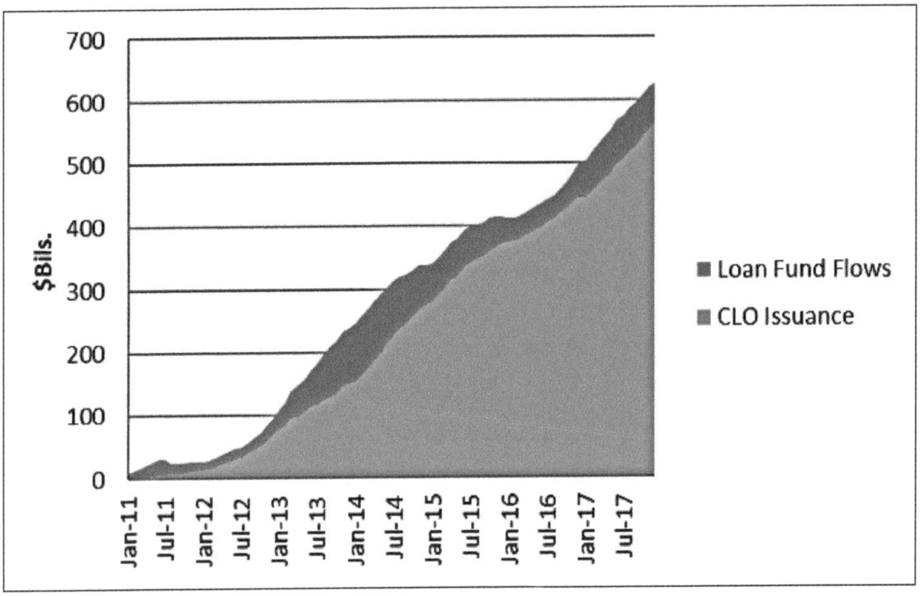

**Source: Thomson Reuters LPC**

In fact, between January 2011 and December 2017, more than $64bn flowed into loan mutual funds dedicated to syndicated loans. While impressive, these flows are dwarfed by the nearly $600bn of cumulative CLO issuance during that time (exhibit 2.42). But while impressive, these figures miss the less-easily measured demand from other sources like separately managed accounts (SMAs) as well as hedge funds and bond funds invested in loans. While CLOs hold roughly half of all outstanding loans and loan mutual funds hold roughly 15%, these other, more enigmatic investors hold another 35% of outstandings, exhibit 2.43.

**Exhibit 2.43: US Institutional Loan Investor Base (Dec. 2017)**

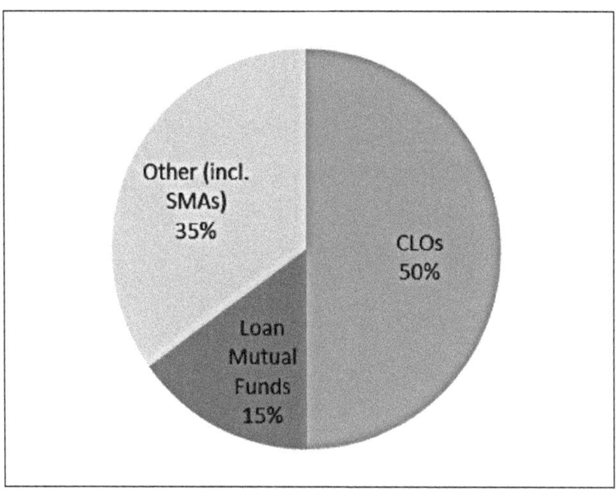


Source: Thomson Reuters LPC

The acceleration of growth in the loan market was counterpointed by a deceleration – and then shrinkage – in the HY bond universe. As exhibit 2.44 demonstrates, the size of the S&P/LSTA Leveraged Loan Index and the BAML HY bond index have increasingly converged. At $1.26trn, the high yield bond universe is less than $300bn larger than the $1trn loan universe.

**Exhibit 2.44: Outstandings in US HY Bond and Loan Indices**

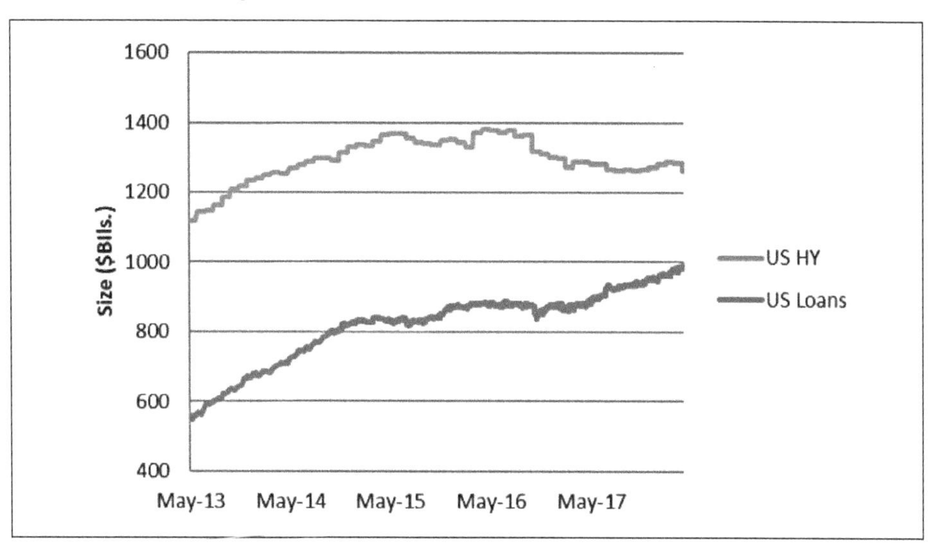


Source: S&P/LCD, Bank of America Merrill Lynch

# KEY LOAN MARKET CHARACTERISTICS

So what are the characteristics of this larger, more mature institutional loan market? It has been marked by spreads that have trended lower, 'coupons' that have been more stable and default rates that have been – at least through early 2018 – benign. But perhaps the most dramatic change in the institutional loan market comes from changing covenants and documentation. As a result, the open question is whether the structural developments in the loan market ultimately will affect their value proposition.

## Loan Yields

#### Exhibit 2.45: TLB Spreads: New Issue vs. Outstanding Loans

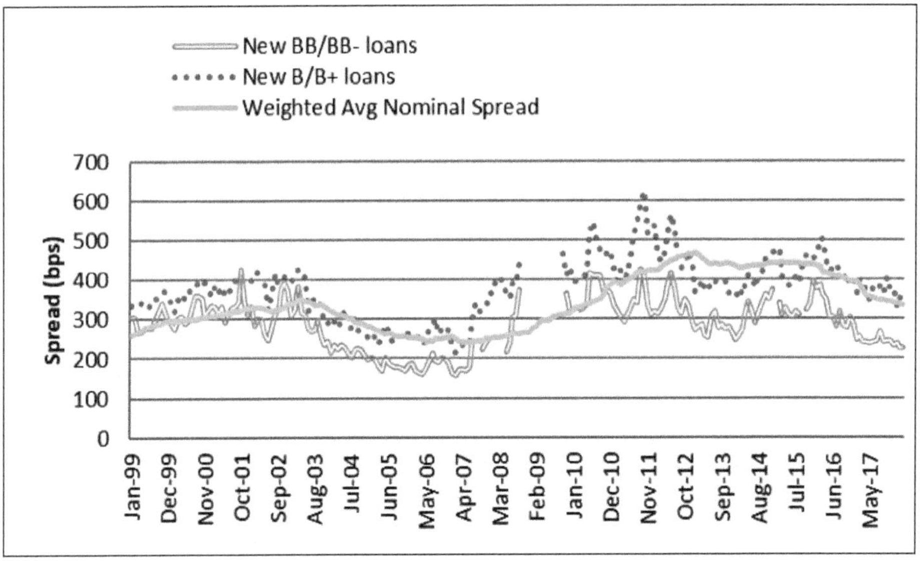

Source: S&P/LCD

Exhibit 2.45 begins the value discussion by considering how institutional loan spreads have evolved during their 20-year life. The pre-GFC period saw loan spreads compressing materially as new investors entered the market. During the GFC, new lending ground to a halt. And, unsurprisingly, once the new issue market reopened after the GFC, loan spreads were exceedingly high. Indeed, the average B+/B rated institutional loan spread topped 600 bps in 2011, while spreads on BB/BB- rated loans touched 400 bps periodically in 2010, 2011 and 2012. New issue loan spreads then dropped quickly, sliding below 400 bps and 300 bps, respectively, by mid-2013. However, as the energy and commodities sector began to soften in 2015, so did the loan market – even though the two sectors combined accounted less than 7% of outstanding loans. By early 2016, BB/BB- loan spreads were again approaching LIB+400 and B+/B loan spreads had again topped LIB+500. But as the commodities and energy pain was contained and default rates generally remained modest (exhibit 2.41), investors piled back into the loan market. In turn, loan spreads again compressed. By early 2018, BB/BB- loan spreads were around LIB+200, while B+/B loan spreads were in the LIB+350 context.

### Exhibit 2.46: Spreads vs. Yields on Outstanding Institutional Term Loans

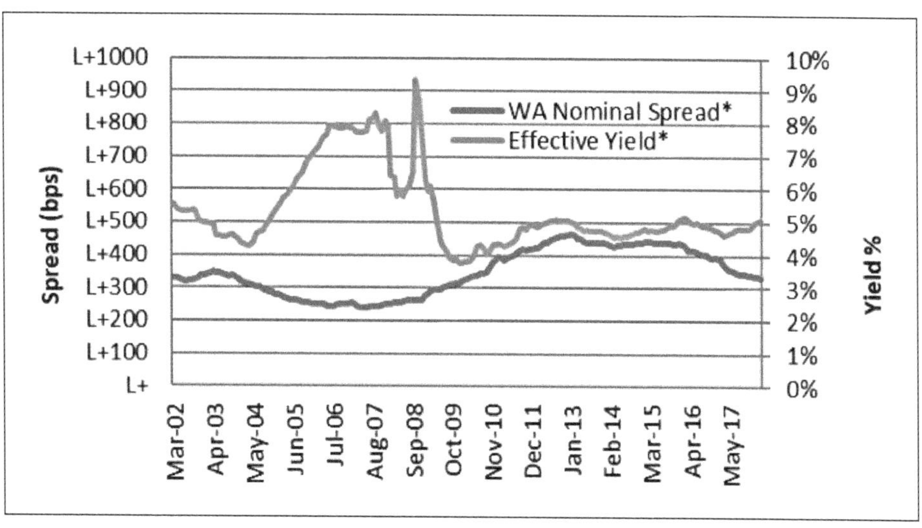


Source: S&P/LSTA Leveraged Loan Index

But while new issue loan spreads gyrated, the yield on loans moved far less. This is demonstrated on both exhibit 2.45 and 2.46. First, new issue spreads are just the 'marginal' spread in a loan portfolio or loan index. While new issue spreads can move quickly, they pull the average spread on the one-thousand-plus loans in the S&P/LSTA Loan Index far more slowly. This is illustrated in exhibit 2.45 where the weighted average nominal spread is less volatile and lags changes in the new issue spread. This lag stabilizes loan portfolio returns. Second, the behavior of LIBOR itself very much impacts the yield on a loan portfolio. This is demonstrated in exhibit 2.46, which compares the weighted average nominal spread to the S&P/LSTA Loan Index's Effective Yield. As the Effective Yield includes LIBOR (or a LIBOR floor), it can behave very differently from the loan spreads. For instance, in the GFC, LIBOR spiked, driving up the Effective Yield, even as the Weighted Average Nominal Spread barely moved. Similarly, since late 2011, the Index's Effective Yield has sat in the 5% context, while spreads rose and fell. Importantly, even as loan spreads have compressed sharply in 2017 and early 2018, rising LIBOR has more than compensated – and the yield on the Index actually increased.

## Credit Considerations

After the loan market recovered from the GFC, loan default rates remained benign – for the most part. Exhibit 2.41 compares loan default rates by dollar volume and by count. Though the default rate by volume jumped above 4% in 2014 – due primarily to the default of Energy Futures Holding, a 2007 mega-LBO in the energy space – the default rate by count averaged 1.3% between 2012 and early 2018. In addition, post-GFC recovery given default averaged roughly 76%. Combined this meant that experienced loan loss rates were below 1%.

Though they are excellent for returns, low default/loss rates married to strong investor appetite do not necessarily bode well for maintaining conservative loan structures. And, indeed, the post-GFC period may be chiefly characterized by evolving loan structures and documentation.

The first major change in post-GFC loans was the excision of maintenance covenants. As their name suggests, maintenance covenants require a borrower to maintain certain financial levels, such as a debt to EBITDA ratio of less than 5:1 or an interest coverage ratio of more than 1.5:1. These maintenance covenants have long been a feature of the leveraged loan market. However in the GFC, many borrowers violated their covenants and, in the process of securing covenant waivers, saw the spread on their loans repriced (way) up to market levels. After the GFC, many borrowers – particularly sponsored borrowers – looked to do new deals without maintenance covenants. As this generally was not a huge sticking point with institutional lenders, the market shifted quickly to a 'covenant lite' structure.

**Exhibit 2.47: Number of Maintenance Covenants in Institutional Term Loans**

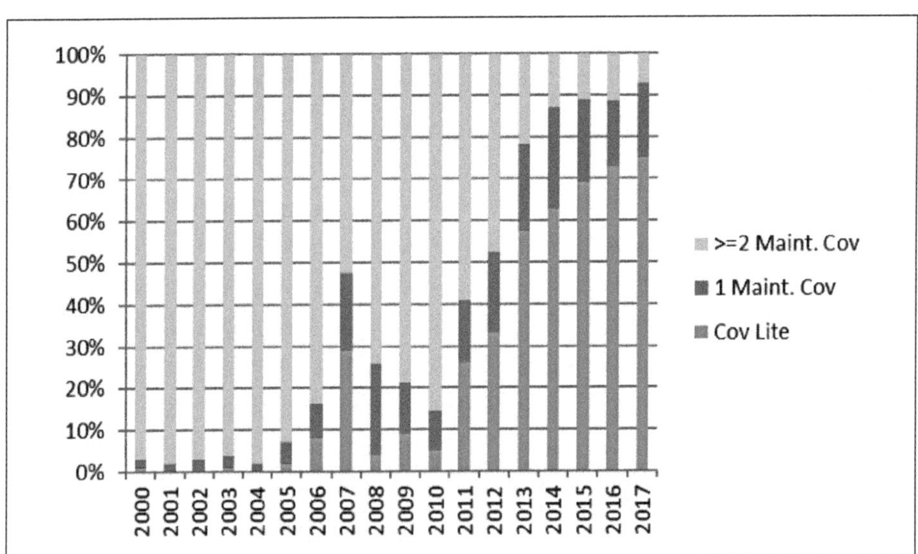


**Source: S&P/LCD**

As exhibit 2.47 illustrates, through 2010, most institutional term loans had two (or more) maintenance covenants. However, starting in 2011, an increasing number of institutional loans were 'covenant lite', e.g., they had incurrence covenants, but not maintenance covenants. By 2015, roughly 70% of institutional loans were covenant lite. Moreover, most of the remaining loans had just one maintenance covenant.

Though sorry to lose the opportunity to reprice a deteriorating loan, most institutional lenders did not see maintenance covenants as critical to loan loss rates. As a result, they did not vociferously protest the rise of covenant lite loans. However, they became more concerned about i) rising leverage, ii) shrinking subordination and iii) loosening documents.

**Exhibit 2.48: Average Debt Multiples of Large Corporate Leveraged Loans**

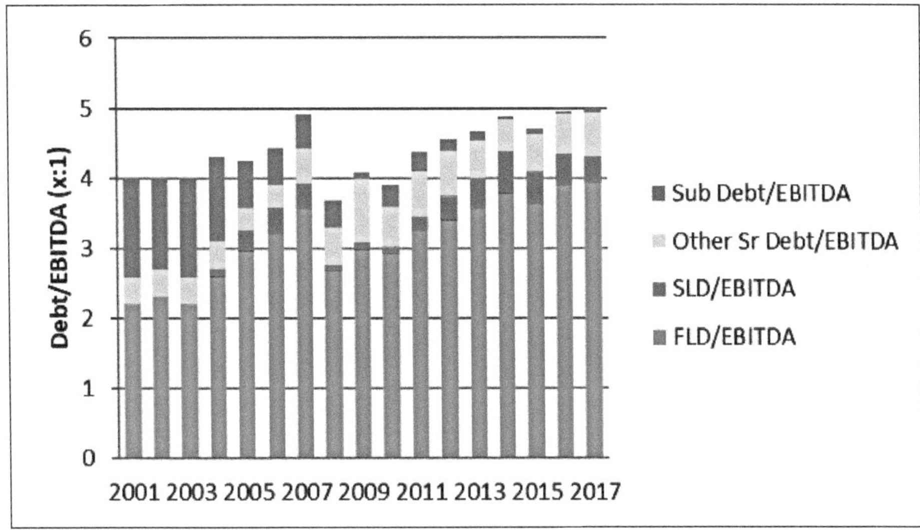


**Source: S&P/LCD**

Exhibit 2.48 shows the average debt multiples of new large corporate leveraged loans from 2001 through 2017. Leverage levels climbed through 2007, declined sharply during and after the GFC, and then rose fairly steadily from 2011 through 2017. By the end of 2017, the average debt/EBITDA multiple of a new large corporate leveraged loan was roughly where it was in 2007. But there were two differences. First, as exhibit 2.48 also demonstrates, senior leverage was higher and there was practically no subordinated debt in 2017's capital structures. Because loans were cheaper and prepayable, many corporate borrowers chose to utilize more first lien/second lien loan capital structures. While this brought more investible debt to the loan market, subordinated debt cushion typically helps the recovery given default of senior, secured first-lien loans. As subordinated debt erodes, this could potentially lead to lower recoveries in the future.

The other major change in loan structures post crisis is that, thanks to EBITDA adjustments and incremental facility capacity, it can be difficult to determine exactly how leveraged a company actually is. Exhibit 2.49 attempts to tease out this relationship by considering the financials of fourth quarter 2017 institutional loans. The left hand bars reflect leverage multiples based on **reported** financials of the companies – in other words before any EBITDA adjustments are made. The bars on the right look at exactly the same companies and leverage multiples, but base them off the companies' **adjusted** EBITDA figures – in other words, after adjustments for items such as synergies.

**Exhibit 2.49: Loan Structure: Accordions and EBITDA Adjustments Make Metrics Fuzzier in 2017**

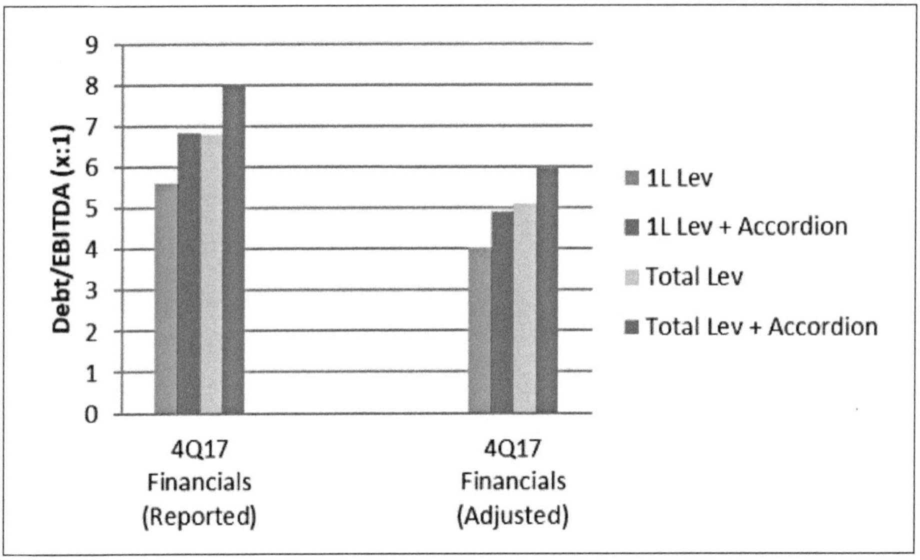

**Source: Covenant Review**

The adjusted EBITDA figures are the ones that are typically reported in the press and used for tests, so we begin with those. The adjusted first lien leverage on fourth quarter 2017 companies was a modest 4.05x. However, add in the incremental debt that the company is permitted to issue, and first lien leverage would climb to 4.92x. All told, the companies' initial total leverage was 5.09x. But again, add in incremental debt the company could take on and total leverage climbs to 5.96x. So, the incremental loan facility itself adds one turn of leverage to these companies – if the borrowers choose to utilize the incremental capacity.

Of course, these leverage multiples are meaningful only if one accepts the validity of all the EBITDA adjustments from the company. If one chooses to use 'reported' EBITDA – e.g., excluding the adjustments – leverage is significantly higher. Looking at reported EBITDA, the fourth quarter companies' first lien leverage climbs from 4.05x to 5.6x. Add in the accordion, which permits the company to issue incremental debt, and the first lien leverage increases to 6.84x. Total leverage is 6.81x, and total leverage including incremental capacity tops 8x.

Clearly there is a material swing from total starting leverage of 5.09x using adjusted EBITDA and assuming no incremental usage to 8.03x using unadjusted EBITDA and assuming accordion usage. Lenders point to this change as one that could affect default rates and recoveries– and thus something that could affect the value proposition of institutional term loans. Counterbalanced against that less-than-ideal trend is the fact that the companies in the loan market in 2017 and 2018 typically are very solid companies with track records of performance. In order for higher loss rates to materialize, these strong and well-performing companies would need to deteriorate materially and ultimately default. The key questions going forward are i) whether these strong companies will be able to avoid default and ii) if they default, how they will behave. That outcome has yet to be determined.

## WHAT DOESN'T KILL YOU MAKES YOU STRONGER?

The experience of the GFC was harrowing in every asset class. Uncharacteristically, it was also nerve-wracking in the loan market. But despite unprecedented – and hopefully unrepeatable – price volatility, ultimate loan performance remained within historical norms. As the loan market recovered, borrowers drew the lesson that they needed greater flexibility and optionality in their loans. Lenders were grudgingly willing to accept looser documents and more flexibility. Whether borrowers use this flexibility to better navigate downturns or to capture value for themselves will determine whether loans continue to fulfill their promise of moderate returns tied to low losses. The next down cycle will tell.

# SUPPLEMENT 7: EXPLAINING LOAN AND RECOVERY RATINGS

**Cameron Andrews**

*Director, Product Management, EMEA, Standard and Poor's*

**Chris Porter**

*Head of Loan, Recovery and CLO Business Development, EMEA, Standard and Poor's*

## INTRODUCTION

S&P Global Ratings began rating loans at the beginning of 1996. Since then there has been consistent growth in ratings assigned across both the investment-grade and leveraged space, most notably in the latter with coverage consistently being above 80% of the market.

There are several reasons for the growth in syndicated loan ratings that centre on the continuous evolution of financial markets as well as the development of the loan rating product itself. Europe has long had a competitive loan market, with banks' regulatory capital requirements providing for higher risk-adjusted returns where they can generate upfront fees by arranging transactions and distributing the risk rather than participating in loans and using their balance sheets. Operating alongside, but with quite different business models and return requirements to the banks, have been institutional investors (such as collateralised loan obligation (CLO) vehicles as well as 'managed accounts' (typically money given by insurance companies and pension funds to fund managers to place on their behalf)). With a fragmented market, the CLO bid has never dominated the European leveraged loan market in the same way as in the US where their market share peaked at 80% to 85% in mid-2007, however CLO money is a significant part of the sponsor-driven syndicated loan market in Europe. Meanwhile, until the liquidity crunch hit in 2007, the highly competitive nature of the European bank market translated into increasingly borrower-friendly terms and conditions for loan funding.

However, irrespective of this history of change; including the degree to which various loan market segments have disintermediated the banks' traditional lending function and the current volatility in the market, corporate credit and loan ratings continue to play a valuable role in supplementing lenders' existing credit processes. By establishing independent benchmarks for credit quality and providing detailed analytical reports, ratings increase the transparency of information and support risk management of portfolios and the secondary market liquidity that participants require.

# RATING DEFINITIONS AND RATING SCALE

A long-term issuer credit rating (ICR) is an opinion of an obligor's overall capacity and willingness to meet its financial commitments when due. The issuer credit rating is the anchor for any associated long-term issue ratings of the company. A separate short-term scale is provided for obligations considered short-term in the relevant market, typically with maturities of less than 365 days.

A long-term *issue* credit rating is a current opinion of the credit risk pertaining to a specific financial obligation. Particular features such as position in the capital structure of the obligor, security, covenants, guarantees and other forms of credit enhancement are considered to see if the rating on the debt instrument should be higher, lower, or the same as the issuer credit rating.

For many years S&P Global Ratings has been undertaking a fundamental, scenario-based analysis of post-default recovery prospects for specific debt instruments, mainly for speculative-grade companies. The recovery ratings (see 'Introduction to loan and recovery ratings' below) assigned to these debt issues form the basis for notching the long-term issue rating relative to the issuer rating. Some of the differences and considerations between issuer and issue ratings are discussed in greater detail below. The traditional long- and short-term rating symbols used for issuer and issue ratings are set out in exhibit 2.50.

S&P Global Ratings' glossary explains (in relation to the long-term ratings) that:

### Investment grade

Companies rated 'AAA' to 'BBB-' by S&P Global Ratings are considered investment grade, that is, their ability to honor financial obligations ranges from highest to adequate.

### Speculative grade

Companies rated 'BB+' to 'CCC-' by S&P Global Ratings are considered speculative grade, meaning they exhibit vulnerability to default.

However, while investors may use credit ratings in making investment decisions, ratings by S&P Global Ratings are NOT indications of investment merit. In other words, the ratings are not buy, sell, or hold recommendations, or a measure of asset value. Nor are they intended to signal the suitability of an investment. They speak to one aspect of an investment decision—credit quality—which, in some cases, may include our view of what investors can expect to recover in the event of default. In evaluating an investment, investors should consider, in addition to credit quality, the current make-up of their portfolios, their investment strategy and time horizon, their tolerance for risk, and an estimation of the security's relative value in comparison to other securities they might choose.

**Exhibit 2.50: Symbols used in short term and long term rating**

| Short term rating | Long term rating |
|---|---|
| A-1+ | AAA |
| | AA+ |
| | AA |
| | AA- |
| A-1 | A+ |
| | A |
| A-2 | A- |
| | BBB+ |
| A-3 | BBB |
| | BBB- |
| B | BB+ |
| | BB |
| | BB- |
| | B+ |
| | B |
| | B- |
| C | CCC+ |
| | CCC |
| | CCC- |
| | CC |
| D | CC |
| | SD |
| | D |

**Source: S&P Global Ratings**

# METHODS OF DISTRIBUTION

S&P Global Ratings issues ratings for use in many different markets. To meet the varying needs of participants the ratings distribution process may also differ.

## Public, private & confidential ratings

S&P Global Ratings standard ratings distribution is public, available to any interested party via S&P Capital IQ (S&P Global Market Intelligence's portal), our website, www.capitaliq.com, and various news media. Ratings that issuers wish to disclose on a confidential basis to a limited number of third parties are called private ratings. Third parties authorised by the issuer are able to access a private rating and related reports on a dedicated password-protected Web site. S&P Global Ratings does not allow issuers to have a mix of private and public ratings. So, if a privately rated issuer chooses to issue publicly rateable debt, all ratings must be public.

Private ratings differ from public ratings only in their form of distribution. While public ratings are widely disseminated, prior to dissemination the issuer may request its initial counterparty rating, and ratings on private debt facilities, to be distributed as a private rating via a third-party private document exchange to a limited number of third parties identified by the issuer (currently limited to 75).

Private ratings are available to issuers with less than €750m (for Europe, Middle East, and Africa) or $1bn (for the Americas, Asia and Pacific regions) of combined privately rated debt. If there is a bond component in the capital structure (excluding US Private Placements), private ratings are generally not available.

Third parties interested in viewing a private rating must contact the issuer and ask to be added to the document exchange's list of approved third-party recipients of the private rating. Once approved by the issuer, and subject to having agreed to certain terms and conditions with S&P Global Ratings, third parties can access, via the document exchange, the private rating and any related research or updates. Issuers that request private ratings cannot disclose any information to interested third parties outside of the document exchange process.

Where there is no distribution of a rating required, for example, if a company wishes to have an independent benchmark for its own internal management process, S&P Global Ratings may also assign a confidential rating at the issuer's request. These are communicated directly to the issuer and are typically provided as issuer-level ratings only.

## Preliminary Ratings

Under certain circumstances, it may also be appropriate to provide an initial credit rating on a preliminary basis. Preliminary ratings are rating opinions that may be assigned to issuers or issued obligations in the following circumstances:

- where a previously unrated issuer is undergoing a well-formulated, significant financing, restructuring, recapitalisation or other transformative event, generally at the point that investor or lender commitments are invited. The preliminary rating may be assigned to the issuer and to its proposed obligation(s). These preliminary ratings consider the anticipated general credit quality of the issuer, as well as attributes of the anticipated obligation(s), assuming successful completion of the transformative event. Should the transformative event not occur within a 90 day period, S&P Global Ratings would likely withdraw these preliminary ratings;
- where an issuer is being formed or is in the process of being independently established when, in S&P Global Ratings' opinion, documentation is close to final. Preliminary ratings may also be assigned to the issuer's obligations;
- where the issuer emerges from bankruptcy or similar reorganisation, based on late-stage reorganisation plans, documentation and discussions with the issuer. Preliminary ratings may also be assigned to the obligations that the issuer will likely issue. These ratings consider the anticipated general credit quality of the reorganised or post-bankruptcy issuer as well as attributes of the anticipated obligation(s).

A preliminary recovery rating (see 'Introduction to loan and recovery ratings', below) may also be assigned to an obligation that has a preliminary issue rating. Preliminary ratings are disseminated to investors through our usual distribution process for ratings–via both public and private channels.

# THE RATING PROCESS

The entire rating process, illustrated in exhibit 2.51, typically takes between four and six weeks to complete from the initial rating request. However, where necessary, S&P Global Ratings will make every effort to meet a desired timetable.

The following describes the key stages in the process of assigning an ICR.

**Exhibit 2.51: The rating process, sequence**

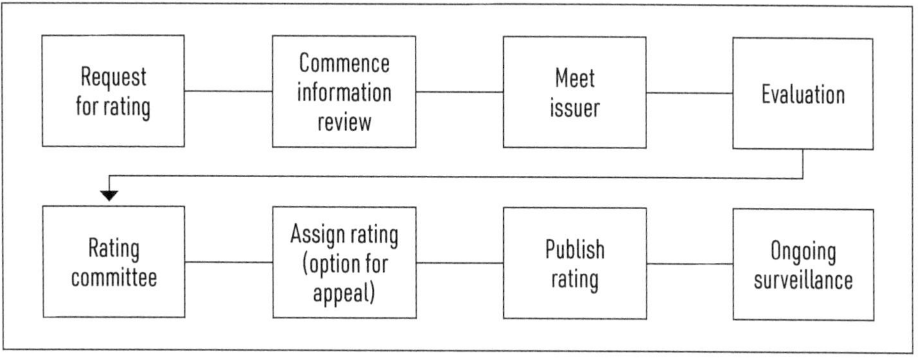


**Source: S&P Global Ratings**

## Rating request

When an organisation first requests a rating, an S&P Global Ratings analyst in that company's sector is assigned to lead the rating team, and schedules a meeting with management. Coordinating diaries to schedule the management meeting at an early stage is critical if the timetable is tight. (For industrial corporations, the sectors are divided into teams, for example, such as consumer products, telecoms, technology or media and leisure.) Several weeks in advance of the meeting, the company will be expected to provide the following information:

- three years of audited annual financial statements;
- the last several interim financial statements;
- narrative descriptions of operations and products;
- if available, a draft registration statement, offering memorandum, or equivalent;
- any other documentation that analysts deem pertinent to a particular rating determination.

Where a loan rating is requested, typical documentation required would include the information memorandum, loan agreements, financial model, details of security package (including legal opinions) and, where appropriate, any intercreditor agreement.

## Management meeting

Typically, a week or two after S&P Global Ratings' analytical team has had an opportunity to review the materials and has identified the key analytical issues to be addressed, the team meets with senior management (usually the CFO and operating executives and sometimes the CEO). They review historical results, of course, but the focus is on the company's future prospects. A meeting with a new issuer typically lasts two to four hours or longer if the company's operations are particularly complex and addresses issues such as:

- industry environment and prospects;
- major business segment review and outlook, including operating statistics and comparisons with competitors and industry norms;
- management's financial policies and performance goals;
- distinctive accounting practices;
- management's projections, including income and cash flow statements and balance sheets, together with the underlying market and operating assumptions;
- capital spending plans;
- financing alternatives and contingency plans.

Management's financial projections are a valuable tool in the rating process because they reflect management's plans, highlight the major challenges, and provide a roadmap for achieving key objectives. Management projections also incorporate the company's financial strategy in terms of anticipated reliance on internal cash flow or outside funds, and help to articulate financial objectives and policies. All that being said, it should be understood that our ratings are not based on management's financial projections or management's view of what the future may hold. Rather, our ratings are based on our own assessment of the firm's prospects. Comparing the company's projections with our analysts' own independent views of the company's and industry's prospects also helps us to evaluate whether its management style is conservative, realistic, or aggressive.

## S&P Global Ratings evaluation

Once S&P Global Ratings has held the management meeting, the lead analyst reviews and analyses the information obtained in accordance with our ratings criteria, both quantitatively and qualitatively, in terms of business risks, such as growth and cyclicality; those risks peculiar to the company's industry and competitive position within that industry; and the quality of the company's management and accounting. Profitability is now considered as part of the business risk analysis and provides a good sanity check on the company's financial health and competitive position. Then the company's financial risks are considered: its characteristics, policies, capital structure, cash flow and asset protection, financial flexibility, and, importantly, liquidity. This review and analysis process usually takes a couple of weeks and culminates in the Rating Committee Meeting.

## Rating committee

A rating by S&P Global Ratings is never assigned by just one analyst. All our ratings are determined by a committee of experienced analysts. The rating committee, typically comprising five experienced members, including the primary analyst, is convened, and the committee discusses the lead analyst's recommendations and the facts and expectations supporting the rating in relation to our criteria and methodologies. Finally, the voting members of the committee vote on the recommendation.

## The appeal period

The issuer subsequently is notified of the rating and the major considerations supporting it. A rating can be appealed prior to its publication–if meaningful new or additional information is to be presented by the issuer. Obviously, there is no guarantee that the new information will alter the rating committee's decision. Once a final rating is assigned, after the issuer has had the opportunity to review for factual errors or any inadvertent disclosure of confidential information, it is disseminated together with the research, on a public or private basis (see 'Methods of distribution').

An important point to emphasise is that, while confidential information provided by the company is integral to the rating assessment, non-public or commercially sensitive information is not disclosed directly in any of the analysis that is subsequently published.

## Surveillance and review are ongoing

The rating process does not end when the rating and outlook are assigned–it is ongoing. Through regular dialogue with management, S&P Global Ratings maintains surveillance on all the companies it rates. If there is a specific event that S&P Global Ratings perceives might have an effect on the rating, we review it immediately, and either make an announcement that the rating or its outlook is being changed or the rating placed on CreditWatch or release a bulletin stating that we see no reason to change the rating. Absent material financial events, issuer ratings are reviewed regularly and updated as necessary.

## Outlooks and CreditWatch listings

Rating outlooks and CreditWatch listings address the possibility that future performance can vary from initial expectations by focusing on the scenarios that can cause a rating change. Ratings appear on CreditWatch when events or developing trends create a significant likelihood (roughly 50% or more) that a rating change is required. Generally, if feasible we seek to complete CreditWatch reviews within 90 days. A CreditWatch may have positive, negative, or developing implications.

In the absence of a CreditWatch listing, a rating outlook is assigned to all long-term debt issuers and assesses the potential for an issuer rating change. Outlooks have a longer time frame than CreditWatch listings–typically two years for investment-grade entities, and one year for speculative grade entities–and incorporate trends or risks with less certain implications for credit quality.

# INTRODUCTION TO LOAN AND RECOVERY RATINGS

Following the introduction of the recovery rating scale in December 2003, S&P Global Ratings started to assign recovery ratings to secured corporate debt issues including loans. Recovery ratings were extended to unsecured debt issues for speculative-grade corporate entities in March 2008. The scale is independent from S&P Global Ratings' long-term issuer credit rating scale that focuses on the likelihood of default in timely payment. Instead, recovery ratings estimate the likely recovery of principal plus interest in the event of default. S&P Global Ratings' recovery ratings utilise a numerical scale with 1+, the highest rating, denoting the likelihood that an issue will fully recover principal plus accrued interest in the event of default. Ratings below that level, 1 through 6, denote varying levels of expected recovery, of principal plus interest from just below 100% down to negligible recovery levels, in 5% increments, e.g., a two (75%) or a three (65%). The recovery ratings scale is set out in exhibit 2.52.

Where recovery ratings are assigned, the foundation for the associated issue rating is the issuer credit rating but it is adjusted to reflect the specific issue's recovery expectations relative to the long-term average recovery rate for unsecured debt. If we can confidently project recovery prospects exceeding 70% for an individual debt obligation, that issue is typically 'notched up' or rated higher than the issuer rating; conversely, if we project recovery for a given security to be under 30%, the issue is typically 'notched down' or rated lower than the issuer rating.

**Exhibit 2.52: Recovery Rating Scale and Issue Rating Criteria**

| Issue Rating Notches v ICR* | S&P Global Ratings Recovery Rating** | | Recovery Expectations |
|---|---|---|---|
| +3 notches | 1+ | Highest expectation of full recovery*** | 100% |
| +2 notches | 1 | **Very high** recovery | 95%<br>90% |
| +1 notch | 2 | **Substantial** recovery | 85%<br>80%<br>75%<br>70% |
| 0 notches | 3 | **Meaningful** recovery | 65%<br>60%<br>55%<br>50% |
| 0 notches | 4 | **Average** recovery | 45%<br>40%<br>35%<br>30% |
| -1 notch | 5 | **Modest** recovery | 25%<br>20%<br>15%<br>10% |
| -2 notches | 6 | **Negligible** recovery of principal | 5%<br>0% |

* ICR = Issuer Credit Rating.

** Recovery of principal plus accrued but unpaid interest at the time of default.

*** Very high confidence of full recovery resulting from significant overcollateralisation or strong structural features.

**Source: S&P Global Ratings**

# RECOVERY RATING METHODOLOGY

At the outset, let us be clear what the recovery rating analysis is trying to determine. Essentially, a recovery rating provides S&P Global Ratings' opinion on the estimated recovery potential for a tranche of debt based on a fundamental, scenario-based analysis of what may cause a company to default on their debt at some point in the future and an assessment of the residual value that might be available to repay creditors at that time. In Europe, as our recovery analysis is mainly undertaken for sub-investment-grade corporations, the typical default horizon is assumed to be between two and five years.

In summary, the analytical process consists of the following steps:

- Review of the borrower's projections.
- Establishing a simulated default path.
- Forecasting the borrower's free cash flow at default, based on our simulated default scenario and default proxy.
- Determining whether the company would be liquidated or sold as a going concern.
- Identifying priority debt claims and value.
- Reviewing the transaction structure and jurisdiction issues.
- Determining the distribution of value to claimants.
- Assigning the recovery rating and conveying the recovery analytics to the issuer and investment community.

## Review of the borrower's projections

The preparatory work is to deconstruct the borrower's cash flow projections by understanding management's business, industry, and economic expectations through the period when the debt instrument will be outstanding. Once we understand the management's perspective, we make any adjustments to future cash flows that we believe are appropriate.

## Establish simulated path to default

Having deconstructed management's cash flow projections, we then identify the economic, industry, and firm-specific factors that would primarily contribute to the borrower's payment default. While there could be many possible foreseen and unforeseen factors contributing to a default scenario, we believe that most contribute to default only at the margin. Frequently, only a few key operating factors meaningfully contribute to default.

The simulated default scenario is our assessment of the borrower's most likely path to a payment default, typically at a point in the future when funds available plus free cash flow are insufficient to pay fixed charges.

## Forecasting cash flow at default

During this step, we attempt to quantify the effect of each factor in the simulated path to default. This analytical step is crucial in estimating the residual value and determining the recovery rating; because here we simulate default-level EBITDA and the free cash flow that underpins our going-concern distressed valuation of the enterprise.

In this analysis, we are not suggesting that such adverse events will occur, or are even suggesting that if a specific factor does occur, that we know the exact effect on the borrower's cash flow. Rather, our analysis attempts to understand the most likely effect on a given borrower if a specific factor does occur. Our simulated default scenario also includes non-operating model assumptions, such as rising interest rates and management's projected uses of cash flow, which we evaluate and include on a conservative basis.

## Determining valuation

We utilise a variety of valuation methodologies, including: discrete asset analysis, transaction multiple, and discounted cash flow (DCF) analysis. We use discrete asset valuation most often when our simulated default scenario indicates that the borrower's liquidation is the most likely outcome of insolvency, or when we believe that recovery depends on the value of specific assets, rather than on the borrower's enterprise value.

We use a combination of transaction multiple and a DCF valuation analysis when our simulated default scenario indicates that the borrower's reorganisation is the most likely outcome.

## Identifying priority debt claims and recovery value

After establishing the borrower's emergence, enterprise or residual value, whether through valuing the firm's cash flow or discrete assets, we then identify liabilities that we expect would be priority claims; that is, claims that we assume must be satisfied before each relevant class of creditors. Claims that we consider to be potential priority debt include:

- Super-priority administrative claims associated with the bankruptcy, such as professional fees.
- Tax claims.

- Mortgage debt.
- Certain financial contracts, such as swap agreements.
- Rejected operating lease claims relative to general unsecured creditors.
- Securitisation liabilities only to the extent that the securitised assets are the borrower's future cash flows, such as future royalties.
- Third-party debt instruments at subsidiaries that are clearly structurally senior to the debt.

## Review transaction structure

After determining the residual value and the relevant priority claims, the next step is to determine the distribution of that value. We first identify the basics, including borrowers, guarantors, commitment amount, tenor, and scheduled amortisation of outstanding debt. We then consider the effect of covenants, intercreditor issues, corporate and capital structures, and the bankruptcy process in the jurisdiction governing borrowers and guarantors. Once these structural details are identified, we then estimate the potential value of each debt instrument's collateral.

Many senior secured obligations limit collateral to specific assets such as accounts receivable, inventory, or specific components of property or equipment. Limitations on pledged collateral do not affect the future value of cash flows used to derive the enterprise value. However, such limitations will diminish recovery values available to the senior secured claimants, relative to a pledge of all assets. It is likely that other claimant classes will benefit from the value of assets not securing the senior secured lenders. Debt instruments that have specific collateral limitations require us to focus our analysis on the value of those discrete assets.

Many other senior secured debt instruments are secured by a pledge of all assets and, by implication, the underlying cash flows generated by the borrower. Other transactions limit collateral to only the stock pledge of subsidiaries. Our review of this collateral is borrower-specific and reflects the simulated default scenario.

## Review jurisdiction issues/legal considerations

Access to collateral and the timing of its realisation depend on how a particular legal regime resolves bankruptcies. Creditor rights vary greatly, depending on the legal jurisdiction. Although there is still somewhat limited empirical bankruptcy and post-default recovery data available publicly in Europe, S&P Global Ratings evaluates and publishes reports on the security and insolvency regimes of the key European jurisdictions.

The key question is whether the creditor will actually benefit from having collateral, by receiving the value of the security. In some jurisdictions court procedures that may impair security rights also require consideration, such as:

- Whether commercial benefit hurdles limit access to security that can severely restrict enforceability of upstream and cross-stream guarantees.
- The extent to which the courts set aside security provided during 'hardening' or 'preference' periods.
- The strength of the rights and protections available to secured creditors when exercising their security rights during insolvency or in a moratorium.
- Who controls the proceedings.
- Whether the controlling parties are looking after the rights of the secured creditors or all creditors.

Greater recovery potential clearly exists in those jurisdictions that are more secured-creditor oriented.

To ensure that lenders have access to their collateral if the borrower goes bankrupt, they should have perfected security interests in the collateral. Typically, lenders should obtain legal opinions to assess the perfection of security interests in each relevant legal system. The nature of the assets is also important. It can be difficult to perfect security interests on intangible assets such as patents and trademarks. These can also be quite difficult to evaluate in a default scenario. Similarly, assets that are easily valued may be difficult to trace and recover if they are in several countries or locations at the time of bankruptcy. Uncertainty about repossessing some of the security can be offset by providing various degrees of lender overcollateralisation.

## Determining collateral value and assigning recovery ratings

To determine the recovery prospects for lenders, we subtract any priority debt from the emergence, enterprise or residual value. Then, usually, the recovery expectation and recovery rating can be determined by comparing the nominal value expected to be received at the end of the workout period or bankruptcy to the exposure at default, the latter defined as principal plus accrued and unpaid interest at the point of default. To the extent that senior lenders are fully covered then the process will be repeated for junior lenders. Unless there are specific restrictions that would apply, we would usually assume that revolvers are fully drawn at the time of default. Also, generally we assume that the outstanding debt at default is reduced by the amount of any scheduled amortisation. The mapping of the recovery expectation to the recovery rating is detailed in exhibit 2.52.

# SUPPLEMENT 8: FINANCIAL REGULATION AND THE SYNDICATED LOAN MARKET

**Simon Crown, Partner**

*Clifford Chance*

Chapter 1 of this book deals with LIBOR and chapter 2 covered aspects of prudential regulation relevant to the syndicated loan market, such as regulatory capital requirements. This supplement covers a range of other non-prudential regulatory issues. In terms of scope, it focusses on issues relevant to the European wholesale syndicated loan market. This means that it does not address the substantial body of consumer credit regulation.

Traditionally, the syndicated loan market has not been a top priority for legislators and regulators at an EU or domestic level. Some of the regulatory developments covered in this supplement affect the market indirectly and perhaps inadvertently, while others show attempts by regulators to address specific areas of concern with the market (e.g., restrictions on tying clauses) or specific attempts to alter the competitive landscape (e.g., moves by some EU member states to enable lending by alternative investment funds which are managed by alternative investment fund managers).

The overall impression of the set of regulatory issues relevant to this market is that there is no grand plan by which regulators and legislators are co-ordinating their efforts, even at the level of the EU.

# PART 1 – EU DEVELOPMENTS

## Brexit and the role of English law

At the time of writing, Brexit is subject to significant uncertainty in terms of its impact on the wholesale lending market. Most lenders actively involved in cross-border lending into and out of the UK are preparing for a loss of passporting rights (that is rights of credit institutions regulated in one EU member state to carry on their lending business throughout the EU) on 29 March 2019. There may be a transitional arrangement which enables lenders to continue to operate as before in respect of the UK until the end of 2020. The licensing regime applicable to lenders after that date, and the ongoing availability of passporting rights, is uncertain.

A loss of passporting rights in respect of lending would not, under the current UK licensing regime, be problematic for non-retail lending on a cross-border basis into the UK, as such lending is not licensed in the UK. But it would be problematic for UK lenders seeking to lend into a number of EU member states, such as France, in light of domestic licensing regimes applicable even to wholesale lending.

In the absence of any agreement at an EU level which would extend passporting rights many participants in the syndicated loan market are planning to reorganise their businesses in such a way that they can continue to lend throughout the EU (and in the UK).

The question of the continuing common use of English law as the governing law of loan documentation arose quickly once the Brexit referendum result was announced in June 2016.

The Rome I Regulation requires courts in EU member states to give effect to the parties' choice of contractual governing law, whether or not that governing law is that of an EU member state. Prior to the Rome I Regulation and the Rome Convention which it replaced, the English courts recognised the parties' choice of contractual governing law. There is no reason to doubt that the English courts will continue to do so after Brexit.

Parties may want to consider the enforceability of judgments from an English court in EU member states, and vice versa. Such enforceability is currently provided for under the Brussels I Regulation. Its replacement post-Brexit is unclear. At worst, judgments of English courts would face the same enforceability issues as judgments of New York courts, i.e., enforceability will depend on the domestic law of the relevant EU member state.

Further, lenders will need to consider whether existing contractual provisions (e.g., references to EU law) are problematic post-Brexit, and should address this in new contracts to the extent possible (e.g., including transfer provisions in respect of EU affiliates of the lender).

## Article 55 BRRD (Bank recovery and resolution directive 2014/59/EU)

The BRRD harmonises the EU framework for the resolution of banks and investment firms. The Directive was implemented in stages in January 2015 and January 2016. The Commission published proposals for reform of the BRRD in November 2016.

The BRRD contains a number of measures. In terms of crisis prevention, it requires institutions at a solo and group level to prepare recovery plans and to take steps to improve resolvability. It gives regulators powers to intervene pre-resolution to require firms to take remedial steps (e.g., to restructure debt). It also gives regulators a broad range of powers to take resolution action prior to the firm's insolvency (e.g., requiring sale of all or part of the business, arranging for a bridge bank to intermediate, providing for asset separation and giving regulators powers to bail-in institutions by writing down or converting certain liabilities of a failing institution into equity).

Article 55 of the BRRD requires EU firms to include contractual recognition of bail-in clauses in a wide range of contracts which have non-EU governing law. Without such a clause, EU resolution authorities could face difficulties in exercising their resolution powers. Article 55 aims to ensure that resolution authorities will be able to exercise their bail-in powers within the EU.

There is a risk that a court in a non-EU jurisdiction would fail to give effect to a bail-in by an EU resolution authority, particularly where the governing law of the relevant agreement is non-EU. Article 55 attempts to tackle this risk by requiring the inclusion of a contractual provision in contracts governed by the law of a non-EU jurisdiction, where such contracts give rise to a liability for the in-scope firm. Article 55 requires the contractual term to include: acknowledgement and acceptance by the in-scope firm's counterparty that such liability is subject to the bail-in powers of relevant EU resolution authorities; a description of the relevant bail-in powers; a clause enabling variation of the contract as necessary to give effect to a bail-in; and acknowledgement that equity interests may be issued to the counterparty in place of the liability.

Where a firm wishes to count a particular liability towards its 'minimum requirement for own funds and eligible liabilities' (MREL) under Article 45 of the BRRD, it will need to comply with Article 55 in respect of the liability and is likely to need to obtain a legal opinion on the effectiveness of the bail-in clause from counsel in the relevant non-EU jurisdiction.

A loan facility constitutes an asset of the lender (from an accounting perspective) and is not a liability for the purposes of the BRRD. However, a bank's commitment to extend credit under a facility agreement, and potential liabilities to other syndicate members may be in scope, just as letters of credit, indemnities and guarantees can be in scope. Accordingly, lenders should have a process in place for identifying when a relevant liability will be created, so that the Article 55 bail-in clause can be included. Some industry associations (including the LMA for syndicated loans) have created standard wording for use in their industry standard documentation.

## ECB guidance on leveraged transactions

The ECB published guidance in May 2017 on leveraged transactions. The guidance entered into force on 16 November 2017 and applies to banks supervised by the ECB under the Single Supervisory Mechanism (SSM), but not to banks in non-eurozone member states such as the UK.

The guidance is designed to help banks to improve risk management of leveraged transactions. By defining in-scope transactions, the guidance requires banks' senior management to focus on a broad range of leveraged lending activities, and to benchmark risk management and reporting in respect of transactions against the standards set out in the guidance. The guidance also encourages banks to apply the guidance to other types of transaction, where relevant.

The guidance requires banks to include in their policies a single definition of leveraged transactions, consistent with the definition in the guidance. This definition includes: all types of loan where the borrower's post financing leverage exceeds a total debt to EBITDA ratio of 4.0 times. In this context, total debt includes drawn and undrawn debt and any additional debt that the loan agreement may permit – calculated on a gross debt basis and without cash being netted against debt; and all types of loan where the borrower is owned by a financial sponsor (i.e., an investment firm that deploys a private equity strategy).

The guidance excludes certain transactions from the definition of leveraged transactions, such as loans to banks, specialised lending (e.g., commodities finance), trade finance and loans to investment grade borrowers.

The guidance indicates that banks should define their risk appetite for leveraged transactions as part of their risk management framework, with appropriate governance arrangements. In respect of syndication, the guidance states that banks should create a comprehensive risk framework, including the setting of underwriting limits. The ECB's expectation is that syndicating transactions with high levels of leverage (total debt to EBITDA ratio of 6 or more) should be exceptional and be subject to an escalation process within the bank's risk management framework.

The ECB also requires banks to implement a credit approval process for new leveraged transactions and renewals and refinancing of existing transactions, to ensure that the transactions are consistent with each bank's risk framework. In addition, banks should engage in ongoing monitoring of syndication activities (e.g., to identify failed syndications) and exposures in the 'hold book'. Banks are expected to stress test such exposures, mimicking the impact of market-wide disruptions on underwriting and syndication.

In respect of loan origination, banks are required to focus on a borrower's debt repayment capacity (with a borrower having adequate capacity to repay if it can fully amortise senior secured debt or repay at least 50% of total debt over a five to seven year period).

The guidance allows implementation to be proportionate to the size and risk profile of the transactions relative to the assets, earnings and capital of the bank in question. The guidance will be enforced by existing supervisory arrangements (e.g., by joint supervisory teams made up of ECB and member state regulator representatives).

The ECB guidance is similar but not identical to leveraged lending guidance published by US authorities (the Office of the Comptroller of the Currency, the Federal Deposit Insurance Corporation and the Federal Reserve) in March 2013.

## Proposed EU regulation on non-performing loans

The Commission consulted in March to June 2018 on a new Directive and Regulation aimed at reducing the burden on EU banks of their non-performing loans. However, the package of reforms would also have implications for the primary loan market as well as the secondary loan market. At the time of writing the proposals are still subject to consultation and a number of syndicated loan market participants (including the LMA) have responded to the consultation in a manner intended to ensure that the proposals do not adversely impact the market. The description of the proposed Directive and Regulation below relates to the proposals *before* the effect of the consultation becomes apparent.

In this context, a loan is classified as a non-performing loan (NPL) if payment is overdue by more than 90 days or if the lender has concluded that the loan is unlikely to be repaid.

The proposed EU legislation takes the form of a Directive and a Regulation, and it contains a number of measures.

The Regulation would amend the CRR to create an incentive for banks to address NPLs earlier than at present and thereby to avoid an excessive accumulation of NPLs.

The Directive provides for the establishment in each EU member state of a non-court based security enforcement mechanism. This would be designed to provide a more efficient means of enforcing obligations under secured loans.

There are several measures designed to encourage secondary markets in NPLs.

First, the Directive introduces a set of new requirements designed to increase the role of non-bank lenders, such as CLOs and other funds, in the secondary market. The new measures apply to all transfers of loans to non-bank lenders, not just NPLs, and have a significant extra-territorial effect, in that they apply wherever the original lender is an EU bank, regardless of the location of the parties to the secondary market transaction. It is not certain how this applicability provision would work in respect of a syndicate of lenders where only some members are established in the EU.

In contrast to the current 'buyer beware' standard of loan sale disclosure, the Directive would require the lender to provide the non-bank lender with 'all necessary information' needed for the non-bank lender to assess the value of the loan and the likelihood of recovery of the debt. Where the original lender is a bank, it will be required to present this information using a template prepared by the EBA. This measure is designed to tackle the information asymmetry that some see as an impediment to a greater role for non-bank lenders in the secondary loan market for performing and non-performing loans. But there are significant concerns with the proposed information requirement, e.g., legal liability for the information provided.

Secondly, the proposed Directive requires that on completion of transfer of a loan to a non-bank lender, the bank must notify the relevant national authorities that the transfer has taken place and disclose the identity of the loan purchaser. The authorities would use this data to monitor activities in the secondary loan markets.

The legislation also proposes new requirements for non-bank lenders, in part to address potential risks that would arise with the increasing role of non-bank lenders in a market currently dominated by highly regulated banks.

First, a non-bank to which a NPL has been transferred would be required to notify the relevant national authorities of its intention to enforce its rights under the facility agreement, in advance of doing so. The notification must also specify the type of asset securing the loan, the value of the loan, and details of the lender and borrower. One of the aims of this notification is to enable regulators to ensure that borrowers are not disadvantaged in terms of a lender's approach to enforcement, once the loan has been transferred to a non-bank lender, by comparison to the protections that would have applied in respect of enforcement by a bank lender.

Secondly, where a loan is transferred to a non-bank lender which is not established in the EU, the lender will be required to appoint an EU based representative which will be responsible for the non-bank lender's obligations under the legislation. Again, this measure is designed to reduce the scope for consumer protections of borrowers to be avoided by non-EU, non-bank lenders (although the measure is not confined to consumer loans). However, the requirement to appoint an EU representative may have the effect of reducing the involvement of non-EU, non-bank lenders from the secondary market in NPLs.

In addition, a non-bank lender to which a loan is transferred (whether or not it is a NPL) will be required to inform the relevant national authorities of the identity of any institution appointed to carry out credit servicing in respect of the loan (in respect of a syndicated loan, this will often be the facility agent and security agent).

The Directive also creates a new regulatory framework for non-bank credit servicers, i.e., entities which, on behalf of a lender, monitor the performance of the loan, inform the borrower of changes in interest rates or enforce the lender's rights under the loan (which could include non-bank facility agents and trustees). Member states will be required to apply licensing to credit servicers and ongoing compliance requirements, including prescribed documentation standards, limits on outsourcing and a requirement to be incorporated in the EU. This new regime would apply to any credit servicer of a loan which was originally made by an EU bank. The new regime for credit servicers would apply to some asset managers of credit funds.

## Restrictions on contractual auditor controls

Lenders commonly scrutinise a borrower's audited annual accounts. Accordingly, the competence of the auditor is important to lenders. Lenders sometimes required borrowers to appoint auditors from a specified list, to give the lender some comfort as to the quality of the audit that would be conducted on the borrower's accounts. In most circumstances, clauses seeking to restrict a company's choice of auditor are since 17 June 2016 incompatible with EU law.

The EU provision (Directive 2014/56 and Regulation 537/2014, which amend the Statutory Audit Directive 2006/43) has been implemented in the UK in the form of the Statutory Auditors and Third Country Auditors Regulations 2017/516 (see regulation 14). The regulation applies to a term which, in relation to the conduct of a statutory audit of an audited person, provides for the restriction of the audited person's choice of statutory auditor to certain categories or lists of auditors. The regulation provides that such clauses have no legal effect. This applies to existing as well as new contracts, as there are no grandfathering provisions in the legislation.

There may be some scope for continuing influence by lenders in respect of a borrower's selection of auditor (e.g., requiring the borrower to appoint an auditor which has been approved in advance by the lender), if the borrower can be persuaded to agree to such a restriction, although such restrictions would be inconsistent with the spirit of the prohibition and so may be vulnerable to legal and regulatory challenge. In addition, the legislation requires 'public interest entities' to report to relevant national authorities any attempt by lenders to impose a banned auditor clause or otherwise improperly to influence the choice of auditor.

## Domestic licensing regimes for lending: liberalisation

There is little EU level harmonisation of the licensing of wholesale lending. A credit institution authorised by a member state will have passporting rights under the Capital Requirements Directive 2013/36/EU which enable it to provide lending in each EU member state. But there is no equivalent for non-banks. Some EU member states, such as France, have domestic licensing regimes which are highly restrictive on lending by entities which are not EU banks. But there has been some liberalisation in recent years in respect of lending by alternative investment funds in a small number of member states.

Ireland established a specific regulatory framework for loan originating investments funds in 2014. The L-QIAIF (loan originating qualifying investor alternative investment fund) is permitted to issue and participate in loans. It takes the form of an alternative investment fund under the Alternative Investment Fund Managers Directive 2011/61/EU and can be marketed solely to 'qualifying investors'.

In May 2015, the German regulator (the BaFin) announced that closed-ended alternative investment funds could grant and restructure loans to German borrowers, and that open-ended funds can restructure loans that they acquire, without the manager of such funds breaching the German licensing regime applicable to lending and other banking services. The manager must be authorised as an alternative investment fund manager in an EU member state.

France's Ordinance No. 2017–1432 of 4 October 2017 provides for the creation of a new type of alternative investment fund, the 'specialised finance organisation'. This type of organisation (an OFS), and the existing type of securitisation organisation (the OT) will benefit from a new exemption to French banking monopoly rules. Both types of vehicle may carry out lending activities in France, subject to certain restrictions.

### Benchmarks regulation

From 1 January 2018, regulated EU entities (e.g., banks) have been prohibited by the Benchmarks Regulation (2016/1011/EU) from using indices as a benchmark in the EU unless the index in question has been produced by an EU administrator which is included on ESMA's register of administrators, or is a non-EU index qualified for use in the EU under the regulation's third country regime.

However, in respect of lending, this requirement only applies in respect of loans which are credit agreements for the purposes of the Consumer Credit Directive or the Mortgage Credit Directive, i.e., to consumer loans and not to wholesale syndicated loans.

# PART 2 - UK DOMESTIC REGULATION

## Bank structural reform (ring-fencing)

The UK's bank ring-fencing regime is set out in the Financial Services (Banking Reform) Act 2013. The majority of the ring-fencing measures apply from 1 January 2019. These measures apply to any UK institution (excluding non-bank institutions and building societies) with core deposits exceeding a threshold of £25bn.

Under the ring-fencing rules, certain core services and activities (such as the acceptance of retail deposits) may only be provided by ring-fenced banks, and such banks may not conduct excluded activities, such as dealing in investments as principal.

Ring-fenced banks will also be subject to specific prohibitions, such as accepting certain forms of exposure to financial institutions. Exposures to banks, investment firms, structured finance vehicles and funds are subject to this prohibition, subject to some exceptions (e.g., where the exposure is for risk management purposes). A ring-fenced bank is permitted to act as a trustee or agent in connection with a syndicated loan, as long as the borrower is not a relevant financial institution.

This means that a ring-fenced bank will be subject to restrictions in respect of its involvement in syndicated loans, depending on the nature of the borrower. While such a bank could lend to a large corporate borrower, it would not be able to lend to a broker/dealer. Such restrictions apply even if the exposure is taken by way of sub-participation. The restrictions on the ability of a ring-fenced bank to establish or maintain a branch or subsidiary outside of the EEA may also limit the involvement of some ring-fenced banks in the syndicated loan market.

## The UK's PSC register

Since 6 April 2016, all UK companies and LLPs (with some exceptions) are required to maintain a register of persons exercising significant control (PSC) over them. The main issue for the loan market is that in some circumstances security may not be able to be taken or enforced over shares in a company with a PSC register. Lenders may also need to be included on the company's PSC register, as well as actively provide information on their interests in the company.

The PSC regime is set out in Part 21A of the Companies Act 2006. It specifies that a legal entity has significant control over a company or LLP where it meets one or more of the following conditions: it holds more than 25% of the shares or voting rights in the company; has the right to appoint a majority of the board of directors; or has the right to exercise significant influence or control over the company.

Only some legal entities which exercise significant control are required to be included in the company's PSC register, e.g., those which are themselves subject to PSC requirements or are listed on an EU regulated market. Accordingly, an unlisted non-UK company would not be included in the register.

A legal entity which is required to be included in a company's PSC register must notify the company of its status, keep the company up to date on any changes and respond to requests for information from the company.

If a company makes a request from an in-scope legal entity which is a PSC and it fails to respond to two such requests, the company may issue a restriction notice. The notice has the effect of freezing the entity's interest (e.g., voting rights under the shares it holds), so that no rights are exercisable in respect of the frozen interest. This mechanism could affect a loan arrangement where there is security over shares and a restriction notice has been issued to the chargor in respect of those shares. The notice can be lifted by the company if the information request is satisfied, or by order of a court.

Where shares are the subject of a restriction notice, it would be difficult to grant and enforce security over such shares. Lenders would mitigate this risk by undertaking searches of the relevant company's PSC register before taking and enforcing security, obtaining representations from the chargor (and possibly the company) that no restriction notices are in place, and obtaining undertakings from the chargor and company to the effect that the former will comply with information requests from the company and from the latter that it will only issue a restriction notice if required by law.

It is possible that a syndicate's security agent could become a PSC in the context of a share charge, where the agent becomes the registered holder of 25% or more of a company's shares or voting rights. There is a specific exception from the PSC registration requirements for rights attached to shares held by way of security where the rights are only exercisable in the chargor's interests, but this would not apply where the agent is the registered holder of the shares (i.e., where the agent does more than hold the rights to the shares).

It is also possible that lenders could become PSCs, if the set of representations and undertakings they obtain from a borrower amount to the lenders exercising significant influence or control over the borrower. There is a specific exception from the PSC registration requirements for third party commercial or financial agreements, which should extend to loans to the company. Accordingly, it should only be the case that a lender risks being a PSC if the features of the loan agreement give the lender a significantly greater degree of control over the borrower than is normally provided in industry standard loan documentation.

## Money Laundering

Money laundering rules applicable to UK lenders are set out under the Money Laundering Regulations 2017 (the MLR). The MLR implement the Fourth Money Laundering Directive (2015/849) and the Funds Transfer Regulation (2015/847).

As with the previous UK rules under the Money Laundering Regulations 2007, the MLR state that a court must decide whether industry guidance was following when determining whether a person has complied with the MLR. This guidance is produced by the Joint Money Laundering Steering Group (JMLSG). Chapter 17 of the current guidance (dated 17 May 2018) contains guidance specifically for the syndicated lending market. The guidance acknowledges that money laundering and terrorist financing risks in this market are comparatively low.

The guidance confirms which parties to a lending arrangement are subject to the obligation to verify the identity of a customer. For example, the syndicate's agent should verify the identity of the borrower and the lenders. The guidance indicates that some parties may take account of identity verification conducted by another party to the transaction. For example, a lender may take into account due diligence on the borrower which has been conducted by the lead manager of the syndicate, where the lead manager is subject to the MLR or equivalent money laundering rules.

The guidance confirms that a lender may decide to confirm the identity of a guarantor of the borrower's obligations either prior to entering into the loan, or prior to calling upon the guarantee. Where the latter approach is taken, the guidance suggests that as a minimum the lender may wish to check whether the guarantor is subject to sanctions restrictions. In respect of checks on the borrower, the guidance confirms that the lender can take into account the checks it conducts for the purpose of commercial credit risk analysis and reputational risk assessment.

The guidance also covers the checks that should be conducted by parties to secondary market transactions. For example, if a firm purchases a participation in a loan from a lender by way of novation or legal assignment, it will have a contractual relationship with the borrower and will be obliged by the MLR to identify the borrower. The guidance indicates that where the firm does not have a direct contractual relationship with the borrower (e.g., where there has been an equitable assignment of an interest in the loan), the firm may not need to identify the borrower (but would want to check that the original lender was subject to rules equivalent to the MLR).

## Prohibition on restrictive contractual clauses: investment and corporate banking

The FCA Handbook (COBS 11A.2) contains rules which ban the use of clauses that restrict a client's choice of future providers of primary market services (i.e., equity and debt capital markets transaction services provided to an issuer, and corporate finance advice). These rules came into effect on 3 January 2018. The effect is to prevent firms which are authorised by the FCA from entering into agreements which give them a right to provide future primary market services to their clients.

This is relevant to the syndicated loan market, as banks would often develop a relationship with a client by offering lending services, with a view subsequently to offer primary market services to the client, such as mergers and acquisitions advice. Some banks sought to 'tie' the client by making use of the bank's primary market services an obligation under the loan agreement, or giving the bank a right of first refusal should the client wish to use primary market services. The FCA conducted a market study, published in October 2016, which identified that these forms of tying could restrict a client's choice of supplier and thereby hinder effective competition between suppliers of primary market services.

The FCA prohibition does not apply to tying clauses included in an agreement for a bridging loan, where the tying only involves the firm which would provide the primary market services to which the bridging loan relates. A bridging loan is a loan provided to a client for the purpose of providing short-term financing, with the commercial intention that it be replaced with a different form of financing, such as a share or bond issuance.

# *Chapter 3*

# STRUCTURE, CONTENT AND COST ANALYSIS OF OFFERS TO ARRANGE SYNDICATED TRANSACTIONS

# STRUCTURING A TERM SHEET

Deal origination occurs in several different ways which will vary depending upon the type of borrower and nature of the transaction. A transaction may arise because a borrower has maturing instruments which need refinancing or because it has to finance new investments, projects or acquisitions. Whatever the reason, the borrower will need to consider a range of submitted bids and propose indicative financing terms before any transaction can commence.

The approach adopted by borrowers in seeking bids also varies widely: some borrowers are prepared to consider bids from any bank prepared to make one, whereas others choose to receive bids only from a small group of banks which have a track record of successful activity in the syndicated market. It is now rare that a borrower solicits bids on the basis of open competitive bidding; it is more usual to rely on the syndication skills of a smaller core group of relationship banks. However, as with any competitive bidding situation, timing – and to a certain extent – luck, can play a key role in the eventual winning of a mandate for the business. In this respect even the most sophisticated offer and related marketing plan developed by a relationship bank cannot provide a perfect hedge against a competitor's unforeseen success.

Notwithstanding the relatively small number of banks that have the resources to mount a bid for a mandate, banks bid extremely competitively against each other in order to secure mandates. To assist the borrower in making comparisons, a common language and format for setting out an offer have been developed over the years which makes the task relatively easy. Terminology has taken the form of a specialised jargon and the purpose of the two sample term sheets, which constitute the body of this chapter, is to examine the commercial and technical implications of the language in an offer.

Market practice requires an offer document to form the basis of the contract with regards to commercial parameters such as pricing, maturity and covenants; however such an offer usually embodies a caveat whereby it is made 'subject to satisfactory documentation mutually acceptable to all parties' (or similar wording). This caveat can in fact be viewed as providing protection for both borrowers and banks, since it means that neither party is committed until negotiations on the language in the facility agreement are successfully concluded. From the borrower's perspective, it means that once funds are committed by banks in the market subject only to satisfactory documentation, the borrower has the opportunity of securing those funds simply by agreeing to the documentation prepared by the banks, however onerous that documentation may be. This is not the usual way of conducting business, but there are extreme circumstances, such as corporate debt restructuring, when this approach may be necessary. Banks are also protected if documentation cannot be agreed since an offer usually has a latest date for reaching agreement (longstop date) after which its terms and conditions may either be reconfirmed or amended to satisfy the then prevailing market conditions or the deal pulled from the market (withdrawn).

In most cases, however, borrowers and banks know and understand the underlying market principles. Frequent borrowers will be familiar with the standard phrase 'the facility agreement will contain customary clauses for this type of facility'. This is a shorthand way to describe the *boilerplate* clauses found in all loan agreements. Such clauses are not generally negotiated in detail at the offer stage but the arranger and legal counsel will always explain them to borrowers unfamiliar with their purpose. These clauses include such matters as conditions precedent to drawings, voluntary prepayment, cancellation, illegality and increased costs. Normally, these clauses will be based upon the provisions of the *Recommended Form of Primary Documents* (LMA Recommended Forms) launched by the LMA in October 1999 and subsequently regularly updated. The clauses and LMA Recommended Forms are examined fully in the annotated facility agreement in chapter 5.

A borrower should negotiate, prior to awarding a mandate, the specific covenants which may be contentious during the negotiation of the facility agreement. For instance, a corporate borrower will need to reach agreement with the potential arranger bank on such issues as the levels of any financial covenant(s) (and the constituent parts of the test(s)) and any 'permitted security interests' under the negative pledge clause. It is essential from the point of view of both the borrower and the lenders to clarify and, so far as possible, to reach broad agreement on these critical items prior to the award of a mandate if negotiations (and relationships) are not going to be in danger of breaking down at a later stage.

It should not be interpreted from this that the credit issues of a syndicated loan differ substantially from those that a prudent lender would seek when making a bilateral loan available to a borrower. Nevertheless, because the terms of a syndicated transaction are subject to the scrutiny of, and have to be acceptable to, a multitude of lenders they may be weighted more in favour of the lenders than those available on bilateral deals.

From the syndication viewpoint, it is vital to include all the principal terms and conditions of the transaction in the invitation that is sent to potential participants so that, once committed, a participant lender does not have to seek a second credit approval because of a late change in the proposal. In practice, this cannot always be avoided since mandates are sometimes awarded prior to agreement on the exact terms of certain covenants. This means that participating lenders generally obtain some flexibility in their credit approval in order to be able to respond positively to evolving situations.

From a pricing perspective, it is rare, though not unheard of, for terms and conditions to change after a mandate has been awarded. This could occur after a deal has failed in syndication because it was mispriced or because of an adverse change in market conditions or in the credit quality of the borrower. Any pricing revisions arising from such circumstances generally result in a shift in favour of the banks. In the late 1990s, arranger banks started to introduce the concept of *marketflex* into their term sheets which allows the arranger banks to change unilaterally the terms, pricing and structure, if the market reacts adversely to a transaction in syndication. This practice is now commonly adopted particularly in the fields of leveraged and acquisition finance. One consequence of its introduction has been to stimulate a response from borrowers demanding *reverseflex* where the pricing of a transaction is reduced if the deal is oversubscribed. Lenders have accepted this principle and there have been many instances during borrower friendly market conditions of transactions being signed at levels of pricing below those set out in the original term sheet.

- A further issue for the borrower when seeking bids is to decide whether these bids are required to be made on a committed (that is, fully underwritten basis), on a partially committed (partially underwritten basis), or on a totally 'best efforts' basis:
    - Bids required on a committed basis assure the borrower that the funds will be available on pre-determined terms and conditions. This is so because, in the absence of a marketflex provision, even if no other banks are prepared to commit to the facility, the bank or banks which gave the underwritten commitment will provide the facility or funds in what will be, in effect, a bilateral or club deal.
    - Bids required on a partially committed basis assure the borrower that at least part of the funds required are committed on pre-determined terms and conditions, but the borrower is prepared to take the risk with the arranger that the remainder can be found in the market on the same terms and conditions.
    - Bids sought on a 'best efforts' basis reflect the preparedness of the borrower to take the risk that the funds can be raised in the market without a firm commitment from the arranger, but recognise that, at worst, the mandate will be returned, the market having rejected the deal.

A borrower needs, however, to take a cautious approach even to a fully underwritten offer particularly as it will usually be subject to 'satisfactory documentation mutually acceptable to all parties'. Such an offer is clearly worth less than one which has a fully negotiated and agreed facility agreement attached as a schedule to the offer; for some transactions, such as the Project Tennis case study used in this chapter, only the certainty of a signed facility agreement will suffice. Market practice requires negotiation of the documentation of fully underwritten deals in good faith in order to meet the objectives of the borrower and the lenders but it is essential that all critical commercial issues for the borrower, as well as for the lenders, be resolved prior to the award of the mandate. A lender would find itself highly embarrassed to receive a mandate on the basis of a fully underwritten offer only to find later that the borrower's understanding of the terms of certain covenants or indeed marketflex was inconsistent with the credit approval that had been obtained. Such occurrences put enormous pressure on banks and generally lead at least to a loss of internal credibility for the bank professionals involved, if not a far worse fate.

A fully underwritten deal which fails in syndication is generally an unexpected and unacceptable result for both the underwriting bank(s) and the borrower. The result for the bank(s) is exposure to a borrower in excess of the anticipated level and this severely damages the credibility of the syndication department if alternative placement is not quickly found. An underwritten deal which fails to syndicate well is highly unsatisfactory, though not disastrous, for the borrower as well. Despite the fact that the borrower has achieved its presumed principal objective of securing the financing, the market will be aware that the deal was a *dog*. This awareness will colour the market's perception of the borrower and may well lead to higher pricing when the borrower next approaches the market. Furthermore, the borrower may also be concerned about its exposure concentration with the underwriting bank(s) if the transaction is an undrawn or a standby facility.

In deciding whether to seek underwritten or best efforts offers, a borrower needs to evaluate a number of factors. These include the timing of the mandate in relation to the need for funds, any additional costs for obtaining an underwritten offer which may be reflected in both the front-end fee and in the margin, the prevailing market conditions and any requirement for certainty of funds for an anticipated acquisition.

It is worth noting that in the early to mid-2000s, banks were prepared to underwrite investment grade transactions quite readily for little or no additional cost because the substantial liquidity and appetite in the market reduced the risk of a failed syndication to virtually zero. After the sub-prime crisis and subsequent credit crunch of mid-2007–08, the market environment changed radically due to banks' increasing losses and focus on survival. This translated into behaviour where banks would shun underwriting opportunities for everything except the highest quality opportunities with their most valued customers.

Due to the strong supply to the market and the relationship nature of the majority of transactions coming to the market in recent years, in all but event driven situations where certain funds are necessary, underwriting tends to be unusual. That having been said, this also has led to the cost of underwriting in the majority of situations coming down substantially. Actually, having a transaction underwritten where that isn't strictly necessary could be seen as a sign of weakness by the borrower which is "so uncertain that it required the certainty provided though an underwriting".

In general only a very small percentage of transactions which an active arranging bank leads in any year are underwritten.

## SAMPLE TERM SHEETS

The two sample term sheets which follow illustrate two common types of syndicated transaction and incorporate structures commonly used. Both of the transactions have been set out in the form of a term sheet which a borrower might receive from a bank bidding to win the mandate to arrange the deal. The usual commercial terms and conditions are included as well as sample covenants, but (as noted earlier) all pricing and other commercial terms are indicative only and not necessarily representative of current market terms.

Both of these term sheets have been annotated with explanatory text highlighting the key commercial issues. If an issue is common to both transactions, the issue is covered in the first term sheet only. Where there are alternatives which are commonly found in practice, they feature in one or other of the term sheets and are discussed in the related explanatory text. It is recommended that the first term sheet for DutchCo SPV B.V. (DutchCo) be read in conjunction with chapter 5, which provides a sample facility agreement, incorporating explanatory text, for the intended financing.

In a real life situation, these term sheets would be accompanied by a mandate letter and/or preamble which would state whether the offer was being made on a fully underwritten, partially underwritten or best efforts basis. In the case of an underwriting, such a letter is likely to include other provisions aimed at protecting the underwriting bank (including possibly drop-dead fees and marketflex). The mandate letter for Project Tennis provides an example of this.

The first term sheet is for a corporate borrower, DutchCo, set up as a special purpose vehicle incorporated in The Netherlands and guaranteed by its parent, Parent Company S.A., an 'A+' name, domiciled in France. This structure, which is typical of corporate structures found in the market, has been chosen deliberately for this example so that the cross-border issues can be highlighted and discussed in the chapter on documentation.

The facility is in the amount of $1bn and it has a maturity of 12 months (but provides for the possibility of an extension for a further 12 months). Its purpose is principally to provide backup to the borrower's US commercial paper programme but the revolving facility may also be used for general corporate purposes. The facility is structured to be fully revolving and there is a swingline available to refinance maturing commercial paper under certain circumstances.

The second proposal is an acquisition finance proposal consisting of a combined mandate letter and a term sheet for Project Tennis. This is the code name chosen by the team working on the deal and is used by all parties to the transaction. A code name is necessary as the proposed acquisition is market sensitive meaning that the transaction team will be *insiders* on the transaction. Any leakage of the actual names of the parties could lead to prosecution of offending individuals or institutions. The financing proposal is issued by Top Bank to Bidco plc ('Bidco'), which intends to raise finance to support its bid for the acquisition of Target plc ('Target'). The amount of the facility is £1bn, spread across three tranches as outlined in the mandate letter and term sheet which follow. The amount is intended to cover the cost of the acquisition, that is, the purchase of the shares of Target which it needs to acquire to secure control, as well as to refinance the existing debt of Target plc. The financing proposal has been structured to take account of the post-acquisition strategy of Bidco which is to refinance rapidly (within 12 months) a significant part of the facility either by a disposal programme or by issuing bonds or a combination of both. The bank submitting the bid, Top Bank, is interested in securing the mandates for the asset disposal programme and/or the bond issues and decides to try to differentiate itself by proposing aggressive terms for the short-term tranche (Facility A) which has a 12 month maturity but with a precautionary term out option (and term out fee). Top Bank offers tight pricing for Facility A, with margin and fees well below the pricing for the other tranches, and agrees to hold the full amount of Facility A on its books for up to one year. Top Bank will only syndicate Facility A if the term out option has been exercised, an event which both Bidco and Top Bank do not expect to happen. In return, Top Bank expects to be well placed for the asset disposal and bond mandates although there is no contractual obligation tying these related transactions (such contractual obligations (so-called "tying clauses") are discussed in supplement 8 to chapter 2).

The facility is denominated in sterling as Target is presumed to be a listed company on the UK stock exchange. It includes a provision for *certain funds* which will enable the relevant advisors acting for Bidco to confirm that the funding is committed and available. It also incorporates a multi-currency clause to provide for the refinancing of Target's debt in currencies other than sterling.

It is worth noting that, although there is no standard or uniform wording for term sheets and each bank has its own style and glossary (and in relation to leveraged buy outs, some equity sponsors have also developed their own form of term sheets), the LMA strongly encourages the use of its recommended forms. The term sheet for DutchCo might have been created by a banker using a house style whereas the mandate letter and term sheet for Project Tennis follow closely the LMA recommendations for offers of acquisition finance. The two case studies in this chapter have been designed to illustrate certain differences in style yet both seek to protect fully the commercial position of the arranger and syndicate banks.

The final section of this chapter provides a methodology for calculating the all-in cost to the borrower of the transactions contemplated by these term sheets. The first transaction, for DutchCo is expected to remain undrawn since it backs up commercial paper, normally a cheaper source of funds for a quality borrower than bank advances. The emphasis therefore is on calculating the all-in cost of maintaining the facility undrawn. On the other hand, the three tranche structure for Project Tennis has been designed to meet the expected needs of Bidco with varying levels of drawdown in each of them. In selecting the most competitive bid, Bidco will need to make assumptions on the amount of the facility that will be drawn, and for how long, when calculating the effective overall cost.

# DUTCHCO

**Term sheet for US$1bn revolving credit facility**

DUTCHCO SPV B.V.

UNCONDITIONALLY GUARANTEED BY PARENT COMPANY S.A.

US$1 BILLION REVOLVING CREDIT FACILITY WITH SWINGLINE OPTION

[DATE]

Summary of terms and conditions

**Borrower**: DutchCo SPV B.V. (DutchCo)

The borrower, which is the issuer of US dollar commercial paper, has been incorporated in The Netherlands on account of the favourable tax regime. Some companies arrange for the relevant issuer to be incorporated in the US (normally in the State of Delaware) in order to enlarge the investor base. Certain US investors of commercial paper have restricted appetite for commercial paper issued by a non-US domiciled issuer.

**Guarantor**: Parent Company S.A.

The guarantor (which is a French company) will provide a full and unconditional guarantee in favour of the syndicate banks. It will as a separate matter also provide such a guarantee to holders of outstanding commercial paper. The banks will advance funds only in accordance with the terms of the facility agreement. The banks are not providing a guarantee of repayment to the holders of commercial paper issued by the borrower (holders of such paper, in the event of a default, must look to the guarantor under the commercial paper programme for redemption of maturing paper). It should be noted that a guarantor is not always a requirement in a syndicated facility if the borrower is of a sufficient creditworthy quality in its own right. However, in this case, DutchCo is established as a special purpose company and would not usually be considered to be sufficiently creditworthy in its own right for the amount involved in this transaction.

**Arrangers**: Arranger Bank Limited, Top Bank plc and XYZ Bank Limited.

A group of banks has been mandated to arrange the transaction and each of them has been listed as arrangers in alphanumerical order. In this case, the banks will arrange the transaction on a "best efforts" basis (rather than underwriting it) such that the size of the facility will be subject to the arrangers' ability to solicit sufficient interest from other banks to ensure that the transaction is fully subscribed.

If a group of banks is mandated to arrange a transaction, just one of them will be nominated to be the agent, usually after negotiations between them on the sharing of roles as described in chapter 4. If there is a sole arranger then it would usually take on the role of facility agent (although that is not always the case). (The 'administrative agent' in US domestic syndications is the term usually used to describe the arranger of the transaction).

**Facility Agent**: XYZ Bank Limited.

The facility agent will administer the facility and handle all payments between the borrower and the syndicate, operating so that they are made on a timely basis. Although a facility agent under an LMA facility agreement is under no obligation to make a payment to a party until it has been able to establish that it has received funds from the relevant other party, in practice it may be difficult for the facility agent to ensure that all moneys have been received prior to making payments to the parties (in particular on multicurrency deals where payments will be made through financial centres in different time zones). LMA facility agreements therefore provide that where a facility agent does decide to advance funds to a borrower before it has been put in funds by a lender and such lender fails to reimburse the facility agent, then the borrower is required to refund to the facility agent the sum advanced together with any funding costs. Agent banks also rely heavily on the clawback provision in facility agreements in the event that any of the parties fails to make a timely payment and that failure is not rectified with good value.

In order to reflect the normal practice of many banks when acting as facility agents, LMA facility agreements provide that where one revolving facility loan is being repaid by way of a simultaneous drawing of another revolving facility loan in the same currency and in the same amount, such "rollover" may be effected on a "cashless" basis.

Swinglines are an essential component of commercial paper back up facilities. They are intended to be activated when the reason for a borrower's inability to refinance maturing paper is not linked to a credit deterioration of the borrower (since, if there were an event of default under the facility agreement, the swingline would not be available), but is a result of dysfunction of the commercial paper market. The swingline agent may be a branch of the facility agent, a sister company or even a different institution. In the sample agreement the facility agent delegates the swingline functions to its branch in New York so that a separate swingline agent is not appointed.

The swingline agent is responsible for the administration of the funding of same day funds to meet maturing commercial paper that cannot be refinanced in the commercial paper market on the same day. Timeliness is of the essence and swingline agents must be able to provide the service levels stipulated in the documentation of the transaction

**Facility Amount**: US$1bn (of which US$500m may be available by way of the Swingline (as defined below)).

The facility amount is defined as US$1bn – as mentioned above, this amount will be subject to the transaction being fully subscribed in syndication. If syndication is successful such that aggregate commitments from the market exceed US$1bn, the arrangers will usually invite the borrower to increase the amount of the facility to take advantage of the level of oversubscription. If the terms and conditions are attractive in the prevailing market, the borrower often accepts the increase. The fixed costs of the transaction, such as legal fees and the preparation of an information memorandum, are then amortised more cost effectively. However, if the syndication strategy dictates that no increase in the facility amount is required on an oversubscription, then the commitments of the arrangers and the other lenders will usually be scaled back on a *pro rata* basis.

**Facility**:

(a) a Revolving Credit Facility (the "Revolving Credit Facility") providing for short-term Loans (the "Loans") in US Dollars, euro and Canadian dollars or other agreed optional currencies with LIBOR (or EURIBOR in relation to Loans in euro or CDOR in relation to loans in Canadian dollars) interest periods of up to six months;

(b) a Swingline (the "Swingline") providing for same day utilisations in US Dollars ("Swingline Loans") with maturities of up to five business days, subject to a maximum amount of US$500m.

Amounts borrowed and repaid under (a) and (b) may subsequently be re-borrowed until the Final Maturity of the Facility subject to the terms and conditions set out herein.

Paragraph (a) provides for drawings under a committed facility for periods which can be determined by the borrower in accordance with the choices specified in the offer with interest calculations based on LIBOR (or EURIBOR in relation to Loans drawn in euro or CDOR in relation to Loans drawn in Canadian dollars).

In 2013 LIBOR was discontinued for a number of currencies and tenors (including Australian dollars, Canadian dollars, Danish Kroner, New Zealand dollars and Swedish Kronor) on account of there being insufficient transaction data available for interbank lending in such currencies and maturities to produce a reliable rate. See chapter 1. Alternative interest rate benchmarks are now used for those currencies and tenors where LIBOR is no longer available. In light of these changes, in 2014, the LMA revised its facility agreements to include optional wording where an alternative benchmark rate is being used for a "Non-LIBOR Currency". As part of these changes, the LMA published an optional standalone slot-in schedule (*"Domestic Interest Rate Benchmark Schedules for use in conjunction with the Recommended Form of Primary Documents"*) which contains suggested drafting for certain interest rate benchmarks for currencies where LIBOR is no longer available.

In this case, it has been agreed that CDOR (the Canadian Dealer Offered Rate) will be used as the interest rate benchmark for loans in Canadian dollars.

Paragraph (b) provides for same-day drawings in the US domestic market which will bear interest at a rate determined in that market, namely the higher of prime rate announced by the facility agent or the Federal Funds rate plus a margin, often 0.25%. (See Interest Rate below).

The revolving nature of the credit facility is described: amounts can be drawn, repaid and redrawn in accordance with the needs of the borrower. The constraints are the commercial and operational terms of the offer. The borrower is also required to agree to repeat certain of the representations required for first drawdown on each subsequent drawing.

**Purpose**: The Facility is for general corporate purposes and, in the case of the Swingline only, to refinance maturing commercial paper issued by the Borrower. The Swingline Loans are to be used to repay a maturing tranche of US Dollar commercial paper, if for some reason (e.g., market disruption) such tranche cannot be reissued. Swingline Loans may be refinanced by Loans drawn under the Revolving Credit Facility.

The purpose clause specifies the uses to which the funds may be put. The purpose of the swingline is clearly defined: it is to be used only to refinance a maturing tranche of US Dollar commercial paper if the tranche cannot be reissued due to market disruption or any other reason. The swingline is not to be seen as an alternative funding source to commercial paper and it would not normally be in the economic interest for the borrower to use it as such. It should be noted that at times of market turbulence, the borrower may find that the total cost of borrowing under the revolving credit facility is lower than the cost of issuing commercial paper but this is very unusual for top rated borrowers and has rarely happened.

When considering whether to provide a swingline facility, one of the factors that banks will take into account is the impact on their own liquidity requirements. In particular, under the Liquidity Coverage Ratio (LCR) requirements set out in Basel III, banks are required to hold certain levels of high quality liquid assets against undrawn commitments under certain facility agreements (including swingline facilities) in order to ensure that they have sufficient liquidity to meet borrowers' requests to draw down credit lines at times when there is a short-term liquidity crisis.

Basel III envisaged a graduated implementation of the LCR from 2015, with full compliance from 2019. In practice, the Basel Committee on Banking Supervision (BCBS) reported that all 27 member jurisdictions had implemented rules relating to the LCR by the end of March 2016. (See chapter 2 for further discussion of Basel III).

The LCR requires banks to assume that specified percentages of all undrawn commitments which they have made available for drawing to meet liabilities maturing within 30 days under (i) "liquidity facilities" and (ii) "credit facilities" will be drawn in a liquidity crisis and therefore banks will be required to ensure that such undrawn commitments are wholly or partially backed by segregated high quality assets such as cash, central bank reserves and sovereign paper and (in more limited circumstances) other paper such as corporate bonds, mortgage backed securities and equities. A "liquidity facility" would include a facility (such as a swingline) which would be used for the purpose of refinancing the borrower's debt facilities in situations where the borrower is unable to obtain its ordinary course of business funding requirements

The LCR requires banks to assume that only 10% of undrawn commitments made available for drawing within 30 days under "credit facilities" to "non-financial corporates" will be drawn and therefore such "credit facilities" will require a lower level of segregated high quality assets to be held against them in order to satisfy the LCR than "credit facilities" provided to financial institutions or any "liquidity facilities" (where the percentage assumed drawn is higher). Basel III states that general working capital facilities provided to corporate entities (such as revolving credit facilities provided for general corporate or working capital purposes) will be treated as "credit facilities" rather than "liquidity facilities".

There was initially a concern that the implementation of the LCR would impact the documentary terms of such facilities, for example to require the purpose clause of revolving facility agreements to state that only a specified portion of the total undrawn commitments may be used as a "liquidity facility" or to require information about the maturity profile of any commercial paper issued by the borrower that could be refinanced by the swingline facility (as the LCR only applies to the extent that the relevant commercial paper matures within 30 days). However, in practice, this has not proved to be the case and the documentary terms of "liquidity facilities" have been largely unaffected by the implementation of the LCR. However, their popularity has decreased as the cost of providing them has risen as a result of the LCR.

**Final Maturity**: 12 months from the date of signing ("Signing Date") of the Facility Agreement. The Borrower shall have the option to request the banks to extend the facility for 12 Months provided that notice of such request shall be given between 60 and 30 days prior to Final Maturity.

This specifies the date at which, under normal conditions, the contract between the parties will expire. Banks will need to obtain credit approval through to this date notwithstanding the fact that tenors of individual instruments used under the terms of the facility are of shorter maturity. The decision to *request* the extension is at the discretion of the borrower. However, the decision to *extend* commitments under the extension option is at the sole discretion of each syndicate bank. Until the implementation of Basel II, banks often made available revolving credit facilities with 364-day commitment periods. This practice developed because of the favourable capital treatment of this type of facility under the Basel Accord but the implementation of Basel II meant that a 0% risk weighting was no longer available for 364-day facilities and therefore this became less important. (See chapter 2 for discussion of capital risk weightings and the Basel Accords). It is usual to expect requests for an extension to be given towards the end of the contractual term, in this case between 60 and 30 days prior to the Final Maturity.

During periods of low pricing, borrowers are often keen to incorporate extension options to lock in favourable margins for as long as possible.

**Utilisations**: Loans may be drawn in minimum principal amounts of US$50m on a fully revolving basis for one, three and six months. Notice of utilisation is to be given to the Facility Agent no later than three business days prior to the date of drawing.

Swingline Loans shall have a maximum tenor of five business days with notice of such utilisations to be given to the Swingline Agent no later than 11.00 a.m. Eastern Standard Time (EST) on the date of drawing.

Interest periods available to the borrower under the revolving credit facility are one, three and six months. As discussed in chapter 1, in 2013 LIBOR ceased to be published for certain tenors. However ICE LIBOR is still available for US dollars for these periods. Notice of drawing is to be given three days in advance so that the agent bank can, on a timely basis, notify all the syndicate banks of the borrower's intention to draw and permit each bank to fix its participation in that drawing two days prior to value date in accordance with market practice for fixing the rate of LIBOR-based US dollar loans as well as EURIBOR-based loans.

The maturity of swingline advances is limited to five business days, since it is intended that these advances will be refinanced by the re-issuance of commercial paper or by a drawing of LIBOR loans under the Revolving Credit Facility. Notice is to be given to the Swingline Agent in New York by 11.00 a.m. EST so that notices for same-day drawdown can be given to syndicate banks to enable them to make the funds transfer on a timely, same-day, basis.

The minimum size of individual drawings offered to the borrower is negotiable but is chosen so that the individual participation of each syndicate bank in each drawing is at least a minimum market amount, usually US$1m.

**Repayment**: The principal amount of each Loan shall be repaid (and may be redrawn) at the maturity of the related interest period. The principal amount of each Swingline Drawing shall be repaid no later than five business days from the date of such utilisation.

This specifies that revolving loans are to be repaid at the end of each interest period and may simultaneously be redrawn. The purpose of this is two-fold: first, banks benefit when they sell an advance in the secondary market if it is sold to its maturity; second, if the borrower redraws, certain representations and warranties are reconfirmed in such drawdown notice. Term loans, by way of contrast, may be of an amortising or bullet nature, as covered in chapter 2.

**Maximum Outstandings**: The Borrower may utilise the Facility as follows:

(a) Revolving Credit up to US$1bn

and

(b) Swingline up to US$500m

**provided that** the aggregate outstandings from time to time under (a) and (b) do not exceed US$1bn.

This provision allows the borrower to switch outstandings from time to time between the LIBOR/EURIBOR/CDOR-based revolving credit facility loans and Swingline Loans, subject to the aggregate amount outstanding not exceeding US$1bn (and the amount of swingline loans not exceeding a sub-limit of US$500m). This sets an upper limit on the committed credit exposure for the transaction and equally for the syndicate banks. It is assumed in this transaction that the banks making the revolving and swingline facilities available will be the same banks although a bank will usually for convenience (given the short time period for swingline banks to make funds available) make the swingline available through its New York branch or even through a separate US corporate entity.

**Voluntary Prepayment**: The Borrower may prepay at any time, without penalty, Loans or Swingline Loans in whole or in part in minimum amounts of US$50m subject to five business days' prior written notice, provided that Loans prepaid at any time other than at maturity of an interest period shall be subject to reimbursement of breakfunding costs and related expenses, if any.

In a revolving credit facility without scheduled amortisation or reduction of commitments and where advances may be repaid and redrawn at will by the borrower, prepayment provisions are only relevant in the circumstances where the date of prepayment does not align with the maturity of an interest period. In such a case, syndicate banks will reserve the right to obtain compensation for break funding, which is explained in more detail in the sample facility agreement in chapter 5.

**Voluntary Cancellation**: On the giving of five business days' prior written notice to the Facility Agent, the borrower may cancel undrawn amounts of the Revolving Credit Facility in minimum amounts of US$100m. Any amount so cancelled shall permanently reduce the amount available under the Facility.

The option for the borrower to cancel all or part of the facility, which is undrawn, provides the borrower with an opportunity to save the commitment fee on the amount cancelled. Any cancellation notice is irrevocable. Five business days' notice is given so that the facility agent can notify all the relevant parties of the cancellation and verify that outstandings do not exceed the reduced amount of the facility. The minimum amount and notice period are usually negotiable.

In this case however, the borrower is using this facility to support the issuance of commercial paper and the borrower's ratings may depend in part, at least, on the size and quality of this facility. The rating agencies will reserve the right to modify the ratings or even remove them altogether if the liquidity line is cancelled without either (i) the substitution of an alternative liquidity line or (ii) a permanent commensurate reduction in the amount of commercial paper outstanding.

**Mandatory Prepayment**: On the occurrence of a Change of Control (as defined below), any Lender may by not less than ten days' prior written notice, cancel its commitments and declare that its portion of any Loans or Swingline Loans, together with accrued interest and all other amounts accrued to it, immediately due and payable.

A 'Change of Control' shall occur if any person or group of persons acting in concert gains control of more than one-half of the issued share capital of the Guarantor or otherwise gains control of the right to appoint or remove all or the majority of the directors of the Guarantor.

**Commitment Fee**: A Commitment Fee equal to 35% of the Applicable Margin is payable quarterly in arrear on the undrawn, uncancelled amount of the Facility, calculated on the basis of actual number of days elapsed and a 360-day year.

A commitment fee is payable on the undrawn, uncancelled part of a facility to compensate banks for the ongoing commitment to provide funds under the facilities.

The use of a 360-day year for the calculation of the commitment fee charges is market practice for the calculation of all fees charged on a per annum basis on US Dollar denominated (and most other Eurocurrency) facilities of this type.

An alternative construction uses a facility fee which is payable regardless of whether the facility is drawn or not. In such cases the applicable margin is usually reduced to recognise that part of the lenders' margin remuneration comes from this fee.

**Applicable Margin**: 0.30% per annum.

The applicable margin is expressed as a percentage and is added to the relevant interest rate benchmark to make up the total interest rate. The applicable margin can also be variable, sometimes referred to as a *grid*, which is determined from time to time by reference to different levels of financial ratios or credit ratings. This can act as an incentive to borrowers by reducing their borrowing costs as performance improves. More importantly from the banks' point of view, is that a grid allows banks to be compensated immediately in a worsening credit situation, without requiring the borrower to renegotiate the whole transaction which might be necessary, say, because of a breach of a covenant.

Where multicurrency facilities are provided, the applicable margin may also vary according to the currency of the loans. For example, in 2011-2012 some European banks encountered difficulties in obtaining US Dollar funding (as they were unable to access the market for US Dollar commercial paper) and therefore demanded a higher margin (referred to as a US Dollar premium) for loans made available to corporate borrowers in US Dollars rather than in euro or other European currencies.

Previously, mandatory costs were also a component of the total interest rate. These were regulatory costs imposed on lenders by the Bank of England, the Prudential Regulatory Authority and the Financial Conduct Authority (for lenders with a facility office in the UK) and the European Central Bank (for lenders with a facility office in any member state of the European Union that has adopted the euro as its lawful currency).

However, facility agents found it operationally difficult to calculate mandatory costs particularly where syndicates contained a wide range of financial institutions who charged differing levels of mandatory cost. There has therefore been an increasing move away from charging these costs such that it is now very uncommon for banks to charge them. As a result of this, in April 2013 the LMA withdrew its mandatory costs schedule from the LMA facility agreements.

**Interest Rate**:

Loans drawn under the Revolving Credit Facility shall accrue interest at the rate of:

(a) the Applicable Margin; and

(b) the interest rate benchmark.

**Interest rate benchmark(s)**:

(a) in relation to any Loan in euro, EURIBOR;

(b) in relation to any Loan in Canadian dollars, CDOR; and

(c) in relation to any Loan in any other currency, LIBOR, set, in each case, by reference to Thomson Reuters (and, if necessary the use of linear interpolation) or, if not available, by specified fallbacks

and if, in each case, the rate is less than zero, it shall be deemed to be zero.

Interest will be payable at the maturity of each Loan. Interest shall be calculated on the basis of actual number of days elapsed and a 360-day year.

Swingline Loans shall accrue interest at the rate which is the higher of:

(a) the prime commercial lending rate in US Dollars announced by the Facility Agent; and

(b) 0.25%. per annum over the federal funds effective rate (as published by the Federal Reserve Bank of New York) or, if not available, the rate which is the average of quotations on overnight federal funds transactions provided by depository institutions selected by the Facility Agent

and if, in each case, the rate is less than zero, it shall be deemed to be zero.

When Loans are drawn under the Revolving Credit Facility, they will accrue interest at LIBOR (for the relevant currency), EURIBOR (for loans in euro) or CDOR (for loans in Canadian dollars) for the same interest period plus a margin. LIBOR rates are set at 11:00 a.m. (London time) each day (and are then published on the relevant Thomson Reuters page at approximately 11:55am. (London time)). 11:00 a.m. (London time) is the time conventionally adopted for LIBOR rate fixings in the London market and the rate is the relevant LIBOR to which the margin will be added. Similarly, EURIBOR rate fixings are made at 11:00 a.m. CET and CDOR at 10:00am. (Toronto time).

If there are errors during the process of producing a benchmark rate on a particular day then the administrators of certain benchmarks including ICE LIBOR may require correction by means of refixing and republishing an originally published screen rate intra-day. This raises difficult operational questions as to whether to reference the refixed and republished rate rather than the originally published rate – see the further discussion in the definition of "Screen Rate" in the sample agreement in chapter 5.

The actual amount of interest is calculated in the conventional way (on the actual number of days elapsed for the period on a 360-day year).

If the Thomson Reuters screen rate is unavailable then the facility agreement sets out a waterfall of fallback options that are to be used to calculate the interest rate. These fallbacks were an area of focus in the loan market following the discontinuation of LIBOR for certain tenors and currencies in 2013. See the further discussion in Clause 15 (*Changes to the calculation of interest*) in the sample agreement in chapter 5.

The interest rate benchmark is expressed to have a "zero floor" meaning that if the relevant benchmark is negative, then for the purposes of the facility agreement, it will be deemed to be zero. This zero floor is designed to protect the lenders' return by preserving the margin. Negative interest rates have been an important issue in the loan market since 2011 when Swiss Franc LIBOR briefly turned negative. In recent years, central bank activity has resulted in EURIBOR and euro LIBOR rates also falling below zero on a number of occasions. See the further discussion in the definition of "LIBOR" in the sample agreement in chapter 5.

Swingline Loans will accrue interest at the higher of prime rate, as determined by the agent, or the Federal Funds Rate plus a margin of 0.25% per annum. The reason for this alternative is to protect banks against the possibility of unusual fluctuations in the Federal Funds Rate which might occur at certain periods of the year, for example at year end.

**Utilisation Fee**: A Utilisation Fee will be payable quarterly in arrear on the total aggregate outstandings under the Revolving Credit Facility and Swingline, calculated at a percentage rate of:

(a) 0.15% per annum for each day on which there are any Loans outstanding but the total aggregate outstandings are less than or equal to 33%. of the Facility Amount;

(b) 0.30% per annum for each day on which the total aggregate outstandings exceeds an amount equal to 33%. (but are less than or equal to 66%.) of the Facility Amount; and

(c) 0.50% per annum for each day on which the total aggregate outstandings exceeds an amount equal to 66%. of the Facility Amount.

As the facility is principally a commercial paper back-up facility, it is not expected to be drawn and the margin may not fully reflect the price that banks would require if the facility had been structured as a term loan. In order to ensure that banks receive an adequate return should the facility be fully drawn, a utilisation fee is incorporated in the structure. This becomes payable if the facility is utilised and steps up to a higher percentage rate if the facility is more than 33%. drawn with a further step up to a higher percentage rate if the facility is more than 66%. drawn. The facility agent will determine whether or not such utilisation fee is due and make the appropriate claim on the borrower.

The economic basis for charging this fee is extremely rational, since the borrower is not expected to draw unless either its credit quality has deteriorated to such an extent that commercial paper investors are no longer prepared to take the paper, or the market has deteriorated such that commercial paper generally cannot be issued. To mitigate the risk of a shortage of funds in the event of an occurrence of either of these circumstances, the committed banks provide liquidity insurance, and the cost to the borrower must reflect this.

The reader may wonder why the margin is not simply increased by the amount of the utilisation fee. The answer is that banks are generally willing to offer the borrower the occasional use of the committed options at margins which reflect low usage of the facility. It is only when that drawn usage is high that the utilisation fee is invoked and it accrues retrospectively.

**Arrangement Fee**: 0.10% flat on the Facility Amount payable to the Arrangers on the Signing Date. This fee will be used to pay underwriting and participation fees to syndicate banks.

The arrangement fee is one of the most critical commercial terms to negotiate at the mandate stage because it incorporates both the flat fee payable to the arrangers as well as the fees to be paid to participating banks. It will also include underwriting fees if the deal is underwritten. Negotiation of the arrangement fee is sensitive because the arrangers are balancing the level of remuneration needed to be paid to participating banks to ensure that the deal syndicates successfully with the level of their own remuneration for winning the mandate. A more detailed discussion of this is given in chapter 4 as this is one of the key issues in the syndication business.

The arrangement fee is normally calculated on the basis of the final facility amount, which may be greater than the amount originally planned if the deal is over-subscribed and the amount of the deal increased. For this reason, it is essential to express the arrangement fee as a percentage of the final facility amount rather than as a single monetary amount.

The arrangement fee is conventionally paid on the signing date but a borrower may negotiate to pay on the earlier of (i) the date of first drawing, in which case it is common to withhold the amount of such fees from the disbursement to the borrower, or (ii) a certain number of days after the date of signing.

The arrangers usually aim to keep a given proportion (sometimes known as the "skim" or – more historically – the "praecipium") of the arrangement fee for themselves and then use the remainder to pay underwriting and participation fees to other banks. In some term loan facilities, participation fees may be paid to other banks by way of an original issue discount such that these banks acquire their participations in the facilities at a discount to their par value. The skill of the arrangers in syndication is to judge just how much or how little of the arrangement fee needs to be paid to those banks without jeopardising the success of the transaction. The residual fee retained by the arrangers adds to the final reward for the market risk taken. (See chapter 4 for an example of the relevant calculations).

**Agency Fee**: The Borrower will pay an annual agency fee of US$37,500 per annum. Initial Agency Fee is payable no later than 30 days after the Signing Date and thereafter on the anniversary of the Signing Date if the Facility is extended.

> The agency fee may be charged in many different ways. Here it is contemplated as a fixed annual fee. Agency fees should cover at the very least the administrative and money transfer costs of the facility agent.

**Expenses**: Out-of-pocket expenses, including legal fees (subject to any caps, if agreed), incurred in connection with the preparation and syndication of the Facility are to be paid by the Borrower.

> Final resolution and the agreement by the borrower to pay all legal expenses will be facilitated by regularly monitoring the level of legal costs incurred and reporting to the borrower, so that at the end of the transaction there are no surprises when the expenses are submitted for reimbursement.

**Documentation**: The Facility is to be made available on condition that a Facility Agreement governing it is negotiated to the mutual satisfaction of the Borrower, the Guarantor, the Facility Agent and the syndicate banks which Agreement shall be based upon the LMA Recommended Form of multicurrency syndicated facilities agreement for investment grade transactions and the Borrower's other recent syndicated facilities and shall incorporate:

Customary provisions including, inter alia:

Representations and warranties of the Borrower and Guarantor:

- Legal (due incorporation, authorisations, etc.)
- Material adverse change
- Information Memorandum is true and accurate
- Obligations do not conflict with any laws or any other agreement
- No material litigation
- Pari passu

Conditions precedent to Loans and Swingline Loans:

- legal opinions from English, French and Dutch counsel to the Arranger
- copies of constitutional documents

- appropriate board and shareholder resolutions
- delivery of last available accounts
- no actual or potential event of default is outstanding
- consents and authorisations
- confirmations that the representations and warranties are correct

Affirmative and negative covenants on the Guarantor standard for a financing of this type including, inter alia:

- interest coverage ratio of a minimum of [ ] to 1
- ratio of Net Debt/EBITDA not to exceed [ ] to 1
- negative pledge and disposals restriction on the Group
- sanctions and anti-corruption

Events of default including, inter alia:

- failure to pay
- misrepresentation
- breach of contract
- cross-default, subject to an agreed threshold amount
- insolvency/creditors' process
- material adverse change provision

Increased costs including those arising out of future changes to the regulatory environment or similar.

The importance of each of these items is explained in the relevant section of the related facility agreement in chapter 5. It should be noted that detailed definitions and levels for the financial covenants will normally be agreed before a mandate is awarded. The number and type of financial covenants will vary from deal to deal but we have included two common ones here for illustrative purposes.

The increased costs provisions have been an area of particular focus in the loan market following the implementation of Basel III. See chapter 2 for further detail. It remains to be seen whether any increased costs that lenders incur as a result of changes in the regulatory landscape following Brexit could be recouped under the increased costs provisions in facility agreements.

Sanctions and anti-corruption is another area of focus in the loan market. Previously lenders mitigated risk in this area by carrying out their own internal due diligence and KYC processes. However, lenders are now increasingly looking to enhance their protection by including sanctions and anti-corruption-related provisions (usually specific representations and covenants) in facility agreements. This is in part due to the large civil and/or criminal penalties that can be imposed on lenders by sanctions authorities as well as the risk of reputational damage should lenders be found to be involved in a transaction which breached sanctions.

If included, sanctions provisions are negotiated on a case-by-case basis and will depend on a variety of different factors including the parties involved, the nature of the borrower's business and the countries in which it operates. Many banks and financial institutions have their own form of wording for inclusion on lending transactions. The LMA has not therefore sought to include suggested wording in its primary facility agreements. See the further discussion in Clause 26 (*General undertakings*) in the sample agreement in chapter 5.

**Amendments/Waivers**: Amendments to or waivers under the Facility Agreement will require the approval of Majority Lenders (representing 66.6% or more of the Facility Amount) with certain exceptions which shall require the consent of all the Banks.

The Majority Lenders concept is a very important commercial element for both the borrower and the banks. Neither side wishes to be held to ransom by a minority participant yet both sides recognise that there are legitimate commercial issues that will require broad acceptance for the relationship to be maintained in harmonious fashion. The level of Majority Lenders included here is frequently found in corporate deals although different levels are sometimes used in more complex deals or in deals syndicated to US lenders.

A mechanism will be included in the Facility Agreement pursuant to which the Borrower may, subject to certain conditions, replace: (i) a Lender which has not consented to a waiver or amendment requiring the consent of all Lenders and to which Lenders holding an aggregate of [90]%. of the Facility Amount have consented; and/or (ii) a Lender to which the Borrower or the Guarantor becomes obliged to pay an amount pursuant to the illegality, increased costs or tax gross-up provisions of the Agreement in excess of amounts payable to the other Lenders generally; and/or (iii) a Defaulting Lender.

If a Lender fails to respond to a request for consent to amendments or waivers (other than in respect of certain amendments and waivers to be agreed), within [15] business days, that Lender's commitment or participation will not be included in calculating whether the consent of the relevant percentage of the Facility Amount and/or participations has been obtained to approve that request.

The above provisions (known colloquially as the "yank-the-bank" and the "snooze you lose" provisions respectively) are included in many LMA facility agreements as a means of allowing borrowers to deal with unresponsive or non-cooperative Lenders.

The "yank-the-bank" provision allows the borrower to find another bank or financial institution to replace an existing Lender which (a) refuses to consent to an "all Lender" amendment or waiver request to which a specified majority of the other Lenders have already consented, (b) has exercised its rights under the increased costs and/or tax gross up provisions, or (c) is a Defaulting Lender (see further below).

The "snooze you lose" provision allows the facility agent and the borrower to disregard the votes of Lenders which have failed to respond to an amendment or waiver request within a given time period when calculating whether Majority Lender or all Lender consent has been obtained for such amendment or waiver request.

**Transfer/Assignment**: Transfer Certificates/Assignment Agreements in customary form enabling the transfer or assignment of participations by syndicate banks to other banks and financial institutions subject to the prior written consent of the Borrower (unless the assignment or transfer is to another Lender or an Affiliate of a Lender or is made when an Event of Default is continuing), such consent not to be unreasonably withheld and to be deemed granted if not refused within five business days of the date when the request for consent was made. Transfers/assignments shall be in minimum amounts of US$10m.

Transferability is a requirement for most syndicated transactions in today's market. However, borrowers may have legitimate concerns over the quality of their banking syndicate, particularly in a standby facility or a revolving credit facility. If a bank is unable to fulfil its obligations under the terms of the facility agreement for any reason, the arrangers will generally, but without commitment, assist the borrower either to find a replacement bank or to reallocate the amount of the failed bank's participation among the syndicate. If this cannot successfully be achieved, the amount of the facility is reduced commensurately, which can have severe consequences for a borrower. Therefore a borrower usually requires the right to give consent for transfers to take place. The usual requirement of the lenders is for such consent not to be unreasonably withheld or delayed (and the LMA recommends that it be agreed that consent be deemed given if not expressly refused within five days). Any potential transferee must be able to book its commitment or asset such that the borrower can make payments free of withholding taxes or other deductions.

Since the 2008 financial crisis, LMA facility agreements have included a "Defaulting Lender" concept to deal with banks or other financial institutions which have failed to make their participation in a utilisation available to the facility agent (or have informed the facility agent they will not be able to do so) or are subject to insolvency proceedings or related events. If a bank or financial institution becomes a Defaulting Lender the LMA facility agreements provide for the following:

(a) The borrower can cancel the undrawn Commitments of the Defaulting Lender, which can then be assumed by another bank selected by the Borrower pursuant to the increase provision.

(b) The participations of the Defaulting Lender in any revolving facility may be converted into a separate term loan with a maturity which is the same as the relevant termination date for the Revolving Credit Facility and may be prepaid by the borrower at any time. This provision allows the borrower to deal with a situation where it would not be possible to rollover a revolving loan at the end of an interest period because a Defaulting Lender would be unable to fund its participation in a new revolving loan.

(c) The borrower can require the Defaulting Lender to transfer to a replacement bank.

(d) No commitment fee is payable to the Defaulting Lender.

(e) The Defaulting Lender will be disenfranchised in respect of its undrawn commitments.

(f) The Commitments of a Defaulting Lender can be disregarded if it fails to respond to an amendment or waiver request within a given time period (see explanation on "snooze and lose" provisions above).

LMA facility agreements also include a "Security over Lenders' rights" provision which allows members of the syndicate to assign their rights in respect of drawn participations under syndicated facilities in favour of central banks (without the consent of the borrower) as collateral for the receipt of funding under central bank liquidity programmes. The credit rating of the borrower, the currency of the facilities and governing law of the relevant facility agreement will generally determine whether lenders' participations constitute eligible collateral under such liquidity programmes.

In many other types of transactions, particularly those connected with acquisition finance whether investment grade or leveraged such as the Project Tennis transaction which follows in the next section, transfers are usually permitted to funds or other entities which are regularly engaged in or established for the purpose of making, purchasing or investing in loans, securities or other financial assets. DutchCo is unlikely to permit transfers to such entities as the ratings for its commercial paper programme will have been obtained, in part, on the basis of the quality of the participants in the syndicate. Furthermore, the pricing of this transaction will not generally be of interest to funds which typically target returns in excess of 150 basis points over LIBOR or EURIBOR.

Transfer certificates are incorporated in most syndicated facility agreements to permit the transfer to take place by novation with the minimum of extra documentation, but documentation will also permit transfers by way of assignment (see chapter 6 for an explanation of the different mechanisms). There will normally be a fee charged by the facility agent for documenting and implementing a transfer of a participation in the facility. This fee will be payable either by the transferor or by the transferee, depending on the result of their commercial negotiations.

In order to keep the syndicate to a manageable size for DutchCo, individual transfers are restricted to minimum amounts of US$10m.

**English Counsel for the Arrangers**: [English law firm].

This law firm will act for the arrangers in the negotiations with the borrower and the syndicate banks and will often be responsible for drafting the documentation (although sometimes the borrower's law firm will draft the documentation). At closing, the firm will issue its opinion to the Arranger, the Banks and the Facility Agent which will satisfy one of the conditions precedent. French and Dutch lawyers will also be required to give opinions on the Guarantor and Borrower.

**Governing law and jurisdiction**: The Facility Agreement will be subject to English law. The Borrower and Guarantor will submit to the non-exclusive jurisdiction of the courts of England & Wales.

Issues related to this provision (including the impact of Brexit) are discussed in chapter 5 and (in relation to Brexit) supplement 8 to chapter 2.

**Taxes**: All payments made under the Facility will be made free and clear of any taxes, duties, withholdings or other deductions whatsoever.

Lenders expect to receive all payments in full without any deductions at all. If the borrower and/or guarantor becomes obliged by law to make withholdings on any payments, they are required to gross up the payment so that the net amount is equal to the amount owing to the banks. Borrowers in withholding jurisdictions offer such protection only to lenders that are Qualifying Lenders (i.e., lenders that are able to receive payments without any withholding). The effect is that the borrowers take the change of law risk that withholding obligations would be extended or exemptions amended.

In 2013, the Organisation for Economic Co-operation and Development (the "OECD") published its Action Plan on Base Erosion and Profit Shifting ("BEPS"). BEPS comprises 15 Actions aimed at tackling tax planning strategies that shift profits from high tax jurisdictions to low tax ones.

Action 6 is aimed at counteracting "treaty shopping" which, broadly, targets structures designed to access artificially *double tax treaty* benefits where a person would otherwise be unable to. A typical structure which tax authorities may view as abusive would consist of an entity resident in a tax haven (or other non-treaty jurisdiction) establishing a conduit vehicle in a jurisdiction that has a double tax treaty with the borrower jurisdiction and does not itself impose withholding on interest. The lender would route the loan through the conduit, intending to eliminate or reduce the rate of withholding tax. Action 6, once fully implemented, would make such structures ineffective by denying treaty relief.

The implementation of Action 6 and certain other BEPS recommendations is achieved through a multilateral instrument (the "MLI"). At the time of writing, over 70 countries have signed the MLI which amends the terms of bilateral double tax treaties among the signatories. Although the take up has been significant, only a handful of those countries have yet completed the ratification process, meaning that only the treaties between these countries have been effectively amended.

This leaves most of the countries in the peculiar position of the rules being published but not yet effective. At the point they become effective, the application of treaties will change and that will likely be regarded as a change of law by most LMA-standard loan documents. Consequently, the borrowers are concerned as signing a loan agreement today means that they bear the risk that their lenders are, at some future point, excluded from treaty relief as a result of the implementation of Action 6. The borrowers, by contrast, have no visibility or control over their lenders' treaty positions and argue that, as a result, the lenders should bear this risk.

Lenders are equally concerned. The rules are fairly general and, aside from the most egregious examples, the exact application and scope is still unclear and so other perfectly commercial and non-tax driven structures may be inadvertently caught. It is, furthermore, unclear how tax authorities will interpret the MLI, and different tax authorities may take an entirely different approach.

Brexit is another uncertainty facing the loan market. In most cases it will have no tax impact on lending. However, in some cases (and in particular for Italian borrowers), a withholding tax exemption may be adversely affected by the UK leaving the EU. Lenders and borrowers alike should consider carefully whether the UK leaving the EU would affect lenders' Qualifying Lender status and result in such borrowers' being obliged to withhold taxes from interest payments to UK based lenders.

**Clear Market**: From the date of acceptance of this proposal until the Signing Date, the Borrower and the Guarantor will ensure that no other debt issue will be syndicated, distributed or privately placed which might, in the Arranger's sole opinion, have a detrimental effect on the successful completion of this transaction.

When syndication starts, the arrangers need to ensure that the borrower and/or guarantor has no other competing transaction in the market at the same time. This is to prevent confusion in the market which may be detrimental to both deals and ultimately affect the success of the syndication. It also prevents the borrower from appearing to be adopting a disorganised approach to the market. However, the arrangers need to adopt a realistic and pragmatic approach. For instance, a yen-denominated private placement in Tokyo could only with great difficulty be argued to breach the clear market provisions for a US Dollar-denominated standby facility.

The terms of the clear market provision are such that a breach will permit the arrangers to pull (withdraw) the transaction from the marketplace and not to proceed further until appropriate renegotiations have taken place if, in their sole opinion, another transaction is launched which would interfere with the market reception accorded to the transaction contemplated by the term sheet. If the borrower is a frequent user of the market, it is in the interest of both the borrower and the arrangers to expedite the transaction through the market to permit the borrower to return to the market if so desired. A borrower may seek to negotiate release from the clear market provision upon completion of the syndication process. The arrangers must negotiate the precise event which signifies that the syndication process is complete. In some cases this may be the end of the syndication window, meaning the end of the period during which the transaction is actually in the market. It may also be defined as the date when a fixed amount has been raised from the market. The latter is a lot less certain for the borrower as the date by which amounts are raised from the market will depend to a large extent on the market's reception of the facility.

**Syndication Strategy**: It will be the intention to seek participations in this transaction from a group of major international banks having an existing relationship with the Guarantor and to form a syndicate of 15 to 25 banks from that group.

The syndication strategy must be briefly discussed if it is to be a condition of the offer. This transaction is structured as a relationship deal, and the borrower will have significant input over the choice of banks to be invited. Given that this deal is principally to be used as a back up line for commercial paper, there may be an additional condition limiting the choice of banks – for instance to those that have qualifying short term debt ratings such as an A-1 and/or P-1 rating from Standard & Poor's and Moody's respectively. This is to ensure that the quality of the banks providing the back up line does not detract from the ratings that the issuer itself is otherwise able to enjoy when it issues commercial paper.

Where there is more than one arranger, each of the arrangers will normally agree to comply with "no front running" provisions in the mandate or commitment letter, which prohibit any arranger from seeking to sell down its exposure in any manner which is contrary to the agreed syndication strategy (and which could prejudice the position of the other arrangers).

**Information**: The Borrower and the Guarantor will provide financial and other information as required by the Arrangers for distribution to prospective syndicate banks.

In order to assist banks in making their decision to join the syndicate it is always necessary to provide potential participants with detailed information about the borrower and, as in this case, the guarantor as well. This paragraph merely provides the arrangers with the right to demand information from the borrower and guarantor and to confirm that such information may be disseminated to potential participant banks. The contents of an information memorandum and the issues involved in organising its distribution are discussed in chapter 4.

**Expiry Date**: If not accepted in writing by the Borrower, this offer will expire five days from the date of this offer unless previously extended in writing by the Arrangers.

In the event that the Facility Agreement is not signed within three months of the date of acceptance of this offer by the Borrower, the Arrangers reserve the right to renegotiate the terms and conditions set out in this term sheet and, if agreement with the Borrower cannot be reached, to withdraw this offer. In such an event, the Borrower will indemnify the Arrangers for their Expenses.

An expiry date is essential since it enables the arrangers to achieve two goals; first, it permits the arrangers to limit their exposure to the vagaries of the market, the risk that market conditions may change thereby causing the offer to become off-market. More importantly, it puts pressure on the borrower to make a decision since there is no certainty that the offer will be renewed after the expiry date.

If the offer is fully underwritten, i.e., with fixed terms and conditions, the time limit will normally be very short, yet sufficient for the borrower to obtain whatever internal approvals are necessary to award a formal mandate. If the offer is partially underwritten or on a best efforts basis only, the time for acceptance may be longer since the market risk is reduced. Nevertheless, for the transaction to be a success, the terms and conditions must reflect those of the prevailing market and, if the expiry date is extended unduly, there is an ever-increasing risk of it being adversely affected by market movement or sentiment.

The second part of this provision sets the latest date for closing the transaction and stipulates that the commercial terms will be subject to renegotiation if the transaction has not in fact closed by that date. In normal circumstances, three months from the start of syndication is sufficient to close a correctly priced transaction.

If a transaction does not close within the stipulated period (after three months in this example) and agreement on revised terms is not reached by the parties, legal and other out-of-pocket expenses will in all probability have already been incurred by the arrangers. The language in this offer calls for the borrower to indemnify the arrangers for these costs. It does not contemplate covering the cost of management time expended by the arrangers.

**Market Conditions**: No events or circumstances (including any material adverse change or the continuation of any circumstance(s)) occurring from the date of acceptance of this offer until the Signing Date in the condition or rating of the Borrower or Guarantor, or in the international capital markets which, in the sole opinion of the Arranger, might affect (directly or indirectly) the relevant syndicated credit market(s) for this transaction and require its withdrawal from such market(s). In the event that such an event takes place the obligation of the Arrangers to arrange the Facility on the terms proposed will cease and the Arrangers shall be entitled, after consultation with the Borrower and Guarantor, to change the structure, terms and pricing of the Facility.

The borrower and guarantor can be expected to have knowledge of any impending situation which may affect the credit. It is therefore logical for any arranger to seek protection from the circumstance where, having launched a transaction, it finds that events occur which adversely affect the credit quality of the borrower. In such a case, the deal may be withdrawn entirely from the market, or it may be repriced and relaunched, depending upon circumstances.

A key issue for an arranger is to ensure that out-of-pocket expenses can be recovered if the deal is withdrawn from the market for whatever reason. Arrangers may also wish to negotiate a drop dead fee, to remunerate them for their commitment and allocation of resources to an aborted transaction although this will be a matter for negotiation. These issues are usually dealt with in a separate legally binding letter between the arranger, the borrower and/or guarantor.

**Legal Status**: This summary term sheet does not constitute a legally binding offer, undertaking or commitment on the part of Arranger Bank Limited, Top Bank plc, XYZ Bank Limited or any of their affiliates to arrange, underwrite or make available the Facility described above.

This makes clear, for the avoidance of doubt, the exact status of this summary term sheet.

# PROJECT TENNIS

As described above, Project Tennis is the code name given to the proposed acquisition of Target plc ('Target') by Bidco plc ('Bidco'). The code name is necessary to prevent inadvertent leakage of the deal to non-team members and/or the market. The team itself is constituted by named individuals who are registered with their compliance unit as being *insiders* on the deal.

The offer by Top Bank to arrange finance for this transaction consists of two parts: a mandate letter and a term sheet attached as an appendix. Together they form the proposal submitted to Bidco. This separation is for convenience and clarity only and in no way adds to or diminishes the legal basis for the ultimate contractual arrangements between the parties. The mandate letter contains clauses forming the basis of the mandate with Top Bank and those which relate specifically to the execution of the transaction, for example, market flex, clear market and publicity. The term sheet contains the principal terms and conditions of the facilities and related covenants, undertakings and events of default, etc.

The borrower, Bidco, is expected to sign and date the mandate letter. Thereafter, Top Bank can begin the process of arranging the transaction, preparing the information memorandum, advising and discussing with Bidco which banks to invite into the transaction. In parallel, Top Bank will confirm the mandate to its legal advisers and request that the first draft of the facility agreement and related documentation be prepared. Depending on the timing of the announcement of the bid, this may be required within a day or two or over a week or two. In any case, Top Bank is ready to enter into a fully underwritten bilateral agreement with Bidco to support its bid for Target. Top Bank may decide to sub-underwrite the transaction once the bid has been officially announced and invite the sub-underwriters to await the final outcome before proceeding to a general syndication.

In other circumstances, more commonly observed for large transactions in today's market, the borrower may feel that the appointment of more than one bank may be prudent: it may be that the credit exposure is too high for Top Bank by itself or that the market will value the names of two banks working on the transaction. The borrower may prefer this route too as it provides a fallback if one bank does not get the requisite approvals or even to ensure there is not too much dependency upon one bank only. In addition it may also prevent the second bank from supporting a rival bid for Target. Banks, however, do not necessarily wish to tie themselves to just one bid when there are competing bids for a target as the probability of success reduces with each additional bid. Banks have therefore designed internal Chinese walls to enable them to support simultaneous bids for a target company by several of their clients, a process which is normally documented and controlled by a bank's compliance department.

Bidco in this case is an established corporate entity which is able to borrow based on its own credit standing. Other structures seen in the market may include a bidco/borrower which is a special purpose vehicle (SPV) requiring support from its parent company by way of guarantee or where the SPV is separately capitalised and the borrowing obligations "ring-fenced" from its shareholders (who do not provide guarantees). In this latter case the lenders would normally expect to receive substantial security over the SPVs shares and assets.

**Project Tennis – mandate letter**

| The offer to arrange finance comprises this mandate letter and the term sheet attached as an Appendix. |
|---|

To:

[Bidco plc] (the "**Company**")
[*Address*]
For the attention of:

[Date]

Dear Sirs

**£1,000,000,000 Term Loan and Revolving Credit Facility (the "Facility")**

We Top Bank (the "**Mandated Lead Arranger**" and the "**Underwriter**") are pleased to set out in this letter the terms and conditions on which we are willing to arrange, manage the primary syndication of and underwrite the Facility.

| Top Bank is emphasising its commitment to be the mandated lead arranger and underwriter of the transaction even though in practice it is often the same legal entity that is fulfilling both roles as is the case here. Top Bank is showing its desire to arrange and manage the transaction and is prepared to commit its balance sheet in support. In contrast to the DutchCo term sheet, here Top Bank is agreeing to underwrite the financing rather than arranging it on a "best efforts" basis. This means that they are agreeing to provide the financing themselves if other lenders cannot be found (subject to the terms and conditions of the mandate letter). |
|---|

In this letter:

"**Affiliate**" means in relation to a person, a subsidiary or holding company of that person and a subsidiary of any such holding company.

"**Business Day**" means a day (other than a Saturday or Sunday) on which banks are open for general business in London.

"**Close of primary syndication**" means the time the Mandated Lead Arranger and Underwriter close syndication under paragraphs 8.2 or 8.3.

"**Facility Documents**" means a facility agreement and related documentation (based on the terms set out in the Term Sheet and this letter) in form and substance satisfactory to the Mandated Lead Arranger and Underwriter.

"**Fee Letter**" means any fee letter between the Mandated Lead Arranger, the Underwriter and/or the Agent and the Company dated on or about the date of this letter.

"**Mandate Documents**" means this letter, the Term Sheet and any Fee Letter.

"**Successful syndication**" means the underwriter reduces its participation in Tranches B and C only of the Facility to a final hold of not more than £100,000,000 (in aggregate).

"**Term Sheet**" means the term sheet attached to this letter as an appendix.

Unless a contrary indication appears, a term defined in any Mandate Document has the same meaning when used in this letter.

Some other definitions are to be found elsewhere in the mandate letter and term sheet.

1. **Appointment**

1.1 The Company appoints:

(a) the Mandated Lead Arranger as exclusive arranger of the Facility;

(b) the Underwriter as exclusive underwriter of the Facility;

(c) the Mandated Lead Arranger as exclusive bookrunner in connection with syndication of the Facility; and

(d) the Mandated Lead Arranger as facility agent in connection with the Facility.

1.2 Until this mandate terminates in accordance with paragraph 15 (*Termination*):

(a) no other person shall be appointed as mandated lead arranger, underwriter, bookrunner or facility agent;

(b) no other titles shall be awarded; and

(c) except as provided in the Mandate Documents, no other compensation shall be paid to any person, in connection with the Facility without the prior written consent of the Mandated Lead Arranger.

## 2. Conditions

Below are general conditions which govern the validity of the offer to arrange finance and include a specific reference to client identification procedures.

This offer to arrange, manage the primary syndication of and underwrite the Facility is made on the terms of the Mandate Documents and is subject to satisfaction of the following conditions:

(a) compliance by the Company with all the terms of each Mandate Document;

(b) the conditions set out in paragraph 3 (*Material Adverse Change*);

(c) each of the representations and warranties made by the Company or any other member of the Group in connection with the transaction contemplated in the Mandate Documents (including, but not limited to, those set out in paragraph 9 (*Information*)) being correct;

(d) the preparation, execution and delivery of the Facility Documents by no later than [•] or any later date agreed between the Company and each of the Mandated Lead Arranger and the Underwriter;

(e) completion by each of the Mandated Lead Arranger and the Underwriter of client identification procedures (including, if necessary, identification of directors and major shareholders of the Company and all other Obligors) in compliance with applicable money laundering rules;

(f) each of the Mandated Lead Arranger and Underwriter obtaining credit committee and all other relevant internal approvals with respect to the company, the Group and the Facility;

(g) no public offer in respect of the shares of the Company or a merger by the Company and another person being announced and no person or group of persons acting in concert gaining control of the Company;

(h) completion of legal, regulatory and financial, due diligence in respect of the Company and the Group, the results being in all respects satisfactory to each of the Mandated Lead Arranger and Underwriter; and

(i) the Company and all other Obligors obtaining all necessary regulatory approvals in connection with the Facility from any relevant authorities in any relevant jurisdictions.

3. **Material Adverse Change**

> The Material Adverse Change clause protects Top Bank from material adverse changes until the signature of the credit agreement. It does not affect the certain funds provision post signature which is governed by the negotiated terms of the credit agreement.

The obligations of each of the Mandated Lead Arranger and the Underwriter under the Mandate Documents are subject to the absence, in its opinion, of any event(s) or circumstance(s) (including any material adverse change or the continuation of any circumstance(s)) which, in its opinion, has (have) adversely affected or could adversely affect:

(a) the business, condition (financial or otherwise), operations, performance, assets or prospects of the Group since the date as at which the latest consolidated audited financial statements were prepared;

(b) the ability of the Company or any other Obligor to perform its obligations under any Mandate Document or Facility Document; or

(c) the international or any relevant domestic syndicated loan, debt, bank, capital or equity market(s) which in the opinion of the Mandated Lead Arranger or Underwriter could prejudice syndication of the Facility, during the period from the date of this letter to the date of signing of the Facility Documents.

4. **Clear Market**

4.1 During the period from the date of this letter to the date, following close of primary syndication, on which all the Lenders subject to such syndication become party to the Facility Documents, the Company shall not and shall ensure that no other member of the Group shall announce, enter into discussions to raise, raise or attempt to raise any other finance in the international or any relevant domestic syndicated loan, debt, bank, capital or equity market(s) (including, but not limited to, any bilateral or syndicated facility, bond or note issuance or private placement) without the prior written consent of the Mandated Lead Arranger and the Underwriter.

4.2 Paragraph 4.1 does not apply to:

(a) the Facility;

(b) any commercial paper issued under a programme existing on the date of this letter and notified in writing to the Mandated Lead Arranger and the Underwriter prior to the date of this letter; or

(c) the renewal of any existing bilateral facility with the same lender, on substantially the same terms and for the same or a smaller amount.

This clause is intended to ensure that the Mandated Lead Arranger is not trying to syndicate this facility at the same time as another competing financing by the same group is in the market.

5. **Market Flex**

The market flex clause permits changes to pricing and structure if it is proving difficult to attract potential lenders as part of syndication. Such clauses are often unpopular with borrowers and they therefore often seek to limit their scope. For instance, here there are caps on the increase in fees and margin.

5.1 During the period from the date of this letter to the date, following close of primary syndication, on which all the Lenders subject to such syndication become party to the Facility Documents, each of the Mandated Lead Arranger and the Underwriter shall be entitled to change the pricing, terms and/or structure (but not the total amount) of the Facility if that Mandated Lead Arranger or Underwriter determines that such changes are advisable in order to enhance the prospects of a successful syndication of the Facility.

5.2 Paragraph 5.1 above shall not result in an increase in:

(a) the Margin by more than 0.30% at each Margin level listed in the Term Sheet; or

(b) each fee referred to in paragraph 6.2(a) by more than 0.35%.

5.3 The Company agrees to, and shall ensure that each other Obligor shall, amend the Facility Documents to reflect any changes made under paragraph 5.1.

6. **Fees, Costs and Expenses**

The Fees, Costs and Expenses clause provides for fees to be paid on a phased basis as the acquisition process proceeds. The front-end fees could be paid upfront as a single amount, but in practice most borrowers seek to defer payment until they see how the acquisition is progressing. From the mandated bank's point of view, it is essential to have at least staged payments if sub-underwriting is expected as fees will be needed to pay to these banks for their underwriting commitments.

6.1 All fees shall be paid as set out in the Term Sheet and paragraph 6.2.

6.2

(a) A front-end fee is payable by the Company to the Mandated Lead Arranger comprising the following amounts, in each case calculated on the amount of commitments (to the extent not cancelled or reduced as at the date such amounts are payable) in the relevant Tranche (if any).

*Tranche A*

(i) 0.50% flat on Tranche A in the following instalments:

(A) [•]% payable on the first Business Day following signing the Facility Agreement; and

(B) [•]% payable on the earlier of three months from the date of signing of the Facility Agreement and the date of first utilisation under the Facility Agreement.

(ii) If the Term Out Option is exercised, a fee will be payable by the Company at that time to facilitate the syndication of Tranche A (in addition to the fees in (i) above and the Term Out Fee of 0.25% flat referred to in the Term Sheet). This additional fee will be specified by us to the Company and will reflect our judgement of fees that would be required to be paid to potential syndicate participants to ensure that this Tranche A is successfully syndicated.

*Tranches B & C*

1.00% flat on the aggregate amount of Tranches B and C in the following instalments:

(i) 0.20% flat on the first Business Day following signing of the Facility Agreement;

(ii) 0.25% flat on the earlier of 14 days from the date of the Offer Press Release and the launch of syndication;

(iii) 0.25% flat on the earlier of [•] and the date of first utilisation under the Facility Agreement; and

(iv) 0.30% flat on the date that the Offer becomes or is declared unconditional in all respects.

This fee includes the arrangement, underwriting and participation fees payable to the Lenders in syndication at the sole discretion of the Mandated Lead Arranger.

(b) An annual agency fee of £30,000 per annum, payable to the Agent for the first year within 30 days of signing of the Facility Agreement and on each anniversary of that date thereafter.

6.3 The Company shall promptly on demand pay the Agent and the Mandated Lead Arranger and the Underwriter the amount of all costs and expenses (including legal fees) reasonably incurred by any of them in connection with:

(a) the negotiation, preparation, printing and execution of the Facility Documents and the Mandate Documents; and

(b) the syndication of the Facility,

whether or not the Facility Documents are signed.

7. **Payments**

| Payments are to be made in the currency of invoice and without deduction. |
|---|

All payments to be made under the Mandate Documents:

(a) shall be paid in the currency of invoice and in immediately available, freely transferable cleared funds to such account(s) with such bank(s) as the Mandated Lead Arranger or the Underwriter (as applicable) notifies to the Company;

(b) shall be paid without any deduction or withholding for or on account of tax (a "**Tax Deduction**") unless a Tax Deduction is required by law. If a Tax Deduction is required by law to be made, the amount of the payment due shall be increased to an amount which (after making any Tax Deduction) leaves an amount equal to the payment which would have been due if no Tax Deduction had been required; and

(c) are exclusive of any value added tax or similar charge ("**VAT**"). If VAT is chargeable, the Company shall also and at the same time pay to the recipient of the relevant payment an amount equal to the amount of the VAT.

## 8. Syndication

This clause sets out the arrangements and obligations of the mandated lead arranger and the borrower in connection with the syndication. It also contains a commercially crucial clause 8.8 overriding the Margin set out in the Term Sheet. As Top Bank plans to hold Facility A on its own books, it can set whatever margin it deems appropriate. By offering this aggressive margin, Top Bank hopes to secure asset disposal and bond mandates. For more information on "future service restrictions" i.e., clauses which oblige borrowers to award or offer future services to particular banks, please see supplement 8 to chapter 2.

As the Target is a listed plc, it is of paramount importance that confidentiality is maintained before the offer is publicly announced. Any syndication would therefore most likely take place after the date of announcement of the proposed offer. To the extent syndication occurs before the date of public announcement then the "Rule of Six" will need to be complied with – this is a Takeover Code rule which states that an announcement may be required (following consultation with the Panel) if more than six external parties (including any potential finance providers, but excluding immediate advisers) have been approached about a possible takeover offer. The Market Abuse Regulation would also need to be considered in the case of a takeover offer for a company with shares admitted to trading on a regulated market.

8.1 The Mandated Lead Arranger shall, in consultation with the Company, manage all aspects of syndication of the Facility, including timing, the selection of potential Lenders, the acceptance and allocation of commitments and the amount and distribution of fees to Lenders. Subject to any applicable confidentiality agreement between the Company and the Mandated Lead Arranger, the Company authorises the Mandated Lead Arranger to discuss the terms of the Facility with and to disclose those terms to, potential Lenders to facilitate the syndication.

Under UK competition law, conduct such as price-fixing and market sharing between competing arrangers and potential lenders can give rise to individual criminal liability (this is the so-called cartel offence) and the inappropriate disclosure or exchange of sensitive competitive information can constitute such conduct. There is a defence to the cartel offence if the borrower is made aware of the agreement between the arrangers and potential lenders. The language at the end of clause 8.1 therefore makes it clear that the arrangers will need to interact with potential lenders and the borrower authorises this legitimate competitive interaction. In recent years, there has been an increased focus on competition issues in the loan markets. In particular, in April 2017 the Directorate General for Competition of the European Commission launched a study into the impact of loan syndication on competition in credit markets. This study has not resulted in any legislation as at the date of writing, but market participants are very aware that their behaviour must be such as to be in compliance with applicable competition/anti-trust laws. In particular, the market has seen an increased focus on the careful design of internal policies to avoid excessive restrictions on efficient price formation and to take into account factors such as the type and timing of information exchange, the role of borrower consent and the importance of documentation and records.

8.2 At any time after the Mandated Lead Arranger has received sufficient commitments that (when reflected as participations in the Facility) would result in a successful syndication, the Mandated Lead Arranger may:

(a) close syndication; and

(b) accept the commitments received and allocate resulting participations in the Facility (in a way that will result in a successful syndication)

8.3 If by [•] the Mandated Lead Arranger has not received sufficient commitments that (when reflected as participations in the Facility) would result in a successful syndication, the Mandated Lead Arranger may:

(a) close syndication; and

(b) accept any commitments received and allocate resulting participations in the Facility.

8.4 The Mandated Lead Arranger may not close syndication, accept commitments received or allocate participations in the Facility other than in accordance with either of paragraphs 8.2 or 8.3.

8.5 The Company shall, and shall ensure that the other members of the Group, give any assistance which the Mandated Lead Arranger reasonably requires in relation to the syndication of the Facility including, but not limited to:

(a) the preparation, with the assistance of the Mandated Lead Arranger, of an information memorandum containing all relevant information (including projections) including, but not limited to, information about the Group and how the proceeds of the Facility will be applied (the "**Information Memorandum**"). The Company shall approve the Information Memorandum before the Mandated Lead Arranger distributes it to potential Lenders on the Company's behalf;

(b) providing any information reasonably requested by the Mandated Lead Arranger or potential Lenders in connection with syndication;

(c) making available the senior management and representatives of the Company and other members of the Group for the purposes of giving presentations to, and participating in meetings with, potential Lenders at such times and places as the Mandated Lead Arranger may reasonably request;

(d) using best efforts to ensure that syndication of the Facility benefits from the Group's existing lending relationships;

(e) agreeing to such shorter Interest Periods during the syndication process as are necessary for the purposes of syndication;

(f) entering into a syndication agreement in substantially the same form as the current LMA recommended form of syndication and amendment agreement; and

(g) making any minor amendments to the Facility Documents which the Mandated Lead Arranger reasonably requests on behalf of potential Lenders.

8.6 The Underwriter hereby confirms its intention that, as at the completion of primary syndication, it will hold Tranche B and Tranche C commitments of an amount not less than any other Lender, unless otherwise agreed. Subject to paragraph 8.7 below, the Underwriter will hold 100% of the Tranche A commitments.

8.7 The Mandated Lead Arranger shall be entitled to syndicate Tranche A following exercise of the Term Out Option. The Company will use all reasonable endeavours to complete the refinancing of Tranche A during the six-month period commencing on the date which is six months from the date of signing the Facility Agreement, but in any event with a view to completing such refinancing by no later than a date which is approximately nine months from the date of signing the Facility Agreement.

8.8 Notwithstanding the provisions for Margin adjustment in the Term Sheet, the Margin for Tranche A during the period commencing on the date of signing the Facility Agreement and ending on the date the Term Out Option is exercised shall be 0.70% per annum.

9. **Information**

9.1 The Company represents and warrants that:

(a) any factual information provided to the Mandated Lead Arranger by or on behalf of it or any other member of the Group (including for the purposes of preparing the Information Memorandum) (the "**Information**") is true and accurate in all material respects as at the date it is provided or as at the date (if any) at which it is stated;

(b) nothing has occurred or been omitted and no information has been given or withheld that results in the Information being untrue or misleading in any material respect; and

(c) any financial projections contained in the Information have been prepared in good faith on the basis of recent historical information and on the basis of reasonable assumptions.

9.2 The representations and warranties set out in paragraph 9.1 are deemed to be made by the Company daily by reference to the facts and circumstances then existing commencing on the date of this letter and continuing until the date the Facility Documents are signed.

9.3 The Company shall immediately notify the Mandated Lead Arranger in writing if any representation and warranty set out in paragraph 9.1 is incorrect or misleading and agrees to supplement the Information promptly from time to time to ensure that each such representation and warranty is correct when made.

9.4 The Company acknowledges that the Mandated Lead Arranger and Underwriter will be relying on the Information without carrying out any independent verification.

10. **Indemnity**

10.1

(a) Whether or not the Facility Documents are signed, the Company shall within three business days of demand indemnify each Indemnified Person against any cost, expense, loss or liability (including without limitation legal fees) incurred by or awarded against that Indemnified Person in each case arising out of or in connection with any action, claim, investigation or proceeding commenced or threatened (including, without limitation, any action, claim, investigation or proceeding to preserve or enforce rights) in relation to:

(i) the use of the proceeds of the Facility;

(ii) any Mandate Document or any Facility Document; and/or

(iii) the arranging or underwriting of the Facility.

(b) The Company will not be liable under paragraph (a) above for any cost, expense, loss or liability (including without limitation legal fees) incurred by or awarded against an Indemnified Person if that cost, expense, loss or liability results directly from any breach by that Indemnified Person of any Mandate Document or any Facility Document which is in each case finally judicially determined to have resulted directly from the gross negligence or wilful misconduct of that Indemnified Person.

(c) For the purposes of this paragraph 10: "**Indemnified Person**" means the Mandated Lead Arranger, the Underwriter, the Agent, each Lender, in each case, any of their respective Affiliates and each of their (or their respective Affiliates') respective directors, officers, employees and agents.

10.2 No Mandated Lead Arranger or Underwriter shall have any duty or obligation, whether as fiduciary for any Indemnified Person or otherwise, to recover any payment made or required to be made under paragraph 10.1.

10.3

(a) The Company agrees that no Indemnified Person shall have any liability (whether direct or indirect, in contract or tort or otherwise) to the Company or any of its Affiliates for or in connection with anything referred to in paragraph 10.1 above except, following the Company's agreement to the Mandate Documents, for any such cost, expense, loss or liability incurred by the Company that results directly from any breach by that Indemnified Person of any Mandate Document or any Facility Document which is in each case finally judicially determined to have resulted directly from the gross negligence or wilful misconduct of that Indemnified Person.

(b) Notwithstanding paragraph (a) above, no Indemnified Person shall be responsible or have any liability to the Company or any of its Affiliates or anyone else for consequential losses or damages.

(c) The Company represents to the Mandated Lead Arranger and Underwriter that:

(i) it is acting for its own account and it has made its own independent decisions to enter into the transaction contemplated in the Mandate Documents (the "**Transaction**") and as to whether the Transaction is appropriate or proper for it based upon its own judgement and upon advice from such advisers as it has deemed necessary;

(ii) it is not relying on any communication (written or oral) from the Mandated Lead Arranger or Underwriter as investment advice or as a recommendation to enter into the Transaction, it being understood that information and explanations related to the terms and conditions of the Transaction shall not be considered investment advice or a recommendation to enter into the Transaction. No communication (written or oral) received from the Mandated Lead Arranger or Underwriter shall be deemed to be an assurance or guarantee as to the expected results of the Transaction;

(iii) it is capable of assessing the merits of and understanding (on its own behalf or through independent professional advice), and understands and accepts, the terms, conditions and risks of the Transaction. It is also capable of assuming, and assumes, the risks of the Transaction; and

(iv) no Mandated Lead Arranger or Underwriter is acting as a fiduciary for or as an adviser to it in connection with the Transaction.

10.4 The Contracts (Rights of Third Parties) Act 1999 shall apply to this paragraph 10 but only for the benefit of the other Indemnified Persons, subject always to the terms of paragraphs 18.2 and 20 (*Governing Law and Jurisdiction*).

11. **Confidentiality**

For transactions of this type, confidentiality is crucial and a requirement for the deal team who become insiders owing to their access to market sensitive information. This clause is also designed to prevent the borrower shopping the deal to other competing banks in an attempt to secure more favourable terms.

The Company acknowledges that the Mandate Documents are confidential and the Company shall not, and shall ensure that no other member of the Group shall, without the prior written consent of each of the Mandated Lead Arranger and the Underwriter, disclose the Mandate Documents or their contents to any other person except:

(a) as required by law or by any applicable governmental or other regulatory authority or by any applicable stock exchange; and

(b) to its employees or professional advisers for the purposes of the Facility who have been made aware of and agree to be bound by the obligations under this paragraph or are in any event subject to confidentiality obligations as a matter of law or professional practice.

12. **Publicity/Announcements**

12.1 All publicity in connection with the Facility shall be managed by the Mandated Lead Arranger in consultation with the Company.

12.2 No announcements regarding the Facility or any roles as arranger, underwriter, lender or agent shall be made without the prior written consent of the Company and each of the Mandated Lead Arranger and Underwriter.

13. **Conflicts**

This clause recognises the reality that many banks may have internal conflicts of interest over their support for a transaction. For this reason "Chinese Wall" or "information barrier" procedures have been adopted in most banks to ensure that they can simultaneously support multiple bids for the same target.

13.1 The Company, the Mandated Lead Arranger and the Underwriter acknowledge that the Mandated Lead Arranger or its Affiliates and the Underwriter or its Affiliates may provide debt financing, equity capital or other services to other persons with whom the Company or its Affiliates may have conflicting interests in respect of the Facility in this or other transactions.

13.2 The Company, the Mandated Lead Arranger and the Underwriter acknowledge that the Mandated Lead Arranger or its Affiliates and the Underwriter or its Affiliates may act in more than one capacity in relation to this transaction and may have conflicting interests in respect of such different capacities.

13.3 The Mandated Lead Arranger and the Underwriter shall not use confidential information obtained from the Company or its Affiliates for the purposes of the Facility in connection with providing services to other persons or furnish such information to such other persons.

13.4 The Company acknowledges that the Mandated Lead Arranger and the Underwriter have no obligation to use any information obtained from another source for the purposes of the Facility or to furnish such information to the Company or its Affiliates.

14. **Assignments**

The Company shall not assign any of its rights or transfer any of its rights or obligations under the Mandate Documents without the prior written consent of the Mandated Lead Arranger and the Underwriter.

15. **Termination**

15.1 If the Company does not accept the offer made by the Mandated Lead Arranger and the Underwriter in this letter before close of business in London on [•], such offer shall terminate on that date.

15.2 The Mandated Lead Arranger or the Underwriter may terminate its obligations under this letter with immediate effect by notifying the Company if:

(a) in its opinion, any of the conditions set out in paragraph 2 (*Conditions*) is not satisfied; or

(b) the Company fails or has failed to disclose to the Mandated Lead Arranger or the Underwriter information which could be relevant to their decision to arrange or underwrite the Facility.

16. **Survival**

16.1 Except for paragraphs 2 (*Conditions*), 3 (*Material Adverse Change*) and 15 (*Termination*) the terms of this letter shall survive and continue after the Facility Documents are signed.

16.2 Without prejudice to paragraph 16.1, paragraphs 6 (*Fees, Costs and Expenses*), 7 (*Payments*), 10 (*Indemnity*), 11 (*Confidentiality*), 12 (*Publicity/ Announcements*), 13 (*Conflicts*) and 15 (*Termination*) to 20 (*Governing Law and Jurisdiction*) inclusive shall survive and continue after any termination of the obligations of the Mandated Lead Arranger or the Underwriter under the Mandate Documents.

17. **Entire Agreement**

17.1 The Mandate Documents set out the entire agreement between the Company the Mandated Lead Arranger and the Underwriter as to arranging and underwriting the Facility and supersede any prior oral and/or written understandings or arrangements relating to the Facility.

17.2 Any provision of a Mandate Document may only be amended or waived in writing signed by the Company, the Mandated Lead Arranger and the Underwriter.

18. **Third Party Rights**

18.1 Unless expressly provided to the contrary in this letter, a person who is not a party to this letter has no right under the Contracts (Rights of Third Parties) Act 1999 to enforce or to enjoy the benefit of any of its terms.

18.2 Notwithstanding any term of this letter, the consent of any person who is not a party to this letter is not required to rescind or vary this letter at any time.

19. **Counterparts**

This letter may be executed in any number of counterparts and this has the same effect as if the signatures on the counterparts were on a single copy of this letter.

20. **Governing Law and Jurisdiction**

20.1 This letter (including the agreement constituted by your acknowledgement of its terms) and any non-contractual obligation arising out of it (or out of such agreement) are governed by English law.

20.2 The courts of England have non-exclusive jurisdiction to settle any dispute arising out of or in connection with this Letter

If you agree to the above, please acknowledge your agreement and acceptance of the offer by signing and returning the enclosed copy of this letter to [•] at Top Bank.

Yours faithfully

..................................

For and on behalf of

**Top Bank**

as Mandated Lead Arranger and Underwriter

We acknowledge and agree to the above:

..................................

For and on behalf of

**Bidco plc**

## Appendix: Project Tennis – term sheet

## £1bn multi-currency facilities for Bidco plc for the proposed acquisition of Target

As stated above, the mandate letter and term sheet appended to it constitute together the offer to arrange this financing. The structure and language used for this case study closely follow the standard forms developed under the auspices of the LMA.

The term sheet comprises six principal sub-sections as follows:

| | |
|---|---|
| **The Parties** | A list of all the relevant parties to the transaction. |
| **Facility A** | Principal terms and conditions of a £300m one-year revolving credit facility with Term Out Option. |
| **Facility B** | Principal terms and conditions of a £300m five-year amortising term loan. |
| **Facility C** | Principal terms and conditions of a £400m five-year revolving credit facility. |
| **Pricing** | Relevant pricing components for the Facilities. Note that there is an override in the mandate letter relating to the Margin on Facility A (Clause 8.8). |
| **Other Terms** | Details of clauses for documentation including covenants, undertakings, events of default, conditions precedent, transferability, governing law and jurisdiction, etc. |

This standardised format enables the reader to review the terms of the proposal in an organised and comprehensive manner. Defined terms are set out at the end of the term sheet.

*Please note that the terms set out in this term sheet are indicative only and do not constitute an offer to arrange or finance the Facilities. The provision of the Facilities is subject to due diligence, credit committee approval, the terms and conditions of the Mandate Letter and satisfactory documentation.*

This caveat will be removed when the terms and conditions have been agreed.

[Date]

**Parties**

| | |
|---|---|
| **Original Borrower:** | Bidco plc |
| **Borrowers:** | In addition to the Original Borrower, any subsidiaries of the Original Borrower which comply with the requirements for Additional Obligors (see below). |
| **Guarantors:** | Any member of the Group which is a Material Subsidiary from time to time.<br><br>The aggregate of earnings before interest, tax, depreciation and amortisation (calculated on the same basis as EBITDA) excluding intra-Group items and the aggregate gross assets of the Guarantors (calculated on an unconsolidated basis and excluding intra-Group items and investments in any other members of the Group) must exceed [90]% of EBITDA/consolidated gross assets of the Group. |
| **Material Subsidiary:** | Any member of the Group: (i) which has earnings before interest, tax, depreciation and amortisation (calculated on the same basis as EBITDA) which exceed 5% of the Group's EBITDA; or (ii) whose gross assets (calculated on an unconsolidated basis and excluding intra-Group items and investments in any other members of the Group) exceed 5% of the Group's gross assets (determined by reference to the latest annual and semi-annual accounts). |
| **Mandated Lead Arranger and Bookrunner:** | Top Bank |
| **Underwriter:** | Top Bank |
| **Lenders:** | As selected by the Mandated Lead Arranger in consultation with the Original Borrower. |
| **Issuing Bank:** | Top Bank |
| **Agent:** | Top Bank |
| **Obligors:** | The Borrowers and the Guarantors. |

**Additional Obligors:** A mechanism will be included in the Agreement to enable any subsidiary of the Original Borrower which has been approved by the Majority Lenders to accede as a Borrower and/or a Guarantor. A mechanism will also be included to enable Borrowers and Guarantors to resign (subject to certain conditions).

**Group:** The Original Borrower and each of its subsidiaries for the time being.

## £300 MILLION MULTICURRENCY REVOLVING LOAN FACILITY WITH TERM OUT OPTION ("FACILITY A")

This short-term facility is expected to be refinanced before the exercise of the Term Out Option as Bidco intends to raise funds through an asset disposal programme and/or by issuing instruments in the capital markets. The funds qualify as part of the certain funds requirement for the acquisition. As the Target is a UK listed company, the conduct of the Offer is regulated by the Takeover Code. Under Rules 2.7 and 24.8 of the Takeover Code, when an Offer is made for cash or includes an element of cash, the Offer Press Release and the Offer Document must include a "cash confirmation" by an appropriate third party (usually Bidco's bank or financial adviser) that sufficient resources are available to Bidco to satisfy full acceptance of the Offer. In order to comply with this requirement, Bidco and its financial adviser will normally require that the facility agreement providing the facilities to fund the cash consideration for the Offer is made available on a "certain funds" basis. This means that many of the usual "draw-stop" provisions in the loan documentation (being the provisions which make the lending of a loan conditional, i.e., conditions precedent, accuracy of representations which are repeated, no Event of Default) should not apply during the period when loans will be needed to fund the cash consideration due to accepting shareholders of the Target.

**Facility:** Revolving Loan Facility.

**Amount:** £300m to be drawn in sterling and any currency (each an "**Optional Currency**") which is readily available and freely convertible into sterling in the London interbank market and, in relation to the euro, the European interbank market and which has either been approved by all the Lenders or is one of the following currencies:

(i) euro;

(ii) US Dollars.

**Termination Date:** 12 months from signing of the Agreement subject to the Term Out Option.

**Purpose:** Financing:

(i) part of the payment of the consideration for the Target Shares pursuant to the Offer and the Squeeze-Out;

(ii) the refinancing of part of the existing financial indebtedness of the Target Group; and

(iii) the costs, fees, commissions and expenses incurred by the Original Borrower in connection with the Acquisition (including debt breakage costs).

**Availability Period:** From the date of the Agreement to the date falling one month before the Termination Date.

**Minimum Amount of each Loan:** £5m or appropriate equivalent minimum amounts for Optional Currencies.

**Maximum Number of Loans:** No more than five Facility A Loans may be outstanding at any time.

**Repayment:** Each Facility A Loan shall be repaid on the last day of its Interest Period. During the Availability Period, amounts repaid may be reborrowed. No amount may be outstanding after the Termination Date.

**Voluntary Prepayment:** Facility A Loans may be prepaid in whole or in part on five business days' prior notice (but, if in part, by a minimum of £5m (or equivalent)). Any prepayment shall be made with accrued interest on the amount prepaid and, subject to breakage costs, without premium or penalty.

**Term Out Option:** The Original Borrower may, at any time prior to the then current Facility A Termination Date, request that Facility A is converted into a term loan facility. Upon such a request, Facility A shall be available for drawing in one advance and shall be drawn in full. Each Facility A Loan then outstanding shall be converted into a term loan. The term loans shall be repayable on the date which falls 1 year after the date of exercise of the Term Out Option.

## £300 MILLION MULTICURRENCY TERM LOAN FACILITY ("FACILITY B")

Facility B is core funding for this transaction and is expected to be fully drawn. It is used directly for the acquisition of shares and provides also for the issuance of bank guarantees if a loan note option is made available pursuant to the Offer. On UK public takeovers, all or part of the consideration offered to Target shareholders can comprise loan notes; this may be attractive to certain Target shareholders from a tax perspective. Facility B also qualifies as certain funds for the acquisition. Note that any outstanding bank guarantees are cash collateralised if there is a prepayment or cancellation of the facility.

**Facility:** Term Loan Facility.

**Amount:** £300m to be drawn in sterling and any Optional Currency.

**Termination Date:** Five years from signing of the Agreement.

**Purpose:**

(i) financing part of the consideration for the Target Shares by the Original Borrower pursuant to the Offer and the Squeeze-Out;

(ii) issuing bank guarantees ("**Bank Guarantees**") in respect of any loan notes issued pursuant to the Offer; and

(iii) refinancing part of the existing financial indebtedness of the Target Group.

**Availability Period:** From the date of the Agreement to the end of the Certain Funds Period, provided, however, that in respect of any utilisation of Facility B for the purpose stated in (iii) above, the Availability Period shall end on the last day of the Clean-Up Period.

**Minimum Amount of each Loan:** £5m or appropriate equivalent minimum amounts for Optional Currencies.

**Maximum Number of Loans:** No more than five Facility B Utilisations may be outstanding at any time.

**Bank Guarantees:** As for L/Cs (see "Facility C" below).

**Repayment:** The Facility B Loans will be repaid in instalments as follows:

| Repayment Date | Repayment Instalment |
|---|---|
| 18 months from signing: | £37.5m |

| | | |
|---|---|---|
| | 24 months from signing: | £37.5m |
| | 30 months from signing: | £37.5m |
| | 36 months from signing: | £37.5m |
| | 42 months from signing: | £37.5m |
| | 48 months from signing: | £37.5m |
| | 54 months from signing: | £37.5m |
| | Termination Date: | All remaining outstandings |

**Voluntary Prepayment:** Facility B Utilisations shall only be prepaid if the whole of the Facility A Loans have been prepaid or will be prepaid at the same time.

Facility B Utilisations may be prepaid after the last day of the Availability Period in relation to Facility B in whole or in part on five business days' prior notice (but, if in part, by a minimum of £5m (or equivalent)). Any prepayment shall be made with accrued interest on the amount prepaid and, subject to breakage costs, without premium or penalty.

If a Facility B Utilisation is repaid, prepaid or is cancelled prior to the Facility B Termination Date, outstanding Bank Guarantees forming part of that Utilisation will be cash collateralised by the applicable Borrower.

Any amount prepaid may not be redrawn and shall be applied pro rata against scheduled repayments.

## £400 MILLION MULTICURRENCY REVOLVING CREDIT FACILITY ("FACILITY C")

Facility C provides working capital facilities to the Group which can also be used to refinance existing indebtedness of the Target group. Bidco has asked for £400m but only plans to use 50% of the facility (see Bidco's assumptions in the cost calculations later in this chapter). The remainder is a backstop for emergencies during the acquisition process. It can be expected that once the acquisition is consummated and the new group has stabilised, Bidco will cancel excess capacity in this facility.

| | |
|---|---|
| **Facility:** | Revolving Credit Facility which may be utilised by way of:<br>(i) the drawing of loans; and<br>(ii) the issue of letters of credit ("**L/Cs**"). |
| **Amount:** | £400m to be drawn in sterling and any other Optional Currency. |
| **Termination Date:** | Five years from signing of the Agreement. |
| **Purpose:** | To:<br>(i) finance working capital and general corporate purposes of the Group;<br>(ii) assist with the refinancing of part of the existing financial indebtedness of the Group; and<br>(iii) assist with the refinancing of the existing financial indebtedness of the Target Group to the extent that Facility A and Facility B have been fully drawn. |
| **Availability Period:** | From the date of the Agreement to the date falling one month before the Termination Date. |
| **Minimum Amount of each Loan:** | £5m or appropriate equivalent minimum amounts for Optional Currencies. |
| **L/Cs and Bank Guarantees (issued under Facility B):** | Each L/C and Bank Guarantee will be:<br>(i) in a form to be approved by the Issuing Bank;<br>(ii) a minimum of £5m or equivalent minimum amounts for Optional Currencies;<br>(iii) issued by the Issuing Bank which will be counter-indemnified by the Lenders;<br>(iv) issued on behalf of a Borrower in favour of [•] or any other beneficiary approved by all the Lenders;<br>(v) if denominated in an Optional Currency, revalued by the Agent at six monthly intervals from the date of the L/C or Bank Guarantee (as applicable); and<br>(vi) issued with an expiry date falling on or before the applicable Termination Date. |

| | |
|---|---|
| | The Agreement (as defined below) will include a provision to allow the Issuing Bank to request that to the extent any Lender has a long-term credit rating which is below an agreed threshold, cash collateral must be provided in respect of such Lender's participation in any L/C or Bank Guarantee. |

LMA facility agreements include an option for the Issuing Bank to request that "Non-Acceptable L/C Lenders" (being banks whose long-term credit rating is below an agreed level) provide cash collateral in respect of their proportionate share in any L/Cs or Bank Guarantees issued by the Issuing Bank. This provision requires such cash collateral to be provided by the borrower to the extent that the relevant Non-Acceptable L/C Lender fails to so do.

| | |
|---|---|
| **Maximum Number of Facility C Utilisations:** | No more than five Facility C Utilisations may be outstanding at any time. |
| **Repayment:** | Each Facility C Loan shall be repaid on the last day of its Interest Period. During the Availability Period, amounts repaid may be reborrowed. No amount may be outstanding after the Termination Date. |
| **Voluntary Prepayment:** | Facility C Utilisations may be prepaid in whole or in part on five business days' prior notice (but, if in part, by a minimum of £5m (or equivalent)). Any prepayment shall be made with accrued interest on the amount prepaid and, subject to breakage costs, without premium or penalty.<br>L/C's will be repaid or prepaid by being cash collateralised by the applicable Borrower. |

**PRICING**

The key pricing components are set out in this section but note that the front end fee is dealt with in the mandate letter as that fee is not to be disclosed to the syndicate as a whole (since at least part of it is for the account of Top Bank only). As mentioned earlier, Top Bank has overridden the Margin for Facility A (see clause 8.8 of the mandate letter) until the exercise of the Term Out Option.

| | |
|---|---|
| **Commitment Fee:** | Facility A: 0.20%. per annum;<br>Facility B: 45%. of the Margin per annum; and<br>Facility C: 45%. of the Margin per annum,<br>in each case on the unused and uncancelled amount of the applicable Facility from and including the date falling 45 days after the date of the Agreement until the last day of the applicable Availability Period. Accrued commitment fee is payable quarterly in arrear during the relevant Availability Period, on the last day of the relevant Availability Period and on the cancelled amount of any Facility at the time a full cancellation is effective. |
| **Ticking Fee:** | 0.225%. per annum on the unused and uncancelled amount of each Facility from and including the date of the Agreement until the date falling 45 days thereafter, payable in arrear. |
| **Term Out Fee:** | 0.25%. flat payable to the Agent (for the account of each Lender under Facility A) on the aggregate Facility A Commitments of the Lenders on the date on which the Term Out Option is exercised (if the Term Out Option is exercised). |
| **Issuing Bank Fee:** | 0.125%. per annum (or such other rate as may be agreed between the Issuing Bank and the Original Borrower from time to time) on the outstanding amount which is counter-indemnified by the Lenders of each L/C or Bank Guarantee requested by a Borrower. |
| **Margin:** | 1.25%. per annum provided that the Margin will be adjusted by reference to the Margin Ratchet. |
| **Margin Ratchet:** | The Margin shall be reduced or increased with reference to the ratio of Consolidated Net Borrowings to EBITDA (as defined below) as follows: |

| Net Borrowings: EBITDA | Applicable Margin |
|---|---|
| Greater than or equal to 3.00:1.00 | 1.25% p.a. |
| Less than 3.00:1.00 but greater than or equal to 2.50:1.00 | 1.00% p.a. |
| Less than 2.50:1.00 but greater than or equal to 2.00:1.00 | 0.75% p.a. |
| Less than 2.00:1.00 | 0.60% p.a. |

| | |
|---|---|
| | The above ratio is to be tested semi-annually with the reduction/increase to apply to all new Interest Periods commencing after delivery to the Agent of a compliance certificate showing the revised ratio. Each existing Loan will continue at the previous Margin. If an Event of Default has occurred and is continuing, the Margin will be 1.25%. per annum.<br><br>No reduction in the Margin shall occur prior to the date which is six months after the first utilisation date. |
| **Interest Periods for Loans:** | One, three or six months or any other period agreed between the Original Borrower and the Lenders (in relation to the relevant Loan). |
| **Interest on Loans:** | The aggregate of the applicable:<br><br>(i) Margin; and<br><br>(ii) LBOR or, in relation to any Loan in euro, EURIBOR set, in each case, by reference to Thomson Reuters (and, if necessary, the use of linear interpolation) or, if not available, by reference to specified fallbacks and, if the rate is less than zero, it shall be deemed to be zero. |

For a detailed discussion regarding developments in LIBOR, please see chapter 1.

| | |
|---|---|
| **Payment of Interest on Loans:** | Interest is payable on the last day of each Interest Period (and, in the case of Interest Periods of longer than six months, on the dates falling at six-monthly intervals after the first day of the Interest Period). |
| **L/C and Bank Guarantee Commission (the "Commission")** | The Commission shall be equal to the applicable Margin and shall be payable quarterly in arrear on the aggregate face value amount of Facility C Utilisations (excluding Facility C Loans) and Facility B Utilisations (excluding Facility B Loans). Accrued Commission is also payable on the cancelled amount of any Lender's participation in any L/C or Bank Guarantee at the time a cancellation in full is effective. |

## OTHER TERMS

**Documentation:**

The Facilities will be made available under a facilities agreement (the "**Agreement**") based on the current recommended form of LMA multicurrency syndicated term/revolving facilities agreement amended as necessary to reflect the terms of this term sheet and otherwise in form and substance satisfactory to the Mandated Lead Arranger and the Lenders.

**Certain Funds**

During the Certain Funds Period:

(i) in relation to a Certain Funds Utilisation, the drawstop conditions in the Agreement will apply as if they referred only to Major Representations and Major Defaults; and

(ii) the Finance Parties shall be restricted from exercising certain rights which would prevent a Certain Funds Utilisation.

**Prepayment and Cancellation:**

(i) **Illegality**

A Lender may cancel its commitment and/or require prepayment of its share of the Utilisations. An Issuing Bank shall not be required to issue L/Cs or Bank Guarantees and the Original Borrower shall procure that each outstanding L/C or Bank Guarantee is released.

(ii) **Change of Control**

Upon a change of control of the Original Borrower, a Lender may by not less than 5 days' notice cancel its Commitment and require repayment of its share of the Utilisations.

(iii) **Increased Costs, Tax Gross Up and Tax Indemnity**

The Original Borrower may cancel the commitment of and prepay any Lender that makes a claim under these provisions.

(iv) **Voluntary Cancellation**

The Original Borrower may, on not less than five business days' prior notice, cancel the whole or any part (being a minimum of £5m (or equivalent)) of an Available Facility.

**Mandatory Prepayment:**

In the event of:

(i) an Applicable Disposal where the Net Proceeds exceed the Pre-determined Limit, such Net Proceeds received by the Group in excess of the Pre-determined Limit shall be applied in mandatory prepayment of the Facilities in the following order:

**first** against Facility B (pro rata against repayment instalments), **second** against Facility A, **third** against Facility C, **provided that**

(a) no amount shall be applied in mandatory prepayment of Facility A prior to the exercise of the Term Out Option; and

(b) where the Net Proceeds of an Applicable Disposal do not exceed £10m but the Pre-determined Limit has been exceeded, then those Net Proceeds in excess of the Pre-determined Limit shall only be required to be applied in mandatory prepayment once the aggregate of those Net Proceeds, together with the Net Proceeds of any other Applicable Disposal not already applied in prepayment, exceeds £10m; or

(ii) a Debt or Equity Issue where the Net Proceeds exceed the Pre-determined Limit, such Net Proceeds received by the Group in excess of the Pre-determined Limit shall be applied in mandatory prepayment of Facility A.

Any prepayment pursuant to paragraphs (i) or (ii) above shall be made at the end of the then current Interest Period. Any prepayment shall be made with accrued interest on the amount prepaid and, subject to breakage costs, without premium or penalty.

"**Pre-determined Limit**" means:

(i) in respect of an Applicable Disposal, Net Proceeds of:

(a) £30m in aggregate in respect of any calendar year; and

(b) £120m in aggregate during the life of the Facilities; and

(ii) in respect of a Debt or Equity Issue, Net Proceeds of £30m.

"**Applicable Disposal**" means any disposal by any member of the Group, excluding:

(i) any disposals in the ordinary course of trading of the disposing entity and on arm's length terms;

(ii) any disposal, the proceeds of which cannot be upstreamed as a result of applicable law provided that the Group has used best efforts to circumvent restrictions under applicable laws;

(iii) any exchange of assets for other assets of a similar nature of value; and

(iv) any intra-Group disposal.

"**Debt or Equity Issue**" means an issue of bonds, notes, debentures, loan stock or similar instruments by any member of the Group or an issue of shares in the issued share capital of the Original Borrower.

"**Net Proceeds**" means:

(i) in the case of an Applicable Disposal, the consideration receivable after deducting reasonable expenses incurred and any Tax incurred and required to be paid by the seller in connection with the Applicable Disposal (as reasonably determined by the seller, on the basis of existing rates and taking account of any available credit, deduction or allowance); and

(ii) in the case of a Debt or Equity Issue, the cash proceeds raised from such issue, net of taxes and all costs, expenses, commissions and fees incurred in connection with such issue.

**Representations:**

Each Obligor will make representations which will include, without limitation, each of the following representations on the date of the Agreement and on the date of the completion of the acquisition of the Target and, in the case of certain representations, on the date of each Utilisation Request and the first day of each Interest Period:

(i) status;

(ii) binding obligations;

(iii) non-conflict with other obligations;

(iv) power and authority;

(v) validity and admissibility in evidence;

(vi) insolvency;

(vii) governing law and enforcement;

(viii) no deduction of tax;

(ix) no filing or stamp taxes;

(x) no default;

(xi) no misleading information (with respect to the Information Memorandum, representation to be given upon approval by the Original Borrower of the Information Memorandum and on the Syndication Date);

(xii) financial statements (UK GAAP including IFRS);

(xiii) pari passu ranking;

(xiv) no proceedings pending or threatened against it or a member of the Group which, if adversely determined, are reasonably likely to have a Material Adverse Effect;

(xv) environmental compliance and no environmental claims which, if adversely determined, are reasonably likely to have a Material Adverse Effect;

(xvi) taxation;

(xvii) group structure chart;

(xviii) sanctions and anti-corruption;

(xix) no material adverse change has occurred in the financial condition of the Group since the date of the last audited accounts provided to the Lenders; and

(xx) Acquisition Documents – Offer Press Release and Offer Document contain all the material terms of the Offer and comply with the Takeover Code in all material respects.

| | |
|---|---|
| **Material Adverse Effect:** | "**Material Adverse Effect**" means a material adverse effect on:<br>(i) the business, operations, property or condition (financial or otherwise) of the Group taken as a whole; or<br>(ii) the ability of an Obligor to perform its payment obligations under any of the Finance Documents and/or its obligations with respect to the Financial Covenants; or<br>(iii) the validity or enforceability of the Finance Documents or the rights or remedies of any Finance Party under any of the Finance Documents. |
| **Information Undertakings:** | The Original Borrower shall supply each of the following:<br>(i) as soon as they become available, but in any event within 180 days of the end of its financial years its audited consolidated financial statements together with those of each Obligor;<br>(ii) as soon as they become available, but in any event within 120 days of the end of the first half of its financial half years its consolidated financial statements;<br>(iii) with each set of consolidated financial statements, a compliance certificate signed by two directors of the Original Borrower and, in the case of the audited consolidated financial statements reported on by the Original Borrower's auditors in the form agreed by the Original Borrower and the Lenders prior to the date of the Agreement;<br>(iv) all documents dispatched by the Original Borrower to its shareholders (or any class of them) or its creditors generally;<br>(v) details of any material litigation, arbitration or administrative proceedings or any material judgment; and<br>(vi) such other information regarding the financial condition, business and operations of any member of the Group as any Finance Party may reasonably request. |

The accounting reference date of the Original Borrower shall not be changed without the consent of the Majority Lenders.

The Original Borrower may satisfy its obligations to deliver information to those Lenders who agree by posting such information onto an electronic website.

**Financial Covenants:**

(i) **Interest Cover**: Consolidated earnings before interest, Tax, depreciation and amortisation and ignoring any exceptional items or project finance vehicle contributions ("**EBITDA**") to be a minimum of 3.00 times the level of Consolidated Net Interest Expenditure. Tested semi-annually on a rolling 12 month basis.

(ii) **Leverage**: Total Consolidated Net Borrowings to be no more than 3.50 times the level of EBITDA. Tested semi-annually on a rolling 12 month basis.

> It often is the case that borrowers accept more onerous covenants (and indeed higher pricing) when undertaking acquisition finance than would be the case for a normal facility agreement in order to secure the balance sheet commitment rapidly and with a minimum number of banks.

**General Undertakings:**

Undertakings usual for transactions of this nature (subject to such qualifications and exceptions as may be agreed) in respect of each Obligor (and, where applicable in relation to the Group) including, without limitation, the following:

(i) authorisations;

(ii) compliance with laws;

(iii) undertaking to ensure that the Target and each member of the Target Group which is a Material Subsidiary accedes to the Agreement as a Guarantor during the Clean-Up Period (subject to any restrictions as a matter of law) and that members of the Group do all that is necessary (including re-registering public companies as private companies) in order to ensure that the relevant company can become a Guarantor;

(iv) restriction on disposals by any Group company subject to agreed exceptions and a basket of £5m per financial year;

(v) restriction on "Class One Transaction" acquisitions by any Group company;

Under the UK Listing Rules "Class One Transactions" are transactions carried out by a listed company which are of a sufficient size that a 25% threshold is reached under any of the class tests set out in the UK Listing Rules.

(vi) negative pledge (to apply to all Group companies) subject to agreed exceptions and a basket (with respect to UK subsidiaries) of £100m, provided that prior ranking indebtedness of the Original Borrower's subsidiaries shall not at any time exceed 30%. of total Consolidated Tangible Net Worth;

(vii) restriction on mergers;

(viii) no change of business;

(ix) notification of default;

(x) pari passu ranking;

(xi) each Group company to effect and maintain insurance;

(xii) environmental compliance;

(xiii) hedging – obligation on the Original Borrower to enter into interest rate hedging arrangements in accordance with the Hedging Letter only (and not for speculative purposes);

(xiv) sanctions and anti-corruption;

(xv) maintenance of pension schemes where failure to maintain would have a Material Adverse Effect; and

(xvi) acquisition indemnity in favour of each Finance Party.

Below are common examples of offer-related undertakings. It will be a matter of negotiation on each deal as to how much control over the offer process the bidder is willing to give to the financing banks.

**Undertakings relating to the Offer:**

The Original Borrower shall ensure that:

(i) the Offer Press Release is issued within seven days after the date of the Agreement and that the Offer Document is posted within 28 days after the date of the Offer Press Release;

(ii) the Offer Press Release and the Offer Document shall contain all the material terms and conditions of the Offer;

(iii) it shall not, without the prior consent of the Majority Lenders, make any material amendments to the terms of the Offer including making any material amendments to the Offer Press Release, the Offer Document or increasing the amount of cash payable by it in connection with the Offer;

(iv) it shall not, without the prior consent of the Majority Lenders, waive or treat as satisfied any condition of the Offer where such waiver or treatment would materially and adversely affect the interests of the Lenders;

(v) it shall not issue any publicity which makes reference to the Facilities or any of the Finance Parties unless required to do so by the Takeover Code or by law;

(vi) it does not take any action and shall use reasonable endeavours to procure that neither it nor any person Acting in Concert (as defined in the Takeover Code) with it shall become obliged to make an offer to the shareholders of the Target under Rule 9 of the Takeover Code;

(vii) it complies with the Takeover Code (subject to any applicable waivers by the Panel) and with other applicable laws and regulations in the context of the Offer;

(viii) it shall keep the Mandated Lead Arranger and the Agent informed as to the status and progress of the Offer and the Squeeze-Out and promptly provide the Mandated Lead Manager and the Agent with such information concerning the Offer as the Mandated Lead Arranger and the Agent may reasonably request (including details of the current level of acceptances of the Offer);

(ix) it shall initiate the compulsory acquisition procedures set out in chapter 3 of Part 28 of the Companies Act 2006 to acquire the minority shareholding in connection with the Offer as soon as reasonably practicable and in any event within seven business days after becoming entitled to do so; and

(x) it shall not, without the prior agreement of the Majority Lenders declare the Offer unconditional as to acceptances until it has acquired or unconditionally contracted to acquire not less than 90%. of the shares in the Target to which the Offer relates.

For the purpose of this term sheet, we have assumed that Bidco will seek to acquire Target by using a contractual offer regulated by the UK City Code on Takeovers and Mergers (the "**Takeover Code**"). The Takeover Code sets out detailed requirements for the timetable, documentation and procedures to be used by companies making such offers, including in situations where there are two or more competing offers for the same company. The detailed terms of the offer would be set out in the Offer Document (as defined below).

As an alternative to a contractual offer, in some situations a bidder might seek to acquire another English company by way of a scheme of arrangement. This is a statutory procedure available under Part 26 of the Companies Act 2006 whereby the target company (subject to court approval) makes an arrangement with its shareholders for the transfer of target's shares to the bidder in consideration for the bidder paying the offer consideration to target shareholders. A scheme of arrangement requires the approval of a majority in number representing 75% by value of the target shareholders who vote at the relevant shareholders' meeting. Once a scheme becomes effective, it binds all shareholders whether or not they have voted in favour of the scheme. The Takeover Code also applies (with certain adaptations) to an offer made by way of a scheme of arrangement. The use of schemes of arrangement is increasingly common for takeover bids. A scheme is proposed by the target company to its shareholders (whereas a contractual offer is made by the bidder). This means that it is therefore difficult to implement a scheme without target co-operation.

It is possible to include provisions in a facilities agreement to envisage the offer being made by way of either a contractual offer or a scheme of arrangement and to allow scope for the bidder to switch between the two types of offer (subject to the terms of the Takeover Code).

| | |
|---|---|
| **Events of Default:** | Events of Default usual for transactions of this nature (subject to such qualifications and exceptions as may be agreed) in respect of each Obligor (and, where applicable, in relation to the Group) including, without limitation, the following:<br>(i) non-payment of principal, interest or other amounts due under the Finance Documents unless failure to pay is caused by: (a) administrative or technical error or (b) a Disruption Event and payment is made within three business days of its due date in the case of (a) or five business days of its due date in the case of (b);<br>(ii) any financial covenant not satisfied;<br>(iii) failure to comply with any other obligations;<br>(iv) misrepresentation;<br>(v) cross default, subject to a *de minimis* threshold of £10m;<br>(vi) insolvency;<br>(vii) insolvency proceedings;<br>(viii) creditors' process;<br>(ix) unlawfulness and invalidity;<br>(x) repudiation and rescission; and<br>(xi) any event or circumstance occurs which has or is reasonably likely to have a Material Adverse Effect. |
| **Clean-Up Period:** | Clean-Up Period to apply in respect of events or circumstances that would otherwise constitute an Event of Default on the terms set out in the Agreement. |

> The Original Borrower is unlikely to be able to conduct extensive due diligence on the Target Group prior to making the Offer and, therefore, is likely to request that the Lenders allow a "Clean-Up Period" of 60-120 days after completing the acquisition of the Target Group. During the Clean-Up Period, the Original Borrower will seek to identify any breaches of certain provisions of the Agreement arising as a result of actions/omissions by the Target Group and will seek to remedy these breaches. As long as any such breach is capable of remedy, steps are being taken to remedy the relevant breach and the circumstances giving rise to the breach have not been procured or approved by the Original Borrower, the Lenders will not be entitled to call an Event of Default in respect of such breaches.

**Hedging:** An interest rate hedging policy is to be set out in the Hedging Letter in respect of the interest rate liabilities of the Borrowers under the Facilities.

**Majority Lenders:** 66.6%. or more of the Total Commitments or if any Utilisations are outstanding, 66.6%. or more of Utilisations. Provisions requiring all Lender consent to certain amendments and waivers will be included.

**Assignments and Transfers by Lenders:** A Lender may assign any of its rights or transfer by novation any of its rights and obligations to another bank or financial institution or to a trust, fund or other entity which is regularly engaged in or established for the purpose of making, purchasing or investing in loans, securities or other financial assets.

Subject to minimum transfer amount of £5m.

The consent of the Original Borrower will be required (not to be unreasonably withheld or delayed) unless the transfer or assignment:

(a) is to another Lender or an Affiliate of any Lender;

(b) is to a fund which is a Related Fund of that Lender; or

(c) is made when an Event of Default is continuing.

The Original Borrower will be deemed to have given its consent if no express refusal is received within five business days.

| | |
|---|---|
| | The consent of the Issuing Bank will be required to any assignment or transfer of its rights or obligations under Facility B or Facility C. |

The reason for the Issuing Bank having the right to give consent in relation to Facility B and Facility C is that it is counter-indemnified by the syndicate banks and may have restrictions on which banks are acceptable as counterparty risk. Other syndicate banks may seek to negotiate that the Issuing Bank's consent should not be unreasonably withheld and given on a timely (ten business days) basis. Bidco and the financial adviser giving the cash confirmation statement may seek to have tighter restrictions on lender transfers during the Certain Funds Period (for instance, by including a ratings requirement for transferees) as they will want to ensure that there is no risk of funds not being made available by any new lender.

| | |
|---|---|
| **Snooze and lose:** | If a Lender fails to respond to a request for consent to amendments or waivers (other than in respect of certain amendments and waivers to be agreed), within [15] business days, that Lender's Commitment or participation will not be included in calculating whether the consent of the relevant percentage of the Total Commitments and/or participations has been obtained to approve that request. |
| **Replacement of Lender:** | A mechanism will be included in the Agreement pursuant to which the Original Borrower may, subject to certain conditions, replace: (i) a Lender which has not consented to a waiver or amendment requiring the consent of all Lenders and to which Lenders holding an aggregate of [90]%. of the Total Commitments have consented; and/or (ii) a Lender to which an Obligor becomes obliged to pay an amount pursuant to the illegality, increased costs or tax gross-up provisions of the Agreement. |

In order to increase the certainty of funds, the financial adviser giving the cash confirmation statement will require as many conditions precedent as possible to be satisfied before it gives the cash confirmation statement. To the extent any of the conditions precedent are not capable of being satisfied prior to the date of the cash confirmation statement, then these will need to be within the control of Bidco.

**Conditions Precedent:** Conditions precedent usual for transactions of this nature in relation to each Obligor in form and substance satisfactory to the Agent including, without limitation, the following:

(i) constitutional documents;

(ii) resolutions of the board of directors;

(iii) a director's certificate including specimen signatures;

(iv) shareholder resolutions in relation to each Guarantor (if required);

(v) borrowing/guaranteeing certificate;

(vi) certification of copy documents;

(vii) legal opinions of counsel to the Lenders;

(viii) evidence of process agent (if required);

(ix) a copy of any other document, authorisation, opinion or assurance specified by the Agent;

(x) latest audited consolidated financial statements relating to the Original Borrower and each Obligor;

(xi) evidence of payment of all fees, costs and expenses then due from the Original Borrower under the Agreement;

(xii) a copy of the financial model for the combined group;

(xiii) a copy of the Hedging Letter; and

(xiv) a copy of the accountants' report (subject to the provision of a reliance letter).

**Additional Offer Related Conditions Precedent:**

(i) a copy of the Offer Press Release;

(ii) a copy of the Offer Document;

(iii) if required under applicable law, evidence of the approval of the shareholders of the Original Borrower in relation to the Offer;

(iv) a copy of any shareholder circular sent to the shareholders of the Original Borrower in relation to the Offer;

(v) a copy of the announcement that the Offer has become or has been declared unconditional in all respects;

(vi) a copy of the certificate from the Original Borrower's receiving agent for the purposes of Note 7 to Rule 10 of the Takeover Code; and

(vii) evidence that all necessary regulatory and competition authority approvals for the Acquisition have been obtained.

**Miscellaneous Provisions:** The Agreement will contain provisions relating to, among other things, default interest, market disruption, breakage costs, tax gross up (including FATCA) and indemnities, (including, without limitation, in relation to the Acquisition), increased costs, Defaulting Lenders, set-off and administration.

**Costs and Expenses:** All costs and expenses (including legal fees) reasonably incurred by the Agent and the Mandated Lead Arranger in connection with the preparation, negotiation, printing, execution and syndication of the Agreement and any other document referred to in it shall be paid by the Original Borrower promptly on demand whether or not the Agreement is signed.

**Governing Law:** English.

**Jurisdiction:** Courts of England.

**Definitions:** "**Acquisition**" means the acquisition by the Original Borrower of all the Target Shares pursuant to the Offer, (including, if applicable, any Squeeze-Out).

"**Certain Funds Period**" means the period beginning on the date of this Agreement and ending on the earliest of:

(i) the date which is 30 days after the Unconditional Date or if the Original Borrower has issued Squeeze-Out Notices before such date, such longer period as is necessary to enable the Original Borrower to implement the Squeeze-Out;

(ii) unless the Unconditional Date has occurred, the date which is six months after the date of issue of the Offer Press Release;

(iii) the date on which the Offer lapses, terminates or is withdrawn;

(iv) the date on which the Target becomes a direct or indirect wholly owned subsidiary of the Original Borrower and the Original Borrower has paid for all Target shares beneficially owned by it; and

(v) the date on which the Offer lapses in accordance with Rule 12 of the Takeover Code as a result of the European Commission initiating Phase II Proceedings or the Acquisition being referred to the UK Competition and Markets Authority (where such date occurs before the first closing date of the Offer or the date on which the Offer becomes or is declared unconditional as to acceptances, whichever is the later).

"**Certain Funds Utilisation**" means a Utilisation made or to be made during the Certain Funds Period where such Utilisation is to be made solely for the purpose of financing the purchase price for the Target Shares.

"**Clean-Up Period**" means the period commencing on the date of this Agreement until the day falling 90 days after the Closing Date.

"**Closing Date**" means the date on which Completion takes place.

"**Completion**" means the date on which the Target becomes a subsidiary of the Original Borrower.

"**Hedging Letter**" means the letter dated on or about the date of the Agreement between the Arranger and the Original Borrower describing the hedging arrangements to be entered into in respect of the interest rate liabilities of the Borrowers.

"**Loan**" means a Facility A Loan, a Facility B Loan or a Facility C Loan.

"**Major Default**" means with respect to the Original Borrower and its Subsidiaries only (and not, for the avoidance of doubt, relating to any member of the Target Group), any circumstance constituting an Event of Default under any of paragraphs (i), (iii) (but only in relation to a breach of any of the obligations relating to the following: negative pledge, disposals, merger, change of business, sanctions and anti-corruption, acquisitions and offer undertakings), (iv) (but only in relation to a Major Representation), (vi), (vii), (viii), (ix) or (x) of the "Events of Default" listed above in this term sheet.

"**Major Representation**" means a representation or warranty with respect to the Original Borrower and its Subsidiaries only (and not, for the avoidance of doubt, relating to any member of the Target Group) under any of paragraphs (i) to (v) inclusive and paragraphs (xviii) and (xx) of the "Representations" listed above in this term sheet.

"**Offer**" means the offer made by the Original Borrower (or on its behalf) for all the Target Shares not already owned by the Original Borrower on the terms set out in the Offer Press Release as such offer may from time to time be varied, amended or waived in accordance with the terms of this Agreement.

"**Offer Document**" means the offer document containing terms of the Offer which is consistent with the terms of the Offer Press Release (or as may be varied, amended or waived in accordance with the terms of the Agreement) and which is to be sent by the Original Borrower to the Target Shareholders and any other document designated as an "Offer Document" by the Agent and the Original Borrower.

"**Offer Press Release**" means the press announcement in the agreed form (or as may be varied, amended or waived in accordance with the terms of this Agreement) to be issued by the Original Borrower (or on its behalf) to announce the terms of the Offer pursuant to Rule 2.7 of the Takeover Code.

"**Panel**" means the Panel on Takeover and Mergers.

"**Squeeze-Out**" means the squeeze-out procedures set out in chapter 3 of Part 28 of the Companies Act 2006 pursuant to which the Original Borrower may acquire any remaining Target Shares the subject of the Offer.

The Companies Act 2006 provides a procedure by which a person who has acquired 90% of the shares in a target company to which the takeover offer relates can compulsorily acquire the remaining shares from the non-assenting minority shareholders and therefore become the sole shareholder of the target company. This is known as the squeeze-out procedure.

"**Takeover Code**" means the UK City Code on Takeovers and Mergers issued by the Panel from time to time.

"**Target**" means Target plc (registered number [•]).

"**Target Group**" means Target and each of its Subsidiaries for the time being.

"**Target Shares**" means all the issued or unconditionally allotted ordinary share capital in the Target and any further such shares which may be issued or unconditionally allotted pursuant to the exercise of any subscription or conversion rights or otherwise.

"**Unconditional Date**" means the date on which the Offer is declared or becomes unconditional in all respects.

"**Utilisation**" means a Loan, a Letter of Credit or a Bank Guarantee.

## All-in cost analysis of the sample term sheets

Before committing to use the syndicated credit market, a borrower will examine other ways of raising finance. It may be that a long-dated private placement in the US domestic markets, a Schuldschein or a fixed-rate Eurobond issue swapped into floating-rate funds provides a cheaper source of funds or satisfies a maturity need unavailable in the syndicated loans market. However, there may be a loss of flexibility for the borrower in using alternative instruments when compared with a syndicated bank credit, for example:

- the single drawdown of a bond compared with multiple drawdowns available in a syndicated loan;
- the fixed final maturity of a bond compared with flexible prepayment options without penalty;
- the single currency of a bond issue as opposed to multi-currency options; and
- the relative inflexibility of bond documentation compared with the relative ease of amending terms and obtaining extensions to the final maturity during the life of a syndicated credit.

Before selecting a market or choosing between competing bids, a borrower needs to establish the all-in cost of each possibility. A critical issue is the way in which the facility is to be used. If it is expected to remain undrawn (for example, to be used as commercial paper backup) the critical cost is that of maintaining the facility undrawn. If it is to be drawn or partly drawn, the cost of the funding is the critical determinant. The key parameters of the offer or the term sheet which are required for the cost analysis are amount, margin, front-end fees, utilisation fees, commitment fees, facility fees, agency fees, expenses, tenor and amortisation schedule. In many cases, the overall amount of the agency fees and expenses is so small in comparison with the other fees and the margin that it is considered irrelevant to include them in an analysis of all-in cost.

A comparison of pricing alone would be an error however, as there is a trade-off between the pricing elements, the strength of the covenants and the maturity. Therefore, before the all-in cost of alternatives can be accurately compared, it is necessary to ensure that all other conditions of competing offers are the same. If a borrower is considering fully underwritten offers, it is necessary to identify any caveat or other escape clauses in the submissions, as these could affect the pricing by being reflected in the level of fees and margin. A borrower also needs to be aware of the implications of an offer which includes a marketflex provision as this could result in the final costs of a transaction being substantially different than those of the original offer.

The term sheet submitted to DutchCo is made on the understanding that the committed facility is not intended to be drawn, rather it is to be used as a standby facility to support the issuance of commercial paper. Therefore, the appropriate cost for this borrower to calculate is the cost of keeping the facility undrawn and in place as liquidity insurance in the event that market disruption should occur. The fully drawn cost is of secondary importance. (Indeed, in pricing such facilities, it is common to establish a fully drawn cost which is higher than the margin would be for a comparable term loan. This approach can be explained since if such a borrower needs to draw under the facility and keep it substantially drawn over a period of time, the financial markets, including the commercial paper markets, will, in all probability be in a state of turbulence resulting in higher costs for all borrowers. It is therefore defensive pricing for the banks.)

In the case of the transaction for Bidco, the borrower and the banks expect the loan to be substantially drawn as the purpose of the Facilities is to finance an acquisition. Thus, while the undrawn cost is not to be neglected, the period during which it is relevant is short. The borrower in this case is far more interested in the drawn cost of the loan than in the undrawn cost and in the prepayment and cancellation options.

In order to make the necessary cost comparisons, a common language understood readily by all parties has become established. It is common practice to express the all-in cost of a transaction as a number of basis points per annum.

It should be noted here that, when comparing the cost of alternative variable rate financing offers, or of variable rate instruments in different financial markets, in the way described below, the borrower is not evaluating the total cost of the financing. This is because the evaluation of the all-in cost of the offers submitted ignores the underlying level of interest rates which will apply. These are properly assumed to be the same for each proposal. When a borrower is in the process of deciding whether or not to finance a project or acquisition, the total cost – which will obviously require forecasts of the absolute levels of interest rates – will be needed to evaluate financial viability. Such analysis is outside the scope of this book but bankers must not lose sight of the importance of this in the decision-making process of their clients.

The methodology for accurately determining the all-in cost of a financing proposal is to use a discounted cash flow (DCF) analysis to calculate the net present value (NPV) of all cash outflows and inflows (excluding Libor or any other benchmark rate) and then annualise the result over the average life of the facility. A simpler approximate method is to ignore the time value of these cash outflows and inflows by calculating the result on a straightline basis (which is equivalent to a 0.00% discount rate in DCF analysis).

The all-in cost can now be calculated for the transactions formulated in the term sheets. The key parameters for each transaction are set out in exhibit 3.1. (If unfamiliar with the level of agency fees and expenses which will be incurred, a borrower may seek estimates from the banks submitting the term sheets. Alternatively, a borrower may insist on a cap – a maximum amount for each of these items.) As mentioned previously all fee, rate and cost levels are indicative only and do not necessarily reflect current market pricing.

## Exhibit 3.1: Key transaction parameters for calculating the all-in costs of the two deals

| Deal Parameter | DutchCo | Project Tennis |
|---|---|---|
| Amount | $1,000m | Facility A: £300m<br>Facility B: £300m<br>Facility C: £400m |
| Margin | 30bps per annum | Facility A: 70bps per annum until exercise of Term Out Option then as Facilities B and C<br>Facilities B and C: 125bps per annum with grid |
| Front-end Fees | 10bps flat | Facility A: 50bps flat<br>Facility B: 100bps flat<br>Facility C: 100bps flat |
| Utilisation Fees | 15bps per annum ≤33%<br>30bps per annum >33%≤66%<br>50bps per annum >66% | None |
| Commitment Fees | 35% of Margin (per annum) | Facility A: 20bps per annum<br>Facility B: 45% of Margin (per annum)<br>Facility C: 45% of Margin (per annum) |
| Agency Fees | $37,500 per annum | £30,000 per annum |
| Expenses | $100,000 flat[1] | £150,000 flat[2] |
| Tenor | 12 Months | Facility A: 1 year<br>Facility B: 5 years<br>Facility C: 5 years |
| Grace Period | Not applicable | Facility A: Not applicable<br>Facility B: 18 months<br>Facility C: Not applicable |
| Repayments | Each loan is to be repaid on the last day of its interest period | Facility A: Each loan is to be repaid on the last day of its interest period<br>Facility B: Semi-annually after expiry of Grace Period<br>Facility C: Each loan is to be repaid on the last day of its interest period |

1 This estimate takes account of the complexity of the transaction, recognising that the borrower and guarantor are incorporated in different jurisdictions but acknowledging that precedent documents are to be used. It would also include the costs of legal opinions.

2 This estimate could be based on the cost of previous transactions under English law and would include the cost of legal opinions.

# COST ANALYSIS FOR DutchCo

The facility for DutchCo is designed to be a back-up line in as much as the borrower does not expect to have any advances outstanding under the facility. It expects to use the facility as liquidity insurance for its commercial paper programme.

Given its purpose (and many such transactions have been arranged and used in this way), the most important cost for the borrower to consider is the cost of maintaining the facility undrawn. This is calculated by adding the principal running cost, which is the commitment fee of 35% of the Margin (10.5bps per annum), to the annualised equivalent of the front-end costs as shown in exhibit 3.2.

### Exhibit 3.2: DutchCo – Total equivalent front-end costs calculated

| | DCF basis ($) | Straightline basis ($) |
|---|---|---|
| Front-end fees | 1,000,000 | 1,000,000 |
| Expenses[1] | 100,000 | 100,000 |
| Agency fees[1] | 37,500 | 37,500 |
| Total equivalent front-end costs | 1,137,500 | 1,137,500 |

1 Based on the data in exhibit 3.1. Note that agency fees are customarily payable annually in advance. For a one-year deal, as all these items are payable on signing or shortly thereafter, the equivalent front-end costs are the same under both methods of calculation. If this deal is extended, there will be further costs to take into account but as this is a lender's rather than a borrower's option, it is not possible to incorporate these costs at this stage as they are not fully pre-determined.

These equivalent front-end costs are then converted to an equivalent number of basis points flat on the amount of the facility, in this case calculated as follows:

$$\frac{1{,}137{,}500}{1{,}000{,}000{,}000} \times 100 = 0.11375\% = 11.375\,\text{bp flat}$$

In this case the average life is one year as there are no scheduled reductions in the amount of the facility prior to its final maturity. The total undrawn cost of the facility for the borrower on a straightline basis is therefore equal to 21.875bps per annum (10.5bps per annum commitment fee plus 11.375bps per annum equivalent front-end costs). If the DCF method is used, the annualised value of the front-end costs using a 2% reinvestment rate on a quarterly basis is 11.715bps per annum giving a total all-in cost of 22.215bps per annum.

(NB: the extension option is for the borrower to request if necessary but for the lenders to grant. It therefore cannot be factored into the calculations by the borrower at this stage as the exact terms that the lenders may require for extending may be subject to further negotiation. If the borrower needs a two-year facility then a two-year facility should be negotiated from the outset.)

Should the facility be fully drawn, the all-in fully drawn cost would be equal to the sum of the equivalent front-end costs (11.375bps per annum), the margin (30bps per annum) and the utilisation fee (50bps per annum) making a total 91.375bps per annum on a straightline basis or 91.715bps per annum on a DCF basis.

As previously stated, this facility is not structured to be used as a bullet loan. Nonetheless, if it is drawn consistently, there is an abrupt change in pricing once any loans are drawn and further changes once pricing exceeds 33% and 66% of the facility amount when the utilisation fee bites. This leads to some startling results.

To explain this we consider an example transaction where at the undrawn level, the margin is 30bps per annum (as per DutchCo) but where the utilisation fee structure is simplified with a utilisation fee (20bps per annum) when outstandings are in excess of 50%. The interaction of the margin and utilisation fee can be examined independently of the other pricing elements of the transaction that will remain the same regardless of the level of outstandings under the facility.

At levels of outstandings up to 50%, the margin is 30bps per annum. However, once average outstandings in a three-month period exceed 50%, the margin on all outstandings is 50bps per annum, being the sum of the margin (30bps per annum) and the utilisation fee (20bps per annum).This means that there is a serious economic incentive for a borrower to find an alternative source of funds rather than borrow under this facility if a small incremental amount of borrowings in excess of 50% is required. If, for example, the borrower has total outstandings equal to 55% of the amount of the facility, the borrower is indifferent (economically) to drawing the full 55% under the facility or drawing 50% under the facility at 30bps per annum and paying a margin (the *breakeven margin*) of 250bps per annum on the incremental 5%. This equates mathematically to 50bps per annum on the full 55%. A graph of breakeven margin against levels of utilisation is given in exhibit 3.3. From this graph it can be seen that if the facility is fully drawn the breakeven margin is 70bps per annum. The borrower will logically choose any other source of funds (such as by soliciting bids from banks for advances) which carries a margin lower than the breakeven margin to fund drawings in excess of 50%.

**Exhibit 3.3: Breakeven margin for DutchCo**

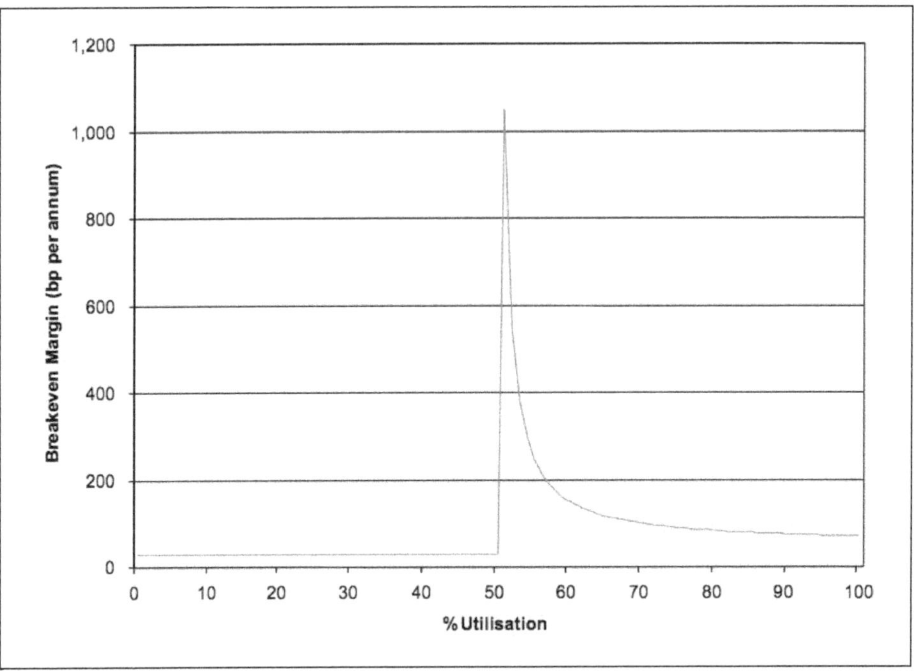


In order to compare alternative offers for financing, Bidco needs to establish its most likely utilisation scenario for the facility and apply the parameters of this scenario to each proposal received. In this case, Bidco intends to utilise Facilities A and B of the facility in order to finance the acquisition of shares of Target and to refinance the debt in Target. Facility C is intended for working capital. The facility is multi-currency allowing Bidco to borrow money in any one or more of the optional currencies if required. This feature is especially useful for facilities where a proportion of a borrower's revenue is in a currency other than the one in which the facility is denominated as it provides a natural hedge for drawings under the facility in the same currency. However, from a borrower's point of view, this does not change the overall calculation of the cost of the facility as the same benefits would apply to all multi-currency offers it receives.

Bidco makes the following assumptions which it will apply to each bid received:

- Facilities A and B are to be drawn down in full after 60 days.
- Bidco hopes to refinance Facility A by a bond issue after about 10 months (comfortably after closing the acquisition) but conservatively considers that Facility A may be outstanding to its normal maturity date (12 months) but that the Term Out Option will not be needed.

- Facility B is repaid in accordance with the contractual repayment schedule.
- Facility C is drawn to a maximum of 50% after 90 days, rolled over at this level continuously and repaid at final maturity.
- Front-end fees, the first agency fee and transaction expenses (estimated) will be assumed to be paid upfront. Subsequent agency fees will be paid annually in advance when due and discounted accordingly. (It should be noted that transaction expenses in this context only relate to this financing proposal and not to the overall transaction expenses which also include the corporate finance aspects of the transaction, that is the acquisition advice and related execution costs.)
- Absolute rates of interest (LIBOR in this case) can be ignored as they will be the same for each financing proposal. However, quarterly periods will be selected for the purpose of this analysis.
- Margin on Facilities B and C remains constant at 1.25%, that is no variation with the grid. (Bidco may take the view that refinancing the whole facility will be a better option if its credit standing improves rather than just take the reduction in margin and commitment fee.)
- Discount rate chosen is 4.5%, applied quarterly when relevant.

The principal terms and conditions are summarised in exhibit 3.1. In order to calculate the discounted all-in-cost for a multi-tranche transaction such as this, Facilities A, B and C need to be analysed separately to take account of the subtle differences embedded in each of them. The payments to be made by Bidco over the life of the facility under these various assumptions are shown in exhibit 3.4.

For each Facility, Bidco must make the following calculations:

| **Front-end fee** | = Fee payable upfront and therefore not discounted. |
|---|---|
| | = Front-end fee × facility amount |
| *Example from Facility A* | *= (.50 / 100) × 300,000,000* |
| | *= £1,500,000* |
| **Commitment fee** | = payable on the undrawn amount of the facility for the period in question. |
| | = Commitment fee × undrawn amount × period undrawn/365 |
| *Facility A: quarter 1* | *= (.20 / 100) × 300,000,000 × (60/365[1])* |
| | *= £98,630* |
| *Discounted for one quarter* | *= 98,630 / 1.01107[2] = £97,551* |
| **Margin** | = Interest on all amounts drawn payable quarterly. |
| | = Margin × drawn amount × period drawn (assumed to be a maximum of 3 months)/365 |
| *Facility A: quarter 2* | *= (.70/ 100) × 300,000,000 × (92/365)* |
| | *= £529,315* |
| *Discounted two quarters* | *= 529,315 / 1.022252 = £517,793* |

1 For sterling transactions, the denominator is 365 (even in a leap year).

2 Relevant quarterly discount factor for the annual discount rate selected.

### Exhibit 3.4: Bidco's cost analysis of Top Bank's proposal for Project Tennis

a. Facility A: £300m revolving credit facility with Term Out Option

| *Quarter* | *Days* | *Available amount (£m)* | *Commit-ment fees (£)* | *Discounted Commit-ment fees (£)* | *Drawn amount (£m)* | *Amount repaid (£m)* | *Margin (£)* | *Discounted Margin (£)* |
|---|---|---|---|---|---|---|---|---|
| 1 | 60 | 300 | 98,630 | 97,551 | 0 | 0 | 0 | 0 |
| 1 | 31 | 0 | | 0 | 300 | 0 | 178,356 | 176,404 |
| 2 | 92 | 0 | | 0 | 300 | 0 | 529,315 | 517,793 |
| 3 | 92 | 0 | | 0 | 300 | 0 | 529,315 | 512,126 |
| 4 | 90 | 0 | | 0 | 300 | 300 | 517,808 | 495,510 |
| Total | | | | 97,551 | | | | 1,701,834 |

**Exhibit 3.4 continued: Bidco's cost analysis of Top Bank's proposal for Project Tennis**

b. Facility B: £300m amortising term loan

| *Quarter* | *Days* | *Available amount (£m)* | *Commit-ment fees (£)* | *Discounted Commit-ment fees (£)* | *Drawn amount (£m)* | *Margin (£)* | *Discounted Margin (£)* |
|---|---|---|---|---|---|---|---|
| 1 | 60 | 300[1] | 277,397 | 274,361 | 0 | 0 | 0 |
| 1 | 31 | 0 | | 0 | 300.00 | 318,493 | 315,008 |
| 2 | 92 | 0 | | 0 | 300.00 | 945,205 | 924,630 |
| 3 | 92 | 0 | | 0 | 300.00 | 945,205 | 914,511 |
| 4 | 90 | 0 | | 0 | 300.00 | 924,658 | 884,840 |
| 5 | 93 | 0 | | 0 | 300.00 | 955,479 | 904,328 |
| 6 | 90 | 0 | | 0 | 300.00 | 924,658 | 865,579 |
| 7 | 91 | 0 | | 0 | 262.50 | 818,065 | 757,416 |
| 8 | 92 | 0 | | 0 | 262.50 | 827,055 | 757,359 |
| 9 | 91 | 0 | | 0 | 225.00 | 701,199 | 635,081 |
| 10 | 92 | 0 | | 0 | 225.00 | 708,904 | 635,034 |
| 11 | 91 | 0 | | 0 | 187.50 | 584,332 | 517,714 |
| 12 | 91 | 0 | | 0 | 187.50 | 584,332 | 512,048 |
| 13 | 90 | 0 | | 0 | 150.00 | 462,329 | 400,703 |
| 14 | 93 | 0 | | 0 | 150.00 | 477,740 | 409,529 |
| 15 | 91 | 0 | | 0 | 112.50 | 350,599 | 297,252 |
| 16 | 91 | 0 | | 0 | 112.50 | 350,599 | 293,999 |
| 17 | 91 | 0 | | 0 | 75.00 | 233,733 | 193,854 |
| 18 | 92 | 0 | | 0 | 75.00 | 236,301 | 193,840 |
| 19 | 92 | 0 | | 0 | 37.50 | 118,151 | 95,859 |
| 20 | 90 | 0 | | 0 | 37.50 | 115,582 | 92,749 |
| Total | | | | 274,361 | | | 10,508,584 |

1 £300m drawn down after 60 days.

**Exhibit 3.4 continued: Bidco's cost analysis of Top Bank's proposal for Project Tennis**

c. Facility C: £400m revolving credit facility with bullet repayment

| *Quarter* | *Days* | *Available amount (£m)* | *Commit-ment fees (£)* | *Discounted Commit-ment fees (£)* | *Drawn amount (£m)* | *Margin (£)* | *Discounted Margin (£)* |
|---|---|---|---|---|---|---|---|
| 1 | 91 | 400 | 560,959 | 554,820 | 0 | 0 | 0 |
| 2 | 92[1] | 200 | 283,562 | 277,389 | 200 | 630,137 | 616,420 |
| 3 | 92 | 200 | 283,562 | 274,353 | 200 | 630,137 | 609,674 |
| 4 | 90 | 200 | 277,397 | 265,452 | 200 | 616,438 | 589,893 |
| 5 | 93 | 200 | 286,644 | 271,298 | 200 | 636,986 | 602,885 |
| 6 | 90 | 200 | 277,397 | 259,674 | 200 | 616,438 | 577,052 |
| 7 | 91 | 200 | 280,479 | 259,685 | 200 | 623,288 | 577,079 |
| 8 | 92 | 200 | 283,562 | 259,666 | 200 | 630,137 | 577,035 |
| 9 | 91 | 200 | 280,479 | 254,033 | 200 | 623,288 | 564,517 |
| 10 | 92 | 200 | 283,562 | 254,013 | 200 | 630,137 | 564,474 |
| 11 | 91 | 200 | 280,479 | 248,503 | 200 | 623,288 | 552,228 |
| 12 | 91 | 200 | 280,479 | 245,783 | 200 | 623,288 | 546,185 |
| 13 | 90 | 200 | 277,397 | 240,422 | 200 | 616,438 | 534,271 |
| 14 | 93 | 200 | 286,644 | 245,717 | 200 | 636,986 | 546,038 |
| 15 | 91 | 200 | 280,479 | 237,802 | 200 | 623,288 | 528,448 |
| 16 | 91 | 200 | 280,479 | 235,199 | 200 | 623,288 | 522,665 |
| 17 | 91 | 200 | 280,479 | 232,625 | 200 | 623,288 | 516,945 |
| 18 | 92 | 200 | 283,562 | 232,608 | 200 | 630,137 | 516,906 |
| 19 | 92 | 200 | 283,562 | 230,062 | 200 | 630,137 | 511,249 |
| 20 | 90 | 200 | 277,397 | 222,598 | 200 | 616,438 | 494,662 |
| Total | | | | 5,079,105 | | | 10,053,966 |

1 £200m drawn down at end of first quarter.

**Exhibit 3.4 continued: Bidco's cost analysis of Top Bank's proposal for Project Tennis**

d. Front-end Costs

| | |
|---|---|
| Front-end Fees on Facility A | £1,500,000 |
| Front-end Fees on Facility B | £3,000,000 |
| Front-end Fees on Facility C | £4,000,000 |
| Legal Expenses | £150,000 |
| Agency Fees (future payments discounted) | £137,626 |
| Total | £8,787,626 |

e. Summary

| | |
|---|---|
| Discounted Commitment Fees on Facility A | £97,551 |
| Discounted Margin on Facility A | £1,701,834 |
| Discounted Commitment Fees on Facility B | £274,362 |
| Discounted Margin on Facility B | £10,508,584 |
| Discounted Commitment Fees on Facility C | £5,079,105 |
| Discounted Margin on Facility C | £10,053,966 |
| Front-end Costs | £8,787,626 |
| **Total Cost of Facilities** | **£36,503,027** |

It is clear that any number of different assumptions could have been made by the borrower and indeed the assumptions used here penalise a bank offering to defer all or part of the front-end fees as is the case in Top Bank's proposal. However, provided the borrower is cognisant of these imperfections in the approach, the borrower is able to use this methodology to compare quantitatively, on a cost basis, the bids it receives for the financing.

# *Chapter 4*

# THE TRANSACTION CYCLE FOR A SYNDICATED CREDIT

# PRINCIPAL PHASES, MILESTONES AND DUTIES

This chapter takes the reader through the cycle of bidding for, executing and administering a mandate as well as describing in detail the duties and responsibilities of the borrower, the arranger, the agent and the participant banks. For the sake of clarity, although titles such as Mandated Lead Arranger & Bookrunner or simply Mandated Lead Arranger (MLA) are now commonly used to refer to the mandated bank or banks, this chapter uses the term 'arranger' generically to refer to the mandated bank or banks when describing duties to be undertaken by such bank or banks. In practice, when a multi-bank group is mandated it is normal for the banks to share the syndication duties (roles) on a basis that relates to the competence, desires and aspirations of each member of the group. This can be the cause of much interbank negotiation at the bidding stage, well before an offer is first submitted to the borrower.

The use of the term 'banks' as potential participants in new transactions occurs frequently in this chapter and should be interpreted in this context as a collective noun for 'banks and other financial institutions including funds', in other words lenders. Equally, the use of the words 'sent' and 'dispatched' are used frequently when describing transaction processes but this should be interpreted to include secure web-based transmission services such as those provided by Debtdomain where 'clicking' is an acceptable way of confirming acceptance and progressing along the transaction cycle.

## Principal phases

There are three principal phases to a syndicated transaction. The first is the pre-mandate phase during which the details of the proposed transaction are pitched, discussed and finalised. This pre-mandate phase is rarely shorter than one month and can be as long as one year depending on factors such as transaction complexity, market conditions and borrower sentiment. The second phase is the post-mandate phase during which the syndication itself takes place, and the facility agreements along with associated documentation are negotiated. It is concluded by the signing of the agreements and associated documentation. This phase is usually completed in a period of six to eight weeks. The third and final phase is the post-signing phase, which lasts for the life of the facility itself and is rarely shorter than six months (in the case of a bridge loan for example) or longer than 7 years for standard syndicated transactions, although syndicated transactions on some aircraft and project financings have been contracted for a period of up to 18 years.

In many acquisition financings, this scenario is varied: the facility agreements are signed and the transaction sometimes funded prior to the general syndication. This enables the borrower to negotiate the deal with one bank, or a small group of banks, prior to announcing a bid thereby protecting confidentiality. General syndication in such cases rarely begins until the acquisition is consummated or definitely committed.

## Milestones and timetable

In each of these phases, there are certain events, or milestones, which occur in all syndicated transactions and it is these milestones that will form the basis of the discussion here.

In the pre-mandate phase, the principal milestones are:

- the identification and articulation of the borrower's need from the syndicated credit market;
- the decision by the borrower on its approach in seeking bids;
- the decision on a bidding configuration and strategy by the banks;
- the internal approval of the credit by the potential arranger;
- the submission of a bid and the award of the mandate.

In the post-mandate phase, the principal milestones are:

- completion of the information memorandum, bank presentation and invitation letter;
- launching the syndication;
- (if relevant) exercising market flex or reverse flex;
- closing the books;
- making allocations and (where relevant) declaring the deal free to trade;
- completing negotiation of the documentation;
- the signing.

The final, post-signing, phase contains less well-defined milestones, since it is essentially an operational phase. Nonetheless, principal milestones are:

- satisfaction by the borrower of conditions precedent;
- issuance of utilisation requests;
- the payment of accrued interest, fees and principal amounts;
- provision to the syndicate of necessary financial and other information on a timely basis.

The timetable for the pre-mandate phase is largely governed by the urgency of the financing need of the borrower. In merger and acquisition finance, it is sometimes necessary to assemble a group of banks rapidly and discreetly, sometimes over two or three days only. In the interest of achieving this goal, a borrower may decide not to solicit competitive bids but to select a small number of relationship banks to work together on a negotiated basis. This approach can considerably reduce the time required to award a mandate. However, without such special circumstances, a borrower will typically discuss a transaction with interested banks over a period of a few weeks prior to awarding a mandate.

It is for the post-mandate phase that a timetable is most essential because during it both the borrower and the mandated bank(s) have committed themselves to raise funds from the market and are therefore at risk. A failure during this phase can result in financial penalties for both sides, as well as loss of reputation and credibility for the parties concerned. It is therefore highly advisable to establish a detailed timetable with target dates for reaching each of the milestones.

In order for this to be achieved, there are tasks which have to be completed either sequentially or in parallel. For instance, during the post-mandate phase the negotiation of the documentation between the arranger and the borrower can take place in parallel with the syndication (that is, when banks are actually in possession of an invitation to participate in the transaction). By contrast, the syndication process itself will not (usually) commence until after the information memorandum, bank presentation and invite letter have been completed and approved and are ready for distribution to prospective bank participants. A typical transaction will have the following timetable during this phase (although no two transactions will be exactly alike in this respect):

### Initiate Process

- Initial meeting to agree post-mandate process

### Week one

- Agree syndication strategy
- Commence work on the information memorandum and bank presentation.

- Instruct counsel to prepare first drafts of the facility agreement and associated documentation.
- Prepare invite letter to be sent to potential participants.

### Week two

- Review the facility agreement, along with associated documentation, and instruct counsel to prepare second drafts for dispatch to the borrower.
- Finalise information memorandum and bank presentation with the borrower.
- Send confidentiality agreement and invitation letter to banks.

### Weeks three to five

- Send information memorandum and bank presentation to interested banks.
- Negotiate the facility agreement and associated documentation with the borrower.
- Coordinate Q&A session for potential lenders
- Control the release of transaction information to the financial press.

### Weeks six to seven

- Obtain credit approval from potential lenders, subject to documentation
- Send the facility agreement and associated documentation to banks for review.
- Negotiate documentation with banks (and borrower if necessary).
- (if necessary) exercise market flex or reverse flex.
- Make final allocations.
- Obtain administrative details and power of attorney from participating banks.
- Make arrangements for closing and if required arrange signing ceremony.

### Week eight

- Execute documentation.
- Borrower to satisfy conditions precedent.

This is illustrated schematically in exhibit 4.1.

## Exhibit 4.1: Typical timetable of events

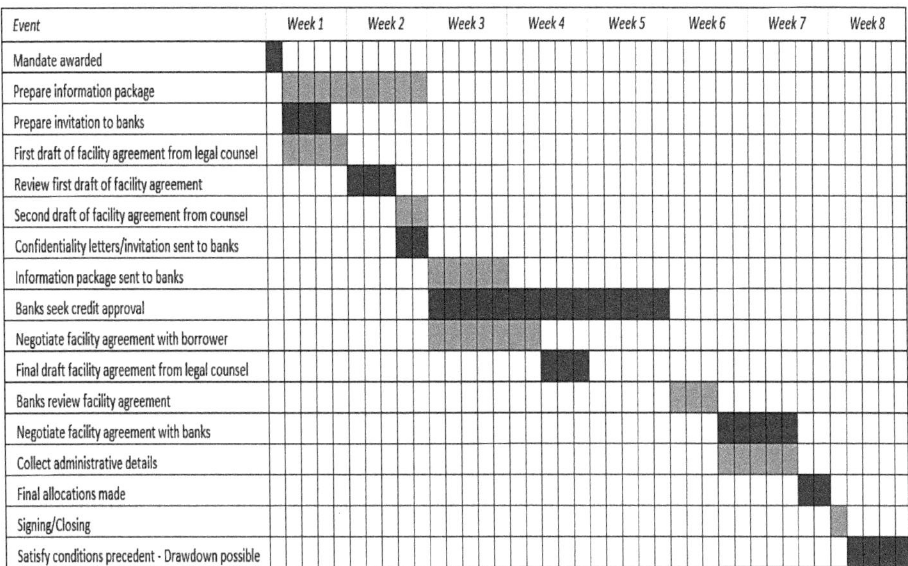


For most of the history of the syndicated loan market much of the process within the post-mandate phase which involves the interaction between arrangers, bookrunners, underwriters and other lenders has been carried out in accordance with practices which market practitioners have developed over time without any formal framework ever being written down or agreed. However, in recent years there has been some demand for a more formalised and consistent approach to some of the processes. This demand has to some extent resulted from the growing involvement in the market of institutional investors who are more used to the more formalised practices of the bond markets (as well as from insistences of unsuccessful deals in the market where it proved difficult to reach agreement between the parties as to how to deal with the problem).

In 2018 the LMA published a number of documents aimed at encouraging more consistent methods of managing various events and scenarios arising in the syndicated process.

In particular, the LMA produced two Decision Charts (one dealing with "Successful Syndication" and the other with "Unsuccessful Syndication") which provide guidelines for how market practitioners should deal with the decisions and information flow around matters like syndication strategy; syndication status reports; the exercise of market flex or reverse flex; the closing or cancellation of syndication; allocations and declaring the deal free to trade; and the sharing of proceeds from general syndication. It is important to note that these Decision Charts are guidelines only and not binding on any parties unless formalised in contractual agreements.

This trend towards greater formalisation of syndication practices was also reflected in the production by the LMA in 2018 of a Recommended Timeline for Settlement of Primary Syndication which seeks to remedy some of the delays in the syndication process by providing a standard (and alternative fast-track) set of recommended timings for various activities in the process. It will be noted that the Recommended Timetable is more extended than that indicated in Exhibit 4.1 (where the time between the final allocations and signature is very short). The transaction referred to in Exhibit 4.1 is likely to be a relationship deal for an investment grade borrower (such as the DutchCo transaction) whereas the Recommended Timetable has to cater for more complex transactions with larger syndicates.

The Recommended Timeline also incorporates (in certain circumstances) a requirement for the underwriters of a deal to pay delayed settlement compensation to the investors/participants if the timetable is not met. Again, the Recommended Timetable (and the delayed settlement compensation requirement) are not binding on the parties unless a specific agreement is reached that they will be.

The principal issue which the Timetable seeks to address is the situation in transactions with substantial numbers of institutional investors (such as leveraged finance deals) where the investors commit to participate in the transaction, but they have to wait for a significant period of time before they formally sign in to the documentation (and start to receive fees and interest).

The Timetable recommends a period of 27 Business Days between the day (AD) on which allocation occurs and close of syndication (or 14 Business Days under the fast track timetable).

In order to assist with meeting the Timetable, the LMA has produced a number of documents which aim to standardise and streamline parts of the process. These include standardised forms for communication of Administrative Details and Agency Details as well as standardised forms of commitment letters under which participating lenders commit to participate in the transaction.

As in all processes, a critical path can be established to focus the attention of both the arranger and the borrower on timing if timing is of the essence. The critical path may change over time if unforeseen events occur, such as failure of the arranger and borrower to agree documentation within the allotted time. This would result in a delay in the dispatch of the documents to the banks joining the deal and would thus delay the review, negotiation and incorporation of their comments, if any, in the final documents. Pressure may be brought to bear on all parties to reduce the time allocated to documentation review and this usually means that the participant banks have less time than originally envisaged. Moreover, the increasing use of secure web-based transmission services, has resulted in many syndicated transactions being executed in a number of counterparts, with each bank signing and sending separate documents which are then combined to form a conformed copy.

The post-signing phase, which lasts until the later of the final maturity date or the date of prepayment or cancellation of the facility by the borrower, is characterised by operational events. These events are both discretionary and non-discretionary on the part of the borrower. Discretionary events for the borrower include the issuance of utilisation requests, selection of interest periods and switching currencies in multi-currency facilities. Non-discretionary events would include payment of fees, interest and repayment of principal, the supply of financial and other information on a timely basis and the delivery of covenant compliance certificates on the relevant due dates.

## Duties/roles

Before considering the pre-mandate phase in detail, it is necessary to understand the duties and roles to be undertaken by banks in the post-mandate phase because if bidding for the mandate means working with other banks as partners, the allocation of these duties and roles between banks is usually a critical element in forming a cohesive bidding group.

The principal roles in the post-mandate phase are in connection with the execution of the following activities: bookrunning, acting as facility agent, coordinating, preparing the information memorandum, acting as technical agent (or security agent) and preparing and negotiating documentation. Minor duties include arranging a signing and handling publicity.

The duties and responsibilities associated with each of these roles are described further on in this chapter. However, it is important for the reader to understand the status and workload of these roles as they can form an integral part of the bidding process as well. It is obvious that, where a bank bids alone and is successful in winning the mandate, all of the work involved in each of the roles is undertaken by that bank. But if banks are bidding together for a mandate, each one needs to establish its position and role within the group prior to the award of a mandate.

In multi-bank bidding situations, the roles will usually be shared among the members of the bidding group. The choice of the bank(s) to be nominated as bookrunner(s), which is generally perceived to be the most prestigious position, will depend on the reputation and the resources of each of the candidate banks in the bidding group. The final choice will also depend heavily on each bank's relationship with the borrower.

The second most prestigious role is that of the facility agent. This has less market visibility during the syndication phase, but provides a long-term operational and commercial relationship with the borrower after the signing. The bank acting as facility agent is well positioned for the next mandate and it is usually the only role which benefits from incremental remuneration (agency fees).

A further role that has become increasingly prevalent in recent years and is highly regarded by banks is that of the coordinator(s). The coordinator(s) supervises the syndication process and undertakes preparation tasks on behalf of the borrower and members of the bidding group.

A technical agent is sometimes needed on project finance deals, such as mining or energy deals, and a security agent is required for aircraft, shipping, property and leveraged finance deals. The facility agent may also take on these duties but often in multi-bank bidding groups the agency roles will be split between two banks. The bank taking on the responsibility of technical or security agent will need specialist staff to execute the functions. These specialist roles are sometimes remunerated by the borrower for the services provided.

Other roles will be allocated according to the desires, aspirations and negotiating skills of the banks in a bidding group. Some banks have decided that, other than for the major roles, the commitment of resources is not worthwhile and prefer, if they do not obtain a major role, to decline the transaction or to take a passive position in the lead group.

If only two banks are bidding together, it is logical to give the task of preparing the information memorandum and lender presentation to the bookrunner and for the facility agent to handle the documentation. This becomes clear when one considers that the role of bookrunning can include the dissemination of all relevant information to the potential participant banks, when a coordinator is not appointed, and the bookrunner has a vested interest in ensuring that the information memorandum and bank presentation are as complete as possible. Again, the facility agent has every interest in ensuring that the documentation is as clear and efficient as possible since it will be operating in accordance with its provisions for several years into the future.

Signing and publicity are junior roles but can be used to provide status to other members of a bidding group if its size exceeds four banks; in other cases these roles are usually allocated either to the bookrunner or to the facility agent.

Although the above-mentioned roles are the ones found in most transactions, other roles can occur from time to time such as the role of the regional bookrunner for a deal which will be syndicated globally. This role granted to a senior regional bank in a bidding group is to take the responsibility of running the books for the selected regional banks for example, banks located in the Middle East, or banks located in Central and Eastern Europe.

# THE PRE-MANDATE PHASE

## Identifying and understanding the borrower's needs

Deal origination occurs in several ways. The opportunity to bid can arise in the course of a joint marketing call involving the relationship officer and a member of the syndications unit. More often, the opportunity or need to borrow has been well established in advance through a careful analysis and review of the borrower's requirements. Corporate and financial institutions (FI) as borrowers are also more opportunistic in nature and most often initiate discussions with their lead banks in seeking competitive offers.

The key information which a potential arranger must determine at an early stage is:

- the amount of the facility required;
- the purpose of the facility;
- the issues affecting the maturity and borrower's desired maturity;
- the likely drawdown schedule (if the loan is to be drawn down in instalments);
- sensitive covenant issues;
- target pricing levels;
- the timing (both for award of mandate and for availability of funds);
- other markets under consideration and other borrowing plans;
- the probability of the transaction proceeding;
- competition and the borrower's approach in seeking bids;
- other factors likely to influence the borrower in awarding the mandate;
- the receptiveness of the borrower to unconventional or innovative ideas.

## A borrower's approach to seeking bids

Unless a banker is aware in advance of a borrowing need or has come upon a bidding situation through a well-timed marketing initiative, the borrower is likely to advise its principal banks of its intention to seek competitive bids. There are three usual methods: selective bidding with key relationship banks; selective bidding with banks having speciality knowledge and expertise; and open bidding.

In nearly all bidding situations the borrower stipulates several conditions, such as amount and timing, and in some cases suggests a range of acceptable rates, terms and conditions, or circulates an indicative term sheet. The borrower may request a fully underwritten offer or partially underwritten offer or an offer on a best efforts basis. A borrower will not often disclose which banks have been asked to submit offers, although this information will usually surface through leaks in the market.

The experience of Dufry in putting together its lending syndicates since 2006 is described in supplement 1 to chapter 2.

### Bidding by relationship banks

The borrower may seek bids from only three to eight banks, who may be given the discretion to form a group or make an independent bid although, most commonly, individual bids are sought prior to putting a group together. Unless the information concerning a proposed bid is closely held, the borrower is likely to receive a number of unsolicited offers as well. Although such unsolicited bids rarely result in a mandate, borrowers often use them as a basis for negotiating a more favourable position with one of the acknowledged contenders.

### Speciality bank bidding

An alternative to seeking bids from key relationship banks is to seek offers from banks which are acknowledged leaders in a specialised field such as infrastructure, utility or energy-related finance, aircraft or leveraged loans, or which have particular knowledge of a unique pricing formula or unusual structure. Product capability is often viewed as having considerable benefit to the borrower; since the invitation to bid is extended on the basis of the bank's expertise in a given field, rather than on an established relationship. Such a strategy would see the borrower benefit from the bank's in-depth sector knowledge and a strong understanding of underlying pricing dynamics.

### Open bidding

Some borrowers seek as many offers as possible causing bidding chaos. This leads certain banks to decline to bid altogether, while others will submit sole bids. Still others seek to form groups, something the borrower probably wished to avoid through extending multiple invitations to bid.

Over the years, banks in the syndication market have mastered the art of creating bidding order out of the chaos. Techniques have been developed and refined with a self-policing mechanism which has now become standard market practice. When seeking to form a group, the bank initiating the calls will say 'A group is being formed to bid for a $300m financing for Borrower X. Are you interested?' The recipient bank, if part of another group, should respond: 'We are forming/have joined a competing syndicate. Thanks for your call.' End of conversation. Banks will need to be sensitive to competition law issues when seeking to form bidding groups.

## Alternative bidding configurations

Once information about the transaction has been obtained and the probable approach being adopted by the borrower in seeking bids is understood, a potential arranger will need to consider the appropriate bidding configuration and strategy in order to secure the mandate to arrange the transaction.

Several bidding configurations have emerged over the years. From an arranger's point of view, the preferred bidding configuration is normally a sole bid, resulting in an unrestricted mandate, which grants the winning bank sole decision-making authority regarding fee distribution and discretion to form an underwriting or sub-underwriting group, to distribute roles, if appropriate, and then to syndicate the transaction in the marketplace.

A less satisfactory alternative for an arranger is a multi-bank bidding group. It is less satisfactory for a number of reasons:

- The bid for the transaction is no longer managed by one bank and all parties to the bid must consent to changes in the bid as it progresses. This can create some logistical difficulties if the bidding group comprises more than two or three banks with some operating in different time zones.
- The members of multi-bank bidding groups tend to jockey for position in terms of both role allocation and prominence with the borrower and in publicity. (Various rules have evolved with regard to publicity – this is discussed later in this chapter.) The jockeying for position can be time consuming, counter-productive for the banks and the borrower and potentially result in a member of the group declining the transaction if not handled by experienced practitioners.
- The fee allocation becomes an item for intense debate. In most cases, banks bidding in a group agree to split the fees on an equal basis if their bid is successful. There are occasions, however, when one bank is clearly in pole position and is able to command a premium either through its relationship with the borrower or because of a feature of the bid which the other banks are unable to match. This feature could be product innovation or simply industry expertise.

If these reasons illustrate why multi-bank bidding groups are less satisfactory than single bank bids, there is one situation when they become essential. This occurs when a borrower seeks a fully underwritten bid for an amount which is too high for any of the bidders to commit to alone. It may be too high simply because of the size of underwriting in relation to the capital base of the bank making the bid; it may be too high because the market risk is considered too great by the bidding bank's management, because the chance of not selling the transaction in the market from the initial underwriting commitment to the final asset retention target is unacceptably high; or it may be that the likely level of pricing will not meet internal targets for the risk/reward ratio. Whatever the reason, in such circumstances, it is necessary to form a group to make a multi-bank bid which is underwritten by the members of the group on a several basis, that is, each bank is solely responsible for its part and not for the part of the others.

A multi-bank bid is more desirable for borrowers in conditions of tight money and rising spreads, where an over-zealous bid by a single bank may result in a lowest offer mandate and possibly a difficult or failed deal. Conversely, in a market where spreads are declining, such consortium bidding generally works against the borrower's interests in that the benefit of potentially finer terms from one competing institution is masked by the group offer.

In forming a multi-bank bidding group, it is essential to create strength for the group by capturing geographic diversity, borrower relationship, syndication skill and market stature. Nonetheless, even with all of these attributes, bidding groups often fail to secure the mandate, usually losing to a competing bank, or group of banks, willing and able to take a more aggressive stance on either pricing or structure, or both.

For the most part, the leading banks in the syndications market tend to be prudent and willing to compromise on the grounds that one-half or one-third of a deal is better than none of it. As borrowers have become more sophisticated in managing their relationships with a group of banks they have more commonly been brought back together as a group or it has even become more prevalent for financings to be organised by way of a club loan, under which there is no expectation of a formal syndication process with all members of the arranging group being expected to keep their original commitments on a "take and hold" basis.

As mentioned above, status with the borrower and the distribution of syndicate roles are key issues and often inhibit competitive group bidding. In terms of fee income, a major drawback is the adverse effect of group bidding on total return, since any arrangement fee is usually shared equally rather than allocated to a single arranger. The decision to bid alone or join a group is one of the most critical early decisions that a bidding bank must make when assessing the trade-off between market risk and financial return.

When banks join to submit a collective underwritten bid, it is sometimes found that the combined total of underwriting amounts approved by the respective credit committees of the bidding banks exceeds the amount of the transaction. In such a case, each of the banks committing to the transaction will be scaled back so that the final underwritten amount equals the total amount required by the borrower. The initial underwriting commitment is converted into an allocated underwriting commitment and it is on this amount that underwriting fees are calculated for each bank. It is also on the amount of the allocated underwriting commitment that the share in the syndication pool is determined.

Even more important in forming an equal bank bidding group, when an equal fee split is agreed as a condition of a group bid, is that one or more of the banks is likely to accept a syndicate role which creates a mismatch between its commitment of human resources and technical skills to the transaction and the undifferentiated level of fee compensation. At one extreme, certain banks will accept such tasks for reasons of visibility with the client or for the status which syndicate roles are believed to convey within the market. At the other end of the activity spectrum, a bank may opt to take no role in the syndication process provided that there will be an equal fee distribution among the arrangers. These issues are normally resolved at a meeting between the banks forming the bidding group.

## Pricing the transaction

Once the borrower's needs have been thoroughly understood, the structuring and pricing of the transaction can start. This will involve various skills from within the bidding bank, in particular those of the relationship manager, the syndication (or distribution) unit, the origination team and the credit approval department. A transaction team must be formed which will strike a balance, after some brainstorming, between the objectives of winning the mandate, organising a successful syndication and maintaining the credit standards of the bank. The relationship manager is required to understand fully the sensitive issues for the borrower and be able to coordinate an active dialogue with the borrower as the transaction starts to take shape. The relationship manager knows the business of the client, in particular its position among its peer group, and should be aware of the likely competition for the mandate as well as having an understanding of the borrower's pricing expectations. The syndication unit is required to provide input regarding the market appetite for the risk by assessing the structure, maturity and price which will be acceptable to potential participating banks, while remaining acutely aware of the trade-off between these variables. The syndication unit will also be required to confirm that, on the basis of prevailing market conditions, the proposed transaction can be sold in the marketplace permitting the bank to meet its desired final hold target. The origination team will work closely with the syndication unit, having had active dialogue with the borrower prior to being mandated and provide input regarding key documentation points as the transaction progresses. The credit department is ultimately required to approve the transaction thereby allowing an offer to be made.

The syndication unit and origination team concentrate on a number of key variables when considering the price for a transaction:

- The purpose of the facility.
- The amount and proposed final maturity of the facility, taking into consideration structural details such as the availability period and amortisation schedule which will affect the length of the average life of the facility.
- The quality of the credit covenants.
- The credit quality of the borrower
- Any ancillary business opportunities
- The strength of the relationship banking group
- Prevailing market conditions

Failure to focus on the quality of credit covenants can lead to disaster, as banks in the market will reject a deal if the covenants are inappropriate and the risk unacceptable. In general, yield enhancement cannot overcome this, whereas an underpriced but sound transaction can be sold in the market if the mandated bank supports the transaction by sacrificing all or part of the arrangement fees or has the opportunity to exercise a marketflex clause. An understanding of the purpose of the facility is critical because it will strongly influence the manner in which pricing for the transaction develops. A commercial paper back-up facility of the type envisaged for DutchCo in chapter 3 must be priced to ensure that the undrawn cost is acceptable to the market, whereas the pricing for Project Tennis places more emphasis on the fully drawn cost with less attention to the undrawn cost.

The amount and final maturity of the transaction are important factors when determining the price for a transaction. Account must be taken of: the likely level of existing bank exposure to the borrower; the appetite for the risk of the bidding bank itself; the number of banks and size of commitments likely to be required to raise the funds from the market; whether there are any competing transactions currently in the market, or likely to be in the market when the transaction is launched; whether it will be a relationship-driven syndication; and whether the period to final maturity is likely to breach the internal policy guidelines for any members of the potential bank group. Another factor to be taken into account is whether the borrower has decided to use the market for deliberate oversubscription: if it is the borrower's intention to increase the final amount of the deal by marketing the transaction more widely and obtaining more commitments than are strictly necessary, the borrower may be prepared to pay a slightly higher price in order to attract more than a minimum number of banks into the syndicate. In recent years ancillary business opportunities have become increasingly important with banks funding costs remaining elevated and banks subsequently often lending at a loss. If significant ancillary opportunities can be identified the borrower may be able to pay slightly lower pricing as banks factor these opportunities into their return. While these issues are being assessed and the probable response of banks is evaluated, attention must continue to be given to the normal credit issues associated with the transaction.

The covenant package, pricing and structure are inter-related. A tightly negotiated covenant package can lead to lower pricing than would otherwise be the case. For longer-dated transactions (three years and above), it is not uncommon to introduce a pricing grid which links changes in pricing either with specific changes in performance under the covenant package or with publicly quoted credit ratings. Nonetheless, the market is not uniform in its requirements and a bidding bank needs to anticipate the proposals likely to emerge from competitors when constructing its offer.

A number of banks have introduced computer models to assist in solving the pricing equation. These models are based on historical analysis of deals in each sector and take account of the actual loss or provisioning experience in each sector. Inevitably, such models can only give a general guideline as to the level of pricing that should apply in any particular case, and it remains with the transaction team to fine tune an offer to the point where it is sufficiently competitive to win the mandate.

The syndication unit and origination team will use all types of market intelligence to assist in forming a view of the most appropriate structure and price for a particular deal. If the borrower is a frequent user of the capital or syndication markets, there may be some ready-made pricing benchmarks which can be found using the sources of information described in chapter 2. Most often, the borrower is not a frequent user of the market and a proxy must be found to provide an insight into the level of pricing that the market will accept. This usually involves identifying transactions that have been arranged for broadly comparable borrowers. Details must be found, if possible, of transactions for borrowers of the same category, of the same nationality, in the same industry, having similar ownership (private sector or public sector), and of similar status and credit quality. It also means finding transactions of similar amount, maturity and purpose to the one under consideration. Databases such as Dealogic's Loan Manager are frequently used for this type of analysis. As can be expected, there is rarely a perfect fit, which is why the expertise of an experienced syndication unit is vital when new situations arise.

Other sources of data are the secondary loan market, the secondary bond market using asset swaps (fixed-rate bond issues swapped into floating-rate assets) and the credit default swap market. The secondary loan market has become quite liquid in the large loans (>$1bn) space, although ad-hoc trades frequently take place in smaller loans as well (see chapter 6). However, secondary loan trades do not necessarily reflect the return requirements for a new transaction as the price in the primary market frequently includes a 'relationship' element which means that banks will participate as a defensive measure, either to protect or generate other relationship business, on a lower yield than might be available in the secondary market. Secondary loan pricing usually reflects the arm's-length yield required by loan investors for the risk and maturity. Although some fixed-rate bonds are priced deliberately to provide a specific return on a floating-rate asset-swapped basis once the paper has been placed, little active trading takes place because of the cost of unwinding the linked swap. Furthermore, the documentation for the underlying bond may be substantially different (weaker) than that contemplated for the new loan.

In their quest for accurate information, the syndication unit can undertake some discreet market soundings. For this information to be of much use, it may be necessary to be very precise about the quality and nationality of the borrower, but it is important to ensure that the market does not deduce the name of the borrower and that the press should not hear of the enquiries and publish its findings, to the embarrassment of the parties concerned. Enquiries with other banks can thus be undertaken only in accordance with a Bank's internal policies (aimed at ensuring compliance with competition law by avoiding inappropriate exchange of competitive information) and on the basis of trust between the individuals concerned and it is this feature of the market which is perhaps the most important for a syndication unit - the establishment of a rapport with competitors which does not breach the competitive spirit of the market (any collusion as to pricing being, of course, unacceptable and contrary to competition law) and yet provides for a two-way flow of information.

The reader will realise by now that pricing a transaction is more of an art than a science, although scientific method is essential if transactions are to be syndicated successfully in the market.

## Liquidity analysis

Having determined the likely pricing parameters, it is important now to assess the capacity in the market and this is done using a liquidity analysis so-called because it helps evaluate the liquidity in the market. The process starts with the syndication unit developing (usually on an iterative basis) a syndication strategy for the transaction which will include initial underwriting amounts, may include sub-underwriting amounts and will include the tickets chosen for the general syndication. Based on its research, the syndications unit will identify a list of potential participant banks and other investors and will assign each of them to a ticket based on their past performance in the market. For instance, a bank that is usually found in a lead role will be assumed to be interested in participating at the top level in the transaction. A bank that typically makes only small commitments in transactions will be assigned to one of the tickets of general syndication. However these assignments are intelligent guesses and not certainties so a probability of the likelihood of the bank actually coming into the deal at these levels needs to be applied in each case.

An example of a liquidity analysis for a $1bn loan is shown in exhibit 4.2.

In this example, the syndication strategy is to form a lead group of four MLA & bookrunners to underwrite the deal at $250m each. This will be followed by a sub-underwriting phase with banks invited in as MLAs to underwrite $125m. General syndication will follow with two tickets at $40m and $25m carrying the titles of lead arrangers and arrangers respectively. The objective for each of the MLA and bookrunners is to hold $75m at the end of primary syndication and for each of the MLAs to hold $55m.

**Exhibit 4.2: Liquidity analysis for $1bn loan**

| *Title* | *MLA & Bookrunners* | *MLA* | *Lead Arranger* | *Arranger* |
|---|---|---|---|---|
| **Selected banks for each ticket (based on research)** | Our bank, Citibank, NatWest, HSBC, Others... (n1) *say n1=5* | SMBC, SG, UniCredit, UBS, Others... (n2) *say n2=10* | RZB, Mizuho, Lloyds,<br><br>Others... (n3) *say n3=15* | Rabobank, Fifth Third Bank, Natixis, Others... (n4) *say n4=15* |
| **Ticket: u/w**<br>**hold** | $250m<br>$75m (h1) | $125m<br>$55m (h2) | n/a<br>$40m (h3) | n/a<br>$25m (h4) |
| **Hit ratio (based on experience and research)** | 80% (p1) | 75% (p2) | 55% (p3) | 35% (p4) |
| **Expected contribution** | n1xh1xp1 | n2xh2xp2 | n3xh3xp3 | n4xh4xp4 |
| **Expected contribution** | $300m | $412.5m | $330m | $131.25m |

In choosing the banks to act as MLA & bookrunners, account will be taken of the banks having the capital to underwrite the amount (in this example $250m) as well as their relationship with the borrower as far as can be determined from public knowledge. Research showing a past history of doing deals with the borrower would be a good sign of potential interest. The syndication unit expects a high hit ratio at this level and plans to contact four other banks (the assumption being that the bidding bank (our bank) will do the deal) with a probability of 80% (p1) assigned to this ticket.

The next level may be less certain as some banks may feel peeved at not being included at the top level and so the syndication unit assigns a lower probability of 75% to this ticket. The chance to take some underwriting risk, albeit not at the top level, and earn underwriting fees will be attractive to some banks.

The research for banks in general syndication, apart from known relationship banks, will focus on institutions interested in the industry sector, the geography and the type of transaction. It will also focus on their known level of commitments in similar deals in the past so that there is a realistic expectation that, if interested in the deal, the amount offered will fall within their comfort zone.

It is now possible to calculate the expected contribution from each ticket being the product of the number of banks approached for each ticket (n), the final hold for that ticket (h) and the probability that a bank for that ticket actually joins the deal (p).

In this example, the expected contributions are $300m, $412.5m, $330m and $131.25m for the MLA & bookrunner, MLA, lead arranger and arranger ticket respectively. The total contribution is $1,173.75m, that is, a 17.4% oversubscription. Although this is no guarantee that the actual process of syndication will produce this result, the syndication unit can at least take comfort that there is oversubscription rather than under-subscription which would clearly indicate a defective strategy from the outset. Indeed, if the expected contribution is less than the amount required by the borrower, a new syndication strategy will need to be developed as it is not appropriate merely to change the probabilities!

The liquidity analysis must also be examined carefully to ensure that, on the basis of the retention targets (be they the underwritten amounts or final holds), each stage meets the financing requirement. For instance, the MLA & bookrunner ticket fails if five banks are offered an underwriting amount of $250m and the assigned probability is 60% as the expected contribution from this ticket at the initial underwriting stage would then only be $750m.

In general terms, an oversubscription of 20% does give the syndication unit a degree of comfort in confirming the sell down to the credit and portfolio management committees within their institution.

A well structured liquidity analysis is a document that can serve a bidding bank well in discussions with the borrower. First of all it demonstrates how the amount of the loan can be raised and sits well with a discussion on pricing. Secondly, the use of bank names for the various tickets helps the borrower focus on this particular aspect of the proposal. If one of the banks included is not one that the borrower wants in the syndicate for any particular reason, the borrower may indicate this and suggest an alternative. This helps validate the probabilities. Thirdly, some borrowers may be targeting a larger amount than the initial amount requested. A liquidity analysis can be used to create the framework for a larger amount (by increasing the number of institutions approached, or the amount of the tickets) and then, if the strategy is successful, being able to announce an increase in the size of the facility.

## Initial negotiations with the borrower

It is sometimes said by frustrated bankers that banking would be a wonderful business if the borrowers would leave the bankers in peace! Such comments evaporate in the face of a serious new business opportunity when bankers bid aggressively to win business in a highly competitive marketplace. The difference in all-in cost between a winning and a losing bid on a transaction of several hundreds of millions of dollars can be as little as a basis point or even a fraction of a basis point, which is perhaps only a few thousand dollars. This difference may manifest itself in such items as the arrangement fee or the agency fee or, indeed, in the willingness of a bank to cap expenses by setting a maximum monetary limit on the borrower's liability to pay transaction costs. In such a competitive environment, a bank bidding for new business must ensure that it presents itself in the most favourable light and uses whatever resources it has at its disposal to secure the mandate.

Once the borrower's needs and requirements have been identified and explored in some considerable depth, a bidding bank must commence its marketing in support of the offer which it hopes to make. Before the offer can be made, a bank will need to organise internal credit approval or, if not a formal credit approval, at least a green light to proceed. The terms of this approval will influence the type of bid that is made. There are, however, many other factors which a borrower will look for in choosing the lead bank and any serious candidate needs to be acutely aware of these criteria.

One of the most important factors for a borrower to consider is the track record of the bidding banks. Evidence of the track record of individual banks can be found in the league tables, although if the period covered by such league tables is too short, distortions can occur as described in chapter 2. League tables taken over a period of years do give a measure of a bank's activity in terms of both volume (amount) and number of deals. The evidence of significant market activity also gives comfort to a borrower that the bank's knowledge of the appetite of potential participant banks for different types of transaction is up to date. This is particularly valuable if a borrower is attempting to widen its universe of banks through the syndication process.

Another factor which is vital for successful syndication is for the mandated bank to have specialised knowledge of the industry sector in which the borrower operates. Specialised sectors include acquisition finance, leveraged finance, shipping, aircraft, property and project finance. The mandates for deals in these sectors are most frequently awarded to banks with a history of providing finance to the sector, so that the appointed bank will have credibility when explaining the transaction to other banks during the syndication process.

Syndication strategy is of vital importance for a borrower as well as the arranger. A number of borrowers have found that successful syndication of a transaction is much easier if this aspect of a transaction is clarified at the outset. If a borrower is ready to 'twist arms' and cajole relationship banks into a finely priced deal, it is important for the arranger to assess how real this relationship (collateral) business really is if making an underwritten offer. Borrowers sometimes inaccurately assess the depth of their bank relationships and this can lead to difficult negotiations later on if banks expected by the borrower to join the deal ultimately decline. A misunderstanding between the parties can have a negative impact in the market. Banks eventually entering such transactions will remember the circumstances and may decline to do further business or exact a much higher price on the next occasion. Borrowers will have the impression that they are doing much of the syndication themselves and will question the arranger's added value. Equally, if having awarded an underwritten mandate the borrower allows the choice of banks to be entirely at the discretion of the arranger, that is, with unrestricted access to any banks it may choose, this must be agreed at the outset. The arranger needs to establish the syndication strategy from the outset so that the approach to the market is tightly managed without the need to change tack halfway through. In practice, it is not possible to predict with absolute certainty the market response to a new transaction, so an arranger and borrower need to monitor progress closely and take corrective action if necessary.

In reality, once a mandate has been awarded, the borrower and the arranger are partners in seeking a satisfactory result in the market. If the deal is a *dog* the reputation of the arranger(s) suffers but so does that of the borrower, since the market will note the failure and price upwards on the next occasion.

## Issues in seeking approval to bid

### Credit approval

Regardless of how a bank has learned of a bidding situation, several simultaneous events now occur in each competing institution. The collective energies of the relationship managers, portfolio managers, syndication team, origination team and credit officers focus on four central issues with regard to the potential deal: credit, price, internal appetite and the ability to syndicate relative to the market. The relationship manager, portfolio manager, treasury and credit officers within the bank are essential to the deal presentation as they usually have responsibility for business development, portfolio credit risk, return on assets, cost of funding, risk adjusted return on capital (RAROC) and management of lending capacity and concentrations. They will be accountable for the continuous monitoring of the quality of the asset resulting from the syndication, unless the asset is to be transferred post-closing to another lender using the secondary market.

In the case of corporate borrowers and Financial Institutions (FI's), the credit process will require that an in-depth financial analysis be performed and an industry review undertaken, while a sovereign proposal will require the services of the bank's economic department and country credit committee. More established names, whether sovereign, public sector, corporate or FI, will require credit and/or economic analysis and a close review of lending capacity and pricing. This is particularly relevant when a portfolio is close to a bank's self-imposed borrower, industry concentration or regulatory limit, as the bank attempts to maximise the return on marginal portfolio capacity.

In either case, the credit package is then presented for in-house approval. Most banks will require that the recommendation of the syndication unit be an integral part of the credit presentation, although others may allow the credit and marketing team to represent the interests of the syndicate specialists. In any event, the bank often requires the unit(s) ultimately responsible for the deal to concur with all four elements of the approval. The recommendation of the syndication unit is particularly relevant when the bidding situation requires fine pricing, large underwriting positions or both. The degree of success that the syndication unit has in reducing individual underwriting exposure to agreed retention targets helps to establish its in-house credibility as well as to secure, over time, a reputation in the marketplace.

A positive response from the credit approval process is then used as the basis of an offer to the borrower. The results, however, are not always in line with the original expectations and the approval may set objectives or goals which are difficult, if not impossible, to achieve. The approval may result in terms and conditions which do not reflect the borrower's status in the marketplace. For example, an approved yield of 90bps per annum over five years may be inconsistent with the market view that the mandate will be awarded on terms which are closer to 62.5bps per annum for the first three years and 75bps per annum for the last two. The process may establish an unrealistic primary market sell-down target where, for example, a $250m underwriting commitment must be reduced to a $10m final asset at the end of primary syndication. A reduction of this magnitude is, in nearly all cases, beyond the reach of the primary syndication process but may well be achievable in the secondary market. The credit process may overlay asset retention and yield criteria with covenants such as debt/equity coverage, working capital ratios or, in the case of sovereign or public sector borrowers, an obligation to maintain IMF membership *in good standing*, or retain the current public ratings on outstanding debt issues. Other banks may be prepared to bid without some or all of these conditions thereby reducing, or eliminating, the competitiveness of a bid which includes all or any of them. A bank may also decide, on the basis of the constraints imposed by the credit committee, to submit a defensive bid, one which it has no intention or desire of winning.

For most banks, the final credit approval is sought and (hopefully) granted once the borrower's intentions are clearly established, covenants and pricing agreed and a mandate imminent.

### Resultant bidding strategies

A straightforward, unrestrictive response from the credit approval process will quickly result in an offer. On the other hand, if the transaction is declined, with little or no likelihood of reversing the decision, it should be communicated promptly to the borrower, couched in language which preserves access to the borrower in the future.

The more likely result, a conditional approval containing provisos as set out above, requires the syndication specialist to devise a strategy consistent with the bank's objectives.

The client will not have been made aware of the status of the original approval nor the provisos attached to it. In dealing with the conditional approval the following strategies can be employed to mitigate a large underwriting risk and/or low return. It is important to note that all of the following strategies are developed in-house.

### Increasing return on assets

Most banks adhere to a concept of risk adjusted return on assets and risk adjusted return on capital (RAROC), expressed as a per annum yield to the lender. In the circumstances where a 62.5 to 75bps per annum margin is required by the market but a 90bps per annum return is the in-house approved minimum, the front-end fee assists in reaching the required yield. The syndication strategy is a crucial component of this as illustrated in the syndication section of this chapter.

Another potential component in the calculation of the lender's return, the commitment fee, is normally only included if the drawdown schedule is committed in advance, for example, when the facility is used to finance stage payments for an aircraft financing.

The syndication specialist may conclude that the only way to build yield past the minimum required is through unequal distribution of the fees. This implies a mandate completely free of restrictions with the result that a joint bid or a pre-sold deal is a more remote possibility. In this circumstance, the likely bidding strategy could be a sole bid seeking an unrestricted mandate where the distribution of fees is left solely to the discretion of the lead bank.

### Aggressive retention targets

Unrealistic sell-down objectives may put the syndicate manager in an untenable position. If the established goal is judged to be beyond reach, the approved underwriting level, and the proposed strategy for the formation of an underwriting group needs to be reviewed. A $250m underwriting and non-negotiable $10m final retention may necessitate a reduced underwriting commitment ($75m instead of the original proposal of $250m). Alternatively, the secondary market may be used to sell part (or all) of the asset retained by the bank after primary syndication and many credit committees will permit 60 to 180 days after signing to reach the sell-down required. At this stage, however, unless there is a highly confident view of the appetite for the asset in the secondary market, a lower underwriting level is the only alternative that can be considered. The in-house negotiations are designed to obtain the best possible deal for the bank and yet produce a realistic syndication strategy. In the end, the syndicate specialist may feel that a reduced underwriting level of $75m is consistent with the desired retention target. One strategy would be to bid on a sole basis with this smaller underwriting commitment forcing greater market risk on the borrower with respect to securing the amount required in the mandate.

An alternative strategy to cater for the same large deal/small retention dilemma, is to form a multi-bank underwriting and bidding group. In such a case, fee dilution will normally be a by-product of the bid and total return (or yield) will be adversely affected.

### Increased yield coupled with aggressive asset retention targets

The most common circumstance for a syndicate manager is a combination of increased yield coupled with aggressive asset retention. In this case, a sensible bidding strategy would be to form a joint multi-bank bid, with banks which have not been invited to bid. These banks may be less inclined to press for equal treatment and may be content with the prominence accorded a joint arranger slot. The key drawback to this strategy is that the borrower may not feel that the status or the strength of the collective group is of sufficient calibre to justify a mandate.

Conversely, a joint multi-bank bid with a select number of the top-tier market leaders featuring an unequal fee split will meet stiff resistance from within the bidding group. One solution may be to offer active and relevant syndicate roles to such banks as compensation for a lower yield. Banks place much emphasis upon running the books, agency and documentation, or a combination of duties. If a bidding bank is conversant with the operating styles of the competition, it is possible to form a well-constructed, multi-bank bid involving the senior syndicate banks. In such a case, yield is preserved for one institution, in what otherwise appears as a joint and equal effort to underwrite a substantial part, or all, of the proposed transaction. The most likely bidding configuration would be a multi-bank bid, formed from banks of equal status and rank with syndicate tasks dispersed among the group. Fee compensation remains unequal, resulting in differential yields among the bidding banks.

A final alternative, the attempt to induce the borrower to accept substantial over-market or premium pricing, is almost always doomed to failure, although many borrowers consistently award mandates on terms which slightly exceed the finest price offered. Pricing and structural innovations, however, are often mandated at some premium, given the risk and uncertainty inherent in bringing any new concept to market.

### Unacceptable financial or economic covenants

The syndications specialist is treading on dangerous ground with respect to recommending amendments to the underlying credit evaluations. The mission of a syndication unit is to manage the bank's underwriting position, whereas the origination team along with portfolio and credit managers must monitor asset quality through the terms of the loan agreement. There is little that the syndication unit can or should do with regard to onerous covenants imposed by the internal credit process, other than advise what the market will and will not accept. For a syndication group to initiate serious in-house compromise on issues of credit and asset protection is a grievous error. If the credit issue cannot be resolved to the satisfaction of the bank, it is preferable to pass up the opportunity to bid, regardless of the credit standards the market is prepared to accept.

During the period of high liquidity between 2004 and mid-2007 a number of major banks allowed the syndication desk to make their own portfolio decisions on individual assets provided that they were to be used as trading assets and not held long term on the portfolio of the banks concerned. This was a natural consequence of the 'originate and distribute' business model adopted by those banks.

### Defensive bidding

A bank's credit approval process may impose pricing or yield requirements in excess of the levels at which competing lenders are prepared to make offers to a prospective borrower, with the knowledge that such terms are decidedly off-market. On the other hand, syndication units have a duty to provide their institutions with market-based pricing which may, or may not, satisfy the return objectives of senior management. The price for a deal is the minimum price at which it can be satisfactorily syndicated in the marketplace. When this price is the one chosen by the borrower, and the deal is successfully completed in the market, the in-house credibility of the syndication unit is reinforced. This credibility has led to the inclusion of syndication professionals in various in-house pricing committees, with the result that the submission of an over-market bid does not normally result from ignorance of competitive offers, but rather reflects the pricing level which the lending bank is prepared to grant to a given borrower, relative to the other opportunities available in the same risk category.

The question then is what to do with the over-market approval. Should the bank decline to bid or submit the offer? In either case it is incumbent upon the relationship manager and/or the syndication specialist to explain the bank's pricing posture to the client. The decision not to submit a proposal should be communicated quickly to the borrower, as the award of a mandate has often been delayed pending receipt of an offer which never appeared. The decision to submit an over-market proposal should be coupled with arguments which support premium pricing. It will not win the mandate, but is likely to rank along with other over-market bids submitted on a similar basis, and be discarded at an early stage.

## Yield calculations

As the reader will by now realise, the bidding process is dynamic and complex. It is dynamic because the bidding parameters evolve and change with each successive conversation with the borrower, as more information is gleaned about the transaction and the competition. It is complex because not only may it be necessary to keep partner banks in the bidding group totally aware of the evolving situation but it is also necessary continuously to take account of changes in the marketplace. The events which trigger these changes can be macro, such as the devaluation of the Thai baht in 1997 which triggered the late 1990s Asian crisis or the sub-prime crisis and resultant credit crunch of 2007–08 both of which provoked an abrupt change in bank behaviour, or micro, such as the reaction of banks to a comparable transaction launched in the marketplace during the bidding process. These changes will affect the bidder's perception of the likely market reaction to the contemplated transaction and will influence levels of pricing, structure and maturity. Changes in the market are quantified by reference to the yield necessary to attract banks into a transaction. Market intelligence and an understanding of the factors affecting bank appetite for a particular type of risk are essential ingredients for a professional syndication and successful transaction.

When pricing a transaction, it is necessary to examine the yield for each ticket envisaged in the syndication strategy in order to assess whether it will be sufficient to attract the number and quality of lenders that the borrower desires for the syndication to be considered a success. Before the mandate is awarded, the tickets themselves may be defined only roughly because at the award of the mandate it is not uncommon for an arranger to find certain constraints being placed upon the structure of the syndicate by the borrower: for instance, by the inclusion of a special ticket for certain relationship banks.

The two key transaction variables in the yield calculation for a drawn loan are the margin and the front-end fees. If the facility is to remain undrawn (as envisaged in the transaction for DutchCo, described in chapter 3) the key variables are the commitment fee (sometimes the facility fee, depending on the precise nature of the facility) and the front-end fees. Unlike the all-in cost calculation for borrowers, yield calculations for the different tickets do not include agency fees or expenses. The reason for this is that agency fees are only paid to one bank (or two if there is a separate technical or security agent) and are therefore irrelevant to the majority of banks in the syndicate.

The methodology commonly used by market practitioners is illustrated by the simple example set out below. It uses the straight line method which, although undervaluing the front-end fees, nevertheless provides results which are sufficiently accurate for most purposes.

If a more precise result is required, for example for submission to a credit committee, the only difference is to annualise the front-end fees using a reinvestment rate of interest equal or approximately equal to market rates for instruments having a maturity equal to the average life of the transaction under consideration in the currency of the facility.

### Yield calculations – a practical example

A borrower seeks bids for a $300m fully underwritten five-year bullet term loan which will be drawn down within 30 days of signing. The borrower has indicated that its relationship banks can be expected to join the transaction at a senior level.

The bidding bank (the 'bidder' or 'MLA') obtains approval from its credit committee to underwrite the full amount of the loan provided the syndication unit confirms that the final retained asset will be no greater than $30m.

After due consideration of recent market transactions, a review of comparable deals, and an examination of the history of past deals arranged for the borrower, the bidder believes the pricing parameters likely to lead to the mandate are a margin of 100bps per annum, an arrangement fee of 80bps flat and a commitment fee of 35% of the margin (35bps per annum).

### Syndication strategy #1

The bidder decides to underwrite the full amount of the loan and, if successful, to arrange for the transaction to be sub-underwritten by three banks each committing $75m. General syndication will follow with one ticket of $30m with the result that the syndicate will comprise 10 banks in all, each committing $30m. The bidder, expecting to be appointed MLA, decides that the sub-underwriters will enjoy the status of Arrangers and that banks joining during the general syndication will be granted the status of Co-arrangers.

The syndication strategy is:

i. the bidder commits $300m and wins the mandate on a sole arranger, or MLA, basis;

ii. the bidder invites and contracts with three sub-underwriters (entitled Arrangers) to commit $75m each;

iii. general syndication leads to a further six banks (entitled Co-arrangers) joining the transaction, each committing $30m and thereby reducing the bidder and sub-underwriters to $30m each.

The final syndicate is shown in exhibit 4.3.

#### Exhibit 4.3: Breakdown of final syndicate

| Ticket | Allocated commitment ($m) | Total ($m) |
|---|---|---|
| One Bidder/MLA | 30 | 30 |
| Three Arrangers | 30 | 90 |
| Six Co-arrangers | 30 | 180 |
| Total | | 300 |

Next it is necessary to examine the yield for each of these tickets based on the pricing parameters mentioned above. The bidder decides that if successful in winning the mandate with its sole, fully underwritten bid, it will take a skim of 15bps flat (on the full amount of the loan) from the arrangement fee, before dividing the remaining arrangement fee among itself and the other Arrangers. The bidder believes that an underwriting fee of 30bps flat on the amount underwritten ($75m), coupled with a participation fee of 35bps flat on their final commitments, will be sufficient to attract the sub-underwriters (Arrangers), particularly when they learn that the participants (Co-arrangers) will be offered 35bps flat on their $30m commitment. The actual fees earned are set out in exhibit 4.4.

**Exhibit 4.4: Breakdown of fees earned by participants**

| Ticket | Bidder/MLA | Arrangers | Co-arrangers |
|---|---|---|---|
| Number in ticket | 1 | 3 | 6 |
| Skim (bps flat) | 15 | - | - |
| Underwriting fee (bps flat) | 30 | 30 | - |
| Participation fee (bps flat) | 35 | 35 | 35 |
| Skim ($ '000s) | 450 | - | - |
| Underwriting fee ($ '000s) | 225 | 225 | - |
| Participation fee ($ '000s) | 105 | 105 | 105 |
| Total fees (each) ($ '000s) | 780 | 330 | 105 |
| Total fees per ticket ($ '000s) | 780 | 990 | 630 |

Aggregate fees paid out to the banks, in each ticket under this syndication strategy is equal to the total front-end fees to be paid by the borrower of $2,400,000 (80bps on $300m); there is no syndication fee pool.

The equivalent flat yield for banks under each ticket is found by dividing the total fees per bank in each ticket by the amount of that ticket's final participation in the loan. In this case the amount is the same for all tickets at $30m and the fee yield is 260bps flat, 110bps flat and 35bps flat for the bidder/MLA, Arrangers and Co-arrangers respectively.

The equivalent straight line yield on a per annum basis is found by dividing the flat yield by the average life. In this case the average life is five years (see the section on yield calculations which follows in this chapter for details on calculating the average life of a transaction). The borrower has requested a bullet loan and it will be fully drawn within 30 days of signing. (As the borrower has committed to a quick drawdown – maximum 30 days – it is conventional to ignore the period between signing and drawdown, as well as the commitment fee, which will often, in such circumstances, apply only after a grace period of 30 to 60 days.) The annualised fee yield for the three tickets is thus 52bps per annum, 22bps per annum, and 7bps per annum which, when added to the margin of 100bps per annum, gives a total yield of 152bps per annum, 122bps per annum and 107bps per annum respectively.

Thus, this syndication strategy will generate 45bps or $135,000 per annum more for the bidder/MLA than for the Co-arrangers which take no market risk, provide no specialised services to the borrower with regard to this transaction, and will spend little or no time originating the transaction. For this extra remuneration the bidder/MLA is required to take the full underwriting and syndication risk and to execute the transaction with its specialist resources. The sub-underwriters (Arrangers) earn incremental remuneration of just 15bps or $45,000 per annum. Are these rewards adequate? Is there an alternative syndication strategy that will reward the bidder/MLA more lucratively without jeopardising the success of the syndication?

### Syndication strategy #2

The bidder decides that a better return can be obtained for the risks that are being taken but is not prepared to change the underwriting approach. It decides that the general syndication will consist of two tickets: banks committing at $20m (Co-arrangers) and banks committing at $10m (Lead Managers). The final syndicate is assumed to be composed as shown in exhibit 4.5.

#### Exhibit 4.5: Breakdown of final syndicate

| Number | Ticket | Allocated commitment (£m) | Total commitments (£m) |
|---|---|---|---|
| 1 | Bidder/MLA | 30 | 30 |
| 3 | Arrangers | 30 | 90 |
| 5 | Co-arrangers | 20 | 100 |
| 8 | Lead Managers | 10 | 80 |
| Total | | | 300 |

The yield for each of these tickets is calculated on the same pricing parameters except for the front-end fee allocation. The bidder again decides that if successful in winning the mandate with its sole underwritten bid, it will take a skim of 15bps flat (on the full amount of the loan) from the arrangement fee. The bidder believes that an underwriting fee of 30bps flat on the amount underwritten ($75m) is still sufficient to attract the sub-underwriters (Arrangers) and that the bidder and the sub-underwriters will each retain $30m in the transaction with the same participation fees (35bps flat) as under syndication strategy #1. The Co-arrangers will be offered 25bps flat on their $20m commitment and Lead Managers will be offered 15bps flat on their $10m commitment. Each ticket under this scenario is entitled to the fees shown in exhibit 4.6.

**Exhibit 4.6: Breakdown of fees earned by participants**

| Ticket | Bidder/MLA | Arrangers | Co-arrangers | Lead Managers |
|---|---|---|---|---|
| Number in ticket | 1 | 3 | 5 | 8 |
| Skim (bps flat) | 15 | - | - | - |
| Underwriting fee (bps flat) | 30 | 30 | - | - |
| Participation fee (bps flat) | 35 | 35 | 25 | 15 |
| Skim ($ '000s) | 450 | - | - | - |
| Underwriting fee ($ '000s) | 225 | 225 | - | - |
| Participation fee ($ '000s) | 105 | 105 | 50 | 15 |
| Total fees (each) ($ '000s) | 780 | 330 | 50 | 15 |
| Total fees per ticket ($ '000s) | 780 | 990 | 250 | 120 |

Under this syndication strategy, the aggregate fees paid out to all participants in the syndicate based on their commitments is $2,140,000, which is $260,000 less than total fees to be paid by the borrower ($2,400,000). This difference is known as the syndication pool and is available as incremental remuneration for the underwriters of the transaction – in this case the bidder/MLA and Arrangers – and is paid out pro rata to their final allocated underwriting amount. This estimate of the pool can now be included in the yield calculation, giving an extra $65,000 each for the bidder/MLA and the three Arrangers, increasing their total remuneration to $845,000 for the bidder/MLA and $395,000 for each of the Arrangers.

The equivalent flat yield of the fees for each ticket is found by dividing the total fees for each ticket by the amount of each ticket's final participation in the loan, giving a yield of 281.67bps flat for the bidder/MLA, 131.67bps flat for each of the Arrangers, 25bps flat for the Co-arrangers and 15bps flat for the Lead Managers. The equivalent straight line yield per annum calculated as above, is 56.33bps per annum, 26.33bps per annum, 5bps per annum and 3bps per annum respectively, to which the margin of 100bps per annum can be added to give total yields of 156.33bps per annum, 126.33bps per annum, 105bps per annum and 103bps per annum respectively.

Syndication strategy #2 creates an improved yield for the bidder/MLA of 4.33bps per annum when compared to strategy #1. Is it realistic? The syndication specialists working on the transaction are the ones who will be committing their institution and are the ones paid to call the market by ensuring that syndication success is not threatened by an inappropriate allocation of front-end fees to the junior tickets for the amounts they are asked to commit.

### Syndication strategy #3

If the bidder's approval for the transaction is to secure a final hold of $15m instead of $30m, another syndication strategy may be appropriate. A sole fully underwritten bid with a committed final take of 5% of the amount of the transaction is very aggressive for a syndicator. It is achievable but is unusual. One approach is to adopt syndication strategy #1 or #2 and sell off the surplus $15m in the secondary market. This approach may run into some problems with the borrower if the borrower wants to retain some control of the syndicate banks. It is even more problematic for undrawn facilities where the quality of the banks in the syndicate may be critical, for rating agency or other reasons, with any dilution in the quality of banks having a negative impact.

Syndication strategy #3, therefore, is to form a multi-bank bidding group to take the underwriting risk with each bank committing $75m. The target retained asset for each bank is $15m. The terms of the bid to the borrower are identical to those under the previous strategies. However, the fee split is entirely different.

The bidders/MLAs decide that they will take 45bps flat on their underwriting amounts without any one of them taking a skim. The tickets in general syndication will be $15m, $10m and $5m. The flat fees on these commitments will be 35bps, 20bps and 10bps respectively. Banks joining at these levels will have the status of Arranger, Co-arranger and Lead Manager respectively.

The results of syndication are expected to be broadly as shown in exhibit 4.7.

#### Exhibit 4.7: Breakdown of final syndicate

| Number | Ticket | Allocated Commitment (£m) | Total commitments (£m) |
|---|---|---|---|
| 4 | Bidders/MLAs | 15 | 60 |
| 7 | Arrangers | 15 | 105 |
| 9 | Co-arrangers | 10 | 90 |
| 9 | Lead Managers | 5 | 45 |
| Total | | | 300 |

The yield for each of these tickets is calculated using the same pricing parameters except for the front-end fee allocation. Each ticket under this scenario is entitled to the fees shown in exhibit 4.8.

Under this syndication strategy, the aggregate fees paid out to banks on their commitments is $2,152,200 which is $247,500 less than the total fees to be paid by the borrower

($2,400,000). This estimate of the syndication pool is to be shared equally by the four bidding banks giving $61,875 each, thus generating total fees for each one of $451,875.

The equivalent flat fee yield, calculated as above, is 301.25bps for the MLAs, 35bps for the Arrangers, 20bps for the Co-arrangers, and 10bps for the Lead Managers. The equivalent straight line yield per annum now becomes 60.25bps per annum, 7bps per annum, 4bps per annum and 2bps per annum respectively, to which the margin of 100bps per annum can be added to give total yields of 160.25bps per annum, 107bps per annum, 104bps per annum and 102bps per annum respectively.

#### Exhibit 4.8: Breakdown of fees earned by participants

| Ticket | Bidder/MLAs | Arrangers | Co-arrangers | Lead Managers |
|---|---|---|---|---|
| Number in ticket | 4 | 7 | 9 | 9 |
| Underwriting fee (bps flat) | 45 | - | - | - |
| Participation fee (bps flat) | 35 | 35 | 20 | 10 |
| Underwriting fee ($ '000s) | 337.5 | - | - | - |
| Participation fee ($ '000s) | 52.5 | 52.5 | 20.0 | 5.0 |
| Total fees (each) ($ '000s) | 390.0 | 52.5 | 20.0 | 5.0 |
| Total fees per ticket ($ '000s) | 1,560 | 367.5 | 180.0 | 45.0 |

Syndication strategy #3 therefore gives a yield on the retained asset for the bidding banks which is not very dissimilar to the result of syndication strategy #2. The asset retained, however, is half the amount of the previous strategies, fulfilling the requirement of the approving committee. While maintaining the yield, this strategy has also reduced substantially the market risk for the bidding bank when compared with the other strategies. It also provides a satisfactory yield for the junior ticket. While it is true that the yield for the most junior ticket has dropped from 107bps per annum in strategy #1 and 103bps per annum in strategy #2 to 102bps per annum in strategy #3, the amount of the commitment required to secure a place in the primary syndication has been respectively reduced from $30m and $10m to $5m.

The reader will appreciate that there are an infinite number of combinations which can be contemplated at this stage of the bidding process and the skill of the experienced syndication professional is to devise a strategy which meets the objectives of the bank, the borrower and the market.

The modelling of the syndication is undertaken ahead of the award of the mandate. If, as is usual, there are several competing bids, the model will need to be updated constantly with each stage of the negotiation process. At all times, it is essential for a professional syndications specialist to be aware of the internal constraints under which the bid must be made. If a minimum yield is required the syndication strategy may have to change or the final retention target be adjusted downwards to accommodate the situation. This may lead to greater market risk which itself may be unacceptable, so the bidding group may have to be enlarged. This will affect the yield resulting in certain consequential changes; as stated earlier, the situation is dynamic.

In multi-tranche leveraged transactions, where institutional funds will provide a significant proportion of the funding requirement, these calculations are more complex but the same principles of assessing appetite and risk/reward ratios still apply.

# THE POST-MANDATE PHASE

Once a bidding bank has been told it has been successful in its bid and has received a written mandate from a borrower, the MLA, as the bidding bank then becomes (although still called the arranger in this chapter), must commence the work of syndication itself. The first steps include preparing an information memorandum and bank presentation to be ready for dispatch to potential participants, instructing counsel to draw up the first draft of the facility agreement, preparing the syndication book and drafting the invitation letter to be sent to potential participants. These activities are now examined in detail.

## Preparation of the information memorandum

Information on a borrower is made available to potential participants in a syndicated transaction in a number of ways. The first method, suitable only for highly rated borrowers, is to collate copies of publicly available financial information about a borrower with reports issued by the rating agencies, brokers, the press or any other useful source of information. These items are usually made available over the internet.

The second common method of disseminating information about the borrower is to prepare an information memorandum (which is also made available over the internet, using secure systems provided by, for example, Debtdomain described in annexe 2.3, or sent upon request to interested participants). This is a formal document, usually prepared by the arranger in conjunction with the borrower (but formally the document is issued by the borrower). It contains information on all the principal credit issues of the transaction and is one of the most important documents in the syndication process. It is prepared with the caveat that the arranger takes no responsibility for the completeness or otherwise of the information provided and that each bank must take whatever steps it deems necessary to evaluate relevant economic and financial aspects of the credit prior to making its decision to join the transaction. Nevertheless the arranger and the borrower want the information memorandum to assist banks in their evaluation of the transaction and try to ensure that the information is presented in a way that is most beneficial for banks when preparing their internal credit presentation.

So far as is possible, the arranger uses information provided by the borrower (and other official sources, such as a central bank, if the borrower is a sovereign borrower). The information is presented in a form which is factual, eliminates any subjective description from the text and avoids giving any opinions about the data. This is left to the potential participant when making its internal assessment. The information memorandum must cover all the issues which will be important to interested banks in their evaluation of the credit. This makes the syndication process more efficient by providing answers in advance to questions which would otherwise arise from most banks. It is also motivated by a desire to use the resources of the arranger as efficiently as possible since it is more productive to spend time researching the answers to more obscure issues in response to individual bank queries than in responding frequently to queries on the straightforward ones.

The content of an information memorandum varies immensely according to the nature of the transaction. Not all syndicated transactions require one. For instance, when relationship banks are the likely participants in the transaction, the arranger can assume that such banks have access to any information they might require and therefore none is supplied. In general, the minimum requirements for inclusion in an information package for an investment grade borrower will be the annual financial statements over the previous few years. Weaker borrowers will require a more thorough information memorandum. It will incorporate details of recent financial performance, management, industry sector analysis, projections of future cash flow and perhaps broker reports and press articles. For sovereign deals the information requirements will differ again and include data on the economy, the balance of payments and foreign trade, the level of public debt, both domestic and foreign, and the general economic policies in force.

It has become commonplace for the arrangers of transactions to release the information memorandum to potential participating banks only after they have signed letters of confidentiality (or 'clicked' acceptance of the confidentiality provisions on the relevant secure website). The purpose of these letters is to prevent sensitive information from being disseminated in the marketplace to the embarrassment, and ultimately the commercial disadvantage, of the borrower if such information should fall into a competitor's hands. It could be expected that this would be an unnecessary precaution, given that it is a bank's duty to keep details of its clients' affairs confidential, but, when a document is sent to a large number of institutions, it is to be anticipated that copies may go astray without careful control. In particular, care must be taken to prevent the press, which plays an important role in commenting on transactions in the market, from obtaining unguarded copies of these information memoranda and publishing extracts in weekly newsletters or on screen-based services.

The LMA recommended confidentiality letter for primary syndication is set out in the section on bookrunning below.

## Contents of an information memorandum

A typical corporate information memorandum would include the following principal sections:

- disclaimer (see important notice below);
- borrower's letter granting authority to release the information memorandum;
- summary terms and conditions;
- history and business of the borrower and/or guarantor;
- industry review;
- business strategy highlights;
- details of management and management structure;
- financial information on the borrower and/or guarantor including public debt ratings.

A typical sovereign borrower information memorandum would include the following principal sections:

- disclaimer (see 'important notice' below);
- borrower's letter granting authority to release the information memorandum;
- summary terms and conditions;
- general information;
- economic review;
- foreign trade and balance of payments information;
- public finance, foreign debt and foreign exchange reserves.

A typical information memorandum for a project financing transaction would include the following principal sections:

- disclaimer (see important notice below);
- borrower's letter granting authority to release the information memorandum;
- summary terms and conditions;
- background to the project;
- general review of the borrower including management;
- detailed description of the project;
- financial information on the borrower;
- economic evaluation and banking case (financial model);
- appendices covering specific items such as insurance, licensing procedures and other relevant issues.

A typical information memorandum for a leveraged acquisition loan would include the following principal sections (but the borrower may be a 'newco' without any history of borrowing set up purely for the purpose of acquiring the target):

- disclaimer (see important notice below);
- borrower's letter granting authority to release the information memorandum;
- terms and conditions of the transaction;
- background to the acquisition;
- detailed description of the business, its prospects and its industry position;
- financial information on the borrower and details of the new proposed management team;
- economic evaluation and banking case scenarios (financial model);
- accountants' reports and other consultant's reports covering specific items such as pension fund review, insurances, licensing procedures, environmental issues, litigation, and other relevant issues.

### Important notice – the disclaimer

Every professionally produced information memorandum has a disclaimer entitled 'important notice' as its first item. It typically takes a form similar to the following.

**IMPORTANT NOTICE**

[Name of Borrower] (the "Borrower"), has authorised [Name of arranger] (the "Arranger") to arrange a syndicated facility (the "Facility"), the principal terms and conditions of which are described herein, and has authorised the issue of this information memorandum ("Memorandum") to potential participants ("Participants") in the facility. The Borrower has supplied all of the information contained herein and the Arranger has received confirmation from the Borrower that this Memorandum does not contain any misstatement of material fact, nor does it omit any fact which is material for disclosure to a Participant.

Neither the Arranger nor any of its subsidiaries or affiliates has independently verified the information set out in this Memorandum nor makes any representation or warranty, express or implied, as to the accuracy or completeness of such information or that it remains unchanged after the date of issue of this Memorandum. Accordingly, neither the Arranger nor any of its subsidiaries or affiliates has any responsibility for such information.

This Memorandum is not intended to provide the sole basis of any credit or other evaluation and each Participant should make its own independent assessment of the Facility and the Borrower as it may deem necessary to determine its interest in participating in the Facility. Furthermore, the Arranger does not undertake to assess or keep under review the business, financial condition, prospects, creditworthiness, status or affairs of the Borrower or any other person during the life of the Facility, except as specifically provided for in the Facility documentation.

This Memorandum and its contents are confidential and no information, representation or warranty may be given or made on behalf of the Borrower without its consent. This Memorandum may not be reproduced in whole or in part by any recipient, or sent by it to anyone else or used for any other purpose without the consent of the Borrower and the Arranger.

At first glance this disclaimer would appear to negate the whole purpose for which the information memorandum has been written. The statement that the 'document is not intended to provide the sole basis for any credit or other evaluation' would appear to indicate that no value can be placed on its contents. On the contrary, the arranger, normally with the full cooperation of the borrower, will have spent considerable effort in terms of human resources and technical expertise in drawing up the document to the point where it is, in fact, a valuable source of data. The memorandum therefore provides information about the transaction and the borrower which other banks may use at their discretion. It is the role of the arranger to ensure that the borrower has confirmed its agreement with every fact, statistic and element of financial data which is in the document, thereby adding credibility to its contents. If it is impossible for the borrower to confirm certain information, for example, elements of the industry review, then the source of such information must be given.

The requirement to insert the disclaimer into the information memorandum is now a market standard and became so on legal advice in the wake of the so-called Colocotronis Shipping Group case. It dates back to 1975 when certain lenders sued an arranger for allegedly materially misrepresenting the financial condition of a borrower in the information memorandum on the basis of which the transaction had been sold to the participants. The case was settled out of court with each of the lenders being repaid in full by the arranger but the implications and risks associated with the production of an information memorandum were given full publicity. Since that time, prudent arrangers always insert the disclaimer in an information memorandum and also obtain a letter of authority from the borrower allowing them to release it. The letter also contains a representation that the information is complete and that there are no material elements omitted which could affect the evaluation of the data.

Since 1975, there have been a number of legal cases relating to the liability of arrangers for misinformation provided to syndicate members. In 2007, the English Court of Appeal issued a judgment in the case of *IFE Fund SA v Goldman Sachs International* ([2007] EWCA Civ 811) which was favourable to the use of disclaimer notices by arrangers. In 2000, Goldman Sachs arranged and underwrote syndicated facilities which were made available to Autodis SA to fund its acquisition of Finelist Group plc. A few months after the completion of the acquisition, Finelist was put into receivership when it transpired that its management had fraudulently misled its auditors as to the financial position of the company. IFE Fund SA was a participant in the mezzanine bond facility used for the Finelist acquisition and claimed damages from Goldman Sachs (on the grounds of misrepresentation and negligence) because the information memorandum had included misleading financial information about Finelist. The Court of Appeal held that the disclaimer notice in the information memorandum was effective to ensure that Goldman Sachs (as arranger) was not liable for the accuracy of information provided by the borrower. The Court of Appeal also found that, on the facts of this case, the arranger did not have a duty of care to potential participants (such as IFE Fund SA), although an arranger could be held to have made an implied representation of good faith (meaning that an arranger must not act in bad faith by knowingly withholding information which makes the information previously supplied inaccurate). Subsequent cases in the English courts have tended to support the validity of disclaimer notices as per the IFE case.

### Authority from the borrower

Once an information memorandum has been prepared, it is standard practice, and important, to obtain a letter from the borrower authorising the arranger to release the information memorandum to banks. This letter is sometimes, though not always, included as an integral part of the package, but the arranger should in any case obtain written authority from the borrower prior to releasing any part of the information memorandum. The letter should also include a statement from the borrower about the accuracy and completeness of the information provided. This representation (or a similar one) will reappear in the facility agreement.

A typical borrower's letter authorising release of the information memorandum is as follows.

> To: Arranger(s)
>
> Dear Sirs,
>
> We refer to the proposed facility [Facility Description ("the Facility")] which you are arranging for [Name of Borrower], the principal terms of which are reflected in the attached Information Memorandum.
>
> We have studied the Information Memorandum which has been prepared on the basis of information which we have provided to you and we confirm that we are fully responsible for all material statements, facts and opinions in the Information Memorandum, and that the Information Memorandum does not contain any untrue statement of a material fact nor does it omit to state any fact which is material for disclosure to a potential participant (including yourselves) in the context of the proposed facility.
>
> We further confirm that the forecasts contained in such document were made after due and careful consideration on our part based on the best information available to us and are fair and reasonable in the circumstances now prevailing.
>
> We hereby authorise and request of you to submit the Information Memorandum to institutions selected by you as potential participants in the proposed facility.
>
> Very truly yours,
>
> By: [Borrower]
>
> [Date]

### Preparing the information memorandum under multi-bank mandates

If the mandate has been won by a bank acting alone, the information memorandum may be released to potential participating banks once authorised by the borrower. If, however, the mandate has been won by several banks acting together, the bank which is allotted the role of preparing the information memorandum must circulate drafts to the partner banks for comment. Typically these banks will confirm their agreement promptly if the document has been drawn up in compliance with the generally accepted market standards, but they reserve the right to force a redraft if they consider the document to be defective in any way. Members of multi-bank groups will need to agree the position and prominence of their names on the cover and will not usually allow any additional prominence for the bank that actually undertook the work. This bank's consolation is the close working relationship that can develop between itself and the borrower during the long hours of concentrated work that goes into the preparation of an information memorandum. The disclaimer for a transaction which is mandated to a multi-bank group must expressly apply to all the mandated banks not just the one which prepared the text.

### Roadshows

It has become quite commonplace for borrowers to launch their transactions with a roadshow. This is a bank meeting organised by the arranger which provides the borrower with the opportunity to sell itself and its transaction to interested banks. The use of the term 'roadshow' refers to the idea that the presentation can travel from one financial centre to another and some companies do hold such meetings in more than one location.

The format of these meetings is fairly standard. Usually the first item on the agenda is a welcome and introduction by the arranger. Then the borrower makes its presentation about its business(es) and about its recent financial performance. Forecasts and projections will be given for project financing transactions and other transactions that depend on future cash flow for debt servicing. The borrower will normally respond to any questions put forward by the banks in attendance and may finish its presentation with a promotional video.

The arranger will then discuss the nature of the proposed transaction and respond to any questions that may arise. The meeting can be used for the distribution of the information memorandum, if this has not already been sent prior to the meeting.

The roadshow is very useful for borrowers tapping a market for the first time. It permits the officers of the company to meet potential participants and to promote the business opportunities which are available. It also permits banks to make a first judgment of management by direct contact so it is important for any borrower to be thoroughly prepared, in order to ensure that a favourable impression is given. The arranger (or, in a multi-bank group, the mandated bank allocated responsibility for the bank presentation

– which may be the same bank as has responsibility for the information memorandum) should assist the borrower, advise on the contents and form of the material which will constitute the substance of the meeting, and on the choice of location. The arranger must also arrange for whatever equipment is required to be available for the presentation and may also organise an informal lunch or dinner to follow the meeting.

## Instructing counsel

Once the mandate has been awarded, the arranger (or bank responsible for the documentation in a multi-bank bidding group) must instruct legal counsel, which will be acting on behalf of the agent and the banks, to prepare the first draft of the facility agreement. It is usual for the instruction to be accompanied by a copy of the final term sheet agreed with the borrower. In some circumstances, the borrower (or private equity sponsor) will have the documents prepared by its counsel and sent to the banks' counsel for review. This became commonplace in the leveraged acquisition market during the highly competitive period 2004 to mid-2007. However for investment grade borrowers, this is usually an inefficient way to proceed and may lead to higher legal costs for the borrower's account.

The role of counsel to the banks is discussed in chapter 5 as a preamble to the sample facility agreement which is illustrative of the first draft an arranger can expect to send to the borrower, based on the DutchCo term sheet set out in chapter 3.

There are some key issues for the arranger. Perhaps one of the most important is the question of expenses. It is not uncommon for the legal expenses to be of a similar magnitude to the arrangement fee which the mandated bank will earn. If the mandate has been won with the inclusion of an expense cap (that is, the borrower's liability to pay transaction expenses is limited in amount) based on an estimate of the likely amount of legal expenses from the banks' counsel, it is incumbent on the arranger to ensure that counsel remain strictly within their brief, as any cost overrun will be for the arranger's account. This is why it is important at the bidding stage to be as precise as possible about the items that are included in an expense cap: failure to do so can lead to disaster. For instance, a borrower may award the mandate on the basis that the documentation will be substantially the same as that used for previous transactions but, once the negotiations start, enter into prolonged debate about the exclusions to the negative pledge. This can be extremely time-consuming and costly and the arranger can find that if the mandate was loosely worded, the legal expenses start to cat into the arrangement fees. In most cases there will be a legitimate reason for the deviation from the previous documentation and, unless the borrower sets out to deliberately mislead the arranger, the borrower will be ready to accept the increased legal costs if advised on a timely basis by the issuance of cost updates.

## The documentation process

The principal steps in the documentation process are set out below:

(i) The arranger instructs counsel to prepare the first draft of the facility agreement, based on the term sheet.

(ii) Counsel delivers the first draft to the arranger for review and comment.

(iii) The arranger and counsel meet to incorporate comments and prepare the second draft for circulation to the other mandated banks for comment in a multi-bank situation or for dispatch to the borrower if there is a sole arranger.

(iv) The borrower, the arranger and counsel to both parties meet to negotiate the documents. This meeting may take place at a mutually convenient location or it may take the form of a conference telephone call. At the end of these negotiations it is to be hoped that only minor points, if any, remain outstanding.

(v) The document is nearly ready to be dispatched to the banks but before it is sent out the arranger and the borrower must be in final agreement. This will enable the arranger to confirm to banks joining the transaction that the 'documentation has been agreed by the borrower and the arranger and that comments, if any, should be limited to matters of substance'.

(vi) Banks making comments on the document can negotiate them with the arranger and counsel. The pattern of negotiations varies between institutions as some banks prefer to negotiate directly with each bank, while others prefer counsel to perform this function for them. Any changes which arise out of the banks' comments will of necessity be negotiated with the borrower and a mutually acceptable solution found; this may involve compromise on both sides.

(vii) Once all comments from the banks have been received and negotiated satisfactorily, the execution copies can be prepared.

The steps described above set out an almost perfect negotiation process. In practice, there are often more steps and more drafts, particularly if the borrower is new to the market and is negotiating precedent with every point. Borrowers that are frequent users of the market try to use a document which can normally be reproduced rapidly with minimal negotiation. Nevertheless, markets change and the credit quality of a borrower may change. It is always necessary to examine a document used as a precedent to ensure that it still reflects the current situation, even if a borrower claims that any changes to the documentation will be unacceptable.

### Choosing counsel to act for the arranger and the banks

It is normal market practice for arrangers to use one of the major international law firms to act as counsel to the arranger and the lenders. The documentation of the majority of international transactions is governed by English or New York law, although, as would be expected, some domestic syndications are governed by local law (for example, the LMA has produced recommended forms of facility agreements governed by the laws of France, Germany and Spain). In all principal centres of syndication activity the major law firms are represented and will provide experienced professionals to undertake the tasks involved.

The criteria to be used in choosing counsel are many but at a minimum should include solid experience of documenting transactions of the type contemplated, adequate resources at a senior (partner) level as well as at the support level (nothing is worse than finding the partner with whom you are dealing is off on another transaction with his/her team) and a reputation which will satisfy the banks joining the syndicate.

## Running the books

This is perceived by many banks to be the most prestigious role of a syndicated transaction. It certainly is the most visible, since it involves 'selling' the transaction to a chosen group of banks. In fact, it is a demanding activity involving a high degree of technical skill as well as administrative organisation, since the bookrunner is required to maintain regular contact with all the potential participants and to deal with questions that arise on a timely basis. It is for this reason that much attention is given by the bookrunner to the quality of the information memorandum or package that is to be supplied to potential participants to minimise the amount of time spent on straightforward or routine matters.

In the late 1990s, the phenomenon of front running, first prevalent in the US market, became an issue and the major banks agreed that such practice worked generally against the interests of underwriting banks. In order to try to control this activity, the leading practitioners introduced a letter of undertaking to be signed by all underwriters agreeing that no secondary market activity should commence prior to the close of the primary market – including verbal promises of future purchases and sales. The LMA recommended letter covering both confidentiality and front running is set out below.

**This document is intended to be used with all LMA Facility Agreements whether or not they contain the new LMA Confidentiality Undertaking.**

For the avoidance of doubt, this document is in a non-binding, recommended form. Its intention is to be used as a starting point for negotiation only. Individual parties are free to depart from its terms and should always satisfy themselves of the regulatory implications of its use.

**LMA CONFIDENTIALITY AND FRONT RUNNING LETTER[1] FOR PRIMARY SYNDICATION**

**THE CONFIDENTIALITY PROVISIONS CONTAINED IN THIS LETTER HAVE BEEN PRODUCED SPECIFICALLY FOR PRIMARY SYNDICATION. THIS LETTER SHOULD NOT THEREFORE BE USED FOR SECONDARY LOAN TRADING. SEPARATE LMA CONFIDENTIALITY LETTERS ARE AVAILABLE FOR USE WITH SECONDARY TRADES.**

**[Letterhead of Arranger]**

To:

| | *[insert name of Potential Lender]* |
|---|---|

Re: **The Facilit[y/ies]**

*Company:* (the "**Company**")

*Date:*

*Amount:*

*Agent:*

Dear Sirs

We understand that you are considering participating in the Facilit[y/ies]. In consideration of us agreeing to make available to you certain information with the knowledge and approval of the Company[2] and to prevent front-running of the Facilit[y/ies], by your signature of a copy of this letter you agree as follows:

(A) **CONFIDENTIALITY**

1. CONFIDENTIALITY UNDERTAKING

You undertake:

1.1. to keep all Confidential Information confidential and not to disclose it to anyone, save to the extent permitted by paragraph (A)2 below and to ensure that all Confidential Information is protected with security measures and a degree of care that would apply to your own confidential information;

1.2. to keep confidential and not disclose to anyone except as provided for by paragraph (A)4 below the fact that the Confidential Information has been made available or that discussions or negotiations are taking place or have taken place between us in connection with the Facilit[y/ies]; and

1.3. to use the Confidential Information only for the Permitted Purpose.[3]

2. PERMITTED DISCLOSURE

We agree that you may disclose such Confidential Information and such of those matters referred to in paragraph (A)1.2 above as you shall consider appropriate:

2.1. to members of the Participant Group[4] and their officers, directors, employees, professional advisers and auditors if any person to whom the Confidential Information is to be given pursuant to this paragraph (A)2.1 is informed in writing of its confidential nature and that some or all of such Confidential Information may be price-sensitive information, except that there shall be no such requirement to so inform if the recipient is subject to professional obligations to maintain the confidentiality of the information or is otherwise bound by requirements of confidentiality in relation to the Confidential Information;

2.2. to any person to whom information is required or requested to be disclosed by any governmental, banking, taxation or other regulatory authority or similar body, the rules of any relevant stock exchange or pursuant to any applicable law or regulation;

2.3. [to any person with (or through) whom you enter into (or may potentially enter into) any transaction under which payments are to be made or may be made by reference to the Facility Agreement or any Obligor if:

   (a) that disclosure and that transaction are permitted under Part (B) of this letter; and

(b) the person to whom the Confidential Information is to be given pursuant to this paragraph (A)2.3 has entered into a confidentiality agreement substantially in the form of the LMA Confidentiality Undertaking for Disclosure by Potential Initial Lenders/Subscribers to Credit Protection Providers or such other form of confidentiality undertaking agreed between us, the Company and you;] [5]

2.4. [subject to the requirements of the Facility Agreement and with effect from the Free to Trade Time, to any person:

(a) to (or through) whom you assign or transfer (or may potentially assign or transfer) all or any of your rights and/or obligations which you may acquire under the Facility Agreement if the person to whom the Confidential Information is to be given pursuant to this paragraph (a) of paragraph (A)2.4 has entered into a confidentiality agreement substantially in the form of the LMA Confidentiality Letter (Seller) or the LMA Confidentiality Letter (Buyer); and

(b) with (or through) whom you enter into (or may potentially enter into) any sub-participation in relation to, or any other transaction under which payments are to be made or may be made by reference to the Facility Agreement or any Obligor if the person to whom the Confidential Information is to be given pursuant to this paragraph (b) of paragraph (A)2.4 has entered into a confidentiality agreement substantially in the form of the LMA Confidentiality Letter (Seller) or the LMA Confidentiality Letter (Buyer);][6] and

2.5. with the prior written consent of us and the Company.

3. NOTIFICATION OF DISCLOSURE

You agree (to the extent permitted by law and regulation) to inform us:

3.1. of the circumstances of any disclosure of Confidential Information made pursuant to paragraph (A)2.2 above except where such disclosure is made to any of the persons referred to in that paragraph during the ordinary course of its supervisory or regulatory function; and

3.2. upon becoming aware that Confidential Information has been disclosed in breach of this letter.

4. RETURN OF COPIES

If you do not participate in the Facilit[y/ies] and we so request in writing, you shall return or destroy all Confidential Information supplied to you by us and destroy or permanently erase (to the extent technically practicable) all copies of Confidential Information made by you and use your reasonable endeavours to ensure that anyone to whom you have supplied any Confidential Information destroys or permanently erases (to the extent technically practicable) such Confidential Information and any copies made by them, in each case save to the extent that you or the recipients are required to retain any such Confidential Information by any applicable law, rule or regulation or by any competent judicial, governmental, supervisory or regulatory body or in accordance with internal policy, or where the Confidential Information has been disclosed under paragraph (A)2.2 above.

5. CONTINUING OBLIGATIONS[7]

The obligations in this letter are continuing and, in particular, shall survive the termination of any discussions or negotiations between you and us. Notwithstanding the previous sentence, the obligations in Part A of this letter [(other than those set out in paragraph (A)10 below which shall remain in place until the end of the Offer Period (as defined in paragraph (A)10 below))][8] shall cease on the earlier of (a) the date on which you become a party to the Facility Agreement or (b) the date falling [twelve] months after the date of your final receipt (in whatever manner) of any Confidential Information.

6. NO REPRESENTATION; CONSEQUENCES OF BREACH, ETC

You acknowledge and agree that:

6.1. neither we nor any of our officers, employees or advisers (each a "**Relevant Person**") (i) make any representation or warranty, express or implied, as to, or assume any responsibility for, the accuracy, reliability or completeness of any of the Confidential Information or any other information supplied by us or any member of the Group or the assumptions on which it is based or (ii) shall be under any obligation to update or correct any inaccuracy in the Confidential Information or any other information supplied by us or any member of the Group or be otherwise liable to you or any other person in respect of the Confidential Information or any such information; and

6.2. we or members of the Group may be irreparably harmed by the breach of the terms of this letter and damages may not be an adequate remedy; each Relevant Person or member of the Group may be granted an injunction or specific performance for any threatened or actual breach of the provisions of this letter by you.

7. ENTIRE AGREEMENT; NO WAIVER; AMENDMENTS, ETC.

7.1. This letter constitutes the entire agreement between us in relation to your obligations regarding Confidential Information and supersedes any previous agreement, whether express or implied, regarding Confidential Information.

7.2. No failure to exercise, nor any delay in exercising any right or remedy under this letter will operate as a waiver of any such right or remedy or constitute an election to affirm this letter. No election to affirm this letter will be effective unless it is in writing. No single or partial exercise of any right or remedy will prevent any further or other exercise or the exercise of any other right or remedy under this letter.

7.3. The terms of this letter and your obligations under this letter may only be amended or modified by written agreement between us.

8. INSIDE INFORMATION

You acknowledge that some or all of the Confidential Information is or may be price-sensitive information and that the use of such information may be regulated or prohibited by applicable legislation including securities law relating to insider dealing and market abuse and you undertake not to use any Confidential Information for any unlawful purpose.

9. NATURE OF UNDERTAKINGS

The undertakings given by you under Part (A) of this letter are given to us and (without implying any fiduciary obligations on our part) are also given for the benefit of the Company and each other member of the Group.

10. [[STANDSTILL

You acknowledge and agree that neither you nor any other member of the Participant Group:

10.1. hold any shares in [*offeree company*] or are otherwise interested in shares carrying voting rights in [*offeree company*];

10.2. will:

(a) acquire or offer to acquire, or cause any other person to acquire or to offer to acquire, any shares in [*offeree company*] or other interests in shares carrying voting rights in [*offeree company*] until the end of the offer period (as defined in the Takeover Code) (the "**Offer Period**"); or

(b) enter into an agreement or arrangement (whether or not legally binding) that would result in the acquisition of shares in [*offeree company*] or other interests in shares carrying voting rights in [*offeree company*] until the end of the Offer Period,

**provided that** nothing in this paragraph 10.2 shall prevent the acquisition of shares in [*offeree company*] or other interests in shares carrying voting rights in [*offeree company*]:

(c) carried out in a client-serving capacity by any part of the trading operations of an entity in the Participant Group that is a recognised intermediary within the meaning of the Takeover Code; or

(d) with the consent of the Takeover Panel, by a member of the Participant Group as security for a loan in the normal course of business.]/ **OR**

[10. INFORMATION BARRIERS

You acknowledge and agree that:

10.1. you have established information barriers between the persons or entities within the Participant Group which are responsible for:

(a) making decisions in relation to your or their participation in the Facilit[y/ies]; and

(b) trading, or making investment decisions in relation to, equity investments,

and that those information barriers comply with the minimum standards for effective information barriers identified in Practice Statement No. 25 ("Debt Syndication During Offer Periods") published by the Takeover Panel Executive on 17 June 2009 (as amended, supplemented or restated from time to time) (the "**Information Barriers**"); and

10.2. you will maintain the Information Barriers, and ensure that the Confidential Information may not be accessed by any persons or entities within the Participant Group who hold or may acquire shares in [*offeree company*] or who are or may be otherwise interested in shares carrying voting rights in [*offeree company*], until the end of the offer period (as defined in the Takeover Code).]][9]

(B) **FRONT RUNNING – PARTICIPANT**

**No Front Running Undertaking**

You acknowledge and agree that:

(a) you will not, and you will procure that no other member of the Participant Group will engage in any Front Running;

(b) if you or any other member of the Participant Group engages in any Front Running we may suffer loss or damage [and your position in future financings with us and the Company may be prejudiced];*

(c) if you or any other member of the Participant Group engages in any Front Running we retain the right not to allocate to you a participation under the Facilit[y/ies];

(d) [you confirm that neither you nor any other member of the Participant Group has engaged in any Front Running.]*

[When you sign the Facility Agreement and any transfer document under the Facility Agreement (in the case of any transfer document, only if signed within [three/six] months after [the date of signing of the Facility Agreement]/[the Free to Trade Time]), you will, if we so request, confirm to us in writing that neither you nor any other member of the Participant Group has breached the terms of this Part (B) of this letter.]*

[Any arrangement, front-end or similar fee which may be payable to you in connection with the Facilit[y/ies] is only payable on condition that neither you nor any other member of the Participant Group has breached the terms of this Part (B) of this letter. This condition is in addition to any other conditions agreed between us in relation to your entitlement to any such fee.]*

(C) **FRONT RUNNING – ARRANGER**

**No Front Running Undertaking**

On our receipt of a copy of this letter signed by you, we acknowledge and agree that:

(a) we will not, and we will procure that no other member of the Arranger Group will engage in any Front Running;

(b) if we or any other member of the Arranger Group engages in any Front Running you may suffer loss or damage [and our position in future financings with you and the Company may be prejudiced]*;

(c) [we confirm that neither we nor any other member of the Arranger Group has engaged in any Front Running.] *

[When we sign the Facility Agreement and any transfer document under the Facility Agreement (in the case of any transfer document, only if signed within [three/six] months after [the date of signing of the Facility Agreement]/[the Free to Trade Time]), we will, if you so request, confirm to you in writing that neither we nor any other member of the Arranger Group has breached the terms of Part (C) of this letter.]

(D) **MISCELLANEOUS**

1. THIRD PARTY RIGHTS

1.1. Subject to this paragraph (D)1 and to paragraphs (A)6 and (A)9, a person who is not a party to this letter has no right under the Contracts (Rights of Third Parties) Act 1999 (the "**Third Parties Act**") to enforce or to enjoy the benefit of any term of this letter.

1.2. The Relevant Persons and each member of the Group may enjoy the benefit of the terms of paragraphs (A)6 and (A)9 subject to and in accordance with this paragraph (D)1 and the provisions of the Third Parties Act.

1.3. Notwithstanding any provisions of this letter, the parties to this letter do not require the consent of any Relevant Person or any member of the Group to rescind or vary this letter at any time.

2. GOVERNING LAW AND JURISDICTION[10]

2.1. This letter and the agreement constituted by your acknowledgement of its terms (the "**Letter**") and any non-contractual obligations arising out of or in connection with it (including any non-contractual obligations arising out of the negotiation of the transaction contemplated by this Letter)[11] are governed by English law.

2.2. The courts of England have non-exclusive jurisdiction to settle any dispute arising out of or in connection with this Letter (including a dispute relating to any non-contractual obligation arising out of or in connection with either this Letter or the negotiation of the transaction contemplated by this Letter).

3. DEFINITIONS

In this letter (including the acknowledgement set out below):

"**Arranger Group**" means us, each of our holding companies and subsidiaries and each subsidiary of each of our holding companies (as each such term is defined in the Companies Act 2006) and each of our or their directors, officers and employees (including any sales and trading teams) provided that when used in this letter in respect of an Arranger it applies severally only in respect of that Arranger, each of that Arranger's holding companies and subsidiaries, each subsidiary of each of its holding companies and each director, officer and employee (including any sales and trading teams) of that Arranger or any of the foregoing and not, for the avoidance of doubt, those of another Arranger.

"**Confidential Information**" means all information relating to the Company, any Obligor, the Group, [the Target Group,][12] the Finance Documents and/or the Facilt[y/ies] which is provided to you in relation to the Finance Documents or Facilt[y/ies] by us or any of our affiliates or advisers, in whatever form, and includes information given orally and any document, electronic file or any other way of representing or recording information which contains or is derived or copied from such information but excludes information that:

(a) is or becomes public information other than as a direct or indirect result of any breach by you of this letter; or

(b) is identified in writing at the time of delivery as non-confidential by us or our advisers; or

(c) is known by you before the date the information is disclosed to you by us or any of our affiliates or advisers or is lawfully obtained by you after that date, from a source which is, as far as you are aware, unconnected with the Group [or the Target Group][13] and which, in either case, as far as you are aware, has not been obtained in breach of, and is not otherwise subject to, any obligation of confidentiality.

"**Facility Agreement**" means the facility agreement entered into or to be entered into in relation to the Facilit[y/ies].

"**Facility Interest**" means a legal, beneficial or economic interest acquired or to be acquired expressly and specifically in or in relation to the Facilit[y/ies], whether as initial lender or by way of assignment, transfer, novation, sub-participation (whether disclosed, undisclosed, risk or funded) or any other similar method.

"**Finance Documents**" means the documents defined in the Facility Agreement as Finance Documents.

"**Free to Trade Time**" means the time we, or any relevant bookrunner(s), notify the parties participating as lenders of record in Syndication of their final allocations in the Facilit[y/ies].

"**Front Running**" means:

(a) undertaking any of the following activities prior to the Free to Trade Time which is intended to or is reasonably likely to encourage any person to take a Facility Interest except as a lender of record in Syndication:

(i) communication with any person or the disclosure of any information to any person in relation to a Facility Interest; or

(ii) making a price (whether firm or indicative) with a view to buying or selling a Facility Interest[; or]

(b) [entering into (or agreeing to enter into) prior to the Free to Trade Time any agreement, option or other arrangement, whether legally binding or not, giving rise to the assumption of any risk or participation in any exposure in relation to a Facility Interest],[14]

excluding where any of the foregoing is:

(A) made to or entered into by you with another member of the Participant Group (in the case of the undertaking made by you in this letter) or by us with another member of the Arranger Group (in the case of the undertaking made by us in this letter);

(B) an act of a member of the Participant Group (in the case of the undertaking made by you in this letter) or the Arranger Group (in the case of the undertaking made by us in this letter) who in each case is operating on the public side of an information barrier unless such person is acting on the instructions of a person who has received Confidential Information and is aware of the proposed Facilit[y/ies]; or

(C) in the case of the undertaking made by us in this letter, made to, or entered into by us (or another member of the Arranger Group) with, a member of another Arranger Group in connection with the facilitation of either Syndication or initial drawdown under the Facilit[y/ies].

"**Group**" means the Company and its subsidiaries for the time being (as such term is defined in the Companies Act 2006).

["**interests in shares**" shall have the same meaning as "interests in securities" under the Takeover Code.][15]

"**Obligor**" means a borrower or a guarantor under the Facility Agreement.

"**Participant Group**" means you, each of your holding companies and subsidiaries and each subsidiary of each of your holding companies (as each such term is defined in the Companies Act 2006) and where such term is used in Part (B) of this letter and the definition of "Front Running" each of your or their directors, officers and employees (including any sales and trading teams).

"**Permitted Purpose**" means considering and evaluating whether to enter into the Facilit[y/ies].

"**Syndication**" means the primary syndication of the Facilit[y/ies].

["**Takeover Code**" means The City Code on Takeovers and Mergers.][16]

["**Takeover Panel**" means the Panel on Takeovers and Mergers.][17]

["**Target**" means [ ].][18]

["**Target Group**" means the Target and its subsidiaries (as such term is defined in the Companies Act 2006).][19]

Please acknowledge your agreement to the above by signing and returning the enclosed copy.

Yours faithfully

..................................

For and on behalf of

[Arranger]

To: [Arranger]

The Company and each other member of the Group

We acknowledge and agree to the above:

..................................

For and on behalf of

[Potential Lender]

1. Please note this document is for use on primary syndication and therefore does not include language dealing with indirect transfers of loan facility interests such as sub-participations etc. Please see the other LMA forms of Confidentiality Undertaking if you wish to cover these interests.

2. Please note that this document **does not** constitute permission from the Company to the Arranger for the Arranger to disclose this information to the potential lender. Arrangers should ensure that adequate permissions from the Company are in place before entering into this document and making any such disclosure.

3. Please note that if the potential lender does not participate in the Facilit[y/ies], it is not permitted to use any Confidential Information it has acquired for any purpose other than the Permitted Purpose.

4. The concept of Participant Group has been retained in this letter and has not been replaced with the concept of Affiliates which is used in the LMA Secondary Confidentiality Letters and the LMA Primary Facility Agreement. This reflects its use in the front running provisions and also avoids the requirement for both concepts particularly since the definitions of Participant Group and Affiliate are substantively the same.

5. Paragraph (A)2.3 is primarily intended to allow the Potential Lender to disclose information to providers of credit protection which it may wish to take steps to put in place prior to the Free to Trade Time. It should be included only if paragraph (b) of the definition of "*Front Running*" is **not** included.

In any event paragraph (A)2.3 should not be included if the Facilit[y/ies] are being made available to finance a transaction which is subject to the City Code on Takeovers and Mergers.

6. Paragraph (A)2.4 allows the Potential Lender to disclose information to a potential trading counterparty during any gap between the Free to Trade Time and the Potential Lender becoming a lender of record under the Facility Agreement. Its inclusion may not be appropriate if the Facilit[y/ies] are being made available to finance a transaction which is subject to the City Code on Takeovers and Mergers and users should seek advice before including paragraph (A)2.4 in such circumstances.

7. This paragraph assumes that primary syndication takes place in two ways: (i) the lender becomes a party to the Facility Agreement by signing up to it or (ii) the lender becomes party to the Facility Agreement by way of novation.

8. This wording should be included if one of the two options provided in paragraph (A)10 is used. One of those two options should be included if the Facilit[y/ies] are being made available to finance a transaction which is subject to the City Code on Takeovers and Mergers. Explanation and background for the inclusion of those provisions is contained in the Users Guide to the LMA Confidentiality Undertakings (English law).

9. One of the two options provided in paragraph (A)10 should be included if the Facilit[y/ies] are being made available to finance a transaction which is subject to the City Code on Takeovers and Mergers. Explanation and background for the inclusion of these provisions is contained in the Users Guide to the LMA Confidentiality Undertakings (English law).

The first option is intended for use where the Potential Lender does not hold shares in the offeree company and is not otherwise interested in shares carrying voting rights in the offeree company. The second option is intended for use where the Potential Lender holds or may hold shares in the offeree company or is otherwise interested or may become interested in shares carrying voting rights in the offeree company.

- Optional

10. The references to non-contractual obligations in this paragraph assume that any commitment letter in respect of the participant's participation and the Facility Agreement will be governed by English law. If this is not the case these references may need to be considered in the context of the relevant transaction.
11. The reference to non-contractual obligations arising out of the negotiation of the contemplated transaction is intended to specifically apply the governing law (and jurisdiction) clause to any non-contractual obligations arising out of negotiations where the transaction breaks down before the proposed participant becomes party to any commitment letter in respect of its participation or to the Facility Agreement.
12. Include if financing is to be used in connection with an acquisition.
13. Include if financing is to be used in connection with an acquisition.
14. Paragraph (b) of the definition of "*Front Running*" is optional and is designed to include within the definition of "*Front Running*" credit derivatives and credit risk insurance in relation to the Facilit[y/ies]. Include paragraph (b) of the definition of "*Front Running*" if the intention is for such activities to be subject to the restrictions on Front Running under Parts B and C of this letter.
15. Include if either of the provisions in paragraph (A)10 are included.
16. Include if either of the provisions in paragraph (A)10 are included.
17. Include if either of the provisions in paragraph (A)10 are included.
18. Include if financing is to be used in connection with an acquisition.
19. Include if financing is to be used in connection with an acquisition.

## Preparing the invitation for banks

Once the mandate has been awarded and the terms and conditions fully agreed for the transaction, the arranger (or bookrunner in a multi-bank group) must convert the term sheet into an invitation letter that can be distributed to all the potential participant banks.

Before the invitation letter can be prepared, a final decision on the parameters for each ticket must be taken. This means deciding on the amount of commitment, status and associated front-end fees which will be offered to the market, taking into account other opportunities which are available to banks in both the primary and secondary markets.

Typical ticket definitions might be as shown in exhibit 4.9.

### Exhibit 4.9: Typical ticket definitions

| Amount | Status | Front-end fees |
|---|---|---|
| $30m | Co-arranger | 35bps flat |
| $20m | Lead Manager | 25bps flat |
| $10m | Manager | 15bps flat |

It is usual in the syndications market for the level of front-end fees paid to participating banks to be directly linked to the amount of their commitment. This means that banks making the highest commitments earn the highest fees. The relationship between the size of commitment and associated fees is usually left to the discretion of the arranger. Judgment plays an important part in determining the level of fees which will attract the required number of banks into each ticket.

Status is important for a bank committing to a transaction because it determines each bank's rank in the transaction vis-à-vis the borrower and other syndicate members as well as its position in any publicity which may be contemplated, in particular for the tombstone. Once a bank commits at, say, the $30m level (its initial commitment), to a transaction offering the tickets defined above, the bank can only be certain that it will carry the status of Co-arranger. Its final amount may turn out to be less than $30m if the syndication is oversubscribed and the commitment of each bank scaled back (reduced). The front-end fees which will be paid out to each bank are, however, calculated at the *rate* associated with its initial commitment. This can sometimes lead to the situation where the final commitment of a bank is reduced to a level equal to that of a lower status, yet the front-end fees earned are calculated at the higher rate associated with the ticket at which the bank made its initial commitment. In this example, a bank may commit for $30m but be reduced at the end of syndication to $20m because of oversubscription. The front-end fees for this bank would be calculated on $20m at the rate of 35bps flat, not 25bps flat which is the level of fees associated with an initial commitment of $20m.

Once the decision on the ticket has been taken, the arranger or bookrunner is in a position to edit the term sheet to convert it into an invitation. This will require an introductory paragraph which, using the transaction contemplated for DutchCo in chapter 3 and assuming it is fully underwritten by Arranger Bank Limited, would be formulated along the lines:

DutchCo has requested Arranger Bank Limited to arrange on its behalf a syndicated revolving credit facility for a total amount of US$1bn, the principal terms of which are outlined below. The facility has been fully underwritten by Arranger Bank Limited.

On behalf of DutchCo, Arranger Bank Limited is pleased to invite you to participate in the facility at one of the following levels:

| Amount | Status | Fees |
|---|---|---|
| $75m | Co-arranger | 6.0bps flat |
| $50m | Lead Manager | 3.5bps flat |

The front-end fees will be payable on the amount of your allocated participation at one of the above ticket levels.

The terms and conditions of the body of the invitation letter are a restatement of the term sheet on which the mandate was awarded. It nevertheless excludes those items that concern only the borrower and the arranger(s) such as the total amount of the arrangement fee, agency fees, reimbursement of expenses, expiry date of the offer, clear market protection and remedies if other conditions change.

After the principal commercial terms and conditions of the transaction have been set out, there remain a few critical items which must be included in the invitation.

Firstly, banks must be advised how the information memorandum or package can be obtained. If it is to be made available only after receipt by the arranger of a signed confidentiality letter (or 'clicked' acceptance to its provisions), it is appropriate to incorporate a pro forma text of such letter with the invitation.

Secondly, potential participants must be advised of the names of the individuals who can be contacted to answer any questions which may arise. These individuals will normally be the members of the bookrunner's syndication unit and may sometimes include an individual from another team if the transaction has features which are best explained by someone with specialised expertise. Their job is to ensure that any issues raised by potential participating banks are rapidly resolved. Time is of the essence, since any delay in answering questions may result in a bank missing its internal deadline for submitting the transaction to its credit committee and losing, in some cases, a critical seven to ten days.

Thirdly, banks must be clearly advised of the date when the books will officially close. This will normally be two to three weeks after the invitations are dispatched. It is, however, quite common to extend the date for responses from a particular bank if requested to do so. The invitation letter will state that the arranger(s) have the right to close syndication at any time at its (their) sole discretion. This gives the arranger the right to close the syndication early to prevent a hot deal, heading for substantial oversubscription with little chance of an increase, resulting in minute participations after anticipated scale back.

Fourthly, the invitation letter must specify to whom responses are to be sent giving the name of the individual(s) and the correct numbers for telephone, fax and email.

Fifthly, the invitation letter must specify the order in which banks will appear in any publicity. The status of a bank is determined by the amount of the initial commitment, regardless of any adjustments made by the arranger(s) to the size of its final commitment (reductions only) after syndication has closed. Within each ticket size, the order is usually alphanumeric (alphabetic by amount). If the arranger(s) expect to have final commitment(s) equal to that of lead managers, the arranger(s) may appear out of order. This will be specified in the invitation letter with a statement to the effect that in any publicity, banks joining at the lead manager level will appear after the arranger(s).

The way of expressing these points for the DutchCo transaction would be:

A package containing information about the Facility can be obtained upon request from

[names of individuals] at Arranger Bank Limited.

Any questions should be addressed to one of the following

[name of individual] [telephone number] [email address]

[name of individual] [telephone number] [email address]

[name of individual] [telephone number] [email address]

We look forward to receiving your response as soon as possible but in any case no later than [final date for responses].

Your response should be directed to [name of individual] at Arranger Bank Limited by email on [email address].

> Arranger Bank Limited reserves the right to close syndication at any time and to allocate final participations at its sole discretion.
>
> In any publicity, banks will appear by status in alphanumerical order after Arranger Bank Limited. Any publicity or information released to the press is to be issued exclusively by DutchCo and/or Arranger Bank Limited
>
> Regards
>
> Arranger Bank Limited

The introductory and closing paragraphs set out above are based on the supposition that Arranger Bank Limited is the sole arranger and therefore has all the roles. If a multi-bank group is mandated, essentially the same language, modified slightly, is used to represent the position of all the banks. Specifically, in the introductory paragraph, 'Arranger Bank Limited' would be replaced by, for example, 'British Bank Limited, German Bank and Japanese Bank (the "Joint Arrangers")' where it first appears and by the 'Joint Arrangers' thereafter. In the closing paragraph, the bank nominated to be the bookrunner would be substituted for 'Arranger Bank Limited' where the context relates to the bookrunning role, namely the dissemination of information memoranda, contact with the banks and collection of responses, but elsewhere the substitution would be 'the Joint Arrangers'.

## Selecting the banks

Once a mandate has been won, whether by a sole bid or by a multi-bank group, the arranger(s) will need to select the banks to which invitation letters are to be sent. In most cases there are some special factors which need to be taken into account. It may be a corporate borrower's desire to syndicate a transaction exclusively among banks with which it enjoys an existing relationship. It may be the publicly quoted debt ratings which each bank must carry if the purpose of the facility is to provide credit enhancement of the borrower in favour of a third party offering attractive funds not available through the commercial banks. Yet another factor may be the desire of the borrower to tap banks from specific markets not previously accessed, such as Middle Eastern based banks.

If there are no special factors, the arranger(s) will be free to choose the banks to be approached in syndication. The choice will take account of the appetite available from different nationalities of banks. It will also take account of the ancillary business which may be available to banks in the syndicate and the interest in the transaction that this may generate for certain banks. The list of banks to be approached will also include banks that have solicited such invitations from the leading players. Another way of selecting banks for a transaction is to examine the records of recent transactions to identify the banks that are active in a particular sector and are therefore likely to have an interest. Two of the most widely used databases for this purpose are Loan Manager provided by Dealogic (see annex 2.1 of chapter 2) and LoanConnector provided by LPC (see annex 2.2 of chapter 2).

However, if a transaction has been fully underwritten, the underwriter(s) will reserve the right to approach the market as widely as is required to achieve their sell-down targets.

Judgement is required in determining the number of invitation letters to issue. Too many invitations for an attractive deal can lead to oversubscription, with the result that, in the absence of an increase in the amount of the facility, the participations of banks have to be scaled back. This can be a major disappointment for some banks planning to book an asset in the amount close to that to which they originally committed. On the other hand, too few invitations may result in under-subscription, meaning that the arranger(s) may be left with a final participation in the deal above their target and the market with the impression that the deal has flopped. It is difficult to give general guidance, but a broad syndication usually attracts commitments from about two-thirds of the banks approached.

## The syndication book

In order to manage the process efficiently, the bookrunner needs to establish the syndication book and this is usually carried out using one of the syndication solutions provided by providers such as FIS Syndtrak or Dealogic's DealManager Loans. It incorporates the details of each invited bank in a consistent format to facilitate follow-up with each bank. A typical syndication book will have the following information for each bank: its name and mailing address, contact name(s), telephone and email, the date the information memorandum was sent, the date of last contact, the response (acceptance/decline) and any other comments.

A typical page from a syndication book for the DutchCo transaction is shown in exhibit 4.10.

**Exhibit 4.10: Syndication book for DutchCo $1bn facility**

| Name of bank | Location | Contact name | Telephone number | Acceptance (US$m) | Information Memorandum | Decline | Comment |
|---|---|---|---|---|---|---|---|
| Banca de la Creme | Milan | Adele Bechamel | | | Yes | | 11/9 – currently reviewing |
| Bank of Good Hope | London | Horatio Cape | | | Yes | | 11/9 – Seeking US$75m |
| Banque de Tremble | Paris | Marie Brave | | | Yes | 11/9 | Exposure |
| Bargain Banking Co | Atlanta | Terry Basement | | | Yes | 28/8 | Pricing |
| Best Bank NA | Amsterdam | Gerald Venty | | 75 | Yes | | |
| Bonanza Banking Corp | New York | Walter Gold | | | | 27/8 | Pricing |
| First and Best Bank NA | London | Gordon Highest | | 50 | Yes | | |
| First and Last Banking Corp | New York | Ingrid Stayer | | | Yes | | Decision on US$50m 23/9 |
| Flash Banking Corp | London | James Gordon | | | | 11/9 | Sector |
| Forever Bank | London | George True | | 50 | Yes | | |
| Leading Bank NA | Frankfurt | Harry First | | 50 | | | |
| Looking Good Bank | Amsterdam | Miranda Glass | | | Yes | | 10/9 – Likes deal |
| National Bank of Good Credit | New York | Joseph Savewell | | | Yes | | 15/9 – Wants more info |
| Nononsense Credit Bank | London | Jane Plaine | | | Yes | | 15/9 – Looking at US$50m |
| Perhaps Banking Corp | Luxembourg | Robert le Farceur | | | | 15/9 | Cannot meet deadline |
| Possible Bank NA | London | Gerry Thinkalot | | | | 15/9 | Pricing |
| Premier Bank and Trust Co | Luxembourg | Philip Toppe | | | Yes | | 9/9 – Exposure problem |
| Resolute Banking Corp | Zurich | Anthony Strong | | 50 | Yes | | |
| Sometimes Bank Ltd | London | Sam Dithers | | | | 28/8 | Exposure |
| Strong Bank NA | London | Tom Hearty | | | Yes | | 8/9 – Processing US$75m |
| Summit Bank | London | Rosemary Topp | | 75 | | | |
| Sure Banking Inc | Nassau | Roland Firmin | | | Yes | | 9/9 – Positive Responding 29/9 |
| Tip Top Bank | London | George Sharp | | 75 | Yes | | |
| Treble Chance Bank | Geneva | Hugh Roller | | | | 27/8 | Fees too low |
| Wonder Bank | Dusseldorf | Max Marvel | | 50 | Yes | | |

During the syndication process, the bookrunner will keep the borrower and other mandated or underwriting banks, if any, abreast of progress by issuing regular status reports. The frequency of issue will be a function of the response of the market to the deal and may be daily towards the end of syndication but otherwise will be once or twice a week. The LMAs Decision Chart makes recommendations on frequency of delivery and whether reports should be full or summary for leveraged and non-leveraged deals.

These reports will include the number of lenders invited, the number of acceptances and declines and the number of lenders outstanding followed by any commentary or market intelligence which the bookrunner feels is relevant. This status report will also periodically list the names of the lenders in each category.

A sample status report for syndication of the transaction for DutchCo is set out in exhibit 4.11.

## Marketing the transaction

The principal responsibility of the bookrunner is to ensure that the transaction receives the best possible response in the market. This involves issuing invitation letters to the selected banks, dealing with questions on the credit or structure of the transaction on a timely basis, explaining how the transaction works in the case of a multi-tranche or multi-option facility and responding to any other matters which are important for any potential participant.

The bookrunner will also need to manage the information which is made available to the press since opinion is influenced by the weekly reports. If the press report that a transaction is proceeding slowly at the time when several credit committees are about to make their decision on whether or not to participate, it may dampen their enthusiasm for the deal and ultimately lead to a decline. On the other hand a report that a transaction is syndicating well is positive and can be beneficial to the marketing efforts.

Running the books takes considerable effort in terms of human resources and technical expertise. Banks that are active in the syndication business have specialised teams who know the market and the key players and understand the responsibility. The importance of resource commitment and competence when taking on the role of bookrunning comes to the fore in situations where other banks are dependent on the bookrunner to achieve their sell-down. An example of this is in underwritten deals where the mandate is awarded to a multi-bank group. Each of the winning banks must be satisfied that the bookrunner will be able to achieve the best syndication result in the market. They will contribute to the process with suggestions of suitable bank names to be invited and may selectively follow up with certain banks in coordination with the bookrunner.

In some circumstances the bookrunning role can be split between the mandated banks. This may lead to an inefficient syndication. If the role is split, one bank must be the principal bookrunner, with overall responsibility for the coordination of the various syndication efforts and must ensure that all banks are adequately covered during the syndication period.

Regardless of whether the role is split or not, it is essential for banks acting in a bookrunning capacity to understand the internal credit approval process in the banks they are following. This is key to running an efficient syndication and means that the quality of the information which is fed back to the borrower will be enhanced. This intelligence comes from the regular conversations that the bookrunner has with each potential participant. The bookrunner learns at an early stage whether the relationship manager is going to recommend the deal and in what amount and later discovers the precise date when the credit committee is going to meet to decide on the transaction.

**Exhibit 4.11: Syndication status report for DutchCo**

**DutchCo**
**US$1bn**
**Revolving credit facility**
**Syndication Status Report number 4**
**Date: 15 September**

| | | | |
|---|---|---|---|
| Number of banks approached | | | 25 |
| Number of banks accepted | | | 8 |
| Number of banks declined | | | 8 |
| Number of banks outstanding | | | 9 |
| *Banks accepted* | | *Amount (US$m)* | |
| Summit Bank | | | 75 |
| Best Bank | | | 75 |
| Tip Top Bank | | | 75 |
| Wonder Bank | | | 50 |
| First and Best Bank NA | | | 50 |
| Forever Bank | | | 50 |
| Leading Bank NA | | | 50 |
| Resolute Banking Corp | | | 50 |
| Total | | | 500 |
| *Banks Outstanding* | | *Comment* | |
| Banca de la Creme | 11/9 | Currently reviewing | |
| Bank of Good Hope | 11/9 | Gone for approval on US$75m | |
| First and Last Banking Corporation | 11/9 | Decision on US$50m 23/9 | |
| Looking Good Bank | 10/9 | Like deal, going for approval | |
| National Bank of Good Credit | 15/9 | Have sought additional information | |
| Nononsense Credit Bank | 15/9 | Looking positively at US$50m | |
| Premier Bank and Trust Co | 9/9 | Still reviewing but exposure problem | |
| Strong Bank NA | 9/8 | Processing US$75m participation | |
| Sure Banking Inc | 9/9 | Will respond 29/9. Positive | |
| *Banks Declined* | | *Comment* | |
| Banque de Tremble | 11/9 | Exposure | |
| Banque Banking Company | 28/8 | Pricing | |
| Bonanza Banking Corp | 27/8 | Pricing | |
| Flash Banking Corp | 11/9 | Out of sector | |
| Perhaps Banking Corp | 15/9 | Unable to meet deadline | |
| Possible Banking NA | 15/9 | Pricing too low | |
| Sometimes Banking NA | 28/8 | Exposure problem | |
| Treble Chance Bank | 27/8 | Fees too low | |

## Responding to an invitation

Once a bank has obtained its internal approval to participate in a transaction, it is customary for an officer of that bank to contact the bookrunner by telephone to advise of the acceptance and to indicate the amount of the participation. This is confirmed in writing in the following way (using the relevant LMA recommended form).

To: Arranger Bank Limited

Re: **The Facility**

*Borrower*: DutchCo

*Amount*: US$1bn revolving credit facility

*Agent*: XYZ Bank Limited

Dear Sirs

We refer to the Facility. We undertake, subject only to satisfactory documentation, to commit [ ] to the Facility (the "**Commitment**"). This Commitment will expire on [ ].

This Commitment is provided on the basis that copies of the latest drafts of the relevant facility agreement (the "**Facility Agreement**") are provided to us within [ ] days of the date of this letter.

Subject only to the terms of any confidentiality and/or front-running letter entered into by us in connection with the Facility, this letter sets out the full extent of our obligations in relation to our Commitment to the Facility until such time as we enter into the relevant Facility Agreement. The terms of this letter and our obligations under this letter may only be amended or modified by written agreement between us.

The terms of this letter may be enforced and relied upon only by you and us and the operation of the Contracts (Rights of Third Parties) Act 1999 is excluded.

This letter and any non-contractual obligations arising out of or in connect with it (including any non-contractual obligations arising out of the negotiation of the transaction contemplated by this letter) are governed by and construed in accordance with the laws of England and the parties submit to the non-exclusive jurisdiction of the English courts.

Yours faithfully

..................................

For and on behalf of

[Potential Lender]

It should be noted that the acceptance by a participating bank can have two provisos. The one used most frequently, as indicated above, is to make the acceptance subject to satisfactory documentation. The exception to this is found in some acquisition finance, project finance and other structured finance transactions where the arranger or group of underwriters is required to sign all the relevant documentation prior to general syndication. In such a case, the participant bank is offered the transaction on a take-it-or-leave-it basis.

The other proviso set out above provides a limit on the date for final signature of the relevant documentation. This is particularly relevant for transactions which absorb a scarce resource of a bank such as a scarce country limit. In such a case, the bank will wish to have the right to extricate itself from a transaction that appears to be going nowhere and use its scarce resource in another transaction. If there is no particular issue of scarce resources, the setting of a time limit is merely a professional discipline which permits the efficient management of portfolio exposure to the relevant borrower, sector, industry or country.

If a bank decides to decline the invitation, it is helpful to the bookrunner to make this known as early as possible. A typical response declining a transaction takes the following form.

To: Arranger Bank Limited

Re: DutchCo SPV B.V.

US$1bn revolving credit facility

We thank Arranger Bank Limited for the invitation to join the subject transaction but regret that on this occasion we shall decline.

[name]

[title]

[name of bank]

Refusals invariably reach the bookrunner ahead of the acceptances because the latter require more work on the part of each invited bank. The first few status reports can therefore tend to suggest that the transaction has been poorly received. Any true syndication specialist will confirm that this is the period when nerves of steel are required, as borrowers and colleagues unfamiliar with the syndication process will tend to panic. Excellent interpersonal skills are required during this period.

## Allocations

It is rare to find that the total amount committed by banks during general syndication exactly matches the amount being sought from the market. It is therefore necessary to plan a formal allocation of commitments once the books are closed, so that the aggregate amount provided by the banks equals the amount required by, and agreed with, the borrower.

The process of allocation consists of balancing fairly the demand for the credit from the banks in the syndicate with the total amount required by the borrower from the facility and this may lead to changes in the level of commitment associated with each ticket. Such changes, if made, always result in a reduction in the level as the arranger has no authority unilaterally to increase the amount of a participant bank's commitment. As a general rule, the reductions in commitment level are made in approximately equal proportions for each ticket (pro rata). The aim is to allocate a rounded amount to each bank avoiding, if possible, odd amounts. The definition of rounded amount varies according to the circumstances: for instance $12.5m is a more common level than say $13m or $11m. At larger levels of commitment, $37.5m or $35m are more usual amounts than $36m or $36.5m. In practice, the final allocated amounts in any transaction are a function of the number of banks for each ticket, with the possibility that the arithmetic of allocation may lead to strange looking amounts.

At each ticket level, banks expect equal treatment and equal allocations in the transaction. At the arranger level, banks may voluntarily rescind their right to equal levels of allocation if it suits their particular portfolio, as might be the case for a bank having substantial exposure to the borrower through other transactions. The final allocation to each ticket is at the discretion of the bookrunner(s) (usually by a ⅔ majority where there is more than one – as suggested in the LMA's Successful Syndication Decision Chart) after consultation with the borrower.

The fees paid to banks for their participation will be calculated at the rate offered to participants at the ticket level to which they commit but only on the amount of their final allocation. This method of fee calculation is market practice but nevertheless must be specified clearly in the invitation letter sent to potential participating banks. (An exception to this practice has occurred for certain leveraged acquisition deals when fees are sometimes paid on the basis of the amount committed rather than the allocated amount. The potential extra fees required to be paid if oversubscription occurs being for the borrower's account.)

As suggested above, the result of general syndication will rarely be that the amount raised exactly matches the amount required. Usually the result is either over- or under-subscription. In the case of oversubscription, the syndication has clearly been a success, with commitments perhaps 20 to 100% higher than required. Possible explanations for this are many. It may be that the deal was too richly priced, resulting in a higher proportion of banks accepting the invitation than expected. It may be that some particularly positive information about the borrower or its business emerged during the syndication. It may equally be that the arranger and the borrower both took a conservative view of the market and simply invited too many banks for the amount of the deal. Another explanation may be that it was a deliberate syndication strategy to present the borrower with a hugely successful deal and an opportunity to increase the amount of the facility.

Whatever the reason, the borrower and the arranger need to agree now on the next step. If the borrower is in a position to accept the increase, then this may be an attractive opportunity to do so, since all expenses of the transaction will be amortised more cost-effectively. The borrower will in any case decide on the final amount to be taken from the aggregate subscriptions. The allocation process will consist of a determination of suitable rounded participation levels for each ticket level to reach the amount that the borrower requires. If the borrower cannot accept the amount of the oversubscription, or can accept only a part of it, the normal procedure is to scale back each ticket level approximately in proportion to the final agreed amount of the loan to total subscriptions then making minor rounding adjustments as appropriate. The final allocations are, however, at the discretion of the arranger and each ticket level may be reduced in unequal or arbitrary proportions. The economic interest of the arranger will be to retain lower ticket levels at a higher committed amount than would be achieved on the basis of proportional reduction because the participation fees associated with such tickets are lower and generate a higher amount for the syndication pool.

In recent years, some borrowers have managed to negotiate a reverse-flex clause in the mandate letter giving them the option to negotiate a price reduction in the pricing if the deal is unexpectedly oversubscribed. Such provisions are most prevalent in leveraged finance transactions. The participating lenders will not be obliged to accept any reduced pricing which may be agreed, but if sufficient lenders do agree to the reduced pricing then participations will be allocated to those who do agree rather than the remaining lenders.

The case of under-subscription is more problematic for the arranger. If the transaction was underwritten by the arranger or a group of joint-arrangers, each of them will be required to take up a share of the shortfall pro rata to the amount that their final allocated underwriting commitment bears to the total amount of the deal. This will result in the arranger and/or underwriting banks retaining a larger asset than anticipated and may require a further approach to the credit committee if the surplus asset cannot be sold quickly in the secondary market. If the transaction was mandated on a best efforts basis, the borrower can take the transaction in a reduced amount, or adjust the terms and conditions and/or structure (increase the pricing, shorten the final maturity, strengthen the covenants) to attract further commitments to make up the shortfall. This last course of action can also be applied to an underwritten deal if the borrower believes that it is in its best interests. Under the now common use of *marketflex*, the mandated bank(s) can also invoke some or all of these changes, depending on the terms negotiated with the borrower at the outset, if the syndication process fails to attract sufficient interest from participant banks. All of these situations have been seen in the syndicated market in recent years.

## Negotiations with the borrower

During the syndication period, the arranger needs to be constantly in contact with the borrower, not only to provide up-to-date information on the progress of the transaction in the market but also to ensure adherence to the transaction timetable. The borrower is also responsible with the arranger for ensuring that the transaction proceeds smoothly by being available for negotiation of the facility agreement and obtaining timely approval for any changes in the documentation which might constitute a deviation from its own internal approvals.

It is the responsibility of the arranger to ensure that documents are available for review on a timely basis, that agreed changes are incorporated and 'blacklined' to highlight them in the next draft. The arranger must also ensure that any comments received from the banks joining the transaction are recorded, negotiated and raised with the borrower if necessary. A real commitment of resources is required to ensure that this part of the process is handled efficiently and it requires extremely close cooperation between the arranger and counsel.

As the syndication progresses, the arranger has the duty to keep the borrower informed of the level of commitments and to provide an early warning if borrower support is needed to help obtain commitments from certain key banks. This support typically takes the form of direct contact between the borrower and the target banks and will usually rely on discussions about current and future business opportunities. The arranger also has the responsibility of providing the borrower with an early indication of a possible increase in the facility if this is likely as a result of a successful syndication. This will permit the borrower to initiate and obtain on a timely basis any internal approvals it requires in order to accept an increase in the facility amount.

# CLOSING THE TRANSACTION

Once the syndication has been closed, allocations made and the documentation reviewed and agreed by all of the banks committed to the transaction, the next event is to organise the execution of the relevant documents by all of the relevant parties.

## Preparing for the signing

In the run-up to the signing a number of specific tasks must be accomplished. First, any outstanding points on the documentation must be negotiated to the satisfaction of all parties. The final stages often require a degree of brinkmanship and a last minute decision by a bank to drop out of the transaction is to be avoided if at all possible. Sometimes it is not possible however, and it has been known, albeit rarely, for major banks to drop out of a syndication within hours of signing, over the failure to resolve a documentation issue.

To expedite the preparation of the execution copies of the documents, an administration information request is sent to every bank. It requires each bank to provide details of the booking office(s), the names of contacts for credit and operational matters, the details of the account to which payments are to be made and the precise way in which the bank wishes to appear in any publicity. Many banks require that the payment of front-end fees be made to a different account to the one to be used for the collection of interest and for the repayment of principal. Some banks wish to appear differently in publicity as arranger etc from their appearance as a provider of funds. This information is captured by the information request. In May 2018 the LMA and LSTA jointly issued a Standard Administrative Details Form which aims to ensure that information is provided in a consistent manner capable of being easily incorporated into the relevant IT systems.

## Signing arrangements

The arrangements for a signing ceremony are part of syndication folklore, with every practitioner able to recall the most memorable occasion in his or her experience but it is not necessary to hold a signing ceremony to close a syndicated transaction. Indeed, it is now far more common for syndicated transactions to be closed electronically and executed in a number of counterparts, with each bank signing and sending (via email) separate documents which are then combined to form a conformed copy. Nevertheless, a signing ceremony can provide an opportunity for the borrower and the lenders to meet in a setting that is both formal and informal.

However, when a transaction is signed without ceremony with the agent acting under a power of attorney on behalf of all the banks or via an electronic closing, it is quite common for the borrower shortly thereafter to host a function for the banks in the syndicate. This occurs mainly when the borrower and the banks are separated by significant distances, for instance when a US or Australian borrower taps the London market. In such cases the documents may be executed to permit the facility to become operational ahead of the ceremony, which would be arranged to coincide with the borrower's next visit to London.

At the same time as the invitations are dispatched to the banks in the syndicate to attend the signing, it is prudent to ask for a power of attorney to be issued in favour of the agent so that, in the unlikely event that a bank's representative fails to appear at the signing, the agent can nevertheless execute the documents on behalf of that bank. This will ensure that there is no danger of the borrower and the transaction being frustratingly held up by a missing signature.

A typical power of attorney would be formulated as follows.

**POWER OF ATTORNEY**

[name of borrower]

[amount of facility]

[description of facility]

We, [name of financial institution] of [address] hereby appoint [name of representative] failing whom [name], failing whom [name], all of [Agent Bank Limited], as our true and lawful attorney-in-fact (the "Attorney"), acting jointly or severally, with full power and authority in our name and on our behalf to sign and deliver the Facility Agreement and any other documents in connection with the Facility of [amount of facility] for [name of borrower], such document to be in such form as the attorney may approve (such approval to be conclusively evidenced by the execution thereof by the attorney), and to do any and all other matters or things necessary or desirable in connection with the foregoing.

We hereby agree to ratify anything done or purported to be done by the attorney by virtue of this power of attorney.

This power of attorney shall be irrevocable for the period of one month from the date hereof.

In witness whereof this power of attorney has been duly executed this [date].

[Name of financial institution]

By:

Title:

## Publicity

The signing signifies the end of the second phase with the transaction now completed. Many borrowers wish to use a successful transaction to obtain publicity for themselves as well as show the quality and geographic diversity of the banks which support their financing needs. The most common form of publicity is the tombstone, so called because of its appearance. However, more recently, the use of tombstones has declined as alternative methods of publicising bank groups have become prevalent – for example screen-based information services.

Tombstones record the name of the borrower (and guarantor, if any), the date, the amount and type of transaction, the names of the banks (or sometimes only the lead banks) that committed to the transaction and the name of the agent(s). The position of banks in the tombstone is strictly determined by the status accorded to each bank based on its initial commitment. Banks may appear several times in the tombstone: for instance a sole arranger may appear as the arranger, a provider of funds and as the agent.

Arrangers have their own distinctive styles for tombstones which are used whenever possible. A sole mandate clearly gives the winning bank the right to use its corporate style for the tombstone since all other banks will be in more junior positions. However, multi-bank groups usually insist on a neutral tombstone so that the publicity will not give undue prominence to any one of the mandated banks. This neutrality will extend to the outline as well as the typeface used in the tombstone.

More recently, borrowers have preferred tombstones to promote their own business rather than the colours and style of the arranger. As a result house styles are seen less frequently than in the past and often the tombstone will embody an image or product line of the borrower.

However, tombstones are rarely published in the financial press nowadays and are used for the production of lucites as souvenirs of the transaction – see below.

One example is shown on the following page.

The tombstone relates to the EUR8.74bn Syndicated Term Loan and Revolving Credit Facilities arranged for HeidelbergCement by Commerzbank, Deutsche Bank, Nordea and RBS. RBS acted also as Facility Agent on the transaction and could therefore appear twice on the tombstone. The complete bank group included many more institutions than the 4 lead banks but the tombstone did not reflect the whole group. As this transaction was signed in June 2009, this transaction has long since been refinanced in both the High Yield markets and through a EUR3bn Revolving Credit Facility. The style of the tombstone was in line with other recently produced tombstones for HeidelbergCement, using their corporate green and an unusual shape.

**Exhibit 4.12: Tombstone for HeidelbergCement**

As a final souvenir of the transaction, it is sometimes the case that a number of lucites are ordered embodying the tombstone. The total number varies, but it is usual for all the individuals who played a significant role in the transaction to receive one as well as the key individuals from the participant banks. This is, however, entirely discretionary and will need special budget sanction between the borrower and the arranger before the orders are placed.

# THE POST-SIGNING PHASE

## After sales service

Once the transaction has been signed and the euphoria has dissipated, the next step is to make the facility operational. The first step is for the borrower to satisfy the conditions precedent (CPs) in order to activate the facility. These requirements are stipulated in the facility agreement and the borrower needs to examine them carefully at the negotiation stage to ensure that none are inadvertently incorporated that cannot be fulfilled. The borrower's counsel is responsible for ensuring that this circumstance does not arise but it remains possible for the lenders to waive a CP for a period of time or completely.

Once the CP documents have been submitted to the agent and the agent has confirmed to both the borrower and the lenders that the CPs have been satisfied, the borrower may then use the facility in accordance with its terms. It is from this point and for the life of the facility that the agent has a full role to play in servicing the borrower and the lenders.

The relationship between the agent bank and participating banks is set out in a section of the facility agreement and most banks which act regularly as an agent have developed language (based on LMA standards) which has received internal approval and from which the agent is rarely willing to accept any deviation whatsoever. A sample agency clause is examined in detail in chapter 5.

### Operational efficiency

One of the key elements for success as an agent bank is for the operational side (that is, limit validation, cash settlements, accounting, deal management and reporting, both financial and regulatory) to be robust, eliminating as far as possible human intervention. A number of banks have invested in systems which allow all relevant static data of a transaction (for example, names of parties, SWIFT information, limits, availability and repayment dates, account details, and so on) to be input once at the outset with the non-static data (for example, interest periods, currencies chosen in multi-currency facilities) to be input as and when the borrower utilises the facilities. Safeguards for checking and mechanisms for payment authorisation can be incorporated into such systems. Reports can be tailor-made to suit the particular transaction or client requirements and payments handled as straight through processing. Once armed with such a system, an agent bank is able to offer an efficient and competitive service to borrowers and to syndicate banks.

### Duties and responsibilities of an agent

Although the agent is normally selected by the borrower, the responsibilities and duties of an agent bank are specified in the facility agreement under the terms of which it must act as agent for the banks and co-ordinate the administration of the facility. Notwithstanding that the agent is acting for the lenders (not the borrower), the agent has a regular service relationship with the borrower, as it is the borrower that uses the facility and who pays for the agent's services.

The relationship between the agent and the banks is one of agent and principal. The agreement will clearly define whether the agent is allowed to make certain decisions, or whether it is to abide by the directions of the majority banks (usually based upon 2/3rd of current commitments or outstandings). Although the agent is acting as agent for the lenders, it has no responsibility to them for the documentation, as each party is expected to review documentation to its own satisfaction. The agent is not obliged to monitor or enquire upon an event of default, but if the agent becomes aware of such default it must inform all parties to the agreement on a *timely* basis. The agent must *promptly* forward any information or notices it receives to the syndicate of lenders. It is clearly stated within the facility documentation that the agent is allowed to have other commercial relationships with the borrower, but it is important for the agent to distinguish between its agency work and any lending activity. The agent is able to rely on any notices and documents that it receives as long as they appear genuine, for instance being on the borrower's headed paper, but unless specifically required to do so, the agent is not obliged to check authenticity.

The use of electronic communication and the use of websites has greatly enhanced the communication between borrowers, banks, the agent and the security trustee (when required).

### Recommended operational practices

The LMA's Loan Operations Committee (and its Agency Sub-Committee) have developed and agreed a framework of operations/practices aimed to increasing the efficiency of the syndicated loan market. This framework has been aligned to legal documentation developed as standard form by the LMA to ensure a consistent approach across the marketplace with respect to the operational aspects of loan agreements. The LMA's website (members only) contains a number of guides to the operational side of the market.

### Know Your Customer (KYC)

Most jurisdictions have requirements designed to minimise the risks of money laundering under which the agent and lending banks are required to hold documentation demonstrating that appropriate investigations have taken place to obtain appropriate and relevant information about the customer (borrower or investor). These investigations differ in detail from one jurisdiction to another (and, indeed, may deviate significantly depending on the identity of the lender and the regulation or risk/control environment) but financial institutions (for example, lending banks in syndicates and banks when acting as agent) are obliged to abide by the relevant procedures and requirements which will normally include the completion of identification checks on the borrower(s) and/or guarantor(s), and for the agent on the members of the lending syndicate. The checks will include obtaining a copy of the latest audited accounts and evidence of incorporation, in the case of an entity listed on a recognised exchange, and, in addition, in the case of a private company, information regarding shareholders and directors, such as inspecting passports and obtaining evidence of residence (and retaining copies of those documents).

The KYC process is managed under the auspices of the Financial Action Task Force against money laundering and the legal framework for the UK is set out in the Proceeds of Crime Act 2002 and also in the UK's Money Laundering Regulations. For more on this topic see supplement 8 to chapter 2.

### Conditions precedent

As previously mentioned, when the agreement has been signed, one of the first duties of the agent will be to ensure that the conditions precedent have been satisfied. The conditions precedent will be as listed in a schedule to the facility agreement and are a pre-condition to any utilisation of the facility. The agent will expect lenders' counsel to collect and confirm that the legal conditions precedent have been satisfied and will then advise the banks or, occasionally if necessary, will seek a waiver from the participant banks. Conditions precedent of a commercial nature (such as the acceptability of due diligence reports) can only be approved by the lenders and the agent will require confirmation from the lenders that these are acceptable.

### Utilisation requests

When the conditions precedent have been satisfied, the facility is available for drawing. The agent will receive a utilisation request in the form specified in the facility agreement, which will be fully completed and signed in accordance with the borrower's board resolution/mandate. A typical utilisation request will detail the name of the borrower, tranche (if applicable), currency and amount, interest period, purpose of the drawing, payment instructions, and a representation that no event of default has occurred. The timing of the submission of the utilisation request to the agent will usually be one day prior to the utilisation date for sterling, and three days prior to the utilisation date for other Eurocurrencies. The reason for this difference is that the rate for sterling is fixed on the utilisation date, and for other currencies two business days prior to the utilisation date. The agent has to ensure that the utilisation request falls within the availability period and is for the purpose specified in the facility agreement. If amounts are to be drawn in a currency other than a base currency, the agent has to obtain notional foreign exchange rates to ensure that facility limits are not exceeded. Each syndicate bank will then be advised of the borrower's utilisation request together with the amount of its participation to be paid to the agent for the account of the borrower.

### Interest Rate

Two days prior to the utilisation date for currencies other than sterling, and on the utilisation date for sterling, the interest rate will be fixed in accordance with the terms in the facility agreement. The rate will usually be a taken from the relevant Reuters Screen.

When fixing interest rates, the agent has to refer to the business days definition in the facility agreement and the Libor clause to ascertain when and how the rate has to be fixed. This is particularly important following the introduction of the euro. Euro rates are fixed by reference to TARGET business days (Trans-European Automated Real-time Gross settlement Express Transfer systems), and the Euromarket is open on some days that coincide with national public holidays. This means that a bank acting as an agent bank for a facility denominated in euro must provide its services for all TARGET business days even when these clash with public holidays. For currencies other than the euro, London must be open for business on the fixing day if the rate is fixed in London. Furthermore, London and the country of payment must be open for business on the value date.

The facility agreement will detail how the rate is to be fixed in the event of any market disruption, and when the banks are able to claim increased costs.

### Payments

The next step for the syndicate of banks is to pay their participation in the drawing to the agent bank on the payment date for the account of the borrower. The agent will pay one amount to the borrower in accordance with the payment instructions given in the utilisation request. Under the terms of the facility agreement, the agent does not have to pay the funds to the borrower until it has received the funds from the syndicate of banks, but in practice some agents will sometimes (assessed on a case-by-case basis) pay the funds to the borrower in the belief that they will be receiving the funds from each member of the syndicate. If the agent does not do so, it will have the right to claim the funds from the party from whom they were due with good value but, if the defaulting party still fails to pay, to seek repayment (claw back) of the funds advanced to the borrower.

### Collections

The agent is responsible for collecting all moneys due under the agreement including front-end/arrangement fees, participation fees, commitment fees, agency fees, utilisation and other fees as well as interest and repayments of principal. Any syndicate member receiving moneys directly from the borrower must make them available to the agent to ensure adherence to the terms of the agreement, in particular to the concept of sharing (see chapter 5).

### Awareness of taxes

The borrower, each syndicate member and the agent must be aware of the potential withholding tax implications on interest payments. The following sets out, in broad terms, the basic gross-up obligation in a market standard facility agreement. For a fuller treatment of UK withholding tax, please refer to the 'withholding tax' section in chapter 6.

A market standard facility agreement will specify that the borrower is obliged to gross up any interest amounts that are subject to withholding taxes so that lenders receive the gross amount of interest expected, provided such lenders are Qualifying Lenders. At the outset, lenders are usually required to lend from a jurisdiction that obviates the need for grossing up of interest payments. If future changes in tax law oblige the borrower to gross up interest payments for a particular lender, most facility agreements require such lender to take reasonable steps to mitigate this and if all else fails, the borrower may have the right to terminate a lender's participation by selective prepayment.

Recently, this fairly entrenched allocation of risk in respect of changes in law is being challenged at least to the extent such changes relate to BEPS and, more precisely, Action 6 (which is dealt with in more detail in the 'Taxes' section of the Dutchco Term Sheet in chapter 3).

The implementation of Action 6 is still ongoing which means that, although the general rules have been published, they are not yet effective as the process of amending the numerous bilateral double tax treaties is not complete. When the rules become effective, the application of treaties will change and that is likely to be regarded as a change of law by most LMA-standard loan documents. As a result, borrowers are concerned about the potential consequences for them where they accept the change of law risk. Whether treaty relief is denied depends on the lender's internal arrangements and structures. The borrowers, therefore, have no visibility or control over their lenders' treaty positions and increasingly argue that any change of law risks relating to Action 6 should be for the lenders to bear.

Lenders are equally concerned. The rules are fairly general and, aside from the most egregious examples, the exact application and scope is still unclear which may lead to other, perfectly commercial and non tax driven structures, being inadvertently caught. Furthermore, it is unclear how tax authorities will interpret the MLI, and different tax authorities may take an entirely different approach.

Brexit is another uncertainty facing the loan market. In most cases it will have no tax impact on lending. However, in some cases (and in particular for Italian borrowers), a withholding tax exemption may be adversely affected by the UK leaving the EU. Lenders and borrowers alike should consider carefully whether the UK leaving the EU would affect lenders' Qualifying Lender status and result in such borrowers' being obliged to withhold taxes from interest payments to UK based lenders.

Both lenders and borrowers need to be aware of the continuing changes in this area and evaluate the level of risk associated with this issue for each transaction.

### Dissemination of information

The agent is responsible for receiving and then distributing financial information which is to be provided under the terms of the facility agreement. It is not usually a requirement for the agent to review the financial information as this is the responsibility of each syndicate member. However, the agent will undertake such financial checks as are required under the terms of the agreement if they have an effect on the level of margin or fees to be charged, for instance, when a pricing grid has been incorporated in the facility.

With the introduction of 'electronic communication' and 'use of website' provisions in loan agreements, more agents are now using web-based platforms, such as those provided by Debtdomain (see chapter 2, annex 2.3) to store and disseminate documentation and information. The benefit of using the website is primarily that once posted that piece of documentation/information is always available to those individuals at the lenders/borrower who have been granted access. For amendments and waivers the agent can monitor who has viewed the request/additional information and can chase those lenders who have not. One of the frequent requests agents received in the past was for further copies of information previously sent. This was time consuming and costly and is eliminated now by the use of websites. Those few lenders that do not wish to receive information via a website are known as 'paper lenders' and the agent must provide them with hard copies. Of great importance in using the widely-used web systems is the ability to mark lenders as either 'public' or 'private' thereby ensuring that institutional investors who only wish to receive publicly available information are not mistakenly sent private information.

### Waivers and amendments

Experience has shown that very rarely does a transaction run to final maturity without a request from the borrower for an amendment or waiver to the terms of the facility agreement such as a change to the final maturity date, a change to the pricing or perhaps relief from one or more of the covenants. The agent normally receives such a request from the borrower but the borrower may ask a bank which is a member of the syndicate to advise on the likely response of the syndicate as a whole. This can be done by some judicious soundings with a representative sample from the syndicate; alternatively, it can be assessed using the recent experience that bank may have had in similar situations with other borrowers. After advice, the borrower will need to determine whether or not it wishes to proceed with a formal request. If the decision is to proceed, the agent will transmit the request to the banks with a fixed date for responses. The agent will provide the borrower with status reports from time to time as responses are received. It may be necessary for the borrower to make contact with certain banks, if they prove hesitant, in order to *market* the proposal. During this type of exercise, it should be noted that the agent is always acting as agent for the banks and not as agent for the borrower. This distinction needs to be maintained at all times.

When appropriate, an agent must seek direction or approval from all or a majority of banks (commonly consisting of banks with commitments or outstandings in excess of 66.67% of the amount of the facility) depending on the nature of the borrower's request before taking any action on behalf of the lenders.

As the range and type of lender has widened, it has been found that some lenders are slow to respond to the agent for waiver/amendment requests or do not respond at all. In order to enable the syndicate to function effectively, a concept has been introduced into some loan agreements, particularly leveraged and M&A transactions, called 'snooze and lose'. This allows the agent to remove any lender who has failed to respond in a specified time from the voting percentage and thereby obtain majority or unanimous approval from those lenders that do reply. For example, suppose there are 100 lenders in a syndicate each with 1% of the commitment and they are requested to consent to a waiver request by a certain date. If only half respond by the due date, the agent would only need 34 of the lenders to vote *yes* to obtain majority lender (66.67%) consent even though this is actually only 34% of the total commitments.

In 2016 the LMA published "Dealing with Requests for Amendment" which is a useful guide to the roles of the various parties in an amendment process.

### Protection for the agent

The role of the agent normally lasts throughout the life of the facility and is extremely important for the syndicate. Some banks will participate in transactions only where the agent is a bank experienced in syndicated transactions. Others will take comfort if the agent, or the agent's lending affiliate, retains a commitment in the transaction for its own account since, in the event of difficulties with the transaction at a later date, the agent will have an economic interest pari passu with the remainder of the syndicate.

The documentation will typically protect the agent legally except for gross negligence or wilful misconduct. The agent has to exercise such skill and care in the performance of its duties as is usual for a bank in performing these duties, or as is reasonably necessary for the due performance of its duties. The agent will disclaim responsibility and limit its liability through the terms of the agreement.

### Default

The agent will be obliged to follow instructions given by the lenders after the occurrence of an event of default. Instructions may be given by the majority lenders, but if the borrower is seeking a waiver or amendment of some of the fundamental terms of the agreement (e.g., an extension of maturity) the agent will need to obtain the unanimous consent of the lenders and this can be a time consuming and arduous process. For this reason, the agent should ensure that the reasonable cost for the work involved is covered either by the facility agreement or in the agent's fee letter signed at the closing of the transaction.

# DUTCHCO AND PROJECT TENNIS: SAMPLE SYNDICATION STRATEGIES AND YIELD CALCULATIONS

This section takes the reader through a typical syndication scenario, illustrates a possible outcome of syndication and then demonstrates the relevant yield calculations for the two sample transactions set out in chapter 3.

## DutchCo: $1bn facility

The term sheet provided in chapter 3 states that the transaction for DutchCo would be syndicated among 15 to 25 relationship banks. The assumption is, therefore, that the borrower will have considerable influence over the choice of banks to be invited and will also be soliciting participations from them on the basis of the overall business relationship which they enjoy.

After discussions with the borrower, the arranger recommends that an approach should be made to 25 banks, if the desired number in the syndicate is 15 to 20 banks. A syndication success is highly probable, provided the business relationship which the borrower has with its banks proves to be real rather than imaginary. The arranger decides to establish two ticket levels, given the type and capacity of banks which are identified as the targets for the syndication. The ticket levels chosen are shown in exhibit 4.13.

### Exhibit 4.13: Ticket levels chosen by the arranger

| Ticket | Amount | Front-end fees |
|---|---:|---:|
| Co-arranger | $75m | 6.0bps flat |
| Lead Manager | $50m | 3.5bps flat |

The arranger decides to retain a skim of 4bps flat as compensation for the commitment of resources to the transaction and also agrees to hold up to $80m in order to provide the transaction with an initial momentum.

At the end of syndication, with $925m raised from the market, the commitments of the syndicate members are shown in exhibit 4.14.

### Exhibit 4.14: Commitments of the syndicate members ($m)

| Number | Ticket | Amount | Aggregate commitments |
|---|---|---|---|
| 1 | Arranger | $75m | $75m |
| 5 | Co-arranger | $75m | $375m |
| 11 | Lead Manager | $50m | $550m |

### Calculation of the syndication pool fees

The fee allocations can now be calculated as shown in exhibit 4.15.

### Exhibit 4.15: Calculation of the syndication pool fee (US$)

| | | |
|---|---|---|
| Total fees paid by borrower | | 1,000,000 |
| *Less:* | | |
| (i) skim for arranger | | (400,000) |
| (ii) participation fees:<br>arranger and co-arrangers<br>lead managers | <br>270,000<br>192,500 | |
| | | (462,500) |
| *Leaving:*<br>syndication pool | | 137,500 |

The reader will recall that the purpose of this facility is to provide liquidity support to the borrower's commercial paper programmes; therefore the return or yield which is of most interest is the return on the undrawn commitment.

This yield is calculated on a straight line basis by annualising the front-end fee, dividing it by the average life of the facility (one year in this case) and adding it to the commitment fee of 10.5bps per annum, which is the relevant rate stipulated in the term sheet (35% of 30bps per annum). For the Co-arrangers, the annualised front-end fee is 6bps per annum and for the Lead Managers, it is 3.5bps per annum. The return on commitment is therefore 16.5bps per annum and 14bps per annum for these ticket levels respectively.

The Arranger is able to benefit from the syndication pool as well as the skim of 4bps flat. Front-end fees for the Arranger are therefore the sum of the skim of $400,000, the front-end fee on its commitment (6bps on $75m) of $45,000 and the syndication pool of $137,500 making a total of $582,500.

This is equivalent to 77.7bps flat on the final commitment of the Arranger which therefore provides for a total return on the Arranger's undrawn commitment of 88.2bps per annum.

The reader may wish to calculate the fully drawn yield for each ticket based on the terms summarised in exhibit 3.1. However, the chances of earning such a yield are minimal if this borrower maintains its ratings and continues to access the commercial paper markets successfully.

## Project Tennis

Although the appointment letter and term sheet issued by Top Bank were based on the assumption that Top Bank would be the sole MLA, it often happens that the borrower appoints more than one bank at the top level. Appointing more than one bank as MLA allows the borrower to meet the expectations of its 'top relationship banks' and perhaps shows an element of prestige in the market if, say, four top banks are acting as MLA. Clearly a bank such as Top Bank can walk away from the deal on the grounds that its conditions have not been met (to be the sole MLA) but if it is a strong relationship bank of Bidco, it is likely to agree to the request of Bidco to share the mandate. For the purposes of this case study, Bidco requests Top Bank and one other bank to provide the facilities set out in the appointment letter and term sheet issued by Top Bank on the basis of equal economics, that is, equal remuneration for each of the MLAs. Bidco, in appointing the second bank as MLA, adds the proviso that it is to adopt the terms and conditions proposed by Top Bank. Both banks are appointed MLA and Bookrunner with Top Bank being appointed the Agent as well. The underwriting of £1bn is shared equally and the strategy for holding Facility A for up to 12 months is agreed on the basis that each MLA holds 50% or £150m of that facility.

### Syndication strategy

The syndication strategy adopted by the two MLAs is to go straight to the market for facilities B and C (this is known as going to general syndication). A list of 20 banks to approach is agreed between the MLAs and the Borrower. Before dispatching the invitation, the Bookrunners decide which one of them will be responsible for syndicating the deal to each potential invitee. The initial step is to find out if these targeted banks are interested in participating in the loan (this is known as 'sounding out' the banks). If a potential bank indicates appetite for the transaction, it will first be formally invited to sign a confidentiality letter and then, having done so, to participate at one of the ticket levels on offer from the MLAs. In this case, the two ticket levels are shown in exhibit 4.16.

#### Exhibit 4.16: Syndication ticket levels

| Ticket | Commitment | Front-end fee |
|---|---|---|
| Arrangers | £50m | 40bps flat |
| Co-arrangers | £30m | 25bps flat |

The market is receptive to the transaction and 12 banks accept the invitation at the Arranger level and seven accept at the Co-arranger level with only one decline. This gives total subscription from general syndication of £810m as shown in exhibit 4.17.

#### Exhibit 4.17: Breakdown of subscription

| Ticket | Commitment | Number | Cumulative commitment |
|---|---|---|---|
| Arrangers | £50m | 12 | £600m |
| Co-arrangers | £30m | 7 | £210m |

Bidco's total requirement from facilities B and C is £700m (and because this is acquisition finance an increase in the amount is not required) which is also to include the commitments from the MLAs. Although the appointment letter made it clear that the MLAs would hold up to £100m in these facilities, the purpose of this was to provide Bidco with strong balance sheet commitment at the outset to protect against a poor reception in the market. This has proved not to be the case. The MLAs decide to commit at £70m each and to reduce the Arrangers and Co-arrangers to £35m and to £20m each respectively. The final syndicate for facilities B and C is as shown in exhibit 4.18.

#### Exhibit 4.18: Final syndicate for facilities B and C

| Ticket | Allocated commitment | Number | Cumulative ticket commitment | Reduction from original commitment |
|---|---|---|---|---|
| MLAs | £70m | 2 | £140m | 30% |
| Arrangers | £35m | 12 | £420m | 30% |
| Co-arrangers | £20m | 7 | £140m | 331/3% |

The banks joining the transaction have no say in the final allocations although if the MLAs stretch too far from normal market practice, an appeal could be made to the borrower. When, however, as in this case, the MLAs have underwritten the transaction they have the right to determine how the final allocations are made but most MLAs will listen to the borrower if there are serious grievances. This might arise if, for instance, the MLAs attempted to hold less than the Co-arrangers at the end of general syndication. In this example, the MLAs are acting responsibly reducing all ticket sizes by an approximately equal proportion as shown in Exhibit 4.18. The cutback in commitments does imply extra appetite for the deal and a healthy secondary market can be expected.

The allocated commitment is split between the Facilities as shown in exhibit 4.19.

**Exhibit 4.19: Breakdown of allocated commitment**

| Allocated commitment | | | |
|---|---|---|---|
| | Facility A | Facility B | Facility C |
| MLAs | £150m | £30m | £40m |
| Arrangers | 0 | £15m | £20m |
| Co-arrangers | 0 | £8.57m | £11.43m |

### Yield calculations

Banks joining the transaction expect that Bidco has built in some surplus capacity into the Facility but at this stage generally do not know how much of it will be utilised. A commonly used approach is to assume that the facilities will be fully drawn. The front-end fees paid to each ticket level are paid on the allocated amount of their commitment at the rate offered to that ticket.

In order to calculate the yield for the banks participating in Facility B, it is necessary to calculate the average life of this amortising facility. The outstanding profile based on the term sheet is illustrated in exhibit 4.20.

**Exhibit 4.20: Outstandings under Facility B**

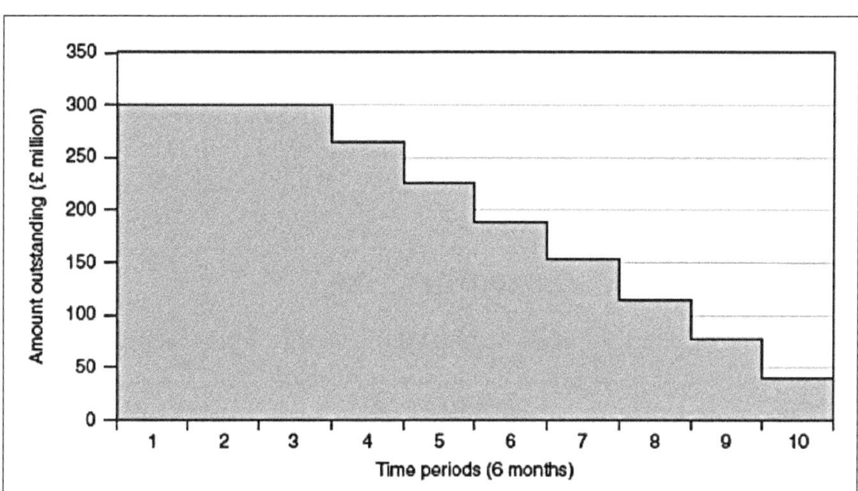


The average life of the loan is calculated by dividing the area under the envelope of the loan shown in exhibit 4.20 by the total amount of the loan. The area under the envelope is calculated by multiplying the amount outstanding by the period for which it is outstanding and then dividing the aggregate result by the total amount of the Facility.

Mathematically this is represented by $\sum a_n t_n / A$ for n=1 to m

where

A is the amount of the facility, in this case £300m;

m is the number of time periods to maturity of the facility, in this case 10;

t is the time period, in this case chosen as six months to match the repayment schedule;

$a_n$ is the amount outstanding in period n; and

$t_n$ is the nth time period.

In this case, the result of these calculations gives an average life for Facility B of 3.25 years. (Both Facility A and C are bullet repayments for which, on the assumption that the facility is drawn down as soon as it is available, the average life is equal to the final maturity, that is, one and five years respectively.)

The equivalent per annum front-end fee yield on a straight line basis (that is, ignoring discounting) can now be calculated by dividing the front-end fee (flat) by the average life of the relevant facility.

As the assumption is that the loan is fully drawn as soon as available (that is, after satisfaction of conditions precedent), it is also assumed for this type of yield calculation that the commitment fee earnings for the period between signing and drawdown are *de minimis*, that is, zero.

The tables in exhibit 4.21 illustrate the calculation of total yield for each ticket on a straight line basis for each of the facilities.

### Exhibit 4.21: Calculation of total yield for each ticket by Facility

**Facility A**: £300m shared equally between the MLAs (assumes Term Out not exercised)

| | Ticket | Top Bank/Other MLA | Calculation |
|---|---|---|---|
| | Number in ticket level | 2 | |
| (A) | Commitment (£) each | £150,000,000 | |
| (B) | Average Life of Facility A | 1 year | |
| (C) | Participation fee | 50bps flat | |
| (D) | Participation fee (£) | £750,000 | (A) x (C) |
| (E) | Participation fee yield | 50bps per annum | (C) / (B) |
| (F) | Margin | 70bps per annum | |
| | Total yield on Facility A | 120bps per annum | (E) + (F) |

The total yield for the two MLAs on their commitment in Facility A is 120bps per annum.

**Facility B**: £300m amortising term loan

| | Ticket | Arranger | Co-arranger | Calculation |
|---|---|---|---|---|
| | Number in ticket | 12 | 7 | |
| (A) | Commitment (£) | £15,000,000 | £,8,571,429 | |
| (B) | Average Life of Facility B | 3.25 years | 3.25 years | |
| (C) | Participation fee | 40bps flat | 25bps flat | |
| (D) | Participation fee (£) | £60,000 | £25,714.29 | (A) x (C) |
| (E) | Participation fee yield | 12.31bps per annum | 7.69bps per annum | (C) / (B) |
| (F) | Margin | 125bps per annum | 125bps per annum | |
| | Total yield on Facility B | 137.31bps per annum | 132.69bps per annum | (E) + (F) |

The total (straight line) yield on Facility B for Arrangers and Co-arrangers is 137.31bps per annum and 132.69bps per annum respectively.

The MLAs have front-end fees from Facility B calculated as follows:

- Total front-end fees on Facility B are £3,000,000 (100bps flat on £300m).
- Total front-end fees paid to Arrangers and Co-arrangers are £900,000 (12 x £60,000 + 7 × £25,714.29).
- Front-end fees for MLAs are £2,100,000 (£3,000,000 – £900,000) or £1,050,000 each.
- The yield (straight line) for the MLAs of this fee is 107.69bps per annum (£1,050,000 / £30,000,000 / 3.25).
- The total yield for the MLAs from Facility B is 232.69bps per annum (margin of 125 + 107.69).

**Facility C**: £400m RCF

| | Ticket | Arranger | Co-arranger | Calculation |
|---|---|---|---|---|
| | Number in ticket | 12 | 7 | |
| (A) | Commitment (£) | £20,000,000 | £11,428,571 | |
| (B) | Average Life of Facility C | 5 years | 5 years | |
| (C) | Participation fee | 40bps flat | 25bps flat | |
| (D) | Participation fee (£) | £80,000 | £28,571.43 | (A) x (C) |
| (E) | Participation fee yield | 8bps per annum | 5bps per annum | (C) / (B) |
| (F) | Margin | 125bps per annum | 125bps per annum | |
| | Total Yield on Facility C | 133bps per annum | 130bps per annum | (E) + (F) |

The total (straight line) yield on Facility C for Arrangers and Co-arrangers is 133bps per annum and 130bps per annum respectively.

The MLAs have front-end fees from Facility C calculated as follows:

- Total front-end fees on Facility C are £4,000,000 (100bps flat on £400m).
- Total front-end fees paid to Arrangers and Co-arrangers are £1,160,000 (12 x £80,000 + 7 × £28,571.43).
- Front-end fees for MLAs are £2,840,000 (£4,000,000 – £1,160,000) or £1,420,000 each.
- The yield (straight line) for the MLAs of this fee is 71bps per annum (£1,420,000 / £40,000,000 / 5).
- The total yield for the MLAs from Facility C is 196bps per annum (margin of 125 + 71).

In summary, the yield for each ticket level for each facility of this case is shown in exhibit 4.22.

### Exhibit 4.22: Yield for each ticket for Facilities A, B and C

| Facility | MLA | Arranger | Co-arranger |
|---|---|---|---|
| A | 120bps per annum | n/a | n/a |
| B | 232.69bps per annum | 137.31bps per annum | 132.69bps per annum |
| C | 196bps per annum | 133bps per annum | 130bps per annum |

As the reader will realise, the utilisation scenario described above is unlikely to be exactly the one adopted by the borrower. Nonetheless, the results of these yield calculations can be used by banks as part of the decision-making process before committing to the transaction.

# *Chapter 5*

# THE DOCUMENTATION PROCESS

As seen in chapter 3, the successful arranging banks will agree a basic set of commercial terms for a loan and will record these in a term sheet. These basic terms must then be properly documented and any remaining issues negotiated and recorded. This is the documentation process.

The process is usually undertaken by an experienced firm of lawyers. This is in contrast to the preparation of the term sheet which is often prepared solely by an arranging bank or its in-house counsel (although a greater emphasis on the mandate or underwriting phase means that increasingly outside counsel are being involved at this stage). The term sheet is fairly standard in nature and either does not produce legal commitments or, if it does, such commitments are invariably tempered by their being made 'subject to satisfactory documentation mutually acceptable to all parties'. The term sheet is concluded by a minimum of parties, namely, the arranging banks, the borrower and, perhaps, the guarantor. The documentation process, on the other hand, will be fully binding and will involve the participation of all the parties to the term sheet together with all the syndicate members. These may number 30 or more and be from many different jurisdictions.

Where the loan is to be guaranteed, the guarantor will normally be heavily involved in the documentation process. The reason for this is that the guarantor will be the ultimate obligor under the loan agreement. The extent to which the borrower will be involved will depend on the relationship between the borrower and the guarantor. If the borrower is a mere finance vehicle which has been set up to raise funds for a parent company or a whole group of companies then its involvement will be limited to more formal acts such as the delivery of board resolutions and other condition precedent documents and the execution of documentation. On the other hand, if the borrower is the head of a group of companies and its debt is being guaranteed by its own subsidiaries then it will usually lead the negotiations from the companies' point of view.

The documentation process normally has a number of stages. The first stage, as mentioned above, is the instruction of a firm of lawyers to prepare the necessary documents. Traditionally this was almost invariably the task of the arranging banks' lawyers. More recently some borrowers have sought to give their lawyers the responsibility of preparing a first draft agreement as a means of taking more control of the process. Although the majority of transactions still involve the arranging banks' lawyers being in charge of drafting documentation, it is important to ensure that the parties are clear at an early stage as to who will handle this aspect of the process.

There will often be a long-standing working relationship between an arranging bank and its lawyers and this will be reflected both by the ability of the lawyers to produce documentation quickly in line with the bank's expectations and by the extent of the role undertaken by the lawyers. In most cases even when there are multiple arranging banks only one law firm is appointed to act as counsel for the lenders since, generally speaking, the interests of all lenders are aligned. It is, therefore, important that the law firm acting for the lenders should be one which is likely to be acceptable to all. The role of lenders' counsel can be important in the process both in relation to reaching a satisfactory compromise with the borrower and because an experienced law firm will know the extent to which terms requested by a borrower will be acceptable to the wider syndicate of lenders.

In addition to drafting the main loan agreement, the lawyers will be instructed to draft necessary secondary legal documents such as separate guarantees or security documents and may also be instructed to draft various side letters (including letters detailing the fees to be paid). External lawyers are rarely instructed to draft documentation used in the syndication process such as invitation letters or information memoranda.

Sometimes one arranging bank will be appointed as documentation agent to coordinate the documentation process. If this is the case then that bank will take the lead role in instructing the law firm and in the process of reviewing and negotiating the documentation.

In transactions governed by English law, the documentation will now normally be based on the Loan Market Association's (LMA's) Recommended Forms of Primary Documentation (see the section below describing the development of these documents although it may also be based on documents used in the borrower's previous syndicated financings). These first drafts will then be sent to the arranging banks for comments. If changes are needed these will be made and the revised draft will then be distributed to the arranging banks, the borrower and any guarantor. It is possible, depending on the time-frame of the deal and the position which the syndication process has reached, that this draft will also be circulated to the syndicate members. However, where the other lenders are consulted at this early stage they will usually not be invited to participate directly in the next stage of the process.

This next stage is the negotiation of any outstanding provisions. Although the term sheet and any invitation letters will almost certainly have stated that the documentation will contain 'customary clauses for this type of loan' (or words to that effect) some of these clauses, such as representations, covenants and events of default, will need to be tailored to the particular deal. This 'tailoring' may well give rise to lengthy discussion. In order to try to reduce the scope of these discussions, term sheets increasingly tend to set out in some detail provisions which are of particular concern to borrowers and lenders. However, some amount of negotiation will always be required. As mentioned above, these negotiations will generally take place with only the arranging banks, the borrower, any guarantor and their respective lawyers. The arranging banks' role in these discussions is often a balancing act of interests. On the one hand one of them will almost invariably become the agent of the syndicate of which each arranging bank will probably be a member and they will, in any event, want the documentation to be in form acceptable to proposed members of the syndicate. On the other hand the arranging banks do not want to make the documentation too restrictive on the borrower so that the borrower may decide not to continue with the deal or alternatively may continue with the deal but find that it is unable to run its business efficiently and profitably because of the constraints of the documentation. The arranging banks, in co-operation with the lawyers, will try to find a compromise to these conflicting interests and enable a revised draft to be agreed.

The lawyers will then prepare and circulate a revised draft to all the parties. The other lenders will be invited to submit their comments on the document. Depending on the relationship between the arranging banks and their lawyers, the other lenders will either forward their comments directly to the lawyers or will be encouraged to send them via the arranging banks (or the documentation agent) who will then have an opportunity to review and filter those comments. A flow of revisions and comments may then take place between the parties and, if these are substantial, further negotiation meetings may be required. It is vital to keep all the parties up to date with amendments and proposed amendments. Depending on the number of lenders and the complexity of the documentation, this stage of the documentation process can be difficult. It requires not only the legal and commercial understanding of the people involved but also efficient logistical organisation.

Once all the documents have been agreed, a signing will be arranged. At one time signings were typically "in person" and involved some ceremony. Increasingly now they will take place via electronic means (albeit that final "hard" copies of the documents are usually produced) although some in person signings do still take place and, in some circumstances (for example where notarial certificates are required), are needed. The total documentation process commonly takes between one and six weeks.

As will be seen from this short description, the role of the lawyers and their working relationship with the arranging banks are crucial to the smooth running of negotiations and the associated organisational challenges.

# SUBSEQUENT SYNDICATION

Subsequent syndication refers to another way of arranging a syndicated loan which is partially covered by the mandate letter for Project Tennis. This means that instead of a syndicate agreeing in advance to share the commitment to a facility in agreed proportions, one or more lender(s) will underwrite the whole transaction and will then seek to place its/ their commitment(s) with other lenders after signing and, if possible, before drawdown. It is often used in acquisition finance where secrecy is crucial and the time-frame of deals very short.

The documentation is quite similar to ordinary syndication. The main difference is that the full syndicate is not listed in the facility agreement. Instead there is an original lender(s) which is/are party to the agreement, a definition of lenders which covers the original lender(s), and any other institutions which take part of the commitment and/or advances of the original lender(s).

The facility agreement (or, more usually, a so-called 'syndication side letter') may contain provisions more frequently found in term sheets (such as clear market, syndication strategy, and so on).

The transfer provisions may restrict which banks can join the syndication in order to satisfy genuine concerns of the borrower or the agent. In addition, in order to induce prime banks to be initial transferees, the agent/arranger (who is likely to be the same entity as the original lender) may agree to waive any right it has to transfer fees in respect of transfers from the original lender.

# THE LMA RECOMMENDED FORM OF PRIMARY DOCUMENTS

## Background

From the inception of the international syndicated loan market until the late 1990's the loan agreements used to document the transactions differed in form depending on the preferences of the arranger of the transaction, the borrower and the law firms involved.

This led to a number of inefficiencies. In particular:

- There were a number of provisions common to all transactions which did not need to differ from deal to deal. An example would be the clauses dealing with the giving of notices by one party to another. Although these were usually non-controversial, different lenders/lawyers had their own favourite wording and this could often lead to time and legal fees being wasted upon a (largely academic) discussion of the relative merits of two substantially similar provisions.

- Each participant in a syndicate had to review every clause of the draft agreement afresh prior to signing it in order to be sure of what its rights and obligations under the document might be.
- If the signed agreement needed to be reviewed at some later stage (for example on the sale by an original lender of its participation to a lender which wishes to 'buy in' to the debt) then again all the document had to be reviewed.

## The Recommended Form Project

The LMA sought to overcome these inefficiencies by sponsoring the production of a set of 'Recommended Forms' of English law loan agreement (also called the 'Primary Documents').

It was recognised from the outset that it would not be sufficient simply to produce an excellent document. What was needed was an excellent document which the participants in the market (borrowers as well as lenders) would be willing to use.

With this in mind a Working Party was set up which contained representatives from:

- the Lenders – bankers and internal lawyers from banks, including representatives of the British Bankers' Association (BBA);
- the Borrowers – representatives of the UK Association of Corporate Treasurers (ACT); and
- the Lawyers – five leading City of London law firms.

The documents, which were finally launched on 28 October 1999, were 'endorsed' by way of a Joint Statement made by the LMA, the BBA and the ACT.

## The documents

The documentation produced consisted of three basic forms.

### Multi-currency term and revolving facilities agreement

This agreement allows the borrower to request loans in any agreed currency under both:

- a term facility; and
- a revolving facility.

### Multi-currency term facility agreement

This is an agreement allowing the borrower to request loans under a term facility in any agreed currency.

### Multi-currency revolving facility agreement

This is an agreement allowing the borrower to request loans under a revolving facility in any agreed currency.

Since 1999 the LMA's suite of recommended loan documents has expanded greatly to include:

- single currency versions of the above;
- swingline and letter of credit options;
- leveraged finance documents;
- a real estate finance document;
- private placement documentation;
- developing markets, commodity finance and export finance variants; and
- versions for use in other jurisdictions (including France, Germany, Spain, South Africa, Kenya, Nigeria, Tanzania, Uganda, Zambia and Zimbabwe).

However, in this description of the documentation process the focus is on the English law Primary Documents used typically for facilities for investment grade rated companies.

## Approach

The LMA documentation has been drafted using a 'plain English' approach aimed at avoiding as far as possible the plethora of provisos and further provisos which can make legal documentation unintelligible to the non-lawyer. This was an important aspect of the LMA's project because the syndicated loan market is a very international one and the readers of these documents will very often not have English as their first language.

## Even-handed drafting

In order to gain ready, widespread acceptance for the documents it was particularly important for them to be drafted so as to pay equal regard to the interests of all participants in the market – arrangers, lenders and borrowers.

With this in mind those working on the documentation sought to identify those issues in relation to syndicated loan agreements which were often a source of debate between borrower and lender. The stance taken was to try to cut short this discussion by inserting the usual compromise into the first draft.

However, it quickly became apparent that not all issues were so easily resolved. Certain provisions of syndicated loan agreements were so dependent on the circumstances of the particular transaction (the credit quality of the borrower; the transaction being financed, and so on) that no attempt to standardise them would succeed.

The response of the Working Party to this was to divide the documents into:

- those provisions (the so-called 'hard' provisions) which are not dependent on the circumstances of the particular deal and which are not expected to be amended in the ordinary course (although clearly even these may be subject to change in appropriate circumstances); and
- those other provisions (the 'soft' provisions) where the Recommended Forms could do no more than set out a starting point for negotiation – it being recognised that amendment is likely to be required on a case-by-case basis.

## The hard provisions

Examples of these are:

- the clauses providing for the mechanics of making the loan, paying interest and principal, and so on;
- withholding tax 'gross-up' clauses and indemnities for taxes and regulatory and other costs;
- provisions dealing with the relationships between the agent bank and the lenders and between the lenders themselves;
- notice clauses; and
- governing law and jurisdiction clauses.

## The soft provisions

The intention of those behind the project was that the standardisation of the hard provisions of the documentation would enable market participants to concentrate more on these provisions which form the commercial core of any transaction (and are always the most keenly negotiated on any deal). They consist of the following:

### Representations

Basic legal representations as to the legal status, powers and authority of the borrower and the validity of the documents are included together with factual representations about the financial and other information provided by the borrower to the lenders. There are also some minimal representations relating to the borrower's business – most of which are qualified by a materiality standard. It is expected that for any particular deal these may need to be supplemented.

### Undertakings

The Recommended Forms contain basic undertakings by the borrower to provide annual and interim financial information together with other information reasonably requested by the Agent. Again it is expected that these may need to be supplemented as, for example, sometimes quarterly information is required. The Recommended Forms also include positive and negative undertakings by the borrower as to the way in which it will run its business. In particular, there are restrictions on the creation of security (negative pledge) and on the disposal of assets. Each of these will need to be carefully tailored to meet the demands of a particular transaction.

### Financial covenants

It was recognised that the subject of financial covenants was too complex to be dealt with in the Recommended Forms and so a blank space was left to be filled in by the responsible law firm. The LMA does include financial covenants in its Recommended Forms of Agreement for Leveraged Finance, but these are not necessarily appropriate for investment grade facilities.

### Events of default

The Recommended Forms contain all the basic events of default occurrence of which will result in acceleration of the loan (or in an undrawn facility ceasing to be available). Options are provided for grace periods to be agreed for the defaults to be remedied and for materiality standards to be applied. The much debated material adverse change (MAC) clause was found to be too controversial to be included except as a blank to be filled in (or not, as appropriate) for each deal.

### Transferability

The ability of a lender to sell its participation in the loan is often a source of controversy. The Recommended Forms provide a mechanism for this, but expressly do not recommend the extent to which a borrower may restrict the lender's ability to sell. A provision requiring borrower approval for sale (not to be unreasonably withheld and to be deemed given if not refused within five Business Days) is included, but only as an option. It was expected that some agreements will continue to allow banks to sell without approval while some would not allow sales at all.

### Conditions precedent

Clearly the conditions which must be satisfied before the borrower can draw the loan will differ significantly from deal to deal. The Recommended Forms provide only the most basic of conditions (corporate authorisations, legal opinions, and so on) and will need adding to depending on circumstances.

## Effect on existing practice

It will be clear from the above that the introduction of the Recommended Forms did not obviate the need for lawyers and their clients to draft and negotiate the documentation for each syndicated loan transaction separately. Indeed it would have been surprising if the position were otherwise. The syndicated loan's distinguishing characteristic is its flexibility and if the documentation project had resulted in one immutable standard form of agreement it would have destroyed this.

However, the Recommended Forms have reduced the amount of time spent negotiating the transactions and their use has become invariable in transactions in EMEA (and in transactions in the Asia Pacific region where a similar form of documentation has been introduced by the Asia Pacific Loan Market Association).

As might be expected the Recommended Forms have evolved to meet changing market practice and legal and regulatory requirements with updates being regularly made.

# THE SAMPLE DOCUMENT

The following sample loan agreement is based on the terms of the sample term sheet for the DutchCo transaction which are described in detail in chapter 3 (but for reasons of – relative – brevity and to avoid repetition no sample loan agreement corresponding to the Project Tennis term sheet is included). For the purposes of this chapter 5, the reader can assume that the commercial terms of the DutchCo term sheet have been accepted by the borrower and the guarantor. The reader can also assume that the sample agreement is a draft agreed between the arranging banks and their lawyers and is ready for delivery to the borrower. In other words, it is a draft at an early stage in the documentation process.

The sample agreement is based on the Recommended Form of LMA Primary Documents (with the optional swingline wording) but has been amended to take account of the requirements of the term sheet and the arrangers.

Annotations are made in the agreement to explain each of its important provisions but a clause-by-clause explanation of the agreement is beyond the scope of this book.

The use of square brackets ([ ]) is a convention to signify that information is to be inserted, clarified or agreed between the parties.

DATED [•]

FOR

DUTCHCO SPV B.V.
AS BORROWER

WITH

PARENT COMPANY S.A.
AS GUARANTOR

ARRANGED BY
ARRANGER BANK LIMITED
TOP BANK PLC
AND
XYZ BANK LIMITED

WITH

XYZ BANK LIMITED
ACTING AS AGENT

---

$1,000,000,000
MULTICURRENCY REVOLVING FACILITY
AGREEMENT INCORPORATING A DOLLAR
SWINGLINE FACILITY

---

# CONTENTS

**THIS AGREEMENT** is dated [date] and made

The first part of a syndicated facility agreement lists all parties to the Agreement. Each party is defined by reference to its specified function, e.g., guarantor, arranger, agent. The reason for this way of defining parties is to avoid confusion where, for example, the Agent changes identity pursuant to Clause 30 (*Role of the Agent, the Arranger and the Reference Banks*) or a transferee becomes a "**Lender**" pursuant to Clause 28 (*Changes to the Lenders*). In Clause 1.2 (*Construction*) each "**Party**" is construed so as to include its successors in title, permitted assigns and permitted transferees. The borrower is referred to as the "**Borrower**" throughout this sample agreement. The lenders are split into different groups in accordance with the different facilities. The lenders are called "**Lenders**" under the Revolving Facility and "**Swingline Lenders**" under the Swingline Facility.

**BETWEEN**:

(1) **DUTCHCO SPV B.V.** (the "**Borrower**");

This party will issue the commercial paper which is intended to be sold in the US market. In this case, Parent Company S.A. has chosen to tap the US commercial paper market through a special purpose vehicle subsidiary incorporated in The Netherlands (which has traditionally had a favourable tax regime for cross-border borrowing (amongst other things)). In some cases, foreign corporations may choose instead to use a US special purpose company, which has the advantage that some US buyers of commercial paper are restricted in the amount of non-US paper they are able to buy. Using a US special purpose company therefore enlarges the potential market of the issuer. However, this comes at the cost (in terms of time and expense) of having to set up the US special purpose company.

(2) **PARENT COMPANY S.A.** (the "**Guarantor**");

(3) **ARRANGER BANK LIMITED, TOP BANK PLC and XYZ BANK LIMITED** as mandated lead arrangers (whether acting individually or together the "**Arranger**");

(4) **THE FINANCIAL INSTITUTIONS** listed in Part II (*The Original Lenders*) and Part III (*The Original Swingline Lenders*) of Schedule 1 (*The Original Parties*) as lenders (the "**Original Lenders**"); and

The Swingline Lenders must be able to provide same day funds in dollars in accordance with the timetable set out in Schedule 9 (*Timetables*). Accordingly, they will be US banks or US branches of non-US banks. The syndicate of Swingline Lenders may differ from the syndicate in respect of the Revolving Facility as some banks may not be able to make domestic funds available other than through an affiliate. For example, sometimes two separate legal entities from within the same bank group will act as lender under the Revolving Facility and the Swingline Facility (e.g., the London branch of an English bank and its US incorporated subsidiary).

(5) **XYZ BANK LIMITED** as agent of the other Finance Parties (the "**Agent**").

Because of the late notice of borrowing permitted in a swingline facility (see Schedule 9 (*Timetables*)), a separate New York entity is often appointed to act as agent for the Swingline Lenders. In this case, the Agent delegates the swingline functions to its branch in New York (so that a separate swingline agent is not appointed).

**IT IS AGREED** as follows:

# SECTION 1

## INTERPRETATION

### 1. DEFINITIONS AND INTERPRETATION

The interpretation section defines those terms of an agreement which are constantly used throughout the agreement and which are of significance for its functions. Usually, all defined terms are written with a first capital letter, except those general terms as referred to in paragraph (a) of Clause 1.2 (*Construction*) of the sample agreement. Many of these defined terms appear in the Glossary, where further explanations can be found.

#### 1.1. Definitions

In this Agreement:

"**Acceptable Bank**" means:

(a) a Lender;

(b) any bank or financial institution which has a rating for its long-term unsecured and non-credit-enhanced debt obligations of [A–] or higher by Standard & Poor's Ratings Services or Fitch Ratings Ltd or [A3] or higher by Moody's Investor Services Limited or a comparable rating from an internationally recognised credit rating agency; or

(c) any other bank or financial institution approved by the Agent (acting reasonably).

"**Affiliate**" means, in relation to any person, a Subsidiary of that person or a Holding Company of that person or any other Subsidiary of that Holding Company.

"**Agent's Spot Rate of Exchange**" means:

(a) the Agent's spot rate of exchange; or

(b) (if the Agent does not have an available spot rate of exchange) any other publicly available spot rate of exchange selected by the Agent (acting reasonably),

for the purchase of the relevant currency with the Base Currency in the London foreign exchange market at or about 11:00 a.m. on a particular day.

"**Assignment Agreement**" means an agreement substantially in the form set out in Schedule 5 (*Form of Assignment Agreement*) or any other form agreed between the relevant assignor and assignee.

"**Authorisation**" means an authorisation, consent, approval, resolution, licence, exemption, filing, notarisation or registration.

"**Availability Period**" means the period from and including the date of this Agreement to and including the Business Day:

(a) falling one Month prior to the Termination Date in relation to the Revolving Facility; and

(b) immediately preceding the Termination Date in relation to the Swingline Facility.

"**Available Commitment**" means (but without limiting Clause 8.4 (*Relationship with the Revolving Facility*)) a Lender's Commitment minus (subject as set out below):

(a) the Base Currency Amount of its participation in any outstanding Revolving Facility Loans; and

(b) in relation to any proposed Utilisation, the Base Currency Amount of its participation in any Revolving Facility Loans that are due to be made on or before the proposed Utilisation Date.

For the purposes of calculating a Lender's Available Commitment in relation to any proposed Utilisation, that Lender's participation in any Revolving Facility Loans that are due to be repaid or prepaid on or before the proposed Utilisation Date shall not be deducted from a Lender's Commitment.

"**Available Facility**" means the aggregate for the time being of each Lender's Available Commitment.

"**Available Swingline Commitment**" of a Swingline Lender means (but without limiting Clause 8.4 (*Relationship with the Revolving Facility*)) that Lender's Swingline Commitment minus (subject as set out below):

(a) the amount of its participation in any outstanding Swingline Loans; and

(b) in relation to any proposed Utilisation under the Swingline Facility, the amount of its participation in any Swingline Loans that are due to be made under the Swingline Facility on or before the proposed Utilisation Date.

For the purposes of calculating a Swingline Lender's Available Swingline Commitment in relation to any proposed Utilisation under the Swingline Facility, that Lender's participation in any Swingline Loans that are due to be repaid or prepaid on or before the proposed Utilisation Date shall not be deducted from a Swingline Lender's Swingline Commitment.

"**Available Swingline Facility**" means the aggregate for the time being of each Swingline Lender's Available Swingline Commitment.

"**Base Currency**" means dollars.

"**Base Currency Amount**" means, in relation to a Loan, the amount specified in the Utilisation Request for that Loan (or, if the amount requested is not denominated in the Base Currency, that amount converted into the Base Currency at the Agent's Spot Rate of Exchange on the date which is three Business Days before the Utilisation Date or, if later, on the date the Agent receives the Utilisation Request) as adjusted to reflect any repayment, prepayment, consolidation or division of a Loan.

"**Benchmark Rate**" means in relation to any Loan in a Non-LIBOR Currency:

(a) the applicable Screen Rate as of the Specified Time for the currency of that Loan and for a period equal in length to the Interest Period of that Loan; or

(b) as otherwise determined pursuant to Clause 15.1 (*Unavailability of Screen Rate*),

and if, in either case, that rate is less than zero, the Benchmark Rate shall be deemed to be zero.

In response to the recommendations included in the Wheatley Report on LIBOR, the publication of LIBOR rates for certain currencies (Australian dollars, Canadian dollars, Danish Kroner, New Zealand dollars and Swedish Kronor) was discontinued in 2013 on account of the limited transaction data for interbank lending in such currencies. As a result of this, alternative benchmark rates need to be used for these currencies. The LMA has included optional drafting in its facility agreements for "Non-LIBOR Currencies". This is supplemented by a separate slot-in schedule containing suggested drafting for certain benchmark rates. In this sample agreement, Revolving Facility Loans can be drawn in Canadian Dollars (which is one of the rates for which LIBOR is no longer published). In the sample agreement, it has therefore been agreed that CDOR will be used as the relevant interest rate.

"**Break Costs**" means the amount (if any) by which:

(a) the interest (excluding any Margin) which a Lender should have received for the period from the date of receipt of all or any part of its participation in a Loan or Unpaid Sum to the last day of the current Interest Period in respect of that Loan or Unpaid Sum, had the principal amount or Unpaid Sum received been paid on the last day of that Interest Period;

exceeds:

(b) the amount which that Lender would be able to obtain by placing an amount equal to the principal amount or Unpaid Sum received by it on deposit with a leading bank for a period starting on the Business Day following receipt or recovery and ending on the last day of the current Interest Period.

"**Business Day**" means a day (other than a Saturday or Sunday) on which banks are open for general business in London, Amsterdam and New York and:

(a) (in relation to any date for payment or purchase of a currency other than euro or a Non-LIBOR Currency) the principal financial centre of the country of that currency;

(b) (in relation to any date for payment or purchase of euro) any TARGET Day; or

(c) (in relation to any date for payment or purchase of (or the fixing of an interest rate in relation to) a Non-LIBOR Currency) any day specified as such in respect of that currency in Schedule 11 (*Other Benchmarks*).

"**Cash**" means, at any time, cash in hand or at bank denominated in dollars, euro or sterling and (in the case of cash at bank) credited to an account in the name of a member of the Group with an Acceptable Bank and to which a member of the Group is alone (or together with other members of the Group) beneficially entitled and for so long as:

(a) that cash is repayable on demand;

(b) repayment of that cash is not contingent on the prior discharge of any other indebtedness of any member of the Group or of any other person whatsoever or on the satisfaction of any other condition;

(c) there is no Security over that cash except for any Security constituted by a netting or set-off arrangement entered into by any member of the Group in the ordinary course of its banking arrangements; and

(d) the cash is freely and immediately available to be applied in repayment or prepayment of the Facilities.

"**Cash Equivalent Investments**" means at any time:

(a) certificates of deposit maturing within one year after the relevant date of calculation and issued by an Acceptable Bank;

(b) any investment in marketable debt obligations issued or guaranteed by the government of the United States of America, the United Kingdom or any Participating Member State which in each case has a credit rating of [AA] or higher by either Standard & Poor's Rating Services or Fitch Ratings Ltd or [Aa2] or higher by Moody's Investor Services Limited or by an instrumentality or agency of any of them having an equivalent credit rating, maturing within one year after the relevant date of calculation and not convertible or exchangeable to any other security;

(c) commercial paper not convertible or exchangeable to any other security:

(i) for which a recognised trading market exists;

(ii) issued by an issuer incorporated in the United States of America, the United Kingdom or any Participating Member State;

(iii) which matures within one year after the relevant date of calculation; and

(iv) which has a credit rating of either A-1 or higher by Standard & Poor's Rating Services or F1 or higher by Fitch Ratings Ltd or P-1 or higher by Moody's Investor Services Limited, or, if no rating is available in respect of the commercial paper, the issuer of which has, in respect of its long-term unsecured and non-credit enhanced debt obligations, an equivalent rating;

(d) any investment in money market funds which (i) have a credit rating of either [A-1] or higher by Standard & Poor's Rating Services or [F1] or higher by Fitch Ratings Ltd or [P-1] or higher by Moody's Investor Services Limited and (ii) which invest substantially all their assets in securities of the types described in paragraphs (a) to (c) above, **provided that** such investment can be turned into cash on not more than 30 days' notice; or

(e) any other debt security approved in writing by the Majority Lenders,

in each case, denominated in dollars, euro or sterling and to which any member of the Group is alone (or together with other members of the Group) beneficially entitled at that time and which is not issued or guaranteed by any member of the Group or subject to any Security.

"**Code**" means the US Internal Revenue Code of 1986.

"**Commitment**" means:

(a) in relation to an Original Lender, the amount in the Base Currency set opposite its name under the heading "**Commitment**" in Part II (*The Original Lenders*) of Schedule 1 (*The Original Parties*) and the amount of any other Commitment transferred to it under this Agreement or assumed by it in accordance with Clause 2.2 (*Increase*); and

(b) in relation to any other Lender, the amount in the Base Currency of any Commitment transferred to it under this Agreement or assumed by it in accordance with Clause 2.2 (*Increase*),

to the extent not cancelled, reduced or transferred by it under this Agreement.

"**Compliance Certificate**" means a certificate substantially in the form set out in Schedule 6 (*Form of Compliance Certificate*).

"**Confidential Information**" means all information relating to the Borrower, the Guarantor, the Group, the Finance Documents or a Facility of which a Finance Party becomes aware in its capacity as, or for the purpose of becoming, a Finance Party or which is received by a Finance Party in relation to, or for the purpose of becoming a Finance Party under, the Finance Documents or a Facility from either:

(a) any member of the Group or any of its advisers; or

(b) another Finance Party, if the information was obtained by that Finance Party directly or indirectly from any member of the Group or any of its advisers,

in whatever form, and includes information given orally and any document, electronic file or any other way of representing or recording information which contains or is derived or copied from such information but excludes:

(i) information that:

(A) is or becomes public information other than as a direct or indirect result of any breach by that Finance Party of Clause 40 (*Confidential Information*); or

(B) is identified in writing at the time of delivery as non-confidential by any member of the Group or any of its advisers; or

(C) is known by that Finance Party before the date the information is disclosed to it in accordance with paragraph (a) or (b) above or is lawfully obtained by that Finance Party after that date, from a source which is, as far as that Finance Party is aware, unconnected with the Group and which, in either case, as far as that Finance Party is aware, has not been obtained in breach of, and is not otherwise subject to, any obligation of confidentiality; and

(ii) any Funding Rate or any Reference Bank Quotation.

"**Confidentiality Undertaking**" means a confidentiality undertaking substantially in a recommended form of the LMA as set out in Schedule 8 (*LMA Form of Confidentiality Undertaking*) or in any other form agreed between the Borrower and the Agent.

"**CRR**" means the Council Regulation (EU) No 575/2013 of the European Parliament and of the Council of 26 June 2013 on prudential requirements for credit institutions and investment firms and amending Regulation (EU) No 648/2012.

"**Default**" means an Event of Default or any event or circumstance specified in Clause 27 (*Events of Default*) which would (with the expiry of a grace period, the giving of notice, the making of any determination under the Finance Documents or any combination of any of the foregoing) be an Event of Default.

"**Defaulting Lender**" means any Lender:

(a) which has failed to make its participation in a Loan available (or has notified the Agent or the Borrower (which has notified the Agent) that it will not make its participation in a Loan available) by the Utilisation Date of that Loan in accordance with Clause 6.4 (*Lenders' participation*) or Clause 8.3 (*Swingline Lenders' participation*);

(b) which has otherwise rescinded or repudiated a Finance Document;

(c) with respect to which an Insolvency Event has occurred and is continuing; or

(d) an Affiliate of which is a Defaulting Lender,

unless, in the case of paragraph (a) above:

(i) its failure to pay is caused by:

(A) administrative or technical error; or

(B) a Disruption Event; and

payment is made within three Business Days of its due date; or

(ii) the Lender is disputing in good faith whether it is contractually obliged to make the payment in question.

"**Disruption Event**" means either or both of:

(a) a material disruption to those payment or communications systems or to those financial markets which are, in each case, required to operate in order for payments to be made in connection with the Facilities (or otherwise in order for the transactions contemplated by the Finance Documents to be carried out) which disruption is not caused by, and is beyond the control of, any of the Parties; or

(b) the occurrence of any other event which results in a disruption (of a technical or systems-related nature) to the treasury or payments operations of a Party preventing that, or any other Party:

   (i) from performing its payment obligations under the Finance Documents; or

   (ii) from communicating with other Parties in accordance with the terms of the Finance Documents,

(and which (in either such case)) is not caused by, and is beyond the control of, the Party whose operations are disrupted.

LMA facility agreements include wording to address how to deal with Defaulting Lenders (as defined above). This wording was introduced in response to events in 2008-09 when certain banks (including certain Lehman Brothers entities and some Icelandic banks) entered into insolvency processes and/or were unable to comply with their obligations under syndicated facility agreements. In this sample agreement, if a Lender becomes a Defaulting Lender, then:

(a) the Borrower can cancel the Defaulting Lender's undrawn Commitments;

(b) the Defaulting Lender's participations in drawn Revolving Facility Loans can be "termed" out, such that its participations are no longer required to be repaid at the end of the then current Interest Period (recognising that if a Defaulting Lender receives such a repayment, it may not be capable of funding the "rollover" of its participation in the relevant Loan);

(c) the Defaulting Lender will cease to have a vote to the extent of its undrawn Commitments and cease to be entitled to receive a commitment fee in respect of its undrawn Commitments;

(d) the Borrower can require the Defaulting Lender to transfer all of its rights and obligations to a replacement bank; and

(e) the Defaulting Lender's Commitments can be disregarded if it fails to respond to an amendment or waiver request within a given time period.

"**Eligible Institution**" means any Lender or other bank, financial institution, trust, fund or other entity selected by the Borrower and which, in each case, is not a member of the Group.

"**Environmental Claim**" means any claim, proceeding or investigation by any person in respect of any Environmental Law.

"**Environmental Law**" means any applicable law in any jurisdiction in which any member of the Group conducts business which relates to the pollution or protection of the environment or harm to or the protection of human health or the health of animals or plants.

"**Environmental Permits**" means any permit, licence, consent, approval and other authorisation and the filing of any notification, report or assessment required under any Environmental Law for the operation of the business of any member of the Group conducted on or from the properties owned or used by the relevant member of the Group.

"**EURIBOR**" means, in relation to any Loan in euro:

(a) the applicable Screen Rate as of the Specified Time for euro and for a period equal in length to the Interest Period of that Loan; or

(b) as otherwise determined pursuant to Clause 15.1 (*Unavailability of Screen Rate*),

and if, in either case, that rate is less than zero, EURIBOR shall be deemed to be zero.

"**Event of Default**" means any event or circumstance specified as such in Clause 27 (*Events of Default*).

"**Facility**" means the Revolving Facility or the Swingline Facility.

"**Facility Office**" means the office or offices notified by a Lender to the Agent in writing on or before the date it becomes a Lender (or, following that date, by not less than five Business Days' written notice) as the office or offices through which it will perform its obligations under this Agreement.

"**Fallback Interest Period**" means one week or, if the Loan is in a Non-LIBOR Currency, the period specified as such in respect of that currency in Schedule 11 (*Other Benchmarks*).

"**FATCA**" means:

(a) sections 1471 to 1474 of the Code or any associated regulations;

(b) any treaty, law or regulation of any other jurisdiction, or relating to an intergovernmental agreement between the US and any other jurisdiction, which (in either case) facilitates the implementation of any law or regulation referred to in paragraph (a) above; or

(c) any agreement pursuant to the implementation of any treaty, law or regulation referred to in paragraph (a) or (b) above with the US Internal Revenue Service, the US government or any governmental or taxation authority in any other jurisdiction.

"**FATCA Application Date**" means:

(a) in relation to a "withholdable payment" described in section 1473(1)(A)(i) of the Code (which relates to payments of interest and certain other payments from sources within the US), 1 July 2014; or

(b) in relation to a "passthru payment" described in section 1471(d)(7) of the Code not falling within paragraph (a) above, the first date from which such payment may become subject to a deduction or withholding required by FATCA.

"**FATCA Deduction**" means a deduction or withholding from a payment under a Finance Document required by FATCA.

"**FATCA Exempt Party**" means a Party that is entitled to receive payments free from any FATCA Deduction.

See Clause 17 (*Tax Gross-Up and Indemnities*) for further information on FATCA.

"**Federal Funds Rate**" means, in relation to any day, the rate per annum equal to:

(a) the rate on overnight federal funds transactions calculated by the Federal Reserve Bank of New York as the federal funds effective rate as published for that day (or, if that day is not a New York Business Day, for the immediately preceding New York Business Day) by the Federal Reserve Bank of New York; or

(b) if a rate is not so published for any day which is a New York Business Day, the average of the quotations for that day on overnight federal funds transactions received by the Agent from three depository institutions of recognised standing selected by the Agent, and if in either case, that rate is less than zero, the Federal Funds Rate shall be deemed to be zero.

"**Fee Letter**" means any letter or letters dated on or about the date of this Agreement between the Arranger and the Borrower (or the Agent and the Borrower) setting out any of the fees referred to in Clause 16 (*Fees*).

"**Finance Document**" means this Agreement, the Mandate Letter, any Fee Letter and any other document designated as a "Finance Document" by the Agent and the Borrower.

"**Finance Lease**" means any lease which would, in accordance with GAAP, be treated as a balance sheet liability (other than any liability in respect of a lease or hire purchase contract which would, in accordance with GAAP in force prior to 1 January 2019, have been treated as an operating lease).

In January 2016 significant changes to lease accounting rules were published. IFRS16 will require most leases (including those that are currently classified as operating leases) to appear as balance sheet liabilities in relation to accounting periods from 1 January 2019. This will have a significant impact on the balance sheets of certain borrowers.

Previously under LMA facility agreements, liabilities under leases were only caught within the definition of "Financial Indebtedness" and included for financial covenant purposes if they were in respect of "Finance Leases". The distinction between finance leases and operating leases became much less relevant after 1 January 2019 given the balance sheet recognition of most operating lease commitments. In light of IFRS 16, the LMA published optional wording (also used in the sample agreement) excluding from the definition of "Finance Leases" those leases that were classified as operating leases prior to the implementation of IFRS 16. This wording is intended to ensure that operating lease liabilities are excluded from the debt definitions so that debt figures are not increased for financial covenant and other purposes once operating lease liabilities are brought on balance sheet.

"**Finance Party**" means the Agent, the Arranger or a Lender.

"**Financial Indebtedness**" means any indebtedness for or in respect of:

(a) moneys borrowed;

(b) any amount raised by acceptance under any acceptance credit facility or dematerialised equivalent;

(c) any amount raised pursuant to any note purchase facility or the issue of bonds, notes, debentures, loan stock or any similar instrument;

(d) the amount of any liability in respect of any Finance Lease;

(e) receivables sold or discounted (other than any receivables to the extent they are sold on a non-recourse basis);

(f) any amount raised under any other transaction (including any forward sale or purchase agreement) of a type not referred to in any other paragraph of this definition having the commercial effect of a borrowing;

(g) any derivative transaction entered into in connection with protection against or benefit from fluctuation in any rate or price (and, when calculating the value of any derivative transaction, only the marked to market value (or, if any actual amount is due as a result of the termination or close-out of that derivative transaction, that amount) shall be taken into account);

(h) any counter-indemnity obligation in respect of a guarantee, indemnity, bond, standby or documentary letter of credit or any other instrument issued by a bank or financial institution;

(i) any amount raised by the issue of redeemable shares which are redeemable (other than at the option of the issuer) before the Termination Date;

(j) any amount of any liability under an advance or deferred purchase agreement if one of the primary reasons behind the entry into the agreement is to raise finance; and

(k) (without double counting) the amount of any liability in respect of any guarantee or indemnity for any of the items referred to in paragraphs (a) to (j) above.

"**Funding Rate**" means any individual rate notified by a Lender to the Agent pursuant to paragraph (a)(ii) of Clause 15.4 (*Cost of funds*).

"**GAAP**" means generally accepted accounting principles in The Netherlands (in the case of the Borrower) and in France (in the case of the Guarantor), in either case including IFRS.

"**Group**" means the Guarantor and its Subsidiaries for the time being.

"**Historic Screen Rate**" means, in relation to any Loan, the most recent applicable Screen Rate for the currency of that Loan and for a period equal in length to the Interest Period of that Loan and which is as of a day which is no more than one Business Day before the Quotation Day.

For information on interest rate fallbacks, please see Clause 15 (*Changes to the calculation of interest*).

"**Holding Company**" means, in relation to a person, any other person in respect of which it is a Subsidiary.

"**IFRS**" means international accounting standards within the meaning of the IAS Regulation 1606/2002 to the extent applicable to the relevant financial statements.

"**Impaired Agent**" means the Agent at any time when:

(a) it has failed to make (or has notified a Party that it will not make) a payment required to be made by it under the Finance Documents by the due date for payment;

(b) the Agent otherwise rescinds or repudiates a Finance Document;

(c) (if the Agent or the Swingline Agent is also a Lender) it is a Defaulting Lender under paragraph (a) or (b) of the definition of "Defaulting Lender"; or

(d) an Insolvency Event has occurred and is continuing with respect to the Agent or the Swingline Agent;

(e) unless, in the case of paragraph (a) above:

(i) its failure to pay is caused by:

(A) administrative or technical error; or

(B) a Disruption Event; and

payment is made within three Business Days of its due date; or

(ii) the Agent is disputing in good faith whether it is contractually obliged to make the payment in question.

LMA facility agreements include optional wording to address how to deal with a situation where (i) an Insolvency Event (as defined below) occurs in relation to an agent, (ii) an agent informs the other Parties that it will not be able to make payments as required under the Finance Documents or (iii) an agent otherwise becomes a Defaulting Lender. If an Agent becomes an Impaired Agent as a result of the occurrence of one of these events, then the Majority Lenders are entitled to replace the Agent and may use alternative means of making payments under the Finance Documents (in order to avoid the situation where payments are made by other Parties to an Impaired Agent which is unable to make the corresponding payments out to the relevant recipients as required under the Finance Documents).

"**Increase Confirmation**" means a confirmation substantially in the form set out in Schedule 10 (*Form of Increase Confirmation*).

"**Increase Lender**" has the meaning given to that term in Clause 2.2 (*Increase*).

"**Indebtedness for Borrowed Money**" means Financial Indebtedness save for any indebtedness for or in respect of paragraphs (g) and (h) of the definition of "Financial Indebtedness".

"**Information Memorandum**" means the document in the form approved by the Borrower concerning the Group which, at the Borrower's request and on its behalf, was prepared in relation to this transaction and distributed by the Arranger to selected financial institutions before the date of this Agreement.

"**Insolvency Event**" in relation to a Finance Party or the Swingline Agent means that the Finance Party or the Swingline Agent:

(a) is dissolved (other than pursuant to a consolidation, amalgamation or merger);

(b) becomes insolvent or is unable to pay its debts or fails or admits in writing its inability generally to pay its debts as they become due;

(c) makes a general assignment, arrangement or composition with or for the benefit of its creditors;

(d) institutes or has instituted against it, by a regulator, supervisor or any similar official with primary insolvency, rehabilitative or regulatory jurisdiction over it in the jurisdiction of its incorporation or organisation or the jurisdiction of its head or home office, a proceeding seeking a judgment of insolvency or bankruptcy or any other relief under any bankruptcy or insolvency law or other similar law affecting creditors' rights, or a petition is presented for its winding-up or liquidation by it or such regulator, supervisor or similar official;

(e) has instituted against it a proceeding seeking a judgment of insolvency or bankruptcy or any other relief under any bankruptcy or insolvency law or other similar law affecting creditors' rights, or a petition is presented for its winding-up or liquidation, and, in the case of any such proceeding or petition instituted or presented against it, such proceeding or petition is instituted or presented by a person or entity not described in paragraph (d) above and:

(i) results in a judgment of insolvency or bankruptcy or the entry of an order for relief or the making of an order for its winding-up or liquidation; or

(ii) is not dismissed, discharged, stayed or restrained in each case within 30 days of the institution or presentation thereof;

(f) has a resolution passed for its winding-up, official management or liquidation (other than pursuant to a consolidation, amalgamation or merger);

(g) seeks or becomes subject to the appointment of an administrator, provisional liquidator, conservator, receiver, trustee, custodian or other similar official for it or for all or substantially all its assets (other than, for so long as it is required by law or regulation not to be publicly disclosed, any such appointment which is to be made, or is made, by a person or entity described in paragraph (d) above);

(h) has a secured party take possession of all or substantially all its assets or has a distress, execution, attachment, sequestration or other legal process levied, enforced or sued on or against all or substantially all its assets and such secured party maintains possession, or any such process is not dismissed, discharged, stayed or restrained, in each case within 30 days thereafter;

(i) causes or is subject to any event with respect to it which, under the applicable laws of any jurisdiction, has an analogous effect to any of the events specified in paragraphs (a) to (h) above; or

(j) takes any action in furtherance of, or indicating its consent to, approval of, or acquiescence in, any of the foregoing acts.

"**Interest Period**" means, in relation to a Loan, each period determined in accordance with Clause 14 (*Interest Periods*) and, in relation to an Unpaid Sum, each period determined in accordance with Clause 13.3 (*Default interest*).

"**Interpolated Historic Screen Rate**" means, in relation to any Loan, the rate (rounded to the same number of decimal places as the two relevant Screen Rates) which results from interpolating on a linear basis between:

(a) the most recent applicable Screen Rate for the longest period (for which that Screen Rate is available) which is less than the Interest Period of that Loan; and

(b) the most recent applicable Screen Rate for the shortest period (for which that Screen Rate is available) which exceeds the Interest Period of that Loan,

each for the currency of that Loan and each of which is as of a day which is no more than one day before the Quotation Day.

"**Interpolated Screen Rate**" means, in relation to any Loan, the rate (rounded to the same number of decimal places as the two relevant Screen Rates) which results from interpolating on a linear basis between:

(a) the applicable Screen Rate for the longest period (for which that Screen Rate is available) which is less than the Interest Period of that Loan; and

(b) the applicable Screen Rate for the shortest period (for which that Screen Rate is available) which exceeds the Interest Period of that Loan,

each as of the Specified Time for the currency of that Loan.

"**Legal Reservations**" means:

(a) the principle that equitable remedies may be granted or refused at the discretion of a court and the limitation of enforcement by laws relating to insolvency, reorganisation and other laws generally affecting the rights of creditors;

(b) the time barring of claims under the Limitation Acts, the possibility that an undertaking to assume liability for or indemnify a person against non-payment of UK stamp duty may be void and defences of set-off or counterclaim; and

(c) similar principles, rights and defences under the laws of any Relevant Jurisdiction.

"**Lender**" means:

(a) any Original Lender; and

(b) any bank, financial institution, trust, fund or other entity which has become a Party as a "Lender" in accordance with Clause 2.2 (*Increase*) or Clause 28 (*Changes to the Lenders*),

which in each case has not ceased to be a Party as such in accordance with the terms of this Agreement.

"**LIBOR**" means, in relation to any Loan:

(a) the applicable Screen Rate as of the Specified Time for the currency of that Loan and for a period equal in length to the Interest Period of that Loan; or

(b) as otherwise determined pursuant to Clause 15.1 (*Unavailability of Screen Rate*),

and if, in either case, that rate is less than zero, LIBOR shall be deemed to be zero.

The definition of LIBOR (and the equivalent definition for EURIBOR) states that the rate will be fixed by reference to the "**Screen Rate**". Clause 15 (*Changes to the calculation of interest*) then contains a series of fallbacks if the relevant screen rate is unavailable. This waterfall of fallbacks was included in the LMA facility agreements in 2014 after the discontinuation of the publication of LIBOR for certain currencies and tenors emphasised the importance of having a series of fallbacks available should a Screen Rate cease to exist. For details of the interest rate fallbacks, please see Clause 15 (*Changes to the calculation of interest*).

As mentioned in the term sheet in chapter 3, EURIBOR and euro LIBOR rates have fallen below zero in recent years. The definitions of LIBOR, EURIBOR and Benchmark Rate in the sample agreement therefore include wording such that if the relevant Screen Rate shows that LIBOR/EURIBOR/Benchmark Rate is negative, then for the purposes of the sample agreement, it will be deemed to be zero. This wording is designed to protect Lenders' return as it ensures that a negative benchmark rate cannot erode the Margin.

In July 2017 the Chief Executive of the FCA, Andrew Bailey, made a speech ("The Future of LIBOR") which most commentators believe signalled the beginning of the end for LIBOR as an interest rate benchmark. For a discussion regarding the future of LIBOR, please see chapter 1.

"**Limitation Acts**" means the Limitation Act 1980 and the Foreign Limitation Periods Act 1984.

"**LMA**" means the Loan Market Association.

"**Loan**" means a Revolving Facility Loan or a Swingline Loan.

"**Majority Lenders**" means a Lender or Lenders whose Commitments aggregate more than 66.66%. of the Total Commitments (or, if the Total Commitments have been reduced to zero, aggregated more than 66.66%. of the Total Commitments immediately prior to the reduction).

"**Mandate Letter**" means the letter dated [*DATE*] between the Arranger, the Borrower and others.

"**Margin**" means 0.30%. per annum.

"**Material Adverse Effect**" means a material adverse effect on:

(a) the business, operations, property, condition (financial or otherwise) or prospects of the Group taken as a whole;

(b) the ability of an Obligor to perform its obligations under the Finance Documents; or

(c) the validity or enforceability of the Finance Documents or the rights or remedies of any Finance Party under the Finance Documents.

"**Month**" means a period starting on one day in a calendar month and ending on the numerically corresponding day in the next calendar month, except that:

(a) other than where paragraph (b) below applies:

(i) (subject to paragraph (iii) below) if the numerically corresponding day is not a Business Day, that period shall end on the next Business Day in that calendar month in which that period is to end if there is one, or if there is not, on the immediately preceding Business Day;

(ii) if there is no numerically corresponding day in the calendar month in which that period is to end, that period shall end on the last Business Day in that calendar month; and

(iii) if an Interest Period begins on the last Business Day of a calendar month, that Interest Period shall end on the last

Business Day in the calendar month in which that Interest Period is to end; and

(b) in relation to an Interest Period for any Loan (or any other period for the accrual of commission or fees) in a Non-LIBOR Currency for which there are rules specified as Business Day Conventions in respect of that currency in Schedule 11 (*Other Benchmarks*), those rules shall apply.

The rules in paragraph (a) above will only apply to the last Month of any period.

"**New Lender**" has the meaning given to that term in Clause 28 (*Changes to the Lenders*).

"**New York Business Day**" means a day (other than a Saturday or Sunday) on which banks are open for general business in New York.

"**Non-Cooperative Jurisdiction**" means a "non-cooperative state or territory" (*Etat ou territoire non coopératif*) as set out in the list referred to in article 238-0 A of the French *Code général des impôts*, as such list may be amended from time to time.

"**Non-LIBOR Currency**" means Canadian Dollars.

"**Obligors**" means the Borrower and the Guarantor.

"**Optional Currency**" means a currency (other than the Base Currency) which complies with the conditions set out in Clause 5.3 (*Conditions relating to Optional Currencies*).

"**Original Financial Statements**" means:

(a) in relation to the Borrower, its audited financial statements for its financial year ended [•]; and

(b) in relation to the Guarantor, the audited consolidated financial statements of the Group for the financial year ended [•].

"**Original Swingline Lender**" means an Original Lender listed in Part III (*The Original Swingline Lenders*) of Schedule 1 (*The Original Parties*) as a Swingline Lender.

"**Original Termination Date**" means the date falling 12 months after the date of this Agreement.

"**Overall Commitment**" of a Lender means:

(a) its Commitment; or

(b) in the case of a Swingline Lender which does not have a Commitment, the Commitment of a Lender which is its Affiliate.

"**Participating Member State**" means any member state of the European Union that has the euro as its lawful currency in accordance with legislation of the European Union relating to Economic and Monetary Union.

"**Party**" means a party to this Agreement.

"**Quotation Day**" means, in relation to any period for which an interest rate is to be determined:

(a)

(i) (if the currency is sterling) the first day of that period;

(ii) (if the currency is euro) two TARGET Days before the first day of that period; or

(iii) (for any other currency (other than a Non-LIBOR Currency)), two Business Days before the first day of that period,

(unless market practice differs in the Relevant Market for that currency, in which case the Quotation Day for that currency will be determined by the Agent in accordance with market practice in the Relevant Market (and if quotations would normally be given on more than one day, the Quotation Day will be the last of those days)); or

(b) (if the currency is a Non-LIBOR Currency) the day specified as such in respect of that currency in Schedule 11 (*Other Benchmarks*).

"**Reference Bank Quotation**" means any quotation supplied to the Agent by a Reference Bank.

"**Reference Bank Rate**" means:

(a) the arithmetic mean of the rates (rounded upwards to four decimal places) as supplied to the Agent at its request by the Reference Banks:

(i) in relation to LIBOR as either:

(A) if:

(1) the Reference Bank is a contributor to the applicable Screen Rate; and

(2) it consists of a single figure, the rate (applied to the relevant Reference Bank and the relevant currency and period) which contributors to the applicable Screen Rate are asked to submit to the relevant administrator; or

(B) in any other case, the rate at which the relevant Reference Bank could fund itself in the relevant currency for the relevant period with reference to the unsecured wholesale funding market; or

(ii) in relation to EURIBOR:

(A) (other than where paragraph (B) below applies) as the rate at which the relevant Reference Bank believes one prime bank is quoting to another prime bank for interbank term deposits in euro within the Participating Member States for the relevant period; or

(B) if different, as the rate (if any and applied to the relevant Reference Bank and the relevant period) which contributors to the applicable Screen Rate are asked to submit to the relevant administrator; or

(b) in relation to a Benchmark Rate for a Loan in a Non-LIBOR Currency, the rate specified as such in respect of that currency in Schedule 11 (*Other Benchmarks*).

"**Reference Banks**" means, in relation to LIBOR the principal London offices of [•], [•] and [•] and, in relation to EURIBOR, the principal office in [•] of [•], [•] and [•] and in relation to the Benchmark Rate for a Loan in a Non-LIBOR Currency, the entities specified as such in respect of that currency in Schedule 11 (*Other Benchmarks*) or in each case, such other entities as may be appointed by the Agent in consultation with the Borrower.

The Reference Bank mechanism is included as a fallback if the Screen Rate is unavailable – see Clause 15 (*Changes to the calculation of interest*). The Reference Bank Rate definition for LIBOR requires (in some circumstances only) Reference Banks to provide their quotations on the same basis as they would if they were contributing to ICE LIBOR. In other circumstances, quotations are required to be based on a more general question.

Following the LIBOR scandal, some banks became much more reluctant to take on the role of Reference Bank. In the LMA facility agreements, the Reference Bank mechanism is now marked as optional. In addition, the LMA have introduced a number of protections for those banks that do agree to act as Reference Banks – see Clause 30.19 (*Role of Reference Banks*) and Clause 41 (*Confidentiality of Funding Rates and Reference Bank Quotations*).

"**Related Fund**" in relation to a fund (the "**first fund**"), means a fund which is managed or advised by the same investment manager or investment adviser as the first fund or, if it is managed by a different investment manager or investment adviser, a fund whose investment manager or investment adviser is an Affiliate of the investment manager or investment adviser of the first fund.

"**Relevant Market**" means in relation to euro, the European interbank market, in relation to a Non-LIBOR Currency, the market specified as such in respect of that currency in Schedule 11 (*Other Benchmarks*) and, in relation to any other currency, the London interbank market.

"**Relevant Nominating Body**" means any applicable central bank, regulator or other supervisory authority or a group of them, or any working group or committee sponsored or chaired by, or constituted at the request of, any of them or the Financial Stability Board.

"**Relevant Jurisdiction**" means in relation to an Obligor:

(a) its jurisdiction of incorporation; or

(b) any jurisdiction where it conducts its business.

"**Repeating Representations**" means each of the representations set out in Clauses 23.2 (*Status*) to 23.7 (*Governing law and enforcement*), Clause 23.10 (*No default*), paragraph (d) of Clause 23.11 (*No misleading information*), Clause 23.13 (*Pari passu ranking*) and Clause 23.14 (*No proceedings*).

Certain representations are repeated on the date of each Utilisation Request, on each Utilisation Date and the first day of each Interest Period. These are representations which are not duplicated elsewhere in the document by an ongoing undertaking.

"**Replacement Benchmark**" means a benchmark rate which is:

(a) formally designated, nominated or recommended as the replacement for a Screen Rate by:

(i) the administrator of that Screen Rate (**provided that** the market or economic reality that such benchmark rate measures is the same as that measured by that Screen Rate); or

(ii) any Relevant Nominating Body,

and if replacements have, at the relevant time, been formally designated, nominated or recommended under both paragraphs, the "Replacement Benchmark" will be the replacement under paragraph (ii) above;

(b) in the opinion of the Majority Lenders and the Obligors, generally accepted in the international or any relevant domestic syndicated loan markets as the appropriate successor to that Screen Rate; or

(c) in the opinion of the Majority Lenders and the Obligors, an appropriate successor to a Screen Rate.

A Replacement Benchmark is an interest rate which replaces a Screen Rate used to calculate interest under the agreement. At the time of writing it is probable that the LIBOR based screen rates will be replaced by alternative benchmark rates (and see chapter 1 and Clause 39.4 (*Replacement of Screen Rate*)).

"**Representative**" means any delegate, agent, manager, administrator, nominee, attorney, trustee or custodian.

"**Revolving Facility**" means the revolving loan facility made available under this Agreement as described in Clause 2.1 (*The Revolving Facility*).

"**Revolving Facility Loan**" means a loan made or to be made under the Revolving Facility or the principal amount outstanding for the time being of that loan.

"**Rollover Loan**" means one or more Revolving Facility Loans:

(a) made or to be made on the same day that a maturing Revolving Facility Loan is due to be repaid;

(b) the aggregate amount of which is equal to or less than the amount of the maturing Revolving Facility Loan;

(c) in the same currency as the maturing Revolving Facility Loan (unless it arose as a result of the operation of Clause 10.2 (*Unavailability of a currency*)); and

(d) made or to be made for the purpose of refinancing a maturing Revolving Facility Loan.

"**Sanctions**" means the economic or financial sanctions laws, regulations, trade embargoes or other restrictive measures enacted, administered, implemented and/or enforced from time to time by any of the following (and including through any relevant Sanctions Authority):

(a) the United Nations;

(b) the European Union;

(c) any member state of the European Union; and

(d) the government of the United States of America.

"**Sanctions Authority**" means any agency or person which is duly appointed, empowered or authorised to enact, administer, implement and/or enforce Sanctions, including (without limitation):

(a) the Department of the Treasury's Office of Foreign Assets Control of the United States of America;

(b) the United States Department of State or the United States Department of Commerce;

(c) the European Union (and any member state thereof); and

(d) Her Majesty's Treasury of the United Kingdom.

See Clause 26 (*General Undertakings*) for further information on anti-corruption and sanctions provisions.

"**Screen Rate**" means:

(a) in relation to LIBOR, the London interbank offered rate administered by ICE Benchmark Administration Limited (or any other person which takes over the administration of that rate) for the relevant currency and period displayed on pages LIBOR01 or LIBOR02 of the Thomson Reuters screen (or any replacement Thomson Reuters page which displays that rate); and

(b) in relation to EURIBOR, the euro interbank offered rate administered by the European Money Markets Institute (or any other person which takes over the administration of that rate) for the relevant period displayed on page EURIBOR01 of the Thomson Reuters screen (or any replacement Thomson Reuters page which displays that rate),

or, in each case, on the appropriate page of such other information service which publishes that rate from time to time in place of Thomson Reuters. If such page or service ceases to be available, the Agent may specify another page or service displaying the relevant rate after consultation with the Borrower; and

(c) in relation to a Benchmark Rate, the rate specified as such in respect of the relevant currency in Schedule 11 (*Other Benchmarks*).

Following the publication of the Wheatley Report, ICE Benchmark Administration Limited took over the administration of LIBOR from the British Bankers' Association in 2014.

In the event that there are errors in the submission or calculation processes for benchmark rates then certain administrators have put in place intraday refixing policies which enable them to refix and republish rates on the same day. In light of this, the LMA has included optional drafting in its facility agreements which can be included to exclude the effects of a refixing and republication of LIBOR or EURIBOR. This optional wording has not been included in this sample agreement and therefore if there were an intra-day refix and republication of LIBOR or EURIBOR, then the refixed and republished rate would be used rather than the originally published rate. Using a refixed and republished rate may cause operational difficulties as the new rate would be published later on in the day and the loan market is accustomed to LIBOR and EURIBOR rates being published at particular times.

"**Screen Rate Replacement Event**" means, in relation to a Screen Rate:

(a) the methodology, formula or other means of determining that Screen Rate has, in the opinion of the Majority Lenders, and the Obligors materially changed;

(b)

(i)

(A) the administrator of that Screen Rate or its supervisor publicly announces that such administrator is insolvent; or

(B) information is published in any order, decree, notice, petition or filing, however described, of or filed with a court, tribunal, exchange, regulatory authority or similar administrative, regulatory or judicial body which reasonably confirms that the administrator of that Screen Rate is insolvent,

**provided that**, in each case, at that time, there is no successor administrator to continue to provide that Screen Rate;

(ii) the administrator of that Screen Rate publicly announces that it has ceased or will cease, to provide that Screen Rate permanently or indefinitely and, at that time, there is no successor administrator to continue to provide that Screen Rate;

(iii) the supervisor of the administrator of that Screen Rate publicly announces that such Screen Rate has been or will be permanently or indefinitely discontinued; or

(iv) the administrator of that Screen Rate or its supervisor announces that that Screen Rate may no longer be used; or

(c) the administrator of that Screen Rate determines that that Screen Rate should be calculated in accordance with its reduced submissions or other contingency or fallback policies or arrangements and either:

(i) the circumstance(s) or event(s) leading to such determination are not (in the opinion of the Majority Lenders and the Obligors) temporary; or

(ii) that Screen Rate is calculated in accordance with any such policy or arrangement for a period no less than the period opposite that Screen Rate in Schedule 12 (Screen Rate contingency periods); or

(d) in the opinion of the Majority Lenders and the Obligors, that Screen Rate is otherwise no longer appropriate for the purposes of calculating interest under this Agreement.

"**Security**" means a mortgage, charge, pledge, lien or other security interest securing any obligation of any person or any other agreement or arrangement having a similar effect.

"**Separate Loan**" has the meaning given to that term in Clause 11 (*Repayment*).

"**Specified Time**" means a day or time determined in accordance with Schedule 9 (*Timetables*).

"**Subsidiary**" means any person (referred to as the "**first person**") in respect of which another person:

(a) holds a majority of the voting rights in that first person or has the right under the constitution of the first person to direct the overall policy of the first person or alter the terms of its constitution; or

(b) is a member of that first person and has the right to appoint or remove a majority of its board of directors or equivalent administration, management or supervisory body; or

(c) has the right to exercise a dominant influence (which must include the right to give directions with respect to operating and financial policies of the first person which its directors are obliged to comply with whether or not for its benefit) over the first person by virtue of provisions contained in the articles (or equivalent) of the first person or by virtue of a control contract which is in writing and is authorised by the articles (or equivalent) of the first person and is permitted by the law under which such first person is established; or

(d) is a member of that first person and controls alone, pursuant to an agreement with other shareholders or members, a majority of the voting rights in the first person or the rights under its constitution to direct the overall policy of the first person or alter the terms of its constitution; or

(e) has the power to exercise, or actually exercises dominant influence or control over the first person; or

(f) together with the first person are managed on a unified basis,

and for the purposes of this definition, a person shall be treated as a member of another person if any of that person's Subsidiaries is a member of that other person or, if any shares in that other person are held by a person acting on behalf of it or any of its Subsidiaries. A subsidiary undertaking shall include any person the shares or ownership interests in which are subject to Security and where the legal title to the shares or ownership interests so secured are registered in the name of the secured party or its nominee pursuant to such Security.

"**Swingline Agent**" means any branch or Affiliate of the Agent through which the Agent performs its duties in respect of the Swingline Facility pursuant to Clause 9.6 (*Swingline Agent*).

"**Swingline Commitment**" means:

(a) in relation to an Original Swingline Lender, the amount in dollars set opposite its name under the heading "Swingline Commitment" in Part III (*The Original Swingline Lenders*) of Schedule 1 (*The Original Parties*) and the amount of any other Swingline Commitment transferred to it under this Agreement or assumed by it in accordance with Clause 2.2 (*Increase*); and

(b) in relation to any other Swingline Lender, the amount of any Swingline Commitment transferred to it under this Agreement or assumed by it in accordance with Clause 2.2 (*Increase*),

to the extent not cancelled, reduced or transferred by it under this Agreement.

"**Swingline Facility**" means the dollar swingline loan facility made available under this Agreement as described in Clause 7 (*Swingline Facility*).

"**Swingline Lender**" means:

(a) an Original Swingline Lender; or

(b) any other person which has become a Party as a "Lender" in respect of a Swingline Commitment or a participation in a Swingline Loan in accordance with Clause 2.2 (*Increase*) or Clause 28 (*Changes to the Lenders*),

which in each case has not ceased to be a Party as such in accordance with the terms of this Agreement.

"**Swingline Loan**" means a loan made or to be made under the Swingline Facility or the principal amount outstanding for the time being of that loan.

"**Syndication Date**" means the day specified by the Arranger as the day on which primary syndication of the Facilities is completed.

"**TARGET2**" means the Trans-European Automated Real-time Gross Settlement Express Transfer payment system which utilises a single shared platform and which was launched on 19 November 2007.

"**TARGET Day**" means any day on which TARGET2 is open for the settlement of payments in euro.

"**Tax**" means any tax, levy, impost, duty or other charge or withholding of a similar nature (including any penalty or interest payable in connection with any failure to pay or any delay in paying any of the same).

"**Tax Authority**" means any government, state municipality or any local, state federal or other fiscal, revenue, customs or excise authority, body or official anywhere in the world.

"**Termination Date**" means the Original Termination Date or any subsequent date to which the Original Termination Date is extended pursuant to Clause 4 (*Extension Option*).

"**Total Commitments**" means the aggregate of the Commitments, being $1,000,000,000 at the date of this Agreement.

"**Total Swingline Commitments**" means the aggregate of the Swingline Commitments, being $500,000,000 at the date of this Agreement.

"**Transfer Certificate**" means a certificate substantially in the form set out in Schedule 4 (*Form of Transfer Certificate*) or any other form agreed between the Agent and the Borrower.

"**Transfer Date**" means, in relation to an assignment or a transfer, the later of:

(a) the proposed Transfer Date specified in the relevant Assignment Agreement or Transfer Certificate; and

(b) the date on which the Agent executes the relevant Assignment Agreement or Transfer Certificate.

"**Unpaid Sum**" means any sum due and payable but unpaid by an Obligor under the Finance Documents.

"**US**" means the United States of America.

"**Utilisation**" means a utilisation of a Facility.

"**Utilisation Date**" means the date of a Utilisation, being the date on which the relevant Loan is to be made.

"**Utilisation Request**" means:

(a) in the case of a Utilisation of the Revolving Facility, a notice substantially in the form set out in Part I (*Utilisation Request - Revolving Facility Loans*) of Schedule 3 (*Requests*); and

(b) in the case of a Utilisation of the Swingline Facility, a notice substantially in the form set out in Part II (*Utilisation Request - Swingline Loans*) of Schedule 3 (*Requests*).

"**VAT**" means:

(a) any tax imposed in compliance with the Council Directive of 28 November 2006 on the common system of value added tax (EC Directive 2006/112); and

(b) any other tax of a similar nature, whether imposed in a member state of the European Union in substitution for, or levied in addition to, such tax referred to in paragraph (a) above, or imposed elsewhere.

**1.2. Construction**

(a) Unless a contrary indication appears any reference in this Agreement to:

(i) the "**Agent**", the "**Arranger**", any "**Finance Party**", any "**Lender**", any "**Obligor**" or any "**Party**" shall be construed so as to include its successors in title, permitted assigns and permitted transferees to, or of, its rights and/or obligations under the Finance Documents;

(ii) "**assets**" includes present and future properties, revenues and rights of every description;

(iii) a "**Finance Document**" or any other agreement or instrument is a reference to that Finance Document or other agreement or instrument as amended, novated, supplemented, extended, replaced or restated;

(iv) a "**group of Lenders**" includes all the Lenders;

(v) "**indebtedness**" includes any obligation (whether incurred as principal or as surety) for the payment or repayment of money, whether present or future, actual or contingent;

(vi) an "**Interest Period**" includes each period determined under this Agreement by reference to which interest on a Swingline Loan is calculated;

(vii) a "**Lender**" includes a Swingline Lender unless the context otherwise requires;

(viii) a "**person**" includes any individual, firm, company, corporation, government, state or agency of a state or any association, trust, joint venture, consortium, partnership or other entity (whether or not having separate legal personality);

(ix) a "**regulation**" includes any regulation, rule, official directive, request or guideline (whether or not having the force of law) of any governmental, intergovernmental or supranational body, agency, department or of any regulatory, self-regulatory or other authority or organisation;

(x) a provision of law is a reference to that provision as amended or re-enacted; and

(xi) a time of day is a reference to London time.

(b) The determination of the extent to which a rate is "**for a period equal in length**" to an Interest Period shall disregard any inconsistency arising from the last day of that Interest Period being determined pursuant to the terms of this Agreement.

The definitions of "Business Day" and "Month" in facility agreements can cause there to be a mismatch between the length of a particular Interest Period and the corresponding period for which a Screen Rate is quoted. The wording above is therefore intended to clarify that any such mismatch should be ignored (and thus minimise the likelihood that an Interpolated Screen Rate would need to be used).

(c) Section, Clause and schedule headings are for ease of reference only.

(d) Unless a contrary indication appears, a term used in any other Finance Document or in any notice given under or in connection with any Finance Document has the same meaning in that Finance Document or notice as in this Agreement.

(e) A Default (other than an Event of Default) is "**continuing**" if it has not been remedied or waived and an Event of Default is "**continuing**" if it has not been waived.

### 1.3. Currency Symbols and Definitions

"**$**" and "**dollars**" denote the lawful currency of the United States of America, "**€**" and "**EUR**" and "**euro**" denote the single currency of the Participating Member States and "**£**" and "**sterling**" denote the lawful currency of the United Kingdom. "**CAD**" and "**Canadian Dollars**" denote the lawful currency of Canada.

### 1.4. Dutch Terms

In this Agreement, where it relates to a Dutch entity, a reference to:

(a) a necessary action to authorise, where applicable, includes without limitation:

(i) any action required to comply with the Dutch Works Council Act (*Wet op de ondernemingsraden*); and

(ii) obtaining unconditional positive advice (*advies*) from each competent works council;

(b) a security interest includes any mortgage (*hypotheek*), pledge (*pandrecht*), retention of title arrangement (*eigendomsvoorbehoud*), privilege (*voorrecht*), right of retention (*recht van retentie*), right to reclaim goods (*recht van reclame*), and, in general, any right *in rem* (*beperkte recht*), created for the purpose of granting security (*goederenrechtelijk zekerheidsrecht*);

(c) a winding-up, administration or dissolution includes a Dutch entity being:

(i) declared bankrupt (*failliet verklaard*);

(ii) dissolved (*ontbonden*);

(d) a moratorium includes *surseance van betaling* and granted a moratorium includes *surseance verleend*;

(e) a trustee in bankruptcy includes a *curator*;

(f) an administrator includes a *bewindvoerder*;

(g) a receiver or an administrative receiver does not include a *curator* or *bewindvoerder;* and

(h) an attachment includes a *beslag.*

### 1.5. French terms

In this Agreement, where it relates to the Guarantor or any other French entity, a reference to:

(a) "**acting in concert**" has the meaning given in article L.233-10 of the French *Code de commerce*;

(b) "**control**" has the meaning given in article L.233-3 of the French *Code de commerce*;

(c) "**gross negligence**" means "*faute lourde*";

(d) a "**guarantee**" includes any "*cautionnement*", "*aval*" and any "*garantie*" which is independent from the debt to which it relates;

(e) "**merger**" includes any "*fusion*" implemented in accordance with articles L.236-1 to L.236-24 of the French *Code de commerce*;

(f) a "**reconstruction**" includes, in relation to any company, any contribution of part of its business in consideration of shares (*apport partiel d'actifs*) and any demerger (*scission*) implemented in accordance with articles L.236-1 to L.236-24 of the French *Code de commerce*;

(g) a "**security interest**" includes any type of security (*sûreté réelle*), transfer or assignment by way of security and *fiducie-sûreté*; and

(h) "wilful misconduct" means "*dol*".

**1.6. Third party rights**

(a) Unless expressly provided to the contrary in a Finance Document a person who is not a Party has no right under the Contracts (Rights of Third Parties) Act 1999 (the "**Third Parties Act**") to enforce or to enjoy the benefit of any term of this Agreement.

(b) Subject to Clause 39.3 (*Other exceptions*) but otherwise notwithstanding any term of any Finance Document, the consent of any person who is not a Party is not required to rescind or vary this Agreement at any time.

This provision has been included in light of the UK Contracts (Rights of Third Parties) Act 1999 which enables persons who are not parties to a contract to enforce rights under the contract. It is assumed that lenders will not wish third parties to obtain rights under syndicated facility agreements in this case except where this is expressly provided for in the facility agreement. In the sample agreement, those third parties who are entitled to rights under the agreement are the officers and employees of the Agent and the Reference Banks (to the extent they are not Lenders).

# SECTION 2

## THE FACILITY

## 2. THE REVOLVING FACILITY

### 2.1. The Revolving Facility

The committed Revolving Facility which is made available under this Clause 2.1 is limited to a maximum available amount of $1bn. The Swingline Facility operates as a sub-limit of $500m within the Revolving Facility (see definition of Total Swingline Commitments in Clause 1.1 (*Definitions*)). Utilisations of the Swingline Facility operate to reduce the Commitments available under the Revolving Facility. The drawdown procedure for each Facility is set out in sections 2 and 3 of the sample agreement.

Many agreements which offer both a revolving facility and a swingline facility will restrict the amount of the swingline facility to a proportion of the revolving amount (depending on the size of the commercial paper programme and the purposes for which the revolving credit is to be put). Whether the amount of the swingline facility should be restricted will also be determined by the fee structure i.e., whether the borrower will be paying additional fees for a facility amount which it will never utilise or if the lenders have a commitment for which they are not being adequately compensated.

The key provisions in relation to the Swingline Facility are included in Clauses 7 (*Swingline Facility*) to 9 (*Swingline Loans*).

For further commentary see chapter 3.

(a) Subject to the terms of this Agreement, the Lenders make available to the Borrower a multicurrency revolving loan facility in an aggregate amount equal to the Total Commitments.

(b) The aggregate amount of all Loans outstanding under this Agreement shall not exceed the Total Commitments.

### 2.2. Increase

This provision deals with the consequences of a situation where the Borrower has chosen to cancel the Available Commitments/Available Swingline Commitments of one or more Lenders because they are Defaulting Lenders or (for example) have exercised their rights to charge Increased Costs or request that interest payments are "grossed up" to take account of a Tax Deduction. In such a scenario, the Borrower may choose to reinstate those Commitments, **provided that** it is able to find a bank or financial institution which is (or are) willing to assume the rights and obligations of the Lenders whose Available Commitments/Available Swingline Commitments were cancelled.

(a) The Borrower may by giving prior notice to the Agent after the effective date of a cancellation of the Commitments and/or Swingline Commitments of a Lender in accordance with:

(i) Clause 12.1 (*Illegality*); or

(ii) paragraph (a) of Clause 12.5 (*Right of replacement or repayment and cancellation in relation to a single Lender*),

request that the Commitments and/or Swingline Commitments relating to any Facility be increased (and the Commitments and/or Swingline Commitments relating to that Facility shall be so increased) in an aggregate amount in the Base Currency (or in the case of a Swingline Commitment, in dollars) of up to the amount of the Commitments or Swingline Commitments (in each case, as applicable) relating to that Facility so cancelled as follows:

(iii) the increased Commitments and/or Swingline Commitments will be assumed by one or more Eligible Institutions (each an "**Increase Lender**") each of which confirms in writing (whether in the relevant Increase Confirmation or otherwise) its willingness to assume and does assume all the obligations of a Lender corresponding to that part of the increased Commitments and/or Swingline Commitments which it is to assume, as if it had been an Original Lender in respect of those Commitments and/or those Swingline Commitments (as applicable);

(iv) each of the Obligors and any Increase Lender shall assume obligations towards one another and/or acquire rights against one another as the Obligors and the Increase Lender would have assumed and/or acquired had the Increase Lender been an Original Lender in respect of that part of the increased Commitments and/or increased Swingline Commitments (as applicable) which it is to assume;

(v) each Increase Lender shall become a Party as a "Lender" and any Increase Lender and each of the other Finance Parties shall assume obligations towards one another and acquire rights against one another as that Increase Lender and those Finance Parties would have assumed and/or acquired had the Increase Lender been an Original Lender in respect of that part of the increased Commitments and/or increased Swingline Commitments (as applicable) which it is to assume;

(vi) the Commitments and Swingline Commitments of the other Lenders shall continue in full force and effect; and

(vii) any increase in the Commitments and/or Swingline Commitments relating to a Facility shall take effect on the date specified by the Borrower in the notice referred to above or any later date on which the Agent executes an otherwise duly completed Increase Confirmation delivered to it by the relevant Increase Lender.

(b) The Agent shall, subject to paragraph (c) below, as soon as reasonably practicable after receipt by it of a duly completed Increase Confirmation appearing on its face to comply with the terms of this Agreement and delivered in accordance with the terms of this Agreement, execute that Increase Confirmation.

(c) The Agent shall only be obliged to execute an Increase Confirmation delivered to it by an Increase Lender once it is satisfied it has complied with all necessary "know your customer" or other similar checks under all applicable laws and regulations in relation to the assumption of the increased Commitments and/or Swingline Commitments by that Increase Lender.

(d) Each Increase Lender, by executing the Increase Confirmation, confirms (for the avoidance of doubt) that the Agent has authority to execute on its behalf any amendment or waiver that has been approved by or on behalf of the requisite Lender or Lenders in accordance with this Agreement on or prior to the date on which the increase becomes effective in accordance with this Agreement and that it is bound by that decision to the same extent as it would have been had it been an Original Lender.

(e) The Borrower shall promptly on demand pay the Agent the amount of all costs and expenses (including legal fees) reasonably incurred by it in connection with any increase in Commitments and/or Swingline Commitments under this Clause 2.2.

(f) The Increase Lender shall, on the date upon which the increase takes effect, pay to the Agent (for its own account) a fee in an amount equal to the fee which would be payable under Clause 28.4 (*Assignment or transfer fee*) if the increase was a transfer pursuant to Clause 28.6 (*Procedure for transfer*) and if the Increase Lender was a New Lender.

(g) The Borrower may pay to the Increase Lender a fee in the amount and at the times agreed between the Borrower and the Increase Lender in a letter between the Borrower and the Increase Lender setting out that fee. A reference in this Agreement to a Fee Letter shall include any letter referred to in this paragraph (g).

(h) Neither the Agent nor any Lender shall have any obligation to find an Increase Lender and in no event shall any Lender whose Commitment is replaced by an Increase Lender be required to pay or surrender any of the fees received by such Lender pursuant to the Finance Documents.

(i) Clause 28.5 (*Limitation of responsibility of Existing Lenders*) shall apply *mutatis mutandis* in this Clause 2.2 in relation to an Increase Lender as if references in that Clause to:

  (i) an "**Existing Lender**" were references to all the Lenders immediately prior to the relevant increase;

  (ii) the "**New Lender**" were references to that "**Increase Lender**"; and

  (iii) a "**re-transfer**" and "**re-assignment**" were references to respectively a "**transfer**" and "**assignment**".

### 2.3. Finance Parties' rights and obligations

(a) The obligations of each Finance Party under the Finance Documents are several. Failure by a Finance Party to perform its obligations under the Finance Documents does not affect the obligations of any other Party under the Finance Documents. No Finance Party is responsible for the obligations of any other Finance Party under the Finance Documents.

A syndicate of lenders does not constitute a partnership under English law. It is an administrative arrangement whereby a group of lenders co-operate in the extension of credit and the handling of receipts in relation to that credit and ancillary technical matters.

It should be noted that the Lenders' Commitments and rights are several, not joint. (See "**several liability**" in the Glossary.)

(b) The rights of each Finance Party under or in connection with the Finance Documents are separate and independent rights and any debt arising under the Finance Documents to a Finance Party from an Obligor is a separate and independent debt in respect of which a Finance Party shall be entitled to enforce its rights in accordance with paragraph (c) below. The rights of each Finance Party include any debt owing to that Finance Party under the Finance Documents and, for the avoidance of doubt, any part of a Loan or any other amount owed by an Obligor which relates to a Finance Party's participation in a Facility or its role under a Finance Document (including any such amount payable to the Agent on its behalf) is a debt owing to that Finance Party by that Obligor.

In 2015, a court in Hong Kong ruled that a Hong Kong law governed facility agreement did not give individual lenders the right to sue for their debt independently. Following that ruling, the LMA supplemented the drafting of this Clause to put beyond doubt the established position that individual lenders have an individual debt claim.

(c) A Finance Party may, except as specifically provided in the Finance Documents, separately enforce its rights under or in connection with the Finance Documents.

## 3. PURPOSE

Depending on the jurisdiction where a borrower is incorporated or located, difficult legal questions may occur where the purpose is *ultra vires* the company or where the purpose fails or becomes impossible.

### 3.1. Purpose

The Borrower shall apply all amounts borrowed by it under the Revolving Facility towards its general corporate and working capital purposes and the refinancing of Swingline Loans.

### 3.2. Monitoring

No Finance Party is bound to monitor or verify the application of any amount borrowed pursuant to this Agreement.

## 4. EXTENSION OPTION

As mentioned in the term sheet for this sample agreement, under Basel I, banks were able to take advantage of a favourable regulatory capital treatment for loans with a tenor of less than a year. This favourable treatment would also apply in respect of an extended loan if a firm offer to extend the commitment was only given in the final thirty days (or sixty days if syndicated as in the case of the sample agreement) of the initial commitment period, following a full credit assessment of the customer. This often led to banks offering their customers a facility with a 364 day tenor, which could be extended for a further 364 days at the option of the lenders.

Although this favourable capital treatment no longer applies, it remains common for banks to offer financings on the basis of an initial maturity (12 months in this case), together with an option for the borrower to request that the lenders extend the maturity for a further period of 12 months, with such extension being at the discretion of each lender.

### 4.1. Extension Option

(a) The Borrower may request that the Original Termination Date be extended by 12 Months by giving the Agent written notice not less than 30 days (and not more than 60 days) before the Original Termination Date (the "**Extension Request**").

(b) A notice served by the Borrower pursuant to paragraph (a) above is irrevocable.

(c) The Agent shall promptly notify each Lender of any Extension Request.

(d) Each Lender shall notify the Agent of its decision (which shall be in its sole discretion) whether or not to agree to the Extension Request not later than 30 days prior to the Original Termination Date (and, if any such Lender fails to notify the Agent of its acceptance of the

Extension Request on or before such date, it shall be deemed to have refused the Extension Request).

(e) The Agent shall notify the Borrower whether or not each Lender has agreed to the Extension Request promptly, and in any event no later than five Business Days after (i) receipt by it of a notification from a Lender as to whether or not it has agreed to the Extension Request or (ii) the deemed refusal of a Lender to the Extension Request (as applicable).

(f) By no later than the date falling five Business Days prior to the Original Termination Date, the Borrower may elect by notice to the Agent to accept the extension offered by all of the relevant Lender(s), in which case the Termination Date shall be extended in relation to the Commitments and/or Swingline Commitments of such Lender(s) who have agreed to the Extension Request.

(g) There may only be one extension of the Termination Date pursuant to this Clause 4.

(h) If any Lender does not agree to the Extension Request, its participation in any outstanding Utilisation shall be repaid on the Original Termination Date and its Commitments and Swingline Commitments shall be reduced to zero.

## 5. CONDITIONS OF UTILISATION

The Lenders' obligation to lend is contingent upon satisfaction of conditions precedent, including delivery of documents evidencing the existence and powers of the Borrower and the Guarantor and the taking by the Borrower and the Guarantor of the corporate action required to authorise execution of the agreement.

A list of the documents required, including opinions of counsel, is set out in Schedule 2 (*Conditions Precedent to Initial Utilisation*). For present purposes it suffices to mention that the advice of the lenders' counsel in the jurisdiction of incorporation of each borrower and guarantor should be sought in order to establish a definitive list of the documents to be required of a company incorporated and/or carrying on business in a given jurisdiction.

**5.1. Initial conditions precedent**

(a) The Borrower may not deliver a Utilisation Request unless the Agent has received all of the documents and other evidence listed in Schedule 2 (*Conditions Precedent to Initial Utilisation*) in form and substance satisfactory to the Agent. The Agent shall notify the Borrower and the Lenders promptly upon being so satisfied.

(b) Other than to the extent that the Majority Lenders notify the Agent in writing to the contrary before the Agent gives the notification described in paragraph (a) above, the Lenders authorise (but do not require) the Agent to give that notification. The Agent shall not be liable for any damages, costs or losses whatsoever as a result of giving any such notification.

**5.2. Further conditions precedent**

Subject to Clause 5.1 (*Initial conditions precedent*), the Lenders will only be obliged to comply with Clause 6.4 (*Lenders' participation*) if on the date of the Utilisation Request and on the proposed Utilisation Date:

(a) in the case of a Rollover Loan, no Event of Default is continuing or would result from the proposed Rollover Loan and, in the case of any other Loan, no Default is continuing or would result from the proposed Loan; and

(b) the Repeating Representations to be made by each Obligor are true in all material respects.

**5.3. Conditions relating to Optional Currencies**

(a) A currency will constitute an Optional Currency in relation to a Loan if it is euro, Canadian Dollars or if:

(i) it is readily available in the amount required and freely convertible into the Base Currency in the wholesale market for that currency on the Quotation Day and the Utilisation Date for that Loan; and

(ii) it has been approved by the Agent (acting on the instructions of all the Lenders) on or prior to receipt by the Agent of the relevant Utilisation Request for that Loan.

(b) If the Agent has received a written request from the Borrower for a currency to be approved under paragraph (a)(ii) above, the Agent will confirm to the Borrower by the Specified Time:

(i) whether or not the Lenders have granted their approval; and

(ii) if approval has been granted, the minimum amount for any subsequent Utilisation in that currency.

**5.4. Maximum number of Loans**

(a) The Borrower may not deliver a Utilisation Request if as a result of the proposed Utilisation [•] or more Loans would be outstanding.

(b) Any Loan made by a single Lender under Clause 10.2 (*Unavailability of a currency*) shall not be taken into account in this Clause 5.4.

(c) Any Separate Loan shall not be taken into account in this Clause 5.4.

# SECTION 3

## UTILISATION

### 6. UTILISATION – REVOLVING FACILITY LOANS

#### 6.1. Delivery of a Utilisation Request

The Borrower may utilise the Revolving Facility by delivery to the Agent of a duly completed Utilisation Request not later than the Specified Time.

#### 6.2. Completion of a Utilisation Request

(a) Each Utilisation Request is irrevocable and will not be regarded as having been duly completed unless:

(i) the proposed Utilisation Date is a Business Day within the Availability Period;

(ii) the currency and amount of the Utilisation comply with Clause 6.3 (*Currency and amount*); and

(iii) the proposed Interest Period complies with Clause 14 (*Interest Periods*).

(b) Only one Revolving Facility Loan may be requested in each Utilisation Request.

#### 6.3. Currency and amount

(a) The currency specified in a Utilisation Request must be the Base Currency or an Optional Currency.

(b) The amount of the proposed Revolving Facility Loan must be:

(i) if the currency selected is the Base Currency, a minimum of \$50,000,000 or if less, the Available Facility; or

(ii) if the currency selected is euro, a minimum of EUR50,000,000 or if less, the Available Facility; or

(iii) if the currency selected is Canadian Dollars, a minimum of CAD50,000,000 or if less, the Available Facility; or

(iv) if the currency selected is an Optional Currency other than euro or Canadian Dollars, the minimum amount specified by the Agent pursuant to paragraph (b)(ii) of Clause 5.3 (*Conditions relating to Optional Currencies*) or, if less, the Available Facility; and

(v) in any event such that its Base Currency Amount is less than or equal to the Available Facility.

**6.4. Lenders' participation**

(a) If the conditions set out in this Agreement have been met, and subject to Clause 11 (*Repayment*), each Lender shall make its participation in each Revolving Facility Loan available by the Utilisation Date through its Facility Office.

(b) The amount of each Lender's participation in each Revolving Facility Loan will be equal to the proportion borne by its Available Commitment to the Available Facility immediately prior to making the Revolving Facility Loan.

(c) The Agent shall determine the Base Currency Amount of each Revolving Facility Loan which is to be made in an Optional Currency and shall notify each Lender of the amount, currency and the Base Currency Amount of each Revolving Facility Loan, the amount of its participation in that Revolving Facility Loan and if different, the amount of that participation to be made available in accordance with Clause 33.1 (*Payments to the Agent*), in each case by the Specified Time.

**6.5. Cancellation of Commitment**

The Commitments which, at that time, are unutilised (taking into account a utilisation of the Revolving Facility by way of Swingline Loan) shall be immediately cancelled at the end of the Availability Period.

**7. SWINGLINE FACILITY**

**7.1. General**

(a) Clauses 5.2 (*Further conditions precedent*) and 5.3 (*Conditions relating to Optional Currencies*);

(b) Clause 6 (*Utilisation – Revolving Facility Loans*);

(c) Clause 10 (*Optional Currencies*);

(d) Clause 13 (*Interest*) as it applies to the calculation of interest on a Loan but not default interest on an overdue amount;

(e) Clause 14 (*Interest Periods*); and

(f) Clause 15 (*Changes to the Calculation of Interest*),

do not apply to Swingline Loans.

**7.2. Swingline Facility**

Subject to the terms of this Agreement, the Swingline Lenders make available to the Borrower a dollar swingline loan facility in an aggregate amount equal to the Total Swingline Commitments.

**7.3. Purpose**

The Borrower shall apply all amounts borrowed by it under the Swingline Facility towards refinancing any note or other instrument maturing under a dollar commercial paper programme of the Borrower. A Swingline Loan may not be applied in repayment or prepayment of another Swingline Loan.

## 8. UTILISATION – SWINGLINE LOANS

The Swingline Facility is required solely in relation to the commercial paper programme of the issuer. Such programmes are routinely rated by a recognised rating agency. In order to obtain an appropriate rating the issuer will normally need to show that it has access to same day funds in the US to meet any obligations which arise on the maturity of the paper (and, therefore, the rating agency will wish to see evidence of the existence of the Swingline Facility).

**8.1. Delivery of a Utilisation Request for Swingline Loans**

(a) The Borrower may utilise the Swingline Facility by delivery to the Agent of a duly completed Utilisation Request not later than the Specified Time.

(b) Each Utilisation Request for a Swingline Loan must be sent to the Agent to the address, fax number or, if relevant, electronic mail address or other such information in New York notified by the Agent to the Borrower for this purpose, with a copy to its address, fax number or, if relevant, electronic mail address or other such information referred to in Clause 35 (*Notices*).

**8.2. Completion of a Utilisation Request for Swingline Loans**

(a) Each Utilisation Request for a Swingline Loan is irrevocable and will not be regarded as having been duly completed unless:

(i) it specifies that it is for a Swingline Loan;

(ii) the proposed Utilisation Date is a New York Business Day within the Availability Period;

(iii) the Swingline Loan is denominated in dollars;

(iv) the amount of the proposed Swingline Loan is not more than the Available Swingline Facility and is a minimum of $50,000,000 or, if less, the Available Swingline Facility; and

(v) the proposed Interest Period:

(A) does not extend beyond the Termination Date;

(B) is a period of not more than five New York Business Days; and

(C) ends on a New York Business Day.

(b) Only one Swingline Loan may be requested in each Utilisation Request.

**8.3. Swingline Lenders' participation**

(a) If the conditions set out in this Agreement have been met, each Swingline Lender shall make its participation in each Swingline Loan available through its Facility Office in New York.

(b) The Swingline Lenders will only be obliged to comply with paragraph (a) above if on the date of the Utilisation Request and on the proposed Utilisation Date:

(i) no Default is continuing or would result from the proposed Utilisation; and

(ii) the Repeating Representations to be made by each Obligor are true in all material respects.

(c) The amount of each Swingline Lender's participation in each Swingline Loan will be equal to the proportion borne by its Available Swingline Commitment to the Available Swingline Facility immediately prior to making the Swingline Loan, adjusted to take account of any limit applying under Clause 8.4 (*Relationship with the Revolving Facility*).

(d) The Agent shall determine the Base Currency Amount of each Swingline Loan and notify each Swingline Lender of the amount of each Swingline Loan and its participation in that Swingline Loan in each case by the Specified Time.

### 8.4. Relationship with the Revolving Facility

(a) This Clause 8.4 applies when a Swingline Loan is outstanding or is to be borrowed.

(b) The Revolving Facility may be used by way of Swingline Loans. The Swingline Facility is not independent of the Revolving Facility.

(c) Notwithstanding any other term of this Agreement a Lender is only obliged to participate in a Loan to the extent that it would not result in the Base Currency Amount of its participation (and that of a Lender which is its Affiliate) in the Loans exceeding its Overall Commitment.

(d) Where, but for the operation of paragraph (c) above, the Base Currency Amount of a Lender's participation (and that of a Lender which is its Affiliate) in the Loans would have exceeded its Overall Commitment, the excess will be apportioned among the other Lenders required under this Agreement to make available a participation in the relevant Loan *pro rata* according to their Commitment or, as the case may be, Swingline Commitment. This calculation will be applied as often as necessary until participations in the Loan are apportioned among the relevant Lenders in a manner consistent with paragraph (c) above.

### 8.5. Cancellation of Swingline Commitment

The Swingline Commitments which, at that time, are unutilised shall be immediately cancelled at the end of the Availability Period.

## 9. SWINGLINE LOANS

### 9.1. Repayment of Swingline Loans

The Borrower shall repay each Swingline Loan on the last day of its Interest Period.

### 9.2. Loss sharing

This Clause 9.2 has been included to ensure that the credit risk in respect of a Swingline Loan is spread between the Lenders proportionately to their share of the Total Commitments (even if they do not participate in the Swingline Facility). The effect of this is that where the Borrower fails to pay an amount in respect of a Swingline Loan when due, each of the other Lenders will make a payment (via the Agent) to the relevant Swingline Lenders of an amount equal to that Lender's proportion of the Total Commitments multiplied by the overdue amount. Inclusion of the loss sharing provision in facilities agreements which incorporate a swingline facility is not invariable. Some lenders take the view that, if they do not share in the economics of a swingline facility, they should not be required to share in any losses associated with it.

(a) If a Loan (including a Swingline Loan) or interest on a Loan (including a Swingline Loan) is not paid in full on its due date, the Agent (if requested to do so in writing by any affected Lender) shall calculate the amount (if any) which needs to be paid or received by each Lender with a Commitment to place that Lender in the position it would have been in had each Lender (or its Affiliate) with a Commitment participated in that Loan in the proportion borne by its Commitment to the Total Commitments and, if the Total Commitments are then zero, the proportion borne by its Commitment to the Total Commitments immediately prior to their reduction to zero.

(b) The calculation of the Agent is designed solely to allocate the unpaid amount proportionally between the Lenders with a Commitment according to their Commitments and will not take into account any commitment fee or other amount payable under the Finance Documents.

(c) The Agent will set a date (the "**Loss Sharing Date**") on which payments must be made under this Clause 9.2. The Agent shall give at least three Business Days' notice to each affected Lender of this date and the amount of the payment (if any) to be paid or received by it on this date.

(d) On the Loss Sharing Date:

(i) each affected Lender who has to make a payment shall pay to the Agent the relevant amount set out in the notice referred to in paragraph (c) above; and

(ii) out of the amounts the Agent receives, the Agent shall pay to each affected Lender who is entitled to receive a payment the amount set out in that notice.

(e) If the amount actually received by the Agent from the Lenders under paragraph (d) above is insufficient to pay the full amount required to be paid under that paragraph, the Agent shall distribute the amount it actually receives among the affected Lenders *pro rata* to the amounts they are entitled to receive under that paragraph.

(f) If a Lender makes a payment to the Agent under this Clause 9.2 then, to the extent that that payment is distributed by the Agent under paragraph (d) or (e) above, as between the relevant Obligor and that Lender an amount equal to the amount of that distributed payment will be treated as not having been paid by the relevant Obligor.

Any payment under this Clause 9.2 will not reduce the obligations in aggregate of any Obligor.

**9.3. Voluntary Prepayment of Swingline Loans**

(a) The Borrower may prepay at any time the whole of any Swingline Loan.

(b) Unless a contrary indication appears in this Agreement, any part of the Swingline Facility which is prepaid or repaid may be re-borrowed in accordance with the terms of this Agreement.

**9.4. Interest**

Interest is charged on each Swingline Loan at the higher of the prime commercial rate for dollars announced by the Agent and the rate on that date determined by the Agent to be the Federal Funds Rate plus a margin of 0.25%.

(a) The rate of interest on each Swingline Loan for any day during its Interest Period is the higher of:

(i) the prime commercial lending rate in dollars announced by the Agent at the Specified Time and in force on that day; and

(ii) 0.25%. per annum over the rate per annum determined by the Agent to be the Federal Funds Rate for that day.

(b) The Agent shall promptly notify the Swingline Lenders and the Borrower of the determination of the rate of interest under paragraph (a) above.

(c) If any day during an Interest Period is not a New York Business Day, the rate of interest on a Swingline Loan on that day will be the rate applicable to the immediately preceding New York Business Day.

(d) The Borrower shall pay accrued interest on each Swingline Loan on the last day of its Interest Period.

**9.5. Interest Period**

(a) Each Swingline Loan has one Interest Period only.

(b) The Interest Period for a Swingline Loan must be selected in the relevant Utilisation Request.

**9.6. Swingline Agent**

(a) The Agent may perform its duties in respect of the Swingline Facility through an Affiliate acting as its agent.

(b) Notwithstanding any other term of this Agreement and without limiting the liability of any Obligor under the Finance Documents, each Lender shall (in proportion to its share of the Total Commitments or, if the Total Commitments are then zero, to its share of the Total Commitments immediately prior to their reduction to zero) pay to or indemnify the Agent, within three Business Days of demand, for or against any cost, loss or liability (including, without limitation, for negligence or for any other category of loss whatsoever) incurred by the Agent or its Affiliate (other than by reason of the Agent's or the Affiliate's gross negligence or wilful misconduct or, in the case of any cost, loss or liability pursuant to Clause 33.11 (*Disruption to payment systems etc.,*) notwithstanding the Agent's or the Affiliate's negligence, gross negligence or any other category of liability whatsoever but not including any claim based on the fraud of the Agent or the Affiliate in acting as Agent for the Swingline Facility under the Finance Documents) unless the Agent or its Affiliate has been reimbursed by an Obligor pursuant to a Finance Document.

**9.7. Partial payments – Swingline Loans**

(a) If the Agent receives a payment in respect of the Swingline Facility that is insufficient to discharge all the amounts then due and payable by an Obligor under the Finance Documents in respect of the Swingline Facility, the Agent shall apply that payment towards the obligations of that Obligor under the Finance Documents in respect of the Swingline Facility in the following order:

(i) **first**, in or towards payment *pro rata* of any amount owing to the Agent or its Affiliate under the Finance Documents incurred in respect of the Swingline Facility;

(ii) **secondly**, in or towards payment *pro rata* of any accrued interest on a Swingline Loan due but unpaid under this Agreement;

(iii) **thirdly**, in or towards payment *pro rata* of the principal of any Swingline Loan due but unpaid under this Agreement; and

(iv) **fourthly**, in or towards payment *pro rata* of any other sum due but unpaid under the Finance Documents in respect of the Swingline Facility.

(b) The Agent shall, if so directed by all the Swingline Lenders, vary the order set out in paragraphs (a)(ii) to (a)(iv) above.

(c) Paragraphs (a) and (b) above will override any appropriation made by an Obligor and Clause 33.6 (*Partial payments*) does not apply to the Swingline Facility.

## 10. OPTIONAL CURRENCIES

### 10.1. Selection of currency

The Borrower shall select the currency of a Loan in a Utilisation Request.

### 10.2. Unavailability of a currency

If before the Specified Time on any Quotation Day:

(a) a Lender notifies the Agent that the Optional Currency requested is not readily available to it in the amount required; or

(b) a Lender notifies the Agent that compliance with its obligation to participate in a Loan in the proposed Optional Currency would contravene a law or regulation applicable to it,

the Agent will give notice to the Borrower to that effect by the Specified Time on that day. In this event, any Lender that gives notice pursuant to this Clause 10.2 will be required to participate in the Loan in the Base Currency (in an amount equal to that Lender's proportion of the Base Currency Amount or, in respect of a Rollover Loan, an amount equal to that Lender's proportion of the Base Currency Amount of the Rollover Loan that is due to be made) and its participation will be treated as a separate Loan denominated in the Base Currency during that Interest Period.

### 10.3. Participation in a Loan

Each Lender's participation in a Loan will be determined in accordance with paragraph (b) of Clause 6.4 (*Lenders' participation*).

# SECTION 4

## REPAYMENT, PREPAYMENT AND CANCELLATION

### 11. REPAYMENT

Each revolving loan must be repaid by the Borrower at the end of its Interest Period. The Borrower can choose the period for which it wishes to make drawings under each of the facilities. The chosen period has to be specified in each request for a Loan and this period is defined as an "**Interest Period**". The Interest Period for drawings under the Revolving Facility may be one, three or six months.

More flexibility could be negotiated by the Borrower. However, periods which are not whole numbers of months are not traded in large volume and so the rates at which they trade may be on the high side. In addition, it is unlikely that the applicable benchmark rate will be available for that tenor and the interest rate would therefore need to be calculated by linear interpolation (see Clause 15.1 (*Unavailability of Screen Rate*)).

All sums repaid under the facilities may be re-borrowed in accordance with the provisions of the sample agreement.

Paragraph (b) below allows the Agent to carry out "cashless rollovers" – this is to say, if a Revolving Facility Loan is being made available to the Borrower on the same day that a maturing Revolving Facility Loan is due to be repaid, then to the extent that the amounts and currencies of such Revolving Facility Loans are the same, then there is no need for the Borrower and the Lenders (via the Agent) to make actual cash payments.

This provision reflects normal operating procedure of many banks when acting as Agent. If rollovers are conducted by way of actual cash payments, from the Borrower's perspective, there remains a risk that the Borrower will repay the maturing Revolving Facility Loan but a member of the syndicate will be a Defaulting Lender and fail to fund its participation in the new Revolving Facility Loan which has been requested on the same day.

(a) Subject to paragraph (c) below, the Borrower shall repay each Revolving Facility Loan on the last day of its Interest Period.

(b) Without prejudice to the Borrower's obligation under paragraph (a) above, if:

(i) one or more Revolving Facility Loans are to be made available to the Borrower:

(A) on the same day that a maturing Revolving Facility Loan is due to be repaid by the Borrower;

(B) in the same currency as the maturing Revolving Facility Loan (unless it arose as a result of the operation of Clause 10.2 (*Unavailability of a currency*)); and

(C) in whole or in part for the purpose of refinancing the maturing Revolving Facility Loan; and

(ii) the proportion borne by each Lender's participation in the maturing Revolving Facility Loan to the amount of that maturing Revolving Facility Loan is the same as the proportion borne by that Lender's participation in the new Revolving Facility Loans to the aggregate amount of those new Revolving Facility Loans,

the aggregate amount of the new Revolving Facility Loans shall, unless the Borrower notifies the Agent to the contrary in the relevant Utilisation Request, be treated as if applied in or towards repayment of the maturing Revolving Facility Loan so that:

(A) if the amount of the maturing Revolving Facility Loan exceeds the aggregate amount of the new Revolving Facility Loans:

(1) the Borrower will only be required to make a payment under Clause 33.1 (*Payments to the Agent)* in an amount in the relevant currency equal to that excess; and

(2) each Lender's participation in the new Revolving Facility Loans shall be treated as having been made available and applied by the Borrower in or towards repayment of that Lender's participation in the maturing Revolving Facility Loan and that Lender will not be required to make a payment under Clause 33.1 (Payments to the Agent) in respect of its participation in the new Revolving Facility Loans; and

(B) if the amount of the maturing Revolving Facility Loan is equal to or less than the aggregate amount of the new Revolving Facility Loans:

(1) the Borrower will not be required to make a payment under Clause 33.1 (*Payments to the Agent*); and

(2) each Lender will be required to make a payment under Clause 33.1 (*Payments to the Agent*) in respect of its participation in the new Revolving Facility Loans only to the extent that its participation in the new Revolving Facility Loans exceeds that Lender's participation in the maturing Revolving Facility Loan and the remainder of that Lender's participation in the new Revolving Facility Loans shall be treated as having been made available and applied by the Borrower in or towards repayment of that Lender's participation in the maturing Revolving Facility Loan.

(c) At any time when a Lender becomes a Defaulting Lender, the maturity date of each of the participations of that Lender in the Revolving Facility Loans then outstanding will be automatically extended to the Termination Date applicable to the Revolving Facility and will be treated as separate Revolving Facility Loans (the "**Separate Loans**") denominated in the currency in which the relevant participations are outstanding.

(d) If the Borrower makes a prepayment of a Revolving Facility Loan pursuant to Clause 12.4 (*Voluntary prepayment of Revolving Facility Loans*), the Borrower may prepay any outstanding Separate Loan by giving not less than five Business Days' prior notice to the Agent. The Agent will forward a copy of a prepayment notice received in accordance with this paragraph (d) to the Defaulting Lender concerned as soon as practicable on receipt.

(e) Interest in respect of a Separate Loan will accrue for successive Interest Periods selected by the Borrower by the time and date specified by the Agent (acting reasonably) and will be payable by the Borrower to the Agent (for the account of that Defaulting Lender) on the last day of each Interest Period of that Loan.

(f) The terms of this Agreement relating to Revolving Facility Loans generally shall continue to apply to Separate Loans other than to the extent inconsistent with paragraphs (c) to (e) above, in which case those paragraphs shall prevail in respect of any Separate Loan.

## 12. PREPAYMENT AND CANCELLATION

### 12.1. Illegality

This Clause 12.1 allows a Lender to cancel its Commitment and Swingline Commitment if it becomes illegal for that Lender to lend to the Borrower after it has entered into the agreement. The possible types of illegality that most concern lenders are (a) situations where diplomatic relations deteriorate between the government of the country of a lender and that of a borrower and (b) situations where newly imposed laws (for example, foreign exchange controls or political changes such as Brexit) make it impossible for a lender to make or maintain its loan.

If it becomes unlawful, in any applicable jurisdiction, for any Lender to perform any of its obligations as contemplated by this Agreement or to fund or maintain its participation in any Loan or at any time it becomes unlawful for any Affiliate of a Lender for that Lender to do so:

(a) that Lender shall promptly notify the Agent upon becoming aware of that event;

(b) upon the Agent notifying the Borrower, the Available Commitment and the Available Swingline Commitment of that Lender and of any Affiliate of that Lender which is a Swingline Lender will be immediately cancelled (to the greatest extent possible which does not result in that Lender (or its Affiliate) failing to meet requirement set out in paragraph (e) of Clause 28.3 (*Other conditions of assignment or transfer*)); and

(c) to the extent that the Lender's (and any such Affiliate's) participation has not been transferred pursuant to paragraph (d) of Clause 12.5 (*Right of replacement or repayment and cancellation in relation to a single Lender*), the Borrower shall repay that Lender's (and any such Affiliate's) participation in the Loans made to the Borrower on the last day of the Interest Period for each Loan occurring after the Agent has notified the Borrower or, if earlier, the date specified by the Lender in the notice delivered to the Agent (being no earlier than the last day of any applicable grace period permitted by law) and that Lender's (and any such Affiliate's) corresponding Commitment(s) and Swingline Commitment(s) shall be cancelled in the amount of the participations repaid.

**12.2. Change of control**

(a) If any person or group of persons acting in concert gains control of the Guarantor:

(i) the Borrower shall promptly notify the Agent upon becoming aware of that event;

(ii) a Lender shall not be obliged to fund a Utilisation (except for a Rollover Loan); and

(iii) any Lender may, by not less than ten days' notice to the Borrower, cancel its Commitment and Swingline Commitment and declare its portion of all outstanding Loans, together with accrued interest, and all other amounts accrued to it under the Finance Documents immediately due and payable, whereupon its Commitment and Swingline Commitment will be cancelled and all such outstanding Loans and amounts will become immediately due and payable.

(b) For the purposes of paragraph (a) above:

(i) "**acting in concert**" means a group of persons who, pursuant to an agreement or understanding (whether formal or informal) actively co-operate (through the acquisition by any of them, either directly or indirectly, of shares in the Guarantor, or otherwise) to obtain or consolidate control of the Guarantor.

(ii) "**control**" means:

(A) the power (whether by way of ownership of shares, proxy, contract, agency or otherwise) to:

(1) cast, or control the casting of, more than one-half of the maximum number of votes that might be cast at a general meeting of the Guarantor; or

(2) appoint or remove all, or the majority, of the directors or other equivalent officers of the Guarantor; or

(3) give directions with respect to the operating and financial policies of the Guarantor which the directors or other equivalent officers of the Guarantor are obliged to comply with; or

(B) the holding of more than one-half of the issued share capital of the Guarantor (excluding any part of that issued share capital that carries no right to participate beyond a specified amount in a distribution of either profits or capital).

**12.3. Voluntary cancellation**

Besides the right to prepay certain amounts under each Facility, the Borrower may cancel Commitments under the Available Facility. The Borrower's benefit from such cancellation is normally a reduction of the fees it has to pay under a committed facility agreement, (in this case the commitment fees under Clause 16.1 (*Commitment fee*)). On the other hand, a cancellation leads to a deterioration of the Borrower's liquidity since a cancelled Commitment may not be reinstated afterwards (see paragraph (e) of Clause 12.6 (*Restrictions*)). This is in contrast to any prepayment which entitles the Borrower to re-borrow those amounts (see paragraph (c) of Clause 12.6 (*Restrictions*)). Usually, a cancellation reduces the Commitments of the Lenders rateably except in the case of cancellations in accordance with Clause 12.5 (*Right of replacement or repayment and cancellation in relation to a single Lender*) in relation to a single Lender which provides for cancellations of Commitments of individual Lenders who are required to be grossed up for withholding tax or who claim for increased costs or under the tax indemnity.

(a) Subject to paragraph (b) below, the Borrower may, if it gives the Agent not less than five Business Days' (or such shorter period as the Majority Lenders may agree) prior notice, cancel the whole or any part (being a minimum amount of $100,000,000) of the Available Facility or the Available Swingline Facility. Any cancellation under this Clause 12.3 shall reduce the Commitments or Swingline Commitments of the Lenders rateably under that Facility.

(b) The Borrower may not make a cancellation pursuant to paragraph (a) above to the extent that that cancellation would result in a Lender (or its Affiliate) failing to meet the requirement set out in paragraph (e) of Clause 28.3 (*Other conditions of assignment or transfer*).

### 12.4. Voluntary prepayment of Revolving Facility Loans

English law does not give a borrower a general right to prepay a loan. Therefore, if a borrower requires such a right it must be negotiated, agreed and recorded in the loan documentation. An indemnity for "Break Costs" that Lenders may incur as a result of a prepayment is included in Clause 15.6 (*Break Costs*) of the sample agreement. This is based on the theoretical assumption that Lenders match fund an advance for its full term. Therefore, if a borrower were to prepay a Loan part way through the relevant term then there would be a risk that the Lenders would be unable to obtain a sufficient return on the sum prepaid in order to meet their liabilities to their sources of funds. The indemnity for losses as a result of prepayment will not be relevant for Swingline Loans as they are funded on an overnight basis and the Swingline Lenders will not normally suffer any funding losses from early prepayment.

The Borrower may, if it gives the Agent not less than five Business Days' (or such shorter period as the Majority Lenders may agree) prior notice, prepay the whole or any part of a Revolving Facility Loan (but if in part, being an amount that reduces the Base Currency Amount of the Revolving Facility Loan by a minimum amount of $50,000,000).

### 12.5. Right of replacement or repayment and cancellation in relation to a single Lender

(a) If:

(i) any sum payable to any Lender by an Obligor is required to be increased under paragraph (c) of Clause 17.2 (*Tax gross-up*);

(ii) any Lender claims indemnification from the Borrower under Clause 17.3 (*Tax indemnity*) or Clause 18.1 (*Increased costs*); or

(iii) any amount payable to any Lender by an Obligor under a Finance Document is not, or will not be (when the relevant corporate income tax is calculated) treated as a deductible charge or expense for French tax purposes for that Obligor by reason of that amount being (A) paid or accrued to a Lender incorporated, domiciled, established or acting through a Facility Office situated in a Non-Cooperative Jurisdiction, or (B) paid to an account opened in the name of or for the benefit of that Lender with a financial institution situated in a Non-Cooperative Jurisdiction, the Borrower may, whilst the circumstance giving rise to the requirement for that increase, indemnification or non-deductibility for French tax purposes continues, give the Agent notice of cancellation of the Commitment(s) and/or Swingline Commitment(s) of that Lender and of any Affiliate of that Lender which is a Swingline Lender and its intention to procure the repayment of that Lender's and any such Affiliate's participation in the Loans or give the Agent notice of its intention to replace that Lender (together with any Affiliate of that Lender) in accordance with paragraph (d) below.

(b) On receipt of a notice of cancellation referred to in paragraph (a) above, the Commitment(s) and/or Swingline Commitment(s) (as the case may be) of that Lender and any such Affiliate shall immediately be reduced to zero.

(c) On the last day of each Interest Period which ends after the Borrower has given notice of cancellation under paragraph (a) above (or, if earlier, the date specified by the Borrower in that notice), the Borrower shall repay that Lender's participation in that Loan.

(d) If:

(i) any of the circumstances set out in paragraph (a) above apply to a Lender; or

(ii) an Obligor becomes obliged to pay any amount in accordance with Clause 12.1 (*Illegality*) to any Lender,

the Borrower may, on five Business Days' prior notice to the Agent and that Lender, replace that Lender (together with any Affiliate of that Lender) by requiring that Lender and that Affiliate to (and to the extent permitted by law, that Lender and that Affiliate shall) transfer pursuant to Clause 28 (*Changes to the Lenders*) all (and not part only) of its rights and obligations under this Agreement to an Eligible Institution which confirms its willingness to assume and does assume all the obligations of the transferring Lender and transferring Affiliate in accordance with Clause 28 (*Changes to the Lenders*) for a purchase price in cash payable at the time of the transfer in an amount equal to the outstanding principal amount of such Lender's and such Affiliate's participation in the outstanding Loans and all accrued interest (to the extent that the Agent has not given a notification under Clause 28.10 (*Pro rata interest settlement*)), Break Costs and other amounts payable in relation thereto under the Finance Documents.

(e) The replacement of a Lender pursuant to paragraph (d) above shall be subject to the following conditions:

(i) the Borrower shall have no right to replace the Agent;

(ii) neither the Agent nor any Lender shall have any obligation to find a replacement Lender;

(iii) in no event shall the Lender replaced under paragraph (d) above be required to pay or surrender any of the fees received by such Lender pursuant to the Finance Documents;

(iv) the Lender shall only be obliged to transfer its rights and obligations pursuant to paragraph (d) above once it is satisfied that it has complied with all necessary "know your customer" or other similar checks under all applicable laws and regulations in relation to that transfer; and

(v) a Lender shall not be obliged to transfer its rights and obligations pursuant to paragraph (d) above to the extent that the transfer would result in the Lender (or its Affiliate) failing to meet the requirement set out in paragraph (e) of Clause 28.3 (*Other conditions of assignment or transfer*).

(f) A Lender shall perform the checks described in paragraph (e)(iv) above as soon as reasonably practicable following delivery of a notice referred to in paragraph (d) above and shall notify the Agent and the Borrower when it is satisfied that it has complied with those checks.

(g)

(i) If any Lender becomes a Defaulting Lender, the Borrower may, at any time whilst the Lender continues to be a Defaulting Lender, give the Agent five Business Days' notice of cancellation of each Available Commitment and/or Available Swingline Commitment (as the case may be) of that Lender.

(ii) On the notice referred to in paragraph (i) above becoming effective, each Available Commitment and/or Available Swingline Commitment (as the case may be) of the Defaulting Lender shall, other than as set out in paragraph (iv) below, immediately be reduced to zero.

(iii) The Agent shall as soon as practicable after receipt of a notice referred to in paragraph (i) above, notify all the Lenders.

(iv) That Lender's Overall Commitment shall immediately be reduced to the lowest amount possible which does not result in that Lender (or its Affiliate) failing to meet the requirement set out in paragraph (e) of Clause 28.3 (*Other conditions of assignment or transfer*).

**12.6. Restrictions**

(a) Any notice of cancellation or prepayment given by any Party under this Clause 12 shall be irrevocable and, unless a contrary indication appears in this Agreement, shall specify the date or dates upon which the relevant cancellation or prepayment is to be made and the amount of that cancellation or prepayment.

(b) Any prepayment under this Agreement shall be made together with accrued interest on the amount prepaid and, subject to any Break Costs in relation to the prepayment of Revolving Facility Loans, without premium or penalty.

(c) Unless a contrary indication appears in this Agreement, any part of a Facility which is prepaid or repaid may be reborrowed in accordance with the terms of this Agreement.

(d) The Borrower shall not repay or prepay all or any part of the Loans or cancel all or any part of the Commitments or the Swingline Commitments except at the times and in the manner expressly provided for in this Agreement.

(e) Subject to Clause 2.2 (*Increase*), no amount of the Total Commitments cancelled under this Agreement may be subsequently reinstated.

(f) If the Agent receives a notice under this Clause 12 it shall promptly forward a copy of that notice to either the Borrower or the affected Lender, as appropriate.

(g) If all or part of any Lender's participation in a Loan is repaid or prepaid and is not available for redrawing (other than by operation of Clause 5.2 (*Further conditions precedent*)), an amount of that Lender's Commitments and/or Swingline Commitments (equal to the Base Currency Amount of the amount of the participation which is repaid or prepaid) will be deemed to be cancelled on the date of repayment or prepayment.

**12.7. Application of prepayments**

Any prepayment of a Loan pursuant to Clause 12.4 (*Voluntary prepayment of Revolving Facility Loans*) shall be applied *pro rata* to each Lender's participation in that Loan.

# SECTION 5

## COSTS OF UTILISATION

## 13. INTEREST

The interest rate payable on each revolving loan will be determined under this section 5 in accordance with the definition of "**LIBOR**", "**EURIBOR**" or in relation to Loans in Canadian Dollars, "**CDOR**". Each LIBOR, EURIBOR or CDOR determination will be determined on the Quotation Day which refers to the day on which, in accordance with market practice for the relevant currency, rates are quoted. In this case, the "Relevant Markets" are the London interbank market, the European interbank market (in the case of EURIBOR) and the market for Canadian bankers' acceptances (in the case of CDOR). Quotations are ordinarily given two Business Days before the disbursement of the funds (or on the same day as disbursement in the case of sterling loans).

In the case of revolving loans, the Lenders' profit will be the Margin (on the assumption that they can fund themselves at the applicable LIBOR, EURIBOR or CDOR rate). During the period from 2010 to 2012 a number of European banks found it difficult to fund themselves in certain currencies at the applicable LIBOR rate. As a result, in some transactions a premium was added to the rate for borrowing in those currencies. This was sometimes expressed as an additional margin and sometimes was calculated by reference to a benchmark rate (such as, for dollar loans, the dollar/euro basis swap rate). A premium is not included in the sample agreement.

Clause 36.3 (*Day count convention*) states that each determination of interest will be calculated on the basis of the actual number of days elapsed and a year of 360 days.

### 13.1. Calculation of interest

The rate of interest on each Revolving Facility Loan for each Interest Period is the percentage rate per annum which is the aggregate of the applicable:

(a) Margin; and

(b) LIBOR or, in relation to any Revolving Facility Loan in euro, EURIBOR or, in relation to any Loan in a Non-LIBOR Currency, the Benchmark Rate for that currency.

### 13.2. Payment of interest

On the last day of each Interest Period the Borrower shall pay accrued interest on the Revolving Facility Loan to which that Interest Period relates (and, if the Interest Period is longer than six Months, on the dates falling at six Monthly intervals after the first day of the Interest Period).

### 13.3. Default interest

The rate at which default interest is charged will usually be 1%. or (sometimes) 2%. per annum above the normal rate charged on the loan. This is justified by the lenders on the basis that they suffer additional costs in time and money when there is a default and it is appropriate to charge more for the increased risk of lending, or continuing to lend, to a deteriorated credit. To the extent that the construction of the default interest Clause and the circumstances at the date of the facility agreement show that the interest charged under this Clause 13.3 is a genuine pre-estimate of the loss likely to be suffered by the Lenders on a default, the Clause will stand. However, if the Clause requires 'a payment of money stipulated as *in terrorem* of the offending party' so that he is discouraged from breaching the contract, the Clause will be void as being a penalty. The case of *Lordsvale Finance Plc v Bank of Zambia* TLR (1996) decided that an additional rate of 1%. was too modest to be construed as a penalty.

(a) If an Obligor fails to pay any amount payable by it under a Finance Document on its due date, interest shall accrue on the overdue amount from the due date up to the date of actual payment (both before and after judgment) at a rate which, subject to paragraph (b) below, is 1%. per annum higher than the rate which would have been payable if the overdue amount had, during the period of non-payment, constituted a Loan in the currency of the overdue amount for successive Interest Periods, each of a duration selected by the Agent (acting reasonably). Any interest accruing under this Clause 13.3 shall be immediately payable by the Obligor on demand by the Agent.

(b) If any overdue amount consists of all or part of a Loan which became due on a day which was not the last day of an Interest Period relating to that Loan:

(i) the first Interest Period for that overdue amount shall have a duration equal to the unexpired portion of the current Interest Period relating to that Loan; and

(ii) the rate of interest applying to the overdue amount during that first Interest Period shall be 1%. per annum higher than the rate which would have applied if the overdue amount had not become due.

(c) Default interest (if unpaid) arising on an overdue amount will be compounded with the overdue amount at the end of each Interest

Period applicable to that overdue amount but will remain immediately due and payable.

### 13.4. Notification of rates of interest

(a) The Agent shall promptly notify the Lenders and the Borrower of the determination of a rate of interest under this Agreement.

(b) The Agent shall promptly notify the Borrower of each Funding Rate relating to a Loan.

## 14. INTEREST PERIODS

### 14.1. Selection of Interest Periods

(a) The Borrower may select an Interest Period for a Loan in the Utilisation Request for that Loan.

(b) Subject to this Clause 14, the Borrower may select an Interest Period of one, three or six Months if the Loan is not in a Non-LIBOR Currency or, if the Loan is in a Non-LIBOR Currency, of any period specified in respect of that currency in Schedule 11 (*Other Benchmarks*) or, in either case, of any other period agreed between the Borrower, the Agent and all the Lenders in relation to the relevant Loan.

(c) An Interest Period for a Loan shall not extend beyond the Termination Date.

(d) Each Interest Period for a Loan shall start on the Utilisation Date.

(e) A Loan has one Interest Period only.

(f) Prior to the Syndication Date, Interest Periods shall be one Month or such other period as the Agent and the Borrower may agree and any Interest Period which would otherwise end during the Month preceding or extend beyond the Syndication Date shall end on the Syndication Date.

### 14.2. Non-Business Days

(a) Other than where paragraph (b) below applies, if an Interest Period would otherwise end on a day which is not a Business Day, that Interest Period will instead end on the next Business Day in that calendar month (if there is one) or the preceding Business Day (if there is not).

(b) If the Loan is in a Non-LIBOR Currency and there are rules specified as "Business Day Conventions" for that currency in Schedule 11 (*Other Benchmarks*), those rules shall apply to each Interest Period for that Loan.

## 15. CHANGES TO THE CALCULATION OF INTEREST

### 15.1. Unavailability of Screen Rate

Clauses 15.1 – 15.5 sets out a series of intermediate interest rate fallbacks which apply if the screen rate is unavailable. The LMA primary facility agreements contain two different approaches for the waterfall of fallbacks - the first approach (which is the approach included in this sample agreement) includes the use of historic screen rates as an intermediate step whereas the second approach does not use historic screen rates.

The first fallback is the use of an "Interpolated Screen Rate". It is customary to include this fallback to cover the scenario where "non-standard" interest periods are requested i.e., an interest period for which no screen rate is quoted. This is particularly relevant given that in 2013 LIBOR was discontinued for certain tenors - as at the date of publication, LIBOR is available for overnight, 1 week, 1, 2, 3, 6 and 12 month tenors.

In 2014, the LMA included optional additional fallbacks based on Historic Screen Rates and shortened Interest Periods. To the extent the Historic Screen Rate fallback is included, market practice is for such rate to be relatively recent, typically between 1 Business Day and 1 week old. If shortened Interest Periods are used then the relevant Fallback Interest Period should be the shortest time period possible for which the relevant Screen Rate is available. These additional fallbacks were introduced to reduce the likelihood that cost of funds would need to be relied upon.

If those fallbacks do not resolve the absence of a benchmark rate, the sample agreement provides for the use of Reference Bank Rates and if a Reference Bank Rate is not available then the Lenders' cost of funds is used (either on an individual basis or a weighted average of all Lenders' cost of funds). Relying on individual Lenders' costs of funds would clearly be very difficult from an operational perspective (as it requires the calculation of multiple rates) and is therefore only intended to be used for a short period in exceptional circumstances.

(a) *Interpolated Screen Rate*: If no Screen Rate is available for LIBOR or, if applicable, EURIBOR or, if applicable, the Benchmark Rate for the Interest Period of a Loan, the applicable LIBOR or EURIBOR or Benchmark Rate shall be the Interpolated Screen Rate for a period equal in length to the Interest Period of that Loan.

(b) *Shortened Interest Period*: If no Screen Rate is available for LIBOR or, if applicable, EURIBOR or, if applicable, the Benchmark Rate for:

(i) the currency of a Loan; or

(ii) the Interest Period of a Loan and it is not possible to calculate the Interpolated Screen Rate,

the Interest Period of that Loan shall (if it is longer than the applicable Fallback Interest Period) be shortened to the applicable Fallback Interest Period and the applicable LIBOR or EURIBOR or Benchmark Rate for that shortened Interest Period shall be determined pursuant to the relevant definition.

(c) *Shortened Interest Period and Historic Screen Rate*: If the Interest Period of a Loan is, after giving effect to paragraph (b) above, either the applicable Fallback Interest Period or shorter than the applicable Fallback Interest Period and, in either case, no Screen Rate is available for LIBOR or, if applicable EURIBOR or, if applicable, the Benchmark Rate for:

(i) the currency of that Loan; or

(ii) the Interest Period of that Loan and it is not possible to calculate the Interpolated Screen Rate,

the applicable LIBOR or EURIBOR or Benchmark Rate shall be the Historic Screen Rate for that Loan.

(d) *Shortened Interest Period and Interpolated Historic Screen Rate:* If paragraph (c) above applies but no Historic Screen Rate is available for the Interest Period of the Loan, the applicable LIBOR or EURIBOR or Benchmark Rate shall be the Interpolated Historic Screen Rate for a period equal in length to the Interest Period of that Loan.

(e) *Reference Bank Rate*: If paragraph (d) above applies but it is not possible to calculate the Interpolated Historic Screen Rate, the Interest Period of that Loan shall, if it has been shortened pursuant to paragraph (b) above, revert to its previous length and the applicable LIBOR or EURIBOR or Benchmark Rate shall be the Reference Bank Rate as of the Specified Time for the currency of that Loan and for a period equal in length to the Interest Period of that Loan there shall be no LIBOR or EURIBOR or Benchmark Rate for that Loan and Clause 15.4 (*Cost of funds*) shall apply to that Loan for that Interest Period.

(f) *Cost of funds*: If paragraph (e) above applies but no Reference Bank Rate is available for the relevant currency or Interest Period there shall be no LIBOR or EURIBOR or Benchmark Rate for that Loan and Clause 15.4 (*Cost of funds*) shall apply to that Loan for that Interest Period.

**15.2. Calculation of Reference Bank Rate**

(a) Subject to paragraph (b) below, if LIBOR or EURIBOR or a Benchmark Rate is to be determined on the basis of a Reference Bank Rate but a Reference Bank does not supply a quotation by the Specified Time, the Reference Bank Rate shall be calculated on the basis of the quotations of the remaining Reference Banks.

(b) If at or about:

(i) noon on the Quotation Day; or

(ii) in the case of a Benchmark Rate, the time specified in respect of the relevant currency in Schedule 11 (*Other Benchmarks*),

none or only one of the Reference Banks supplies a quotation, there shall be no Reference Bank Rate for the relevant Interest Period.

**15.3. Market disruption**

(a) If before:

(i) close of business in London on the Quotation Day for the relevant Interest Period; or

(ii) in the case of a Loan in a Non-LIBOR Currency, the time specified in respect of that currency in Schedule 11 (*Other Benchmarks*),

the Agent receives notifications from a Lender or Lenders (whose participations in a Loan exceed 35%. of that Loan) that the cost to it of funding its participation in that Loan from whatever source it may reasonably select would be in excess of LIBOR or, if applicable, EURIBOR or, if applicable, the Benchmark Rate then Clause 15.4 (*Cost of funds*) shall apply to that Loan for the relevant Interest Period.

**15.4. Cost of funds**

(a) If this Clause 15.4 applies, the rate of interest on each Lender's share of the relevant Loan for the relevant Interest Period shall be the percentage rate per annum which is the sum of:

(i) the Margin; and

(ii) the rate notified to the Agent by that Lender as soon as practicable and in any event within one Business Day of the first day of that Interest Period (or, if earlier, on the date falling three Business Days before the date on which interest is due to be paid in respect of that Interest Period), to be that which expresses as a percentage rate per annum the cost to the relevant Lender of funding its participation in that Loan from whatever source it may reasonably select.

(b) If this Clause 15.4 applies and the Agent or the Borrower so requires, the Agent and the Borrower shall enter into negotiations (for a period of not more than thirty days) with a view to agreeing a substitute basis for determining the rate of interest.

(c) Any alternative basis agreed pursuant to paragraph (b) above shall, with the prior consent of all the Lenders and the Borrower, be binding on all Parties.

(d) If this Clause 15.4 applies pursuant to Clause 15.3 (*Market disruption*) and:

(i) a Lender's Funding Rate is less than LIBOR or, in relation to any Loan in euro, EURIBOR or, in relation to any Loan in a Non-LIBOR Currency, the Benchmark Rate; or

(ii) a Lender does not supply a quotation by the time specified in paragraph (a)(ii) above,

the cost to that Lender of funding its participation in that Loan for that Interest Period shall be deemed, for the purposes of paragraph (a) above, to be LIBOR or, in relation to a Loan in euro, EURIBOR or, in relation to a Loan in a Non-LIBOR Currency, the Benchmark Rate.

(e) If this Clause 15.4 applies pursuant to Clause 15.1 (*Unavailability of Screen Rate*) but any Lender does not supply a quotation by the time specified in paragraph (a)(ii) above the rate of interest shall be calculated on the basis of the quotations of the remaining Lenders.

### 15.5. Notification to the Borrower

If Clause 15.4 (*Cost of funds*) applies the Agent shall, as soon as is practicable, notify the Borrower.

### 15.6. Break Costs

This Clause 15.6 is based on the assumption that for each Interest Period for which a principal amount is outstanding under the agreement, each Finance Party will fund itself in the relevant interbank market with a matching deposit. Accordingly, it is **provided that** if all or any part of a revolving loan or Unpaid Sum (which is unpaid default interest) is received otherwise than at the end of its current Interest Period the Borrower will pay to each relevant Finance Party the amount by which:

(i) the interest which a Lender should have received for the period from the date of receipt of prepayment to the end of the Interest Period, exceeds

(ii) the amount (if any) which the Lender would be able to obtain by depositing the same amount for the remainder of the Interest Period

The assumption which underlies this Clause 15.6 may not always be true. In the case of the Swingline Facility it clearly is untrue and, therefore, this facility is excluded from the ambit of the Clause. So far as the Revolving Facility is concerned, although many Lenders will not fund themselves with matching deposits, the methodology appears to be generally accepted in the loan market as a simple way of estimating a Lender's likely loss.

(a) The Borrower shall, within three Business Days of demand by a Finance Party, pay to that Finance Party its Break Costs attributable to all or any part of a Loan or Unpaid Sum being paid by the Borrower on a day other than the last day of an Interest Period for that Loan or Unpaid Sum.

(b) Each Lender shall, as soon as reasonably practicable after a demand by the Agent, provide a certificate confirming the amount of its Break Costs for any Interest Period in which they accrue.

## 16. FEES

### 16.1. Commitment fee

(a) The Borrower shall pay to the Agent (for the account of each Lender) a fee in the Base Currency computed at the rate of 35%. of the Margin on that Lender's Available Commitment for the Availability Period.

(b) The accrued commitment fee is payable on the last day of each successive period of three Months which ends during the Availability Period, on the last day of the Availability Period and, if cancelled in full, on the cancelled amount of the relevant Lender's Overall Commitment at the time the cancellation is effective.

(c) No commitment fee is payable to the Agent (for the account of a Lender) on any Available Commitment of that Lender for any day on which that Lender is a Defaulting Lender.

### 16.2. Utilisation fee

(a) The Borrower shall pay to the Agent (for the account of each Lender) a utilisation fee computed at the rate of:

(i) 0.15%. per annum for each day on which there are any Loans outstanding but the aggregate amount of Loans outstanding is less than or equal to 33.33%. of the Total Commitments as at the date of this Agreement;

(ii) 0.30%. per annum for each day on which the aggregate amount of Loans outstanding exceeds an amount equal to 33.33%. (but is less than or equal to 66.66%.) of the Total Commitments as at the date of this Agreement; and

(iii) 0.50%. per annum for each day on which the aggregate amount of Loans outstanding exceeds an amount equal to 66.66%. of the Total Commitments as at the date of this Agreement.

(b) The utilisation fee is payable on the aggregate amount of Loans outstanding on the relevant date for the account of each Lender in an amount equal to the proportion borne by such Lender's participation in the Loans outstanding on that date to such aggregate amount.

(c) The accrued utilisation fee is payable quarterly in arrear and is also payable to the Agent for the account of any Lender on the date that such Lender's Overall Commitment is cancelled and/or its share in the Loans prepaid or repaid in full.

### 16.3. Arrangement fee

The Borrower shall pay to the Arranger an arrangement fee in the amount and at the times agreed in a Fee Letter.

### 16.4. Agency fee

The Borrower shall pay to the Agent (for its own account) an agency fee in the amount and at the times agreed in a Fee Letter.

> The benefit of detailing the fees such as the arrangement fee and the agency fee in a separate letter rather than in the agreement is that the agent and arranger may keep confidential certain fees they are obtaining from a borrower. See the example fee letter at the end of this sample agreement.

# SECTION 6

## ADDITIONAL PAYMENT OBLIGATIONS

## 17. TAX GROSS-UP AND INDEMNITIES

### 17.1. Definitions

The purpose of this section 6 is to preserve the profit margin of each lender. The justification for this is that since lenders charge on a cost plus margin basis they have the right to be indemnified against all costs, no matter how incurred, other than overheads and overall net income taxes. However, in order not to impose an excessive charge on a borrower for the length of a deal, the borrower is customarily given the right to repay an individual lender if that lender makes certain claims under these provisions. Clause 12.5 (*Right of replacement or repayment and cancellation in relation to a single Lender*) of the sample agreement gives the Borrower this right in relation to paragraph (c) of Clause 17.2 (*Tax gross-up*), Clause 17.3 (*Tax indemnity*) and Clause 18.1 (*Increased costs*).

Paragraph (c) of Clause 17.2 (*Tax gross-up*) covers the imposition of a withholding tax on the Obligors, i.e., a tax levied by deduction at source. It is dealt with by requiring that, unless one of the circumstances set out in paragraph (d) of Clause 17.2 (*Tax gross-up*) applies, the payment from which the tax is deducted is to be grossed up so that after the appropriate deduction the lender receives a net sum equal to the sum which it would have received had no such deduction been required. It should be noted that the application of paragraph (c) of Clause 17.2 (*Tax gross-up*) is not restricted to changes which occur after the date of the agreement. In a deal involving many jurisdictions it is often not possible to be certain even at the date of the agreement that there are no withholding tax problems in any of these jurisdictions and the lenders insist that this small risk is borne by borrowers. Concerned borrowers can reduce this risk by incorporating a definition of "**Qualifying Lender**" which imposes restrictions as to which Lenders may claim the benefit of the gross-up provisions (essentially by requiring that each Lender should organise its participation in the Facilities in such a way as to meet any requirement of the relevant taxation laws (as at the date of the agreement) in order for the Borrower to be able to make payments without withholding tax). A "Qualifying Lender" concept has been included in the sample agreement even though, at the time of writing, The Netherlands does not impose a withholding tax on interest payments. This is because legislative changes have been announced by The Netherlands government introducing a withholding tax in certain types of abusive situations with effect from 2021. The "Qualifying Lender" wording should only impact certain (non-qualifying or non-compliant) Lenders who become a party to the Agreement after the introduction of withholding tax in The Netherlands, as before such date, all Lenders should qualify as "Dutch Qualifying Lenders".

Clause 17.3 (*Tax indemnity*) covers a tax (other than normal corporation tax) imposed on or in relation to sums received by any party or by the Agent on its behalf under the agreement.

The LMA's facility agreements provide that all parties are entitled to withhold tax when required to do so by the Foreign Account Tax Compliance Act (FATCA) and do not need to gross-up payments if a FATCA deduction is required. This means that any economic loss in respect of FATCA payments would be borne by the payee.

(a) In this Agreement:

"**Dutch Qualifying Lender**" means, in respect of any payment made under the Finance Documents by the Borrower, a Lender which is entitled to interest payable to that Lender in respect of an advance under a Finance Document and:

(i) is a Dutch Treaty Lender; or

(ii) is otherwise entitled to receive a payment of interest under this Agreement without any Tax Deduction imposed by The Netherlands.

"**Dutch Treaty Lender**" means, in relation to the Borrower, a Lender which:

(i) is treated as a resident of a Dutch Treaty State for the purposes of the Dutch Treaty;

(ii) does not carry on a business in The Netherlands through a permanent establishment with which that Lender's participation in the Loan is effectively connected; and

(iii) fulfils any other conditions (other than the completion of necessary procedural formalities) which must be fulfilled under the Dutch Treaty or Dutch domestic law by residents of that Dutch Treaty State for such residents to obtain a full exemption from Tax on interest imposed by The Netherlands.

"**Dutch Treaty State**" means a jurisdiction having a double taxation agreement (a "**Dutch Treaty**") with The Netherlands which makes provision for a full exemption from tax imposed by The Netherlands on interest.

"**Protected Party**" means a Finance Party which is or will be subject to any liability, or required to make any payment, for or on account of Tax in relation to a sum received or receivable (or any sum deemed for the purposes of Tax to be received or receivable) under a Finance Document.

"**Tax Credit**" means a credit against, relief or remission for, or repayment of any Tax.

"**Tax Deduction**" means a deduction or withholding for or on account of Tax from a payment under a Finance Document other than a FATCA Deduction.

"**Tax Payment**" means either the increase in a payment made by an Obligor to a Finance Party under Clause 17.2 (*Tax gross-up*) or a payment under Clause 17.3 (*Tax indemnity*).

(b) Unless a contrary indication appears, in this Clause 17 a reference to "**determines**" or "**determined**" means a determination made in the absolute discretion of the person making the determination.

**17.2. Tax gross-up**

(a) Each Obligor shall make all payments to be made by it without any Tax Deduction, unless a Tax Deduction is required by law.

(b) The Borrower shall promptly upon becoming aware that an Obligor must make a Tax Deduction (or that there is any change in the rate or the basis of a Tax Deduction) notify the Agent accordingly. Similarly, a Lender shall notify the Agent on becoming so aware in respect of a payment payable to that Lender. If the Agent receives such notification from a Lender it shall notify each Obligor.

(c) If a Tax Deduction is required by law to be made by an Obligor, the amount of the payment due from that Obligor shall be increased to an amount which (after making any Tax Deduction) leaves an amount equal to the payment which would have been due if no Tax Deduction had been required.

(d) A payment by the Borrower shall not be increased under paragraph (c) above by reason of a Tax Deduction on account of Tax imposed by The Netherlands, if on the date on which the payment falls due:

(i) the payment could have been made to the relevant Lender without a Tax Deduction if the Lender had been a Dutch Qualifying Lender, but on that date that Lender is not or has ceased to be a Dutch Qualifying Lender other than as a result of any change after the date it became a Lender under this Agreement in (or in the interpretation, administration, or application of) any law or Dutch Treaty, or any published practice or published concession of any relevant taxing authority; or

(ii) the Obligor making the payment is able to demonstrate that the payment could have been made to the Lender without the Tax Deduction had that Lender complied with its obligations under paragraph (g) below.

(e) If an Obligor is required to make a Tax Deduction, that Obligor shall make that Tax Deduction and any payment required in connection with that Tax Deduction within the time allowed and in the minimum amount required by law.

(f) Within thirty days of making either a Tax Deduction or any payment required in connection with that Tax Deduction, the Obligor making that Tax Deduction shall deliver to the Agent for the Finance Party entitled to the payment evidence reasonably satisfactory to that Finance Party that the Tax Deduction has been made or (as applicable) any appropriate payment paid to the relevant Tax Authority.

(g) A Lender and each Obligor which makes a payment to which that Lender is entitled shall co-operate in completing any procedural formalities necessary for that Obligor to obtain authorisation to make that payment without a Tax Deduction.

**17.3. Tax indemnity**

(a) The Borrower shall (within three Business Days of demand by the Agent) pay to a Protected Party an amount equal to the loss, liability or cost which that Protected Party determines will be or has been (directly or indirectly) suffered for or on account of Tax by that Protected Party in respect of a Finance Document.

(b) Paragraph (a) above shall not apply:

(i) with respect to any Tax assessed on a Finance Party:

(A) under the law of the jurisdiction in which that Finance Party is incorporated or, if different, the jurisdiction (or jurisdictions) in which that Finance Party is treated as resident for tax purposes; or

(B) under the law of the jurisdiction in which that Finance Party's Facility Office is located in respect of amounts received or receivable in that jurisdiction, if that Tax is imposed on or calculated by reference to the net income received or receivable (but not any sum deemed to be received or receivable) by that Finance Party; or

(ii) to the extent a loss, liability or cost:

(A) is compensated for by an increased payment under Clause 17.2 (*Tax gross-up*);

(B) would have been compensated for by an increased payment under Clause 17.2 (*Tax gross-up*) but was not so compensated solely because one of the exclusions in paragraph (d) of Clause 17.2 (*Tax gross-up*) applied; or

(C) relates to a FATCA Deduction required to be made by a Party.

(c) A Protected Party making, or intending to make a claim under paragraph (a) above shall promptly notify the Agent of the event which will give, or has given, rise to the claim, following which the Agent shall notify the Borrower.

(d) A Protected Party shall, on receiving a payment from an Obligor under this Clause 17.3, notify the Agent.

**17.4. Tax Credit**

If an Obligor makes a Tax Payment and the relevant Finance Party determines that:

(a) a Tax Credit is attributable to an increased payment of which that Tax Payment forms part, to that Tax Payment or to a Tax Deduction in consequence of which that Tax Payment was required; and

(b) that Finance Party has obtained and utilised that Tax Credit,

the Finance Party shall pay an amount to that Obligor which that Finance Party determines will leave it (after that payment) in the same after-Tax position as it would have been in had the Tax Payment not been required to be made by that Obligor.

**17.5. Lender Status Confirmation**

(a) Each Lender which is not an Original Lender shall indicate, in the documentation which it executes on becoming a Party as a Lender, and for the benefit of the Agent and without liability to any Obligor, which of the following categories it falls in:

(i) not a Dutch Qualifying Lender;

(ii) a Dutch Qualifying Lender (other than a Dutch Treaty Lender); or

(iii) a Dutch Treaty Lender.

If such a Lender fails to indicate its status in accordance with this paragraph (a) then that Lender shall be treated for the purposes of this Agreement (including by each Obligor) as if it is not a Dutch Qualifying Lender until such time as it notifies the Agent which category applies (and the Agent, upon receipt of such notification, shall inform the Borrower). For the avoidance of doubt, the documentation which a Lender executes on becoming a Party as a Lender shall not be invalidated by any failure of a Lender to comply with this paragraph (a).

(b) Such a Lender shall also specify, in the documentation which it executes on becoming a Party as a Lender, whether it is incorporated or acting through a Facility Office situated in a Non-Cooperative Jurisdiction. For the avoidance of doubt, the documentation which a Lender executes on becoming a Party as a Lender shall not be invalidated by any failure of a Lender to comply with this paragraph (b).

**17.6. Stamp taxes**

The Borrower shall pay and, within three Business Days of demand, indemnify each Finance Party against any cost, loss or liability that Finance Party incurs in relation to all stamp duty, registration and other similar Taxes payable in respect of any Finance Document.

**17.7. VAT**

(a) All amounts expressed to be payable under a Finance Document by any Party to a Finance Party which (in whole or in part) constitute the consideration for any supply for VAT purposes are deemed to be exclusive of any VAT which is chargeable on that supply, and accordingly, subject to paragraph (b) below, if VAT is or becomes chargeable on any supply made by any Finance Party to any Party under a Finance Document and such Finance Party is required to account to the relevant tax authority for the VAT, that Party must pay to such Finance Party (in addition to and at the same time as paying any other consideration for such supply) an amount equal to the amount of the VAT (and such Finance Party must promptly provide an appropriate VAT invoice to that Party).

(b) If VAT is or becomes chargeable on any supply made by any Finance Party (the "**Supplier**") to any other Finance Party (the "**Recipient**") under a Finance Document, and any Party other than the Recipient (the "**Relevant Party**") is required by the terms of any Finance Document to pay an amount equal to the consideration for that supply to the Supplier (rather than being required to reimburse or indemnify the Recipient in respect of that consideration):

(i) (where the Supplier is the person required to account to the relevant tax authority for the VAT) the Relevant Party must also pay to the Supplier (at the same time as paying that amount) an additional amount equal to the amount of the VAT. The Recipient must (where this paragraph (i) applies) promptly pay to the Relevant Party an amount equal to any credit or repayment the Recipient receives from the relevant tax authority which the Recipient reasonably determines relates to the VAT chargeable on that supply; and

(ii) (where the Recipient is the person required to account to the relevant tax authority for the VAT) the Relevant Party must promptly, following demand from the Recipient, pay to the Recipient an amount equal to the VAT chargeable on that supply but only to the extent that the Recipient reasonably determines that it is not entitled to credit or repayment from the relevant tax authority in respect of that VAT.

(c) Where a Finance Document requires any Party to reimburse or indemnify a Finance Party for any cost or expense, that Party shall reimburse or indemnify (as the case may be) such Finance Party for the full amount of such cost or expense, including such part thereof as represents VAT, save to the extent that such Finance Party reasonably determines that it is entitled to credit or repayment in respect of such VAT from the relevant tax authority.

(d) Any reference in this Clause 17.7 to any Party shall, at any time when such Party is treated as a member of a group for VAT purposes, include (where appropriate and unless the context otherwise requires) a reference to any person who is treated as making the supply, or (as appropriate) receiving the supply, under the grouping rules (as set out in Article 11 of Council Directive 2006/112/EC or as implemented by a member state of the European Union).

(e) In relation to any supply made by a Finance Party to any Party under a Finance Document, if reasonably requested by such Finance Party, that Party must promptly provide such Finance Party with details of that Party's VAT registration and such other information as is reasonably requested in connection with such Finance Party's VAT reporting requirements in relation to such supply.

**17.8. FATCA information**

(a) Subject to paragraph (b) below, each Party shall, within ten Business Days of a reasonable request by another Party:

(i) confirm to that other Party whether it is:

(A) a FATCA Exempt Party; or

(B) not a FATCA Exempt Party;

(ii) supply to that other Party such forms, documentation and other information relating to its status under FATCA as that other Party reasonably requests for the purposes of that other Party's compliance with FATCA; and

(iii) supply to that other Party such forms, documentation and other information relating to its status as that other Party reasonably requests for the purposes of that other Party's compliance with any other law, regulation, or exchange of information regime.

(b) If a Party confirms to another Party pursuant to paragraph (a)(i) above that it is a FATCA Exempt Party and it subsequently becomes aware that it is not or has ceased to be a FATCA Exempt Party, that Party shall notify that other Party reasonably promptly.

(c) Paragraph (a) above shall not oblige any Finance Party to do anything, and paragraph (a)(iii) above shall not oblige any other Party to do anything, which would or might in its reasonable opinion constitute a breach of:

(i) any law or regulation;

(ii) any fiduciary duty; or

(iii) any duty of confidentiality.

(d) If a Party fails to confirm whether or not it is a FATCA Exempt Party or to supply forms, documentation or other information requested in accordance with paragraph (a)(i) or (a)(ii) above (including, for the avoidance of doubt, where paragraph (c) above applies), then such Party shall be treated for the purposes of the Finance Documents (and payments under them) as if it is not a FATCA Exempt Party until such time as the Party in question provides the requested confirmation, forms, documentation or other information.

**17.9. FATCA Deduction**

(a) Each Party may make any FATCA Deduction it is required to make by FATCA, and any payment required in connection with that FATCA Deduction, and no Party shall be required to increase any payment in respect of which it makes such a FATCA Deduction or otherwise compensate the recipient of the payment for that FATCA Deduction.

(b) Each Party shall promptly, upon becoming aware that it must make a FATCA Deduction (or that there is any change in the rate or the basis of such FATCA Deduction), notify the Party to whom it is making the payment and, in addition, shall notify the Borrower and the Agent and the Agent shall notify the other Finance Parties.

**18. Increased Costs**

This Clause sets out the indemnity given by the Borrower in respect of an "Increased Cost" as described in paragraph (b)(i) of Clause 18.1 (*Increased costs*). In order for Lenders to be able to make a claim there must be either a change in law (or its interpretation or application) or there must be some compliance with a law or regulation made after the date of the Agreement. Costs resulting from Basel II are expressly excluded from the increased costs provision on the basis that Basel II has been in force for some time (and therefore Lenders should be able accurately to estimate any costs arising under it in connection with their participation in syndicated loan facilities and incorporate such costs as part of the Margin).

The European legislation which implements Basel III (known as CRD IV) came into force on 1 January 2014. Given that the implementing legislation is in force, borrowers often argue that costs associated with Basel III should already be factored into pricing and therefore such costs should not be capable of being claimed under the increased costs provision. However, lenders often seek expressly to include costs associated with Basel III on the basis that such costs are not yet sufficiently certain to be able to be taken into account when pricing a deal. In this sample agreement, Basel III costs have been expressly included.

To the extent borrowers agree to Basel III costs being included, then they often seek to limit the scope of any claims, for instance by requiring claims to be made within a certain period of time and/or only permitting claims to be made to the extent they relate to costs that were not capable of being determined when the facility agreement was entered into.

Basel III was modified in December 2017 by a package of changes informally known as "Basel IV". Regulators have indicated that they consider Basel IV to be an upgrade of Basel III rather than a separate new capital standard. Despite this, it is possible that some banks may push to include a reference to Basel IV (and CRR2) when carving Basel III back in, to ensure that any increased costs resulting from Basel IV are within scope.

### 18.1. Increased costs

(a) Subject to Clause 18.3 (*Exceptions*) the Borrower shall, within three Business Days of a demand by the Agent, pay for the account of a Finance Party the amount of any Increased Costs incurred by that Finance Party or any of its Affiliates as a result of:

(i) the introduction of or any change in (or in the interpretation, administration or application of) any law or regulation after the date of this Agreement;

(ii) compliance with any law or regulation made after the date of this Agreement;

(iii) the implementation or application of, or compliance with, Basel III or any law or regulation that implements or applies Basel III; or

(iv) compliance with the Dodd Frank Wall Street Reform and Consumer Protection Act or any law or regulation made under, or connected with, that Act.

(b) In this Agreement:

(i) "**Increased Costs**" means:

(A) a reduction in the rate of return from a Facility or on a Finance Party's (or its Affiliate's) overall capital;

(B) an additional or increased cost; or

(C) a reduction of any amount due and payable under any Finance Document, which is incurred or suffered by a Finance Party or any of its Affiliates to the extent that it is attributable to that Finance Party having entered into its Commitment or Swingline Commitment or funding or performing its obligations under any Finance Document; and

(ii) "**Basel III**" means:

(A) the agreements on capital requirements, a leverage ratio and liquidity standards contained in "Basel III: A global regulatory framework for more resilient banks and banking systems", "Basel III: International framework for liquidity risk measurement, standards and monitoring" and "Guidance for national authorities operating the countercyclical capital buffer" published by the Basel Committee on Banking Supervision in December 2010, each as amended, supplemented or restated;

(B) the rules for global systemically important banks contained in "Global systemically important banks: assessment methodology and the additional loss absorbency requirement - Rules text" published by the Basel Committee on Banking Supervision in November 2011, as amended, supplemented or restated; and

(C) any further guidance or standards published by the Basel Committee on Banking Supervision relating to "Basel III".

**18.2. Increased cost claims**

(a) A Finance Party intending to make a claim pursuant to Clause 18.1 (*Increased costs*) shall notify the Agent of the event giving rise to the claim, following which the Agent shall promptly notify the Borrower.

(b) Each Finance Party shall, as soon as practicable after a demand by the Agent, provide a certificate confirming the amount of its Increased Costs.

**18.3. Exceptions**

(a) Clause 18.1 (*Increased costs*) does not apply to the extent any Increased Cost is:

(i) attributable to a Tax Deduction required by law to be made by an Obligor;

(ii) attributable to a FATCA Deduction required to be made by a Party;

(iii) compensated for by Clause 17.3 (*Tax indemnity*) (or would have been compensated for under Clause 17.3 (*Tax indemnity*) but was not so compensated solely because any of the exclusions in paragraph (b) of Clause 17.3 (*Tax indemnity*) applied);

(iv) attributable to the wilful breach by the relevant Finance Party or its Affiliates of any law or regulation;

(v) attributable to the implementation of or compliance with the "International Convergence of Capital Measurement and Capital Standards, a Revised Framework" published by the Basel Committee on Banking Supervision in June 2004 in the form existing on the date of this Agreement (but excluding any amendment arising out of Basel III) ("**Basel II**") or any other law or regulation which implements Basel II (whether such implementation, application or compliance is by a government, regulator, Finance Party or any of its Affiliates); or

(vi) attributable to the United Kingdom bank levy as set out in the Finance Act 2011 or the Dutch bank levy (*Wet bankenbelasting*) or any levy or Tax of a similar nature in force as at the date of this Agreement and imposed in any jurisdiction by reference to the assets or liabilities of a financial institution or other entity carrying out financial transactions.

The above reference to excluding costs relating to certain bank levy costs from the increased costs indemnity is sometimes agreed by lenders at the request of borrowers. If accepted, this exclusion would normally refer only to any bank levy which is in force as at the date of the relevant facility agreement (rather than to any proposed bank levy which has not yet been enacted).

(b) In this Clause 18.3, a reference to a "**Tax Deduction**" has the same meaning given to that term in Clause 17.1 (*Definitions*).

## 19. OTHER INDEMNITIES

It is now well-established practice that English courts will, if requested, give judgments in foreign currencies. However, English courts retain a discretion to substitute a judgment in sterling. In addition, foreign courts (either in enforcing an English judgment or in making their own judgment) may take a different approach. Therefore, provision is made in Clause 19.1 (*Currency indemnity*) for the company to indemnify the other parties against any loss suffered by reason of any discrepancy in the rates of exchange used for the purposes mentioned in the Clause.

It should be noted that English courts might regard a final judgment on an agreement as discharging entirely the obligations created by the agreement including, in the case of the sample agreement, the indemnity on the part of the Borrower contained in Clause 30.3 (*Duties of the Agent*).

### 19.1. Currency indemnity

(a) If any sum due from an Obligor under the Finance Documents (a "**Sum**"), or any order, judgment or award given or made in relation to a Sum, has to be converted from the currency (the "**First Currency**") in which that Sum is payable into another currency (the "**Second Currency**") for the purpose of:

(i) making or filing a claim or proof against that Obligor;

(ii) obtaining or enforcing an order, judgment or award in relation to any litigation or arbitration proceedings,

that Obligor shall as an independent obligation, within three Business Days of demand, indemnify each Finance Party to whom that Sum is due against any cost, loss or liability arising out of or as a result of the conversion including any discrepancy between (A) the rate of exchange used to convert that Sum from the First Currency into the Second Currency and (B) the rate or rates of exchange available to that person at the time of its receipt of that Sum.

(b) Each Obligor waives any right it may have in any jurisdiction to pay any amount under the Finance Documents in a currency or currency unit other than that in which it is expressed to be payable.

### 19.2. Other indemnities

A borrower will be required to give lenders a general indemnity against any losses or expenses which they suffer as a result of the borrower's default. This, like default interest, is clearly applicable regardless of whether an Event of Default is formally declared by the lenders.

Each Obligor shall, within three Business Days of demand, indemnify each Finance Party against any cost, loss or liability incurred by that Finance Party as a result of:

(a) the occurrence of any Event of Default;

(b) a failure by an Obligor to pay any amount due under a Finance Document on its due date, including without limitation, any cost, loss or liability arising as a result of Clause 32 (*Sharing Among the Finance Parties*);

(c) funding, or making arrangements to fund, its participation in a Loan requested by the Borrower in a Utilisation Request but not made by reason of the operation of any one or more of the provisions of this Agreement (other than by reason of default or negligence by that Finance Party alone); or

(d) a Loan (or part of a Loan) not being prepaid in accordance with a notice of prepayment given by the Borrower.

### 19.3. Indemnity to the Agent

The Borrower shall promptly indemnify the Agent against any cost, loss or liability incurred by the Agent (acting reasonably) as a result of:

(a) investigating any event which it reasonably believes is a Default;

(b) acting or relying on any notice, request or instruction which it reasonably believes to be genuine, correct and appropriately authorised; or

(c) instructing lawyers, accountants, tax advisers, surveyors or other professional advisers or experts as permitted under this Agreement.

## 20. MITIGATION BY THE LENDERS

### 20.1. Mitigation

(a) Each Finance Party shall, in consultation with the Borrower, take all reasonable steps to mitigate any circumstances which arise and which would result in any amount becoming payable under or pursuant to, or cancelled pursuant to, any of Clause 12.1 (*Illegality*), Clause 17 (*Tax Gross-up and Indemnities*) or Clause 18 (*Increased Costs*) or in any amount payable under a Finance Document by an Obligor established in France becoming not deductible from that Obligor's taxable income for French tax purposes by reason of that amount being (i) paid or accrued to a Finance Party incorporated, domiciled, established or acting through a Facility Office situated in a Non-Cooperative Jurisdiction or (ii) paid to an account opened in the name of or for the benefit of that Finance Party in a financial institution situated in a Non-Cooperative Jurisdiction, including (but not limited to) transferring its rights and obligations under the Finance Documents to another Affiliate or Facility Office.

(b) Paragraph (a) above does not in any way limit the obligations of any Obligor under the Finance Documents.

### 20.2. Limitation of liability

(a) The Borrower shall promptly indemnify each Finance Party for all costs and expenses reasonably incurred by that Finance Party as a result of steps taken by it under Clause 20.1 (*Mitigation*).

(b) A Finance Party is not obliged to take any steps under Clause 20.1 (*Mitigation*) if, in the opinion of that Finance Party (acting reasonably), to do so might be prejudicial to it.

## 21. COSTS AND EXPENSES

### 21.1. Transaction expenses

The Borrower shall promptly on demand pay the Agent and the Arranger the amount of all costs and expenses (including legal fees subject to any agreed caps) reasonably incurred by any of them in connection with the negotiation, preparation, printing, execution and syndication of:

(a) this Agreement and any other documents referred to in this Agreement; and

(b) any other Finance Documents executed after the date of this Agreement.

### 21.2. Amendment costs

If:

(a) an Obligor requests an amendment, waiver or consent;

(b) an amendment is required pursuant to Clause 33.10 (*Change of currency*); or

(c) any amendment or waiver is contemplated or agreed pursuant to Clause 39.4 (*Replacement of Screen Rate*),

the Borrower shall, within three Business Days of demand, reimburse the Agent for the amount of all costs and expenses (including legal fees subject to any agreed caps) reasonably incurred by the Agent in responding to, evaluating, negotiating, complying with or implementing that request, requirement or actual or contemplated agreement.

> It will need to be agreed on each deal how the responsibility for the costs and expenses relating to any amendment or waiver contemplated by the Replacement of Screen Rate Clause are allocated. In this agreement it has been agreed that the Borrower will cover these costs.

### 21.3. Enforcement costs

The Borrower shall, within three Business Days of demand, pay to each Finance Party the amount of all costs and expenses (including legal fees) incurred by it in connection with the enforcement of, or the preservation of any rights under, any Finance Document.

# SECTION 7

## GUARANTEE

## 22. GUARANTEE AND INDEMNITY

In addition to the principal purpose of ensuring that, if a borrower does not meet its obligations under an agreement then the guarantor will, a guarantee also serves two other purposes: it ensures that the guarantor exercises a supervisory function over a borrower and, in certain circumstances, secures non-interference from the guarantor. The latter purpose would arise, for example, where a central bank is guaranteeing a borrower's obligation and the lenders wish to ensure that it will not impose exchange controls etc., to the detriment of the borrower's ability to repay.

The guarantee in this Clause 22 has two principal obligations: the first is a true guarantee (i.e., secondary undertaking) of the Borrower's observance and performance of its obligations under the agreement and the second is an indemnity (i.e., a primary undertaking to cover the situation where if the Borrower does not have the necessary capacity to enter into the agreement or for some other reason is held by law not to have to meet its obligations under the agreement, then the Guarantor will do so). The indemnity is required in the second situation because without it a guarantor cannot be liable where the underlying debtor is not liable. As a matter of law it is a question of construction whether an agreement which is purported to be made between a number of parties is binding on any of the parties if one party proves not to have had the capacity to enter into the agreement. Paragraph (c) of Clause 22.1 (*Guarantee and indemnity*) is drafted to make it clear that the Guarantor will be under an obligation to the other parties to the agreement should the Borrower be found not to have validly entered the agreement.

The remaining provisions of this Clause 22 are generally referred to as the preservation of rights provisions. These are needed to preserve the rights of beneficiaries against guarantors because the general law gives guarantors certain rights to deny liability under guarantees if, for example, the underlying agreement has been amended without their consent or obligations of the borrower or other sureties have been waived.

### 22.1. Guarantee and indemnity

The Guarantor irrevocably and unconditionally:

(a) guarantees to each Finance Party punctual performance by the Borrower of all the Borrower's obligations under the Finance Documents;

(b) undertakes with each Finance Party that whenever the Borrower does not pay any amount when due under or in connection with any Finance Document, the Guarantor shall immediately on demand pay that amount as if it was the principal obligor; and

(c) agrees with each Finance Party that if any obligation guaranteed by it is or becomes unenforceable, invalid or illegal it will, as an independent and primary obligation, indemnify that Finance Party immediately on demand against any cost, loss or liability it incurs as a result of the Borrower not paying any amount which would, but for such unenforceability, invalidity or illegality, have been payable by it under any Finance Document on the date when it would have been due. The amount payable by the Guarantor under this indemnity will not exceed the amount it would have had to pay under this Clause 22 if the amount claimed had been recoverable on the basis of a guarantee.

### 22.2. Continuing guarantee

The statement that the guarantee is "**continuing**" conveys the parties' agreement that the guarantee will cover a borrower's obligations in respect of loans made from time to time in the future.

This guarantee is a continuing guarantee and will extend to the ultimate balance of sums payable by the Borrower under the Finance Documents, regardless of any intermediate payment or discharge in whole or in part.

### 22.3. Reinstatement

Insolvency and similar laws in some jurisdictions provide for return to a troubled company, or to a trustee or similar official appointed with respect to the company or its property, of certain kinds of payments made by the company, often within specified periods before the filing or commencement of insolvency or similar proceedings. This Clause 22.3 provides for the guarantee to continue in effect, or to be reinstated, if all or part of any payment by the Borrower to the Agent or any of the lenders has to be returned or is rescinded under such circumstances or otherwise.

If any discharge, release or arrangement (whether in respect of the obligations of any Obligor or any security for those obligations or otherwise) is made by a Finance Party in whole or in part on the basis of any payment, security or other disposition which is avoided or must be restored in insolvency, liquidation, administration or otherwise, without limitation, then the liability of the Guarantor under this Clause 22 will continue or be reinstated as if the discharge, release or arrangement had not occurred.

### 22.4. Waiver of defences

The obligations of the Guarantor under this Clause 22 will not be affected by any act, omission, matter or thing which, but for this Clause, would reduce, release or prejudice any of its obligations under this Clause 22 (without limitation and whether or not known to it or any Finance Party) including:

(a) any time, waiver or consent granted to, or composition with, the Borrower or other person;

(b) the release of the Borrower or any other person under the terms of any composition or arrangement with any creditor of any member of the Group;

(c) the taking, variation, compromise, exchange, renewal or release of, or refusal or neglect to perfect, take up or enforce, any rights against, or security over assets of, the Borrower or other person or any non-presentation or non-observance of any formality or other requirement in respect of any instrument or any failure to realise the full value of any security;

(d) any incapacity or lack of power, authority or legal personality of or dissolution or change in the members or status of the Borrower or any other person;

(e) any amendment, novation, supplement, extension or restatement (however fundamental and whether or not more onerous) or replacement of a Finance Document or any other document or security including without limitation any change in the purpose of, any extension of, or any increase in, any facility or the addition of any new facility under any Finance Document or other document;

(f) any unenforceability, illegality or invalidity of any obligation of any person under any Finance Document or any other document or security; or

(g) any insolvency or similar proceedings.

### 22.5. Immediate recourse

The Guarantor waives any right it may have of first requiring any Finance Party (or any trustee or agent on its behalf) to proceed against or enforce any other rights or security or claim payment from any person before claiming from the Guarantor under this Clause 22. This waiver applies irrespective of any law or any provision of a Finance Document to the contrary.

### 22.6. Appropriations

Until all amounts which may be or become payable by the Borrower under or in connection with the Finance Documents have been irrevocably paid in full, each Finance Party (or any trustee or agent on its behalf) may:

(a) refrain from applying or enforcing any other moneys, security or rights held or received by that Finance Party (or any trustee or agent on its behalf) in respect of those amounts, or apply and enforce the same in such manner and order as it sees fit (whether against those amounts or otherwise) and the Guarantor shall not be entitled to the benefit of the same; and

(b) hold in an interest-bearing suspense account any moneys received from the Guarantor or on account of the Guarantor's liability under this Clause 22.

### 22.7. Deferral of Guarantor's rights

Until all amounts which may be or become payable by the Borrower under or in connection with the Finance Documents have been irrevocably paid in full and unless the Agent otherwise directs, the Guarantor will not exercise any rights which it may have by reason of performance by it of its obligations under the Finance Documents or by reason of any amount being payable, or liability arising, under this Clause 22:

(a) to be indemnified by the Borrower;

(b) to claim any contribution from any other guarantor of the Borrower's obligations under the Finance Documents;

(c) to take the benefit (in whole or in part and whether by way of subrogation or otherwise) of any rights of the Finance Parties under the Finance Documents or of any other guarantee or security taken pursuant to, or in connection with, the Finance Documents by any Finance Party;

(d) to bring legal or other proceedings for an order requiring the Borrower to make any payment, or perform any obligation, in respect of which the Guarantor has given a guarantee, undertaking or indemnity under Clause 22.1 (*Guarantee and indemnity*);

(e) to exercise any right of set-off against the Borrower; and/or

(f) to claim or prove as a creditor of the Borrower in competition with any Finance Party.

If the Guarantor receives any benefit, payment or distribution in relation to such rights it shall hold that benefit, payment or distribution to the extent necessary to enable all amounts which may be or become payable to the Finance Parties by the Borrower under or in connection with the Finance Documents to be repaid in full on trust for the Finance Parties and shall promptly pay or transfer the same to the Agent or as the Agent may direct for application in accordance with Clause 33 (*Payment Mechanics*).

Guarantees customarily include limitations on the guarantor's rights of subrogation i.e., the right of the guarantor which has discharged the debt it has guaranteed to step into the shoes of the creditor and take over by subrogation the creditor's rights against the debtor in respect of the debt and all the securities held by the creditor for payment of the debt. This Clause 22.7 effectively constitutes a waiver of such rights until final satisfaction of all sums owing by the borrower to the lenders.

### 22.8. Additional security

This guarantee is in addition to and is not in any way prejudiced by any other guarantee or security now or subsequently held by any Finance Party.

# SECTION 8

## REPRESENTATIONS, UNDERTAKINGS AND EVENTS OF DEFAULT

### 23. REPRESENTATIONS

The functions fulfilled by the representations are: (a) to provide for certain contractual "**internal**" remedies within the framework of the facility agreement, (b) (to a lesser extent) to give the lenders the benefit of certain remedies available under the general law, and (c) to provide the lenders with full information in the course of their negotiations.

(a) *The internal remedies*

(i) *Suspension*: One of the conditions precedent to a borrower's right to draw down any part of the facility is the accuracy of all the representations. Accordingly, on the discovery of the inaccuracy of a representation, lenders may suspend the making of further loans under an agreement until such time as either the circumstances have changed so that the representation concerned is accurate or the lenders agree to waive this condition precedent.

(ii) *Cancellation*: The second remedy provided within the facility agreement is also available only to the extent that the full amount of the facility has not been drawn down. As stated above, it is an Event of Default if any representation made by a borrower proves to have been incorrect or misleading when made (Clause 27.4 (*Misrepresentation*)). In such circumstances one of the remedies available to the lenders will be the cancellation of the undrawn Commitments. The decision to cancel will usually, as in this sample agreement, require a positive decision by a significant grouping of lenders – the "**Majority Lenders**".

(iii) *Acceleration*: The other remedy arising from a misrepresentation Event of Default, again exercisable on the instructions of the Majority Lenders, is the right to declare the loan immediately due and repayable. In other words, the liability of a borrower is rendered immediately current and the borrower is obliged to pay the balance of the loan and accrued interest to the lenders at once. In practice, it is recognised that a borrower may be unlikely to be able to satisfy this obligation and the danger to the borrower is that it may cause its other creditors to accelerate their indebtedness by virtue of cross-default Clauses. However, the power to render the repayment obligation current is needed by the lenders in order that they may speedily take any necessary action against a borrower or any of the borrower's assets so as to protect their position.

(b) *Remedies under general law*

The protection given to lenders in respect of the representations under the general law are less significant than those expressly provided in the facility agreement. In certain circumstances a person who has been induced to enter into a contract by a misleading representation has rights to rescind the contract, treating it as having become void, and/or to claim damages. This area of law is rather complicated, the remedies being different in the cases of fraudulent, negligent and innocent misrepresentations and being, to some extent, discretionary. In cases such as syndicated facility agreements, where representations have been incorporated as terms of the contract, the relationship between the remedies for misrepresentation and those for breach of warranty is unclear. However, such remedies will not usually give lenders any rights against borrowers which they would not otherwise have under a properly drawn facility agreement, and such remedies are unlikely, because of their uncertainty, to be enforced without litigation.

(c) *Investigative function*

One purpose of inserting representations in the draft facility agreement is to give borrowers and their lawyers and lenders' lawyers every opportunity to say that the representation is inaccurate and must be qualified or amended. Once the facility agreement is signed and the money advanced, it is too late to make discoveries of this sort: they must be made as early as possible.

Each Obligor makes the representations and warranties set out in this Clause 23 to each Finance Party on the date of this Agreement.

**23.1. Status**

(a) It is a corporation, duly incorporated and validly existing under the law of its jurisdiction of incorporation.

(b) It and each of its Subsidiaries has the power to own its assets and carry on its business as it is being conducted.

**23.2. Binding obligations**

The obligations expressed to be assumed by it in each Finance Document are, subject to the Legal Reservations, legal, valid, binding and enforceable obligations.

**23.3. Non-conflict with other obligations**

The entry into and performance by it of, and the transactions contemplated by, the Finance Documents do not and will not conflict with:

(a) any law or regulation applicable to it;

(b) its or any of its Subsidiaries' constitutional documents; or

(c) any agreement or instrument binding upon it or any of its Subsidiaries or any of its or any of its Subsidiaries' assets.

### 23.4. Power and authority

This representation is concerned with the capacity of the Borrower and the Guarantor to enter into the agreement. Since it may not be possible to correct a breach of this representation subsequently, its effectiveness is primarily to give rise to an Event of Default to enable the Lenders to get out of their commitment to lend. In deciding whether an Obligor has power to enter into the agreement, the two relevant matters to consider are the constitutional documents of the relevant party and the law of the country of its incorporation. English law, as the proper law of the contract, is only secondary. It is therefore vital to obtain counsel's opinions on the power and authority of the Borrower and the Guarantor.

It has the power to enter into, perform and deliver, and has taken all necessary action to authorise its entry into, performance and delivery of, the Finance Documents to which it is a party and the transactions contemplated by those Finance Documents.

### 23.5. Validity and admissibility in evidence

If extensive governmental authorisations are required, it is useful to list them in a schedule to the facility agreement. If there are formalities that can only be accomplished after the facility agreement is signed, such as registration of the agreement itself with the exchange control authorities in the Obligors' jurisdiction, those formalities should be referred to as exceptions in the representations and the legal opinions, and an undertaking from the Borrower to accomplish them promptly after signature of the facility agreement should be included.

All Authorisations required or desirable:

(a) to enable it lawfully to enter into, exercise its rights and comply with its obligations in the Finance Documents to which it is a party; and

(b) to make the Finance Documents to which it is a party admissible in evidence in its jurisdiction of incorporation,

have been obtained or effected and are in full force and effect.

### 23.6. Governing law and enforcement

(a) The choice of English law as the governing law of the Finance Documents will, subject to the Legal Reservations, be recognised and enforced in its Relevant Jurisdiction.

(b) Any judgment obtained in England in relation to a Finance Document will be recognised and enforced in its Relevant Jurisdiction.

### 23.7. Deduction of Tax

It is not required to make any Tax Deduction (as defined in Clause 17.1 (*Definitions*)) from any payment it may make under any Finance Document to a Finance Party.

### 23.8. No filing or stamp taxes

This representation assumes that no stamp duty is payable under the execution of the agreement. This is currently the case, in relation to UK stamp duty, but it is still necessary to cover (a) the possible future imposition of stamp duty or (b) foreign stamp duty and this is achieved by the indemnity in Clause 17.6 (*Stamp taxes*).

Under the law of its Relevant Jurisdiction it is not necessary that the Finance Documents be filed, recorded or enrolled with any court or other authority in that jurisdiction or that any stamp, registration or similar tax be paid on or in relation to the Finance Documents or the transactions contemplated by the Finance Documents.

### 23.9. No default

(a) No Event of Default is continuing or might reasonably be expected to result from the making of any Utilisation.

(b) No other event or circumstance is outstanding which constitutes a default under any other agreement or instrument which is binding on it or any of its Subsidiaries or to which its (or any of its Subsidiaries') assets are subject which might have a Material Adverse Effect.

### 23.10. No misleading information

(a) Any factual information provided by any member of the Group for the purposes of the Information Memorandum was true and accurate in all material respects as at the date it was provided or as at the date (if any) at which it is stated.

(b) The financial projections contained in the Information Memorandum have been prepared on the basis of recent historical information and on the basis of reasonable assumptions.

(c) Nothing has occurred or been omitted from the Information Memorandum and no information has been given or withheld that results in the information contained in the Information Memorandum being untrue or misleading in any material respect.

(d) All written information (other than the Information Memorandum) supplied by any member of the Group is true, complete and accurate in all material respects as at the date it was given and is not misleading in any respect.

**23.11. Financial statements**

If accounting principles change frequently or if there is no recognised body of generally accepted principles of good accounting practice in the borrower's jurisdiction, it may be appropriate to include a more precise description of the financial reporting that is to be provided.

(a) Its Original Financial Statements were prepared in accordance with GAAP consistently applied unless expressly disclosed to the Agent in writing to the contrary before the date of this Agreement.

(b) Its Original Financial Statements fairly present its financial condition as at the end of the relevant financial year and its results of operations during the relevant financial year (consolidated in the case of the Guarantor) unless expressly disclosed to the Agent in writing to the contrary before the date of this Agreement.

If the Obligors are required to deliver quarterly financial statements, some facility agreements provide that the representation as to the absence of any material adverse change (sometimes called a 'MAC' Clause) should run from the date of the quarterly statements. The more usual practice, however, is to have it run from the date of the most recent audited statements, which are not subject to year-end adjustments. If there has in fact been a material adverse change in the financial condition of the Guarantor or of the Group between the two dates, the relevant circumstances should of course be reviewed in detail between the parties, and the representation should be adapted to reflect those circumstances, assuming the change is not so drastic that the lenders will call off the transaction.

(c) There has been no material adverse change in its business or financial condition (or the business or consolidated financial condition of the Group, in the case of the Guarantor) since the date as at which its Original Financial Statements are stated to have been prepared.

**23.12.** ***Pari passu* ranking**

This provision is an example of a '*pari passu* Clause'. The Clause in effect states that there are no legal provisions which would cause the loans to be subordinated to other indebtedness of the Borrower. The reference to obligations "mandatorily preferred by law" takes account of those classes of creditors which are (in many countries, including England) preferred above all creditors in the liquidation of a company. These preferred creditors are, typically, employees and tax and social security authorities. Until recently the accepted interpretation of the *pari passu* Clause has been that, upon the liquidation (or equivalent) of a company, all unsecured indebtedness will rank equally (subject to the usual statutory preferences referred to above). However, several judicial decisions in Europe and the United States have (in the context of sovereign borrowers) suggested a possible wider interpretation, being that equally ranking debts must be paid equally at all times and not solely on the onset of insolvency. This means that if there are insufficient funds to pay equally ranking creditors in full, then each creditor must receive a rateable share. This wider interpretation has been strongly criticised by academics and is not binding on English courts.

This representation, of course, has no effect against a third party with no knowledge of the provision. In practice it may serve to ensure that the obligors disclose all liabilities that may amount to a breach of it if undisclosed.

Its payment obligations under the Finance Documents rank at least *pari passu* with the claims of all its other unsecured and unsubordinated creditors, except for obligations mandatorily preferred by law applying to companies generally.

**23.13. No proceedings**

(a) No litigation, arbitration or administrative proceedings of or before any court, arbitral body or agency which, if adversely determined, might reasonably be expected to have a Material Adverse Effect has or have (to the best of its knowledge and belief) been started or threatened against any member of the Group (or against the directors of any member of the Group).

(b) No judgment or order of a court, arbitral body or agency which might reasonably be expected to have a Material Adverse Effect has (to the best of its knowledge and belief) been made against it or any of its Subsidiaries.

**23.14. Environmental compliance**

Each member of the Group has performed and observed in all material respects all Environmental Law, Environmental Permits and all other material covenants, conditions, restrictions or agreements directly or indirectly concerned with any contamination, pollution or waste or the release or discharge of any toxic or hazardous substance in connection with any real property which is or was at any time owned, leased or occupied by any member of the Group or on which any member of the Group has conducted any activity where failure to do so might reasonably be expected to have a Material Adverse Effect.

**23.15. Environmental Claims**

No Environmental Claim has been commenced or (to the best of its knowledge and belief) is threatened against any member of the Group where that claim would be reasonably likely, if determined against that member of the Group, to have a Material Adverse Effect.

**23.16. Anti-corruption law**

Each member of the Group has conducted its businesses in compliance with applicable anti-corruption laws and has instituted and maintained policies and procedures designed to promote and achieve compliance with such laws.

**23.17. Sanctions**

No member of the Group nor, any director, officer, agent, employee or Affiliate of any member of the Group, is currently a designated target of, or is otherwise a subject of, Sanctions.

See Clause 26 (*General Undertakings*) for further information on anti-corruption and sanctions provisions.

**23.18. Repetition**

The Repeating Representations are deemed to be made by each Obligor (by reference to the facts and circumstances then existing) on the date of each Utilisation Request and the first day of each Interest Period.

## 24. INFORMATIONAL UNDERTAKINGS

The undertakings in this Clause 24 remain in force from the date of this Agreement for so long as any amount is outstanding under the Finance Documents or any Commitment is in force.

### 24.1. Financial statements

It is normal to provide that a borrower's annual financial statements be audited in a particular manner. It is especially important that the auditing and accountancy principles are applied consistently from year to year, or the task of making meaningful comparisons will be made more difficult. Moreover, certain financial tests may lose some of their value if these principles are changed.

The lenders, having received the financial information from a borrower, have sophisticated financial and asset tests which they can apply to that information in order to assess objectively the condition and performance of a borrower's (or, as in the sample agreement, the Group's) business, and therefore its ability to repay the loan. There is a variety of such tests which are employed from time to time. This is not the place for their detailed discussion, but it should be noted that, in some cases, their significance goes beyond the monitoring function.

The Borrower shall supply to the Agent in sufficient copies for all the Lenders:

(a) as soon as the same become available, but in any event within 120 days after the end of each of its financial years:

  (i) its audited financial statements for that financial year; and

  (ii) the audited consolidated financial statements of the Guarantor for that financial year; and

(b) as soon as the same become available, but in any event within 90 days after the end of each half of each of its financial years:

  (i) its financial statements for that financial half year; and

  (ii) the consolidated financial statements of the Guarantor for that financial half year.

### 24.2. Compliance Certificate

(a) The Borrower shall supply to the Agent, with each set of financial statements delivered pursuant to paragraph (a)(ii) or (b)(ii) of Clause 24.1 (*Financial statements*), a Compliance Certificate setting out (in reasonable detail) computations as to compliance with Clause

25 (*Financial Covenants*) as at the date at which those financial statements were drawn up.

(b) Each Compliance Certificate shall be signed by two directors of the Borrower and, if required to be delivered with the financial statements delivered pursuant to paragraph (a)(ii) of Clause 24.1 (*Financial statements*), shall be reported on by the Guarantor's auditors in the form agreed by the Guarantor's auditors (and approved by the Majority Lenders) before the date of this Agreement.

**24.3. Requirements as to financial statements**

(a) Each set of financial statements delivered by the Borrower pursuant to Clause 24.1 (*Financial statements*) shall be certified by a director of the relevant company as fairly presenting its financial condition as at the date at which those financial statements were drawn up.

(b)

(i) The Borrower shall procure that each set of financial statements of an Obligor delivered pursuant to Clause 24.1 (*Financial statements*) is prepared using GAAP and accounting practices and financial reference periods consistent with those applied in the preparation of the Original Financial Statements for that Obligor unless, in relation to any set of financial statements, it notifies the Agent that there has been a change in GAAP or the accounting practices or reference periods, and its auditors (or, if appropriate, the auditors of the Guarantor) deliver to the Agent:

(A) a description of any change necessary for those financial statements to reflect the GAAP, accounting practices and reference periods upon which that Obligor's Original Financial Statements were prepared; and

(B) sufficient information, in form and substance as may be reasonably required by the Agent, to enable the Lenders to determine whether Clause 25 (*Financial Covenants*) has been complied with and make an accurate comparison between the financial position indicated in those financial statements and that Obligor's Original Financial Statements.

(ii) If the Borrower notifies the Agent of a change in accordance with paragraph (i) above then the Borrower and Agent shall enter into negotiations in good faith with a view to agreeing:

(A) whether or not the change might result in any material alteration in the commercial effect of any of the terms of this Agreement; and

(B) if so, any amendments to this Agreement which may be necessary to ensure that the change does not result in any material alteration in the commercial effect of those terms,

and if any amendments are agreed they shall take effect and be binding on each of the Parties in accordance with their terms.

Any reference in this Agreement to "those financial statements" shall be construed as a reference to those financial statements as adjusted to reflect the basis upon which the Original Financial Statements were prepared.

**24.4. Information: miscellaneous**

The Borrower shall supply to the Agent (in sufficient copies for all the Lenders, if the Agent so requests):

(a) all documents despatched by the Guarantor to its shareholders (or any class of them) or by any Obligor to its creditors generally at the same time as they are dispatched;

(b) promptly upon becoming aware of them, the details of any litigation, arbitration or administrative proceedings which are current, threatened or pending against any member of the Group (or against the directors of any member of the Group), and which might, if adversely determined, have a Material Adverse Effect;

(c) promptly upon becoming aware of them, the details of any judgment or order of a court, arbitral body or agency which is made against any member of the Group, and which might have a Material Adverse Effect; and

(d) promptly, such further information regarding the financial condition, business and operations of any member of the Group as any Finance Party (through the Agent) may reasonably request.

### 24.5. Notification of default

The principal purpose of this Clause 24.5 is to place an obligation on a borrower to give notice to the lenders of the occurrence of events of default that are likely to be known to the borrower before they would otherwise be known to the lenders. The Agent can also request delivery by the Borrower of a certificate to the effect that no Event of Default (or event that could develop into one) exists, and if it does exist, stating what it is and what (if anything) is being done to remedy it.

(a) Each Obligor shall notify the Agent of any Default (and the steps, if any, being taken to remedy it) promptly upon becoming aware of its occurrence (unless that Obligor is aware that a notification has already been provided by another Obligor).

(b) Promptly upon a request by the Agent, the Borrower shall supply to the Agent a certificate signed by two of its directors or senior officers on its behalf certifying that no Default is continuing (or if a Default is continuing, specifying the Default and the steps, if any, being taken to remedy it).

### 24.6. Use of websites

(a) The Borrower may satisfy its obligation under this Agreement to deliver any information in relation to those Lenders (the "**Website Lenders**") who accept this method of communication by posting this information onto an electronic website designated by the Borrower and the Agent (the "**Designated Website**") if:

(i) the Agent expressly agrees (after consultation with each of the Lenders) that it will accept communication of the information by this method;

(ii) both the Borrower and the Agent are aware of the address of and any relevant password specifications for the Designated Website; and

(iii) the information is in a format previously agreed between the Borrower and the Agent.

If any Lender (a "**Paper Form Lender**") does not agree to the delivery of information electronically then the Agent shall notify the Borrower accordingly and the Borrower shall supply the information to the Agent (in sufficient copies for each Paper Form Lender) in paper form. In any event the

Borrower shall supply the Agent with at least one copy in paper form of any information required to be provided by it.

(b) The Agent shall supply each Website Lender with the address of and any relevant password specifications for the Designated Website following designation of that website by the Borrower and the Agent.

(c) The Borrower shall promptly upon becoming aware of its occurrence notify the Agent if:

(i) the Designated Website cannot be accessed due to technical failure;

(ii) the password specifications for the Designated Website change;

(iii) any new information which is required to be provided under this Agreement is posted onto the Designated Website;

(iv) any existing information which has been provided under this Agreement and posted onto the Designated Website is amended; or

(v) the Borrower becomes aware that the Designated Website or any information posted onto the Designated Website is or has been infected by any electronic virus or similar software.

If the Borrower notifies the Agent under paragraph (c)(i) or paragraph (c)(v) above, all information to be provided by the Borrower under this Agreement after the date of that notice shall be supplied in paper form unless and until the Agent and each Website Lender is satisfied that the circumstances giving rise to the notification are no longer continuing.

(d) Any Website Lender may request, through the Agent, one paper copy of any information required to be provided under this Agreement which is posted onto the Designated Website. The Borrower shall comply with any such request within ten Business Days.

### 24.7. "Know your customer" checks

> This Clause 24.7, together with paragraph (c) of Clause 2.2 (*Increase*), paragraph (e)(iv) of Clause 12.5 (*Right of replacement or repayment and cancellation in relation to a single Lender*), Clause 26.2 (*Compliance with laws*), paragraph (b) of Clause 28.6 (*Procedure for transfer*) and paragraph (b) of Clause 28.7 (*Procedure for assignment*) has been included to take account of any "know your customer" (**KYC**) checks to be carried out by a Finance Party in relation to the identity of its "customers". In the UK these checks are required, pursuant to the Money Laundering Regulations 2007 (the **Regulations**), to be carried out where a person, in the course of "relevant financial business" forms a "business relationship" (as such terms are defined in the Regulations). As such, KYC issues arise between the (i) Finance Parties and both Obligors; (ii) the Agent and the Lenders; and (iii) the Original Lenders and any New Lenders.

(a) If:

(i) the introduction of or any change in (or in the interpretation, administration or application of) any law or regulation made after the date of this Agreement;

(ii) any change in the status of an Obligor or the composition of the shareholders of an Obligor after the date of this Agreement; or

(iii) a proposed assignment or transfer by a Lender of any of its rights and obligations under this Agreement to a party that is not a Lender prior to such assignment or transfer,

obliges the Agent or any Lender (or, in the case of paragraph (iii) above, any prospective new Lender) to comply with "know your customer" or similar identification procedures in circumstances where the necessary information is not already available to it, each Obligor shall promptly upon the request of the Agent or any Lender supply, or procure the supply of, such documentation and other evidence as is reasonably requested by the Agent (for itself or on behalf of any Lender) or any Lender (for itself or, in the case of the event described in paragraph (iii) above, on behalf of any prospective new Lender) in order for the Agent, such Lender or, in the case of the event described in paragraph (iii) above, any prospective new Lender to carry out and be satisfied it has complied with all necessary "know your customer" or other similar checks under all applicable laws and regulations pursuant to the transactions contemplated in the Finance Documents.

(b) Each Lender shall promptly upon the request of the Agent supply, or procure the supply of, such documentation and other evidence as is reasonably requested by the Agent (for itself) in order for the Agent to carry out and be satisfied it has complied with all necessary "know your customer" or other similar checks under all applicable laws and regulations pursuant to the transactions contemplated in the Finance Documents.

## 25. FINANCIAL COVENANTS

Financial covenants should be objective and, preferably, capable of determination from information available in the regular statements to be supplied by the obligors. For this reason, properly considered and drafted financial covenants may be more attractive to all parties than the protection afforded by an Event of Default occurring on a material adverse change in the financial condition of a borrower (or, as in the sample agreement's case, the Group). Compliance with such financial covenants should mean that a borrower's business is being directed in a prudent and safe manner, while a breach may be an indication of difficulties to follow. A breach will also, through the occurrence of an Event of Default, entitle the lenders to demand to be repaid early while there is still some prospect of a borrower being able to do so. Alternatively, lenders can use the threat of demanding repayment in order to require the borrower to renegotiate the terms of the agreement including increasing the margin or providing security. Financial covenants do, however, have their shortcomings, the chief of which, aside from the difficulty of setting realistic parameters in the first place, is the inevitable delay in discovering any breach. Annual financial statements will commonly take up to six months in preparation, and so it may be 12 or 18 months after the event that a particular adverse change is discovered in this way. While usually it will be open to the lenders to request financial information of a borrower at any time, normally the lenders will not do this unless they already have reason to suspect that a borrower is in difficulties. Accounting principles and standards vary from time to time and from country to country. This can be partially overcome by the definition of accounting terms and principles in the facility agreement, but the lenders must accept that the protection given by the financial covenants is only as good as the raw information supplied by a borrower in the first place.

### 25.1. Financial definitions

The following definitions are not necessarily applicable to all borrowers since they are too dependent on the circumstances of the particular deal.

It is important that the values to be ascribed to the defined financial terms can be readily ascertained from the financial statements, i.e., that the conditions and the terms in which they are written reflect the layout of the financial statement.

In this Clause 25:

"**Consolidated EBIT**" means, in respect of any Relevant Period, the consolidated operating profit of the Group before taxation (excluding the results from discontinued operations):

(a) before deducting any interest, commission, fees, discounts, prepayment fees, premiums or charges and other finance payments whether paid, payable or capitalised by any member of the Group (calculated on a consolidated basis) in respect of that Relevant Period;

(b) not including any accrued interest owing to any member of the Group;

(c) before taking into account any Exceptional Items;

(d) after deducting the amount of any profit (or adding back the amount of any loss) of any member of the Group which is attributable to minority interests;

(e) after deducting the amount of any profit of any Non-Group Entity to the extent that the amount of the profit included in the financial statements of the Group exceeds the amount actually received in cash by members of the Group through distributions by the Non-Group Entity; and

(f) before taking into account any unrealised gains or losses on any derivative instrument (other than any derivative instrument which is accounted for on a hedge accounting basis),

in each case, to the extent added, deducted or taken into account, as the case may be, for the purposes of determining the operating profit of the Group before taxation.

"**Consolidated EBITDA**" means, in respect of any Relevant Period, Consolidated EBIT for that Relevant Period after adding back any amount attributable to the amortisation, depreciation or impairment of assets of members of the Group (and taking no account of the reversal of any previous impairment charge made in that Relevant Period).

"**Consolidated Net Finance Charges**" means, in respect of any Relevant Period, the aggregate amount of the accrued interest, commission, fees, discounts, prepayment penalties or premiums and other finance payments in respect of Indebtedness for Borrowed Money whether paid, payable or capitalised by any member of the Group in respect of that Relevant Period:

(a) excluding any such obligations owed to any other member of the Group;

(b) including the interest element of payments in respect of any Finance Lease;

(c) including any accrued commission, fees, discounts and other finance payments payable by any member of the Group under any interest rate hedging arrangement;

(d) deducting any accrued commission, fees, discounts and other finance payments owing to any member of the Group under any interest rate hedging instrument; and

(e) deducting any interest payable in that Relevant Period to any member of the Group (other than by another member of the Group) on any Cash or Cash Equivalent Investment.

"**Consolidated Total Net Debt**" means at any time the aggregate outstanding principal, capital or nominal amount of all obligations of the Group for or in respect of Indebtedness for Borrowed Money but:

(a) excluding any such obligations to any other member of the Group;

(b) including, in the case of any Finance Lease, its capitalised value; and

(c) deducting the aggregate amount of freely available Cash and Cash Equivalent Investments held by any member of the Group at that time,

and so that no amount shall be included or excluded more than once.

"**Exceptional Items**" means any material items of an unusual or non-recurring nature which represent gains or losses including those arising on:

(a) the restructuring of the activities of an entity and reversals of any provisions for the cost of restructuring;

(b) disposals, revaluations or impairment of non-current assets; or

(c) disposals of assets associated with discontinued operations.

"**Financial Year**" means the annual accounting period of the Guarantor ending on or about [31 December] in each year.

"**Interest Cover**" means, in respect of any Relevant Period, the ratio of Consolidated EBITDA for that Relevant Period to Consolidated Net Finance Charges for that Relevant Period.

"**Non-Group Entity**" means any investment or entity (which is not itself a member of the Group (including associates and joint ventures)) in which any member of the Group has an ownership interest.

"**Relevant Period**" means each period of twelve months ending on the last day of the Financial Year and each period of twelve months ending on the last day of the first half of the Financial Year.

### 25.2. Financial condition

The elements in each of the financial undertakings require definition in a facility agreement (see Clause 25.1 (*Financial definitions*)) so that it is clear what is to be comprised in the financial tests applicable to a particular group. It will be for the lenders to decide what tests and definitions are appropriate in a particular case. It will also be necessary to decide whether the tests and other covenants are to be applied to a borrower alone or whether there are entities, such as subsidiaries, which should also be covered. Generally, however the tests are applied on a Group-wide basis.

The Guarantor shall ensure that:

(a) Interest Cover for each Relevant Period shall not be less than [•]:1; and

(b) the ratio of Consolidated Total Net Debt to Consolidated EBITDA for any Relevant Period shall not at any time exceed [•]:1.

### 25.3. Financial testing

The financial covenants set out in Clause 25.2 (*Financial condition*) shall be tested by reference to each of the financial statements and/or each Compliance Certificate delivered pursuant to Clause 24.2 (*Compliance Certificate*).

## 26. GENERAL UNDERTAKINGS

The fact that the loan is unsecured and committed puts lenders in a vulnerable position. Lenders seek to use undertakings (together with financial covenants and events of default) to reduce this vulnerability. Their scope will naturally depend upon the circumstances and will be a matter of detailed negotiation between the borrower and the lenders. This situation may be affected by the degree of scrutiny of their customers' affairs which the borrower's main bankers normally adopt.

Lenders may sometimes (for example, in the case of less creditworthy borrowers, special purpose vehicles or limited recourse loans) insist that the undertakings impose severe limits on the management options of the borrower (which is, for example, the case with the LMA's Recommended Form of Facilities Agreement for Leveraged Acquisition Finance Transactions). More often, however, with stronger corporate borrowers they will be willing to leave the borrower's managerial powers largely unfettered **provided that** Events of Default cover a deterioration in the borrower's financial position. This will give lenders the right to demand repayment or, often more importantly in practice, the opportunity to renegotiate the terms of the loan (including imposing more severe undertakings).

The undertakings in this Clause 26 remain in force from the date of this Agreement for so long as any amount is outstanding under the Finance Documents or any Commitment is in force.

### 26.1. Authorisations

This area is primarily the responsibility of local counsel and will be covered by their legal opinion. A principal concern is compliance with any exchange controls, since the sanctions for failure to comply with them can be quite severe and may even render the facility agreement unenforceable. In this case, exchange controls are not relevant as they do not apply in The Netherlands where the Borrower is incorporated.

Each Obligor shall promptly:

(a) obtain, comply with and do all that is necessary to maintain in full force and effect; and

(b) supply certified copies to the Agent of,

any Authorisation required under any law or regulation of its jurisdiction of incorporation to enable it to perform its obligations under the Finance Documents and to ensure the legality, validity, enforceability or admissibility in evidence in its jurisdiction of incorporation of any Finance Document.

### 26.2. Compliance with laws

Each Obligor shall comply in all respects with all laws to which it may be subject, if failure so to comply would materially impair its ability to perform its obligations under the Finance Documents.

### 26.3. Negative pledge

The negative pledge Clause is a companion to the *pari passu* representation (Clause 23.13 (*Pari passu ranking*)). While the repetition of the *pari passu* representation throughout the life of the loan obliges the borrower to maintain parity between its unsecured obligations, the negative pledge Clause seeks to control the borrower's ability to create or maintain secured indebtedness.

The Lenders under this sample agreement, being unsecured creditors of a borrower, will be determined to prevent other creditors being preferred to them, but they also will assert that it is when the borrower is in difficulties that it is most likely that it will be required to give security for its loans, and this is exactly the situation in which the lenders will not be prepared to see particular assets of the borrower pledged to other creditors and taken out of the fund to which the unsecured creditors, including the Lenders, may look.

The negative pledge Clause is only of limited value because it is effective only as long as it is complied with. Once it is breached the lenders will have the right to accelerate the loan and to demand immediate repayment through the events of default, but they will be unable to dislodge any encumbrance already created unless, on the liquidation of a corporate borrower, they are able to point to some fraudulent preference which avoids the offending encumbrance. They may, however, obtain some claim against the secured lenders for inducing a breach of contract if those lenders were aware of the terms of the original lenders' negative pledge.

In this Clause 26.3, "**Quasi-Security**" means an arrangement or transaction described in paragraph (b) below.

(a) No Obligor shall (and the Guarantor shall ensure that no other member of the Group will) create or permit to subsist any Security over any of its assets.

(b) No Obligor shall (and the Guarantor shall ensure that no other member of the Group will):

(i) sell, transfer or otherwise dispose of any of its assets on terms whereby they are or may be leased to or re-acquired by an Obligor or any other member of the Group;

(ii) sell, transfer or otherwise dispose of any of its receivables on recourse terms;

(iii) enter into any arrangement under which money or the benefit of a bank or other account may be applied, set-off or made subject to a combination of accounts; or

(iv) enter into any other preferential arrangement having a similar effect,

in circumstances where the arrangement or transaction is entered into primarily as a method of raising Financial Indebtedness or of financing the acquisition of an asset.

(c) Paragraphs (a) and (b) above do not apply to any Security or (as the case may be) Quasi-Security, listed below:

(i) any Security or Quasi-Security listed in Schedule 7 (*Existing Security*) except to the extent the principal amount secured by that Security or Quasi-Security exceeds the amount stated in that Schedule;

(ii) any netting or set-off arrangement entered into by any member of the Group in the ordinary course of its banking arrangements for the purpose of netting debit and credit balances;

(iii) any payment or close out netting or set-off arrangement pursuant to any hedging transaction entered into by a member of the Group for the purpose of:

(A) hedging any risk to which any member of the Group is exposed in its ordinary course of trading; or

(B) its interest rate or currency management operations which are carried out in the ordinary course of business and for non-speculative purposes only,

excluding, in each case, any Security or Quasi-Security under a credit support arrangement in relation to a hedging transaction;

(iv) any lien arising by operation of law and in the ordinary course of trading;

(v) any Security or Quasi-Security over or affecting any asset acquired by a member of the Group after the date of this Agreement if:

(A) the Security or Quasi-Security was not created in contemplation of the acquisition of that asset by a member of the Group;

(B) the principal amount secured has not been increased in contemplation of, or since the acquisition of that asset by a member of the Group; and

(C) the Security or Quasi-Security is removed or discharged within three months of the date of acquisition of such asset;

(vi) any Security or Quasi-Security over or affecting any asset of any company which becomes a member of the Group after the date of this Agreement, where the Security or Quasi-Security is created prior to the date on which that company becomes a member of the Group, if:

(A) the Security or Quasi-Security was not created in contemplation of the acquisition of that company;

(B) the principal amount secured has not increased in contemplation of or since the acquisition of that company; and

(C) the Security or Quasi-Security is removed or discharged within three months of that company becoming a member of the Group;

(vii) any Security or Quasi-Security entered into pursuant to any Finance Document;

(viii) any Security and/or right of set-off arising under Clause 24 or Clause 25 of the general terms and conditions (*algemene bankvoorwaarden*) of any member of the Dutch Bankers' Association or the equivalent in any other jurisdiction;

(ix) any Security or Quasi-Security arising under any retention of title, hire purchase or conditional sale arrangement or arrangements having similar effect in respect of goods supplied to a member of the Group in the ordinary course of trading and on the supplier's standard or usual terms and not arising as a result of any default or omission by any member of the Group; or

(x) any Security or Quasi-Security securing indebtedness the principal amount of which (when aggregated with the principal amount of any other indebtedness which has the benefit of Security or Quasi-Security given by any member of the Group other than any permitted under paragraphs (i) to (viii) above) does not exceed $[•] (or its equivalent in another currency or currencies).

**26.4. Disposals**

> This covenant attempts to preserve a borrower's assets which would be available for any future distribution, and it applies either to a single transaction or a series of transactions which exceed a particular amount of the book value. It is linked to the undertaking in Clause 26.7 (*Insurance*) to make sure that the preserved assets are adequately insured.

(a) No Obligor shall (and the Guarantor shall ensure that no other member of the Group will), enter into a single transaction or a series of transactions (whether related or not) and whether voluntary or involuntary to sell, lease, transfer or otherwise dispose of any asset.

(b) Paragraph (a) above does not apply to any sale, lease, transfer or other disposal:

(i) made in the ordinary course of trading of the disposing entity;

(ii) of assets in exchange for other assets comparable or superior as to type, value and quality (other than an exchange of a non-cash asset for cash); or

(iii) where the book value of the assets (when aggregated with the book value of the assets for any other sale, lease, transfer or other disposal by the Group, other than any permitted under paragraphs (i) to (ii) above) does not exceed $[•] (or its equivalent in another currency or currencies) in any financial year.

**26.5. Merger**

(a) No Obligor shall (and the Guarantor shall ensure that no other member of the Group will) enter into any amalgamation, demerger, merger or corporate reconstruction.

(b) Paragraph (a) above does not apply to any sale, lease, transfer or other disposal permitted pursuant to Clause 26.4 (*Disposals*).

**26.6. Change of business**

The Guarantor shall ensure that no substantial change is made to the general nature of the business of the Obligors or the Group from that carried on at the date of this Agreement.

**26.7. Insurance**

Each Obligor shall (and the Guarantor shall ensure that each member of the Group will) maintain insurances on and in relation to its business and assets with reputable underwriters or insurance companies against those risks and to the extent as is usual for companies carrying on the same or substantially similar business.

**26.8. Environmental Compliance**

Each Obligor shall (and the Guarantor shall ensure that each member of the Group will) comply in all material respects with all Environmental Law and obtain and maintain any Environmental Permits and take all reasonable steps in anticipation of known or expected future changes to or obligations under the same where failure to do so might reasonably be expected to have a Material Adverse Effect.

**26.9. Environmental Claims**

Each Obligor shall inform the Agent in writing as soon as reasonably practicable upon becoming aware of:

(a) any Environmental Claim that has been commenced or (to the best of its knowledge and belief) is threatened against any member of the Group; or

(b) any facts or circumstances which will or are reasonably likely to result in any Environmental Claim being commenced or threatened against any member of the Group,

where the claim would be reasonably likely, if determined against that member of the Group, to have a Material Adverse Effect.

**26.10. Anti-corruption law**

(a) No Obligor has (and the Guarantor shall ensure that no other member of the Group will) directly or indirectly use the proceeds of the Facilities for any purpose which would breach the Bribery Act

2010, the United States Foreign Corrupt Practices Act of 1977 of other similar legislation in other jurisdictions.

(b) Each Obligor shall (and the Guarantor shall ensure that each other member of the Group will):

(i) conduct its businesses in compliance with applicable anti-corruption laws; and

(ii) maintain policies and procedures designed to promote and achieve compliance with such laws.

**26.11. Sanctions**

No Obligor shall (and the Guarantor shall ensure that no other member of the Group will) directly or indirectly, use the proceeds of the Facilities (or lend, contribute or otherwise make available such proceeds to any person):

(a) to fund or facilitate any activities or business of, with or related to (or otherwise make funds available to or for the benefit of) any person, who is a designated target of or who is otherwise the subject of Sanctions; or

(b) in any manner or for any purpose:

(i) that is prohibited by Sanctions applicable to any Party or any of its Affiliates; or

(ii) that would result in a violation of Sanctions by any Party or any of its Affiliates.

Lenders are increasingly looking to supplement their own due diligence and KYC checks and include sanctions and anti-corruption provisions in facility agreements. The precise wording will be negotiated on a deal by deal basis as it will depend on a number of factors including the geography and sector of the borrower. The LMA has not therefore sought to include suggested wording for sanctions provisions in its primary facility agreements. Many lenders will have their own particular wording that they require to be included. However, broadly speaking, the key areas that lenders look to cover in sanctions provisions are:

(i) a representation that no members of the Group (nor their respective officers) are subject to sanctions;

(ii) a covenant that the proceeds of the Loan will not be used for any purposes prohibited by sanctions; and

(iii) a covenant that the funds used to repay amounts owing under the facility agreement are not derived from any activity with a sanctioned person or sanctioned activity.

In addition, lenders often want to ensure that any amendments to sanctions provisions require all (rather than majority) lender consent. Some lenders also push for no grace period to apply in the event of a breach of a sanctions-related provision.

The LMA does include anti-corruption provisions in the Senior Multicurrency Term and Revolving Facilities Agreement for Leveraged Acquisition Finance Transactions. Anti-corruption provisions tend to be more focused on ensuring that the group is in compliance with anti-corruption laws and has the requisite policies and procedures in place.

## 27. EVENTS OF DEFAULT

Since the events of default can lead to the lenders being relieved of their obligation to lend and being entitled to exercise remedies that include acceleration, a borrower will be concerned to limit the actions or circumstances that will constitute events of default and will also want to include provisions: (a) that give the borrower time to cure events of default and (b) that require notice to be given to a borrower before those cure periods start to run. The lenders, however, will be determined to protect their ability to act quickly to demand repayment of the loan, with accrued interest, if serious problems arise.

The first three events of default cover the whole spectrum of actual breaches of the terms of the facility agreement. However, there are many possible events, the occurrence of any of which would be a warning that a borrower may soon be in breach of a term of the facility agreement. The early warning events of default are very important since by the time an actual default occurs it may be too late for the lenders to protect their position; other creditors may already have protected themselves and left nothing for the lenders.

Each of the events or circumstances set out in this Clause 27 is an Event of Default (save for Clause 27.14 (*Acceleration*)).

### 27.1. Non-payment

The fundamental concept of a loan is the repayment of principal and the payment of interest on the outstanding principal. The first Event of Default is therefore usually non-payment. The payment obligation is fundamental, and its breach may be said to be the last Event of Default as well as the first in the sense that the other events of default are included only because they are indications of a future non-payment. The lenders are therefore unlikely to agree to any significant qualifications of this event.

However, in some cases a grace period is allowed (as in the sample agreement). Any conceded grace period will usually be short and will often only be for delays occurring for purely technical difficulties in effecting payment.

An Obligor does not pay on the due date any amount payable pursuant to a Finance Document at the place at and in the currency in which it is expressed to be payable unless:

(a) its failure to pay is caused by:

(i) administrative or technical error; or

(ii) a Disruption Event; and

(b) payment is made within:

(i) (in the case of paragraph (a)(i) above) three Business Days of its due date; or

(ii) (in the case of paragraph (a)(ii) above) five Business Days of its due date.

**27.2. Financial covenants**

Any requirement of Clause 25 (*Financial Covenants*) is not satisfied.

**27.3. Other obligations**

During negotiations some borrowers may seek to limit this Clause 27.3 by inserting a materiality limitation or by providing that a grace period applies during which certain breaches may be remedied before they become events of default.

(a) An Obligor does not comply with any provision of the Finance Documents (other than those referred to in Clause 27.1 (*Non-payment*) and Clause 27.2 (*Financial covenants*)).

(b) No Event of Default under paragraph (a) above will occur if the failure to comply is capable of remedy and is remedied within 15 Business Days of the earlier of (i) the Agent giving notice to the Borrower and (ii) the Borrower becoming aware of the failure to comply.

**27.4. Misrepresentation**

During negotiations some borrowers will wish to dilute the impact of this Clause 27.4 by inserting a materiality limitation (as in the sample agreement) or by restricting it to those representations and statements which cover key commercial areas. This will usually be resisted by lenders. In addition, some borrowers may seek to include a grace period during which the underlying circumstances which gave rise to the misrepresentation may be remedied.

Any representation or statement made or deemed to be made by an Obligor in the Finance Documents or any other document delivered by or on behalf of any Obligor under or in connection with any Finance Document is or proves to have been incorrect or misleading in any material respect when made or deemed to be made.

**27.5. Cross default**

The first of the early warning events of default is the cross-default Clause, as a default by a borrower under another financing is likely to be followed by defaults on all of its obligations to all of its creditors. Accordingly, and on the principle that all creditors of the same class should be treated alike, lenders attach great importance to cross-default provisions.

The definition of "**Financial Indebtedness**" is deliberately very wide in its scope and includes all financial obligations, whether as principal or as surety, owed to any person. A borrower will often request that this be restricted to, say, indebtedness in respect of borrowed moneys. This would take a borrower's hedging debts out of the ambit of the cross-default. However, hedging debts can be as crippling as any other, so an alternative approach to the problem is to insert, as in this sample agreement, a financial threshold, (which will be dictated by the balance sheet of the borrower) so that defaults which do not exceed a specified aggregate sum will not trigger the cross-default event of default.

The cross-default will always focus on a borrower, but if the lenders are looking at other entities, such as a guarantor or subsidiaries, as part of the credit for a loan, they too will be covered by the cross-default. Thus, in the sample agreement, a default by the guarantor or one of its subsidiaries under some unrelated transaction would lead to an Event of Default under the sample agreement, even though the borrower was not yet in difficulties itself. Some transactions have a cross-acceleration Clause rather than a cross-default Clause. This is weaker for the lenders and is achieved by deleting paragraph (d) from the sample Clause.

(a) Any Financial Indebtedness of any member of the Group is not paid when due nor within any originally applicable grace period.

(b) Any Financial Indebtedness of any member of the Group is declared to be or otherwise becomes due and payable prior to its specified maturity as a result of an event of default (however described).

(c) Any commitment for any Financial Indebtedness of any member of the Group is cancelled or suspended by a creditor of any member of the Group as a result of an event of default (however described).

(d) Any creditor of any member of the Group becomes entitled to declare any Financial Indebtedness of any member of the Group due and payable prior to its specified maturity as a result of an event of default (however described).

(e) No Event of Default will occur under this Clause 27.5 if the aggregate amount of Financial Indebtedness or commitment for Financial Indebtedness falling within paragraphs (a) to (d) above is less than $[•] (or its equivalent in any other currency or currencies).

**27.6. Insolvency**

(a) A member of the Group:

(i) is unable or admits inability to pay its debts as they fall due (including a state of *cessation des paiements* within the meaning of the French *Code de commerce*);

(ii) is deemed to or declared to be unable to pay its debts under any applicable law;

(iii) suspends or threatens to suspend making payments on any of its debts; or

(iv) by reason of actual or anticipated financial difficulties, commences negotiations with one or more of its creditors (excluding any Finance Party in its capacity as such) with a view to rescheduling any of its indebtedness.

This provision works in conjunction with the cross-default Clause but may bite at an earlier stage. For example, the expression "**unable to pay its debts**" is a term of art and can happen before a debt is not paid. By comparison, the expression used in the cross-default Clause ("**is not paid**") may not mean that a borrower/obligor is unable to pay its debts only that it is not willing to pay a particular debt.

(b) The value of the assets of any member of the Group is less than its liabilities (taking into account contingent and prospective liabilities).

(c) A moratorium is declared in respect of any indebtedness of any member of the Group.

(d) Any member of the Group which conducts business in France is in a state of *cessation des paiements* within the meaning of articles L.631-1 *et seq.* of the French *Code de Commerce*, or any member of the Group becomes insolvent for the purpose of any applicable insolvency law.

### 27.7. Insolvency proceedings

Although it is possible that the laws of a number of countries may automatically treat bankruptcy or liquidation of a borrower as an event which would result in an acceleration of the loan, regardless of what is stated in the facility agreement, such an eventuality should still be covered within the events of default, since the relevant legal procedure in the country of a borrower's domicile may be disadvantageous to the lenders or at least not as advantageous as the lenders would wish. Also, the event should be triggered by the start of such proceedings and not by the subsequent making of an order under such proceedings.

Any corporate action, legal proceedings or other procedure or step is taken in relation to:

(a) the suspension of payments, a moratorium of any indebtedness, winding-up, dissolution, administration, the opening of proceedings for *sauvegarde, sauvegarde accélérée, sauvegarde financière accélérée, redressement judiciaire* or *liquidation judiciaire* or a judgment for *cession totale ou partielle de l'entreprise* pursuant to articles L.620-1 to L.670-8 of the French *Code de commerce* or reorganisation (by way of voluntary arrangement, scheme of arrangement or otherwise, including in the context of a *mandat ad hoc* or of a *conciliation* in accordance with articles L.611-3 to L.611-16 of the French *Code de commerce*) of any member of the Group other than a solvent liquidation or reorganisation of any member of the Group which is not an Obligor;

(b) a composition, compromise, assignment or arrangement with any creditor of any member of the Group;

(c) the appointment of a liquidator (other than in respect of a solvent liquidation of a member of the Group which is not an Obligor), receiver, administrative receiver, administrator, *mandataire ad hoc, conciliateur*, compulsory manager or other similar officer in respect of any member of the Group or any of its assets;

(d) enforcement of any Security over any assets of any member of the Group;

(e) any member of the Group which conducts business in France commences proceedings for *conciliation* in accordance with articles L.611-4 to L.611-15 of the French *Code de Commerce*; or

(f) a judgement for *sauvegarde, redressement judiciaire, cession totale de l'entreprise* or *liquidation judiciaire* is entered in relation to any member of the Group which conducts business in France under articles L.620-1 to L.670-8 of the French *Code de Commerce,*

or any analogous procedure or step is taken in any jurisdiction.

This Clause 27.7 shall not apply to any winding-up petition which is frivolous or vexatious and is discharged, stayed or dismissed within [14] days of commencement.

**27.8. Creditors' process**

Any expropriation, attachment, sequestration, distress or execution (including any of the enforcement proceedings provided for in the French *Code des procédures civiles d'exécution*) or any analogous process in any jurisdiction affects any asset or assets of a member of the Group and is not discharged within [14] days.

**27.9. Tax Status**

A notice under Article 36 Dutch Tax Collection Act (*Invorderingswet 1990*) has been given by any member of the Group.

**27.10. Unlawfulness**

It is or becomes unlawful for an Obligor to perform any of its obligations under the Finance Documents.

**27.11. Repudiation**

An Obligor repudiates a Finance Document or evidences an intention to repudiate a Finance Document.

**27.12. Ownership of the Borrower**

The Borrower ceases to be a wholly-owned subsidiary of the Guarantor.

### 27.13. Material adverse change

This is a safety-net provision. The events of default generally are intended to deal with unexpected occurrences, and it is the nature of such occurrences that they do not fall neatly into previously contemplated categories. It is therefore prudent to have such a comprehensive and general event of default in order to pick up adverse events in the light of which the lenders want to review their positions, but which are not expressly contemplated in the facility agreement. However, in order to cover all possibilities, the language will, by definition, be vague and therefore it can make it very difficult for the lenders to be certain that particular circumstances entitle them to rely on this Event of Default. This event is not likely to be relied on in marginal cases but has been used in practice where the position is a clear one and where convincing evidence is available of material adverse change. Where the commercial paper programme of the borrower is being rated, the rating agency may be concerned about the inclusion of a 'MAC' Clause as it may mean that the facility is not available to be used when the borrower's credit condition deteriorates.

Any event or circumstance occurs which might reasonably be expected to have a Material Adverse Effect.

### 27.14. Acceleration

On and at any time after the occurrence of an Event of Default which is continuing the Agent may, without *mise en demeure* or any other judicial or extra judicial step, and shall if so directed by the Majority Lenders, by notice to the Borrower but, in respect of the Guarantor, subject to the mandatory provisions of Book VI *(Difficulties faced by businesses*) of the French *Code de commerce:*

(a) cancel the Total Commitments, at which time they shall immediately be cancelled;

(b) declare that all or part of the Loans, together with accrued interest, and all other amounts accrued or outstanding under the Finance Documents be immediately due and payable, at which time they shall become immediately due and payable; and/or

(c) declare that all or part of the Loans be payable on demand, at which time they shall immediately become payable on demand by the Agent on the instructions of the Majority Lenders.

It is not necessary for all the lenders to agree in order to call a default. The decision in Clause 27.14 (*Acceleration*), among others provided for elsewhere in the sample agreement, is taken by the "**Majority Lenders**". Thus, lenders who have a greater amount at stake have a greater vote in the matter. The actual percentage to be applied will vary from loan to loan, but 66.6%. is quite normal. It is, of course, important that the percentage is at least 50%. since otherwise there would be the possibility of getting two groups of lenders requiring the agent to take contradictory action.

The references above to certain provisions of French law are required given the Guarantor's jurisdiction of incorporation.

# SECTION 9

## CHANGES TO PARTIES

### 28. CHANGES TO THE LENDERS

#### 28.1. Assignments and transfers by the Lenders

For a general commentary on assignments and transfers of loans, see chapter 6 "Secondary market transfer mechanism".

Subject to this Clause 28, a Lender (the "**Existing Lender**") may:

(a) assign any of its rights; or

(b) transfer by novation any of its rights and obligations,

to another bank or financial institution or to a trust, fund or other entity which is regularly engaged in or established for the purpose of making, purchasing or investing in loans, securities or other financial assets (the "**New Lender**").

LMA facility agreements allow for transfers to a wide range of participants in the loan market. In practice, revolving credit facilities with swingline options are not likely to be attractive to "non-bank" lenders such as funds or collateralised loan obligations because they are likely to remain undrawn at most times (and therefore do not offer sufficient yield in terms of interest income) and also require Lenders to be capable of funding their participations in Loans at short notice. "Non-bank" lenders invest primarily in drawn term loan facilities which have been underwritten (and funded) by bank lenders.

#### 28.2. Borrower Consent

(a) The consent of the Borrower is required for an assignment or transfer by an Existing Lender, unless the assignment or transfer is:

(i) to another Lender or an Affiliate of any Lender; or

(ii) made at a time when an Event of Default is continuing.

(b) The consent of the Borrower to an assignment or transfer must not be unreasonably withheld or delayed. The Borrower will be deemed to have given its consent five Business Days after the Existing Lender has requested it unless consent is expressly refused by the Borrower within that time.

(c) Any assignment or transfer of part only of a Lender's Overall Commitment must be in a minimum amount of $10,000,000.

**28.3. Other conditions of assignment or transfer**

(a) An assignment will only be effective on:

(i) receipt by the Agent (whether in the Assignment Agreement or otherwise) of written confirmation from the New Lender (in form and substance satisfactory to the Agent) that the New Lender will assume the same obligations to the other Finance Parties as it would have been under if it had been an Original Lender; and

(ii) performance by the Agent of all necessary "**know your customer**" or other similar checks under all applicable laws and regulations in relation to such assignment to a New Lender, the completion of which the Agent shall promptly notify to the Existing Lender and the New Lender.

(b) A transfer will only be effective if the procedure set out in Clause 28.6 (*Procedure for transfer*) is complied with.

(c) If:

(i) a Lender assigns or transfers any of its rights or obligations under the Finance Documents or changes its Facility Office; and

(ii) as a result of circumstances existing at the date the assignment, transfer or change occurs, an Obligor would be obliged to make a payment to the New Lender or Lender acting through its new Facility Office under Clause 18 (*Increased Costs*),

then the New Lender or Lender acting through its new Facility Office is only entitled to receive payment under that Clause to the same extent as the Existing Lender or Lender acting through its previous Facility Office would have been if the assignment, transfer or change had not occurred. This paragraph (c) shall not apply in respect of an assignment or transfer made in the ordinary course of the primary syndication of any Facility.

(d) Each New Lender, by executing the relevant Transfer Certificate or Assignment Agreement, confirms, for the avoidance of doubt, that the Agent has authority to execute on its behalf any amendment or waiver that has been approved by or on behalf of the requisite

Lender or Lenders in accordance with this Agreement on or prior to the date on which the transfer or assignment becomes effective in accordance with this Agreement and that it is bound by that decision to the same extent as the Existing Lender would have been had it remained a Lender.

(e) Notwithstanding any other term of this Agreement, each Lender shall ensure that at all times its Overall Commitment is not less than:

(i) its Swingline Commitment; or

(ii) if it does not have a Swingline Commitment, the Swingline Commitment of a Lender which is its Affiliate.

(f) Subject to the terms of this Agreement, the obligations of each Obligor under this Agreement will continue in full force and effect following any novation under this Clause 28. A novation under this Clause 28 is a novation (*novation*) within the meaning of Articles 1271 *et seq*. of the French *Code Civil*.

**28.4. Assignment or transfer fee**

The New Lender shall, on the date upon which an assignment or transfer takes effect, pay to the Agent (for its own account) a fee of $[•].

**28.5. Limitation of responsibility of Existing Lenders**

(a) Unless expressly agreed to the contrary, an Existing Lender makes no representation or warranty and assumes no responsibility to a New Lender for:

(i) the legality, validity, effectiveness, adequacy or enforceability of the Finance Documents or any other documents;

(ii) the financial condition of any Obligor;

(iii) the performance and observance by any Obligor of its obligations under the Finance Documents or any other documents; or

(iv) the accuracy of any statements (whether written or oral) made in or in connection with any Finance Document or any other document,

and any representations or warranties implied by law are excluded.

(b) Each New Lender confirms to the Existing Lender and the other Finance Parties that it:

(i) has made (and shall continue to make) its own independent investigation and assessment of the financial condition and affairs of each Obligor and its related entities in connection with its participation in this Agreement and has not relied exclusively on any information provided to it by the Existing Lender in connection with any Finance Document; and

(ii) will continue to make its own independent appraisal of the creditworthiness of each Obligor and its related entities whilst any amount is or may be outstanding under the Finance Documents or any Commitment is in force.

(c) Nothing in any Finance Document obliges an Existing Lender to:

(i) accept a re-transfer or re-assignment from a New Lender of any of the rights and obligations assigned or transferred under this Clause 28; or

(ii) support any losses directly or indirectly incurred by the New Lender by reason of the non-performance by any Obligor of its obligations under the Finance Documents or otherwise.

**28.6. Procedure for transfer**

(a) Subject to the conditions set out in Clause 28.2 (*Borrower Consent*) and Clause 28.3 (*Other conditions of assignment or transfer*) a transfer is effected in accordance with paragraph (c) below when the Agent executes an otherwise duly completed Transfer Certificate delivered to it by the Existing Lender and the New Lender. The Agent shall, subject to paragraph (b) below, as soon as reasonably practicable after receipt by it of a duly completed Transfer Certificate appearing on its face to comply with the terms of this Agreement and delivered in accordance with the terms of this Agreement, execute that Transfer Certificate.

(b) The Agent shall only be obliged to execute a Transfer Certificate delivered to it by the Existing Lender and the New Lender once it is satisfied it has complied with all necessary "know your customer" or other similar checks under all applicable laws and regulations in relation to the transfer to such New Lender.

(c) Subject to Clause 28.10 (*Pro rata interest settlement*), on the Transfer Date:

(i) to the extent that in the Transfer Certificate the Existing Lender seeks to transfer by novation its rights and obligations under the Finance Documents each of the Obligors and the Existing Lender shall be released from further obligations towards one another under the Finance Documents and their respective rights against one another under the Finance Documents shall be cancelled (being the "**Discharged Rights and Obligations**");

(ii) each of the Obligors and the New Lender shall assume obligations towards one another and/or acquire rights against one another which differ from the Discharged Rights and Obligations only insofar as that Obligor and the New Lender have assumed and/or acquired the same in place of that Obligor and the Existing Lender;

(iii) the Agent, the Arranger, the New Lender and the other Lenders shall acquire the same rights and assume the same obligations between themselves as they would have acquired and assumed had the New Lender been an Original Lender with the rights and/or obligations acquired or assumed by it as a result of the transfer and to that extent the Agent, the Arranger and the Existing Lender shall each be released from further obligations to each other under the Finance Documents; and

(iv) the New Lender shall become a Party as a "Lender".

**28.7. Procedure for assignment**

(a) Subject to the conditions set out in Clause 28.2 (*Borrower Consent*) and Clause 28.3 (*Other conditions of assignment or transfer*) an assignment may be effected in accordance with paragraph (c) below when the Agent executes an otherwise duly completed Assignment Agreement delivered to it by the Existing Lender and the New Lender. The Agent shall, subject to paragraph (b) below, as soon as reasonably practicable after receipt by it of a duly completed Assignment Agreement appearing on its face to comply with the terms of this Agreement and delivered in accordance with the terms of this Agreement, execute that Assignment Agreement.

(b) The Agent shall only be obliged to execute an Assignment Agreement delivered to it by the Existing Lender and the New Lender once it is satisfied it has complied with all necessary "know your customer" or other similar checks under all applicable laws and regulations in relation to the assignment to such New Lender.

(c) Subject to Clause 28.10 (*Pro rata interest settlement*), on the Transfer Date:

   (i) the Existing Lender will assign absolutely to the New Lender the rights under the Finance Documents expressed to be the subject of the assignment in the Assignment Agreement;

   (ii) the Existing Lender will be released by each Obligor and the other Finance Parties from the obligations owed by it (the "**Relevant Obligations**") and expressed to be the subject of the release in the Assignment Agreement; and

   (iii) the New Lender shall become a Party as a "Lender" and will be bound by obligations equivalent to the Relevant Obligations.

(d) Lenders may utilise procedures other than those set out in this Clause 28.7 to assign their rights under the Finance Documents (but not, without the consent of the relevant Obligor or unless in accordance with Clause 28.6 (*Procedure for transfer*), to obtain a release by that Obligor from the obligations owed to that Obligor by the Lenders nor the assumption of equivalent obligations by a New Lender) **provided that** they comply with the conditions set out in Clause 28.2 (*Borrower Consent*) and Clause 28.3 (*Other conditions of assignment or transfer*).

**28.8. Copy of Transfer Certificate, Assignment Agreement or Increase Confirmation to Borrower**

The Agent shall, as soon as reasonably practicable after it has executed a Transfer Certificate, an Assignment Agreement or an Increase Confirmation, send to the Borrower a copy of that Transfer Certificate, Assignment Agreement or Increase Confirmation.

**28.9. Security over Lenders' rights**

In addition to the other rights provided to Lenders under this Clause 28.9, each Lender may without consulting with or obtaining consent from any Obligor at any time charge, assign or otherwise create Security in or over (whether by way of collateral or otherwise) all or any of its rights under any Finance Document to secure obligations of that Lender including, without limitation:

(a) any charge, assignment or other Security to secure obligations to a federal reserve or central bank; and

(b) any charge, assignment or other Security granted to any holders (or trustee or representatives of holders) of obligations owed, or securities issued, by that Lender as Security for those obligations or securities,

except that no such charge, assignment or Security shall:

(i) release a Lender from any of its obligations under the Finance Documents or substitute the beneficiary of the relevant charge, assignment or Security for the Lender as a party to any of the Finance Documents; or

(ii) require any payments to be made by an Obligor or grant to any person any more extensive rights than those required to be made or granted to the relevant Lender under the Finance Documents.

**28.10. *Pro rata* interest settlement**

(a) If the Agent has notified the Lenders that it is able to distribute interest payments on a "*pro rata* basis" to Existing Lenders and New Lenders then (in respect of any transfer pursuant to Clause 28.6 (*Procedure for transfer*) or any assignment pursuant to Clause 28.7 (*Procedure for assignment*) the Transfer Date of which, in each case, is after the date of such notification and is not on the last day of an Interest Period):

(i) any interest or fees in respect of the relevant participation which are expressed to accrue by reference to the lapse of time shall continue to accrue in favour of the Existing Lender up to but excluding the Transfer Date ("**Accrued Amounts**") and shall become due and payable to the Existing Lender (without further interest accruing on them) on the last day of the current Interest Period (or, if the Interest Period is longer than six Months, on the next of the dates which falls at six Monthly intervals after the first day of that Interest Period); and

(ii) the rights assigned or transferred by the Existing Lender will not include the right to the Accrued Amounts, so that, for the avoidance of doubt:

(A) when the Accrued Amounts become payable, those Accrued Amounts will be payable to the Existing Lender; and

(B) the amount payable to the New Lender on that date will be the amount which would, but for the application of this Clause 28.10, have been payable to it on that date, but after deduction of the Accrued Amounts.

(b) In this Clause 28.10 references to "Interest Period" shall be construed to include a reference to any other period for accrual of fees.

(c) An Existing Lender which retains the right to the Accrued Amounts pursuant to this Clause 28.10 but which does not have a Commitment shall be deemed not to be a Lender for the purposes of ascertaining whether the agreement of any specified group of Lenders has been obtained to approve any request for a consent, waiver, amendment or other vote of Lenders under the Finance Documents.

**28.11. French law provisions**

In the case of a transfer of rights and/or obligations by the Existing Lender hereunder, the New Lender should, if it considers it necessary to make the transfer effective as against the Guarantor, arrange for such transfer to be notified to, or acknowledged by, the Guarantor.

**29. CHANGES TO THE OBLIGORS**

No Obligor may assign any of its rights or transfer any of its rights or obligations under the Finance Documents.

# SECTION 10

## THE FINANCE PARTIES

## 30. ROLE OF THE AGENT, THE ARRANGER AND THE REFERENCE BANKS

The agreement must contain provisions governing the relationship of the lenders between themselves and between them and the agent (and arranger). In view of difficulties experienced by agents over the years broad exculpatory statements are included in the agency Clause, relieving the agent from responsibility for losses incurred by the lenders as a result of their participations. The agent should generally only be required to perform, in a reasonable manner, those duties specifically delegated to it within the facility agreement, and should not be responsible to any syndicate member unless it fails to perform such functions as a result of gross negligence or misconduct.

Similarly, there should be a confirmation from the lenders to the agent (and arranger) that each lender has made its own independent investigation of the financial condition of the borrowers and has not relied upon information supplied by the agent (or arranger). In essence, the agent performs exclusively mechanical and operational functions, with the limits of its authority defined by the lending syndicate.

### 30.1. Appointment of the Agent

(a) Each of the Arrangers and the Lenders appoints the Agent to act as its agent under and in connection with the Finance Documents.

(b) Each of the Arrangers and the Lenders authorises the Agent to perform the duties, obligations and responsibilities and to exercise the rights, powers, authorities and discretions specifically given to the Agent under or in connection with the Finance Documents together with any other incidental rights, powers, authorities and discretions.

### 30.2. Instructions

(a) The Agent shall:

(i) unless a contrary indication appears in a Finance Document, exercise or refrain from exercising any right, power, authority or discretion vested in it as Agent in accordance with any instructions given to it by:

(A) all Lenders if the relevant Finance Document stipulates the matter is an all Lender decision;

(B) in all other cases, the Majority Lenders; and

(ii) not be liable for any act (or omission) if it acts (or refrains from acting) in accordance with paragraph (i) above.

(b) The Agent shall be entitled to request instructions, or clarification of any instruction, from the Majority Lenders (or, if the relevant Finance Document stipulates the matter is a decision for any other Lender or group of Lenders, from that Lender or group of Lenders) as to whether, and in what manner, it should exercise or refrain from exercising any right, power, authority or discretion and the Agent may refrain from acting unless and until it receives those instructions or that clarification.

(c) Save in the case of decisions stipulated to be a matter for any other Lender or group of Lenders under the relevant Finance Document and unless a contrary indication appears in a Finance Document, any instructions given to the Agent by the Majority Lenders shall override any conflicting instructions given by any other Parties and will be binding on all Finance Parties.

(d) The Agent may refrain from acting in accordance with any instructions of any Lender or group of Lenders until it has received any indemnification and/or security that it may in its discretion require (which may be greater in extent than that contained in the Finance Documents and which may include payment in advance) for any cost, loss or liability which it may incur in complying with those instructions.

(e) In the absence of instructions, the Agent may act (or refrain from acting) as it considers to be in the best interest of the Lenders.

(f) The Agent is not authorised to act on behalf of a Lender (without first obtaining that Lender's consent) in any legal or arbitration proceedings relating to any Finance Document.

**30.3. Duties of the Agent**

(a) The Agent's duties under the Finance Documents are solely mechanical and administrative in nature.

(b) Subject to paragraph (c) below, the Agent shall promptly forward to a Party the original or a copy of any document which is delivered to the Agent for that Party by any other Party.

(c) Without prejudice to Clause 28.8 (*Copy of Transfer Certificate, Assignment Agreement or Increase Confirmation to Borrower*), paragraph (b) above shall not apply to any Transfer Certificate, any Assignment Agreement or any Increase Confirmation.

(d) Except where a Finance Document specifically provides otherwise, the Agent is not obliged to review or check the adequacy, accuracy or completeness of any document it forwards to another Party.

(e) If the Agent receives notice from a Party referring to this Agreement, describing a Default and stating that the circumstance described is a Default, it shall promptly notify the other Finance Parties.

(f) If the Agent is aware of the non-payment of any principal, interest, commitment fee or other fee payable to a Finance Party (other than the Agent or the Arranger) under this Agreement it shall promptly notify the other Finance Parties.

(g) The Agent shall provide to the Borrower, within five Business Days of a request by the Borrower (but no more frequently than once per calendar month), a list (which may be in electronic form) setting out the names of the Lenders as at the date of that request, their respective Commitments and/or Swingline Commitments, the address and fax number (and the department or officer, if any, for whose attention any communication is to be made) of each Lender for any communication to be made or document to be delivered under or in connection with the Finance Documents, the electronic mail address and/or any other information required to enable the sending and receipt of information by electronic mail or other electronic means to and by each Lender to whom any communication under or in connection with the Finance Documents may be made by that means and the account details of each Lender for any payment to be distributed by the Agent to that Lender under the Finance Documents.

(h) The Agent shall have only those duties, obligations and responsibilities expressly specified in the Finance Documents to which it is expressed to be a party (and no others shall be implied).

### 30.4. Role of the Arranger

Except as specifically provided in the Finance Documents, the Arranger has no obligations of any kind to any other Party under or in connection with any Finance Document.

### 30.5. No fiduciary duties

(a) Nothing in any Finance Document constitutes the Agent or the Arranger as a trustee or fiduciary of any other person.

(b) Neither the Agent nor the Arranger shall be bound to account to any Lender for any sum or the profit element of any sum received by it for its own account.

### 30.6. Business with the Group

The Agent and the Arranger may accept deposits from, lend money to and generally engage in any kind of banking or other business with any member of the Group.

### 30.7. Rights and discretions

The Agent may:

(a) rely on:

(i) any representation, communication, notice or document believed by it to be genuine, correct and appropriately authorised;

(ii) assume that:

(A) any instructions received by it from the Majority Lenders, any Lenders or any group of Lenders are duly given in accordance with the terms of the Finance Documents; and

(B) unless it has received notice of revocation, that those instructions have not been revoked; and

(iii) rely on a certificate from any person:

(A) as to any matter of fact or circumstance which might reasonably be expected to be within the knowledge of that person; or

(B) to the effect that such person approves of any particular dealing, transaction, step, action or thing, as sufficient evidence that that is the case and, in the case of paragraph (A) above, may assume the truth and accuracy of that certificate.

(b) The Agent may assume (unless it has received notice to the contrary in its capacity as agent for the Lenders) that:

(i) no Default has occurred (unless it has actual knowledge of a Default arising under Clause 27.1 (*Non-payment*));

(ii) any right, power, authority or discretion vested in any Party or any group of Lenders has not been exercised;

(iii) any notice or request made by the Borrower (other than a Utilisation Request) is made on behalf of and with the consent and knowledge of the Guarantor

(c) The Agent may engage and pay for the advice or services of any lawyers, accountants, tax advisers, surveyors or other professional advisers or experts.

(d) Without prejudice to the generality of paragraph (c) above or paragraph (e) below, the Agent may at any time engage and pay for the services of any lawyers to act as independent counsel to the Agent (and so separate from any lawyers instructed by the Lenders) if the Agent in its reasonable opinion deems this to be desirable.

(e) The Agent may rely on the advice or services of any lawyers, accountants, tax advisers, surveyors or other professional advisers or experts (whether obtained by the Agent or by any other Party) and shall not be liable for any damages, costs or losses to any person, any diminution in value or any liability whatsoever arising as a result of its so relying.

(f) The Agent may act in relation to the Finance Documents through its officers, employees and agents and the Agent shall not:

(i) be liable for any error of judgment made by any such person; or

(ii) be bound to supervise, or be in any way responsible for any loss incurred by reason of misconduct, omission or default on the part, of any such person,

unless such error or such loss was directly caused by the Agent's gross negligence or wilful misconduct.

(g) Unless a Finance Document expressly provides otherwise the Agent may disclose to any other Party any information it reasonably believes it has received as agent under this Agreement.

(h) Without prejudice to the generality of paragraph (g) above, the Agent:

(i) may disclose; and

(ii) on the written request of the Borrower or the Majority Lenders shall, as soon as reasonably practicable, disclose,

the identity of a Defaulting Lender to the Borrower and to the other Finance Parties.

(i) Notwithstanding any other provision of any Finance Document to the contrary, neither the Agent nor the Arranger is obliged to do or omit to do anything if it would, or might in its reasonable opinion, constitute a breach of any law or regulation or a breach of a fiduciary duty or duty of confidentiality.

(j) The Agent is not obliged to disclose to any Finance Party any details of the rate notified to the Agent by any Lender or the identity of any such Lender for the purpose of paragraph (a) of Clause 15.3 (*Market disruption*).

(k) Notwithstanding any provision of any Finance Document to the contrary, the Agent is not obliged to expend or risk its own funds or otherwise incur any financial liability in the performance of its duties, obligations or responsibilities or the exercise of any right, power, authority or discretion if it has grounds for believing the repayment of such funds or adequate indemnity against, or security for, such risk or liability is not reasonably assured to it.

**30.8. Responsibility for documentation**

Neither the Agent nor the Arranger is responsible or liable for:

(a) the adequacy, accuracy or completeness of any information (whether oral or written) supplied by the Agent, the Arranger, an Obligor or any other person in or in connection with any Finance Document or the Information Memorandum or the transactions contemplated in the Finance Documents or any other agreement, arrangement or document entered into, made or executed in anticipation of, under or in connection with any Finance Document;

(b) the legality, validity, effectiveness, adequacy or enforceability of any Finance Document or any other agreement, arrangement or document entered into, made or executed in anticipation of, under or in connection with any Finance Document; or

(c) any determination as to whether any information provided or to be provided to any Finance Party is non-public information the use of which may be regulated or prohibited by applicable law or regulation relating to insider dealing or otherwise.

**30.9. No duty to monitor**

The Agent shall not be bound to enquire:

(a) whether or not any Default has occurred;

(b) as to the performance, default or any breach by any Party of its obligations under any Finance Document; or

(c) whether any other event specified in any Finance Document has occurred.

**30.10. Exclusion of liability**

(a) Without limiting paragraph (b) below (and without prejudice to any other provision of any Finance Document excluding or limiting the liability of the Agent), the Agent will not be liable for:

(i) any damages, costs or losses to any person, any diminution in value, or any liability whatsoever arising as a result of taking or not taking any action under or in connection with any Finance Document, unless directly caused by its gross negligence or wilful misconduct;

(ii) exercising, or not exercising, any right, power, authority or discretion given to it by, or in connection with, any Finance Document or any other agreement, arrangement or document entered into, made or executed in anticipation of, under or in connection with, any Finance Document other than by reason of its gross negligence or wilful misconduct; or

(iii) without prejudice to the generality of paragraphs (i) and (ii) above, any damages, costs or losses to any person, any diminution in value or any liability whatsoever (including, without limitation, for negligence or any other category of liability whatsoever but not including any claim based on the fraud of the Agent) arising as a result of:

(A) any act, event or circumstance not reasonably within its control; or

(B) the general risks of investment in, or the holding of assets in, any jurisdiction,

including (in each case and without limitation) such damages, costs, losses, diminution in value or liability arising as a result of: nationalisation, expropriation or other governmental actions; any regulation, currency restriction, devaluation or fluctuation; market conditions affecting the execution or settlement of transactions or the value of assets (including any Disruption Event); breakdown, failure or malfunction of any third party transport, telecommunications, computer services or systems; natural disasters or acts of God; war, terrorism, insurrection or revolution; or strikes or industrial action.

(b) No Party (other than the Agent) may take any proceedings against any officer, employee or agent of the Agent in respect of any claim it might have against the Agent or in respect of any act or omission of any kind by that officer, employee or agent in relation to any Finance Document and any officer, employee or agent of the Agent may rely on this Clause subject to Clause 1.6 (*Third party rights*) and the provisions of the Third Parties Act.

(c) The Agent will not be liable for any delay (or any related consequences) in crediting an account with an amount required under the Finance Documents to be paid by the Agent if the Agent has taken all necessary steps as soon as reasonably practicable to comply with the regulations or operating procedures of any recognised clearing or settlement system used by the Agent for that purpose.

(d) Nothing in this Agreement shall oblige the Agent or the Arranger to carry out:

(i) any "know your customer" or other checks in relation to any person; or

(ii) any check on the extent to which any transaction contemplated by this Agreement might be unlawful for any Lender or for any Affiliate of any Lender, on behalf of any Lender and each Lender confirms to the Agent and the Arranger that it is solely responsible for any such checks it is required to carry out and that it may not rely on any statement in relation to such checks made by the Agent or the Arranger.

(e) Without prejudice to any provision of any Finance Document excluding or limiting the Agent's liability, any liability of the Agent arising under or in connection with any Finance Document shall be limited to the amount of actual loss which has been finally judicially determined to have been suffered (as determined by reference to the date of default of the Agent or, if later, the date on which the loss arises as a result of such default) but without reference to any special conditions or circumstances known to the Agent at any time which increase the amount of that loss. In no event shall the Agent be liable for any loss of profits, goodwill, reputation, business opportunity or anticipated saving, or for special, punitive, indirect or consequential damages, whether or not the Agent has been advised of the possibility of such loss or damages.

**30.11. Lenders' indemnity to the Agent**

(a) Each Lender shall (in proportion to its share of the Total Commitments or, if the Total Commitments are then zero, to its share of the Total Commitments immediately prior to their reduction to zero) indemnify the Agent, within three Business Days of demand, against any cost, loss or liability (including, without limitation, for negligence or any other category of liability whatsoever) incurred by the Agent (otherwise than by reason of the Agent's gross negligence or wilful misconduct) (or, in the case of any cost, loss or liability pursuant to Clause 33.11 (*Disruption to payment systems etc.,*) notwithstanding the Agent's negligence, gross negligence or any other category of liability whatsoever but not including any claim based on the fraud of the Agent) in acting as Agent under the Finance Documents (unless the Agent has been reimbursed by an Obligor pursuant to a Finance Document).

(b) Subject to paragraph (c) below, the Borrower shall immediately on demand reimburse any Lender for any payment that Lender makes to the Agent pursuant to paragraph (a) above.

(c) Paragraph (b) above shall not apply to the extent that the indemnity payment in respect of which the Lender claims reimbursement relates to a liability of the Agent to the Borrower.

**30.12. Resignation of the Agent**

(a) The Agent may resign and appoint one of its Affiliates acting through an office in the United Kingdom as successor by giving notice to the Lenders and the Borrower.

(b) Alternatively the Agent may resign by giving 30 days' notice to the Lenders and the Borrower, in which case the Majority Lenders (after consultation with the Borrower) may appoint a successor Agent, which shall not be incorporated or acting through an office situated in a Non-Cooperative Jurisdiction.

(c) The Borrower may, on no less than 30 days' prior notice to the Agent, require the Lenders to replace the Agent and appoint a replacement Agent if any amount payable under a Finance Document by an Obligor established in France becomes not deductible from that Obligor's taxable income for French tax purposes by reason of that amount (i) being paid or accrued to the Agent incorporated or acting through an office situated in a Non-Cooperative Jurisdiction or (ii) paid to an account opened in the name of the Agent in a financial institution situated in a Non-Cooperative Jurisdiction. In this case, the Agent shall resign and a replacement Agent shall be appointed by the Majority Lenders (after consultation with the Borrower) within 30 days after notice of replacement was given.

(d) If the Majority Lenders have not appointed a successor Agent in accordance with paragraph (b) above within 20 days after notice of resignation was given, the retiring Agent (after consultation with the Borrower) may appoint a successor Agent.

(e) If the Agent wishes to resign because (acting reasonably) it has concluded that it is no longer appropriate for it to remain as agent and the Agent is entitled to appoint a successor Agent under paragraph (c) above, the Agent may (if it concludes (acting reasonably) that it is necessary to do so in order to persuade the proposed successor Agent to become a party to this Agreement as Agent) agree with the proposed successor Agent amendments to this Clause 30 and any other term of this Agreement dealing with the rights or obligations of the Agent consistent with then current market practice for the appointment and protection of corporate trustees together with any reasonable amendments to the agency fee payable under this Agreement which are consistent with the successor Agent's normal fee rates and those amendments will bind the Parties.

(f) The retiring Agent shall, at its own cost, make available to the successor Agent such documents and records and provide such assistance as the successor Agent may reasonably request for the purposes of performing its functions as Agent under the Finance Documents. The Borrower shall, within three Business Days of demand, reimburse the retiring Agent for the amount of all costs and expenses (including legal fees) properly incurred by it in making available such documents and records and providing such assistance.

(g) The Agent's resignation notice shall only take effect upon the appointment of a successor.

(h) Upon the appointment of a successor, the retiring Agent shall be discharged from any further obligation in respect of the Finance Documents (other than its obligations under paragraph (f) above) but shall remain entitled to the benefit of Clause 19.3 (*Indemnity to the Agent*) and this Clause 30 (and any agency fees for the account of the retiring Agent shall cease to accrue from (and shall be payable on) that date). Any successor and each of the other Parties shall have the same rights and obligations amongst themselves as they would have had if such successor had been an original Party.

(i) After consultation with the Borrower, the Majority Lenders may, by notice to the Agent, require it to resign in accordance with paragraph (b) above. In this event, the Agent shall resign in accordance with paragraph (b) above.

(j) The Agent shall resign in accordance with paragraph (b) above (and, to the extent applicable, shall use reasonable endeavours to appoint a successor Agent pursuant to paragraph (c) above) if on or after the date which is three months before the earliest FATCA Application Date relating to any payment to the Agent under the Finance Documents, either:

  (i) the Agent fails to respond to a request under Clause 17.8 (*FATCA information*) and the Borrower or a Lender reasonably believes that the Agent will not be (or will have ceased to be) a FATCA Exempt Party on or after that FATCA Application Date;

(ii) the information supplied by the Agent pursuant to Clause 17.8 (*FATCA information*) indicates that the Agent will not be (or will have ceased to be) a FATCA Exempt Party on or after that FATCA Application Date; or

(iii) the Agent notifies the Borrower and the Lenders that the Agent will not be (or will have ceased to be) a FATCA Exempt Party on or after that FATCA Application Date,

and (in each case) the Borrower or a Lender reasonably believes that a Party will be required to make a FATCA Deduction that would not be required if the Agent were a FATCA Exempt Party, and the Borrower or that Lender, by notice to the Agent, requires it to resign.

**30.13. Replacement of the Agent**

(a) After consultation with the Borrower, the Majority Lenders may, by giving 30 days' notice to the Agent (or, at any time the Agent is an Impaired Agent, by giving any shorter notice determined by the Majority Lenders) replace the Agent by appointing a successor Agent (acting through an office in the United Kingdom).

(b) The retiring Agent shall (at its own cost if it is an Impaired Agent and otherwise at the expense of the Lenders) make available to the successor Agent such documents and records and provide such assistance as the successor Agent may reasonably request for the purposes of performing its functions as Agent under the Finance Documents.

(c) The appointment of the successor Agent shall take effect on the date specified in the notice from the Majority Lenders to the retiring Agent. As from this date, the retiring Agent shall be discharged from any further obligation in respect of the Finance Documents (other than its obligations under paragraph (b) above) but shall remain entitled to the benefit of Clause 19.3 (*Indemnity to the Agent*) and this Clause 30 (and any agency fees for the account of the retiring Agent shall cease to accrue from (and shall be payable on) that date).

(d) Any successor Agent and each of the other Parties shall have the same rights and obligations amongst themselves as they would have had if such successor had been an original Party.

### 30.14. Confidentiality

(a) In acting as agent for the Finance Parties, the Agent shall be regarded as acting through its agency division which shall be treated as a separate entity from any other of its divisions or departments.

(b) If information is received by another division or department of the Agent, it may be treated as confidential to that division or department and the Agent shall not be deemed to have notice of it.

(c) Notwithstanding any other provision of any Finance Document to the contrary, neither the Agent nor the Arranger is obliged to disclose to any other person (i) any confidential information or (ii) any other information if the disclosure would, or might in its reasonable opinion, constitute a breach of any law or regulation or a breach of a fiduciary duty.

### 30.15. Relationship with the Lenders

(a) Subject to Clause 28.10 (*Pro rata interest settlement*), the Agent may treat the person shown in its records as Lender at the opening of business (in the place of the Agent's principal office as notified to the Finance Parties from time to time) as the Lender acting through its Facility Office:

(i) entitled to or liable for any payment due under any Finance Document on that day; and

(ii) entitled to receive and act upon any notice, request, document or communication or make any decision or determination under any Finance Document made or delivered on that day,

unless it has received not less than five Business Days' prior notice from that Lender to the contrary in accordance with the terms of this Agreement.

(b) Any Lender may by notice to the Agent appoint a person to receive on its behalf all notices, communications, information and documents to be made or despatched to that Lender under the Finance Documents. Such notice shall contain the address, fax number and (where communication by electronic mail or other electronic means is permitted under Clause 35.6 (*Electronic communication*)) electronic mail address and/or any other information required to enable the transmission of information by that means (and, in each case, the department or officer, if any, for whose attention communication is to be made) and be treated as a notification of a substitute address, fax number, electronic mail address (or such other information), department and officer by that Lender for the purposes of Clause 35.2 (*Addresses*) and paragraph (a)(ii) of Clause 35.6 (*Electronic communication*) and the Agent shall be entitled to treat such person as the person entitled to receive all such notices, communications, information and documents as though that person were that Lender.

**30.16. Credit appraisal by the Lenders**

Without affecting the responsibility of any Obligor for information supplied by it or on its behalf in connection with any Finance Document, each Lender confirms to the Agent and the Arranger that it has been, and will continue to be, solely responsible for making its own independent appraisal and investigation of all risks arising under or in connection with any Finance Document, including, but not limited to:

(a) the financial condition, status and nature of each member of the Group;

(b) the legality, validity, effectiveness, adequacy or enforceability of any Finance Document and any other agreement, arrangement or document entered into, made or executed in anticipation of, under or in connection with any Finance Document;

(c) whether that Lender has recourse, and the nature and extent of that recourse, against any Party or any of its respective assets under or in connection with any Finance Document, the transactions contemplated by the Finance Documents or any other agreement, arrangement or document entered into, made or executed in anticipation of, under or in connection with any Finance Document; and

(d) the adequacy, accuracy or completeness of the Information Memorandum and any other information provided by the Agent, any Party or by any other person under or in connection with any Finance Document, the transactions contemplated by any Finance Document or any other agreement, arrangement or document entered into, made or executed in anticipation of, under or in connection with any Finance Document.

### 30.17. Agent's management time

Any amount payable to the Agent under Clause 19.3 (*Indemnity to the Agent*), Clause 21 (*Costs and Expenses*) and Clause 30.11 (*Lenders' indemnity to the Agent*) shall include the cost of utilising the Agent's management time or other resources and will be calculated on the basis of such reasonable daily or hourly rates as the Agent may notify to the Borrower and the Lenders, and is in addition to any fee paid or payable to the Agent under Clause 16 (*Fees*).

### 30.18. Deduction from amounts payable by the Agent

If any Party owes an amount to the Agent under the Finance Documents the Agent may, after giving notice to that Party, deduct an amount not exceeding that amount from any payment to that Party which the Agent would otherwise be obliged to make under the Finance Documents and apply the amount deducted in or towards satisfaction of the amount owed. For the purposes of the Finance Documents that Party shall be regarded as having received any amount so deducted.

### 30.19. Role of Reference Banks

(a) No Reference Bank is under any obligation to provide a quotation or any other information to the Agent.

(b) No Reference Bank will be liable for any action taken by it under or in connection with any Finance Document, or for any Reference Bank Quotation, unless directly caused by its gross negligence or wilful misconduct.

(c) No Party (other than the relevant Reference Bank) may take any proceedings against any officer, employee or agent of any Reference Bank in respect of any claim it might have against that Reference Bank or in respect of any act or omission of any kind by that officer, employee or agent in relation to any Finance Document, or to any Reference Bank Quotation, and any officer, employee or agent of each Reference Bank may rely on this Clause 30.19 subject to Clause 1.6 (*Third party rights*) and the provisions of the Third Parties Act.

### 30.20. Third Party Reference Banks

A Reference Bank which is not a Party may rely on Clause 30.19 (*Role of Reference Banks*), Clause 39.3 (*Other exceptions*) and Clause 41 (*Confidentiality of Funding Rates and Reference Bank Quotations*), subject to Clause 1.6 (*Third party rights*) and the provisions of the Third Parties Act.

## 31. CONDUCT OF BUSINESS BY THE FINANCE PARTIES

No provision of this Agreement will:

(a) interfere with the right of any Finance Party to arrange its affairs (tax or otherwise) in whatever manner it thinks fit;

(b) oblige any Finance Party to investigate or claim any credit, relief, remission or repayment available to it or the extent, order and manner of any claim; or

(c) oblige any Finance Party to disclose any information relating to its affairs (tax or otherwise) or any computations in respect of Tax.

## 32. SHARING AMONG THE FINANCE PARTIES

This provision, known as a "**sharing**", "**redistribution**" or "***pro rata***" Clause, operates together with Clause 34 (*Set-off*), which permits the lenders to set-off against deposits of a borrower and a guarantor. The sharing Clause acquired its current form in light of experience with its use following the freeze of Iranian assets imposed by the United States and following the Falklands/Malvinas crisis, when Argentine borrowers made debt repayments only to non-British lenders. The sharing Clause requires a lender that has exercised set-off rights (or otherwise received more than its "share" of a due payment) to acquire the other lenders' rights to receive payments from a borrower in amounts sufficient effectively to redistribute the amount so obtained by set-off among all the lenders.

The Clause is sometimes written without the provision in paragraph (b) of Clause 32.5 (*Exceptions*). The sharing provision could then be restricted to only cover sums net of the costs of any legal proceedings brought to realise such sums.

### 32.1. Payments to Finance Parties

If a Finance Party (a "**Recovering Finance Party**") receives or recovers any amount from an Obligor other than in accordance with Clause 33 (*Payment Mechanics*) (a "**Recovered Amount**") and applies that amount to a payment due under the Finance Documents then:

(a) the Recovering Finance Party shall, within three Business Days, notify details of the receipt or recovery to the Agent;

(b) the Agent shall determine whether the receipt or recovery is in excess of the amount the Recovering Finance Party would have been paid had the receipt or recovery been received or made by the Agent and distributed in accordance with Clause 33 (*Payment Mechanics*), without taking account of any Tax which would be imposed on the Agent in relation to the receipt, recovery or distribution; and

(c) the Recovering Finance Party shall, within three Business Days of demand by the Agent, pay to the Agent an amount (the "**Sharing Payment**") equal to such receipt or recovery less any amount which the Agent determines may be retained by the Recovering Finance Party as its share of any payment to be made, in accordance with Clause 33.6 (*Partial payments*).

### 32.2. Redistribution of payments

The Agent shall treat the Sharing Payment as if it had been paid by the relevant Obligor and distribute it between the Finance Parties (other than the Recovering Finance Party) (the "**Sharing Finance Parties**") in accordance with Clause 33.6 (*Partial payments*) towards the obligations of that Obligor to the Sharing Finance Parties.

### 32.3. Recovering Finance Party's rights

On a distribution by the Agent under Clause 32.2 (*Redistribution of payments*) of a payment received by a Recovering Finance Party from an Obligor as between the relevant Obligor and the Recovering Finance Party, an amount of the Recovered Amount equal to the Sharing Payment will be treated as not having been paid by that Obligor.

### 32.4. Reversal of redistribution

If any part of the Sharing Payment received or recovered by a Recovering Finance Party becomes repayable and is repaid by that Recovering Finance Party, then:

(a) each Sharing Finance Party shall, upon request of the Agent, pay to the Agent for the account of that Recovering Finance Party an amount equal to the appropriate part of its share of the Sharing Payment (together with an amount as is necessary to reimburse that Recovering Finance Party for its proportion of any interest on the Sharing Payment which that Recovering Finance Party is required to pay) (the "**Redistributed Amount**"); and

(b) as between the relevant Obligor and each relevant Sharing Finance Party, an amount equal to the relevant Redistributed Amount will be treated as not having been paid by that Obligor.

### 32.5. Exceptions

(a) This Clause 32 shall not apply to the extent that the Recovering Finance Party would not, after making any payment pursuant to this Clause, have a valid and enforceable claim against the relevant Obligor.

(b) A Recovering Finance Party is not obliged to share with any other Finance Party any amount which the Recovering Finance Party has received or recovered as a result of taking legal or arbitration proceedings, if:

  (i) it notified that other Finance Party of the legal or arbitration proceedings; and

  (ii) that other Finance Party had an opportunity to participate in those legal or arbitration proceedings but did not do so as soon as reasonably practicable having received notice and did not take separate legal or arbitration proceedings.

# SECTION 11

## ADMINISTRATION

## 33. PAYMENT MECHANICS

### 33.1. Payments to the Agent

(a) On each date on which an Obligor or a Lender is required to make a payment under a Finance Document, that Obligor or Lender shall make the same available to the Agent (unless a contrary indication appears in a Finance Document) for value on the due date at the time and in such funds specified by the Agent as being customary at the time for settlement of transactions in the relevant currency in the place of payment.

(b) Payment shall be made to such account in the principal financial centre of the country of that currency and with such bank as the Agent, in each case, specifies (other than a Non-Cooperative Jurisdiction).

### 33.2. Distributions by the Agent

Each payment received by the Agent under the Finance Documents for another Party shall, subject to Clause 33.3 (*Distributions to an Obligor*), Clause 33.4 (*Clawback and pre-funding*) and Clause 30.18 (*Deduction from amounts payable by the Agent*) be made available by the Agent as soon as practicable after receipt to the Party entitled to receive payment in accordance with this Agreement (in the case of a Lender, for the account of its Facility Office), to such account as that Party may notify to the Agent by not less than five Business Days' notice with a bank specified by that Party in the principal financial centre of the country of that currency (or, in relation to euro, in the principal financial centre of a Participating Member State or London, as specified by that Party), other than a Non-Cooperative Jurisdiction.

### 33.3. Distributions to an Obligor

The Agent may (with the consent of the Obligor or in accordance with Clause 34 (*Set-off*)) apply any amount received by it for that Obligor in or towards payment (on the date and in the currency and funds of receipt) of any amount due from that Obligor under the Finance Documents or in or towards purchase of any amount of any currency to be so applied.

### 33.4. Clawback and pre-funding

(a) Where a sum is to be paid to the Agent under the Finance Documents for another Party, the Agent is not obliged to pay that sum to that other Party (or to enter into or perform any related exchange contract) until it has been able to establish to its satisfaction that it has actually received that sum.

(b) Unless paragraph (c) below applies, if the Agent pays an amount to another Party and it proves to be the case that the Agent had not actually received that amount, then the Party to whom that amount (or the proceeds of any related exchange contract) was paid by the Agent shall on demand refund the same to the Agent together with interest on that amount from the date of payment to the date of receipt by the Agent, calculated by the Agent to reflect its cost of funds.

(c) If the Agent has notified the Lenders that it is willing to make available amounts for the account of the Borrower before receiving funds from the Lenders then if and to the extent that the Agent does so but it proves to be the case that it does not then receive funds from a Lender in respect of a sum which it paid to the Borrower:

(i) the Borrower shall on demand refund it to the Agent; and

(ii) the Lender by whom those funds should have been made available or, if that Lender fails to do so, the Borrower, shall on demand pay to the Agent the amount (as certified by the Agent) which will indemnify the Agent against any funding cost incurred by it as a result of paying out that sum before receiving those funds from that Lender.

As mentioned in the term sheet in chapter 3, this provision protects agents who decide to advance funds to a borrower before they have been put in funds by a lender and such lender then fails to reimburse them. Although this provision can be helpful from a practical perspective (as it means that the agent can transfer funds without it having to wait to receive the relevant funds from the lenders), some agents can still be reluctant to prefund.

### 33.5. Impaired Agent

(a) If, at any time, the Agent becomes an Impaired Agent, an Obligor or a Lender which is required to make a payment under the Finance Documents to the Agent in accordance with Clause 33.1 (*Payments to the Agent*) may instead either:

(i) pay that amount direct to the required recipient(s); or

(ii) if in its absolute discretion it considers that it is not reasonably practicable to pay that amount direct to the required recipient(s), pay that amount or the relevant part of that amount to an interest-bearing account held with an Acceptable Bank within the meaning of paragraph (b) of the definition of "Acceptable Bank" and in relation to which no Insolvency Event has occurred and is continuing, in the name of the Obligor or the Lender making the payment (the "**Paying Party**") and designated as a trust account for the benefit of the Party or Parties beneficially entitled to that payment under the Finance Documents (the "**Recipient Party**" or "**Recipient Parties**").

In each case such payments must be made on the due date for payment under the Finance Documents.

(b) All interest accrued on the amount standing to the credit of the trust account shall be for the benefit of the Recipient Party or the Recipient Parties *pro rata* to their respective entitlements.

(c) A Party which has made a payment in accordance with this Clause 33.5 shall be discharged of the relevant payment obligation under the Finance Documents and shall not take any credit risk with respect to the amounts standing to the credit of the trust account.

(d) Promptly upon the appointment of a successor Agent in accordance with Clause 30.13 (*Replacement of the Agent)*, each Paying Party shall (other than to the extent that that Party has given an instruction pursuant to paragraph (e) below) give all requisite instructions to the bank with whom the trust account is held to transfer the amount (together with any accrued interest) to the successor Agent for distribution to the relevant Recipient Party or Recipient Parties in accordance with Clause 33.2 (*Distributions by the Agent*).

(e) A Paying Party shall, promptly upon request by a Recipient Party and to the extent:

(i) that it has not given an instruction pursuant to paragraph (d) above; and

(ii) that it has been provided with the necessary information by that Recipient Party, give all requisite instructions to the bank with whom the trust account is held to transfer the relevant amount (together with any accrued interest) to that Recipient Party.

**33.6. Partial payments**

(a) Subject to Clause 9.7 (*Partial payments – Swingline Loans*), if the Agent receives a payment that is insufficient to discharge all the amounts then due and payable by an Obligor under the Finance Documents, the Agent shall apply that payment towards the obligations of that Obligor under the Finance Documents in the following order:

(i) **first**, in or towards payment *pro rata* of any unpaid amounts owing to the Agent and the Arranger under the Finance Documents;

(ii) **secondly**, in or towards payment *pro rata* of any accrued interest, fee or commission due but unpaid under this Agreement;

(iii) **thirdly**, in or towards payment *pro rata* of any principal due but unpaid under this Agreement; and

(iv) **fourthly**, in or towards payment *pro rata* of any other sum due but unpaid under the Finance Documents.

(b) The Agent shall, if so directed by the Majority Lenders, vary the order set out in paragraphs (a)(ii) to (a)(iv) above.

(c) Paragraphs (a) and (b) above will override any appropriation made by an Obligor.

**33.7. No set-off by Obligors**

All payments to be made by an Obligor under the Finance Documents shall be calculated and be made without (and free and clear of any deduction for) set-off or counterclaim.

**33.8. Business Days**

(a) Any payment under the Finance Documents which is due to be made on a day that is not a Business Day shall be made on the next Business Day in the same calendar month (if there is one) or the preceding Business Day (if there is not).

(b) During any extension of the due date for payment of any principal or Unpaid Sum under this Agreement interest is payable on the principal or Unpaid Sum at the rate payable on the original due date.

**33.9. Currency of account**

(a) Subject to paragraphs (b) to (e) below, the Base Currency is the currency of account and payment for any sum due from an Obligor under any Finance Document.

(b) A repayment of a Loan or Unpaid Sum or a part of a Loan or Unpaid Sum shall be made in the currency in which that Loan or Unpaid Sum is denominated pursuant to this Agreement on its due date.

(c) Each payment of interest shall be made in the currency in which the sum in respect of which the interest is payable was denominated pursuant to this Agreement when that interest accrued.

(d) Each payment in respect of costs, expenses or Taxes shall be made in the currency in which the costs, expenses or Taxes are incurred.

(e) Any amount expressed to be payable in a currency other than the Base Currency shall be paid in that other currency.

**33.10. Change of currency**

(a) Unless otherwise prohibited by law, if more than one currency or currency unit are at the same time recognised by the central bank of any country as the lawful currency of that country, then:

(i) any reference in the Finance Documents to, and any obligations arising under the Finance Documents in, the currency of that country shall be translated into, or paid in, the currency or currency unit of that country designated by the Agent (after consultation with the Borrower); and

(ii) any translation from one currency or currency unit to another shall be at the official rate of exchange recognised by the central bank for the conversion of that currency or currency unit into the other, rounded up or down by the Agent (acting reasonably).

(b) If a change in any currency of a country occurs, this Agreement will, to the extent the Agent (acting reasonably and after consultation with the Borrower) specifies to be necessary, be amended to comply with any generally accepted conventions and market practice in the Relevant Market and otherwise to reflect the change in currency.

**33.11. Disruption to payment systems etc.**

If either the Agent determines (in its discretion) that a Disruption Event has occurred or the Agent is notified by the Borrower that a Disruption Event has occurred:

(a) the Agent may, and shall if requested to do so by the Borrower, consult with the Borrower with a view to agreeing with the Borrower such changes to the operation or administration of the Facilities as the Agent may deem necessary in the circumstances;

(b) the Agent shall not be obliged to consult with the Borrower in relation to any changes mentioned in paragraph (a) above if, in its opinion, it is not practicable to do so in the circumstances and, in any event, shall have no obligation to agree to such changes;

(c) the Agent may consult with the Finance Parties in relation to any changes mentioned in paragraph (a) above but shall not be obliged to do so if, in its opinion, it is not practicable to do so in the circumstances;

(d) any such changes agreed upon by the Agent and the Borrower shall (whether or not it is finally determined that a Disruption Event has occurred) be binding upon the Parties as an amendment to (or, as the case may be, waiver of) the terms of the Finance Documents notwithstanding the provisions of Clause 39 (*Amendments and Waivers*);

(e) the Agent shall not be liable for any damages, costs or losses to any person, any diminution in value or any liability whatsoever (including, without limitation for negligence, gross negligence or any other category of liability whatsoever but not including any claim based on the fraud of the Agent) arising as a result of its taking, or failing to take, any actions pursuant to or in connection with this Clause 33.11; and

(f) the Agent shall notify the Finance Parties of all changes agreed pursuant to paragraph (d) above.

## 34. SET-OFF

> This Clause 34 contains a provision under which the Borrower authorises each Finance Party to apply credit balances (in whatever currency) in satisfaction of sums due but unpaid under the sample agreement. As such, this Clause 34 constitutes a contractual mandate from the Borrower to the Finance Parties and therefore gives rise to contractual rights and obligations entirely distinct from any rights of set-off which might exist in relation to accounts of the Borrower with the Finance Parties under the laws applicable in the jurisdiction or jurisdictions in which such accounts are maintained.

A Finance Party may set off any matured obligation due from an Obligor under the Finance Documents (to the extent beneficially owned by that Finance Party) against any matured obligation owed by that Finance Party to that Obligor, regardless of the place of payment, booking branch or currency of either obligation. If the obligations are in different currencies, the Finance Party may convert either obligation at a market rate of exchange in its usual course of business for the purpose of the set-off.

## 35. NOTICES

### 35.1. Communications in writing

Any communication to be made under or in connection with the Finance Documents shall be made in writing and, unless otherwise stated, may be made by fax or letter.

### 35.2. Addresses

The address and fax number (and the department or officer, if any, for whose attention the communication is to be made) of each Party for any communication or document to be made or delivered under or in connection with the Finance Documents is:

(a) in the case of the Borrower, that identified with its name below;

(b) in the case of each Lender or any other Obligor, that notified in writing to the Agent on or prior to the date on which it becomes a Party; and

(c) in the case of the Agent, that identified with its name below,

or any substitute address or fax number or department or officer as the Party may notify to the Agent (or the Agent may notify to the other Parties, if a change is made by the Agent) by not less than five Business Days' notice.

### 35.3. Delivery

(a) Any communication or document made or delivered by one person to another under or in connection with the Finance Documents will only be effective:

(i) if by way of fax, when received in legible form; or

(ii) if by way of letter, when it has been left at the relevant address or five Business Days after being deposited in the post postage prepaid in an envelope addressed to it at that address,

and, if a particular department or officer is specified as part of its address details provided under Clause 35.2 (*Addresses*), if addressed to that department or officer.

(b) Any communication or document to be made or delivered to the Agent will be effective only when actually received by the Agent and then only if it is expressly marked for the attention of the department or officer identified with the Agent's signature below (or any substitute department or officer as the Agent shall specify for this purpose).

(c) All notices from or to an Obligor shall be sent through the Agent.

(d) Any communication or document made or delivered to the Borrower in accordance with this Clause will be deemed to have been made or delivered to the Guarantor.

(e) Any communication or document which becomes effective, in accordance with paragraphs (a) to (d) above, after 5.00 p.m. in the place of receipt shall be deemed only to become effective on the following day.

### 35.4. Notification of address and fax number

Promptly upon changing its own address or fax number, the Agent shall notify the other Parties.

### 35.5. Communication when Agent is Impaired Agent

If the Agent is an Impaired Agent the Parties may, instead of communicating with each other through the Agent, communicate with each other directly and (while the Agent is an Impaired Agent) all the provisions of the Finance Documents which require communications to be made or notices to be given to or by the Agent shall be varied so that communications may be made and notices given to or by the relevant Parties directly. This provision shall not operate after a replacement Agent has been appointed.

### 35.6. Electronic communication

(a) Any communication to be made between any two Parties under or in connection with the Finance Documents may be made by electronic mail or other electronic means (including, without limitation by way of posting to a secure website) if those two Parties:

(i) notify each other in writing of their electronic mail address and/ or any other information required to enable the transmission of information by that means; and

(ii) notify each other of any change to their address or any other such information supplied by them by not less than five Business Days' notice.

(b) Any such electronic communication as specified in paragraph (a) above to be made between an Obligor and a Finance Party may only be made in that way to the extent that those two Parties agree that, unless and until notified to the contrary, this is to be an accepted form of communication.

(c) Any such electronic communication as specified in paragraph (a) above made between any two Parties will be effective only when actually received (or made available) in readable form and in the case of any electronic communication made by a Party to the Agent only if it is addressed in such a manner as the Agent shall specify for this purpose.

(d) Any electronic communication which becomes effective, in accordance with paragraph (c) above, after 5.00 p.m. in the place in which the Party to whom the relevant communication is sent or made available has its address for the purpose of this Agreement shall be deemed only to become effective on the following day.

(e) Any reference in a Finance Document to a communication being sent or received shall be construed to include that communication being made available in accordance with this Clause 35.6.

### 35.7. English language

(a) Any notice given under or in connection with any Finance Document must be in English.

(b) All other documents provided under or in connection with any Finance Document must be:

(i) in English; or

(ii) if not in English, and if so required by the Agent, accompanied by a certified English translation and, in this case, the English translation will prevail unless the document is a constitutional, statutory or other official document.

## 36. CALCULATIONS AND CERTIFICATES

### 36.1. Accounts

> Under English law an extract from the accounts of a lender certified under the hand of a duly authorised officer of that lender constitutes *prima facie* evidence of the existence and amounts of the obligations of the debtor which are recorded in that account.
>
> It is not, therefore, necessary (unless local law otherwise requires) that the obligations of a borrower to repay the principal of and to pay interest on the amounts from time to time outstanding under the agreement be evidenced by the issue of promissory notes. However, in certain jurisdictions there may be particular benefits to be obtained from the use of promissory notes and in such circumstances it would be proper, on the basis of appropriate legal advice, to issue promissory notes. It should be mentioned that if such promissory notes incorporate the provisions of an agreement relating to the principal amount outstanding and also the provisions for early repayment, it is unlikely that those promissory notes will be true 'promissory notes'.

In any litigation or arbitration proceedings arising out of or in connection with a Finance Document, the entries made in the accounts maintained by a Finance Party are *prima facie* evidence of the matters to which they relate.

### 36.2. Certificates and determinations

Any certification or determination by a Finance Party of a rate or amount under any Finance Document is, in the absence of manifest error, conclusive evidence of the matters to which it relates.

### 36.3. Day count convention

> The use of a 360-day year is market practice for LIBOR and EURIBOR-based loans (other than sterling LIBOR loans) and it has been adopted from the point of view of convenience although it does produce a higher "true" rate of interest.
>
> In the case of swingline loans, the reference rate is increasingly calculated on a 360-day basis (although a 365 day basis was formerly more prevalent for this rate). Whether a 360 or 365 day basis is agreed may depend on the credit rating of the borrower and the margin which has been agreed in addition to the Federal Funds Rate.

Any interest, commission or fee accruing under a Finance Document will accrue from day to day and is calculated on the basis of the actual number of days elapsed and a year of 360 days or, in any case where the practice in the Relevant Market differs, in accordance with that market practice.

## 37. PARTIAL INVALIDITY

If, at any time, any provision of a Finance Document is or becomes illegal, invalid or unenforceable in any respect under any law of any jurisdiction, neither the legality, validity or enforceability of the remaining provisions nor the legality, validity or enforceability of such provision under the law of any other jurisdiction will in any way be affected or impaired.

## 38. REMEDIES AND WAIVERS

No failure to exercise, nor any delay in exercising, on the part of any Finance Party, any right or remedy under a Finance Document shall operate as a waiver of any such right or remedy or constitute an election to affirm any of the Finance Documents. No election to affirm any Finance Document on the part of any Finance Party shall be effective unless it is in writing. No single or partial exercise of any right or remedy shall prevent any further or other exercise or the exercise of any other right or remedy. The rights and remedies provided in each Finance Document are cumulative and not exclusive of any rights or remedies provided by law.

## 39. AMENDMENTS AND WAIVERS

### 39.1. Required consents

(a) Subject to Clause 39.2 (*All Lender matters*) and Clause 39.3 (*Other exceptions*) any term of the Finance Documents may be amended or waived only with the consent of the Majority Lenders and the

Obligors and any such amendment or waiver will be binding on all Parties.

(b) The Agent may effect, on behalf of any Finance Party, any amendment or waiver permitted by this Clause 38.

(c) Paragraph (c) of Clause 28.10 (*Pro rata interest settlement*) shall apply to this Clause 38.

**39.2. All Lender matters**

(a) Subject to Clause 39.4 (*Replacement of Screen Rate*) an amendment or waiver of any term of any Finance Document that has the effect of changing or which relates to:

(i) the definition of "Majority Lenders" in Clause 1.1 (*Definitions*);

(ii) an extension to the date of payment of any amount under the Finance Documents;

(iii) a reduction in the Margin or a reduction in the amount of any payment of principal, interest, fees or commission payable;

(iv) a change in currency of payment of any amount under the Finance Documents;

(v) an increase in or an extension of any Commitment or the Total Commitments or any requirement that a cancellation of Commitments reduces the Commitments of the Lenders rateably under the Facilities;

(vi) a change to the Borrower or Guarantor;

(vii) any provision which expressly requires the consent of all the Lenders;

(viii) Clause 2.3 (*Finance Parties' rights and obligations*), Clause 6.1 (*Delivery of a Utilisation Request*), paragraph (a) of Clause 8.1 (*Delivery of a Utilisation Request for Swingline Loans*), Clause 12.1 (*Illegality*), Clause 12.2 (*Change of control*), Clause 12.7 (*Application of prepayments*), Clause 28 (*Changes to the Lenders*), Clause 29 (*Changes to the Obligors*), Clause 32 (*Sharing Among the Finance Parties*), this Clause 39, Clause 43 (*Governing Law*) or Clause 44.1 (*Jurisdiction*);

(ix) the nature or scope of the guarantee and indemnity granted under Clause 22 (*Guarantee and Indemnity*); or

(x) (other than as expressly permitted by the provisions of any Finance Document) the release of any such guarantee and indemnity granted under Clause 22 (*Guarantee and Indemnity*) unless permitted by this Agreement,

shall not be made without the prior consent of all the Lenders.

(b) If:

(i) any Defaulting Lender fails to respond to a request for a consent, waiver, amendment of or in relation to any term of any Finance Document or any other vote of the Lenders under the terms of this Agreement within [15] Business Days of that request being made; or

(ii) any Lender which is not a Defaulting Lender fails to respond to such a request (other than an amendment, waiver or consent referred to in paragraph (a)(ii), (a)(iii), (a)(v) or (a)(vi) above) or other vote of the Lenders under the terms of this Agreement within [15] Business Days of that request being made,

(unless, in either case, the Borrower and the Agent agree to a longer time period in relation to any request):

(A) its Commitment(s) shall not be included for the purpose of calculating the Total Commitments when ascertaining whether any relevant percentage (including, for the avoidance of doubt, unanimity) of Total Commitments has been obtained to approve that request; and

(B) its status as a Lender shall be disregarded for the purpose of ascertaining whether the agreement of any specified group of Lenders has been obtained to approve that request.

(c) An amendment or waiver which relates to the rights or obligations of the Agent or the Arranger (each in their capacity as such) may not be effected without the consent of the Agent or the Arranger as the case may be.

**39.3. Other exceptions**

An amendment or waiver which relates to the rights or obligations of the Agent or the Arranger or a Reference Bank (each in their capacity as such) may not be effected without the consent of the Agent, the Arranger or that Reference Bank, as the case may be.

**39.4. Replacement of Screen Rate**

(a) Subject to Clause 39.3 (*Other exceptions*), if a Screen Rate Replacement Event has occurred in relation to any Screen Rate for a currency which can be selected for a Loan, any amendment or waiver which relates to:

(i) providing for the use of a Replacement Benchmark in relation to that currency in place of that Screen Rate; and

(ii)

(A) aligning any provision of any Finance Document to the use of that Replacement Benchmark;

(B) enabling that Replacement Benchmark to be used for the calculation of interest under this Agreement (including, without limitation, any consequential changes required to enable that Replacement Benchmark to be used for the purposes of this Agreement);

(C) implementing market conventions applicable to that Replacement Benchmark;

(D) providing for appropriate fallback (and market disruption) provisions for that Replacement Benchmark; or

(E) adjusting the pricing to reduce or eliminate, to the extent reasonably practicable, any transfer of economic value from one Party to another as a result of the application of that Replacement Benchmark (and if any adjustment or method for calculating any adjustment has been formally designated, nominated or recommended by the Relevant Nominating Body, the adjustment shall be determined on the basis of that designation, nomination or recommendation),

may be made with the consent of the Agent (acting on the instructions of the Majority Lenders) and the Obligors.

(b) If any Lender fails to respond to a request for an amendment or waiver described in paragraph (a) above within [15] Business Days (or such longer time period in relation to any request which the Borrower and the Agent may agree) of that request being made:

(i) its Commitment(s) shall not be included for the purpose of calculating the Total Commitments under the Facilities when ascertaining whether any relevant percentage of Total Commitments has been obtained to approve that request; and

(ii) its status as a Lender shall be disregarded for the purpose of ascertaining whether the agreement of any specified group of Lenders has been obtained to approve that request.

This provision is intended to allow the Majority Lenders and the Obligors to agree upon a Replacement Reference Rate in circumstances where a Screen Rate Replacement Rate has occurred. The LMA published a revised version of this Clause in May 2018 in order to provide for the possible replacement of Ibor-based benchmark rates with so-called Risk Free Rate benchmarks. See chapter 1 for the background.

### 39.5. Disenfranchisement of Defaulting Lenders

(a) For so long as a Defaulting Lender has any Available Commitment, in ascertaining:

(i) the Majority Lenders; or

(ii) whether:

(A) any given percentage (including, for the avoidance of doubt, unanimity) of the Total Commitments; or

(B) the agreement of any specified group of Lenders,

has been obtained to approve any request for a consent, waiver, amendment or other vote of Lenders under the Finance Documents,

that Defaulting Lender's Commitments under the relevant Facility will be reduced by the amount of its Available Commitments under the relevant Facility and:

(1) to the extent that that reduction results in that Defaulting Lender's Total Commitments being zero, that Defaulting Lender shall be deemed not to be a Lender for the purposes of paragraphs (a)(i) and (a)(ii) above; and

(2) to the extent that that reduction results in that Defaulting Lender's Swingline Commitment being zero, that Defaulting Lender shall be deemed not to be

a Swingline Lender for the purposes of paragraph (a)(ii)(B) above.

(b) For the purposes of this Clause 39.5, the Agent may assume that the following Lenders are Defaulting Lenders:

(i) any Lender which has notified the Agent that it has become a Defaulting Lender;

(ii) any Lender in relation to which it is aware that any of the events or circumstances referred to in paragraph (a), (b) or (d) of the definition of "Defaulting Lender" has occurred,

unless it has received notice to the contrary from the Lender concerned (together with any supporting evidence reasonably requested by the Agent) or the Agent is otherwise aware that the Lender has ceased to be a Defaulting Lender.

**39.6. Replacement of Lender**

(a) If at any time:

(i) any Lender becomes a Non-Consenting Lender (as defined in paragraph (d) below); or

(ii) any Obligor becomes obliged to repay any amount in accordance with Clause 12.1 (*Illegality*),

then the Borrower may, on five Business Days' prior written notice to the Agent and such Lender, replace such Lender by requiring such Lender to (and such Lender shall) transfer pursuant to Clause 28 (*Changes to the Lenders*) all (and not part only) of its rights and obligations under this Agreement to a Lender or other bank, financial institution, trust, fund or other entity (a "**Replacement Lender**") selected by the Borrower, and which is acceptable to the Agent (acting reasonably), which confirms its willingness to assume and does assume all the obligations of the transferring Lender (including the assumption of the transferring Lender's participations on the same basis as the transferring Lender) for a purchase price in cash payable at the time of transfer equal to the outstanding principal amount of such Lender's participation in the outstanding Utilisations and all accrued interest, Break Costs and other amounts payable in relation thereto under the Finance Documents.

(b) The replacement of a Lender pursuant to this Clause shall be subject to the following conditions:

(i) the Borrower shall have no right to replace the Agent;

(ii) neither the Agent nor any Lender shall have any obligation to the Borrower to find a Replacement Lender;

(iii) in the event of the replacement of a Non-Consenting Lender, such replacement must take place no later than [90] days after the date the Non-Consenting Lender notifies the Borrower and the Agent of its failure or refusal to give a consent in relation to, or agree to any waiver or amendment to the Finance Documents requested by the Borrower;

(iv) in no event shall the Lender replaced under this paragraph (b) be required to pay or surrender to such Replacement Lender any of the fees received by such Lender pursuant to the Finance Documents;

(v) the Lender shall only be obliged to transfer its rights and obligations pursuant to paragraph (a) above once it is satisfied that it has complied with all necessary "know your customer" or other similar checks under all applicable laws and regulations in relation to that transfer; and

(vi) a Lender shall not be obliged to transfer its rights and obligations pursuant to paragraph (a) above to the extent that the transfer would result in the Lender (or its Affiliate) failing to meet the requirement set out in paragraph (e) of Clause 28.3 (*Other conditions of assignment or transfer*).

(c) A Lender shall perform the checks described in paragraph (b)(v) above as soon as reasonably practicable following delivery of a notice referred to in paragraph (a) above and shall notify the Agent and the Borrower when it is satisfied that it has complied with those checks.

(d) In the event that:

(i) the Borrower or the Agent (at the request of the Borrower) has requested the Lenders to give a consent in relation to, or to agree to a waiver or amendment of, any provisions of the Finance Documents;

(ii) the consent, waiver or amendment in question requires the approval of all the Lenders; and

(iii) Lenders whose Commitments aggregate more than [90]%. of the Total Commitments (or, if the Total Commitments have been reduced to zero, aggregated more than [90]%. of the Total Commitments prior to that reduction) have consented or agreed to such waiver or amendment,

then any Lender who does not and continues not to consent or agree to such waiver or amendment shall be deemed a "**Non-Consenting Lender**".

This Clause 39.6 is known colloquially as the "yank the bank" Clause. It enables the Borrower to replace (at par value) a Non-Consenting Lender which refuses to agree to an amendment or waiver which requires all lender consent, **provided that** a defined majority of the Lenders (in this case [90]%.) have provided their consent already. This allows the Borrower to remove a Non-Consenting Lender, assuming that the Borrower is able to find another Lender which is prepared to replace such Non-Consenting Lender.

### 39.7. Replacement of a Defaulting Lender

(a) The Borrower may, at any time a Lender has become and continues to be a Defaulting Lender, by giving five Business Days' prior written notice to the Agent and such Lender:

(i) replace such Lender by requiring such Lender to (and, to the extent permitted by law, such Lender shall) transfer pursuant to Clause 28 (*Changes to the Lenders*) all (and not part only) of its rights and obligations under this Agreement;

(ii) require such Lender to (and, to the extent permitted by law, such Lender shall) transfer pursuant to Clause 28 (*Changes to the Lenders*) all (and not part only) of:

(A) the undrawn Commitment of the Lender; and

(B) the undrawn Swingline Commitment of that Lender; or

(iii) require such Lender to (and, to the extent permitted by law, such Lender shall) transfer pursuant to Clause 28 (*Changes to the Lenders*) all (and not part only) of its rights and obligations in respect of the Revolving Facility and the Swingline Facility,

to a Lender or other bank, financial institution, trust, fund or other entity (a "**Substitute Lender**") selected by the Borrower, and which confirms its willingness to assume and does assume all the obligations, or all the relevant obligations, of the transferring Lender in accordance with Clause 28 (*Changes* *to the Lenders*) for a purchase price in cash payable at the time of transfer which is either:

(A) in an amount equal to the outstanding principal amount of such Lender's participation in the outstanding Loans and all accrued interest to the extent that the Agent has not given a notification under Clause 28.10 (*Pro rata interest settlement*), Break Costs and other amounts payable in relation thereto under the Finance Documents; or

(B) in an amount agreed between that Defaulting Lender, the Substitute Lender and the Borrower and which does not exceed the amount described in sub-paragraph (A) above.

(b) Any transfer of rights and obligations of a Defaulting Lender pursuant to this Clause 39.7 shall be subject to the following conditions:

(i) the Borrower shall have no right to replace the Agent;

(ii) neither the Agent nor the Defaulting Lender shall have any obligation to the Borrower to find a Substitute Lender;

(iii) the transfer must take place no later than [90] days after the notice referred to in paragraph (a) above;

(iv) in no event shall the Defaulting Lender be required to pay or surrender to the Substitute Lender any of the fees received by the Defaulting Lender pursuant to the Finance Documents;

(v) the Defaulting Lender shall only be obliged to transfer its rights and obligations pursuant to paragraph (a) above once it is satisfied that it has complied with all necessary "know your customer" or other similar checks under all applicable laws and regulations in relation to that transfer to the Substitute Lender; and

(vi) the Defaulting Lender shall not be obliged to transfer its rights and obligations pursuant to paragraph (a) above to the extent that the transfer would result in that Lender (or its Affiliate) failing to meet the requirement set out in paragraph (a) of Clause 28.3 (*Other conditions of assignment or transfer*).

(c) The Defaulting Lender shall perform the checks described in paragraph (b)(v) above as soon as reasonably practicable following delivery of a notice referred to in paragraph (a) above and shall notify the Agent and the Borrower when it is satisfied that it has complied with those checks.

## 40. CONFIDENTIAL INFORMATION

This Clause 40 is included in order to ensure that all Lenders (including both banks and other types of financial institutions) are bound by an express duty of confidentiality in relation to information relating to the Obligors. This confidentiality requirement is subject to the exceptions set out in Clause 40.2 (*Disclosure of Confidential Information*), which allow Lenders to disclose Confidential Information in certain circumstances. For example, a Lender may disclose Confidential Information to a potential Lender to which it may potentially transfer or assign its rights and/or obligations under the Finance Documents, provided such potential Lender signs a Confidentiality Undertaking.

### 40.1. Confidentiality

Each Finance Party agrees to keep all Confidential Information confidential and not to disclose it to anyone, save to the extent permitted by Clause 40.2 (*Disclosure of Confidential Information*) and Clause 40.3 (*Disclosure to numbering service providers*), and to ensure that all Confidential Information is protected with security measures and a degree of care that would apply to its own confidential information.

### 40.2. Disclosure of Confidential Information

Any Finance Party may, without prejudice to the provisions of article L.511-33 of the French *Code monétaire et financier*, disclose:

(a) to any of its Affiliates and Related Funds and any of its or their officers, directors, employees, professional advisers, auditors, partners and Representatives such Confidential Information as that Finance Party shall consider appropriate if any person to whom the Confidential Information is to be given pursuant to this paragraph (a) is informed in writing of its confidential nature and that some or all of such Confidential Information may be price-sensitive information except that there shall be no such requirement to so inform if the recipient is subject to professional obligations to maintain the confidentiality of the information or is otherwise bound by requirements of confidentiality in relation to the Confidential Information;

(b) to any person:

(i) to (or through) whom it assigns or transfers (or may potentially assign or transfer) all or any of its rights and/or obligations under one or more Finance Documents or which succeeds (or which may potentially succeed) it as Agent and, in each case, and to any of that person's Affiliates, Related Funds, Representatives and professional advisers;

(ii) with (or through) whom it enters into (or may potentially enter into), whether directly or indirectly, any sub-participation in relation to, or any other transaction under which payments are to be made or may be made by reference to, one or more Finance Documents and/or one or more Obligors and to any of that person's Affiliates, Related Funds, Representatives and professional advisers;

(iii) appointed by any Finance Party or by a person to whom paragraph (i) or (ii) above applies to receive communications, notices, information or documents delivered pursuant to the Finance Documents on its behalf (including, without limitation, any person appointed under paragraph (b) of Clause 30.15 (*Relationship with the Lenders*));

(iv) who invests in or otherwise finances (or may potentially invest in or otherwise finance), directly or indirectly, any transaction referred to in paragraph (i) or (ii) above;

(v) to whom information is required or requested to be disclosed by any court of competent jurisdiction or any governmental, banking, taxation or other regulatory authority or similar body, the rules of any relevant stock exchange or pursuant to any applicable law or regulation;

(vi) to whom information is required to be disclosed in connection with, and for the purposes of, any litigation, arbitration, administrative or other investigations, proceedings or disputes;

(vii) to whom or for whose benefit that Finance Party charges, assigns or otherwise creates Security (or may do so) pursuant to Clause 28.9 (*Security over Lenders' rights*);

(viii) who is a Party; or

(ix) with the consent of the Borrower,

in each case, such Confidential Information as that Finance Party shall consider appropriate if:

(A) in relation to paragraphs (b)(i), (b)(ii) and (b)(iii) above, the person to whom the Confidential Information is to be given has entered into a Confidentiality Undertaking except that there shall be no requirement for a Confidentiality Undertaking if the recipient is a professional adviser and is subject to professional obligations to maintain the confidentiality of the Confidential Information;

(B) in relation to paragraph (b)(iv) above, the person to whom the Confidential Information is to be given has entered into a Confidentiality Undertaking or is otherwise bound by requirements of confidentiality in relation to the Confidential Information they receive and is informed that some or all of such Confidential Information may be price-sensitive information;

(C) in relation to paragraphs (b)(v), (b)(vi) and (b)(vii) above, the person to whom the Confidential Information is to be given is informed of its confidential nature and that some or all of such Confidential Information may be price-sensitive information except that there shall be no requirement to so inform if, in the opinion of that Finance Party, it is not practicable so to do in the circumstances;

(c) to any person appointed by that Finance Party or by a person to whom paragraph (b)(i) or (b)(ii) above applies to provide administration or settlement services in respect of one or more of the Finance Documents including without limitation, in relation to the trading of participations in respect of the Finance Documents, such Confidential Information as may be required to be disclosed to enable such service provider to provide any of the services referred to in this paragraph (c) if the service provider to whom the Confidential Information is to be given has entered into a confidentiality agreement substantially in the form of the LMA Master Confidentiality Undertaking for Use With Administration/Settlement Service Providers or such other form of confidentiality undertaking agreed between the Borrower and the relevant Finance Party; and

(d) to any rating agency (including its professional advisers) such Confidential Information as may be required to be disclosed to enable such rating agency to carry out its normal rating activities in relation to the Finance Documents and/or the Obligors if the rating agency to whom the Confidential Information is to be given is informed of its confidential nature and that some or all of such Confidential Information may be price-sensitive information.

### 40.3. Disclosure to numbering service providers

> Numbering service providers assign loan identification numbers to individual facilities agreements (and different facilities within such facilities agreements) for the purpose of allowing automation of the servicing and administration of syndicated facilities. Where such loan identification numbers are used, parties such as facility agents and lenders are able to use an online platform to reconcile their respective records as to lenders' participations in a given facilities agreement.

(a) Any Finance Party may, without prejudice to the provisions of article L.511-33 of the French *Code monétaire et financier*, disclose to any national or international numbering service provider appointed by that Finance Party to provide identification numbering services in respect of this Agreement, the Facilities and/or one or more Obligors the following information:

(i) names of Obligors;

(ii) country of domicile of Obligors;

(iii) place of incorporation of Obligors;

(iv) date of this Agreement;

(v) Clause 43 (*Governing Law*);

(vi) the names of the Agent and the Arranger;

(vii) date of each amendment and restatement of this Agreement;

(viii) amounts of, and names of, the Facilities (and any tranches);

(ix) amount of Total Commitments;

(x) currencies of the Facilities;

(xi) type of Facility;

(xii) ranking of Facility;

(xiii) Termination Date for Facility;

(xiv) changes to any of the information previously supplied pursuant to paragraphs (i) to (xiii) above; and

(xv) such other information agreed between such Finance Party and the Borrower,

to enable such numbering service provider to provide its usual syndicated loan numbering identification services.

(b) The Parties acknowledge and agree that each identification number assigned to this Agreement, the Facilities and/or one or more Obligors by a numbering service provider and the information associated with each such number may be disclosed to users of its services in accordance with the standard terms and conditions of that numbering service provider.

(c) Each Obligor represents that none of the information set out in paragraphs (a)(i) to (a)(xv) above is, nor will at any time be, unpublished price-sensitive information.

(d) The Agent shall notify the Borrower and the other Finance Parties of:

(i) the name of any numbering service provider appointed by the Agent in respect of this Agreement, the Facilities and/or one or more Obligors; and

(ii) the number or, as the case may be, numbers assigned to this Agreement, the Facilities and/or one or more Obligors by such numbering service provider.

**40.4. Entire agreement**

Without prejudice to the provisions of article L.511-33 of the French *Code monétaire et financier*, this Clause 40 constitutes the entire agreement between the Parties in relation to the obligations of the Finance Parties under the Finance Documents regarding Confidential Information and supersedes any previous agreement, whether express or implied, regarding Confidential Information.

**40.5. Inside information**

Each of the Finance Parties acknowledges that some or all of the Confidential Information is or may be price-sensitive information and that the use of such information may be regulated or prohibited by applicable legislation including securities law relating to insider dealing and market abuse and each of the Finance Parties undertakes not to use any Confidential Information for any unlawful purpose.

### 40.6. Notification of disclosure

Each of the Finance Parties agrees (to the extent permitted by law and regulation) to inform the Borrower:

(a) of the circumstances of any disclosure of Confidential Information made pursuant to paragraph (b)(v) of Clause 40.2 (*Disclosure of Confidential Information*) except where such disclosure is made to any of the persons referred to in that paragraph during the ordinary course of its supervisory or regulatory function; and

(b) upon becoming aware that Confidential Information has been disclosed in breach of this Clause 40.

### 40.7. Continuing obligations

The obligations in this Clause 40 are continuing and, in particular, shall survive and remain binding on each Finance Party for a period of twelve months from the earlier of:

(a) the date on which all amounts payable by the Obligors under or in connection with this Agreement have been paid in full and all Commitments have been cancelled or otherwise cease to be available; and

(b) the date on which such Finance Party otherwise ceases to be a Finance Party.

## 41. CONFIDENTIALITY OF FUNDING RATES AND REFERENCE BANK QUOTATIONS

### 41.1. Confidentiality and disclosure

(a) The Agent and each Obligor agree to keep each Funding Rate (and, in the case of the Agent, each Reference Bank Quotation) confidential and not to disclose it to anyone, save to the extent permitted by paragraphs (b), (c) and (d) below.

(b) The Agent may disclose:

(i) any Funding Rate (but not, for the avoidance of doubt, any Reference Bank Quotation) to the Borrower pursuant to Clause 13.4 (*Notification of rates of interest*); and

(ii) any Funding Rate or any Reference Bank Quotation to any person appointed by it to provide administration services in respect of one or more of the Finance Documents to the extent necessary to enable such service provider to provide those services if the service provider to whom that information is to be given has entered into a confidentiality agreement substantially in the form of the LMA Master Confidentiality Undertaking for Use With Administration/Settlement Service Providers or such other form of confidentiality undertaking agreed between the Agent and the relevant Lender or Reference Bank, as the case may be.

(c) The Agent may disclose any Funding Rate or any Reference Bank Quotation, and each Obligor may disclose any Funding Rate, to:

(i) any of its Affiliates and any of its or their officers, directors, employees, professional advisers, auditors, partners and Representatives if any person to whom that Funding Rate or Reference Bank Quotation is to be given pursuant to this paragraph (i) is informed in writing of its confidential nature and that it may be price-sensitive information except that there shall be no such requirement to so inform if the recipient is subject to professional obligations to maintain the confidentiality of that Funding Rate or Reference Bank Quotation or is otherwise bound by requirements of confidentiality in relation to it;

(ii) any person to whom information is required or requested to be disclosed by any court of competent jurisdiction or any governmental, banking, taxation or other regulatory authority or similar body, the rules of any relevant stock exchange or pursuant to any applicable law or regulation if the person to whom that Funding Rate or Reference Bank Quotation is to be given is informed in writing of its confidential nature and that it may be price-sensitive information except that there shall be no requirement to so inform if, in the opinion of the Agent or the relevant Obligor, as the case may be, it is not practicable to do so in the circumstances;

(iii) any person to whom information is required to be disclosed in connection with, and for the purposes of, any litigation, arbitration, administrative or other investigations, proceedings or disputes if the person to whom that Funding Rate or Reference Bank Quotation is to be given is informed in writing of its confidential nature and that it may be price-sensitive information except that there shall be no requirement to so inform if, in the opinion of the Agent or the relevant Obligor, as the case may be, it is not practicable to do so in the circumstances; and

(iv) any person with the consent of the relevant Lender or Reference Bank, as the case may be.

(d) The Agent's obligations in this Clause 41 relating to Reference Bank Quotations are without prejudice to its obligations to make notifications under Clause 13.4 (*Notification of rates of interest*) **provided that** (other than pursuant to paragraph (b)(i) above) the Agent shall not include the details of any individual Reference Bank Quotation as part of any such notification.

**41.2. Related Obligations**

(a) The Agent and each Obligor acknowledge that each Funding Rate (and, in the case of the Agent, each Reference Bank Quotation) is or may be price-sensitive information and that its use may be regulated or prohibited by applicable legislation including securities law relating to insider dealing and market abuse and the Agent and each Obligor undertake not to use any Funding Rate or, in the case of the Agent, any Reference Bank Quotation for any unlawful purpose.

(b) The Agent and each Obligor agree (to the extent permitted by law and regulation) to inform the relevant Lender or Reference Bank, as the case may be:

(i) of the circumstances of any disclosure made pursuant to paragraph (c)(ii) of Clause 41.1 (*Confidentiality and disclosure*) except where such disclosure is made to any of the persons referred to in that paragraph during the ordinary course of its supervisory or regulatory function; and

(ii) upon becoming aware that any information has been disclosed in breach of this Clause 41.

### 41.3. No Event of default

No Event of Default will occur under Clause 27.3 (*Other obligations*) by reason only of an Obligor's failure to comply with this Clause 41.

This provision requires the Agent to keep Reference Bank Quotations confidential. It was included by the LMA in their facility agreements in light of the LIBOR Code of Conduct for Contributing Banks which requires contributors to ICE LIBOR to keep their contributions confidential. This code of conduct is relevant given that Reference Banks provide quotations on the same basis as they would if they were contributing to the relevant screen based interest rate benchmark.

## 42. COUNTERPARTS

Each Finance Document may be executed in any number of counterparts, and this has the same effect as if the signatures on the counterparts were on a single copy of the Finance Document.

# SECTION 12

## GOVERNING LAW AND ENFORCEMENT

### 43. GOVERNING LAW

It is essential for a particular system of law to be chosen to govern the interpretation of the contract. In an agreement with parties of several different nationalities, it is difficult to ascertain which law should ultimately prevail if a governing law is not specified at the outset. Normally, the choice of law for international syndicated facility agreements is either that of England or New York because the two legal systems are considered to be well developed in areas of commercial and financial matters but other legal systems may be selected in appropriate circumstances. For a brief discussion of governing law provisions in the light of Brexit please see supplement 8 to chapter 2.

This Agreement and any non-contractual obligations arising out of or in connection with it are governed by English law.

### 44. ENFORCEMENT

Notwithstanding the choice of law, lenders may elect to have disputes heard by courts in various countries. Generally, facility agreements will attempt to enable the lenders to bring disputes before English courts and the courts of the country where a borrower or any guarantor is resident. English courts are chosen not only because the law of the agreement is English but also because the courts are internationally considered to be impartial and competent and experienced in cross-border commercial disputes. This sample agreement does not need to cover submission to the courts of The Netherlands or France (i.e., the jurisdictions of incorporation of the Borrower and the Guarantor) since that is dealt with by a treaty to which England, France and The Netherlands are parties but note the next paragraph in relation to an alternative approach. For a brief discussion of enforcement Clauses in the light of Brexit please see supplement 8 to chapter 2.

Many agreements also submit to the jurisdiction of New York courts. This is not always required but is sometimes sought depending on the nationalities of the parties, whether the obligors have any assets in the United States and whether any payments will be routed through New York. The fact that English law might have been chosen to govern the agreement will not prevent a New York court from hearing any dispute, and from then applying English law and most jurisdictions will do the same.

Another factor which may affect the choice of jurisdiction is the ability of the lenders to ensure that the judgment received is capable of being speedily executed.

**44.1. Jurisdiction**

(a) The courts of England have jurisdiction to settle any dispute arising out of or in connection with this Agreement (including a dispute relating to the existence, validity or termination of this Agreement or the consequences of its nullity or any non-contractual obligations arising out of or in connection with this Agreement) (a "**Dispute**").

(b) The Parties agree that the courts of England are the most appropriate and convenient courts to settle Disputes and accordingly no Party will argue to the contrary.

(c) Subject to paragraph (d) below and notwithstanding paragraph (a) above, no Finance Party shall be prevented from taking proceedings relating to a Dispute in any other courts with jurisdiction. To the extent allowed by law, the Finance Parties may take concurrent proceedings in any number of jurisdictions.

(d) The provisions of paragraph (c) above shall not apply in relation to any proceedings commenced by the Finance Parties against the Guarantor and any such proceedings shall be commenced in the courts of England pursuant to paragraphs (a) and (b) above.

It is established market practice for the exclusive jurisdiction Clauses included in facilities agreements to be stated to be for the benefit of the Finance Parties only so that the parties agree that the English courts will have jurisdiction over disputes but that the Finance Parties may choose to commence legal proceedings in another appropriate jurisdiction. However, in September 2012, the French Supreme Court (*Cour de cassation*) held that a one-sided jurisdiction Clause (i.e., where one party submits to the exclusive jurisdiction of a particular court while another party retains the right to bring proceedings in any court) was invalid on the basis that it was contrary to the Brussels I Regulation on jurisdiction and the recognition and enforcement of judgments in civil and commercial matters. This French decision is not binding on other European courts, although it has persuasive authority. Since that decision, there have been conflicting decisions of courts in other European Union jurisdictions as to whether one-sided jurisdiction Clauses complied with the requirements of the Brussels I Regulation. An English court, at first instance, has held that this type of Clause is effective and complies with the requirements of the Brussels I Regulation. However, until the matter is resolved by the Court of Justice of the European Union, the enforceability of this type of jurisdiction provision remains uncertain.

In this case, there is a one-sided jurisdiction Clause (see paragraph (c)) but this doesn't apply where the relevant proceedings are in relation to the Guarantor (given that it is a French entity and the concerns around the enforceability of one-sided jurisdiction

Clauses have principally stemmed from French case law). Where the Finance Parties wish to bring proceedings in relation to the French Guarantor then paragraph (d) would require them to be brought in England.

Issues related to the impact of Brexit on this provision are briefly discussed in Supplement 8 of chapter 2.

### 44.2. Service of process

The purpose of the appointment of a process agent is, so far as proceedings in England are concerned, to make it unnecessary to apply to the courts for leave to serve process, which leave would otherwise be required where process is to be served on a foreign corporation. Independent process agents are commonly used but a subsidiary of a borrower resident in the relevant jurisdiction may suffice.

Without prejudice to any other mode of service allowed under any relevant law, each Obligor:

(a) irrevocably appoints [•] as its agent for service of process in relation to any proceedings before the English courts in connection with any Finance Document; and

(b) agrees that failure by an agent for service of process to notify the relevant Obligor of the process will not invalidate the proceedings concerned.

If any person appointed as an agent for the service of process is unable for any reason to act as agent for service of process, each Obligor must immediately (and in any event within [•] days of such event taking place) appoint another agent on terms acceptable to the Agent. Failing this, the Agent may appoint another agent for this purpose.

**THIS AGREEMENT** has been entered into on the date stated at the beginning of this Agreement.

# SCHEDULE 1

THE ORIGINAL PARTIES

## PART I

## THE OBLIGORS

| Name of Borrower | Registration number (or equivalent, if any) |
| --- | --- |
| DutchCo SPV B.V. | [•] |

| Name of Guarantor | Registration number (or equivalent, if any) |
| --- | --- |
| Parent Company S.A. | [•] |

## PART II

## THE ORIGINAL LENDERS

| Name of Original Lender | **Commitment** |
| --- | --- |

*[To be inserted]*

## PART III

## THE ORIGINAL SWINGLINE LENDERS

| Name of Original Lender | **Swingline Commitment** |
| --- | --- |

*[To be inserted]*

# SCHEDULE 2

## CONDITIONS PRECEDENT TO INITIAL UTILISATION

### 1. Obligors

(a) A copy of the constitutional documents of each Obligor, including:

(i) in the case of the Borrower, a copy of the articles of association (*statuten*) and deed of incorporation (*oprichtingsakte*), as well as an up-to-date extract (*uittreksel*) from the Dutch Commercial Register (*Handelsregister*) relating to it; and

(ii) in the case of the Guarantor, a copy of its constitutive documents (*statuts*), a copy of its certificate of incorporation (*Extrait K-bis*), a non-bankruptcy certificate (*recherche négative de procédure collective*) and an encumbrance certificate (*état des privilèges et nantissements*) relating to it, in each case dated no more than 15 days prior to the date of this Agreement.

(b) A copy of a resolution of the board of directors (or managing directors) of each Obligor:

(i) approving the terms of, and the transactions contemplated by, the Finance Documents to which it is a party and resolving that it execute the Finance Documents to which it is a party;

(ii) authorising a specified person or persons to execute the Finance Documents to which it is a party on its behalf; and

(iii) authorising a specified person or persons, on its behalf, to sign and/or despatch all documents and notices (including, if relevant, any Utilisation Request) to be signed and/or despatched by it under or in connection with the Finance Documents to which it is a party.

(c) A specimen of the signature of each person authorised by the resolution referred to in paragraph (b) above.

(d) If applicable, a copy of the resolution of the shareholder(s) of the Borrower approving the resolutions of the board of managing directors referred to under (b) above.

(e) If applicable, a copy of the resolution of the board of supervisory directors of the Borrower approving the resolutions of the board of managing directors referred to under paragraph (b) above.

(f) A copy of (i) the request for advice from each works council, or central or European works council with jurisdiction over the transactions contemplated by this Agreement and (ii) the unconditional positive advice from such works council.

(g) A certificate of each Obligor (signed by a director of each Obligor) confirming that borrowing or guaranteeing, as appropriate, the Total Commitments would not cause any borrowing, guaranteeing or similar limit binding on any Obligor to be exceeded.

(h) A certificate of an authorised signatory of the relevant Obligor certifying that each copy document relating to it specified in this Schedule 2 is correct, complete and in full force and effect as at a date no earlier than the date of this Agreement.

**2. Legal opinions**

(a) A legal opinion of [English law firm] legal advisers to the Arranger and the Agent in England, substantially in the form distributed to the Original Lenders prior to signing this Agreement.

(b) A legal opinion of the legal advisers to the Arranger and the Agent in The Netherlands, substantially in the form distributed to the Original Lenders prior to signing this Agreement.

(c) A legal opinion of the legal advisers to the Arranger and the Agent in France, substantially in the form distributed to the Original Lenders prior to signing this Agreement.

**3. Other documents and evidence**

(a) Evidence that any agent for service of process referred to in Clause 44.2 (*Service of process*), if not an Obligor, has accepted its appointment.

(b) A copy of any other Authorisation or other document, opinion or assurance which the Agent considers to be necessary or desirable (if it has notified the Borrower accordingly) in connection with the entry into and performance of the transactions contemplated by any Finance Document or for the validity and enforceability of any Finance Document.

(c) The Original Financial Statements of each Obligor.

(d) Evidence that the fees, costs and expenses then due from the Borrower pursuant to Clause 16 (*Fees*) and Clause 21 (*Costs and Expenses*) have been paid or will be paid by the first Utilisation Date.

# SCHEDULE 3

## REQUESTS

## PART I

## UTILISATION REQUEST – REVOLVING FACILITY LOANS

From: DutchCo SPV B.V.

To: [*Agent*]

Dated:

Dear Sirs

**DutchCo SPV B.V. – [•] Facility Agreement**

**dated [•] (the "Agreement")**

1. We refer to the Agreement. This is a Utilisation Request. Terms defined in the Agreement have the same meaning in this Utilisation Request unless given a different meaning in this Utilisation Request.

2. We wish to borrow a Revolving Facility Loan on the following terms:

| | |
|---|---|
| **Proposed Utilisation Date:** | **[•] (or, if that is not a Business Day, the next Business Day)** |
| **Currency of Revolving Facility Loan:** | [•] |
| **Amount:** | [•] or, if less, the Available Facility |
| **Interest Period:** | [•] |

3. We confirm that each condition specified in Clause 5.2 (*Further conditions precedent*) of the Agreement is satisfied on the date of this Utilisation Request.

4. [This Loan is to be made in [whole]/[part] for the purpose of refinancing [*identify maturing Loan*]. [The proceeds of this Revolving Facility Loan should be credited to [*account*].]] OR

   [The proceeds of this Revolving Facility Loan should be credited to [*account*].]

5. This Utilisation Request is irrevocable.

Yours faithfully

authorised signatory for and on behalf of

**DutchCo SPV B.V.**

**WARNING NOTE: Please seek Dutch legal advice (i) until the interpretation of the term "public" (as referred to in Article 4.1(1) of the CRR) has been published by the competent authority, if the share of a Lender in any Utilisation requested by the Borrower is less than EUR 100,000 (or the foreign currency equivalent thereof) and (ii) as soon as the interpretation of the term "public" has been published by the competent authority, if the Lender is considered to be part of the public on the basis of such interpretation.**

## PART II

## UTILISATION REQUEST – SWINGLINE LOANS

From: DutchCo SPV B.V.

To: [*Agent*]

Dated:

Dear Sirs

**DutchCo SPV B.V. – [•] Facility Agreement**

**dated [•] (the "Agreement")**

1. We refer to the Agreement. This is a Utilisation Request. Terms defined in the Agreement have the same meaning in this Utilisation Request unless given a different meaning in this Utilisation Request.
2. We wish to borrow a Swingline Loan on the following terms:

| | |
|---|---|
| **Proposed Utilisation Date:** | **[•] (or, if that is not a New York Business Day, the next New York Business Day)** |
| **Facility to be utilised:** | Swingline Facility |
| **Amount:** | $[•] or, if less, the Available Swingline Facility |
| **Interest Period:** | [•] |

3. We confirm that each condition specified in paragraph (b) of Clause 8.3 (*Swingline Lenders' participation*) of the Agreement is satisfied on the date of this Utilisation Request.
4. The proceeds of this Swingline Loan should be credited to [*account*].
5. This Utilisation Request is irrevocable.

Yours faithfully

authorised signatory for and on behalf of

**DutchCo SPV B.V.**

**WARNING NOTE: Please seek Dutch legal advice (i) until the interpretation of the term "public" (as referred to in Article 4.1(1) of the CRR) has been published by the competent authority, if the share of a Lender in any Utilisation requested by the Borrower is less than EUR 100,000 (or the foreign currency equivalent thereof) and (ii) as soon as the interpretation of the term "public" has been published by the competent authority, if the Lender is considered to be part of the public on the basis of such interpretation.**

# SCHEDULE 4

## FORM OF TRANSFER CERTIFICATE

See chapter 6 on "Secondary transfer mechanisms" for techniques of and reasons for loan transfers.

To: [•] as Agent

From: [*The Existing Lender*] (the "**Existing Lender**") and [*The New Lender*] (the "**New Lender**")

Dated:

**DutchCo SPV B.V. – [•] Facility Agreement**

**dated [•] (the "Agreement")**

1. We refer to the Agreement. This is a Transfer Certificate. Terms defined in the Agreement have the same meaning in this Transfer Certificate unless given a different meaning in this Transfer Certificate.
2. We refer to Clause 28.6 (*Procedure for transfer*) of the Agreement:
   (a) The Existing Lender and the New Lender agree to the Existing Lender transferring to the New Lender by novation, and in accordance with Clause 28.6 (*Procedure for transfer*) of the Agreement, all of the Existing Lender's rights and obligations under the Agreement and other Finance Documents which relate to that portion of the Existing Lender's Commitment(s) and participations in Loans under the Agreement as specified in the Schedule.

   (b) The proposed Transfer Date is [•].

   (c) The Facility Office and address, fax number and attention details for notices of the New Lender for the purposes of Clause 35.2 (*Addresses*) of the Agreement are set out in the Schedule.
3. The New Lender expressly acknowledges the limitations on the Existing Lender's obligations set out in paragraph (c) of Clause 28.5 (*Limitation of responsibility of Existing Lenders*) of the Agreement.

4. The New Lender confirms, for the benefit of the Agent and without liability to any Obligor, that it is:*

   (a) a Dutch Qualifying Lender (other than a Dutch Treaty Lender);

   (b) a Dutch Treaty Lender; or

   (c) not a Dutch Qualifying Lender,

   and that it [is]/[is not]* incorporated or acting through a Facility Office situated in a Non-Cooperative Jurisdiction.

5. This Transfer Certificate may be executed in any number of counterparts and this has the same effect as if the signatures on the counterparts were on a single copy of this Transfer Certificate.

6. This Transfer Certificate and any non-contractual obligations arising out of or in connection with it are governed by English law.

7. This Transfer Certificate has been entered into on the date stated at the beginning of this Transfer Certificate.

   **NOTE: The New Lender may, in the case of a transfer of rights by the Existing Lender under this Transfer Certificate, if it considers it necessary to make the transfer effective against third parties, arrange for it to be notified by way of *signification* to the Obligors incorporated in France in accordance with Article 1690 of the French *Code Civil.***

   **WARNING NOTE: Please seek Dutch legal advice (i) until the interpretation of the term "public" (as referred to in Article 4.1(1) of the CRR) has been published by the competent authority, if the participation of a Lender in a Loan is less than EUR 100,000 (or the foreign currency equivalent thereof) and (ii) as soon as the interpretation of the term "public" has been published by the competent authority, if a Lender is or would be considered to be part of the public on the basis of such interpretation.**

# THE SCHEDULE

**Commitment/rights and obligations to be transferred**

*[insert relevant details]*

*[Facility Office address, fax number and attention details for notices and account details for payments,]*

| For and on behalf of | For and on behalf of |
|---|---|
| [Existing Lender] | [New Lender] |
| By: | By: |

This Transfer Certificate is accepted by the Agent and the Transfer Date is confirmed as [•].

For and on behalf of
[Agent]

By:

NOTES:

*Delete as applicable – each New Lender is required to confirm which of these three categories it falls within.

# SCHEDULE 5

## FORM OF ASSIGNMENT AGREEMENT

To: [•] as Agent and [•] as Borrower

From: [the *Existing Lender*] (the "**Existing Lender**") and [the *New Lender*] (the "**New Lender**")

Dated:

**DutchCo SPV B.V. – [•] Facility Agreement**

**dated [•] (the "Agreement")**

1. We refer to the Agreement. This is an Assignment Agreement. Terms defined in the Agreement have the same meaning in this Assignment Agreement unless given a different meaning in this Assignment Agreement.

2. We refer to Clause 28.7 (*Procedure for assignment*) of the Agreement:

   (a) The Existing Lender assigns absolutely to the New Lender all the rights of the Existing Lender under the Agreement and the other Finance Documents which relate to that portion of the Existing Lender's Commitment(s) and participations in Loans under the Agreement as specified in the Schedule.

   (b) The Existing Lender is released from all the obligations of the Existing Lender which correspond to that portion of the Existing Lender's Commitment(s) and participations in Loans under the Agreement specified in the Schedule.

   (c) The New Lender becomes a Party as a Lender and is bound by obligations equivalent to those from which the Existing Lender is released under paragraph (b) above.

3. The proposed Transfer Date is [•].

4. On the Transfer Date the New Lender becomes Party to the Finance Documents as a Lender.

5. The Facility Office and address, fax number and attention details for notices of the New Lender for the purposes of Clause 35.2 (*Addresses*) of the Agreement are set out in the Schedule.

6. The New Lender expressly acknowledges the limitations on the Existing Lender's obligations set out in paragraph (c) of Clause 28.5 (*Limitation of responsibility of Existing Lenders*) of the Agreement.

7. The New Lender confirms, for the benefit of the Agent and without liability to any Obligor, that it is:*

   (a) a Dutch Qualifying Lender (other than a Dutch Treaty Lender);

   (b) a Dutch Treaty Lender; or

   (c) not a Dutch Qualifying Lender,

   and that it [is]/[is not]* incorporated or acting through a Facility Office situated in a Non-Cooperative Jurisdiction.

8. This Assignment Agreement acts as notice to the Agent (on behalf of each Finance Party) and, upon delivery in accordance with Clause 28.8 (*Copy of Transfer Certificate, Assignment Agreement or Increase Confirmation to Borrower*) of the Agreement, to the Borrower (on behalf of each Obligor) of the assignment referred to in this Assignment Agreement.

9. This Assignment Agreement may be executed in any number of counterparts and this has the same effect as if the signatures on the counterparts were on a single copy of this Assignment Agreement.

10. This Assignment Agreement and any non-contractual obligations arising out of or in connection with it are governed by English law.

11. This Assignment Agreement has been entered into on the date stated at the beginning of this Assignment Agreement.

    **WARNING NOTE: Please seek Dutch legal advice (i) until the interpretation of the term "public" (as referred to in Article 4.1(1) of the CRR) has been published by the competent authority, if the participation of a Lender in a Loan is less than EUR 100,000 (or the foreign currency equivalent thereof) and (ii) as soon as the interpretation of the term "public" has been published by the competent authority, if a Lender is or would be considered to be part of the public on the basis of such interpretation.**

# THE SCHEDULE

**Rights to be assigned and obligations to be released and undertaken**

*[insert relevant details]*

*[Facility office address, fax number and attention details for notices and account details for payments]*

| For and on behalf of | For and on behalf of |
|---|---|
| [Existing Lender] | [New Lender] |
| ____________________ | ____________________ |
| By: | By: |

This Assignment Agreement is accepted by the Agent and the Transfer Date is confirmed as [•].

Signature of this Assignment Agreement by the Agent constitutes confirmation by the Agent of receipt of notice of the assignment referred to herein, which notice the Agent receives on behalf of each Finance Party.

For and on behalf of
[Agent]

By:

NOTES:

* Delete as applicable – each New Lender is required to confirm which of these three categories it falls within.

# SCHEDULE 6

## FORM OF COMPLIANCE CERTIFICATE

To: [•] as Agent

From: *Borrower/Guarantor*

Dated:

Dear Sirs

**DutchCo SPV B.V. – [•] Facility Agreement**

**dated [•] (the "Agreement")**

1. We refer to the Agreement. This is a Compliance Certificate. Terms defined in the Agreement have the same meaning when used in this Compliance Certificate unless given a different meaning in this Compliance Certificate.

2. We confirm that:

   (a) on the last day of the Relevant Period ending on [•] Consolidated EBITDA were [•] and Consolidated Net Finance Charges for such Relevant Period were [•]. Therefore Interest Cover for such Relevant Period was [•]:1 and the covenant contained in paragraph (a) of Clause 25.2 (*Financial condition*) [has/has not] been complied with; and

   (b) on the last day of the Relevant Period ending on [•] Consolidated Total Net Debt was [•] and Consolidated EBITDA for such Relevant Period was [•]. Therefore the ratio of Consolidated Total Net Debt to Consolidated EBITDA was [•]:1 and the covenant contained in paragraph (b) of Clause 25.2 (*Financial condition*) [has/has not] been complied with.

3. [We confirm that no Default is continuing.]*

| Signed: | ______________________ | Signed: | ______________________ |
|---|---|---|---|
| | Director<br>of<br>*Borrower* | | Director<br>of<br>*Borrower* |

*[insert applicable certification language]*

for and on behalf of
*[name of auditors of the Guarantor]*

NOTES:

* If this statement cannot be made, the certificate should identify any Default that is continuing and the steps, if any, being taken to remedy it.

# SCHEDULE 7

## EXISTING SECURITY

| **Name of Obligor** | **Security** | **Total Principal Amount of Indebtedness Secured** |
|---|---|---|
| Parent Company S.A. | *Hypothèque conventionelle* over building at 9, place Vendôme, Paris | EUR5,000,000 |

# SCHEDULE 8

## LMA FORM OF CONFIDENTIALITY UNDERTAKING

# SCHEDULE 9

## TIMETABLES

| | **Loans in dollars** | **Loans in euro** | **Loans in other currencies** |
|---|---|---|---|
| Agent confirms to Borrower if a currency is approved as an Optional Currency in accordance with paragraph (b) of Clause 5.3 (*Conditions relating to Optional Currencies*) | – | – | U-4 |
| Delivery of a duly completed Utilisation Request (Clause 6.1 (*Delivery of a Utilisation Request*)) | U-3<br>9.30 a.m. | U-3<br>9.30 a.m. | U-3<br>9.30 a.m. |
| Agent determines (in relation to a Utilisation) the Base Currency Amount of the Loan, if required under Clause 6.4 (*Lenders' participation*) | U-3<br>noon | U-3<br>noon | U-3<br>noon |
| Agent notifies the Lenders of the Loan in accordance with Clause 6.4 (*Lenders' participation*) | U-3<br>3.00 p.m. | U-3<br>3.00 p.m. | U-3<br>3.00 p.m. |
| Agent receives a notification from a Lender under Clause 10.2 (*Unavailability of a currency*) | - | Quotation Day<br>10.00 a.m. | Quotation Day<br>10.00 a.m. |
| Agent gives notice in accordance with Clause 10.2 (*Unavailability of a currency*) | - | Quotation Day<br>10.30 a.m. | Quotation Day<br>10.30 a.m. |
| LIBOR or EURIBOR is fixed | Quotation Day as of 11:00 a.m. London time | Quotation Day as of 11.00 a.m. Brussels time | Quotation Day as of 11:00 a.m. London time |
| Benchmark Rate is fixed for a Loan in a Non-LIBOR Currency | - | - | As specified as such in respect of that currency in Schedule 11 (*Other Benchmarks*) |

| | **Loans in dollars** | **Loans in euro** | **Loans in other currencies** |
|---|---|---|---|
| Reference Bank Rate calculated by reference to available quotations in accordance with Clause 15.1 (*Unavailability of Screen Rate*) | Noon on the Quotation Day | Quotation Day 11.30 a.m. (Brussels time) | Noon on the Quotation Day in respect of LIBOR and as specified as such in respect of the relevant currency in Schedule 11 (*Other Benchmarks*) in respect of a Benchmark Rate |

# SWINGLINE LOANS

| | **Dollar Swingline Loans** |
|---|---|
| Delivery of a duly completed Utilisation Request (Clause 8.1 (*Delivery of a Utilisation Request for Swingline Loans*)) | U<br>11.00 a.m. (Eastern Standard Time) |
| Agent announces prime commercial lending rate in dollars under Clause 9.4 (*Interest*) | U<br>11.00 a.m. (Eastern Standard Time) |
| Agent determines (in relation to a Utilisation) the Base Currency Amount of the Swingline Loan, if required under Clause 8.3 (*Swingline Lenders' participation*) and notifies each Swingline Lender of the amount of its participation in the Swingline Loan under Clause 8.3 (*Swingline Lenders' participation*) | U<br>11.00 a.m. (Eastern Standard Time) |

"U" = date of utilisation

"U – X" = X Business Days prior to date of utilisation

# SCHEDULE 10

## FORM OF INCREASE CONFORMATION

To: [•] as Agent and [•] as the Borrower

From: [the *Increase Lender*] (the "**Increase Lender**")

Dated:

**DutchCo SPV B.V. – [•] Facility Agreement**

**dated [•] (the "Agreement")**

1. We refer to the Agreement. This is an Increase Confirmation. Terms defined in the Agreement have the same meaning in this Increase Confirmation unless given a different meaning in this Increase Confirmation.
2. We refer to Clause 2.2 (*Increase*) of the Agreement.
3. The Increase Lender agrees to assume and will assume all of the obligations corresponding to the Commitment and/or Swingline Commitment specified in the Schedule (the "**Relevant Commitment**") as if it was an Original Lender under the Agreement.
4. The proposed date on which the increase in relation to the Increase Lender and the Relevant Commitment is to take effect (the "**Increase Date**") is [ ].
5. On the Increase Date, the Increase Lender becomes party to the relevant Finance Documents as a Lender.
6. The Increase Lender confirms, for the benefit of the Agent and without liability to any Obligor, that it is:*

   (a) a Dutch Qualifying Lender (other than a Dutch Treaty Lender);

   (b) a Dutch Treaty Lender; or

   (c) not a Dutch Qualifying Lender,

   and that it [is]/[is not]* incorporated or acting through a Facility Office situated in a Non-Cooperative Jurisdiction.

7. The Facility Office and address, fax number and attention details for notices to the Increase Lender for the purposes of Clause 35.2 (*Addresses*) of the Agreement are set out in the Schedule.

8. The Increase Lender expressly acknowledges the limitations on the Lenders' obligations referred to in paragraph (g) of Clause 2.2 (*Increase*) of the Agreement.

9. This Increase Confirmation may be executed in any number of counterparts and this has the same effect as if the signatures on the counterparts were on a single copy of this Agreement.

10. This Increase Confirmation and any non-contractual obligations arising out of or in connection with it are governed by English law.

11. This Increase Confirmation has been entered into on the date stated at the beginning of this Agreement.

**WARNING NOTE: Please seek Dutch legal advice (i) until the interpretation of the term "public" (as referred to in Article 4.1(1) of the CRR) has been published by the competent authority, if the participation of an Increase Lender in a Relevant Commitment is less than EUR 100,000 (or the foreign currency equivalent thereof) and (ii) as soon as the interpretation of the term "public" has been published by the competent authority, if a Lender is or would be considered to be part of the public on the basis of such interpretation.**

# THE SCHEDULE

**Relevant Commitment/rights and obligations to be assumed by the Increase Lender**

*[insert relevant details]*

*[Facility office address, fax number and attention details for notices and account details for payments]*

[Increase Lender]

By: ........................................................

This Increase Confirmation is accepted as an Increase Confirmation is accepted by the Agent and the Increase Date is confirmed as [•].

Agent

By: ........................................................

* Delete as applicable – each Increase Lender is required to confirm which of these three categories it falls into.

# SCHEDULE 11

## OTHER BENCHMARKS

| | |
|---|---|
| **CURRENCY:** | Canadian Dollars. |
| ***Definitions*** | |
| **Business Day:** | Any day on which banks are open for general business in Toronto. |
| **Business Day Conventions (definition of "Month" and Clause 14.2** (*Non-Business Days*)): | No rules specified. |
| **Fallback Interest Period:** | One Month. |
| **Quotation Day:** | Two Business Days before the first day of that period. |
| **Reference Bank Rate:** | The arithmetic mean of the rates (rounded upwards to four decimal places) as supplied to the Agent at its request by the Reference Banks:<br>(a) (other than where paragraph (b) below applies) as the rate at which the relevant Reference Bank would be willing to lend (offer) Canadian Dollar funds against primary bankers' acceptances issuances with a term to maturity approximately equal in length to the relevant period (disregarding any inconsistency arising from the last day of that period being determined pursuant to the terms of this Agreement) to clients with existing credit facilities that reference the Canadian Dollar Offered Rate plus a fee; or<br>(b) if different, as the rate (if any and applied to the relevant Reference Bank and the relevant period (disregarding any inconsistency arising from the last day of that period being determined pursuant to the terms of this Agreement)) which contributors to the applicable Screen Rate are asked to submit to the relevant administrator. |
| **Reference Banks:** | The principal Toronto offices of [ ], [ ] and [ ]. |
| **Relevant Market:** | The market for Canadian bankers' acceptances. |

| | |
|---|---|
| **Screen Rate:** | The Canadian Dollar Offered Rate administered by Thomson Reuters Benchmark Services Limited (or any other person which takes over the administration of that rate) for the relevant period displayed on page CDOR of the Thomson Reuters screen (or any replacement Thomson Reuters page which displays that rate) or on the appropriate page of such other information service which publishes that rate in place of Thomson Reuters. If such page or service ceases to be available, the Agent may specify another page or service displaying the relevant rate after consultation with the Borrower. |
| ***Interest Periods*** | |
| **Periods capable of selection as Interest Periods (paragraph (b) of Clause 14.1** (*Selection of Interest Periods*)**):** | One, three or six Months. |
| ***Rate fixing timings*** | |
| **Time at which Benchmark Rate is fixed (Schedule 9** (*Timetables*)**):** | Quotation Day prior to 10:15 a.m. (Toronto time). |
| **Time at which Reference Bank Rate falls to be calculated by reference to available quotations (Schedule 9** (*Timetables*)**):** | Quotation Day 11:00 a.m. (Toronto time). |
| **Deadline for quotations to establish a Reference Bank Rate (paragraph (b) of Clause 15.2** (*Calculation of Reference Bank Rate*)**):** | Quotation Day 11:00 a.m. (Toronto time). |
| **Deadline for Lenders to report market disruption (Clause 15.3** (*Market disruption*)**):** | Close of business in London on the date falling one Business Day after the Quotation Day for the relevant Interest Period. |

# SCHEDULE 12

## SCREEN RATE CONTINGENCY PERIODS

| **Screen Rate** | **Period** |
|---|---|
| LIBOR | [•] |
| EURIBOR | [•] |

## SIGNATURES

**THE BORROWER**

For and on behalf of
**DUTCHCO SPV B.V.**

By: ...................................................................

Address:

Fax:

**THE GUARANTOR**

For and on behalf of
**PARENT COMPANY S.A.**

By: ...................................................................

Address:

Fax:

**THE ARRANGER**

For and on behalf of
**ARRANGER BANK LIMITED**

By: ...................................................................

Address:

Fax:

For and on behalf of
**TOP BANK PLC**

By: ...................................................................

Address:

Fax:

For and on behalf of
**XYZ BANK LIMITED**

By: ..................................................................

Address:

Fax:

**THE AGENT**

For and on behalf of
**XYZ BANK LIMITED**

By: ..................................................................

Address:

Fax:

Attention:

**THE ORIGINAL LENDERS**

For and on behalf of

[•]

By: ..................................................................

For and on behalf of

[•]

By: ..................................................................

# SAMPLE FEES LETTER

To: DutchCo SPV B.V.

[Address]

Date: [•]

Dear Sirs,

**$1BN REVOLVING AND SWINGLINE CREDIT FACILITY AGREEMENT DATED [•] (the "Facility Agreement")**

We refer to the Facility Agreement between DutchCo SPV B.V. as Borrower, Parent Company S.A. as Guarantor, Arranger Bank Limited as Arranger, the Lenders mentioned therein and XYZ Bank Limited as Agent. Terms defined in the Facility Agreement shall have the same meanings when used in this letter.

This letter constitutes the Fee Letter referred to in Clause 16.3 (*Arrangement fee*) and Clause 16.4 (*Agency fee*) of the Facility Agreement. By countersigning and returning the attached copy of this letter the Borrower agrees to pay the following fees:

1. **Agency Fee**

The Borrower shall pay to the Agent an agency fee (the "**Agency Fee**") of $37,500 per annum and shall be paid annually in advance. The Agency Fee shall be payable on the date of the Facility Agreement and on each anniversary of the date of the Facility Agreement until all amounts under the Facility Agreement have been repaid and all Commitments and Swingline Commitments irrevocably cancelled in full.

2. **Arrangement**

The Borrower shall pay to the Agent for the account of the Arrangers and the Lenders an arrangement fee of $1,000,000 being 0.10%. flat on the Total Commitments. Such fee shall be payable on the date of the Facility Agreement.

All fees set out in this letter shall be payable in full without set-off, counterclaim or deduction, and the provisions of Clause 17 (*Tax Gross-up and Indemnities*) of the Facility Agreement apply to any payment of fees.

Yours faithfully

..................................................................................

For and on behalf of

**XYZ Bank Limited**

(on behalf of itself and as Agent and the Arrangers)

To: XYZ Bank Limited

We agree to pay the fees set out in the letter of which the above is a true copy.

..................................................................................

Signed for and on behalf of

**DutchCo SPV B.V.**

..................................................................................

Date:

# *Chapter 6*

# SECONDARY MARKET TRANSFER MECHANISM

# INTRODUCTION

The secondary loan market refers to the secondary market for the activities of buying, selling, dealing, brokering and trading interests in and derived from commercial loans and other credit facilities.

A participant in a syndicated loan may wish to 'sell' or transfer either all or part of its rights and obligations under a credit agreement to a third party via the secondary market. The term 'asset sale' or 'asset transfer' is used in this chapter to cover a wide range of loan transfer techniques, whether funded or unfunded. The term 'secondary market', in contrast to the term 'primary market', signifies any sale or transfer made after the syndication of the loan has been concluded through the arranging bank(s).

Secondary loan market activity in Europe has increased dramatically over the last 25 years as banks have sought to manage their lending portfolios more proactively and as new classes of investors such as funds and collateralised debt obligations (CDOs) have begun to invest in the loan product. This has been aided by the formation of the Loan Market Association (LMA), in December 1996, which has developed standard documentation for par and near par and distressed debt trading and standardised a number of practices in order to promote an orderly secondary market.

In this chapter we explore some of the legal issues affecting secondary transfers and the principal drivers behind the growth in secondary market activity.

# BACKGROUND

The secondary loan market today can be broadly split into two categories, par and near par (which includes leveraged or high yield debt) and distressed debt.

Prior to the formation of the LMA, the secondary market in Europe had been dominated by a small number of US houses, predominantly commercial banks, specialist distressed debt traders and vulture funds with activity focused on the distressed market.

Today, an increasing number of institutional investors as well as investment, commercial and retail banks are active in the secondary market for both par and near par and distressed debt. It is no longer the case that banks are the principal buyers of loans, with institutional investors now regular and active participants in the European leveraged loan market.

The growth of the secondary market can be traced back to the sovereign debt crisis in the 1980s when a distinct market emerged to deal on a discount basis, mainly with rescheduled debt and other weaker credits of sovereign borrowers. This market subsequently expanded to cover distressed and impaired corporate debt.

In the 1990s intense competition between banks and a thriving primary loan market pushed credit spreads to extremely low levels resulting in a more concerted effort by many banks to manage their loan portfolios and banking relationships more proactively, through the secondary market.

The combination of buyers and sellers was consequently responsible for the surge in secondary market activity, leading to an active and orderly loan trading market being established and the greater use of new techniques such as securitisation and credit derivatives. Although the distressed debt market differs in a number of ways from the par and near par market, the legal issues relating to transfer techniques are largely the same.

At the same time, the growth of the CLO (Collateralised Loan Obligation) market and the attraction of the loan asset class (principally leveraged loans) to non-bank investors resulted in substantial new liquidity and a significant increase in portfolio management and loan trading activity in the secondary market.

In conjunction with this, leveraged loan credit default swaps (LCDS) were developed out of the corporate CDS market whilst leveraged loan indices (such as the iTraxx LevX indices) were created as a loan related alternative to the iTraxx crossover index (which is compiled from CDSs for high yield bonds). Although initially used by banks as well as institutional investors and particularly hedge funds as a means of hedging loans and assuming synthetic risk, a lack of liquidity prevented any real growth in the market and today both are rarely traded.

However, the secondary market continues to be used as a means of managing individual exposures and portfolio concentrations, facilitating wider risk distribution, generating new revenue streams and improving economic returns.

# OBJECTIVES

There are various reasons why banks or other financial institutions may want to sell a loan to a third party or to buy it from a lender. These are discussed below from the point of view of both transferor and transferee.

# TRANSFEROR'S OBJECTIVES

### Regulatory constraints

The application of capital ratios imposed by national regulators and EU directives, specifically by way of implementation of Basel II and Basel III, requires banks to maintain capital equivalent to a certain percentage of their risk-weighted assets, so that sufficient capital is available to support the banks against losses. This has encouraged, or even forced, banks to restructure their balance sheets by the sale of assets.

### Reduction and diversification of risks

The seller of an asset may wish to transfer the borrower's credit risk (that is, the risk of the borrower's default) to a third party. The seller may also wish to sell off assets from specific countries where the risks of sovereign default, currency redenomination, nationalisation or expropriation of the borrower, the introduction of transfer restrictions or exchange controls, or, in the case of a sovereign borrower, the inability to collect sufficient hard currency to meet its foreign currency obligations are judged to be unacceptable.

### Exposure management

Linked to the above is the seller's objective of freeing credit lines for new business with special clients, geographical areas or specific countries. A selling bank may wish to use the secondary market for 'selling down' its stake in a syndication by selling assets and transferring commitments to counterparties outside the syndicate.

### Liquidity and trading profits

The seller may simply be looking for an improvement in its liquidity position or the realisation of profits or losses.

# TRANSFEREE'S OBJECTIVES

### Market access and client relationship

A buyer of a loan may wish to use the secondary market to enter the market for Euroloans or to build up specific client relationships or contacts with other financial institutions. Especially for a small bank with less experience in the international field, the purchase of a loan can be used as a marketing tool to make its name better known in the Euromarket, although this is achieved with more effect in the primary syndication market.

### Exposure management

A buyer of an asset may wish for various reasons to concentrate its portfolio on specific clients, geographical areas or countries. It may, for example, already have specialised information or knowledge of these particular clients, countries or areas.

### Debt/equity financing

Corporate investors or, sometimes, banks have used the discount on rescheduled debt to finance investments in highly indebted countries such as Mexico or Venezuela by using the debt/equity swap mechanism provided by rescheduling agreements and national legislation.

### Investment Return

A buyer (particularly an institutional investor) may simply wish to make a return on its investment either through interest payments or via price appreciation.

# TRANSFER TECHNIQUES UNDER ENGLISH LAW

English law provides several legal techniques to transfer a loan to a third party. Generally speaking a transfer agreement will be governed by the law of the country with the closest and most real connection with the agreement, usually the chosen law of the debt, unless the parties choose otherwise. Where a loan is sold through assignment, questions such as assignability, the relationship between the assignee and the debtor, the conditions under which an assignment can be invoked against the debtor and any question as to whether the debtor's obligations have been discharged will be governed by the proper law of the loan agreement (although a draft regulation proposed by the European Commission in 2018 would, if implemented, result in the proprietary effects of an assignment being governed by the laws of the country where the assignor is resident). Inconsistency may therefore arise between the law applicable to the loan agreement and the law applicable to the transfer agreement. For the avoidance of such inconsistency it is advisable that the transfer agreement should contain a choice of law clause ensuring that the transfer is governed by the same law as the loan agreement. Since many syndicated loan agreements are governed by English law, it follows that English law will also have a major impact on transfer agreements.

## Novation

Novation is the cleanest and by far the most commonly used method for transferring a loan to a third party under English law (schematically shown in exhibit 6.1).

Novation involves the cancellation and discharge of the existing rights and obligations of the seller under the loan, in consideration for which the buyer will acquire and assume rights and obligations identical to those previously owed to and by the seller. Novation is the only method by which, as a matter of English law, the obligations owed by the original lender to the borrower can be transferred to the buyer. Therefore, the novation route is used to transfer commitments under revolving credit facilities where new advances will be made at the end of successive roll-over periods.

### Exhibit 6.1: Novation

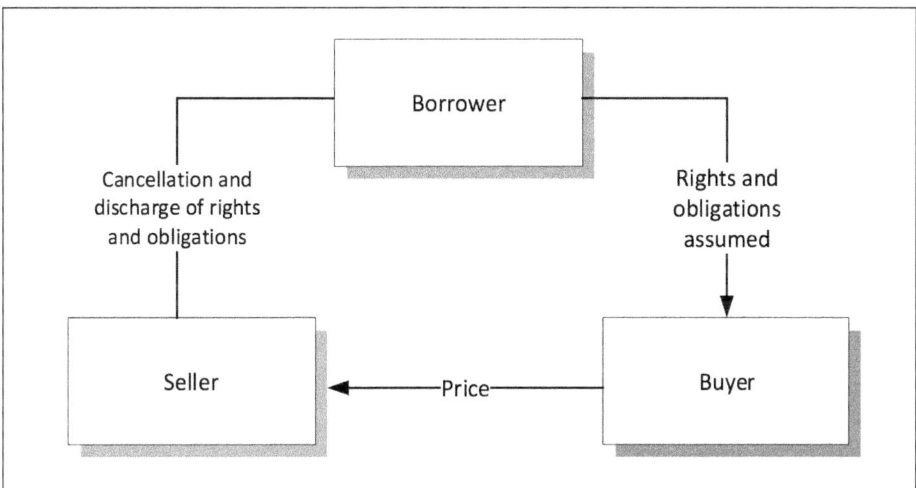


The difficulty of a transfer in the form of a novation is that, in the context of a syndicated loan, there is a requirement to obtain the agreement of all the parties to the loan agreement and this may be extremely cumbersome. If this principle were applied to a syndicated loan arrangement, without modification, the result would be that all parties to the agreement would have to be involved in order for a new lender to assume all the rights and obligations in replacing an old lender. Such an approach might be legally effective, but it is hardly practicable. The problem of how to effect the transfer in a manner which only requires the active participation of those parties directly concerned was solved during the 1980s by an innovative application of an old English law principle, established in the case of Carlill v Carbolic Smoke Ball Company ([1892] 2 Q.B. 484), that an offer may be made 'to the public at large' and such offer may be accepted by anyone who satisfies the conditions specified in this offer. Application of this principle to syndicated loan arrangements gave rise to the idea that parties to a syndicated loan agreement could at the outset offer to accept a limited novation of the original contracts, that is, a novation involving primarily the borrower, the selling bank and the buying bank. The transfer technique usually included in a loan agreement is for the seller and the buyer to execute a transfer certificate in a form which is a schedule to the loan agreement. Once the transfer certificate is executed and delivered to the agent, the novation is effected.

An example of this technique can be found in Clause 28.6 of the sample loan agreement in chapter 5. This clause sets out the framework for a novation, requiring the delivery of a transfer certificate to the agent bank before the novation date. A form of transfer certificate is, as indicated above, scheduled to the agreement (*see* Schedule 5 of the sample agreement). Even if no form of transfer certificate is included, but transfer by novation is permitted, an LMA standard form transfer certificate can be used (see the sample transfer certificate and supporting documentation included within the worked example at the end of this chapter).

Syndicated loan agreements often contain restrictions on a bank's ability to transfer its rights and obligations. It is very common in the market to see a restriction that no transfer may be made without the prior consent of the borrower. This consent is normally required to be in writing but often the borrower may not unreasonably withhold or delay its consent. In the case of an assignment or transfer to an existing syndicate bank, or to a subsidiary or holding company, or subsidiary of a holding company, of an existing syndicate bank, the consent of the borrower is not usually required. Consent is also often not required when an event of default (as defined in the loan agreement) has occurred. As banks have increasingly sought the flexibility to fund themselves through central bank funding schemes they have also tried to ensure that loan agreements allow them to charge or assign their rights by way of collateral to Federal Reserve or central banks.

These restrictions on transfers became particularly relevant in late 2007 and 2008, as arrangers worked hard to syndicate some high-profile acquisition facilities in the face of difficult credit market conditions. In 2008, one bank issued proceedings in the English courts to claim that a borrower had breached the terms of a syndicated loan agreement by unreasonably withholding its consent to a proposed transfer. This claim did not come before the courts because the parties reached a settlement on their dispute before the trial. However, it did shine a light on the transfer provisions commonly used in loan agreements. Lenders remain keen to minimise restrictions on their entitlement to transfer their rights and obligations, but many borrowers in the syndicated lending markets have remained steadfast in their desire to retain some control over the composition of their lending syndicates through these consent mechanisms (in contrast to the bond markets where "free transferability" is the norm). Indeed borrowers in the leveraged finance markets have imposed increasingly stringent controls over the rights of lenders to transfer their interest in loans (including by way of so-called "white lists" and "black lists" as well as prohibitions on transfers to "competitors").

In the case of larger 'jumbo' acquisition facilities, lenders are often keen to ensure that such facilities are 'freely transferable', requiring no borrower consent whatsoever. In addition, in the case of multi-tranche facilities, de-coupling of the tranches is usual so as to allow assignment or transfer on a non pro-rata basis, in order to encourage liquidity in the secondary market.

The LMA has sought to standardise borrower's consent provisions by introducing deemed consent wording, whereby the borrower's consent is deemed to have been given if the borrower does not expressly decline or respond to such a request within a certain period of time, for example, five business days after receipt of the request. In this way, the secondary market can operate more efficiently and the LMA's recommended settlement period of T + 10 (10 business days after the Trade Date) can be adhered to.

A further common restriction concerns the minimum amounts for any transfer. The purpose of this restriction is often to protect the agent from inadequately remunerated administrative work when the loan breaks into pieces that are too small.

Normally the agent bank charges the transferee a fee for its services, often in the range of $1,000 to $2,000.

It should be noted that in certain jurisdictions a loan transfer through novation may cause problems in two ways (both of which stem from the fact that the novation operates to discharge the original debt and create a new one). The issue arises first because so-called 'hardening periods' for the purpose of insolvency provisions may be repeatedly started and secondly because novation may operate as a discharge of the benefit of any security. When these issues arise another legal route to allow transfer (for example, assignment) may need to be used.

# Assignment

Assignments take the form of either a legal or an equitable assignment (schematically shown in exhibits 6.2 and 6.3 respectively). Both give the assignee a direct claim on the borrower (although the assignee may not be able to sue in its own name in the case of an equitable assignment).

## Legal assignment

A legal assignment must satisfy the conditions set out in Section 136 of the Law of Property Act 1925 and must therefore be in writing, the whole of the debt must be transferred absolutely and notice of the assignment has to be given to the debtor. The effect of a legal assignment is to 'pass and transfer' from the seller (assignor) to the buyer (assignee) the legal right to the debt, all legal and other remedies for the debt and the power to give a good discharge for payment. The buyer accordingly acquires the full legal and beneficial interest in the debt and may sue the underlying debtor directly without need to rely upon the seller to assist in the enforcement of the debt.

It should be stressed that only the lender's rights are transferred; the assignment will not be effective to transfer to the assignee any obligations which the lender continues to owe, for example, funding obligations under a roll-over facility or a request by the borrower to reschedule or renegotiate the loan. Furthermore, the rights of the assignee may be impaired by any rights of set-off that exist between the borrower and the assignor.

### Exhibit 6.2: Legal assignment

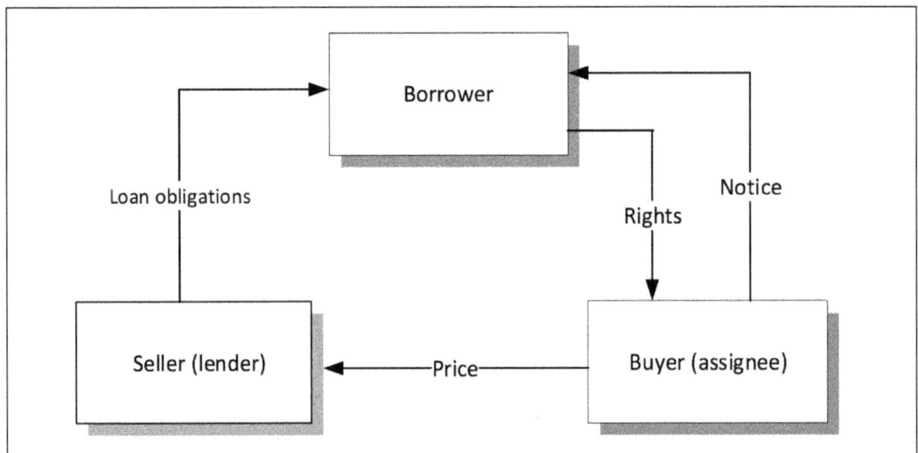

**Exhibit 6.3: Equitable assignment**

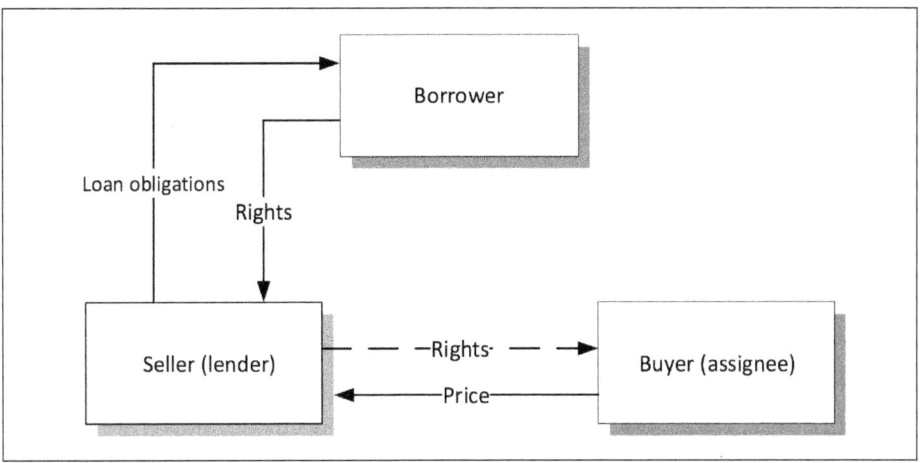


## Equitable assignment

If an assignment does not meet all the conditions set out in Section 136 of the Law of Property Act 1925, it will not constitute a legal assignment but it may nevertheless be effective as an assignment 'in equity'. This means that the buyer will obtain a beneficial interest in the debt and, subject to certain procedural formalities such as giving notice to the borrower, will obtain the right to sue the borrower directly. However, if notice is not given to the borrower, the buyer's interest in the loan will essentially be held "through" the seller (with all payments being made to the seller by the borrower).

The LMA's documentation includes a form of assignment (as a schedule to the facilities agreement – see Schedule 5 of the sample agreement contained in chapter 5). It should be noted that a syndicated loan agreement does not only govern the relationship between the borrower and the lender but also, through the sharing clause and the agency provisions, the rights and obligations among the lenders themselves. Therefore, the LMA's assignment procedure provides that the assignee must agree to be under the same obligations towards the other lenders as it would have been, had it been an original party to the agreement – failing which, the syndicate banks will not be under any obligation to recognise any rights of the assignee towards them (see Clause 28.3(a)(i) of the sample agreement).

Care needs to be taken in relation to those types of facilities involving continuing obligations owed by the lenders to a borrower, for example roll-over loans or multi-currency term loans where lenders may have an obligation to change currency or provide a top-up in case of exchange movements. In these cases an assignment may need to be supplemented in some way to create an effective bridge in relation to these obligations.

## Participation

Under English law a participation is essentially a contractual agreement between the seller and the buyer to make funding arrangements. It is an entirely separate contract from the underlying loan agreement and does not involve the transfer to the buyer of a legal or a beneficial interest* in the debt so that the buyer gets no directly enforceable rights against the borrower. Although it has no technical legal meaning in English law, the term is usually adopted to describe the 'sale' of an asset. This can take place in one of two ways – funded or non-funded.

### Funded sub-participation

Under the funded sub-participation agreement (shown schematically in exhibit 6.4) the buyer of the asset will place with the seller a deposit in the amount agreed between the seller and the buyer and on terms matching the terms of the underlying loan agreement. The participant has a double credit risk on the borrower and the seller. In other words, if the seller went into liquidation, money subsequently received from the borrower would be available to the general body of creditors of the seller and would not be set aside for the participant.

### Non-funded or 'risk participation'

Where the assets being sold are contingent ones, it is common to see the asset being disposed of by way of risk participation (shown schematically in exhibit 6.5). The participant receives a fee in return for the agreement to compensate the seller of the asset for any default on the part of the underlying debtor. Once a default under the loan agreement has occurred and the risk participant has reimbursed the seller, it will either take an assignment of the seller's rights against the debtor or will simply be contractually entitled to any moneys subsequently recovered by the seller from the debtor.

* However, certain types of participation may result in loss of beneficial ownership for tax purposes. This is particularly true in the case of a funded sub-participation where the lender relies on a double tax treaty to eliminate withholding since the 'beneficial ownership' concept here would follow principles established in the Indofood case (*Indofood International Finance Ltd v JP Morgan Chase Bank NA [2006] EWCA Civ 158*)

**Exhibit 6.4: Funded sub-participation**

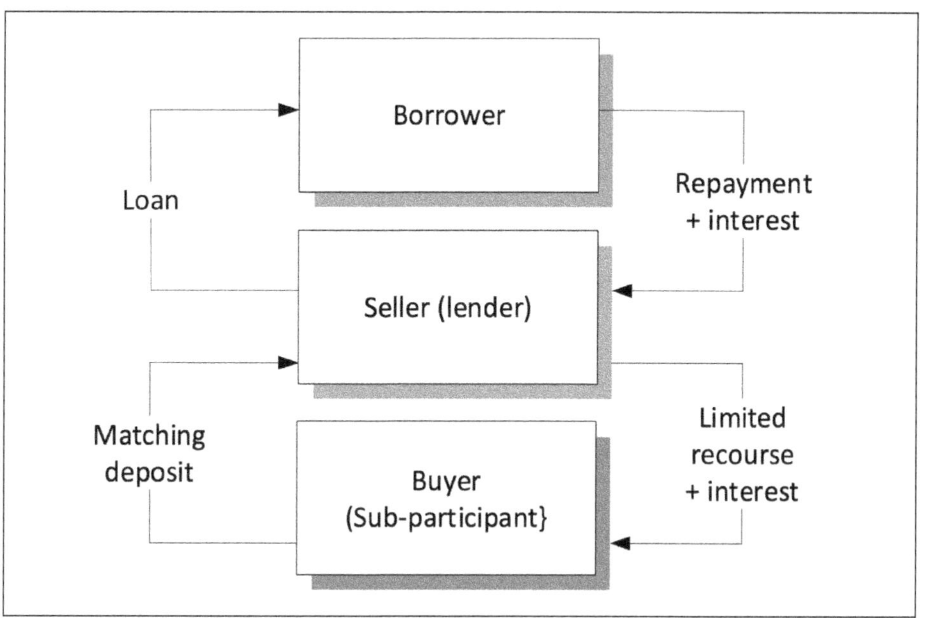


**Exhibit 6.5: Risk sub-participation**

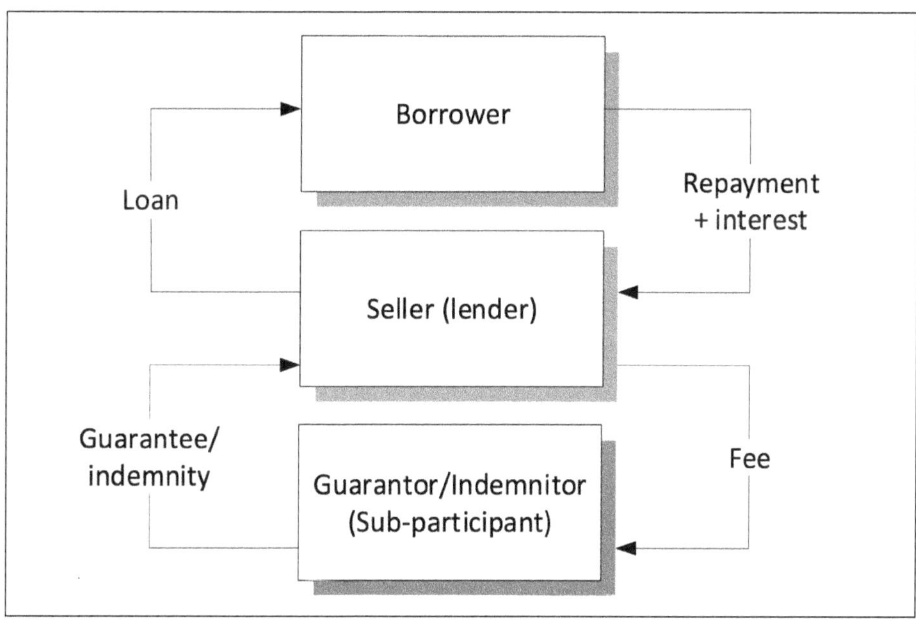

Essentially, a risk participation involves the substitution of issuer risk, that is, the risk of default, with counterparty risk – the credit risk of the guarantor or indemnitor, the risk participant. A risk participation in economic effect is the simplest form of credit derivative or credit default swap (albeit that the structures and documentation adopted in the credit derivative market differ markedly from those used for risk participations).

## Contractual and other legal restrictions on asset sales

The majority of syndicated loan agreements will attempt to regulate and restrict the manner in which assignments of rights or transfers of rights and obligations can take place. Particularly common is a restriction which requires the written consent of a borrower before any assignment or transfer can take place. In addition, many agreements deal with issues such as minimum amounts or multiples in which transfers may be made. The failure to observe these contractual restrictions will mean at least that the assignment or transfer is ineffective against the borrower and/or any guarantor. It may also mean that the assignment or transfer is of no effect even between the seller and the buyer of the assets. In contrast to restrictions on assignments and novations, it is unusual in a loan facility to find restrictions on the granting of participations (although increasingly borrowers are attempting to do so). The reason is that a participation does not affect the original relationship between borrower and lender.

A further restriction under English law, and also in many other legal systems, is that a bank will owe a general duty of confidentiality to its customers. Any disclosure by the lender to a third party of the terms, or even the very existence, of any credit facility or of any information provided to the lender in connection with that facility will, prima facie, involve a breach of this duty of confidentiality. Therefore, and to avoid any damages for breach of contract, many syndicated loan agreements contain express authority to disclose the existence of the loan and such other information about the borrower and any guarantor which the lending bank considers to be appropriate. Increasingly borrowers insist on loan agreements containing provisions expressly requiring information about the borrower to be kept confidential albeit with exceptions to permit asset sales (for an example of which see Clause 40 of the sample agreement in chapter 5).

## The impact of other laws

In addition to these express or implied restrictions, it is important for the parties to a transfer agreement to recognise that, although the transfer agreement itself may be governed by English law, its effectiveness may further depend on the laws of other countries. The law of the country of incorporation or residence of the borrower or of any guarantor, for example, may be relevant in determining the effectiveness of the method of sale adopted, since effective enforcement of the debt and the question of the rights of third parties may ultimately depend on the decision of the courts in that country. The law of the seller's or the buyer's country or the legal regime applicable to the place where the sale occurs cannot be ignored, especially in relation to tax issues such as stamp duty and withholding tax. Assignment or transfers of loans to third parties may therefore increase, or give rise to, withholding taxes which did not previously exist and an assignee may find in these circumstances that the grossing-up provisions in tax clauses or previous tax exemptions do not extend to protect their position. Prudent parties to a transfer agreement will at the very least make enquiries about the local laws and the jurisdiction of the borrower and any guarantor to discover where restrictions may exist in relation to the proposed method of sale. The experience of the international offices of Clifford Chance in carrying out such reviews has revealed that, more often than not local law will have an impact on sales by way of assignment or novation. Indeed, in certain jurisdictions sub-participation is the only feasible method of disposing of assets. However, even the use of sub-participation structures will not always ensure that local law issues can be ignored because increasingly tax authorities will look carefully at structures such as participations which appear to introduce steps into a transaction in order to avoid withholding, or other, taxes.

## Accounting and supervisory treatment of asset sales

From a strict accounting and supervisory perspective it is usually the seller's objective to ensure that the loan to be transferred will be disregarded for banking supervisory and accounting purposes and, therefore, that the assets cease to be counted on the seller's balance sheet. It is evident that, for accounting and supervisory purposes, the law of the place of incorporation or residence of the seller is relevant in order to determine whether off-balance sheet treatment will be achieved and whether the supervisory authorities will acknowledge the asset sale in question. Additionally, or alternatively, the seller may wish to ensure that, when the asset is accounted for in the consolidated balance sheet of its institution, the same accounting and supervisory treatment will be accorded to the asset sale. English law and accounting practices will be relevant if the seller or any of its parent companies is registered in England.

## Regulatory treatment

The Prudential Regulation Authority (PRA), being the supervisory authority for authorised institutions in England, will recognise an asset transfer and therefore exclude the transferred loan from the seller's risk asset ratio (subject to a few conditions which are set out below), if the assets are transferred through a novation. A transfer through assignment, whether legal or equitable, will be recognised if it is duly notified to the borrower and reasonable precautions are made to ensure that the buyer's rights under the assignment are not impaired by an intervening right, for example, a right of set-off between the seller and the borrower. Assignment without notification to the borrower will usually also be recognised as a transfer, provided that the seller recognises and protects itself against additional risks, such as pressure from the borrower to reschedule or to renegotiate the terms of the loan or to advance further funds. The PRA will further recognise funded and non-funded sub-participations. Undrawn commitments will be excluded from the selling bank's risk asset ratio only when the transfer is by novation or by an assignment accompanied by: a release from the borrower of the seller from its obligations; an assumption by the buyer of the seller's obligations; and, a formal acknowledgement by the borrower of the transfer.

The PRA's recognition of an asset transfer is subject to the general conditions that:

- the transfer does not contravene provisions in the underlying loan agreement;
- all necessary consents have been obtained;
- the seller did not keep any residual beneficial interest in the principal amount of the loan;
- the buyer has no formal recourse to the seller for losses;
- there is no obligation on the seller to repurchase the loan;
- the burden of rescheduling or renegotiation will be on the buyer; and
- the seller, if payments are routed through its accounts, will be under no obligation to remit funds to the buyer unless and until they are received from the borrower.

Failure to satisfy one of the conditions will result in the situation where the assets will not only continue to be included in the seller's risk asset ratio but will also be included in the buyer's.

## Accounting treatment

Two conditions must be met in order to achieve off-balance sheet treatment of a loan transfer.

First, it is necessary to ensure that neither the seller nor any parent company is a 'subsidiary undertaking' under the Companies Act 2006 of either the buyer or the buyer's parent company. The basic definition of a 'parent and subsidiary undertaking' relationship is that one company holds or controls a majority of voting rights in the other company or has the right to exercise a dominant influence.

Second, the seller must comply with applicable accounting rules. The International Accounting Standards Board's International Financial Reporting Standard No.9 (*Financial*

*Instruments*) came into force in January 2018 and applies, inter alia, to loan transfers on the secondary market. This standard is very similar to the above-mentioned rules of the PRA. It should, however, be noted that the principles applying on the transfer of securitised mortgages and the factoring of debts may be relevant as well.

If a transfer fails to comply with the rules outlined above, the result will be that the assets will remain either on the balance sheet of the seller's group or on the balance sheet of the seller itself and additionally on the buyer's balance sheet.

In the US, off-balance sheet treatment will be governed by ASC Topic 860, Transfer and Servicing. Please see the section below on transfer techniques under New York law for a further discussion of this

## Tax implications of asset sales

One of the most problematic areas for a buyer or a seller of assets is to appreciate fully the tax implications of the particular sale method adopted. Tax implications of loan sales are different and depend on the true nature and the consequences of the particular asset sale method. Areas of particular relevance for lenders and borrowers operating in the UK are withholding tax, and stamp duty. Set out below is a brief description of the issues, but note that this is a highly complex area on which specialist advice should always be sought.

## Withholding tax

In general, a UK borrower (or a non-UK borrower making UK source payments) is required to deduct tax at the basic rate (currently 20%) from payments of interest that it makes. There are various exemptions from this obligation, of which the most commonly used include: (a) the loan is made by a UK bank, a UK branch of an overseas bank or a UK resident company or UK branch of an overseas entity (Sections 879, 933 and 934 of the Income Tax Act 2007); (b) the borrower is itself a UK bank (Section 878 of the Income Tax Act 2007); (c) the lender is able to benefit from an exemption available under the UK's extensive double taxation treaty network; or (d) the qualifying private placement exemption applies (Section 888A of the Income Tax Act 2007).

No withholding tax arises if the interest is payable on an advance from a 'bank' (as such term is defined in Section 991 of the Income Tax Act 2007) and, at the time the interest is paid, the person beneficially entitled to the interest (which need not necessarily be the bank making the loan) is within the charge to UK corporation tax as respects that interest. UK tax resident companies (such as certain institutional investors) and non-UK tax resident companies acting through UK permanent establishments should be within the charge to UK corporation tax.

No withholding tax arises if the borrower is a bank (again as defined in Section 991 of the Income Tax Act 2007) provided that the interest is paid by the bank in its ordinary course of business.

A non-UK tax resident lender (such as a foreign bank or institutional investor), that is eligible to benefit from a double taxation treaty between the UK and its jurisdiction of tax residence, may be entitled to an exemption from, or a reduction in, the rate of UK withholding tax. The treaty will specify various conditions that the lender must satisfy in order to gain the benefit of such tax relief. If the lender meets these, it may make an application to HM Revenue & Customs to receive interest payments free from withholding tax. If HM Revenue & Customs accepts the application, it will give a direction to the borrower. Once the borrower receives this, it may pay interest to that lender without withholding. It typically takes six months for HM Revenue & Customs to process an application and grant a direction under the standard treaty clearance process.

An alternative route to access treaty benefits is for lenders to register with HM Revenue & Customs for a "Treaty Passport" which, once obtained, enables borrowers to use a streamlined process to obtain treaty clearance in respect of those lenders more quickly.

The qualifying private placement exemption is an exemption which came into force on 1 January 2016 (Section 888A of the Income Tax Act 2007). It eliminates the need to obtain HM Revenue & Customs clearance (and the associated delay) and is broadly available to lenders that are resident in double tax treaty jurisdictions (whether or not such treaty eliminates withholding or merely reduces the rate). In addition to lender related conditions, there are a number of requirements that relate to the borrower and the loan itself which need to be satisfied for the exemption to apply. The scope and application of this new exemption remains unclear and so the take-up has been limited.

Withholding issues under sub-participations are complex and the availability of reliefs, as well as the scope of withholding obligations, depends on the terms of the sub-participation and the identity of all parties. Very broadly, in the context of a sub-participation, where the lender maintains beneficial ownership of the underlying loan, the interest payments from the borrower to the lender and the interest payments from the lender to the sub-participant are each considered separately for the purposes of determining the applicable withholding tax. However, the position may be different if the sub-participation is entered into to facilitate the avoidance of tax.

## Stamp duty and stamp duty reserve tax (SDRT)

UK stamp duty and SDRT are relevant, in the context of loan debt trading, to sales in which a seller passes on existing contractual rights to a buyer. Accordingly, they are, generally speaking, relevant to sales by way of assignment, and not to sales by way of novation or participation. As most sales in the UK are effected by way of novation, this is of limited application.

Despite the similarity suggested by their names, stamp duty and SDRT are separate from each other and are subject to different administrative regimes. Stamp duty is chargeable on instruments transferring property, including stock (a loan is regarded as 'stock' for these purposes). There are financial penalties for late payment and, perhaps more importantly, until the relevant document is duly stamped (and the appropriate duty paid) an instrument which is chargeable to stamp duty may not, generally, be relied on before an English court.

Assignments of certain types of loan capital are, however, exempt from stamp duty. The scope of the exemption is set out in Section 79 of the Finance Act 1986 and the term 'loan capital' is defined in Section 78 of the Finance Act 1986. It covers most standard loans but does not cover loans which are repayable on demand, which carry rights of conversion or acquisition or which carry the right to excessive interest or to interest determined by reference to a business or property or to a premium on redemption. The exemption may also not apply if the assignment purports to transfer other rights of the parties which are not directly associated with the loan asset.

SDRT was introduced by the Finance Act 1986 with the primary aim of capturing transfers of securities taking place in clearing systems. Unlike stamp duty, it is a tax on agreements (irrespective of whether such an agreement is written or oral) to transfer 'chargeable securities'. Chargeable securities are defined to cover loan capital but not loan capital of a non-UK body corporate unless that loan capital is kept in a register in the UK by the body corporate or on its behalf. Fortunately, the Finance Act 1986 provides that, if a particular asset is exempt from stamp duty, it will also be exempt from SDRT.

## Conclusion

English law provides a reasonable framework for asset sales in the secondary market with transfers between lenders now commonplace. Although a great deal in this chapter is about risk aspects of the asset sales market, most of the problems discussed above seem to be manageable.

With the formation of the LMA, and the introduction of standard documentation, there is now an active and orderly market in which the buying and selling of loans takes place. This in turn has seen a thriving trading market develop and the LMA has published a common set of standard terms and conditions for par/near par and distressed debt trading.

Whilst the majority of loan transfers are completed by means of novation using transfer certificates, individual loan sales between banks through the secondary market are just one way banks seek to manage their balance sheets. It should be further mentioned that secondary market transfer techniques are used in different ways to reallocate international capital resources such as by means of securitisation and through the use of credit derivatives, as well as total return swaps and various combinations of different participations.

In the face of changing regulation and legislation, participants in syndicated loans are likely to continue to utilise a variety of secondary transfer mechanisms to achieve risk mitigation and yield enhancement across their portfolios. Care should be taken to consider withholding tax issues in the context of such arrangements.

# TRANSFER TECHNIQUES UNDER NEW YORK LAW

## Introduction

The methods of transfer under New York law are in principle similar to those under English law despite the difference in the nomenclature ascribed to them. An interest in a loan or part of a loan may be transferred by means of novation, assignment or by granting a participation in the loan or part thereof to a third party, although in the US, the two most common techniques for transferring an interest in a loan are assignments and participations.

## Assignment agreements

The description given under the English law analysis of novation above applies equally to novations effected under New York law. Under English law, however, the novation is more commonly used than under New York law where an assignment agreement is the usual means by which a lender assigns specified rights and delegates specified obligations (and novations are rarely if ever used). The purpose of an assignment agreement is to allow for the complete substitution of one lender's obligation to extend all or part of the credit for another lender's obligation under the loan agreement (and its effect is, therefore, similar to that of a novation). A common practice within the US is to 'strip' a loan, by a lender selling different tranches under a loan agreement to different assignees or to even different types of assignees (banks, insurance companies, vulture funds, etc.).

In addition, it is not unknown for a bank, which may also be the agent in the syndicated credit, to assign all of its rights and obligations as a lending bank to another institution, but to retain its administrative rights, including the right to the agent's fee. This practice became more popular as fee income became more important and as banks became more interested in avoiding capital requirements. Again, this often resulted in administrative problems for the lending banks and borrower since sometimes the agent may demonstrate a lack of interest in its administrative duties once it has no remaining economic stake. However, it is rare to find restrictions in either the agency provisions or the assignment provisions on the agent's ability to take this action.

As in the case of novations in respect of loan agreements governed by English law, the 'assignment' or 'assignment and assumption' is used to facilitate transfers of rights and obligations in the secondary loan market. By means of this mechanism, the assignee will be able to rely on a contractual right to enforce the benefits assigned to it and the borrower likewise will have an enforceable right directly against the assignee, rather than each having to depend on a common law doctrine. The Loan Syndications and Trading Association (LSTA), which performs a similar function to the LMA for the US market, has crafted model credit agreement assignment provisions which have been adopted by the major arranging banks and which accomplish the same result. The form of the assignment agreement is usually attached to the loan agreement as an exhibit and contains contractual statements on the part of both the assignor and the assignee.

In the assignment agreement, the assignor will agree to sell and assign to the assignee without recourse, and the assignee will agree to purchase and assume from the assignor, specified rights and obligations under the loan agreement. The assignee will also confirm that it has received and reviewed the underlying loan agreement and has received all information it requires to enable it to make an independent credit decision about the borrower. The assignor will make a specific statement disclaiming any responsibility with respect to any statement, warranty or representation made in or in connection with the underlying loan agreement and will explicitly disclaim responsibility with respect to the financial condition of the borrower. Typically, the assignor represents only that it owns the loan and that it is not subject to any lien or other encumbrance. Representations may be expanded to include references to any payments received by the assignor prior to the effective date of the assignment, any knowledge of the assignor regarding any existing defaults or other similar 'basic' representations. In relation to sales of so-called 'distressed' loans an LSTA Purchase and Sale Agreement will usually be entered into and this will contain a wide variety of additional representations and warranties.

In order to ensure that the assignment agreement is valid with respect to all the parties to the underlying loan agreement, the borrower, the agent and the other lenders in a syndicated facility will have agreed in such loan agreement to transfers by a lender, subject to certain requirements. For example, the loan agreement may provide that transfers will only be permitted to banks or other financial institutions whose ordinary business includes participating in banking facilities, will only be effected by means of an assignment agreement, and will only be effective upon the consent of the borrower (such consent not to be unreasonably withheld or delayed) and the agent (especially if the loan is not fully funded or if there is a letter of credit facility, since the agent under such circumstances also suffers some credit exposure to the new assignee). The LSTA has also sought to standardise borrower's consent provisions by introducing deemed consent wording in the model credit agreement assignment provisions to facilitate faster loan settlements (similar to the LMA approach) and borrower consent will often not be required when a default has occurred and is continuing under the loan agreement. Furthermore, the underlying loan agreement may contain a provision requiring prompt notice of all transfers to be given to each party thereto and the maintenance of a register by the agent for the recording of all transfers. Upon acceptance, notice and recording by the agent, the assignment will take effect, the assignee will become a party to the underlying loan agreement and the assignor will be released from its obligations thereunder (except for certain indemnity provisions which may continue under some circumstances).

Notwithstanding the limitations outlined above, an institution may usually assign its interests to a lender or a lender affiliate without any other party's consent and an institution must be able to pledge or assign a security interest in all or any portion of its rights under the loan agreement to any Federal Reserve Bank in accordance with Regulation A of the Federal Reserve Board with the qualification that no pledge relieves the pledgor of any obligations under the loan agreement.

## Assignment of rights

Strictly speaking, an assignment will only involve the transfer of rights of the assignor to the assignee. Duties are delegated by way of acceptance or assumption of the obligations of the assignor by the assignee, which must be consented to by each party to whom obligations are owed. In US usage, the term 'assignment' is most typically used to refer to both an assignment of rights and a delegation and assumption of obligations. The assignment of an existing right to future payment is permitted under New York law without the requirement of consent from any other party except where it: materially impairs rights of a third party under the loan agreement; is prohibited by statute; increases the risk upon the obligor; or materially changes the duty of the obligor (this is possible, for example, where the assignment may result in increased costs to the borrower); or, where there is an express contractual prohibition upon the assignment of rights. Moreover, contractual restrictions on a sale of a promissory note or payment intangible (for example, the right to mere payment under a loan agreement) are made ineffective under the revised Article 9 of the Uniform commercial Code (Section 9-408).

Where an assignment is permitted, New York law enshrines a similar legal principle to that contained in Section 136 of the English Law of Property Act 1925: namely, that the borrower may continue to make payments to the original lender and deal with it as such until it receives notice of the assignment. In addition, until the borrower has been notified, modification or discharge of the contract is effective as between the borrower and the original obligor. If notice has been given to the borrower, the borrower will be required to make payments directly to the assignee. Conversely, the assignee is not bound by any agreement reached between the borrower and the assignor unless it expressly assumes such agreement nor is the assignor relieved of its obligations to the borrower unless the borrower consents thereto.

## Participations

Like the sub-participation in English law, the participation under New York law is the mechanism by which a lender can transfer the benefit and the risk of all or part of the loan under the loan agreement to a participant without the involvement of any other party to that loan agreement, including the borrower (the principal difference between a properly drafted New York law participation (that is, an "LSTA – style" participation) and an English law sub-participation (that is, an "LMA – style" participation) being that the New York law participation can convey a beneficial interest in the underlying loan to the participant whereas an English law sub-participation implements a back-to-back financing by the participant to the seller and creates a debtor/creditor relationship even when the participation is without recourse to the seller's credit). Nor is notice required to be given to any other party to the loan agreement since the direct relationship between the lender and borrower is not affected by the participation agreement between the lender and the participant. Some strong borrowers have in a minority of cases been able to negotiate to have either consent rights or the right to receive notice when a participation occurs. While it is resisted by lenders (who often sell 'silent' participations to participants which are prohibited from even contacting the borrower, thereby allowing the selling bank to maintain its exclusive relationship with the borrower), several well-published workouts have been hampered by the existence of participants (which were previously unknown to the borrower). Another common response by borrowers has been to limit, in participation provisions set forth in credit documents, the voting rights of a participant so that a participating bank is unable to contract with its participant voting rights greater than those which would require unanimous lender consent under the loan agreement.

Since participations generally give the participant no contractual, statutory or common law rights of action against the borrower, the participant must be careful to protect itself from any adverse consequences from the bankruptcy of the lender, including set-off of the loan revenues against deposit obligations of the insolvent lender to the borrower. This can be done by ensuring in the participation agreement that the transfer is characterised under New York law as a sale rather than a loan.

For the transfer to be characterised as a sale, the participation agreement should explicitly provide that:

- the participant takes the credit risk if the borrower fails to pay and that the obligation of the lender, if any, is only to advance collections actually received from the borrower to the participant;
- the participation matches the underlying loan to the borrower in payments of principal and interest to the participant; and
- the term 'sale' and 'purchase' is used.

The assignee under an assignment and acceptance agreement will, for similar reasons, want to ensure that there has been a 'sale' of the rights and obligations transferred thereunder. Accordingly, it will be explicitly stated in the agreement that the assignment is without recourse.

If the participation (or for that matter the assignment and acceptance) is characterised as a sale, both the lender and the transferee will benefit in the following ways:

- as a financial regulatory and accounting matter, a portion of the underlying loans (in the case of a participation) and all of the underlying loan (in the case of an assignment) is removed from the books of the lender, thereby facilitating compliance with lending limits and reserve and capital adequacy requirements;
- the transferee is protected from claims by creditors of the lender in the case of its insolvency against payments made by the borrower to the lender on the basis that such payment is received by the lender for the benefit of the transferee; and
- in the situation where the loan is secured by collateral of a borrower which subsequently becomes insolvent, the court will recognise the transferee as having an interest in the collateral (provided that where there is a transfer of an interest in a secured loan, all the necessary steps have been taken to perfect the security interest of the transferee).

Another significant risk which a participant should bear in mind is that if the lender becomes insolvent the borrower may have rights to set-off deposits owed to it by the lender, thereby leaving the participant with a specific right only to the net (after set-off) proceeds in the loan and a general claim against the lender for the balance. This is again because the relationship of the lender and the borrower cannot be affected by a participation agreement to which only the lender and the participant are party. The equitable remedy of set-off, however, would not be available to a borrower who has consented to the transfer of all or a portion of the rights and obligations of the lender pursuant to an assignment and acceptance agreement.

Conversely, the participating lender also bears the risk of a participant becoming insolvent. Since the participating lender is still the direct party under the credit document, it will be obliged to perform thereunder even if the participant is in default of the participation agreement or is insolvent. This is usually made even clearer by language in the loan agreement to the effect that the borrower, agent and other lenders may continue to treat the participating lender as the lender for all purposes, notwithstanding the existence of a participation.

Notwithstanding the fundamental differences between an English law sub-participation and New York law participation, as of July 10, 2012, both the U.S. Securities and Exchange Commission and the U.S. Commodity Futures Trading Commission approved joint final rules and guidance defining "swap" and "security-based swap" for the purposes of Title VII of Dodd-Frank Wall Street Reform and Consumer Protection Act (Dodd-Frank) and making it clear that both LSTA-style and LMA-style participations are not swaps and therefore are not subject to any of the Dodd-Frank derivatives regulations. To qualify for exclusion, the final rules require that any excluded loan participation must reflect the transfer of a "current or future direct or indirect ownership interest" in an underlying loan or commitment. The final rules articulate the following four characteristics that should be present, all of which are covered in both the LSTA and the LMA standard forms for funded participations (risk participations may not satisfy all these conditions):

1. The grantor of the loan participation is a lender under, or a participant or sub-participant in, the loan or commitment that is the subject of the loan participation.

2. The aggregate participation in the loan or commitment that is the subject of the loan participation does not exceed the principal amount of such loan or commitment. Further, the loan participation does not grant, in the aggregate, to the participant in such loan participation a greater interest than the grantor holds in the loan or commitment that is the subject of the loan participation.

3. The entire purchase price for the loan participation is paid in full when acquired and is not financed.

4. The loan participation provides the participant all of the economic benefit and risk of the whole or part of the loan or commitment that is the subject of the loan participation.

## Transfer agreements as securities

If the interest of the assignee or participant is characterised as a 'security' for purposes of the Securities Act of 1933 and the Securities Exchange Act of 1934 (collectively, the 'Security Acts'), the lender will be subject to the information requirements and anti-fraud provisions of the Securities Acts, imposing strict standards of disclosure. The lender would, in such case, have a duty to notify the assignee or participant about any material non-public information regarding the creditworthiness of the borrower and the collateral and certain material non-public information about the integrity and management ability of the lender and the parties would be subject to applicable insider trading laws.

A participation or other transfer agreement may be characterised as a 'security' under the Securities Acts if it is found to be in essence an investment contract rather than a commercial loan. Although the matter is not entirely free from legal doubt as there is no bright line test, the market continues to treat loans as non-securities and market participants do not seek to register them under securities laws or to seek an exemption from registration.

## Regulatory treatment

US banking organisations are required to file quarterly Consolidated Reports of Condition and Income ('Call Reports'). For purposes of reporting transfers of financial assets on a Call Report, US banking organisations must follow US generally accepted accounting principles. More specifically, US banking organisations must follow the accounting standards for transfers of financial assets set forth in ASC Topic 860, Transfers and Servicing (formerly FASB Statement No. 140, *Accounting for Transfers and Servicing of Financial Assets and Extinguishments of Liabilities)*. Generally, after the reporting bank transfers financial assets that satisfy the conditions for the transfer to be accounted for as a sale, it recognises the financial and servicing assets it controls and the liabilities it has incurred, removes financial assets from the balance sheet when control has been surrendered, and removes liabilities from the balance sheet when extinguished.

A bank should account for a transfer of an entire financial asset or a group of entire financial assets as a "sale" if generally: (i) the transferred assets have been isolated from the transferor, i.e., are beyond the reach of the transferor or its creditors, even in bankruptcy; (ii) each transferee has the right to pledge or exchange the assets without conditions; and (iii) the transferor does not maintain effective control over the transferred assets. The transfer of a portion of an entire financial asset must also meet the definition of participating interest to qualify for 'sale' treatment. As defined by ASC Topic 860, a 'participating interest' has the following characteristics: (i) from the date of the transfer, it must represent a pro rata ownership interest in an entire financial asset; (ii) from the date of the transfer, all cash flows received from the entire financial asset, except any cash flows allocated as compensation for servicing or other services performed (which must not be subordinated and must not significantly exceed an amount that would fairly compensate a substitute service provider should one be required), must be divided proportionately among the participating interest holders in an amount equal to their share of ownership; (iii) the rights of each participating interest holder (including the lead lender) must have the same priority, no interest is subordinated to another interest, and no participating interest holder has recourse to the lead lender or another participating interest holder other than standard representations and warranties and ongoing contractual servicing and administration obligations; and (iv) no party has the right to pledge or exchange the entire financial asset unless all participating interest holders agree to do so. If a transfer of an entire financial asset or participating interest in a financial asset does not satisfy the criteria for 'sale' treatment, the transfer should be accounted for as a 'secured borrowing' with pledge of collateral. Generally, a 'sale' will take the transferred asset off the balance sheet of the bank whereas a 'secured borrowing' will not.

Assets transferred in transactions that do not qualify as 'sales' under generally accepted accounting principles should be reported as assets on the Call Report balance sheet and are subject to the US bank regulatory agencies' regulatory capital requirements. A transfer of assets that qualifies as a 'sale' under generally accepted accounting principles generally would not be subject to capital requirements. Such transfer may, however, be subject to regulatory capital requirements if the transfer is made with 'recourse'. A recourse obligation typically arises when an institution transfers assets and retains an obligation to repurchase the assets or absorb losses due to a default of principal or interest or any other deficiency in the performance of the underlying obligor or some other party. Recourse may also exist implicitly where a bank provides credit enhancement beyond any contractual obligation to support assets it has sold. There are a number of exemptions but, in general, US banking organisations must hold risk-based capital against the entire outstanding amount of assets sold with recourse.

Loan participations transferred with recourse by a banking organisation are likely not to be considered isolated from the transferor and reclaimed by the Federal Deposit Insurance Corporation ('FDIC') in a receivership or conservatorship proceeding. FDIC's regulations generally limit the FDIC's ability to reclaim loan participations transferred 'without recourse', as defined in the regulations, but do not limit the FDIC's ability to reclaim loan participations transferred with recourse.

Loan participation transfers that meet certain conditions are excluded for purposes of compliance with the regulatory limits on loans to one borrower. The regulations of the

Comptroller of the Currency who is the primary federal regulator for all national banks provide that participation interests do not constitute loans or extensions of credit for the purposes of the lending limits, so long as the participation is transferred on a non-recourse basis, and provided that the participation results in a pro rata sharing of credit risk proportionate to the respective interests of the originating and participating lenders.

## US withholding taxes

Under US federal income tax laws, interest payments to non-US persons by US borrowers are generally subject to withholding tax at a rate of 30% unless the non-US person provides the US borrower with a valid applicable US Internal Revenue Service (IRS) Form W-8 and (i) satisfies the requirements for exemption from, or a reduced rate of, withholding tax pursuant to the provisions of an applicable income tax treaty between the US and the non-US person's country of residence; (ii) is eligible for the 'portfolio interest exemption' (described below), which exempts certain US-source interest from withholding tax; or (iii) receives payments that are effectively connected with such non-US person's conduct of a trade or business in the US.

A non-US person is eligible for the 'portfolio interest exemption' if (i) the loan obligation is in registered form; (ii) the amount of interest under the loan is not determined by reference to certain measures of economic performance of the US borrower, change in the value of property of the borrower or dividend or similar payment made by the borrower; and (iii) the non-US person is not (a) a 10% shareholder of the US borrower, (b) a 'controlled foreign corporation' that is related to the US borrower, or (c) a bank receiving the payments on an extension of credit in the ordinary course of its business. As a result of this last requirement, banks generally cannot rely on the portfolio interest exemption and must instead rely either upon treaty qualification or upon the interest being effectively connected with a US branch.

Borrowers will normally be required to indemnify lenders for withholding taxes pursuant to a 'gross-up' provision, as illustrated in the US dollar sample loan agreement. However, US borrowers usually request that their tax gross-up obligations not extend to non-US persons who are not entitled, on the date they become a party to the loan agreement, to an exemption from withholding tax. Furthermore, since an assignment results in direct payments to the assignee as the substituted lender, assignment and acceptance agreements normally provide for delivery by the assignee to the US borrower of duly completed copies of the relevant IRS Form on the date of the assignment.

## Conclusion

The secondary loan market in the US has become mature and quite well-established. An ever-widening variety of financial institutions now participate in it, including, among others, traditional domestic and foreign banks, finance companies, investment banks, insurance companies, broker-dealers, investment funds, CLOs and CDOs, hedge funds and asset managers. These entities are increasingly looking abroad for loan assets and are increasingly insisting that the liquidity and documentation standards to which they have grown accustomed in the US loan market be available to them in the foreign markets. This is driving an initiative to converge the foreign (especially the UK) and US secondary markets into a single, more seamless global market.

## Other Considerations – The Impact of FATCA

### In general

The US has adopted rules, commonly referred to as FATCA, that are designed to prevent US persons from holding unreported financial assets, and earning unreported income, outside the United States. FATCA attempts to achieve this by having "foreign financial institutions" (or "FFIs"), defined very broadly, report information about their US investors and customers to the IRS. Unless an FFI is specifically exempted from, or deemed compliant, under these rules, it will be subject to a 30% US withholding tax if it does not enter into an agreement to provide this information to the IRS on an annual basis.

FATCA imposes this tax on "withholdable payments" – a broad category of payments from US sources, including among other things "US source interest" and principal on, and gross proceeds from the disposition of, property of a type that "can produce" US source interest. It generally will include interest paid by US borrowers. However, in some circumstances (unusual in the context of Corporate Lenders) interest paid by a non-US borrower can be considered to be US source, particularly if some or all of the interest paid by the non-US borrower is associated with a trade or business conducted by the non-US borrower in the United States.

An FFI that enters into an agreement to report information to the IRS under FATCA will also be required to withhold on certain payments it makes to other FFIs that are themselves subject to withholding under FATCA. This "passthrough withholding" applies even to certain payments that have no obvious US nexus. As indicated above, the definition of FFI is very broad and in addition to banks and other classic financial institutions, can include, among others, holding companies, treasury companies, special purposes vehicles and funds investing in loans.

FATCA contains a rule exempting "grandfathered obligations" even after withholding otherwise is scheduled to start. In the first instance this applied to most obligations funded prior to 1 July 2014 or subject to binding commitments entered into before that date even if funded after. However, if the terms of a loan are considered to be materially modified, as defined for purposes of FATCA, after 30 June 2014, grandfathered status can be lost.

Where payments are being made by or to an FFI, particularly in connection with a loan to a US borrower, FATCA needs to be considered. In the context of the secondary loan market, the following considerations may apply:

### English Law LMA Funded Sub-participation

Where a non-US lender of record enters into a funded sub-participation with another party, it will have to consider whether it will be required to withhold amounts under FATCA if it does not establish that the sub-participant is exempt from withholding under FATCA. In part this will be based on whether FATCA withholding applies to the underlying loan. However, it will also be necessary to determine whether the sub-participation transfers beneficial ownership of an interest in the underlying loan for US federal tax purposes (even though, as a matter of English law, a funded sub-participation does not have that effect). If it does, the determination of whether payments under the sub-participation arrangement are potentially subject to FATCA withholding may be based on the characteristics of the underlying loan. In this case, it is possible that the purchase of a sub-participation interest in a loan that pays US source interest income will be treated as disposition proceeds potentially subject to FATCA withholding when paid to the lender of record, though it is likely as a practical matter that a lender will only continue to be a lender of record on a loan paying US source interest income if it is generally not subject to withholding under FATCA. If the sub-participation does not transfer beneficial ownership of an interest in the underlying loan, the determination of whether FATCA withholding may apply is more complicated. However, there is a possibility that a participation sold by a participating FFI may potentially be subject to FATCA withholding even if direct payments on the underlying loan would not be.

### Novation and Assignment

As noted above, gross proceeds from the disposition after 31 December 2019 of, property of a type that can produce US source interest is potentially subject to withholding under FATCA. Generally, this will apply to a novation or assignment of debt of a US borrower though it can apply to debt of a non-US borrower in certain situations as well. Further guidance is needed to know how to handle the disposition of certain interests in debt obligations of a non-US borrower (starting in 2019) as well as the potential application of foreign passthrough withholding to novations and assignments (starting no earlier than 1 January 2019).

### Risk sub-participation

In addition to the general uncertainty about how various aspects of FATCA will be applied once FATCA withholding goes into effect, the treatment of risk sub-participations is further complicated by it being unclear exactly how these arrangements should be viewed from a US federal income tax perspective. Where the arrangement relates to risk of an underlying US borrower, a US party or the potential for foreign passthrough withholding, advice of US counsel should be sought to determine how to address the potential application of FATCA to these arrangements.

### Intergovernmental Agreements (IGAs)

Many jurisdictions have signed an IGA with the US with a view to improving the compliance obligations for FFIs in the relevant jurisdiction under FATCA. These have greatly reduced the likelihood of counterparties being FFIs.

### LMA Terms

The LMA's standard terms and conditions for trades provide for each party to have the right to withhold any amount it is required to withhold on account of FATCA (and, therefore, any economic loss in respect of FATCA payments would be borne by the payee).

### Secondary Market Documentation

This chapter does not seek to cover the documentation of secondary market trades in detail, but annex 6.1 sets out a case study of a secondary market trade with worked examples and is based on a trade made under LMA Standard Terms and Conditions.

The US and EMEA markets now use relatively standardised terms and conditions for secondary trades (produced by the LSTA and LMA respectively) and, as the EMEA markets have matured, the terms of trade used in these two markets have tended to converge.

The LMA's documentation covers both par/near par and distressed debt sales (through one set of standard terms and conditions covering both market segments) and includes documentation for trading both bank debt and claims in a borrower's insolvency.

The basic framework of the LMA documentation is that a verbal agreement on a trade will be confirmed by a written trade confirmation which will contain the principal terms of the transaction and will incorporate by reference the LMA's standard terms and conditions. There will be a further document to implement the trade in the manner agreed by the parties (eg novation, assignment or participation). The LMA also publishes numerous ancillary documents to assist market participants (including confidentiality agreements, purchase price notices, termination agreements and netting agreements). The LSTA has a similarly compendious library of standard form trading documents.

# ANNEX 6.1

# SECONDARY LOAN TRADING: A CASE STUDY

David Fewtrell

*Director and Portfolio Manager, Investcorp Credit Management EU.*

Updated by Michael Ward

*Manager, Leverage Finance, HSBC*

This supplement takes the reader through a hypothetical worked example with reference to the relevant documentation as recommended by the LMA. Any resemblance to reality is purely coincidental.

## Worked example

Secondary par loan trade subject to LMA Standard Terms & Conditions

Secondary loan trade in Telefónica, S.A. EUR 2,000m Syndicated facilities signed 17 February 2016

Sale of EUR 25m participation of Term Loan A maturing in 17 February 2023 by Bank A to Bank B.

Trade Date: 1 March 2018

Target Settlement Date: T+10 (15 March 2018)

Actual Settlement Date: 20 March 2018

Price: 98.50%

Trade subject to LMA Standard Terms and Conditions for Par and Distressed Trade Transactions (Bank Debt/Claims), including Legal Transfer Only, buyer and seller agreed to split transfer fees

## Anatomy of a trade

Set out below is the LMA's suggested 'time line' for a straightforward secondary market trade. The time line is not definitive, although the LMA recommends a 'T + 10' standard for settlement of par trades, it is clearly possible for the period to the Settlement Date to be longer (or shorter). In addition, the order in which certain steps are taken could differ (for example due diligence may take place before or after the Trade Date). N.B. T = Trade Date and T +/- (number) = number of business days after/before Trade Date.

| | |
|---|---|
| T - x | Buyer and Seller exchange Confidentiality Letter (if necessary) |
| T | Trade Date (telephone or otherwise) |
| T + 1 | Seller sends Confirmation to Buyer; (if required) requests Borrower consent from Agent; and sends Credit Documentation to Buyer |
| T + 2 | Buyer returns Confirmation to Seller; Agent sends consent request to Borrower |
| T + 3 | Seller sends draft Completion Documents to Buyer |
| T + 2 - T + 7 | Buyer's due diligence on Credit Documentation |
| T + 5 | Signing of Completion Documents (subject to any necessary consents) and delivery to Agent (if required) |
| T + 7 | Borrower's approval of trade (or failure to approve trade); and or await settlement date from Agent |
| T + 10 | Settlement Date |
| T + 11 | Giving of any necessary notices; Delay Compensation and Cost of Carry start to accrue |

## LMA TRADE CONFIRMATION (BANK DEBT)

To: Bank B

Date: 2nd March 2018

Attn: [•]

We are pleased to confirm the following transaction, subject to the Standard Terms and Conditions for Par and Distressed Trade Transactions (Bank Debt/Claims) of the Loan Market Association ("**LMA**") as in effect on the Trade Date, which are incorporated in this Confirmation.

1. **Type of transaction:**

   ☑ Par trade transaction

   ❑ Distressed trade transaction

2. **Credit Agreement Details:**

   Borrower(s) Telefónica, S.A.

   Agent Bank: Banco Santander, S.A.

   Date: 17 February 2016

   Total Facility Amount:

   EUR 2,000,000,000.00

3. **Trade Date:** 1st March 2018

4. **Settlement Date:** As soon as reasonably practicable

5. **Delayed Settlement Compensation:**

   This transaction incorporates Delayed Settlement Compensation (*Accrues from 10 Business Days after Trade Date for Par trade transactions and from 20 Business Days after Trade Date for Distressed trade transactions*):

   ☑ Yes ❑ No

6. **Seller: Bank A**

   As ☑ principal

   ❑ agent for ____________________

7. **Buyer: Bank B**

   As ☑ principal

   ❑ agent for ____________________

8. **Details of Traded Portion:**

   Name of Tranche/Facility: A

   Nature (Revolving, Term, Acceptances, Guarantee, Letter of Credit, Other): Term Loan

   *Traded Portion of Commitment: Term Loan A: EUR 25,000,000.00*

9. **Pricing:** Tranche/Facility Tranche/Facility

   Purchase Rate: 98.500%

10. **Accrued Interest (other than PIK Interest)**:

    ☑ Settled Without Accrued Interest

    ❑ Paid on Settlement Date

    ❑ Paid on Settlement Date and Discounted from next roll-over date

    ❑ Trades Flat (accrued interest to Buyer)

11. **Transfer Costs:** Recordation and Transfer fee payable by

    ❑ Buyer ❑ Seller

    ☑ Buyer and Seller in equal shares

12. **Form of Purchase:**

☑ Legal transfer by Transfer Certificate/Assignment Agreement in form prescribed by the Credit Agreement *or* (where there is no form of transfer provided under the Credit Agreement) Novation using LMA standard form of Transfer Agreement (Bank Debt) *or* (where there is no form of transfer provided under the Credit Agreement) Assignment Agreement using LMA standard form of Assignment Agreement (Bank Debt)

❑ Funded Participation using LMA standard form of Funded Participation Agreement (par/distressed)

☑ Legal Transfer only (*applicable only if the Seller and the Buyer do not wish to settle the transaction by a Funded Participation)*

If this transaction settles by Funded Participation, the Participation Agreement will grant:

- Voting rights *(Applicable to Distressed Trade transactions only)*:

❑ Yes ❑ No

- Information rights: ❑ Yes ❑ No

- Collateral for undrawn commitment: ❑ Yes ❑ No

13. **Transaction Documentation:**

To be prepared by: ☑ Seller

❑ Buyer

14. **Credit Documentation to be provided by Seller:**

☐Yes ☑ No

15. **Process Agents:**

Buyer: ❑ Yes ❑ No

If yes, details of process agent:

Name: ____________________

Address: ____________________

____________________

Seller: ❑ Yes ❑ No

If yes, details of process agent:

Name: ____________________

Address: ____________________

____________________

16. **Other Terms of Trade:**

❑ This transaction shall incorporate the additional representations annexed to this Confirmation.

❑ Buy-in/sell-out damages do not apply to this par trade transaction. (*Relevant only if the transaction is a par trade transaction*).

❑ Breakfunding compensation applies to this par trade transaction. (*Relevant only if the transaction is a par trade transaction*)

If so:

❑ as specified in paragraph (b) of Condition 15 (*Breakfunding*) of the Standard Terms and Conditions for Par and Distressed Trade Transactions (Bank Debt/Claims) of the LMA

❑ other (*Specify*) __________

❑ ____________________

## Confirmation

"**Confirmation**" means the confirmation executed and delivered by the Seller and the Buyer in relation to the transaction.

It is designed to record the terms of the actual trade, which takes place on oral agreement. It is therefore expected that the parties will agree, at the time of the oral trade, all of those matters which are required to be decided in order to complete the Confirmation. The above is a recommended form and can be added to where necessary.

**LMA Condition 4:**

(a) Unless otherwise specified in the Agreed Terms, the Responsible Party shall send to the Other Party a form of Confirmation, duly completed, signed on behalf of the Responsible Party and substantially in the form most recently published by the LMA, not later than the close of business on the second Business Day after the Trade Date and the Other Party shall, unless it has raised any disagreement pursuant to paragraph (b) below, sign, and return to the Responsible Party, the Confirmation not later than the close of business on the second Business Day after delivery of that Confirmation becomes effective in accordance with Condition 31 (*Notices*).

(b) The Other Party shall immediately after receipt of that Confirmation and, in any event, not later than the close of business on the second Business Day after delivery of that Confirmation becomes effective in accordance with Condition 31 (*Notices*), raise with the Responsible Party any disagreement with any of the terms of such Confirmation.

"**Responsible Party**" means either the party responsible for preparing the Confirmation as agreed between the Seller and the Buyer on the Trade Date or the party responsible for preparing the Transaction Documentation as specified in the Confirmation, as the context may require.

# LMA TRANSFER CERTIFICATE (PAR)

## (FOR USE WHERE THE CREDIT AGREEMENT CONTAINS TRANSFER PROVISIONS BUT NO TRANSFER CERTIFICATE)

| | | |
|---|---|---|
| LENDER: | **Bank A** | Date: 20 March 2018 |
| TRANSFEREE: | **Bank B** | |

This Transfer Certificate is entered into pursuant to (a) the agreed terms (the "Agreed Terms") evidenced by the Confirmation dated 2 March 2018 between the Lender and the Transferee (acting directly or through their respective agents) and (b) the Credit Agreement.

On the Settlement Date, the transfer by novation from the Lender to the Transferee on the terms set out in this Transfer Certificate and in the Credit Agreement shall become effective subject to:

(a) the schedule to this Transfer Certificate; and

(b) the terms and conditions annexed to this Transfer Certificate, both of which are incorporated in this Transfer Certificate.

| | |
|---|---|
| The Lender | The Transferee |
| Bank A | Bank B |
| By: | By: |

This Transfer Certificate is accepted by the Agent and the Settlement Date is confirmed as 20 March 2018.

**The Agent**

[Agent Bank]

By:

**The Schedule**

**1. Credit Agreement Details:**

| | |
|---|---|
| Borrower(s): | **Telefónica, S.A.** |
| Guarantor(s): | **Telefónica, S.A.** |
| Agent Bank: | **Banco Santander, S.A.** |
| Date: | **17 February 2016** |
| Facility Amount: | **EUR 2,000,000,000.00** |
| Governing Law: | **Spanish** |
| Security: | ——————————No Yes (specify) ___ |
| Additional Information: | ___ |
| **2. Settlement Date:** | **20th March 2018** |
| **3. Transfer Details:** | |
| Name of Tranche/Facility: | **A** |
| Nature (Revolving, Term, Acceptances Guarantee/Letter of Credit, Other): | **Term Loan** |
| Contractual Margin: | **1.25% p.a.** |
| Recurring Fees: | **n/a** |
| Final Maturity: | **17 February 2023** |
| *Participation Transferred* | |
| Commitment transferred[1] | **EUR 25,000,000.00** |
| Drawn Amount (details below)[1]: | **EUR25,000,000.00** |
| Undrawn Amount[1]: | **NIL** |
| *Details of outstanding Credits[1]* | |
| Specify in respect of each Credit: | |
| Transferred Portion (amount): | **EUR 25,000,000.00** |
| Tranche/Facility: | **Term Loan A** |
| Nature: | **Term**<br>Revolver Acceptance<br>Guarantee/Letter of Credit<br>Other (specify) ___ |

[1] As at the date of the Transfer Certificate

**4. Administration Details:**

| Lender's Receiving Account: | Transferee's Receiving Account: |
|---|---|
| **Pay to:** | **Pay to:** |
| **SWIFT:** | **SWIFT:** |
| **Account Name:** | **Account Name:** |
| **SWIFT:** | **SWIFT:** |
| **Account No.** | **Account No.** |
| **Reference:** | **Reference:** |

**5. Addresses:**

| Lender **Bank A** | Transferee **Bank B** |
|---|---|
| Address: **[Address]** | Address: **[Address]** |
| Telephone: **[Tel. No.]** | Telephone**: [Tel. No.]** |
| Facsimile: **[Fax. No.]** | Facsimile: **[Fax. No.]** |
| Attn/Ref: **[Name/Ref]** | Attn/Ref: **[Name/Ref]** |

## Transaction Documentation

"**Transaction Documentation**" means the documentation required to implement the transaction (including the agreed Form of Purchase and any Pricing Letter).

**LMA Condition 8:**

The Responsible Party shall prepare the Transaction Documentation on the agreed basis and, subject to any relevant condition specified in the Agreed Terms, endeavour to deliver it to the Other Party within five Business Days after the Trade Date. The parties shall endeavour to execute the Transaction Documentation and, where appropriate, provide copies to the Agents as required under the Credit Documentation, as soon as reasonably practicable after the Trade Date.

"**Pricing Letter**" means any letter agreement made or to be made between the Seller and the Buyer that specifies the calculations for determining the Settlement Amount with respect to the Purchased Assets.

# Pricing Letter

**SCHEDULE**

| | | | | |
|---|---|---|---|---|
| **Borrower:** | Telefónica, S.A. | | | |
| **Buyer:** | Bank B | | | |
| **Seller:** | Bank A | | | |
| **Trade Date:** | 01-Mar-18 | | | T + 10 date |
| **Settlement Date:** | 20-Mar-18 | | | 15-Mar-18 |
| | | Term Loan | | |
| **Traded Portion:** | EUR 25,000,000.00 | A | | |

**Settlement Calculation**

| | | A |
|---|---|---|
| Purchase rate | % | 98.50000 |
| Upfront fee | EUR | (375,000.00) |
| Cash drawn amount | EUR | 25,000,000.00 |
| Undrawn amount | EUR | 0.00 |
| Transfer fee | EUR | (1,500.00) |
| Delayed Compensation | EUR | (4,340.28) |
| Cost of Carry | EUR | 1,272.29 |
| Breakfunding | EUR | 0.00 |
| Settlement Amount due to Seller | **EUR** | **24,620,432.01** |

Day count basis: 360

Delayed Comp due to Buyer

| *From* | *Settlement* | *Days* | *Rate* | *Drawn Amount* | *Interest Due* |
|---|---|---|---|---|---|
| 15-Mar-18 | 20-Mar-18 | 5 | 1.25% | 25,000,000.00 | 4,340.28 |

Cost of Carry due to Seller

| *From* | *Settlement* | *Days* | *Rate* | *Drawn Amount* | *Interest Due* |
|---|---|---|---|---|---|
| 15-Mar-18 | 20-Mar-18 | 5 | -0.372% | 24,625,000.00 | -1,272.29 |

## Settlement Amount Calculation

"**Settlement Amount**" means the amount payable for the Purchased Assets pursuant to Condition 13 (*Settlement amount calculation*).

**LMA Condition 13**

13.1 **Settlement Amount calculation**

The amount payable for the Purchased Assets shall be determined for:

a) each currency in which the principal amount of the Purchased Assets has been funded;

b) the base currency of any portion of the Purchased Assets which is unfunded as of the Settlement Date; and

c) the currency of any Non-Recurring Fees received by the Seller on or before the Settlement Date to which the Buyer is entitled pursuant to the Agreed Terms,

and shall be equal to the Purchase Rate multiplied by the principal amount of the Purchased Assets funded in the same currency as of the Settlement Date less:

i) (100% minus the Purchase Rate) multiplied by the unfunded portion of the Purchased Assets as of the Settlement Date, where the base currency of such unfunded portion is the same currency as the principal amount of the funded portion of the Purchased Assets;

ii) (100% minus the Purchase Rate) multiplied by any Permanent Reductions (as *defined in Condition 12 (Permanent Reduction)) made in the same currency* as the principal amount of the funded portion of the Purchased Assets and which occur in respect of the Purchased Assets on or after the Trade Date and on or before the Settlement Date; and

iii) without double counting, any Non-Recurring Fees received by the Seller (where the currency of those Non-Recurring Fees is the same currency as the principal amount of the funded portion of the Purchased Assets) on or before the Settlement Date to which the Buyer is entitled pursuant to the Agreed Terms,

adjusted to take account of any Delayed Settlement Compensation and any applicable recordation, processing, transfer or other fee and Agent's Expenses which under the Agreed Terms is to be payable by either party in the same currency as the principal amount of the funded portion of the Purchased Assets.

## Delayed Settlement Compensation

"**Delayed Settlement Compensation**" means any amounts payable pursuant to Condition 10.2 (*Delayed settlement*) (other than pursuant to paragraph (c)(ii) of Condition 10.2 (*Delayed settlement*)).

**LMA Condition 10.2:**

**Delayed Settlement**

If the Agreed Terms specify that the transaction incorporates Delayed Settlement Compensation then, if the transaction settles after the Delay Period Commencement Date, the parties shall pay Delayed Settlement Compensation for each day during the Delay Period as set out below:

"...The Buyer shall pay to the Seller (or if the Seller is required to pay the Buyer the Settlement Amount pursuant to Condition 13 (*Settlement Amount Calculation*), the Seller shall pay the Buyer) on the Settlement Date an amount equal to interest that would accrue for each day during the Delay Period at the Relevant Rate on an amount in respect of each relevant currency (the "**Original Settlement Amount**")... ...equal to the Settlement Amount calculated as of the Delay Period Commencement Date pursuant to Condition 13 (*Settlement Amount Calculation*)..."

# *Chapter 7*

# DEFAULTS, ENFORCEMENT AND WORKOUT

# INTRODUCTION

The lending business goes through alternating cycles of credit expansion and bad debts. The 1980s and 1990s witnessed successive forms of bad debt problems. The 1980s were marked in particular by the sovereign debt crisis; and the latter part of the 1980s and the first half of the 1990s witnessed bad debt problems in a variety of sectors (including leveraged finance and real estate). The second half of the 1990s saw a renewal of sovereign debt crises in Mexico (1994), Asia (1997–98) and Russia (1998). In the late 1990s and early years of the 21st century there was a series of corporate collapses centred around the technology, energy and telecoms industries together with sovereign debt bond exchanges in Pakistan, Ukraine and Ecuador and the default of the emerging market borrower with by far the largest outstanding amounts of debt in the form of bonds, Argentina, in 2001. More recently, the GFC has resulted in the demise of some (Lehman Brothers) and a requirement to restructure other (Northern Rock) financial institutions. The subsequent crisis in the eurozone has returned the topic of sovereign default to the top of many people's agendas.

In chapter 5 we have looked at the forms of default which are provided for in most credit agreements. These describe the prima facie credit concerns of lending banks. What happens if an event of default occurs?

Before looking in detail at the processes by which default situations are handled, it is first of all necessary to investigate the types of remedies that are available to lenders upon the occurrence of an event of default. The following description is based on English law but the situation under New York law and under the laws of many other countries is not very different.

# REMEDIES FOR DEFAULT

## Express remedies

Credit agreements almost invariably provide specific remedies for the creditors upon the occurrence of an event of default or an event of acceleration (as it is sometimes called). The two main remedies are listed below.

### Termination of the obligation to continue to provide credit

The agreement will usually stipulate that upon the occurrence of an event of default the creditors will not be required to extend further credit.

### Acceleration

The main express right of creditors once an event of default has occurred is to declare the principal amounts outstanding to be immediately due and payable.

## Other remedies available

As well as the express rights provided for in the agreement itself, creditors will have other rights following a default.

### Repudiation

A credit agreement is like any other contract and a creditor could repudiate a contract in the context of a repudiatory breach by the debtor. Repudiation would entail cessation of the obligations of the creditors together with rights to sue for damages.

### Damages

Both in the context of repudiation and in the context of a breach which does not amount to repudiatory breach, creditors would have available to them actions for damages. In the context of a credit agreement however, damages would not ordinarily give rise to any greater rights than suing for the amounts outstanding plus accrued interest and expenses.

### Suit for unpaid sums

In relation to any amount which has fallen due for payment and has not been paid, the creditors would have a right to take court action in respect of the debt which has been dishonoured.

### Rescission

If the debtor has been responsible for a misrepresentation then in certain circumstances the creditors would have rights to rescind the contract in accordance with the usual laws of contract.

### Liquidation and insolvency

The creditors would have specific rights under the liquidation or insolvency laws of most jurisdictions if the debtor became insolvent and/or subject to liquidation proceedings, but they generally lose their rights to enforce any claims on their own behalf in the courts.

### Set-off

Following default by a debtor the creditors will often have rights of set-off. The right can only arise if the creditor is in possession of funds which are owned by the defaulting debtor. The extent of the rights of the creditor will depend upon the place where those funds are held. Not infrequently the credit agreement itself seeks to supplement and expand the rights that might be available as a matter of ordinary law. The law relating to set-off is technical and it is inappropriate to deal with it in any detail here. Suffice it to say that the exercise by creditors of rights of set-off has frequently created major impediments in the orderly restructuring of the financial affairs of debtors in difficulty. The reason for this is that an important principle between creditors is that, in an orderly restructuring, creditors should receive comparable treatment and the premature exercise by any creditor of rights of set-off may provide that creditor with a privileged position which will not be acceptable to the other creditors involved. Accordingly, when assessing whether a right of set-off should be exercised or not, a creditor should evaluate not only its immediate individual position, but should also consider the implications of making the set-off in relation to the putting into effect of an orderly rearrangement of the debtor's financial affairs.

### Interference with contractual arrangements

The tort or delict system of most countries provides for potential liability at law if anyone knowingly interferes with a contract between other parties in such a way as to cause one party to the contract to breach its obligations to the others. It is usually necessary to show either intention to cause the breach or some element of recklessness. In seeking to carry out any orderly rearrangement of a debtor's financial affairs attention has to be paid to this area of the law. It is necessary to organise procedures and cast documents in such a way as not to give rise to potential liability in respect of this tortious or delictal action. Clearly the activities of a steering or co-ordination committee of a creditor seeking an orderly restructuring do not involve seeking to interfere with contractual arrangements between the debtor and other creditors which are not party to the restructuring proposals. They are based on an earnest desire to seek to have developed sets of proposals for the agreement of all relevant creditors on their own behalf.

# ENFORCEMENT OR WORKOUT

Following the occurrence of an event of default, the creditor has to choose between taking immediate action to recover the outstandings, and working with the borrower to try to rearrange credits in order to re-establish an orderly situation in which the borrower may be able to pay off its outstandings over time.

This decision is one of the most difficult decisions which lenders have to take in the course of their business. Experience has shown that lenders will generally treat sovereign debtors and corporate debtors differently. Various of the remedies available in a corporate default situation are just not available in respect of a sovereign borrower. Furthermore, there are big differences in the surrounding environment including the support and work performed by the multi-lateral agencies in respect of sovereign states. Over the years we have seen a large number of restructuring processes in relation to different countries. The next section of this chapter will identify the principles governing what happened in these processes.

The restructuring process in relation to corporate borrowers presents commercial creditors with vastly different types of issues. The last section of this chapter seeks to draw out some of the major areas of concern and, as an example, describes the interplay between formal insolvency proceedings and consensual restructurings in the US market.

# THE RESTRUCTURING PROCESS IN RELATION TO SOVEREIGN DEBT

The techniques used to implement Sovereign debt restructurings continue to evolve. Whilst different country cases give rise to arrangements which are individual to the countries concerned, the process which started in the 1980s and culminated in Brady bond exchanges in the mid to late 1990s displayed some degree of uniformity and it is therefore possible to make various general observations with regard to the evolution of the restructuring process over that time horizon.

## Participants in the debt restructuring process

Before drawing out those general observations it is instructive to look at the types of creditors a country is likely to have at the point of commencing a restructuring arrangement.

A country's creditors can be divided into certain broad categories for these purposes (although there are often other types too – such as secured creditors with commodity-linked financings):

1. International financial creditors such as the International Monetary Fund, the World Bank and the European Bank for Reconstruction and Development.
2. Government creditors.
3. Trade creditors.
4. Bank creditors.
5. Bondholders.

The first category of creditors generally do not enter into restructuring arrangements. If further assistance is appropriate and available it has tended to be provided by means of further loans. It is unusual for trade creditors to restructure their claims in any concerted systematic fashion. It is not unusual however for trade creditors to be made subject to a restructuring on a set of bilateral bases.

Up until Pakistan's Eurobond restructuring in 1999, the approach in sovereign debt restructurings was, in the main (but with a few notable exceptions), not to restructure bonds but rather to honour them as they fell due. This was in part because the amounts involved were relatively modest when compared with other categories of debt.

The systematic restructuring process up to 1999 therefore applied to the government creditors, acting usually through the Paris Club, and the bank creditors. Following Pakistan's Eurobond restructuring in 1999, the systematic restructuring process would now be regarded as applicable as well to the fifth category, namely bondholders.

Interestingly, following the adoption of the Highly Indebted Poor Country ("HIPC") initiative, subject to strict conditionality and subject to reaching the so called 'completion point' under the HIPC initiative, claims in the first category were reduced. This is only in the case of a subset of the world's poorest nations who successfully migrate through various phases of conditionality.

## Management of sovereign debt restructuring

In restructurings up to 2000 it was almost invariable that a steering committee (or bank advisory committee) of banks was formed to co-ordinate the formulation of the restructuring proposals with the country concerned. Usually the committee comprised 10-15 banks with a permanent chairman or joint chairman. The committee often created sub-committees as needed, and, almost invariably, an economic sub-committee was established.

The important point is that the process worked with high levels of take up and very little litigation. Many believe that a significant reason that it did so was the existence of the steering or bank advisory committee and there are five main reasons for that as follows:

1. this created an effective interface between the universe of creditors and the debtor;
2. this interface was, in the main, respected and had credibility;
3. committee members broadly had a commonality of interest with fellow creditors;
4. significant creditors took ownership of the problem from the creditors' perspective and harnessed their skills to deliver deals; and
5. deals taken to the market with bank advisory committee endorsement were perceived as being consensual.

These benefits can be substantial but the world has changed and since 2000 there has been a shift away from the use of bank advisory committees. There has also been an increase in litigation.

In the London Club deal for Russia in 2000 there was a creditor committee. In the case of Pakistan there was a creditor committee dealing with trade debt but not in relation to Eurobonds. In the case of Ecuador (2000) there were attempts to form a creditor committee but these were considered largely unsuccessful. In the Ukraine Eurobond exchange (2000) there was no formal attempt to form a committee but rather a financial intermediary was appointed by the debtor who was incentivised to deliver on a deal. In the case of Argentina (2005) multiple creditor committees were formed but most groups felt there was no meaningful negotiation with Argentina. On the other hand, Greece's 2012 restructuring saw a reversion to the earlier model of a creditor committee with direct dialogue with the sovereign debtor.

As will be seen from the above, there is no uniform approach in this context and a number of factors have, over time, affected the desire to use approaches other than creditor committees. One significant ongoing factor has been the increasing migration of economic risk away from bank creditors.

## Credit Derivatives

The 1998 Russian GKO restructuring was the first sovereign debt restructuring exercise in which the existence of credit derivatives materially affected the process. In essence, through credit derivatives structures, the economic risk on the underlying GKOs had been passed to third parties, who, initially at least, felt unrepresented at the discussion table. This had a material bearing on the process for managing the sovereign debt restructuring exercise.

In the majority of deals up to 2000, banks were the main private sector creditors. With the increased use of credit derivatives, the increased prevalence of funds specialising in sovereign debt and certain sovereign bonds being targeted at the retail market, significant holdings of economic claims now reside in the hands of non-banks. The position is therefore now more mixed and it is probably wrong to encourage or seek to impose a single approach to the management of the sovereign debt restructuring process in all circumstances. In some instances a creditor committee approach is likely to serve better than in others.

## Sovereign Debt Restructuring Mechanism

In this changed environment, it is not surprising that there have been various initiatives designed to facilitate the sovereign debt restructuring process and the most noteworthy initiative was the Sovereign Debt Restructuring Mechanism (SDRM).

In November 2001 Anne Krueger, the first deputy managing director of the International Monetary Fund, proposed a new approach to sovereign debt restructuring at a speech given in Washington DC which effectively launched the so-called Sovereign Debt Restructuring Mechanism or SDRM debate. The proposal was to have, at the level of the IMF, a structure under which sovereign debt claims could be made the subject of an internationally recognised court process. A significant part of the purpose of the SDRM was to seek to ensure that the sovereign restructuring process could remain orderly and to have a process through which an overriding majority of creditors could agree on new restructuring terms which would then be binding on all applicable creditors.

## Principles and CACs

Whilst the SDRM was effectively shelved at a meeting of the International Monetary and Finance Committee of the IMF in 2003, it is generally accepted that the SDRM acted as a catalyst for a number of significant market based initiatives and two in particular are worthy of mention.

By the time the SDRM proposal was launched, the levels of issuances of sovereign bonds (particularly from Emerging Markets issuers) had grown considerably and (post Pakistan, 1999) the norm had become to include bonds in sovereign debt restructurings, reflecting the fact that their exclusion would have made deals very difficult to implement (because too high an amount of the stock of debt would otherwise have remained untouched).

In the absence of a Chapter 11 style approach with majority creditor voting, not surprisingly, attention turned to voluntary contractual provisions contained in sovereign bonds which could be used to effect a restructuring through majority action. Such clauses, so called, collective action clauses ("CACs") had been routinely used in English law governed bonds for some years but, for market convention rather than legal reasons, New York law governed bonds did not contain CACs. In February 2003, seven financial industry trade associations released for discussion a draft set of model CACs for New York law governed bonds and then, in March 2003, Mexico issued New York law governed bonds with CACs. Many other sovereign issuances under New York law with CACs then followed.

The second noteworthy development in this period came in November 2004 when the Institute of International Finance ("IIF") published its "Principles for Stable Capital Flows and Fair Debt Restructuring in Emerging Markets". The Principles emphasised the desirability of prompt transparency of information, regular dialogue between debtors and creditors (with a view to avoiding shocks), a voluntary good faith process in instances where a restructuring had become inevitable and the avoidance of any unfair discrimination among affected creditors.

## Eurozone – CACs and PSI

The Eurozone debt crisis, gave rise to a further policy discussion on CACs and the process of restructuring private sector claims. By 2010 a number of sovereign issuers were encountering difficulties. There were subsequent Eurozone sovereign rescue arrangements for Greece, Ireland and Portugal and, in 2012 Greece became the only Eurozone country to restructure its private sector claims.

As a prelude to this step, the Eurogroup issued a statement on 28 November 2010 recognising that in certain circumstances private sector involvement (PSI) through a debt restructuring may be necessary for Eurozone countries. In order to facilitate any such future restructuring, that Eurogroup statement provided that CACs would be included in all debt issuances of Eurozone members with a maturity greater than one year from mid-year 2013 onwards (this date was subsequently brought forward by six months). Interestingly the statement also provided that such CACs were to be identical and to contain aggregation features, under which bonds would be capable of being voted on an aggregated basis. This therefore enhanced the position for the debtor countries.

Greece's PSI transaction, launched in April 2012, was carried out without a payment default. Market standard Credit Default Swap protection was, however, triggered because of the use of CACs to bind those creditors who did not vote in favour of the proposed restructuring and who were within the ambit of CACs where the requisite voting thresholds were achieved. In this context the main rating agencies placed Greece on selective default for a period. The majority of Greece's affected debt was governed by Greek law and Greece chose to make changes in local law so that CACs with aggregation features were included. These "retroactive" CACs were then used as part of the restructuring to boost take up in the deal.

In October 2012, an addendum to the Principles was published by the IIF which was influenced by a number of features of the Greek PSI process. That addendum expressed the view that the appropriate format and role of negotiation vehicles, such as creditor committees, should be determined flexibly and on a case by case basis. This was against the backdrop in Greece of there being a creditor committee in which IIF senior management themselves participated. Other points made included that the distortion of market signals, with the resultant mispricing of risk, should be avoided; that CACs with aggregation features were useful but retroactive CACs should be avoided; there should be no exclusions of relevant debt (to avoid special treatment); and there should be a bias towards a process involving voluntary good faith negotiations. The Principles were also extended (on a voluntary basis) to all sovereigns as opposed to only emerging market sovereigns.

## Litigation Risk

Litigation is now a feature of most sovereign debt restructuring arrangements and Greece is no exception. However, the case of Argentina serves to highlight how a long shadow can be cast over sovereign debt restructurings in certain circumstances.

Argentina went into sovereign debt default in 2001. It launched a restructuring offer, largely perceived as being more unilateral than consensual, in 2005 and achieved a take up level of approximately 76%. Argentina launched a further deal in 2010 and achieved increased participation from creditors. Litigation was a feature of the process from the early stages after payment default, with multiple law suits, multiple judgements but very limited success at the level of enforcement for the litigating creditors. Litigation continued until President Macri took office in 2015 and adopted a policy of seeking to resolve the position with holdout creditors. Noteworthy aspects of the long running litigation against Argentina centre on the *pari passu* provisions in the original debt claims (which were then in arrears) as against the new debt instruments issued in 2005 and 2010, payments on which were being honoured. A significant judgement in 2012 from the United States Court of Appeals for the Second Circuit affirmed an injunction issued by a lower court based on a controversial interpretation of the *pari passu* clause in some of the original debt claims. That interpretation required Argentina to make rateable payments on the original debt claims when it made payments on the restructured bonds (issued by Argentina to its assenting creditors in 2005 and 2010). This injunction caused considerable concern for policy makers, including those seeking to ensure the proper functioning of the international capital markets and also for the financial institutions involved in payment transfers, including the clearing systems. Rather than comply with the terms of the injunction, Argentina chose to default on the restructured bonds.

As will have been seen from the above, much of the recent activity associated with standard contractual provisions in sovereign debt instruments has centred on debt in the form of bonds.

However, the Principles have, throughout their evolution, focussed on sovereign debt in the form of both bonds and loans and many middle income sovereigns continue to raise funds through the loan markets.

In addition, China's policy banks continue to prefer to extend credit through loans and they are significant lenders especially in the emerging market sovereign sphere.

In this context two points are noteworthy for sovereign loan markets. First, it is common for sovereign loans to have *pari passu* provisions. Clearly much will turn on the precise wording and the surrounding facts but if unrestructured loan debt with a broad *pari passu* provision is not being paid whilst new debt issued as part of a restructuring process is being paid and the unrestructured loan ranks *pari passu* with a new debt then difficulties similar to those in Argentina could arise. There is currently no official sector or market based initiative to address this potential difficulty. Secondly, in the context of achieving restructuring outcomes through majority action, whilst most syndicated loans now have amendment clauses, it is almost universal in the loan market place that any alteration to payment terms requires unanimity. Where lenders have entered into repackagings, sub participations and structured credit linked note products, obtaining consents becomes more difficult, if not impracticable, and this is likely to become a problem for sovereign borrowers. However, most syndicated loans incorporate sharing clauses under which, in broad terms, payments and recoveries are shared on a pro rata basis among lenders and this should serve to make syndicated loans less attractive to those who may be looking to trade into a loan with a view to becoming a holdout creditor.

Clearly, however, loans without sharing clauses, including bilateral loans, would be in a different category. Loans from China's policy banks are bilateral loans. Whilst these loans are generally not traded, this can cause problems between lenders because loans from China's policy banks are unlikely to be restructured. China is now consistently an observer at Paris Club negotiations but it is not a member, nor has it committed to become a Paris Club member. In the years ahead, it is likely that China's policy banks will face, in some contexts, challenges with their lending arrangements in countries facing debt distress and China is likely to face calls to develop some type of strategy in this field. Experience to date indicates that some type of credit enhancement is one favoured mechanism of China's policy banks but clearly IBRD and other applicable negative pledges should limit the range of choices in practice.

In a similar vein, the absence of syndicate wide voluntary prepayment provisions is also potentially problematic. If a country, under mounting financial distress, attempts to follow IMF guidance and seek a voluntary sovereign debt restructuring in the absence of a payment default, the inability to prepay existing expensive loans with the proceeds of, say, a new source of funds at low interest rates could be problematic.

More broadly it is possible that the appetite for other bilateral sovereign loans may grow and that could give rise to other challenges in delivering sovereign debt restructurings in the future.

More broadly, one significant impact of the litigation faced by Argentina over many years was the adverse impact on Argentina's ability to re-enter the voluntary international capital markets on post default terms.

## The Challenges Today

Whatever approach is adopted to the process of restructuring sovereign debt claims, creditors will expect the sovereign to:

- Demonstrate that the underlying economic problems which gave rise to the country's financial difficulties are being addressed with a viable and believable plan.
- Show that its financial circumstances justify debt relief from private creditors.
- Explain the basis on which the requested debt relief can be viewed as proportional in the light of the financial needs to the country.
- Explain the intended approach with the other creditor groups.

Importantly, under the differing structures deals have been done. In many cases they were done rapidly. In some cases there were holdout creditors but they did not prevent the debtor country's financing gap from being filled.

However, in this evolving environment, the issue of (i) the process for reaching a consensual arrangement (and this extends to an evaluation of whether to use a creditor committee and how to communicate with creditors), and (ii) managing litigation risk are the real challenges for successful sovereign debt restructurings.

# THE RESTRUCTURING PROCESS IN RELATION TO CORPORATE BORROWERS

It has been possible in the previous section to formulate certain generalisations with regard to the handling of the restructuring process in the context of sovereign borrowers. The reasons for this are various, but include the fact that there is an established framework of practice in relation to any country as to how its debts are to be handled. General experiences lead to general expertise and convention. The internal laws of each country, different as they are, affect only marginally the overall restructuring package. Also, the creditors themselves (or at least the bank creditors) have reacted to the problems of the individual countries with a remarkable degree of consensus (with the exception of so-called "hold-out" creditors).

None of these things can be said in relation to corporate borrowers. Each corporate borrower is the subject of specific domestic law. The different domestic laws with regard to insolvency of each different country provide a different framework for the resolution of financial problems (although a certain amount of coordination has been attempted by EU-wide regulations). Resort to legal remedies and court action do frequently occur in relation to corporate financial problems.

A major part of the process for restructuring a corporate borrower in difficulties comprises an evaluation of the worth of security arrangements that can be put in place in order to act as the basis for restructuring of the existing debt and/or the injection of necessary new funds.

## Trends towards subservience of the creditor's dominant interest

It is possible to observe one general movement, namely a growing tendency for countries to move towards the restriction of the creditor's dominant rights in relation to the insolvency of corporate borrowers. Historically most countries allowed creditors to take immediate steps to terminate the effectiveness of a corporate borrowing in difficulties. Any restructuring was to be carried out in the context only of mutual consensus and with the threat that any dissenting creditor could wreck the restructuring process.

J. H. Dalhuisen in his work *Dalhuisen on International Insolvency and Bankruptcy* from 1979 already commented on the trend:

> *'Under the circumstances it is perhaps correct to sum up the modern tendencies in bankruptcy as follows: bankruptcy liquidation is viewed more and more as an extraordinary measure to be reserved for exceptional situations. The desirability of rehabilitation of the private debtor and reorganisation of the corporate debtor, if feasible from an economic point of view, are recognised*

> *while as a consequence the aims and claims of the creditors are not all dominant. Their will and interests are only one factor in determining the nature of the proceedings against the debtor. Litigation or survival is decided upon by taking into account other factors as well. Once this is accepted, the way is open for an entirely new set of rules under which the interest to the debtor, the creditors and the public may be balanced in accordance with the views reflected of their relative importance prevailing in society from time to time. This may do away with the classic notions in the field of bankruptcy which have been shaped over a long time, of creditors' predominance, and it may not be too hazardous to say that if this happens a whole new era in insolvency law will dawn, the first signs of which are manifest today.'*

One example of this trend is the UK where the Insolvency Act 1986 created for the first time arrangements for the suspension of the creditor's rights in certain circumstances (administration), which have similarities with the arrangements applying in the US. However, the UK remained a very creditor-friendly country and the 1986 Act did not have a significant impact on this. The UK government, therefore, introduced the insolvency provisions of the Enterprise Act 2002 the purpose of which was to strengthen the administration process and to limit the circumstances in which creditors of companies incorporated in the UK could avail themselves of 'self help' remedies such as administrative receivership.

## Basic factors in a corporate workout

The details of the laws of the different countries vary enormously and the tactics for carrying out an effective restructuring with regard to a corporate borrower in difficulties must take account of the specific laws applicable.

They must also take account of the circumstances of the particular borrower concerned, the nature of the business being carried out and the extent to which the provision of security or further security is possible on a co-ordinated basis.

It is possible, however, to identify certain basic factors in a corporate workout (although this section tends to reflect practice in the UK).

### Co-ordination of the creditors

It is necessary to ensure that the relevant creditors are organised. The type of organisation for any corporate borrower will vary. One needs to evaluate whether the different types of creditors need separate representation. They may comprise secured, unsecured, senior or subordinate creditors. If they establish separate organisations then there is a need to provide co-ordination between the different committees. It is also necessary to establish the extent of creditor participation in the management of the corporate borrower. Clearly the creditors should not become involved in the management decisions themselves.

It is important to establish a method by which the creditors understand fully what the management is doing without incurring the legal liabilities associated with a closer involvement in the management decision making. It may also be necessary to set up arrangements with government departments, unions, dealers and other affected parties in order to enable a successful restructuring to take place.

### Management for the debtor

Usually the management of a business is capable of running the business while matters are going well and of coping with temporary downturns or the fluctuations of the business cycle. However, most managements are not able to deal with the pressures of the restructuring process without further support. The restructuring process is very pressurised and puts a great strain on management, especially if they are also expected to attend to ordinary business matters. Usually it is necessary for the management team to be supplemented for a corporate restructuring to progress satisfactorily.

### Shape of the obligor

It is of course necessary to establish precisely what is the appropriate form for the restructuring obligor to take. It is relatively rare for a corporate workout to take place in the context of a single company. Usually there is a need to address the problems of a group as a whole. Often the different members of the group will be incorporated, and functioning, in different countries. Individual solutions will need to be found. The solutions need to take account of the specific functions of captive finance companies and of specific pricing and asset or service transfer arrangements between the different members of the group.

### Consensual or court-imposed solutions

The extent to which there is scope and/or a need to resort to court proceedings to establish a restructuring will depend upon the relevant jurisdictions involved. A basic issue to be addressed is whether there is a benefit or a need to establish new court-based procedures to assist in the restructuring process. The approach (now not commonly followed) known as *the London Approach*, supported by the Bank of England and adopted as a matter of practice, not law, in corporate restructurings in the UK, required ultimately the unanimous consent of all relevant creditors to the restructuring. However, there has in recent years been a clear trend away from restructurings requiring unanimous consent and a consequent reliance upon court-based procedures (such as Schemes of Arrangement (UK) or Chapter 11 (USA)).

Interestingly the World Bank has looked at ways of establishing protocols for cross-border corporate restructurings and has sponsored the production by INSOL International of a set of principles for a 'Global Approval to Multi Creditor Workouts' – which has some similarities to the London Approach. In particular, these:

- support the idea that financial creditors of a borrower should remain supportive of it while necessary information is gathered and disseminated (enabling properly informed decisions as to future actions); and
- require fairness between financial creditors while having regard to the strengths and weaknesses of their respective positions.

### Parity of treatment

It is a fundamental reality of all restructuring, whether sovereign or corporate, that similar creditors should be the subject of similar treatment. The ranking between creditors and different types of debt in relation to a corporate borrower needs to be established by reference to the priorities available as a matter of the general law of the jurisdictions within which the corporate insolvency is handled. The restructuring process will only stand a chance of success if arrangements are formulated which provide *pari passu* treatment to comparable creditors in relation to similar debt.

### Conclusion

Whereas the nature of default under a credit agreement and the remedies available under that contract are as a matter of law subject to a great deal of consistency and precision, the actual way in which defaults are handled as a matter of practice varies enormously.

It is the case that the process of sovereign restructuring has been the subject of such intensive work that a great deal of expertise and many basic techniques have evolved to handle the problems on a case by case basis. These techniques are continuing to develop and the remaining challenges lie basically in the areas of stimulating further growth to the economies involved and the transition of the credit process from the restructuring mode to the recreation of voluntary new financing. Increasingly the conversion of debt to equity is seen as a basic part of this development.

The development of expertise and techniques with regard to corporate restructuring is more diffuse and diverse. Also the dissimilarities between the laws of different jurisdictions prevent the development of co-ordinated processes which can be applied internationally. There is a growing (but slowly growing) convergence of the underlying principles of the bankruptcy codes in different countries and there is a greater awareness of what are the necessary pre-requisites for any form of successful corporate restructuring.

# WORKOUTS AND REORGANISATIONS IN THE US

## Introduction

In the US, out-of-court restructurings of troubled loans take place against the legal backdrop of bankruptcy laws governing debtor-creditor rights as well as the treatment of claims and interests of various creditor and shareholder constituencies. Any proposed out-of-court workout should be compared with the benefits and burdens of a court-supervised process under the US Bankruptcy Code, including liquidation under chapter 7 or reorganisation under Chapter 11.

## Eligibility to be a debtor

Relief under Chapter 7 of the Bankruptcy Code is available to individuals, partnerships, and corporations (which include joint-stock companies, unincorporated companies or associations and business trusts). Chapter 7 is not available to railroads, US insurance companies, banks and certain other financial institutions. Chapter 11 relief is available to any person or entity that may be a debtor under Chapter 7 (except a stockbroker or a commodity broker) as well as railroads, uninsured state member banks and certain entities that operate as multilateral clearing organisations.

## Public perceptions and stigma

There can be a perception that filing for bankruptcy or negotiating an out-of-court restructuring may weaken a company's reputation as well as the confidence of its vendors, customers, employees and others. This is generally not the case in the US; the use of Chapter 11 is more often viewed as a strategic decision that enables a company to take advantage of the myriad benefits of the Bankruptcy Code, allowing a company to restructure its debts and reorganise its business and emerge from bankruptcy as a healthy and financially stable business.

## Continuation of operations

In Chapter 11 proceeding as in an out-of-court restructuring, the company remains in possession of its assets and current management continues to operate and manage its business in the ordinary course. An out-of-court restructuring does not involve the commencement of a formal legal proceeding. Outside of bankruptcy, the board of directors and officers continue to manage and operate the company, without court supervision. The right of shareholders to replace directors and certain corporate governance changes may be negotiated by the parties as part of the restructuring (as discussed below). The company generally retains the power to enter into transactions. Creditors remain free to exercise any contractual, common law or statutory remedies they may have including declaring a default, causing acceleration or, in some circumstances, placing the debtor into an involuntary bankruptcy proceeding.

Typically, under applicable US state law the directors of a corporation owe their fiduciary duties to shareholders. However, in circumstances in which a company may be insolvent, the directors' fiduciary duties may expand to include duties to creditors. In an out-of-court restructuring, secured lenders may require, as a condition to agreeing or to forebear from exercising remedies, that the company retain an independent crisis manager. This person may serve as a chief operating officer, a chief restructuring officer or a consultant, and may report directly to the board of directors. Such professionals often play crucial roles in consummating a restructuring either through an out-of-court restructuring or a Chapter 11 proceeding.

As the goal of a Chapter 11 reorganisation is the rehabilitation and reorganisation of a business, management typically remains in control of the debtor's assets and operations. Generally, a debtor may engage in ordinary course business transactions without court approval and, with the approval of the bankruptcy court, may enter into transactions out of the ordinary course of business such as asset sales and settlements. In certain circumstances, upon the request of creditors or other parties-in-interest management may be removed and replaced with a 'trustee'. A trustee may be appointed by the court as an independent fiduciary typically where there have been instances of fraud, dishonesty, incompetence or gross mismanagement. Replacing current management with a trustee is an exceptional circumstance and the continued cooperation of some or all of the existing management is often viewed as a benefit of the Chapter 11 process. In a Chapter 7 liquidation, existing management is immediately displaced by a trustee upon the entry of an order for relief at the beginning of the case.

### The automatic stay

In an out-of-court workout, absent a forbearance or similar arrangement, creditors are free to sue and to exercise rights and remedies they may have against a company and its property. The exercise of such remedies by creditors may dismember the company's assets, consume the company's resources, distract management and threaten the restructuring process. Creditors may exercise remedies available to them in various forums in multiple jurisdictions or threaten to do so in an attempt to strengthen their bargaining position in workout discussions or to bring the company to the table for negotiations.

The commencement of a bankruptcy proceeding provides a sharp contrast to such a situation and potentially to the parties' relative bargaining positions. Upon the filing of a bankruptcy petition, an injunction referred to as the 'automatic stay' immediately comes into effect and prohibits any action against the debtor and its property, wherever located. Accordingly, with certain exceptions, all suits, actions, attempted foreclosures and the like are stayed unless a creditor obtains an order from the bankruptcy court granting relief from the automatic stay, after notice and a hearing where the debtor and other parties-in-

interest have the opportunity to object. As a result, the automatic stay provides a debtor with breathing room by, among other things, staying creditor remedies and channelling collection efforts into a single venue - the bankruptcy court. Accordingly, all creditors are forced to present their claims in this single forum rather than pursuing remedies in piecemeal litigation in various forums in different jurisdictions. This permits the debtor to concentrate on operating its ongoing business and developing a restructuring plan. Thus, the automatic stay balances the debtor's privilege to pursue reorganisation against its creditors' rights to recovery.

### Funding to continue operations

The accessibility of sufficient cash flow for operations, or the availability of outside financing, is significant in determining the viability of the troubled company. Although a Chapter 11 debtor may continue to operate and incur expenses in the ordinary course of business, new funding generally is available only on a secured basis or a priority basis in the form of debtor-in-possession (DIP) financing or the use of a pre-petition secured creditor's cash collateral. Both DIP financing and the use of cash collateral require court approval, after notice and a hearing, as well as showing that the pre-petition secured creditor's interests in its collateral (including cash collateral) will be adequately protected from diminution of value resulting from DIP financing or use of cash collateral. While adequate protection can take many forms, it typically involves granting replacement liens on post-petition collateral, periodic payment or super priority administrative claim status in the debtor's bankruptcy case.

### Employees

Employee retention is an important part of a debtor's efforts to reorganise. In a bankruptcy proceeding, absent court approval the debtor may not pay employee compensation that has accrued but is unpaid as of the date of filing of the petition. Furthermore, bankruptcy may have an impact on other pre-petition obligations to employees, such as employment contracts, indemnification agreements and continuation of employee benefits. These limitations, combined with the uncertainty of the outcome of any bankruptcy proceeding, can often lead to the loss of key employees.

Thus, to ensure the smooth transition into Chapter 11, a debtor may try and fulfil certain payroll obligations prior to filing its bankruptcy case. In many circumstances this is not possible or appropriate and employees have claims against the debtor when the case is filed. In those instances, to avoid the loss of essential employees and to otherwise engender goodwill, upon the commencement of a Chapter 11 case, a debtor may seek court authorisation to immediately pay employees certain accrued but unpaid wages in an amount equal to the priority that the Bankruptcy Code allows for pre-petition wages. This type of relief, to the extent it is limited to the amounts entitled to priority under the

Bankruptcy Code, is usually not met with much resistance, especially if there is a general consensus among creditors that they are more likely to recover a higher percentage of their claims if the debtor continues operating its business, and that value can be maximised by retaining key employees.

Conversely, with respect to senior managers, a debtor will often seek to incentivise such individuals with retention bonuses or similar payments, which also require court approval. This type of relief can be met with great opposition from creditor constituencies, especially in cases where a successful reorganisation is questionable. The laws governing bankruptcy cases generally place restrictions on the amount of incentives and bonuses that may be paid to senior managers.

### Avoidance actions: voidable preferences and fraudulent transfers

The Bankruptcy Code provides that certain transactions that the debtor engaged in before bankruptcy can be 'avoided', and the assets or value recovered as a means of bringing assets back into the bankruptcy estate to distribute to creditors on a *pro rata* basis in accordance with the priority of their claims. Such transactions may not have been improper at the time they took place (and may even have been perfectly valid) but once the debtor files for bankruptcy, pre-petition transactions often are the subject of scrutiny in an effort by the debtor, the trustee and even some creditors to avoid the transactions for the benefit of all the debtor's creditors.

Transfers of assets by a debtor that took place shortly before bankruptcy, and which favoured one or more creditors over others may be avoided as voidable preferences pursuant to the provisions in the Bankruptcy Code. A voidable preference is a transfer by the debtor of an interest in its property made: (1) to or for the benefit of a creditor, (2) for or on account of an antecedent debt owed by the debtor before such transfer was made, (3) at a time that the debtor was insolvent, (4) within 90 days before the bankruptcy (one year if made to an insider) and (5) which enables the creditor to receive more than it would receive in a liquidation under Chapter 7. There are certain defences to the avoidability of preferential transfers, including situations where the transfers were made in the ordinary course of business or in exchange for value.

The fraudulent transfer provisions in the Bankruptcy Code can be used to avoid certain transfers of a debtor's property or obligations incurred by a debtor within two years before bankruptcy. The Bankruptcy Code provides for avoidance of both actual fraudulent transfers and constructive fraudulent transfers. An actual fraudulent transfer is transfer made by the debtor with actual intent to hinder, delay or defraud creditors. Constructive fraudulent transfers are those made in exchange for less than reasonably equivalent value and (1) the debtor was insolvent or was rendered insolvent thereby, (2) the debtor was engaged or was about to engage in a business or transaction for which its remaining property was an unreasonably small capital, (3) the debtor intended to or believed it would incur debts beyond its ability to pay or (4) the transfer or obligation was to or for the benefit of an insider under an employment contract and not in the ordinary course of business.

### Executory contracts and unexpired leases

The Bankruptcy Code allows a Chapter 11 debtor to assume, assume and assign, or reject executory contracts and unexpired leases subject to court approval. The term 'executory contract' is not defined in the Bankruptcy Code but generally is understood to mean a contract between a debtor and another party under which material performance remains due on both sides, such that if either side were to stop performing it would constitute a breach of the contract.

Pending a determination by the debtor as to whether to assume, assume and assign or reject a contract, the debtor generally must perform post-petition obligations under such contract. Assumption of a contract or unexpired lease permits the debtor or a reorganised debtor to continue to benefit from such contract or unexpired lease. If a debtor elects to assume an executory contract or unexpired lease, it must assume the entire contract or lease. In other words, an executory contract or unexpired lease must be assumed *cum onere* ('with burdens'). As a condition to assumption, the debtor must cure defaults under the contract or lease (except for certain defaults specified in the Bankruptcy Code) and provide adequate assurance of future performance under the contract or lease. With certain exceptions, a debtor also may assume an executory contract or unexpired lease and assign it to a third party notwithstanding provisions in the contract or lease restricting assignment. A debtor also has the option to reject a contract or lease that it views as unfavourable (for example, a burdensome contract or above market lease). Rejection of a contract is treated as a breach of the contract by the debtor as of the petition date and the contract party will be entitled to assert a claim for contract damages as part of the bankruptcy proceeding. Subject to satisfaction of the Bankruptcy Code requirement, bankruptcy courts typically defer to a debtor's business judgment in its determination as to whether to assume or reject contacts and leases.

The Bankruptcy Code further protects a debtor's rights to benefit from favourable contracts and leases by, with certain limited exceptions, prohibiting counterparties from enforcing contractual provisions (referred to as *ipso facto* clauses) that would modify the debtor's rights under or provide for the termination of the contract or lease as a result of the debtor's insolvency or financial condition or the commencement of the bankruptcy case.

### Strategic asset sales

A debtor may also seek to sell some or substantially all of its assets as part of a Chapter 11 proceeding. Bankruptcy is an attractive way to sell assets because the debtor can convey title free and clear of any interest including liens, claims or encumbrances with such interest, if any, to attach to the proceeds of the sale. A debtor in bankruptcy can also sell its business as a going concern, in most cases without successor or pre-sale liabilities being assumed by the buyer. This is appealing to potential buyers and this power may enhance the sale price for the assets because the buyer will have a court order transferring the property unencumbered and without liability. The debtor may only sell assets free and clear of an interest in such property if: (1) applicable non-bankruptcy law permits the sale free and clear of such interest, (2) the entity holding such interest consents, (3) such interest is a lien and the price at which the property is to be sold is greater than the aggregate value of all liens on such property, (4) such interest is in bona fide dispute, or (5) the holder of the interest could be compelled, in a legal or equitable proceeding, to accept a money satisfaction of such interest.

## Negotiating the Workout

### Standstill agreements

Workout negotiations may occur during a period when many, if not all, institutional creditors have acceleration rights on their debt. Often, lenders that enjoy the benefit of financial covenants may receive early warning signs of financial distress due to deteriorating performance and proactively pursue a restructuring. Formal standstill or forbearance agreements that provide that a creditor will not accelerate or exercise remedies for a specified period give parties breathing room, but the standstill agreements may themselves prove difficult and time-consuming to negotiate.

### Analysis of the debtor's business plan

The debtor and its major institutional creditors usually seek to negotiate the restructuring. In large restructurings, it is not uncommon for one or more coordinating or steering committees of lenders or noteholders to be formed. These creditors often hire an investment bank or independent accounting firm to assist them with the restructuring and to analyse the feasibility of the debtor's business plan, which inevitably includes cash flow projections upon which payment schedules are structured.

Issues raised in the business plan and to be negotiated in connection with the restructuring can include future operating and capital expenditures, new or additional collateral, affiliate transactions, management strengths and weaknesses, viability of present lines of business and concessions from other third-party constituencies including, for example, employees, suppliers, and controlling shareholders. Inevitably, creditors often also will seek some compensation if the company successfully recovers, usually in the form of increased interest or warrants.

### New financing

In some out-of-court restructurings, both sides may conclude that new financing is essential to the debtor's continued operations. The most likely financing technique is the encumbering or sale of assets. The debtor may resist granting collateral for various reasons, including:

1. the desire to hold back a bargaining chip in case a second restructuring becomes necessary;
2. the negative reaction of other creditors, including trade and other unsecured creditors (or covenant prohibitions contained in existing agreements); and
3. the concern that, if bankruptcy ultimately ensues the debtor's flexibility in obtaining DIP financing, using cash collateral, selling assets or proposing a plan of reorganisation may be restricted because of protection afforded to secured creditors by the Bankruptcy Code.

### Restrictive covenants

Restrictive financial covenants which may be implemented in a restructuring allow creditors to monitor closely the financial condition of the debtor and to 'return to the table' quickly if the restructuring appears to be failing.

The negotiating process can raise potential lender liability issues for creditors if their actions and asserted leverage cross a line and constitute control over the debtor's management or operations. Lender liability claims include breach of contract claims, tort claims and statutory causes of action. In addition, in a bankruptcy proceeding, bankruptcy courts have the ability to equitably subordinate a creditor's claim upon a showing of inequitable conduct by the creditor that results in harm to other creditors. With respect to creditors who are insiders of a debtor, bankruptcy courts will examine the alleged misconduct more closely than they would for non-insiders. These issues tend to be fact specific inquiries and are determined on a case by case basis.

### Uniformity of treatment amount creditors

Disputes often arise between secured and unsecured creditors, senior and subordinated creditors and creditors of different subsidiaries of a multi-corporate debtor. These issues are negotiated on the basis of creditors' perceptions as to their strength or weakness in liquidation and in litigation.

### Chapter 11 plans under the Bankruptcy Code

If an out-of-court reorganisation is not feasible, the debtor may resort to formal bankruptcy proceedings. This section presents a brief summary of the formulation, requirements and standards for confirmation of Chapter 11 reorganisation plans.

#### Right to file a plan

The debtor may file a plan with the petition commencing a voluntary Chapter 11 case or at any time during the course of the case. Unless the court has appointed a trustee, the debtor has the exclusive right to file a plan within the first 120 days of the case and the exclusive right to gain acceptances of its plan for 180 days from the filing date, subject to any extensions or reductions of time that the bankruptcy court may grant. Since 2005, the Bankruptcy Code has provided that the 120-day and 180-day exclusivity periods may not be extended beyond a date that is 18 months and 20 months, respectively, after the bankruptcy filing date. Parties in interest may ask the court to terminate the debtor's exclusivity period if the debtor is not making sufficient progress towards formulating a reorganisation plan.

Any party in interest may file a plan if either a trustee has been appointed or the debtor's exclusive right to file a plan has expired or been terminated. Parties in interest are any parties that have standing to be heard in the bankruptcy case and include the debtor, the trustee, any official committee appointed in the case, a creditor, an equity security holder or any indenture trustee.

#### Disclosure statement

A plan of reorganisation generally must be accompanied by a disclosure statement when it is sent to creditors for voting. The disclosure statement is subject to court approval and must contain 'adequate information' concerning the plan such that a reasonable creditor or equity holder can 'make an informed judgement about whether to vote to accept or reject the plan'. The court determines what constitutes adequate information on a case-by-case basis depending upon the nature and history of the debtor and the condition of the debtor's books and records. A disclosure statement may be considered analogous to a securities offering prospectus, but it does not have to meet securities law requirements. After the court approves the disclosure statement, the plan proponent must disseminate the plan and the disclosure statement, together with ballots, to all creditors and equity security holders who are 'impaired' and entitled to vote on the plan.

#### Acceptance of a plan by creditors and equity security holders

Every plan must designate 'classes' of claims and interests. A plan may place a claim or interest in a particular class only if such claim or interest is substantially similar to the other claims or interests in the class. Within each class of claims a plan must provide the same treatment for each claim or interest, unless the holder of a particular claim or interest agrees to a less favourable treatment. Except with respect to 'cramdown' (as discussed below), a plan may only be confirmed if each class of claims or interests either has accepted the plan or is not impaired by the plan.

A class is not impaired by a plan if, with respect to each claim or interest in the class, the plan leaves unaltered the legal, contractual and equitable rights to which the holder of the claim or interest is entitled. If a class is not impaired, then it is presumed to accept the plan.

An impaired class accepts a plan if it is accepted as follows: (1) for a class of claims, by creditors holding at least two-thirds in amount and a majority in number of allowed claims in the class or (2) for a class of interests, by holders of at least two-thirds in the amount of the allowed interests in the class. In each case only those holders that actually vote on the plan are counted.

### Confirmation of the plan

The Bankruptcy Code requires that the court, after notice, hold a hearing on confirmation of a plan. The Bankruptcy Code sets forth the basic confirmation standards for Chapter 11 plans, which include among other requirements that the plan was proposed in good faith, that it is accepted by at least one impaired class of claims or interests not counting the acceptance of the plan by any insider and that the plan is not likely to be followed by liquidation or the need for further financial reorganisation of the debtor or any successor to the debtor under the plan, unless such liquidation or reorganisation is proposed in the plan.

If a plan meets the standards for confirmation but has not been accepted by all impaired classes of claims or interests, then so long as at least one impaired class of claims votes to accept the plan, the court may approve the 'cramdown' of the plan upon other dissenting classes as long as the plan does not 'discriminate unfairly' and is 'fair and equitable' with respect to each dissenting class. A plan meets the 'fair and equitable' standard for most creditor classes if the holder of any claim or interest that is junior to the dissenting class receives nothing under the plan on account of its junior claim or interest. This differs, however, for a class of secured claims class the plan must provide for a holder either to receive the equivalent of its lien (in a variety of ways or to retain its lien and receive deferred cash payments in an amount equal to the allowed amount of its claim. Confirmation hearings in contentious cases can be quite lengthy and complex, and parties often file lengthy objections in order to achieve better treatment in the plan.

## Conclusion

In summary, the reality of restructurings and bankruptcy options in the US differs from the common perception that a distressed company's resort to bankruptcy is a last option. Rather, a restructuring effectuated through a bankruptcy proceeding often gives management the option to retain control of the company and hopefully rehabilitate the enterprise and is often viewed by the company, its creditors and even its shareholders as a positive strategic alternative. In order to maximise its own position, a creditor in these circumstances needs to be proactive and well-informed, as a successful workout may lead to a higher recovery than a costly and litigious alternative strategy.

# GLOSSARY OF TERMS

**acceptance:** the standard positive response to an offer seeking participations in a credit facility usually qualified with the proviso 'subject to documentation' unless the full documentation forms part of the invitation.

**acceleration:** when lenders require the immediate repayment of all outstanding debt upon the occurrence of an event of default in a credit agreement prior to its scheduled maturity.

**acceptance commission:** a commission paid to a bank for accepting bills of exchange. Analogous to the margin on a loan.

**acceptance credit:** a credit whose terms involve the drawing of time bills needing acceptance either by the bank issuing the credit or by the customer.

**accordion facility:** an uncommitted facility (often an acquisition facility or revolving credit facility) whereby the borrower has the ability to approach the lenders via the agent after signing and request that the lenders increase their existing commitments. If the lenders agree, and subject to there being no continuing event of default, the increased commitments are added to the existing commitments under the relevant facility. As the concept is pre-approved (at term sheet stage and also in the facilities agreement), only the consent of those lenders who choose to increase their commitment is required.

**accrued interest:** the interest being earned or accruing daily on a loan between two interest payment dates.

**administrative agent:** the arranger of a syndicated transaction in the US market.

**advance:** the amount of a single drawing under a loan facility. In a loan document the term is generally used to identify the various portions of a loan by reference to which interest is being calculated (*see* LIBOR and interest period).

**agency agreement:** a legal agreement between the borrower, the banks and the agent (facility agent, security agent, issuing and paying agent, and/or swingline agent), which governs the rights and responsibilities of the agent(s) in the transaction. Commonly set out in an agency clause in the loan agreement rather than a separate legal document.

**agency fee:** an annual fee, calculated as a lump-sum or per bank per annum, payable by the borrower to compensate the agent for the mechanical and operational work performed under the loan contract.

**agent:** a person who acts on behalf of another party (a principal). In a syndicated loan the agent is the bank which acts on behalf of all lenders and is responsible for administering the loan and acting as a conduit for all payments. Often called the facility agent.

**agent for the service of process:** the person or institution appointed by a borrower to receive legal process (writs, summons, and so on) in a foreign jurisdiction on its behalf.

**all-in cost:** the overall cost of the transaction to the borrower (*see* cost to the borrower).

**allocation:** the final phase of the syndication process. Lenders are advised of their final participation in the transaction which represents the amount each bank will commit at signing.

**alphabet tranches:** components of leveraged loans known as the A, B, C and D tranches, which are normally senior (secured) tranches but of increasing final maturity.

**alternative currency:** *see* multi-currency loan.

**alternative interest rate clause:** a clause usually incorporated in financing documents making provision for interest to be calculated on a different basis (usually the lenders' own cost of funds) where the chosen basis rate (for example, LIBOR) cannot be determined. This clause is also known as the market disruption clause.

**amend and extend (A and E):** extending the maturity of a loan or credit facility by an agreement between the borrower and the syndicate of lenders to amend the terms (rather than simply refinancing the facility with a new syndicate of lenders). This will typically require the agreement of all lenders being required to extend the maturity of their loan (unless the agreement provides for majority lender approvals for the relevant changes).

**amortisation:** gradual repayment of a debt over time, in a series of instalments.

**ancillary business:** business which a lender obtains from a borrower client in addition to the provision of credit facilities. The practice of lending at uneconomically low margins to certain borrowers is often justified by the argument that the use of the lender's balance sheet in this way is the price that has to be paid in order to gain access to the borrower's more lucrative ancillary business.

**ancillary facility:** a facility established on a bilateral basis within a revolving credit facility. A conventional ancillary facility is usually established by a lender under a revolving credit facility agreeing to provide a facility (typically an overdraft, short-term loan or derivatives facility) on a bilateral basis in place of all or part of that lender's unused revolving credit facility commitment.

**arrangement fee:** a fee paid to a mandated bank or group of banks for arranging a transaction. It generally includes underwriting fees and fees to be paid to participating banks.

**arranger:** a bank or other financial institution responsible for originating and syndicating a transaction. The arranger always has a senior role, is often the agent and if required usually underwrites all or part of the transaction as well as participating, although not always, at the most senior level (*see* Ticket).

**asset-backed loan:** a loan which is supported by assets, such as house mortgages, car receivables, credit card receivables, owned by the issuer of the debt and, usually, placed with a trustee.

**asset or liability management:** a process of controlling or matching the cash flows, durations or maturities of assets and liabilities to maximise return and minimise the interest rate risk from mismatching.

**asset swap:** sale of a coupon-bearing bond or floating-rate note, coupled with a swap of the coupon stream, the swap obligations usually being independent of the performance on the bond (*see* synthetic security).

**assets:** all tangible and intangible property of a company including real property, chattels, money and debts owing to such company.

**assignment:** an agreement to transfer all of the rights (but not the obligations) under the contract to a new lender evidenced by an assignment agreement. In the US the term can also denote the transfer of obligations.

**associated costs rate:** *see* mandatory costs.

**AUM:** assets under management.

**authentication:** the verification of signatures for acceptance of drawdown and other official notices.

**authorised institution:** under the Financial Services and Markets Act 2000, no person may in the UK accept a deposit in the course of a deposit-taking business unless that person is an authorised institution under the provisions of the Act.

**availability period:** period of time, between signing of loan agreement and the expiry of lenders' commitment to lend, during which a borrower, having satisfied conditions precedent, is permitted to draw down advances.

**average life:** weighted average maturity of outstandings after taking into account drawdown and amortisation provisions.

**average loan:** the weighted loan amount outstanding under the facility in each year.

**backstop facility:** facility to advance funds only when a borrower cannot obtain funds under short-term instruments, such as commercial paper.

**balloon repayment:** a final repayment instalment of an amortising loan which is substantially larger than earlier instalments, for example, four instalments of 15% followed by a balloon of 40%.

**bankers' acceptance (BA):** a bill of exchange, drawn on and accepted by a bank. Acceptance of a bill of exchange involves the bank in accepting full liability to pay the bill on maturity as primary obligor. US equivalent of an acceptance credit.

**base rate:** the rate quoted by individual banks to customers as the reference point at which they are willing to lend money and pay for deposits. The base rate changes from time to time, usually, in the UK, in response to announcements from the Bank of England Monetary Policy Committee.

**Basel I:** *see* Basel Accord

**Basel II:** the revised Basel Accord, which was finalised and published in 2004, has now largely been implemented and replaced the existing 1988 Basel Accord (Basel I).

**Basel III:** the successor to Basel II and contained in a number of papers issued by the Basel Committee between 2010 and 2012.

**Basel Accord:** framework agreement reached in July 1988 on capital adequacy by the Basel Committee, which contained proposals for the international convergence of capital measurement and capital standards. Also known as the Cooke Report or Basel Capital Accord or Basel I.

**Basel Committee:** the Basel Committee on Banking Supervision (which comprises representatives of the central banks of certain major industrialised nations).

**basis point (bp):** one one-hundredth of 1% (0.01%).

**basket:** a way of describing a general exception to a covenant permitting transactions or arrangements within a financial limit tested annually and/or over the life of the facility (for example, amount of financial indebtedness allowed to be incurred, value of assets allowed to be disposed of, and so on).

**BBA Interest Settlement Rate/BBA LIBOR:** the LIBOR rate as determined by the British Bankers Association (BBA) and published by Reuters. Replaced by ICE LIBOR in 2014.

**bells and whistles:** additional features incorporated in a debt transaction designed to distinguish it from a plain vanilla transaction.

**benchmark rate:** the rate used as a basis for the calculation of interest under a loan facility (for example, LIBOR).

**best efforts:** where a loan facility has not been fully underwritten the arranger will agree to use its best efforts to attract sufficient lenders to complete the transaction in the amount required by the borrower. In contrast to the use of the phrase in other contexts, best efforts in the syndication business does not imply an obligation to do absolutely everything the arranger can to achieve syndication.

**bid bond:** a bond provided by a bank to a buyer promising compensation, usually on demand, in the event that a supplier declines to enter into a contract in conformity with the binding offer put forward.

**bid facility:** facility where syndicate banks compete against each other to provide short-term advances or notes to a borrower (sometimes known as a tender panel facility).

**bidding group:** a group of banks who bid on a bid facility (also known as a tender panel).

**bilateral loan:** a loan where the only parties are the borrower and one bank.

**black list:** a list of institutions which the borrow has specified at the time of signing of the facility agreement as being not authorised as transferees/assignees of its syndicated debt (*see* also "**white list**").

**boilerplate:** clauses found regularly in loan documentation which are standard and vary little from agreement to agreement.

**bookrunner:** *see* running the books.

**borrower:** an institution or individual that raises funds in return for contracting into an obligation to repay those funds together with payment of interest at determinable periods over the life of a facility.

**borrowing base facility:** a facility which has limits on drawings calculated by reference to levels of receivables and/or stock (inventory).

**bracket:** *see* ticket.

**bridge financing:** interim financing.

**broken-funding indemnity/break costs indemnity:** an indemnity given by a borrower to its lender(s) in respect of the costs and losses incurred by the lender in reallocating a deposit taken to fund an advance in the event of that advance being pre-paid other than on the last day of an interest period.

**bullet repayment:** repayment of a debt in a single instalment at its final maturity (that is, no amortisation).

**business day:** a day on which banks are open for business in the relevant financial centres. The relevant financial centres will normally include the place where the rate is set and the principal financial centres of each of the currencies in which any payment is to be made or rate of exchange calculated. Thus, in the case of a dollar-denominated loan with a LIBOR rate, business day would be defined as a day on which banks are generally open for business in London and New York. In the case of the euro, it has now become customary to define a business day as a day on which the TARGET2 system is open.

**buyer credit:** a financing arrangement under which a bank in the supplier's country lends directly to the buyer or to a bank in the buyer's country to enable the buyer to make payments due to the supplier under a contract to supply goods or services.

**cancellation:** the borrower's option to cancel undrawn commitments.

**cap:** agreement between a borrower and a bank imposing a limit on the upward movement of an interest rate or coupon; the price of the cap is paid for by the borrower (*see* floor/ceiling, and expense cap).

**capital markets:** the medium to long-term fixed and floating-rate debt and equity markets. Syndicated loans are sometimes included in this definition.

**cash-flow lending:** lending placing emphasis on the borrower's cash flow.

**cash pay:** interest which is paid in cash, as opposed to 'rolled-up', 'capitalised' or 'PIK' interest (interchangeable terms).

**cash sweep:** a mandatory prepayment obligation requiring the application of all or a specified percentage of *excess cash* generated by a borrower group over a period (usually annual) in prepayment of the outstanding amounts under a loan facility.

**certain funds:** the provision by the lenders to the borrower of a facility with minimal conditions precedent to drawdown (excluding, for example, material adverse change provisions) during a fixed period. Originally these provisions were included to enable borrowers to meet the requirements of the UK Takeover Code in relation to financings of takeover bids for a UK quoted company, but they have since also been used to provide certainty of funding to borrowers in a variety of acquisition related facilities.

**Chapter 11:** US bankruptcy law. A corporation in difficulties may file for Chapter 11 to give it protection from its creditors while it seeks to revitalise its business.

**cherry picking:** an attempt by a borrower to negotiate the final terms of a mandate based on the most advantageous conditions offered by competing banks.

**clawback clause:** a clause commonly found in syndicated loan agreements enabling an agent bank to recover money paid out by it to one party in the mistaken belief that it had received a corresponding payment from another party. The incorporation of this clause means that, for example, an agent bank may distribute a repayment instalment to the syndicate of banks on the relevant repayment date without first verifying receipt of payment from the borrower (which may take up to 24 hours).

**clean down:** a requirement for a revolving credit facility or working capital facility to be undrawn or drawn to below a specified limit for a number of consecutive days during a given period. A clean-down requirement tests that the borrower is using its working capital facilities properly, that is, not as permanent borrowings.

**clean-up period:** a period, often 90 days, during which banks lending for acquisition finance tolerate deviation from certain undertakings with respect to the Target company.

**clear market:** an agreement by the borrower at mandate stage not to engage in other public financings which would compete with the syndicated loan being arranged.

**club loan:** a group of banks, ranging from three up to 20 or 30 in number, which agree to take and hold an asset at the outset of the transaction. There is no intention of reducing the commitment to lend through a subsequent syndication. This is also referred to as a private placement based on a take-and-hold strategy.

**co-arranger:** *see* bracket.

**collar:** agreement containing floor and ceiling.

**collateralised debt obligation (CDO):** a method of securitising a portfolio of loans or 'debt obligations' by transferring the portfolio to a special purpose vehicle, whose liabilities are collateralised by the portfolio.

**collateralised loan obligation (CLO):** *see* collateralised debt obligation.

**commercial paper:** a short-term unsecured promise to repay a debt on a certain future date, usually written as a promissory note and generally sold at a discount. The most active commercial paper market is in the US.

**commercial terms:** the lending conditions which form the basis of an offer to the borrower; or an offer submitted to banks either to form a management group or to seek participations in the general market once the borrower has awarded the mandate.

**commitment fee:** an annual percentage fee payable to a bank on the undrawn portion of a facility made available by it to a borrower. The commitment fee is typically payable quarterly in arrears (*see* facility fee).

**committed facility:** credit arrangement whereby the lenders are obliged to lend or stand by to lend up to a certain limit of money for a specified period subject to satisfaction of previously specified conditions.

**competitive tender:** an open bidding situation where many banks may be encouraged to submit offers.

**conditional acceptance:** a response from a prospective lender which places restrictions on the final agreement to participate, in addition to the customary 'subject to documentation' proviso.

**conditional mandate:** an authority to proceed in the marketplace on a borrower's behalf, subject to certain financial, geographic or syndication restrictions.

**conditions precedent:** the matters which have to be dealt with before a borrower will be allowed to borrow under a facility agreement. These will be listed in the agreement. Most of the conditions precedent will involve the preparation and submission of documents to the agent for the banks (such as evidence of authority for the borrower to execute the facility agreement). Also known as CP's.

**conduit bank:** in a transaction where an international syndicate is lending funds to a borrower which would have to withhold tax on interest payments if borrowing directly from an international syndicate, a branch of a bank in a suitable location may be appointed as the bank through which funds will be made available to the borrower. A facility agreement will be entered into between this conduit bank and the borrower and a separate funding/participation/deposit agreement will be executed between the syndicate of banks and the conduit bank. The aim is to allow payments of interest without withholding of tax (although, increasingly, tax authorities look dimly on such arrangements).

**confidentiality undertaking or confi:** an agreement signed by a potential participant in a loan to observe the confidentiality of information provided to it concerning the financial position of the borrower or other aspects of its business.

**conformed copy:** a copy of a loan agreement where printed names of signatories are substituted for their signatures.

**consolidation of loan:** where separate tranches of a loan are merged to simplify administration.

**contingent liability:** a liability which is uncertain as to its crystallisation (for example, a guarantee).

**coordinator:** a bank chosen from among the mandated banks to oversee and/or implement the various syndication and documentation tasks.

**cost to the borrower:** the five principal costs of a syndicated loan – margin, front-end fee, commitment fee, (out-of-pocket) expenses and agency fee constitute the cost to the borrower of the loan. Since the facility is based upon a floating rate of interest, total cost can only be calculated by making an assumption regarding the average cost of the interest benchmark rate over the life of the loan.

**covenant:** an agreement by a borrower to perform certain acts (such as the provision of financial statements) or to refrain from certain acts (such as incurring further indebtedness beyond an agreed level).

**covenant lite/cove lite:** refers to borrower-friendly leveraged finance loans which were first launched in the London market in 2007 and are now common in leveraged finance facilities. Covenant lite transactions were to some extent modelled on the terms available to issuers in the high yield bond market and originated in the US loan market. The main facet of a covenant lite structure is the use of 'incurrence style' covenants, rather than 'maintenance' covenants and a reduced number of financial covenants.

**coverage ratio:** the ratio of EBITDA-to-debt service requirements used as an indicator of the safety margin for servicing debt.

**credit default swap (CDS):** a derivative product used to hedge the credit risk associated with counterparty default; in the context of a syndicated loan, a CDS typically involves a lender hedging its risk that the obligors do not meet their payment obligations. In its simplest terms the CDS contract usually features one counterparty agreeing to 'sell' protection to another. The 'protected' party pays a fee each year in exchange for a guarantee that if a bond or loan agreement goes into default, the seller of the protection will provide compensation.

**credit facility:** a term used to describe the provision of various credit instruments to a borrower.

**credit process:** the multi-step loan approval procedure within a lending institution.

**CRM:** client (or customer) relationship management, a model for managing a lender's interactions with current or future clients or customers.

**cross-default:** an event of default triggered by a default in the payment of, or the actual or potential acceleration of the repayment of, other indebtedness of the same borrower or of related entities.

**crossover credit:** means different things to different people. Two possible meanings are: (1) a credit which was of investment grade quality at the outset but the credit rating given to the transaction has, over the life of the loan, been revised downwards or (2) a credit made available to an investment grade borrower where the purpose of the credit is, for example, a significant acquisition, as a result of which the credit rating given to the borrower may go down.

**CT Corporation System:** a New York corporation sometimes used by borrowers as their agent for the service of process in New York.

**currency of denomination:** currency in which the borrower pledges to pay interest and repay principal amounts.

**currency swap:** an agreement between two parties to exchange future payments in one currency for payments in a second currency. These agreements are used to transform the currency denomination of assets or liabilities and must include an exchange of principal at maturity. The exchange ensures that neither party is subject to currency risk because exchange rates are pre-determined. (Can be combined with an interest rate swap.)

**current assets:** any asset other than one intended for use on a continuing basis in the company's activities, which will generally turn into cash within one year.

**current liabilities:** liabilities of a company maturing within one year.

**CUSIP:** a 9 character alphanumeric code which uniquely identifies a financial security for the purpose of facilitating clearing and settlement (the acronym is derived from the Committee on Uniform Security Identification Procedures which developed the CUSIP system).

**current ratio:** the ratio of a company's current assets to its current liabilities.

**daylight exposure:** cash payments being made prior to receipt of funds.

**DCM:** debt capital markets.

**debenture:** a document evidencing actual indebtedness. (It should be noted that the exact legal meaning of the term debenture is uncertain and there are differing views on whether or not documents such as loan agreements constitute debentures although the majority of English lawyers will say that they do not.) English lawyers also sometimes refer to a document creating security over all or substantially all of a company's assets as a "debenture".

**debt push-down:** generic term for moving debt in an acquisition financing structure in order to optimise the tax position by moving debt repayment obligations into those companies which earn profits (so that any available tax deductions can be off-set against taxable profits); it can take a number of forms including (1) merging companies, (2) novation of the debt and (3) an arrangement whereby a subsidiary into which debt is to be pushed down declares and pays to its parent company a dividend in the amount of debt pushed down (the proceeds of which are then used to repay debt at the level of the parent) – the subsidiary gets the money through an advance in the appropriate amount made to it by the lenders under the syndicated facility; all of this usually happens on the same day.

**debt-to-EBITDA:** this ratio provides a perspective on an issuer's debt capacity and ability to refinance debt obligations coming due. This ratio is often calculated for total debt and senior debt when assessing a borrower's capacity to service debt of different ranking in its capital structure. Also known as leverage ratio.

**debt-to-equity ratio:** the ratio of a company's debt to its equity used as a measure of the financial stability of such company and its ability to increase its level of total borrowings.

**debt-to-equity swap:** a transaction in which the owner of a debt instrument exchanges it for an equity investment.

**decline:** the standard negative response to an offer seeking participation in a credit facility.

**default:** failure to fulfil the conditions of a contract (*see* event of default and cross default).

**default interest clause:** a clause providing for interest to continue to accrue on an overdue debt, usually at an enhanced rate. The clause may be void as a penalty under English law if the rate of interest imposed does not represent a genuine estimate of the loss being suffered by the lender.

**defeasance:** the pre-payment of financial obligations, usually through a third party, in circumstances where the third party assumes the responsibility to discharge such financial obligations, and the lessor/lender has no recourse to the original obligor therefore.

**delayed compensation:** a component of pricing in the settlement of loan trades which do not close on a timely basis. Delayed compensation is intended to place the parties in the approximate economic position that they would have been if they had closed the trade on a timely basis.

**delivery risk:** when settlement centres are in different time zones.

**disclaimer:** statement made by the arranger(s) as representative(s) for the underwriting syndicate and contained in offering documents, which asserts, *inter alia*, that certain information provided in the prospectus was supplied by the borrower, and is therefore not the responsibility of the arranger(s). Exculpatory language is normally included as part of the information memorandum, to reinforce the importance for each bank of performing its own independent financial and economic analysis of the borrower.

**distressed debt:** loans that have been made to borrowers (which may include governments, companies or financial institutions) that are now either in a form of insolvency or in severe financial distress. They are loans that the market considers unlikely to be repaid in full, which therefore trade for a fraction of their face value. The buyer is betting on the likelihood that either a portion of the debt will be repaid as part of the insolvency settlement or restructuring or that the borrower will recover and the debt will eventually be repaid in full.

**documentation agent:** a member of the group of arranging banks which takes responsibility for coordinating the documentation process.

**Dodd-Frank:** the US Dodd-Frank Wall Street Reform and Consumer Protection Act of 2010.

**dog:** a syndicated loan or other financing which meets an unreceptive response in the market.

**domestic currency:** a currency held by a resident in the country of that particular currency.

**double tax treaties (DTTs):** are agreements between two jurisdictions that allocate the right to tax between them in order to eliminate double taxation. With regards to taxation of interest payments, this is usually achieved by removing or limiting the tax in the borrower jurisdiction. Hence if, for example, a US lender is lending to a UK borrower, they rely on the US/UK double tax treaty to receive the interest free of withholding tax.

**drawdown:** an actual borrowing of money (advance) under the terms of a facility.

**drawdown period:** *see* availability period.

**drop-dead fee:** an agreed fee to be paid to a bank as compensation for its work on a transaction which is ultimately aborted.

**dual currency loans:** a loan denominated in one currency which gives the lenders the right but not the obligation to redenominate the loan at a future date in another currency at a pre-determined exchange rate.

**due date:** date on which payment of interest or principal becomes due and payable. Also referred to as maturity.

**due diligence:** the detailed review of the borrower's overall position, which is sometimes undertaken by, or on behalf of, the arranger(s) of a new financing in conjunction with the preparation of the information memorandum and legal documentation.

**EBIT:** earnings before interest and taxes.

**EBITDA:** earnings before interest, taxes, depreciation and amortisation.

**ECB costs:** additional costs arising as a result of requirements of the European Central Bank.

**eligible bill:** a banker's acceptance which can be rediscounted at the Bank of England. When an instrument is eligible, the accepting bank can sell it without becoming subject to reserve requirements.

**EMEA:** Europe, Middle East and Africa.

**EONIA:** Euro overnight interest average, an overnight interest rate based on unsecured lending in the interbank market.

**equity:** in the context of a company's financial condition, such company's paid-up share capital and other shareholders' funds. Long-term subordinated loans may also be included.

**equity cure:** an umbrella term for the right (but not the obligation) given to a private equity sponsor in a leveraged finance deal to 'cure' a breach of the financial covenants by putting more money (either by way of equity or shareholder loans) into the transaction.

**ERISA:** the US Employee Retirement Income Security Act of 1974. This act regulates a broad range of issues relating to the pension and welfare plans of US companies. Because of the importance of these provisions and the severe penalties which can be incurred if they are breached it is customary in loan agreements with US borrowers to require those borrowers to give certain representations, covenants and events of default as to their compliance with ERISA.

**€STR (or ESTER):** the Euro Short-Term Rate, a wholesale euro unsecured overnight borrowing rate.

**Euribor:** Euro Interbank Offered Rate.

**Eurobond:** a debt instrument denominated in one of the Eurocurrencies and sold in the international bond market.

**Eurocommercial paper:** unsecured debt with a maturity of one year or less issued in the Euromarkets by corporate or sovereign borrowers or financial institutions. It is invariably written as a promissory note and may, or may not, be interest bearing. Also known as EuroCP.

**Eurocurrency:** a currency held by a non-resident of the country of that currency.

**Eurodollars:** US dollars held by a non-resident of the US in an account outside the US.

**Euroloan:** a loan denominated in a Eurocurrency.

**Euromarket:** general term for the international capital markets which encompasses, *inter alia*, the market for Eurobonds, Euro-FRNs, Euro-CDs/FRCDs, Euro-interbank deposits and Euro-syndicated credits.

**Euro-MTN:** *see* medium-term note.

**Euronote:** short-term fully negotiable bearer promissory note usually issued at a discount to face value and typically of one-, three-, or six-months' maturity.

**Euronote facility:** facility that allows a borrower to issue short-term notes via a variety of note distribution mechanisms under the umbrella of a medium-term commitment from a group of banks to purchase notes at a pre-determined rate or maximum margin, usually expressed in relation to LIBOR, if they cannot be placed with investors at or under that margin.

**eurozone crisis:** the market turmoil resulting from fears that one or more countries which had the euro as their currency would choose (or be forced) to revert to their national currencies (thus leaving the eurozone) and/or would default on their sovereign debt obligations.

**event driven:** a loan transaction arising out of a need to finance some other transaction (normally an M&A deal).

**event of default:** one of a list of events, the happening of which entitles the lender(s), under the terms of the relevant credit facility or debt instrument, to cancel the facility and/or declare all amounts owing by the debtor to be immediately due and payable. Events of default typically include non-payment of amounts owing to the lender, breach of covenant, cross-default, insolvency and material adverse change.

**evergreen facility:** a facility which is renewable from year to year.

**excess cash:** in general terms, the amount by which a borrower group's (annual) cash flow exceeds its (annual) total funding costs (interest and principal) under a loan facility.

**expense cap:** agreement by arranger to limit the expenses of arranging a loan agreement that the borrower will be required to pay. Excess expenses are absorbed by the arranger and/or management group.

**expenses (out-of-pocket):** the cost associated with the negotiation and execution of the credit facility. The most significant components are legal fees and travel costs.

**facility agent:** *see* agent.

**facility fee:** an annual percentage fee payable *pro-rata* to banks providing a credit facility on the full amount of the facility, whether or not it is utilised.

**facility office:** the branch of a bank through which a particular credit facility is provided. Also known as lending office.

**FATCA:** the Foreign Account Tax Compliance provisions of the US Hiring Incentives to Restore Employment Act of 2010.

**federal funds:** deposits, mostly by member commercial banks, at the US Federal Reserve. Payments in federal (or fed) funds are available and good on the day payment is made.

**federal funds rate:** the overnight rate of interest at which federal funds are traded among financial institutions; regarded as a key indicator of US domestic interest rates.

**FI:** financial institution.

**final take:** the commitment allocated to a bank. Because of oversubscription, it may be less than the commitment a bank has offered to take.

**finance vehicle:** special company incorporated for the sole purpose of issuing debt securities and on-lending the proceeds to another company or another subsidiary.

**financial advisory fee:** a fee, separate and distinct from all of the other fees associated with a syndicated loan. It is often incidental to a specific financing and is agreed between a client and bank to cover a broad range of services.

**flat:** a commission or fee, calculated as a percentage of the principal amount, which is payable once, usually front end, as opposed to a percentage fee payable annually.

**floating or variable rate interest:** interest on a loan which is not fixed for the term of the loan, but which is periodically determined by an agent bank in accordance with the loan documentation. The rate is usually set at a margin in relation to a specified money market rate (e.g. three- or six-month LIBOR).

**floating-rate notes (FRNs):** bonds at a floating rate of interest, with the coupon normally based upon six-month LIBOR. The instrument can take the form of an actual bond issue or disguised syndicated loan where the paper is placed within commercial banking portfolios.

**floor/ceiling:** agreement under which one party agrees to pay to the other amounts calculated as for interest on a notional principal sum to the extent that an agreed reference rate (for example, LIBOR) falls below (floor) and/or exceeds (ceiling) the agreed rate (*see* collar).

**forward start facility (FSF):** a facility under which lenders under an existing facility agree to provide a new facility upon the maturity of the existing facility (thereby effectively extending the maturity of the existing facility).

**FpML:** Financial products Markup Language – an electronic messaging standard used in the derivatives industry and under consideration for use in relation to syndicated loans.

**front-end fee:** a fee, calculated as a percentage of the principal amount, which is payable once generally at signing of the agreement, to the agent for distribution to the banks usually in an amount related to the size of commitment.

**front running:** the process whereby an arranger or underwriter of a syndicated loan either actively encourages a bank or other investor which is considering a participation in the primary market to wait for the secondary market (on the assumption that better terms will then be available) or actually makes a bid/offer on the syndicated loan before allocations are released.

**fronting bank/institution:** a bank or institution that provides credit to a borrower (for example, by way of issuing a letter of credit on its behalf) but will itself be wholly or partially counter-indemnified by a syndicate of banks.

**FSF:** *see* forward start facility.

**gearing:** a ratio of the net worth of a company to its total level of debt.

**general syndication:** *see* syndication.

**GFC:** *see* Global Financial Crisis.

**Glass Steagall Act:** US Congressional Act of 1933 forbidding US commercial banks to own, underwrite or deal in certain types of securities.

**Global Financial Crisis:** the crisis in the global financial system which arguably started in 2007/8 with problems in the sub-prime mortgage markets in the United States eventually leading to the collapse of various significant financial institutions (including Lehman Brothers) and the sale or whole or partial nationalisation of others (Merrill Lynch, Royal Bank of Scotland, Lloyds Banking Group).

**good standing:** US lenders are accustomed to having their domestic corporate borrowers represent that they are in good standing in the jurisdictions where they are incorporated and licensed to do business. This is so because a corporation that is not in good standing (for example, because it is delinquent in the payment of state franchise taxes) may have jeopardised its corporate status, its ability to do business and its access to the courts or other governmental authorities in the relevant jurisdiction. However, the concept of 'good standing' has no counterpart in many other jurisdictions.

**governing law:** the legal system to which the terms and conditions of a transaction are subject.

**grace period:** the period between signing and first repayment; also, the period which may be allowed to a borrower to remedy an event of default.

**grey market:** activity in relation to a syndicated loan prior to the release of allocations at the end of primary market activity which involves any actual sale or purchase of a loan, any agreement for a future sale or purchase of a loan or any discussions relating to potential sales or purchases of the loan.

**grid:** *see* pricing grid.

**gross up:** additional payments made by a borrower to compensate its creditors for withholding taxes or similar levies that reduce the amounts actually received by the lenders.

**group:** a usual way of defining a specified company and its subsidiaries for the time being. A loan agreement may specify various events which, if they affect any member of the group will give rise to particular rights of the lenders. This means that such rights could arise even if a minor subsidiary were to be affected. The definition, is therefore, sometimes narrowed to include only those subsidiaries which are identified as having key importance for the company or alternatively only those which are material in that they have a specified net aggregate value.

**guarantee:** a statutory or contractual obligation by a parent company or other entity (for example, sovereign or bank) to make interest, principal or premium, if any, payments if the borrower defaults on such payments.

**haircut:** a situation where lenders have agreed to accept a reduction in interest and/or fee and/or principal, to help prevent the borrower falling into bankruptcy.

**headroom:** used to describe the amount of flexibility in a facility or covenant versus the actual or projected level, for example, the available amount of a revolving facility over the actual amount drawn or the scope for deterioration from the base case model permitted when setting financial covenants.

**hedge fund:** a pooled investment vehicle that is privately organised and administered by investment management professionals and not widely available to the public. Hedge funds are generally not constrained by legal limitations on their investment discretion and can adopt a variety of trading strategies.

**hedging:** a device used to obtain protection against loss due to market fluctuation. This is usually done by counterbalancing a current sale or purchase by another, usually future, purchase or sale. The aim is to ensure that any profit or loss on the current sale or purchase will be offset by the loss or profit on the future purchase or sale.

**hell-or-high water clause:** a clause which states an unconditional obligation to make a payment regardless of any event affecting the transaction.

**high-yield bond:** a bond or note issued by an issuer having a less than top quality credit rating which results in the bond or note commanding a high rate of interest or discount. High-yield bonds are mostly used as a method of financing start-up companies, sub-investment grade companies and leveraged acquisitions.

**HLT:** highly leveraged transaction.

**ICE LIBOR:** the LIBOR rate for dollars, sterling, euro, Swiss francs and Japanese yen as administered by Intercontinental Exchange since 2014.

**illegality:** an event which makes it illegal for a bank to lend.

**increased cost clause:** an indemnity usually included in credit facilities designed to protect the banks against any increase in the cost of maintaining a facility or advances thereunder resulting from changes of law or compliance with central bank or official requests or requirements.

**incurrence style covenants:** have historically been the preserve of high yield financings and some of the so-called covenant-lite financings. Incurrence style covenants involve no ongoing compliance by the borrower in the sense of checking whether a particular financial ratio is maintained or a particular action is covered by a specific permission. Instead, an incurrence test covenant (for example, as to the incurrence of financial indebtedness) will typically provide that a borrower may incur whatever financial indebtedness it likes provided it remains in compliance with identified financial ratios after having done so.

**indemnity:** an agreement to protect a person against the consequences (and especially any financial loss) of particular circumstances.

**indicative terms:** the likely commercial terms upon which a bank will lend, subject to its internal credit approval or other conditions. Not a firm offer to lend or arrange a loan.

**information memorandum:** a document prepared in connection with a proposed credit facility containing details of the borrower, its business and financial condition, and a description of the proposed transaction. In complex transactions, the information memorandum may contain substantial amounts of additional information such as, in the case of a project financing, experts' reports on the viability of the relevant project.

**institutional investor:** an organisation whose purpose is to invest its assets or those held in trust for others, for example, pension funds, insurance companies and investment funds (*see* Supplement 3 to Chapter 2).

**instructing group:** *see* majority lenders.

**interbank rate:** the rate at which banks bid for (buy) and offer (sell) deposits to each other.

**inter-creditor agreement:** a legal agreement which governs the relationship between different groups of lenders within the same or different syndicates with respect to the obligations of their common borrower.

**interest cover ratio:** a measurement of a borrower's earnings before interest or taxes which will be available to service interest on its debt.

**interest period:** each of the periods by reference to which interest on a debt is calculated. Where, as in the case of LIBOR, the interest rate of a loan is calculated by reference to the cost to a bank of obtaining deposits of the required amount, the interest period will equal the period for which such deposits are obtained. Typically, interest periods are of three or six months' duration but interest periods of one or 12 months are also fairly common.

**interest rate swap:** the economic transfer between two counterparties of interest rate obligations, one of which normally has an interest rate fixed to maturity, while the other normally varies in accordance with changes in some basis rate. An interest rate swap is an exchange of cash flows only and can be combined with a currency swap.

**interim facility:** a short form (and short term) loan facility encountered in *leveraged buyouts* in particular. An interim facility is often requested by a private equity *sponsor* in advance of long form (or 'full') loan documents in order to demonstrate to the vendor in an auction process that it is well-advanced in terms of putting its funding for the acquisition in place. Neither the sponsor nor the lenders anticipate that the funds available under an interim facility will actually be drawn down, rather the parties anticipate the actual funding will take place under the long form documents which will be drafted in the period between signing of the share purchase agreement and completion.

**internal rate of return (IRR):** the discount rate that equates the present value of a future stream of payments to the initial investment.

**investment grade:** a borrower or a debt instrument is of investment grade status if awarded a credit rating of BBB- or higher by Standard & Poor's or Baa3 or higher by Moodys Investors Service, Inc (or similar ratings by other credit ratings agencies).

**invitation:** a communication to prospective syndicate members from an arranger describing terms and conditions and inviting them to participate in the loan.

**ISIN:** International Securities Identification Number – a 12 character alphanumerical code which serves for uniform identification of a security for the purposes of trading and settlement.

**issuing bank:** a bank that issues a letter of credit on behalf of its client (*see* fronting bank).

**joint and several liability:** in the context of a financial instrument for which there is more than one guarantor, this liability gives rise to one joint obligation and to as many several obligations as there are joint and several promisors. The co-promisors are not cumulatively liable, so that performance by one discharges all (*see* several liability).

**joint arrangers:** a group of mandated banks with equal status.

**judgment currency indemnity:** an indemnity often included in credit facilities to protect the banks against losses suffered as a result of obtaining judgment against the borrower in a currency different to that in which the debt is denominated. (In many countries, it is still only possible to obtain judgment in local currency.)

**jumbo (or mega) loan:** a syndication which, depending on the borrower, exceeds $5bn (in the investment grade market) or $1bn (in the leveraged loan market) or its equivalent in other currencies.

**junk bond:** *see* high-yield bond.

**jurisdiction clause:** the borrower expressly submits to the jurisdiction of particular courts (usually the English and/or New York courts) and waives any sovereign or other similar immunities it may have.

**know your customer (KYC):** checks and investigations required as part of the procedures to prevent money laundering.

**Law Debenture Trust Corporation Plc:** an English company sometimes used by borrowers as an agent for service of process in England.

**lead manager:** *see* ticket.

**leading the market down:** a bid which is below the majority of offers submitted to a borrower.

**league tables:** the multitude of statistical tables and graphs in the financial press which evidence leadership in the syndications business.

**legal opinion:** written opinion of legal counsel concerning the enforceability of the loan documents and other matters.

**lending office:** *see* facility office.

**letter of credit:** a letter of credit is a written undertaking by a bank (issuing bank) given to the seller (beneficiary) at the request and in accordance with the instructions of the buyer (applicant) to effect payment (that is, by making a payment or by accepting and negotiating bills of exchange) up to a stated sum of money within a prescribed time limit and against stipulated documents (*see* standby letter of credit).

**leverage ratio:** a measure of the borrower's ability to service debt (*see* debt-to-EBITDA).

**leveraged buy-out (LBO):** acquisition of a company where the ratio of the debt component of the financing in relation to the equity component is high. Such financings often include mezzanine debt or high-yield bonds.

**LIBOR (London Interbank Offered Rate):** the commonly used measure upon which loan pricing is based. It is the rate at which leading banks in the Euromarkets could borrow funds were they to do so by asking for and then accepting interbank offers for deposits in reasonable market sizes (*see* also BBA Interest Settlement Rate or BBA LIBOR and ICE LIBOR).

**line of credit:** a credit arrangement whereby a bank agrees to lend up to a certain limit (line) of money for a specified period. It is called a committed facility when the bank is obliged to lend, subject to satisfaction of prespecified conditions; an uncommitted line of credit does not oblige the bank to lend.

**loan agreement (contract):** the document that commits the borrower and syndicate of lenders to the terms and conditions of the mandate. The contract governs the disbursement of funds, the repayment of principal, the payment of interest and fees, and serves as a basis for monitoring the financial well-being of the borrower until final maturity of the loan.

**London Club:** an informal group of private creditors of debtor countries.

**loss leader:** an effort to seek a mandate on terms known to be below the accepted market norm. The mandated bank is normally willing to book a substantial asset and accept the market-related risk of raising the remaining portion of the loan.

**LTRO:** the European Central Bank's long-term refinancing operations – funding schemes under which the ECB provides liquidity to European banks at advantageous rates.

**M&A:** merger and acquisition (activity).

**MAC clause:** material adverse change clause.

**maintenance covenants:** financial covenants which require the borrower to maintain specified levels of financial performance in the ordinary course and/or bring its activities within specific permissions in the loan agreement. Most commonly used in all forms of syndicated loan (unless incurrence covenants are to be used).

**majority lenders:** a group of lenders within a syndicate holding a specified percentage (typically 66.6%) of the commitments, with the power to bind the syndicate as a whole in calling events of default and agreeing to certain amendments or waivers. Instructs the facility agent and is sometimes called an instructing group.

**management buy-in (MBI):** occurs when an outside management team (generally identified by an investing institution or venture capitalist) obtains boardroom control, significant shareholdings and, with their financial backers, voting control in the target company.

**management buy-out (MBO):** occurs when managers and/or employees of a business acquire control of that business or a part of the business.

**management fee:** *see* front-end fee.

**management group:** the group of banks committed to underwrite a portion or all of the credit facility. The group would include the arranger(s) (mandate-holder(s)) and other senior brackets.

**manager:** *see* bracket.

**mandate:** the authority to act in the marketplace on behalf of a borrower. The approach to the market is based upon terms and conditions that have been agreed between the arranger and borrower.

**mandated bank:** the bank given the authority to proceed into the marketplace on behalf of the borrower, on the basis of the terms and conditions set out in the mandate letter. As such, the mandated bank is responsible to the borrower for the success of the syndication. Referred to as the arranger in the Euromarkets and administrative agent in the US markets.

**Mandated Lead Arranger (MLA):** usually a mandated bank but also a title given to certain lenders, having no specific role or mandate, that provide a substantial proportion of the loan or facility.

**Mandated Lead Arranger and Bookrunner:** a mandated bank at the highest level with the role of bookrunner (which may or may not be an active one). The use of the title when a bank is not an active bookrunner is for league table purposes only.

**mandatory costs (formerly mandatory liquid asset cost):** a cost of lending, usually for the account of the borrower, to cover the cost to syndicate banks of complying with Bank of England, Financial Conduct Authority, Prudential Regulation Authority and ECB regulations concerning liquid assets which was typically charged on syndicated loans until circa 2013.

**margin:** the extra percentage rate of interest charged by a lender over the relevant basis rate reflecting the credit quality of the borrower.

**margin ratchet:** a margin which is linked directly to the performance of the borrower.

**market disruption clause:** *see* alternative interest rate clause.

**market failure:** *see* dog.

**market flex:** the unilateral right reserved for underwriters to vary the structure and conditions of a mandate (in favour of the lenders) if the syndication process does not raise sufficient funds. Borrowers may negotiate restrictions on this unilateral right limiting variations to price only, hence *price flex*.

**market sentiment:** the perceived view of the majority of banks in the syndicated loans market of market conditions in general or of a certain transaction in particular.

**marking to market:** the process of valuing a portfolio of assets on the basis of the current market value for each asset.

**match fund:** to match a loan (asset) with a deposit (liability) of the same maturity.

**material adverse change (MAC) clause:** a general event of default designed to pick up any change in circumstances that might adversely affect the likelihood of a borrower paying its debts or performing under its covenants. The clause is couched in general language and is used to supplement more specific events of default, such as the cross-default clause.

**maturity:** the date upon which a given credit facility finally expires. Also refers to the last day of the interest period of an advance.

**medium-term notes (MTNs):** unsecured debt instruments with a maturity generally between one and seven years (although it may be longer) issued by high-quality borrowers. These may be issued in domestic markets or in the Euromarkets, hence Euro-MTNs.

**mezzanine:** a type of finance defined by some as the halfway point between debt and equity in terms of the risk and return that it carries. Mezzanine finance is usually made up of debt bearing high interest with little security for the lender if the borrower fails; it is subordinated to senior debt and sometimes carries an equity warrant.

**MNPI:** material non-public information, that is, information of a confidential nature distributed to lenders which is or may be price sensitive.

**money market:** market for deposits, CDs and commercial paper.

**multi-currency loan:** a loan where the borrower has the option to choose to borrow in more than one currency.

**multi-option facility:** a flexible form of financing that can incorporate a number of capital-raising options to be used at a borrower's discretion, such as short-term note issuance, bankers' acceptances and short-term cash advances by tender panels, as well as committed credit.

**multi-tranche loan:** a loan where the borrower has the option of drawing down in several tranches under the same loan document.

**name lending:** a decision to join a transaction based on the name and reputation of the borrower rather than on a detailed credit analysis.

**negative pledge:** a covenant whereby a borrower and its guarantor, if any, undertake that neither party (and, sometimes, no member of their group) will allow the creation or subsistence of secured debt or, if each has the right to issue secured debt in the future, it will not secure such new debt without offering the same security equally to the borrowing to which such a covenant applies. Negative pledges will normally be subject to numerous negotiated exceptions.

**negotiated offer:** an agreement between the borrower and an arranger to negotiate the terms and conditions of a transaction without seeking competitive bids. This is often referred to as having the 'right of first refusal' to each agreement.

**newco:** the name given to the acquiring company created during an acquisition financing.

**note issuance facility (NIF):** medium-term arrangement enabling borrowers to issue short-term paper, typically of three- or six-months' maturity, in their own names. Usually a group of underwriting banks guarantees the availability of funds to the borrowers by purchasing any unsold notes at each issue date, or by providing a standby credit.

**novation:** the transfer of rights and obligations from one contracting party (which is released of those obligations) to a third party with the agreement of each of the other contracting parties.

**novation agreement:** the document which formally concludes the sale and transfer by novation of all rights and obligations to a new lender. Parties to the agreement include the new lender, old lender, agent and borrower.

**NPL:** non-performing loan.

**offer:** a document which sets out the basic terms and conditions upon which an arranger is prepared to syndicate the transaction; or a document submitted to banks either to form a management group, or seek participations in the general market once the borrower has awarded the mandate (*see* invitation).

**offshore:** in respect of taxation, any location where levels of taxation or regulations governing operations are sufficiently favourable to attract borrowers and lenders of funds from major financial centres.

**option:** the right (but not the obligation) to buy or sell a given underlying instrument at a specified price and up to a specific future time.

**original issue discount (OID):** an amount by which the par value of a debt exceeds its offering price at the time of its original issuance. Has a similar effect to an upfront fee.

**out of the box:** the pricing on a facility as notified to the market at the start of primary syndication.

**oversubscription (fabricated):** creating an increase in the deal amount by increasing the management group beyond the number strictly necessary to underwrite the nominal amount of the loan.

**oversubscription (genuine):** raising an amount in excess of the deal target. The unanticipated volume is derived from general market participations above the collective asset retention target of the management group.

**pacman defence:** a pacman defence is said to have occurred when a company, subject to a (hostile) bid, counterbids for the potential acquirer. (Origin: computer games.)

**paper:** colloquially, securities such as bonds, notes and commercial paper.

**parallel debt:** a provision contained in security documents or in an intercreditor agreement whereby an entity granting security covenants to pay all amounts it owes to the lenders to a security trustee. It is a mechanism used in a number of continental European jurisdictions which do not recognise the concept of a trust to enable local law security to be held and administered broadly as if it were held on trust by the security trustee. The debt to the security trustee is reduced by the amount of any payment made to the lenders and vice versa.

***pari passu* clause:** a covenant usually included in credit facilities and debt instruments requiring a borrower to ensure that its indebtedness under the relevant facility or instrument would, in a liquidation, rank at least equally with all other unsecured indebtedness of that borrower. The covenant will normally have exceptions in respect of indebtedness which is preferred by law (such as taxes and wages).

**Paris Club:** a group of officials from major creditor countries whose role is to find co-ordinated and sustainable solutions to the payment difficulties experienced by debtor countries.

**partially underwritten:** an offer to arrange a syndicated loan which is partially but not wholly underwritten by the arranger.

**participant:** *see* ticket.

**participation:** a single lender's share of the overall loan facility.

**participation agreement:** an agreement whereby one bank (sub-participant) agrees to fund another bank's (seller's) share of a loan on terms under which the seller will have to repay the funding only if, and to the extent that, it receives repayment from the borrower. Also known as a sub-participation agreement.

**participation fee:** a credit-related fee, normally paid on or within 30 days of signing, calculated on each bank's final allocated commitment.

**performance bond:** a contract may be awarded by a government department or public authority at home or abroad, subject to the provision by a bank or similar financially acceptable institution on behalf of the contractor of a guarantee of 5% to 10% or more of the value of the contract callable if the contractor fails to fulfil its obligations.

**PE – Private Equity:** funds and investors that directly invest in private companies, or that engage in buyouts of public companies, resulting in the delisting of public companies.

**periphery:** the name applied during the eurozone crisis to states which were eurozone members but which were markets to be at risk of being forced to leave the eurozone or default on their debts.

**PIK:** an abbreviation for '*payment in kind*'. Used to describe interest which is 'paid' by adding the amount of accrued interest to the principal amount of debt already outstanding and on the same terms as the debt on which it is earned. Also referred to as '*capitalised*' or '*rolled-up*' interest.

**placing power:** the ability of an arranger to attract lenders into the syndication.

**plain vanilla:** a straightforward credit facility with no bells and whistles.

**pool:** a residual fee, left after payment of the coordination fee, underwriting fees and all participation fees. The amount is normally shared among the management group *pro-rata* to their underwriting commitments in the transaction.

**portfolio management:** the active management of loan assets using the secondary market and/or the credit derivatives market to optimise returns.

**power of attorney:** a document authorising an individual to commit the entity issuing the power of attorney to a specific loan and up to a maximum amount.

**PPP:** Public/Private Partnership: a range of structures involving government and private sector.

**praecipium:** *see* skim.

**pre-payment:** a repayment of any principal amount owing in respect of a loan prior to the scheduled repayment date.

**pre-sold syndication:** a loan which is partially or fully underwritten before the mandate is awarded.

**price flex:** *see* market flex.

**pricing (through the market):** pricing a transaction below the market norm in anticipation of an across-the-board easing of lending conditions.

**pricing grid:** when a borrower agrees to pay a margin, the level of which varies by reference to specific financial ratios (for example, leverage) or external credit ratings, the transaction is said to contain a pricing grid or matrix (*see* also margin ratchet).

**primary market:** the market for syndicating a loan before loan documentation is signed.

**prime rate (or reference rate):** the rate at which US banks lend US dollars to their most credit-worthy customers. Thus, prime rate contains a small profit element. As a result of a court decision, many US banks now call this rate 'base rate' or 'reference rate' to avoid the implication that it is the lowest rate at which they will lend.

**private placement:** a group of lenders ranging from three up to 20 or 30 in number which agree to take and hold an asset at the outset of the transaction. There is no intention of reducing the commitment to lend through a subsequent syndication. This is often referred to as a 'take-and-hold' strategy, or a 'club loan'. In the US market a private placement will usually refer to the issue of notes to a group of institutional investors and increasingly a European institutional private placement market (sometimes involving an issue of notes) is growing up.

**professionalism:** the perception in the market of whether the arranger is maintaining a high standard of communication and control as well as implementing the appropriate syndication and documentation procedures with respect to the borrower and syndicate of lenders.

**programme:** formal arrangement generally between a single dealer or group of dealers and an issuer for the sale of short-term notes, MTN's, commercial paper or CDs on a best efforts basis. A programme is not generally underwritten.

**project finance:** the financing of a specific project on terms such that the lenders will receive repayment out of the earnings and/or the assets of the project with recourse to the general assets of the project-sponsoring company or group being strictly limited. A project finance transaction may be arranged using a specific single purpose company or by including in the loan documentation contractual restrictions on the lenders' right to claim against the general assets of the project-sponsoring company.

**pro-rata sharing:** an agreement by syndicate banks to share *pro-rata*, according to commitments/outstandings, all amounts received from a borrower.

**prospectus:** another name for information memorandum. It should not necessarily be construed as a prospectus under the Financial Services and Markets Act 2000.

**public to private (P2P):** the acquisition by a private company of ownership of a public company.

**qualifying lender:** a restriction in some syndicated loans on eligibility of banks to participate in a loan.

**qualitative variables:** the (non-financial) criteria the borrower employs in selecting an arranger.

**quotation date:** the date when interest rates are fixed in the relevant interbank market.

**ratchet:** the movement from one pricing level to another on the pricing grid.

**rateably:** in proportion to (usually) commitments or outstandings under syndicated loan documentation.

**rate setting:** the determination by the facility agent of the interest rate applicable to an interest period (*see* quotation date).

**rating:** a notation signifying a debt's investment quality or a borrower's creditworthiness. A rating may change in time with the borrower's anticipated ability to service interest and repayment obligations.

**reciprocity:** the evolving relationship between a borrower and a bank, or between two banks. The meaning of the term can differ considerably between the two parties and often provides grounds for misunderstanding.

**reference banks:** in relation to interest rates calculated by reference to a particular basis rate, the bank or banks whose quote, or the average of whose quotes, for such basis rate is taken as being such basis rate for the purposes of calculating the relevant rate of interest.

**reference rate:** *see* prime rate.

**refinancing (outstanding) loans:** raising new money to meet maturing debt obligations; or renegotiating the terms of existing facilities in order to take advantage of more favourable borrowing conditions.

**regulatory capital:** the capital required to support a portfolio of assets derived by reference to applicable capital requirements.

**regional coordinator:** a bank within the management group assigned the role of coordinating syndication among banks in a certain geographical area.

**relationship lending:** the practice of lending to a borrower on a loss leader basis in the expectation of receiving additional remuneration via ancillary business.

**relationship manager (RM):** the principal client contact point within a bank. This individual is often given the responsibility of orchestrating the various product lines and special units which can be used by the customer.

**relationship yield:** the return on assets enjoyed by a lender from a client relationship involving individual transactions over a specified period of time. This can also be referred to as 'portfolio averaging'.

**repayment schedule:** *see* amortisation.

**representations and warranties:** a series of statements of law and/or fact made by the borrower in a credit facility on the basis of which the lenders agree to provide the facility. The representations will typically cover such matters as the legality and enforceability of the documentation, the financial condition of the borrower and the absence of any material litigation or other proceedings against the borrower. Material inaccuracies in the representations will normally constitute an event of default.

**rescheduling loans:** altering the terms and conditions of existing loan agreements because of the inability of the borrower to meet the established interest and/or principal repayments.

**reserve asset cost:** the expense of syndicate banks complying with reserve asset requirements of regulators (*see also* mandatory costs).

**reserve requirements:** a percentage of different types of deposit which banks are required to hold or deposit at their central bank.

**return on assets (ROA):** a broadly accepted basis for banks to measure the relative profitability of a commitment to lend money. The components of ROA comprise margin, fees, including commitment fee if applicable, and average life of the facility. The resulting ROA is said to produce a specific yield to each bank.

**Reuters screens:** screen-based information provided by or transmitted through Reuters.

**reverse flex:** the inclusion of reverse flex language in commitment documents allows a borrower to seek to have the pricing of its loan facilities revised downwards (that is, in its favour) if there is a material oversubscription for the facilities. It is usually formulated as a best efforts obligation on the arranger to obtain better pricing (rather than any change in the structure of the facilities) with a financial incentive for the arranger if it succeeds.

**revolving credit facility (RCF):** a loan facility that permits the borrower to draw down and repay at its discretion for a specified period of time.

**Risk Adjusted Return on Capital (RAROC):** the return on capital of an asset portfolio taking account of the risk weighting (as determined by capital adequacy guidelines outlined by the Basel Committee) of each asset.

**risk asset weighting:** the weighting of individual assets on or off the balance sheets of commercial banks when determining whether such banks are in compliance with regulatory levels of capital adequacy.

**risk participation:** where another bank (risk participant) agrees to assume from a syndicate bank all or some of the credit risk in a loan but does not fund that syndicate bank's participation.

**ROA:** *see* return on assets.

**roadshow:** a presentation to potential syndicate members by a borrower. Usually organised by the arranger and held in more than one geographic location.

**roles:** various tasks assigned to banks in a management group during the course of a loan syndication.

**roll-over:** the reissue of outstanding short-term money market securities on their date of maturity or the renewal of an advance under a credit facility.

**running the books:** the central task in the execution phase of the syndication. The bank appointed to run the books is responsible for issuing invitations, disseminating information to interested banks and informing both the borrower and management group of daily progress. The role is very visible *vis-à-vis* the borrower and the general market. As such it is generally considered the most desirable syndicate task.

**RWA:** risk weighted asset – *see* risk asset weighting.

**secondary market:** the market for distribution or trading of loan assets after closure of primary market distribution.

**secured debt:** debt backed by specified assets or revenues of the borrower. If there is an event of default, the lenders can force the sale of assets to meet their claims.

**securitisation:** a process whereby bank loans or other non-tradeable financial transactions are consolidated into tradeable securities. The mortgage-backed securities market is an example of securitisation.

**sell-down:** the reduction of an initial commitment in a loan or other syndicated facility.

**sell-down target:** the desired level of each bank's final participation in the loan (also known as target hold).

**senior debt:** debt which has priority of repayment in a liquidation.

**servicing:** the payment by the borrower of interest in accordance with the terms of a loan.

**set-off clause:** a clause commonly included in credit facilities permitting banks to set off any deposits made with them by a borrower against amounts owing to them by such borrower.

**several liability:** in the context of a group of legal entities entering into similar obligations, the basis of the obligation of each such legal entity being stand-alone. This means that the non-performance by one entity of its obligations will not affect or alter the obligations of the other entities.

**Sharpe ratio:** the average return earned by an investment in excess of the risk-free rate per unit of volatility.

**signing:** the execution of the loan documents by the borrower, the management group, the participants, the facility agent and other parties (for example, the guarantor).

**SIV:** a structured investment vehicle – a type of structured credit product popular in the period prior to the GFC.

**skim:** a portion of the front-end fee (also referred to as the *praecipium*) calculated on the nominal amount of the loan and paid to the MLAs and Bookrunners in recognition of the human resources and technical skills commitment required to conclude a successful transaction. In multi-bank bidding groups, any skim is usually shared equally between the MLAs and Bookrunners without regard for the unequal commitment of resources to the transaction.

**snooze and lose:** (also referred to as '*snooze, you lose*' or '*use it or lose it*'). A colloquial (but widely used) term to refer to a provision in a credit agreement which excludes from any vote in relation to an amendment or waiver of the credit agreement the commitments of any lender which does not reply to the request for that waiver or amendment within a fixed period of time (for example, 10 business days).

**SOFR:** the Secured Overnight Financing Rate, an overnight secured reference rate based on transactions in the US Treasury repo market.

**SONIA:** the Sterling Overnight Interest Average, an overnight reference rate for unsecured sterling transactions.

**sovereign immunity:** an historical doctrine of law in certain jurisdictions under which sovereign governments may not be sued or their assets seized. Sovereign governments may waive their immunity, or their immunity in respect of commercial activities may be limited by local law.

**sovereign lending:** lending to sovereign governments or to state entities which carry the explicit or implicit guarantee of the government.

**special purpose vehicle (SPV):** a company set up for a specific purpose (often to acquire an asset or develop a project).

**split pricing:** a margin set at differing levels for specific periods of the loan. For example, an agreement to lend at 0.625%, years one to three; 0.75%, years four to five.

**spread:** *see* margin.

**standard market practice:** informal procedures which govern the syndicated loan business, and have gained broad acceptance among market leaders and participants.

**standby letter of credit:** a letter of credit issued by a bank as a form of guarantee. The beneficiary will normally be entitled to make a drawing under a letter of credit merely by presenting a certificate of non-payment pursuant to the terms of the underlying contract.

**standstill or standstill period:** an arrangement whereby a subordinated or mezzanine creditor is prevented from taking enforcement action for a given period during which the senior lenders decide what to do with a defaulting borrower.

**step-down margin:** a margin which decreases during the term of the loan.

**step-up margin:** a margin which increases during the term of the loan.

**structural subordination:** arises where one class of creditors have debt claims which will in an insolvency of the group rank behind the debt claims of other creditors because of the structure. This may be (for example) because the claims of that class of creditor are only against an entity whose assets consist only of the shares in the subsidiary of that entity but where another class of creditor have debt claims directly against that subsidiary. In that case the first class of creditors are said to be structurally subordinated to the creditors of the subsidiary.

**sub-investment grade:** a borrower or debt instrument is of sub-investment grade status if its credit rating is lower than investment grade (for which see above).

**subordinated loan:** a loan made on terms whereby the lender agrees contractually that some or all payment obligations owed to such lender will rank behind certain other indebtedness of the borrower. In certain circumstances, it is possible to make subordinated arrangements binding on the borrower's liquidator. Subordinated loans will usually be made for long periods and will usually not be callable.

**sub-participation:** the silent sale of an asset where the sub-participant agrees to fund the loan and assume the credit risk but does not obtain any rights and obligations against the borrower. Parties to the agreement are limited to the syndicate bank and the sub-participant.

**subscriptions:** lenders' indication of willingness to commit funds during the course of the general syndication. In theory, a participating lender subscribes for a certain level of assets, while the management group allocates final participations at its discretion upon the close of the general syndication. Unless there is an oversubscription, the participating lender receives a full allocation.

**sub-underwriter:** an underwriter will sometimes sell down a portion of its underwriting commitment to a sub-underwriter.

**supplier credit:** a financing arrangement under which the supplier agrees to accept deferred payment terms from the buyer and funds itself by discounting or selling the bills of exchange or promissory notes so created with a bank in its own country.

**surety bond:** a device, similar to a standby letter of credit, employed in the US to provide the equivalent of a bank guarantee for bonds or notes issued by a corporation. In general, surety bonds are issued by insurance companies.

**swap:** the exchanging of one security, debt, currency or interest rate for another.

**swingline:** a facility usually made available to a borrower in connection with its commercial paper programme. The facility will customarily be available on very short notice and will be designed to ensure that a borrower has sufficient liquidity to pay maturing commercial paper in the event that it is unable to roll-over the commercial paper (that is, fund the repayments out of a new issue of commercial paper).

**swingline agent:** the bank that administers a swingline facility.

**syndicate:** a group of lenders participating in a single credit facility.

**syndicate list:** the list of lenders to be approached in the general syndication, following agreement between the arrangers, the underwriters, if any, and the borrower.

**syndicated loan:** a loan made available by a group of lenders in pre-defined proportions under the same credit facility.

**syndicated loan market:** the medium to long-term floating-rate loan market. The instruments are priced over a basis rate and the loan is then syndicated among commercial lending and other financial institutions.

**syndication:** the formation of a management group in order to underwrite the principal amount of a loan or the distribution of the risk among a group of participating lenders. This latter function is often referred to as the general syndication.

**syndication pool:** *see* pool.

**synthetic security:** generally, a floating-rate instrument created by combining an interest rate swap with a bond. For instance, by using an interest rate swap, floating-rate interest payments can be created and linked to coupon payments under a fixed-interest rate bond. The resulting floating-rate instrument is synthetic, that is, it has been created after issuance of the underlying bond, and its terms might not otherwise be available in the market.

**systemic risk:** an event that could lead to or trigger a collapse of confidence in or of the banking system.

**take and hold:** a strategy which requires that each lender retains its original commitment in the loan, without distributing risk to a broader group of lenders through syndication.

**take or pay contract:** an agreement between a purchaser and a seller that provides for the purchaser to pay specified amounts periodically in return for products or services. The purchaser must make specified minimum payments even if it does not take delivery of the contracted products or services.

**take out:** the means by which a syndicated loan is expected to be repaid (including capital markets issuances; asset disposals; refinancing etc.).

**taker:** any participant in the loan or credit facility.

**TARGET2:** a single, shared technical platform which is the payment system for settlement in real time of predominantly high-value euro payments in central bank money.

**TARGET business day:** a day when the Trans-European Automated Real-time Gross Settlement Express Transfer System is operating.

**target hold:** *see* sell-down target.

**tender panel:** a pre-determined group of lenders from whom an issuer may request competitive bids for the making of short-term advances.

**tender panel agent:** the lender which administers a tender panel.

**termination date:** either the date by which a loan must be drawn down (the last day of the availability period) or the date upon which a loan must be repaid (also referred to as the maturity date).

**term loan:** a loan with a fixed drawdown period and a repayment schedule, where the principal is normally repaid on an equal, semi-annual basis (but *see* also Grace periods and Bullet repayment).

**term sheet:** a document, which is not generally intended to be legally binding until it forms part of a formal offer, setting out the main agreed terms and conditions of a transaction between the borrower and arranger.

**ticket:** a level of commitment (underwriting or final take) and related title offered to banks invited into a syndicated transaction. The usual titles are:

- Mandated Lead Arranger (MLA) and Bookrunner – a mandated bank responsible for originating, syndicating and executing a transaction. Underwriting may be included in the responsibilities;
- joint MLAs – a group of MLAs, sharing roles and underwriting commitments, if any;
- Arranger – generally a title for a second level mandated or underwriting bank or a bank committing to the highest level of participation;
- Co-arranger – generally a title for a bank committing to the second highest level of participation;
- Lead Manager – a bank committing to a senior level of participation; and
- Participant – a bank committing to the most junior level of participation.

Not all of these titles are available on all transactions. Other titles are sometimes offered, such as Co-lead Manager, if the size of a transaction justifies another level of commitment from banks. (In the Euromarkets the term 'Lead Manager(s)' referred to the mandated bank(s) until about 1985 when the term 'Arranger' became more prevalent and this is now replaced with MLA and Bookrunner.) *See also* bracket; title.

**timetable (documentation):** the procedural steps required to secure agreement on a loan contract, to which the borrower, agent and lending syndicate are party. The process covers the entire period from mandate to signing.

**timetable (syndication):** the procedural steps required to underwrite a transaction, and then reduce the underwriting exposure of each lender through syndication to a broad and diverse group of interested lenders. The process covers the period from mandate to the final allocation of assets among syndicate participants.

**title:** *see* ticket.

**toggle:** (also referred to as a '**PIK toggle**') refers to the ability of a borrower to switch between cash pay and PIK interest in respect of subordinated debt. The right to switch is sometimes granted by lenders, often on the basis of an increased margin for any period during which the PIK option is selected.

**tombstone:** an advertisement in the financial press that announces the completion of a financial transaction and contains brief details of the transaction and the names of the parties involved.

**total cost to the borrower:** *see* cost to the borrower.

**tranche:** part of a financial transaction which is split into different portions. Tranches may be used because there are different lenders, instruments, basis rates, currencies or maturities.

**transaction yield:** the ROA on a specific deal.

**transfer certificate:** a certificate issued under a syndicated loan allowing a syndicate member to transfer all or part of its share of that loan to another person by way of novation.

**UCITS:** Undertakings for Collective Investments in Transferable Securities – a form of collective investment scheme.

**underwriter:** a lender which commits in advance of drawdown to take on a portion of the overall facility.

**underwriting commitment:** the maximum amount a lender commits to lend. The purpose of syndication is to reduce this commitment to reach a final retention target.

**underwriting fee:** part of the front-end fee, based upon the initial, or allocated amount of the underwriting commitment.

**utilisation fee:** a fee paid to the lender to increase its return on assets. The payment of the fee is generally linked to the average level of utilisation during a specified period of time.

**variable margin:** a margin which varies during the term of a loan, often in relation to the credit rating of the borrower.

**waiver of sovereign immunity:** agreement by a sovereign borrower that it will not use the principle of sovereign immunity as a shield against a law suit.

**wallet:** the portion of a borrower's income which is available to remunerate its lenders.

**Wheatley Report:** the final report of the Wheatley Review of LIBOR published in September 2012.

**white list:** a list of institutions which the borrower has pre-approved as acceptable transferees/assignees of its syndicated debt (*see* also "**black list**").

**withholding tax:** a tax deductible at source on interest or dividend payments.

**yank the bank:** a colloquial (but widely used) term to refer to a provision in a credit agreement which gives the borrowers the right to force a lender out of the deal if it does not vote in favour of a requested amendment or waiver to the credit documents. In most cases the lender can only be forced out if there is another entity willing to take a transfer of that lender's commitments but in some cases, the borrower may have the right to pre-pay the non-consenting lender.

**yield:** *see* transaction yield.

**YTD:** year to date.

# INDEX

Note: Page numbers in *italic* refer to exhibit examples; references to Notes are indicated as 1n2 (page1 note2)

Lightning Source UK Ltd.
Milton Keynes UK
UKHW051523070220
358268UK00005B/43